THE HISTORY OF THE NAZI PARTY: 1933–1945

THE *History* OF THE NAZI PARTY: 1933-1945

DIETRICH ORLOW

UNIVERSITY OF PITTSBURGH PRESS

Library of Congress Catalog Card Number 72–81795
ISBN 0–8229–3253–9
Media Directions Inc., London
Manufactured in the United States of America

To Ingrid

Contents

Preface

The history of the Nazi Party (NSDAP) in power confronts the historian with a constant and not easily solved dilemma: how to avoid writing a full-scale history of the Third Reich, and yet not present the development of the NSDAP as an autonomous process taking place in a societal vacuum. As a number of reviewers of *The History of the Nazi Party: 1919–1933* noted, my approach there tilted away from a full treatment of the larger aspects of German history in this period. The present volume continues this emphasis, I hope with even more justification. While it is true that there is no definitive history of the Third Reich, a large number of monographs have illuminated various aspects of Nazi society. On the other hand, neither a full-scale study of the NSDAP as an organized political and social entity nor a sufficient number of specialized monographs have appeared to date. As a result, the major focal point of this book is the impact on the internal mechanism of the Nazi Party of obtaining governmental power and managing foreign conquests rather than the transformations wrought by the NSDAP on German and European society as a whole. To be sure, there are numerous instances in which the two emphases cannot be separated because they become interdependent causal agents.

Nonetheless, this approach may result in some unusual, although, it is hoped, not distorting treatments of familiar events in the history of the Third Reich. The Four Year Plan, for example, will receive little attention in this study. It is perfectly true that the plan was a major step on Hitler's road to war, but for the history of the party it is important primarily because it prevented the party's initiatives in the field of economic policy. In contrast, the establishment and the operations of the *Arbeitsbereich* form of NSDAP organization in the conquered areas of Europe were a factor of utmost importance in the history of the

NSDAP. Yet previous studies of German policies in occupied Europe have scarcely recorded the existence of these organizations.

This is not a definitive history of the NSDAP. In part, meaningful sources for several important aspects of the party's development are not available. The Reich treasurer managed to burn most of his detailed records before he gave himself up to the Americans. The bulk of the files from the office of the deputy Führer have been lost. Virtually no Gau (province) archives survived intact. In addition, there are quantitative limitations on the amount of material than can be meaningfully digested in a one-volume history of the NSDAP in the Third Reich. The party's district leaders, some seven hundred strong, are an extremely important group of functionaries, but a full study of the entire contingent was obviously not possible. Many of the party's social control initiatives lay in the hands of the mass welfare organizations—the NSV and DAF[1]—but these organizations left literally millions of documents that remain largely undigested. For the most part, then, this history of the NSDAP is a study of the political and organizational developments in the party. It cannot claim, for example, to provide a definitive sociological typology of the mass of Nazi Party members, though this is an area in which systematic work is urgently needed.

Finally, a word about the sources and their manner of citation. The overwhelming bulk of the documentation for this history consists of the unpublished papers left by various party organizations in the wake of the collapse of the Third Reich. Some of these are available in one archive only, but for a large number both the original documents and microfilm copies are open to researchers. The microfilms are available at and from the National Archives, while the originals either remained in Germany or have been returned to Germany. Since this book was researched and written in about equal parts in Europe and the United States, the citations will be either to the microfilms or to the originals—depending on my residence during that part of the research. The bibliographic note should be helpful in correlating the differing archival sources of the same materials.

1. See the Glossary, pp. 495–98, for an explanation of these abbreviations.

Acknowledgments

It is a pleasant duty to acknowledge the many personal, financial, and institutional acts of kindness that made this book possible. The research and writing could not have been accomplished without several generous faculty research grants awarded by the Social Science Research Council. In addition, I am grateful to the two universities with which I have been associated in the course of writing the book: Syracuse University granted me a sabbatical semester, and Boston University offered a summer research award when the work was in the final stages of preparation.

Numerous colleagues in the profession and among the archival staffs on both sides of the Atlantic have been unfailing in their help and encouragement. Professors Gerhard Weinberg and Robert Koehl permitted me to call upon their time on a number of occasions. Along with numerous others, I have all too frequently taken Dr. Robert Wolfe's unique efficiency and knowledge of the materials at the National Archives for granted, and it is appropriate once more to acknowledge his aid publicly. In addition, the library staffs of Boston University and the University of Michigan responded with admirable dispatch to my requests for "special assistance." In Europe, Dr. Anton Hoch of the Institut für Zeitgeschichte and Dr. Kinder at the Bundesarchiv stood ready with both advice and swift procurement of needed materials. I owe a very special debt of gratitude to Dr. Werner Jochman, of the Forschungsstelle für die Geschichte des Nationalsozialismus in Hamburg, not only for his unfailing archival services and for arranging an interview with the ex-Gauleiter of Hamburg, but, above all, for numerous conversations which helped to put some thematic emphases into focus and to eliminate some possible distortions. In addition, the staffs of the Rijksinstituut voor Oorlogsdokumentatie in Amsterdam, the Centre Documentation Juive Contemporaine in Paris, the Berlin Document Center in Berlin, the Institut für Zeitgeschichte in Munich, the Bayerische Staatsbibliothek, and the Bayerisches Geheimes Staatsarchiv all were unstinting in their helpfulness.

Arthur Madden and Deborah Drosnin aided in the final preparation of the manuscript.

Finally, this book owes more than can be expressed in words to the efforts of my wife. From aids with the research to editorial criticism, the history of the NSDAP could not have been written without her.

D.O.

Chestnut Hill, Massachusetts
February 1972

Abbreviations Used in Notes

Arb. NSDAP	Arbeitsbereich der NSDAP
ARV	*Anordnungen, Rundschreiben, Verfügungen* of the deputy Führer
BA	Bundesarchiv
BDC	Berlin Document Center
BGStA	Bayerisches Geheimes Staatsarchiv
CDJC	Centre Documentation Juive Contemporaine
Forsch. Hbg.	Forschungsstelle für die Geschichte des Nationalsozialismus in Hamburg
GBA	Generalbevollmächtigter für den Arbeitseinsatz
GBK	Generalbevollmächtigter für den Kriegseinsatz
GG	Generalgouvernement
GKzbV (Ni)	Generalkommissar zur besonderen Verwendung in den Niederlanden
GL	Gauleitung or Gauleiter
HAB	Hauptarchiv Berlin
HMB/NBO	Halbmonatsberichte des Regierungspräsidiums von Niederbayern-Oberfranken
HMB/OBB	Halbmonatsberichte des Regierungspräsidiums von Oberbayern
HSSPF	Höherer SS- und Polizeiführer
IB	*Illustrierter Beobachter*
IfZ	Institut für Zeitgeschichte, Munich
Mittbl. Kr. Mü.	*Mitteilungsblatt des Kreises München der NSDAP*
MiU/GAC	University of Michigan German Archival Collection
NA	National Archives
OPG	Oberstes Parteigericht
PK	Parteikanzlei
PKC	Parteikanzlei Correspondenz
Rdschr.	*Rundschreiben des Reichsschatzmeisters*
RFSS	Reichsführer-SS
RK	Reichskommissar
RKO	Reichskommissariat Ostland
RKU	Reichskommissariat Ukraine

RL   Reichsleitung
RMO   Reichsministerium für die besetzten Ostgebiete
ROL   Reichsorganisationsleiter
RPL   Reichspropagandaleitung
Rschm.   Reichsschatzmeister
Rsth.   Reichsstatthalter
RVBl   *Reichsverfügungsblatt*
RVK   Reichsverteidigungskommissar
RvO   Rijksinstituut voor Oorlogsdokumentatie, Amsterdam
SD   Sicherheitsdienst
SS   SS officer personnel records
StdF   Stellvertreter des Führers
T–000   Identifies microfilms of captured German documents
              published by the National Archives, Washington,
              D.C.
TB   Telex-Berichte of the RK for the occupied Netherlands
VAB   *Verfügungen, Anordnungen, Bekanntgaben* of the PK
VB   *Völkischer Beobachter*
VI   *Vertrauliche Informationen* of the PK
Vjh.f.Z.   *Vierteljahrshefte für Zeitgeschichte*
VOBl   *Verordnungsblatt der Reichsleitung der NSDAP*

THE HISTORY OF THE NAZI PARTY: 1933–1945

Introduction

The Nazi era of German history continues to fascinate academic researchers and the public alike. To date literally hundreds of books and articles have systematically, analytically, descriptively, and, at times, sensationally described how a great industrial nation came to be dominated in a few short years by men of demonstrably low human character bringing about indescribable evil. In addition, a flood of memoirs has come from the pens of a large number of prominent and lesser-known contemporaries.

Inevitably, in the twenty-five years since the ignominious death of the Nazi empire, certain focal points of topical and methodological emphasis have characterized various stages of the writings about the Nazis; in a minor way, the Third Reich has developed a historiography of its own. Immediately after World War II, under the impact of the Nuremberg trials, the physical and political brutalities committed by the Nazis received foremost attention, and the Nazi phenomenon came to be described rather too simplistically as no more than a drive for evil power.[1] Greater chronological distance from the subject led to a less diabolical and one-sided interpretation. In the fifties and early sixties, influenced by the reality of the tensions caused by the Cold War, several attempts were made to create a typology of totalitarian political systems,[2] a category broad enough to include at least Nazi Germany and

---

1. See, for example, Erwin Faul, "Hitlers Über-Machiavellismus," *Vierteljahrshefte für Zeitgeschichte* (cited hereafter as *Vjh.f.Z.*), II (Oct. 1954), 344–72; and Helmut Krausnick, "Stationen der Gleichschaltung," in Theodor Eschenburg, ed., *Der Weg in die Diktatur* (Munich, 1962), p. 178.
2. Carl J. Friedrich and Zbigniew K. Brzezinski, *Totalitarian Dictatorship and*

Stalinist Russia, and perhaps Fascist Italy[3] and Communist China as well. Within these attempts at systematization, the single mass party typical of totalitarian systems played a major role; it was one of several prerequisites for assigning the label "totalitarian" to a political system. Despite their momentary popularity, the typologies were not entirely satisfactory. A number of major differences persisted in the seemingly so similar political systems created by Stalin, Mussolini, and Hitler.[4] Partly as a result of these difficulties, there emerged in the mid-sixties what might be called somewhat facetiously the "klein-totalitarian" school of thought. Numerous contributions enlivened the "Fascist" vs. "National Socialist" controversy[5] ushered in by Ernst Nolte's *The Three Faces of Fascism.*[6]

All of these attempts at typological definitions of totalitarianism or fascism shared certain underlying assumptions, although these were often not made explicit. Above all, they presupposed that the totalitarian political systems, like their democratic counterparts, were systems in equilibrium,[7] that is, political systems in which certain qualitative and quantitative values could be assigned to a number of identifiable institutions such as, for example, the totalitarian party, the secret police, the lower-middle class. Unfortunately, the hypotheses became axioms, and the overriding desire for more inclusive typological categorizations all too often resulted in distorted descriptions of historical developments.[8]

Autocracy (Cambridge, Mass., 1956), with several subsequent editions, is the best-known and most successful attempt to create a "typology" of modern totalitarianism.

3. See Dante L. Germino, *The Italian Fascist Party in Power* (Minneapolis, 1959), pp. 125–26, in which the author attempts to apply Friedrich and Brzezinski's characteristics to Italy in order to prove that Mussolini had created a totalitarian political system.

4. See, for example, Willi Boelcke, ed., *Kriegspropaganda 1939–1941* (Stuttgart, 1966), p. 97; and Karl-Dietrich Bracher, *Die deutsche Diktatur* (Cologne, 1969), pp. 257–58.

5. For an excellent review of the more recent literature on "rightist" totalitarianism, see Eugen Weber *et al.*, "Fascisme et National-Socialisme," *Annales*, XXIV (Jan.-Feb. 1969), 195–233.

6. (New York, 1965). The German original is *Der Faschismus in seiner Epoche* (Munich, 1963).

7. Tom Bottomore, "Conservative Man," *New York Review of Books*, XV (8 Oct. 1970), 20–21.

8. See the somewhat ironic comments by Hans-Dietrich Loock, *Quisling, Rosenberg und Terboven* (Stuttgart, 1970), pp. 11–13.

The role played by the Nazi Party (NSDAP) in the development and dynamics of the Third Reich serves as a particularly useful barometer of the difficulties encountered in many of the typological attempts. Perhaps precisely because no full-scale analysis of the NSDAP's history in the Third Reich has appeared, the factor "Nazi Party" has been assigned widely divergent values in a number of studies concerned primarily with other aspects of the Nazi era. There is no agreement, for example, on one of the fundamental characteristics of a totalitarian party: the ingredients and indeed the very existence of a Nazi ideology are a matter of considerable dispute. Some authors have taken the position that the Nazi ideology (or *Weltanschauung*, to use the party's own terminology) consisted of an all-encompassing political pseudoreligion.[9] In contrast, others have denied the existence of a genuine ideology, claiming instead that the NSDAP never went beyond formulating a few intuitive and charismatically useful action-guidelines which could be interpreted as the occasion demanded.[10]

Similarly, a question as basic as the relation of party and state under the Nazi system, surely one of the most fundamental problems of any totalitarian political society, is unclear. The conclusions range from the affirmation that (unlike Stalinist Russia) the NSDAP was never able to challenge the priority of state organs in the struggle for influence over German society[11] to the exact opposite,[12] with a compromise position offered by the statement that party and state engaged primarily in a process of mutual destruction.[13]

Such controversies are of more than minor importance; they are basic to any analysis of the NSDAP itself. If the party had no ideology, it cannot be treated as a genuinely revolutionary movement in German society, so that its activities can be described as little more than a sus-

9. Esp. Joachim C. Fest, *Das Gesicht des Dritten Reiches* (Munich, 1964), p. 257; and Hans-Jochen Gamm, *Der braune Kult* (Hamburg, 1962), pp. 156–90.

10. Among more recent literature, most emphatically in Joseph Nyomarkay, *Charisma and Factionalism in the Nazi Party* (Minneapolis, 1967).

11. David Schoenbaum, *Hitler's Social Revolution* (New York, 1966), pp. xix, 197, and 223. The excellent compendium of articles *Probleme des Zweiten Weltkrieges*, ed. Andreas Hillgruber (Cologne, 1967), does not contain a contribution on the role of the NSDAP during the war.

12. Hildegard Brenner, *Die Kunstpolitik des Nationalsozialismus* (Reinbek b. Hamburg, 1963), p. 36.

13. Hans Mommsen, *Beamtentum im Dritten Reich* (Stuttgart, 1966), p. 13.

tained drive to destroy the *Rechtsstaat* (a society governed by a code of
laws not subject to personal interference by individual political leaders)
norms and institutions on a mass scale.[14] And if the party's role was
wholly subordinate to that of other power components in the Third
Reich, its development can be analyzed as incidental to the history of
the regime, so that the researcher's focal point should properly remain
in the governmental and military spheres.

The widely divergent conclusions result not merely from differing
interpretations of the available documentation, but also from a failure
to define what is meant by the term "Nazi Party." In the totality of its
affiliated organizations after 1933, the NSDAP included virtually all
Germans. Their numbers ranged from conservative and aristocratic
fellow travelers who hoped for a return to pre-1914 times to wild-eyed
proponents of gigantic wars of racial extermination.[15] In terms of organization, the millions of Germans attached to the party in some way or
other were grouped in a three-tiered system of overlapping memberships and jurisdictions. The Nazis themselves termed the three levels
the territorial cadre organization (*Politische Organisation*, PO), the
"divisions" (*Gliederungen*), and the affiliated organizations (*ange-
schlossene Verbände*). The PO consisted primarily of the NSDAP's territorial organization and the staffs of the Reich-level offices concerned
with administering the territorial cadres, notably those of the deputy
Führer, the party treasurer, the Reich organizational leader, and the
intraparty judiciary system. The divisions included the Hitler Youth
(*Hitler-Jugend*, HJ) and the paramilitary organizations, in other words,
the storm troopers (*Sturmabteilung*, SA), the SS (*Schutzstaffel*), the
National Socialist Motor Corps (*Nationalsozialistisches Kraftfahrer-
korps*, NSKK), and the National Socialist Flying Corps (*Nationalsozialistisches Fliegerkorps*, NSFK). Finally, the affiliated organizations were
the large number of professional and interest groups either created
or controlled by the party to influence socioeconomic life in Germany.

14. Hermann Weinkauff, "*Die deutsche Justiz und der Nationalsozialismus—Ein
Überblick*," in Weinkauff *et al.*, *Die deutsche Justiz und der Nationalsozialismus*
(Stuttgart, 1968), I, 41; and Krausnick, "Stationen," p. 179.
15. Manfred Messerschmidt, *Die Wehrmacht im NS-Staat* (Hamburg, 1969),
p. 247.

The most important of this last group was the compulsory single labor organization permitted in Nazi Germany, the German Labor Front (*Deutsche Arbeitsfront*, DAF).

Most of these organizations and their leaders lacked either the desire or the ability (if not both) to convert the groups' power goals into over-all party policy. Political success in Nazi Germany depended upon three factors: access to Hitler by the components' leaders, a set of policy goals designed significantly to alter the relationships among all segments of German society, and the availability of a sufficiently well-developed functionary corps to translate policy goals into regime-wide influence and power.

The most important among these criteria was the relationship and access of the groups' spokesmen to Hitler. Although the Nazi Führer now headed the German government as well as his party, Hitler's conception of himself as a personified historical force standing above abstract ideological principles and possessing the ability to change them at will[16] was not altered by his oath to the constitution on January 30, 1933. Nor did he change the manner of distributing portions of his power. As in the "years of struggle" (*Kampfzeit*), Hitler subcontracted (with the understanding that the contract could be terminated at will) segments of his authority to his individual derivative agents,[17] rather than to offices or institutions. In consequence, the history of the NSDAP in the Third Reich must at times read like a series of interwoven political biographies. This is the only possible answer to the challenge posed by the "personality problem" in the Nazi Party. Not only were institutional dynamics in the NSDAP little more than the personal relationships and clashes of individual party leaders, but the relationship between Hitler and his derivative agents was an intensely personal one.

16. Thus the comment by the governor of Bavaria, Franz v. Epp, on a speech by Hitler that "the Führer repeatedly uses [in his speech to the governors on 28 Sept. 1933] the words 'that is not National Socialist' but he refuses to define . . . what is meant by 'National Socialist'" misses the point. Hitler had no intention of going beyond a very narrow negative definition of individual acts. See Epp, "Besprechung mit den Reichsstatthaltern am 28. September 1933," p. 8, in Bayerisches Geheimes Staatsarchiv, Reichsstatthalter, no. 148.

17. On this concept see Dietrich Orlow, *The History of the Nazi Party: 1919–1933* (Pittsburgh, 1969), pp. 81 ff.

Even the party's national treasurer, Franz X. Schwarz, an able, pedan-
tically bureaucratic man, was nevertheless bound to Hitler in a way
which can only be described as romantic-emotional.[18] Similarly, Hitler
regarded the corps of provincial leaders (the Gauleiters) as his personal
followers whose loyalty he rewarded with well-nigh unassailable positions of power, while ignoring their incompetence and corruption.[19]

Along with retaining his manner of distributing power, Hitler maintained his circle of subcontractors with no major changes. As in the
Kampfzeit, he assigned derivative-agent status to the provincial chiefs
of the party's territorial cadre organization, the Gauleiters (GLs), and
to the division heads of the NSDAP's Reich administration, the Reichsleiters (RLs). The former group was responsible for administering
territorial jurisdictional spheres; the latter group consisted of the officials responsible for executing a policy line that was not territorially
restricted, but applied to a major social or economic interest group
in the Reich as a whole. Also, the agential force included the heads of
the NSDAP's paramilitary organizations and a few men, like Hermann
Göring, who were close to Hitler, but held no major party office. In
theory, all members of this group, numbering some sixty persons at one
point during the Third Reich, possessed the right of direct access to
Hitler; in practice only a much smaller number had the requisite personality traits or the interest to compete for Hitler's personal attention.

Although (at least until 1939) Hitler lived a life of almost constant
public appearances and travel and dreaded to be left alone, his personality has largely eluded biographical analysis. Joachim Fest has
called him "peculiarly flat . . . impressionless, abstract . . . with a femi-
nine streak,"[20] a description that raises more questions than it answers.
As an administrator, the new chancellor was the antithesis of an ef-

18. Ulf Lükemann, "Der Reichsschatzmeister der NSDAP" (Dissertation, Free
University of Berlin, 1963), pp. 17 and 23.

19. Peter Diehl-Thiele, *Partei und Staat im Dritten Reich* (Munich, 1969), p.
201; and Robert Koehl, *RKFDV—German Resettlement Policy 1939–1945* (Cambridge, Mass., 1957), p. 227. Basic for the whole problem of the Gauleiters' relationship to Hitler is Peter Hüttenberger, *Die Gauleiter* (Stuttgart, 1969).

20. Fest's foreword in Jochen v. Lang, ed., *Adolf Hitler, Gesichte eines Diktators*
(Hamburg, 1968), pp. 5–6. The best overall biography of Hitler is still Alan Bullock, *Hitler: A Study in Tyranny*, latest ed. (New York, 1962).

fective bureaucrat. He disliked administrative work intensely, was often unpunctual,[21] seldom used his desk,[22] and preferred to handle most difficult issues by ignoring them. He was, however, unsurpassed as a public speaker, and bathed in the adoration of the crowd. Yet, here, too, he feared failure and spoke only when he could announce an actual or imagined success.[23] Hitler had no close friends, but he did have two overlapping circles of preferred associates, a private one and a more official one. The private group of individuals, with whom the Führer preferred to spend his many nonworking hours, consisted almost entirely of his old Munich entourage. This circle included such obviously apolitical individuals as Eva Braun, Hitler's mistress and wife for one day, but it is noteworthy that the powerful Gauleiter of Upper Bavaria and Munich, Adolf Wagner, and the later whiz-kid Reich minister of munitions, Albert Speer, were also regular members of the private circle.[24]

The membership of Hitler's official circle is more open to question and controversy. A number of mutually contradictory lists have been compiled of those whom Hitler trusted and to whom he gave, at least prior to the outbreak of the war, immediate access to his person. From the available memoir literature it is clear that the circle was quite small and that it included almost entirely men who had supported Hitler since the early days of his political career. None of the figures who became prominent and powerful only after 1933 were received into the core of the official circle. The membership varied considerably during the life span of the Third Reich, but all of the following were members in good standing at least for a considerable time: Hermann Göring,

21. Ernst Hanfstaengl, *Unheard Witness* (Philadelphia, 1957), p. 228; and Albert Speer, *Erinnerungen* (Berlin, 1969), p. 59.

22. A formal portrait of Hitler taken in 1933 shows him sitting at his desk with the drawers facing the camera! See the party's illustrated weekly, *Illustrierter Beobachter* (cited hereafter as *IB*) (special edition, n.d.), p. 60.

23. For an analysis of Hitler as a speaker see Max Domarus, ed., *Hitler, Reden und Proklamationen 1932–1945* (Munich, 1965), I, 44–55; and the introduction in Hildegard v. Kotze and Helmut Krausnick, eds., *Es spricht der Führer!* (Gütersloh, 1966).

24. Otto Dietrich, *Zwölf Jahre mit Hitler* (Cologne, 1955), pp. 161 and 217; and Friedrich Hossbach, *Zwischen Wehrmacht und Hitler*, 2d ed. (Göttingen, 1965), p. 17.

Heinrich Himmler, Joseph Goebbels, Franz Xaver Schwarz, Rudolf Hess, Martin Bormann, Robert Ley, Adolf Wagner, Fritz Sauckel, Erich Koch, Karl Kaufmann, and Josef Bürckel.[25]

All of these men reached the highest positions in the Third Reich, often holding numerous posts simultaneously. (This in itself is an indication of Hitler's reluctance to trust a large circle of associates with positions of potentially independent power.) Göring became prime minister of Prussia, commander-in-chief of the air force, economic czar of Germany after 1936, and from 1939 to 1945 Hitler's designated successor. Himmler added numerous posts to his leadership of the SS; Schwarz served as the party's national treasurer and its executive secretary for administration. Rudolf Hess, Hitler's private secretary, became his deputy in 1933. Bormann was Hess's staff director until May 1941 and then succeeded him. Ley served as chief of the party's organizational apparatus and later was head of the Nazis' compulsory labor union (DAF). Goebbels headed the powerful propaganda ministry, and he was also Gauleiter of Berlin; Gauleiter Wagner was Bavarian minister of the interior; Sauckel was Gauleiter of Thuringia and during World War II chief of labor allocation; Koch served as Gauleiter of East Prussia and Reich commissioner in the Ukraine; and Kaufmann was the party's provincial leader in Hamburg and Reich commissioner for ocean shipping. Finally, Bürckel was Gauleiter in the Palatinate, and also at various times Reich commissioner in the Saar, Austria, and Lorraine.

This group is remarkable in a number of ways. The members were relatively young; in 1933 their average age was thirty-nine years. All were long-time members of the NSDAP; their membership numbers ranged from 6 (Schwarz) to 60,508 (Bormann). Even more significant in the context of this study is the large proportion of "cadre" men among the group. Of the twelve, ten had served solely in the party's political administration prior to 1933 (Goebbels, Schwarz, Hess, Bormann, Ley, Wagner, Sauckel, Koch, Kaufmann, Bürckel), and even after the

25. Dietrich, *Zwölf Jahre*, pp. 247–48 and 259; Hanfstaengl, *Unheard Witness*, pp. 230, 235, and 259; Hossbach, *Zwischen*, p. 24; Speer, *Erinnerungen*, p. 48; Ilse Hess, ed., *England-Nürnberg-Spandau* (Leoni a. Starnberger See, 1952), p. 26; and Fritz Wiedemann, *Der Mann der Feldherr werden wollte* (Velbert, 1964), pp. 58–59.

NSDAP came to power, only Ley and Goebbels identified more strongly with a component outside the cadre organization. In addition, six of the group (Goebbels, Wagner, Sauckel, Koch, Kaufmann, Bürckel) were Gauleiters both before and after 1933. In general, then, Hitler's official circle revealed his clear preference for leaders of the territorial cadre organization. The two major exceptions were Heinrich Himmler and Hermann Göring. Himmler and Göring alone among the non-cadre men were able to construct massive empires, and only Himmler succeeded in maintaining his creation throughout the Third Reich. In the later thirties and during the wartime years, the SS was a distinct rival to the PO. The story of the SS has already been told in some detail,[26] and it will be treated in this study only insofar as it affected the history of other power segments in the NSDAP.

As individuals (never as a group) these men had what Karl-Dietrich Bracher terms "the right of immediate access,"[27] that is, the right to present their wishes and complaints directly to Hitler. As a result, they were in a preferred position to receive a *Führerbefehl* (Führer order), the most important instrument of administrative decision-making in the Third Reich. Quite often such Hitlerian orders took the form of oral expressions thrown out more or less at random in response to a question or request by a member of the official circle.[28] The informal decision-making habits in turn raised Hitler's daily luncheons (when he was in Berlin) to the status of high-level leadership audiences. Since Hitler disliked regular appointments, he issued a blanket invitation to all Gauleiters, the heads of the paramilitary organizations, and the chiefs of the affiliated organizations to join him for luncheon whenever he and they happened to be in the capital.[29] At these meals the party leaders attempted to weave their requests or complaints skillfully into the conversation in the hope—by no means always realized—that Hitler would

26. Most notably, Hans Buchheim *et al.*, *Anatomie des SS-Staates*, 2 vols. (Freiburg i. Br., 1965); and Heinz Höhne, *Der Orden unter dem Totenkopf* (Gütersloh, 1967).

27. Karl-Dietrich Bracher, *Die nationalsozialistische Machtergreifung* (Cologne, 1965), p. 607.

28. Dietrich, *Zwölf Jahre*, pp. 153–54.

29. The custom was formalized in a circular letter from Hess (then deputy Führer) dated 11 June 1934. See National Archives, Microcopy No. T-580, roll 12, folder 169.

express an opinion that might be interpreted as a Führerbefehl.[30] The sessions were in no way akin to actual consultations or genuine discussions; even the party's leaders were informed through the public press of most of Hitler's actions and decrees.[31] Still, since Hitler for the most part resolutely refused to read ministerial memoranda,[32] and no representatives of the traditional civil service groups held regular membership in either his official or his private circle, the Führer's style of administration assured that the party's leaders had greater opportunity than the spokesmen for other societal components to achieve their personal and policy goals.

After Martin Bormann became head of the party chancellery, he attempted systematically to prevent access to Hitler by other party leaders, but even in the thirties relatively few of those invited to luncheon made regular use of their direct access to Hitler. For one thing, there were risks involved. There was always the possibility of arousing Hitler's wrath by venturing forth with an incautious remark that ran counter to the Führer's set opinions on any number of subjects. The actual item mattered little. An "incorrect" view on art or architecture could be as devastating to a career as a misjudgment on questions of constitutional reform. There was also the fear of Goebbels' sarcasm. Particularly in the early years of his rule, Hitler enjoyed the propaganda chief's company at the luncheon table.[33] The Führer appreciated Goebbels' biting attacks on his rivals, which might include other guests at the table; as a result, those derivative agents who were less skilled in the art of repartee soon learned to stay away.

Finally, the scope of policy goals of some of the Reichleiters and Gauleiters was relatively narrow. The affiliate heads for the most part

30. For descriptions of these luncheon sessions see Hanfstaengl, *Unheard Witness*, p. 229; Hossbach, *Zwischen*, p. 23; and Wiedemann, *Der Mann*, pp. 69–70.

31. Dietrich, *Zwölf Jahre*, p. 46.

32. Bernhard Lösener, "Als Rassereferent im Reichsministerium des Innern," *Vjh.f.Z.*, IX (July 1961), 280.

33. Hitler also expressed the wish that Goebbels and his family should live in the "immediate vicinity" of the Reich chancellery. See Darré, "Vermerk" (ca. April 1934), Berlin Document Center (cited hereafter as BDC)/Darré (SS). The BDC's records are grouped under individual names according to various categories, e.g., SS officer personnel records (SS), Oberstes Parteigericht (OPG), and Parteikanzlei Correspondenz (PKC). They will be cited with the provenance following in parentheses after the title of the individual in whose folder the document is located.

fought tenaciously to retain their organizational autonomy and pro-vide material and political benefits for their constituencies, but they had little interest in imposing their values on societal groups that were not organized in their particular affiliate. Moreover, the affiliates' func-tionary corps did not have fully developed vertical and horizontal or-ganizations; accordingly, the farmers' affiliate, for example, had no ef-fective offices in the large urban areas. There is one major exception to this general observation. The membership of the German Labor Front cut across traditional interest group lines and the DAF did develop a massive functionary corps. But since the head of the DAF was also the Reich organizational leader of the party's territorial cadres, the DAF's relationship to the party can be effectively included in a discussion of the cadres.

In effect, then, the term "party" in the sense of the organization typi-cal of twentieth-century totalitarian regimes must in the case of the NSDAP encompass the territorial cadres (PO) and the two major paramilitary organizations, the SA and the SS. After a bitter but sub-dued struggle, the SA in June 1934 dropped out of the ranks of sig-nificant power contestants. The SS stayed in contention until almost literally the final day of the Third Reich; but, as noted above, its story has already been sufficiently told. As a result, this study is primarily an analysis of the development and influence of what in Communist par-ties are called the cadres, and the NSDAP termed the PO. Their per-sonnel may be salaried or hold honorary positions, but in either case, they would fit what Maurice Duverger terms the "militant" element in a mass political party.[34] Their function is both to administer the party apparatus and to "partify" the society, that is, to extend the party's control over governmental administration, economic life, and public opinion through propaganda, personnel control, and administrative influence.[35]

The term "partification" is awkward, but appropriate. In totalitarian regimes words like *parti'nost* or *Parteilichkeit* have quite precisely de-

34. See Maurice Duverger, *Political Parties*, tr. Barbara and Robert North (New York, 1954), pp. 110 ff.
35. Joachim Schultz's succinct discussion of the Communist Party's role in the German Democratic Republic (*Der Funktionär in der Einheitspartei* [Stuttgart, 1956], pp. 22–23 and 30) applies to the NSDAP as well.

fined meanings; they refer to the imposition or applicability of a set of policy goals derived from the party's values or ideological base to the conduct of societal relations. The NSDAP's Weltanschauung was rudimentary in comparison to the far more developed ideologies of totalitarian parties derived from a Marxist base, but it was nonetheless revolutionary. Essentially, partification for the Nazis meant the use of advanced technology and technically competent personnel[36] to attain a completely politicized society[37] in which all human interaction was based upon the racially defined criteria of primitive Social Darwinism. The party's role was both to define the standards of behavior and to control their application.

There was no disagreement among the PO's leaders about the goals of partification, but a bitter controversy emerged over the means to accomplish these aims. All of the men involved in the struggle supported the ruthless suppression and even physical extermination of oppositional and apolitical elements in German society, and every leader worked for the material and political elevation of the cadre organization. But there remained an unbridgeable chasm in the conception of the party's relationship to the new, partified society. The key terms in the differing approaches were "control" and *"Betreuung"* (welfare, taking-care-of), and the major leaders who ranged against each other were Robert Ley with some of the Gauleiters on one side and the combination of Hess and Bormann as well as the Reich treasurer, Franz X. Schwarz, with their forces on the other.

The conflict had its roots in the origins and early history of the NSDAP. Unlike other totalitarian movements, the Nazis emerged in a sophisticated, industrialized, technologically superior societal environment. Moreover, the society at large remained intact through the years of struggle and after the party's seizure of power. Within this larger body social, the NSDAP had at first looked upon itself as a small, syn-

---

36. Ralf Dahrendorf, *Gesellschaft und Demokratie in Deutschland* (Munich, 1966), pp. 431 ff. For a comparison of the Italian situation and Mussolini, see Roland Sarti, "Fascist Modernization in Italy: Traditional or Revolutionary," *American Historical Review*, LXXV (April 1970), 1029–45. On the problem of technology as a sociopolitical force, see also Jacques Ellul, *The Technological Society* (New York, 1964); and Fest's portrait of Albert Speer in *Gesicht*, pp. 271–85.

37. Cf. Hitler's interview with the Nazi author Hanns Johst, 27 Jan. 1934, in Domarus, *Hitler*, I, 349. See also Schoenbaum, *Hitler's Social Revolution*, p. 61.

thetic social system that represented the vanguard of irrestible historical forces. As a result, the party cadres had both propagandistic and
administrative functions; the two tasks (and their personnel) were
interdependent and presupposed each other. As long as the Nazis did
not control the mechanism of the basic decision-making apparatus in
Germany, the relationship of party and society could be construed as
paralleling the classic distinction between *Gemeinschaft* (a close-knit
community, as in the case of a village) and *Gesellschaft* (a society characterized by essentially atomized relationships between individuals).

But what about now? Had not the NSDAP achieved its Kampfzeit
goal of governmental power? According to Robert Ley and his supporters, the relationship between party and society had undergone fundamental changes. After the defeat of the Nazis' political enemies, the
elimination of Jews from societal life in Germany, and so on, the synthetic party-Gemeinschaft should merge with the remaining, now politicized segments of the German social organism and form a *Volksgemeinschaft* (an entire people's community; a national village). The process
would take some time, but its organizational and thematic propellants
were clear. Under the leadership of Robert Ley as head, simultaneously,
of the territorial cadres and the DAF, the party permeated all elements
of German society (always exempting political opponents and apolitical
holdouts, of course) with education and Betreuung. The latter was
Ley's favorite word; it implied a politically motivated welfare state in
which the party "took care of" whatever needs the valuable parts of the
Volksgemeinschaft might have. "Education," of course, was another
term for propaganda. The party took on the responsibility for molding
the thought processes of the German people so that they would adapt
themselves willingly to their function in the Volksgemeinschaft. Organizationally, the most important aspect of Ley's plan was the reduction
of the elite status of the membership and cadre organization of the
NSDAP. The Reich organization leader envisioned himself as head
of a vast, multi-million-member NSDAP-DAF combination which accorded no particular elite status to the members of the party proper.
The cadres remained something of an elite, but here, too, Ley was
unwilling to draw a distinction between the functionary corps of the
PO and that of the DAF.

Hess, Bormann, Schwarz, and their allies rejected all of Ley's ideas.

Quite aside from the fact that they would have disputed the accumulation of power in Ley's hands in any event, they also rejected Ley's
concept of German society under Nazi rule. In their view, far from
becoming a Volksgemeinschaft, Germany should remain a Gesellschaft
in which the key activity of the party was control, not Betreuung. As a
result, Ley's opponents labored to create a tightly knit, centralized,
vertically taut organization, with an elite, co-opted membership and
a fanatic, but technically and administratively competent functionary
corps. In this view the territorial cadres of the NSDAP would become
a decision-making elite that dominated all other societal components—
whether affiliated with the party or not. Specifically, the elitist conception of the party precluded Ley's planned merger between the cadre
organization and the DAF.

Hitler, who alone could have decided the conflict, refused to take a
stand, or, rather, alternately and simultaneously endorsed the views of
both sides. In 1933, Adolf Hitler was a man desperate for power; he
was well aware that he was almost forty-four years old when he became
chancellor. At the beginning of that year[38] his appearance clearly reflected the setbacks of the year before.[39] His face was broader, perhaps
more spongy, and the mustache larger, less well cared for than in later
years. His hair appears to have been seldom well combed. The pictures
usually present a stern, martial-looking Hitler, whose lips seemed to
disappear when he laughed, leaving a disproportionately large mustache. Close-up photographs reveal remarkably large tear sacs under
the eyes, long fingers with closely clipped fingernails, and a pronounced
tendency toward a double chin and paunch. His preference in clothes
still ran to the semimilitary outfits of his earlier years. For his frequent
travels he wore a hip-length double-breasted leather jacket with the
leather cap common for automobile and plane travel in the 1920s. Military boots and riding pants completed the outfit. Almost constantly he
carried a riding whip in his hands. For his public appearances he wore
either the party's brown shirt or an ill-fitting dark suit, a shirt with a

38. The following composite description is drawn from the photographs of Hitler
published in *IB* between 29 October 1932, and February 1933. Significantly, the
IB contained no pictures of Hitler in the issues of 26 November, 3 December, and
10 December 1932.

39. For an analysis of Hitler's trials and triumphs in 1932 see Orlow, *Nazi Party*,
chaps. 6 and 7.

soft, rolled collar, and a dark tie. The changes in appearance after his appointment as chancellor are remarkable. A photo taken shortly after the Nazi seizure of power shows a smiling, confident, almost transcendental Hitler with springy step, wearing a soft overcoat of obviously good quality material and tailoring.[40]

Having attained power, Hitler was determined not to endanger it with far-reaching social experiments. Instead, for most of his twelve-year rule, he insisted that the NSDAP was to be simultaneously a mass-membership organization with primary emphasis on propagandistic and welfare functions and a corps of elitist cadres executing control tasks. That the two facets of party activity were incompatible was of little concern to Hitler; as in the Kampfzeit, his decisions or nondecisions were not governed by considerations of practicality but derived from his overwhelming desire to maintain for himself a position of undisputed personal power in the NSDAP and, later, in the German Reich.

Adolf Hitler's inauguration as chancellor on January 30, 1933, began a unique and, as it eventually turned out, frightful era. For the first time in the history of modern times a totalitarian party had come to power in an advanced, highly industrialized society. A group of personal failures, animated by a desire to destroy liberalism and pluralism in Germany, and grouped around a fanatical, charismatic, unstable leader, took over the reins of one of the most sophisticated governmental structures in Europe. This was the culmination of fifteen years of political struggle for the NSDAP, but also the beginning of the greatest test of its viability: what would be the consequences for both the party and Germany of the interaction of a technologically advanced society with a political grouping that saw societal relations mainly in terms of personal power, racial hatred, and intraparty warfare?

40. Title page of *IB*, 11 Feb. 1933.

"Now It's Our Turn" *

Adolf Hitler became Reich chancellor at noon on January 30; that same evening the NSDAP celebrated the triumph of its Führer with noisy torchlight parades in Berlin and other cities throughout Germany. To a casual observer these victory demonstrations were visible manifestations of the party's self-image: martial, disciplined, enthusiastic, loyal, and numerous. In fact, only the last two adjectives described characteristics of the Nazi Party at the beginning of January. The NSDAP did have the largest membership[1] among German political parties, and there was no doubt about its fanatical devotion to the person of Adolf Hitler. Yet that overriding emotion also marked the limits of cohesion and internal discipline among members and leaders in the party.

At the beginning of 1933, the NSDAP was a highly amorphous political organism whose large membership could not hide either the massive internal discords among its leadership corps or a number of clearly apparent disintegrative tendencies among the membership. The NSDAP was in fact a series of separate territorial organizations and socioeconomic interest groups, united—for the moment—in their loyalty to the

* "Now it's our turn" is part of a statement made by the deputy Gauleiter of Hamburg, Harry Henningsen, during the Nazi take-over of the city's government in early March 1933. Quoted in Henning Timpke, ed., *Dokumente zur Gleichschaltung des Landes Hamburg* (Frankfurt, 1964), p. 41.

1. The NSDAP's actual membership at this time was 849,000, though the cards given out in January were numbered as high as 1.2 million. The discrepancy resulted from the party's custom of continuing to number cards in strict numerical order. The numbers assigned to members who had died or resigned from the party were left blank, sometimes to be assigned to a prominent latecomer (e.g., Hermann Göring's wife in 1937). See Hans Buchheim, "Mitgliedschaft bei der NSDAP," in *Gutachten des Instituts für Zeitgeschichte*, ed. Paul Kluke (Munich, 1958), p. 316.

party's leader. In contrast to other modern mass parties, the NSDAP had not assigned a position of clear superiority to the political cadres over the socioeconomic interest affiliates. In addition, its political cadres were never dominated by the type of disciplined, declassed, and bureaucratized administrator who was, for example, characteristic in Communist parties.[2] Instead, the overwhelming number of the party's administrators still remained attached—though often in perverted form —to their lower-middle-class origins and values. The story of the keeper of a Hamburg notion shop who overnight became borough president[3] is typical of hundreds of cadre administrators. For many the sudden change of fortune in their lives proved unsettling. There was considerable truth in Goebbels' bitter statement about his party comrades: "In the good days [that is, after 1933] many of the old fighters[4] and their wives played popular leader and mother of the country, but now [in 1945] they wish they were back in their cheese shops or plumbing establishments."[5]

The "old fighters" supplied the largest contingent of administrators within the political and territorial cadres of the NSDAP. As a result, Hitler's appointment as chancellor brought to the front ranks of the decision-making machinery in a highly industrialized and sophisticated society a group of alienated political fanatics with few technical or administrative skills. A psychological group portrait of the old comrades reveals a rather unpleasant picture of Germany's new elite. Almost consistently, accounts of the period (by both ex-Nazis and their opponents) use words like "primitive, immature, lack of substance"[6] to characterize the *alte Kämpfer* (old fighters). Typical of an excessive

2. Timpke, *Dokumente*, p. 284.

3. See the de-Nazification prodeedings of Amandus Brandt, district leader of Harvestehude (Gau Hamburg) in Forschungsstelle für die Geschichte des Nationalsozialismus in Hamburg (cited hereafter as Forsch. Hbg.) /PA/12/B. For a similar but less extreme case see the descriptions in William S. Allen, *The Nazi Seizure of Power* (Chicago, 1965).

4. "Old fighters" (*alte Kämpfer*) was a generic term applied to all members of the NSDAP who had joined the party before 30 January 1933. It will be used in this sense throughout the study.

5. Wilfred von Oven, *Mit Goebbels bis zum Ende*, 2d ed. (Buenos Aires, 1949), II, entry for 26 March 1945, p. 284.

6. *Ibid.*, II, entry for 16 April 1945, p. 299; Albert Speer, *Erinnerungen* (Berlin, 1969), p. 39; and Herbert Schwarzwälder, *Die Machtergreifung in Bremen* (Bremen, 1966), p. 31.

concern with externals was the statement of the district leader of
Eisenach (Gau Thuringia) to a friend that surely he would wish to
remain political leader (*Politischer Leiter*, PL)[7] rather than become
city councilor because the PL's uniform was bound to be the "most
handsome."[8] Coupled with the need to possess visible proof of re-
spectability was an easily bruised sense of dignity (the cases of "vio-
lated honor" handled by the party courts ran into the thousands) and a
desire to be both loved and feared. Cases of extreme emotional ego-
centricity were widespread among the cadre administrators. Ironically,
many Nazi leaders could readily diagnose the faults of their comrades.
The Nazi Gauleiter of Hessen-Nassau-Nord, Karl Weinrich, described
the later notorious president of the People's Court, Roland Freisler, as
"unsuited for any position of authority, since . . . he is too subject to
sudden shifts of mood."[9] Goebbels, undoubtedly one of the most intelligent of the Nazi leaders, was equally caustic about his peers, yet
he published an account of the *Machtergreifung* (seizure of power)
which was itself an excellent example of boundless vanity.[10] Other
Nazi leaders, with less literary talent, took to cruder methods of self-
glorification (known in party circles as *Selbstbeweihräucherung*, literally "sprinkling incense on oneself"), and attempts by the *Reichsleitung*
(the party's Reich leadership) to curtail such practices met with little
success.[11]

7. The term *political leader* is unsatisfactory but unavoidable. It designated those
cadre administrators who held positions in either the territorial administrations or
the Reichsleitung of the party proper, as distinguished from those who worked for
the affiliates or the paramilitary groups.

8. Hermann Köhler to . . . , 17 April 1939, in University of Michigan German
Archival Collection (cited hereafter as MiU/GAC), folder 12.

9. Weinrich to RL, 16 April 1927, Berlin Document Center (cited hereafter as
BDC)/Freisler (PKC).

10. The book was *Vom Kaiserhof zur Reichskanzlei*, 12th ed. (Munich, 1936).
Alfred Rosenberg gleefully recorded critical comments about the work in *Das po-
litische Tagebuch Alfred Rosenbergs 1934/35 und 1939/40*, ed. Hans-Günther
Seraphim (Munich, 1964), entry for 7 July 1934, p. 48.

11. In late July 1934 the deputy Führer (on this office see below, p. 70) "for the
last time" prohibited the various types of commanded adulation among the Nazi
leaders. See StdF, "Verfügung," 22 July 1934, National Archives, Microcopy No. T-
(cited hereafter as T-) 580, roll 12, folder 169. The originals of this collection of
orders, directives, and circulars issued by the office of the StdF are now in the
Bundesarchiv (cited hereafter as BA)/NS 8/200 ff. See also Ernst van Meergaard to

The pseudoromantic and protoreligious traits of the average PL were equally important aspects of the PL corps' group psychology. Despite their numerous bitter intraparty rivalries, the NSDAP's cadres in the last analysis did think of themselves as a community of comrades[12] which was committed to a revolutionary restructuring of German values.[13] The activists of the NSDAP never lost the feeling that they were a band of the righteous surrounded by hosts of enemies, past and present. The fact that most of these enemies adopted the protective coloring of fellow travelers only angered and frustrated the cadres. This in turn explains the enthusiasm with which the old comrades participated in the purely destructive actions for which they were "unleashed" from time to time;[14] above all, these were explosions of stored-up anger. For, in essence, the "men of the first hour" knew that without the despised fellow travelers, the NSDAP could neither have come to nor have remained in power. At the beginning of 1933 the Nazi Party had many followers in the technical and administrative occupation groups of Germany,[15] but its own cadres were not only disorganized but disheartened[16] in the aftermath of the crisis that was precipitated by the resignation of Gregor Strasser in early December of 1932 as Reich organizational leader because of his intense disagreement with Hitler's guidance of the NSDAP.[17] In their fury against Strasser, Hitler and his chief

Hitler, 28 March 1933, quoted in Erich Matthias and Rudolf Morsey, eds., *Das Ende der Parteien 1933* (Düsseldorf, 1960), pp. 640–41.

12. Cf. Alfred Rosenberg, *Letzte Aufzeichnungen* (Göttingen, 1955), p. 160.

13. See the excellent overall analysis in Manfred Messerschmidt, *Die Wehrmacht im NS-Staat* (Hamburg, 1969), pp. 1–17.

14. As for example in the anti-Semitic boycott of April 1933. See Helmut Genschel, *Die Verdrängung der Juden aus der Wirtschaft im Dritten Reich* (Göttingen, 1966), p. 72.

15. Hans-Gerd Schumann, *Nationalsozialismus und Gewerkschaftsbewegung* (Hanover, 1958), p. 57; and Karl-Dietrich Bracher *et al.*, *Die nationalsozialistische Machtergreifung* (Cologne, 1965), p. 477.

16. See "Halbmonatsberichte des Regierungspräsidiums von Oberbayern" (cited hereafter as HMB/OBB), 20 Feb. 1933, p. 1, Bayerisches Geheimes Staatsarchiv (cited hereafter as BGStA), MA 106672; and Allen, *Seizure*, p. 168.

17. For an analysis of the NSDAP after Strasser's resignation, see Dietrich Orlow, *The History of the Nazi Party, 1919–1933* (Pittsburgh, 1969), pp. 291–98; Bracher, *Machtergreifung*, p. 31; Hans Mommsen, *Beamtentum im Dritten Reich* (Stuttgart, 1966), p. 31; Peter Diehl-Thiele, *Partei und Staat im Dritten Reich* (Munich, 1969), pp. 205 ff.; and Robert Ley's foreword to *Reichsorganisationsleiter, Organisationsbuch der NSDAP*, 2d. ed. (Munich, 1936), p. xxiii.

lieutenants in the cadre administration, Robert Ley and Rudolf Hess,[18] showed far more enthusiasm for destroying the old than for developing a new programmatic or organizational synthesis. Ley blindly attacked the fairly effective proto-union affiliate of the party, the National Socialist Organization of Factory Cells (*Nationalsozialistische Betriebszellenorganisation*, NSBO), although, he remembered later, the party had nothing to put in its place.[19] Hess's office conducted a quiet but effective purge of those among Strasser's personal friends who had not deserted him quickly enough at the moment of his resignation.[20] What remained was a paradox: Hitler had destroyed the party's only genuine organizational base for systematically saturating German society with Nazi cadre personnel,[21] but many of Strasser's associates continued to hold important cadre positions and his ideas still permeated the party's political and propagandistic activities.[22]

In late January, then, the NSDAP was in no way prepared to assume the responsibility for governing German society. Hitler had just barely managed to prevent the virtual disintegration of the party; only the hunger for power and jobs[23] as well as a vastly overrated image of its own ability to deal with the technical problems of power[24] kept the party's cadres from losing heart altogether.

The blindness of the German conservatives saved the NSDAP from

18. For their division of Strasser's empire in Dec. 1932 see Orlow, *Nazi Party*, pp. 294–96, and below, pp. 72 ff.

19. Robert Ley, "Rechenschaftsbericht des . . . Dr. Ley auf der 5. Jahrestagung der Deutschen Arbeitsfront zu Nürnberg vom 11. September 1937," in Paul Meier-Benneckenstein, ed., *Dokumente der deutschen Politik*, (Berlin, 1938), V, 366–68.

20. See the documents relating to two business associates of Strasser's in the Hauptarchiv Berlin (cited hereafter as HAB)/320/35 and HAB/77/6.

21. Rather ruefully, some Nazi leaders came to this realization in the dying days of the Third Reich. See Heinrich Walkenhorst (of the staff of the PK), "Reichsliste," 10 March 1945, T-580, roll 80, folder 371.

22. Cf. the program for the Gau congress in Kassel, January 1933, *Völkischer Beobachter* (cited hereafter as *VB*), 4 Feb. 1933 with Strasser's organizational scheme, in Orlow, *Nazi Party*, pp. 258 ff.

23. See the documents in HAB/77/32; Timpke, *Dokumente*, p. 41; and Allen, *Seizure*, p. 168.

24. Ley described the party in these terms: "[the NSDAP] is an action-community [*Tatgemeinschaft*] formed to attain certain precisely defined goals whose exact parameters are known." ROL, Dienstvorschrift der PO [mimeographed draft, July 1933] ([Munich, 1933]), pp. 6–7. A copy of this important document is in the

taking the road to political impotence, and suddenly, at the end of January, lack of confidence was no longer a problem for the party. Rather, the NSDAP experienced a state of euphoria that has been aptly compared to the outbreak of World War I.[25] Although Hitler's cabinet included only two Nazi ministers (Wilhelm Frick and Hermann Göring) in addition to the chancellor, the Nazis interpreted the change in administration as a mandate to destroy the Weimar Republic; for the moment they gave little thought to what was to come in its stead.[26] Having returned home from the torchlight parade, tired and hoarse but marvelously elated, the average PL concretized "success" or "power" essentially as follows: he wanted his judicial innocence back[27] (that is, any previous "political" crimes were to be eliminated from the police records), he expected tangible economic benefits (ranging from a job to tax breaks and the reconstruction of the medieval guild system),[28] and he wanted to see the swift elimination of all those institutions and officials that, in his view, had caused Germany's and his own political and socioeconomic failure.[29] In short, the immediate aims of the typical PL were simplistic, egoistic, negative, and punitive.

For the moment, the NSDAP seemed to encounter no difficulties in its establishment of the Nazi dictatorship. The elimination of political opposition groups and the placing of Nazi controls over all aspects of German government and society succeeded so readily because there

---

Centre Documentation Juive Contemporaine/ XLV-514. See also Goebbels, *Kaiserhof*, entry for 6 April 1933, p. 294; and David Schoenbaum, *Hitler's Social Revolution* (New York, 1966), pp. xxi–xxii.

25. Max Domarus, ed., *Hitler Reden und Proklamationen, 1932–1945* (Munich, 1965), I, 283.

26. Goebbels, *Kaiserhof*, entry for 11 Feb. 1933, p. 261.

27. See Göring to police president of Berlin, 17 Feb. 1933 in BDC/Daluege, Kurt (SS); and Hermann Weinkauff *et al.*, *Die Deutsche Justiz und der Nationalsozialismus* (Stuttgart, 1968), pp. 96, 113–15, and 128–29.

28. HMB/OBB, 4 March 1933, BGStA, MA 106670; Allen, *Seizure*, pp. 155–56; and Raimund Rämisch, "Der berufsständische Gedanke als Episode in der Nationalsozialistischen Politik," *Zeitschrift für Politik*, IV, no. 3 (1957), 265–66.

29. Mommsen, *Beamtentum*, p. 46; and Curt Rothenberger, "Sechzehn Monate Berlin" (MS, 4 April 1944), p. A1 [*sic*], Forsch. Hbg./PA/Rothenberger. Rothenberger served as senator for justice in Hamburg after January 1933 and later (1942) as state secretary in the Reich ministry of justice.

was no organized opposition, and even very little unorganized grumbling. It is of course true that the Nazis attempted to hide their destructive aims,[30] but very few groups or individuals even bothered to point out that such aims existed. Prominent Weimar politicians either had already made common cause with the Nazis or did not hesitate to ask the new bosses for favors soon after Hitler's appointment.[31] Whole occupational and professional categories hastened to pin the swastika badge on their lapels. On January 1, only one of the professional judges in the city-state of Hamburg had been a member of the party; five months later more than half (out of some seventy) paid their dues as comrades.[32] Under these circumstances the NSDAP toppled the old Weimar coalition governments in state after state: by mid-February, eight of the *Länder* (federal states) had Nazi administrations, and the rest followed in March.

While the ease of the take-over was in one sense gratifying to the party cadres, the sudden increase of party members among the professional and civil service groups provided something of a stumbling block to many a PL who had hoped to slip into a secure government position on the basis of his party record.[33] To be sure, for the upper echelons of the party leadership there were sufficient jobs to go around. Hermann Göring, the newly appointed prime minister of Prussia, "laid low one provincial governor after the other,"[34] and the Gauleiters took over the

30. See Frick's support of federalism in *VB*, 2 Feb. 1933.

31. The former mayor of Duisburg, Karl Jarres, asked the GL of Westfalen, Terboven, for an appointment as curator of the University of Bonn. See Terboven to Grauert, 10 July 1933, HAB/77/3.

32. Curt Rothenberger, "Im Kampf ums Recht" (MS., 1944–45), p. B1 [*sic*], Forsch. Hbg./PA/Rothenberger; and Werner Johe, *Die gleichgeschaltete Justiz* (Frankfurt, 1967), p. 71.

33. The Nazi *Gleichschaltung* did not lead to a genuine personnel revolution of the Reich and state-level government bureaus. Except for Goebbels' new ministry of propaganda and public enlightenment, the Reich ministries did not fill their ranks with the eager "old fighters." The enthusiasm of the old ruling classes for the Nazi-led "rejuvenation of the nation" created a sufficiently large pool of technically able civil servants which severely reduced the need for the untrained political administrators of the party. Even the Nazi Reich and Prussian minister of the interior, Wilhelm Frick, avoided wholesale appointments of party-book candidates. See Bracher, *Machtergreifung*, pp. 504 and 507–08; Mommsen, *Beamtentum*, p. 27; and Goebbels, *Kaiserhof*, entries for 5 and 9 Feb. 1933, pp. 258–59.

34. Goebbels, *Kaiserhof*, entry for 15 Feb. and 3 March 1933, pp. 262 and 273.

vacant positions. In the other Länder parallel developments took place. The pace of the purges accelerated after the Reichstag fire,[35] but these high-level appointments were of no real concern to the lower cadre personnel, gratified though they might have been that their Gauleiter was now also *Oberpräsident* (head of a state or provincial administration). For the lower personnel, the quickest way to power and position lay in the institution of the *Kommissare* (commissioners) and *Sonderbeauftragte* (special appointees). This type of public official was not a Nazi invention (Franz von Papen had been *Reichskommissar* in Prussia since July 1932), but under the Nazis the system did reach unprecedented proportions. Technically, the commissioners were only interim appointees at various levels of the governmental administration; they were in charge of an office in the interval between the dismissal of its Weimar incumbent and the appointment of a new permanent official. In practice, most commissioners saw the institution as an opportunity to purge the old civil servants and to secure permanent government positions for themselves and their party friends. Hundreds of party functionaries, most of them virtually unqualified for their new positions, suddenly emerged as heads of government offices with far-reaching powers over personnel and administrative decisions.[36]

As was to be expected, the party's Reich and Gau offices soon lost virtually all control over the new commissioners. Especially at the local level, their power to organize terror actions was almost unlimited. Many of the appointees were SA leaders who simply tended to ignore the authority of the Gauleiters.[37] In Bavaria the SA virtually excluded

35. *Ibid.*, entry for 27 Feb. 1933, p. 270. For the controversy surrounding the fire itself, see Fritz Tobias, *Der Reichstagsbrand* (Rastatt, 1962); and the review articles by Martin Broszat, "Zum Streit um den Reichstagsbrand," and Hans Mommsen, "Der Reichstagsbrand und seine politischen Folgen," in *Vierteljahrshefte für Zeitgeschichte* (cited hereafter as *Vjh.f.Z*), VIII (July 1960), and XII (Oct. 1964) 275–79 and 351–413, respectively. For the latest exchange see the letters to the editor by Henri Lichtenstein, Michael Mansfeld, and Hermann Rauschning, in the *Spiegel*, 17 Nov. 1969.

36. Only the highest level positions in the Reich and Länder ministries were generally filled with qualified though politically far-right civil servants. For a full discussion of the various types of commissioners see Bracher, *Machtergreifung*, pp. 461–63.

37. *Ibid.*, p. 462; and Karl Wahl, *Es ist das deutsche Herz* (Augsburg, 1954), p. 87.

the PLs in the appointment of commissioners, and the appointees were specifically instructed to accept orders only from state and SA authorities, not from the political leaders.[38]

In general, the commissioners' activities in the first weeks after the Machtergreifung brought Germany to the brink of chaos. The commissioners in the counties and municipalities tended to ignore all directives, with little regard to their origin in state or party offices.[39] In areas where the Gauleiter's position was firmly established (this was especially true of the smaller Länder and some of the Prussian provinces), the Gauleiter retained control of the situation, but in the larger states the provincial leaders were often mere figureheads. They were particularly resentful because most of the coveted municipal police chief posts went to retired military personnel, many of whom held SA rank and had little sympathy for the NSDAP's political cadres.[40] Attempts to centralize the appointment of commissioners within the party met with little success. On February 17, Ley established a special office of political appointments within the office of the Reich organization leader (ROL) to serve as a clearing-house for all requests for personnel purges originating from party offices in Prussia. The new office was headed by a Gauleiter, Wilhelm Kube of Ostmark-Brandenburg. In practice, however, Kube was unable to assert his authority; local party groups continued to approach Göring directly, leaving the Gauleiter frustrated and helpless.[41]

For the moment, the commissioners at the local level remained virtually undisturbed as they proceeded to put a Nazi social revolution into effect. The NSDAP and its economic and social affiliates were not content to dismiss a few mayors and city councilors; they sought also to

38. See Röhm's "Befehl," 1 April 1933, BGStA, MA 105255. See also *VB*, 14 Feb. 1933. The PLs did not in fact go completely empty-handed since the GL of Munich–Upper Bavaria, Adolf Wagner, was appointed Bavarian minister of interior. The best secondary account of the Nazi seizure in Bavaria is Edward N. Peterson, *The Limits of Hitler's Power* (Princeton, N.J., 1969), pp. 157 ff.

39. See "Halbmonatsberichte des Regierungspräsidiums von Niederbayern-Oberfranken (cited hereafter as HMB/NBO), 20 April 1933, BGStA, MA 106672.

40. An unsigned memo in Grauert's file (HAB/77/1) dating from this period specifically noted that one of the tasks of the SA-affiliated police officials was to prevent excesses by the NSDAP's political cadres. A list of new police chiefs appointed in the first six months of 1933 is in Kluke, *Gutachten*, pp. 307–08.

41. *VB*, 17 Feb. 1933; and the documents in HAB/77/32.

restructure German economic life and subject it to the control of the party.[42] Many of the PLs had become active in the NSDAP precisely because it promised relief from the pressure of an industrialized and impersonal system of economics. Gregor Strasser, while he was in office, had been the most vocal exponent of the party's anti-industrial stand. He advocated a return to a pseudomedieval system of guild-dominated economics. After his resignation, the leadership of the anticapitalist wing of the party was passed to Otto Wagener, a somewhat enigmatic individual who sank to oblivion rapidly after 1933. Before the Nazis came to power, however, Wagener was by no means an unknown official in the inner circles of the NSDAP. Born in 1888, he had served as interim SA chief of staff from 1930 to 1932 (between Franz von Pfeffer and Ernst Röhm) and at the time of the Machtergreifung was described as one of Hitler's "closest associates."[43] Wagener never developed an economic theory of his own, but simply combined the totalitarian power aspirations of the NSDAP with Othmar Spann's ideas of a revitalized *Ständestaat* (a society governed by representatives of the various occupational groups) based on small retailers and business firms.[44] In practice, this meant that Wagener and the men around him wanted to place German economic life within the organizational framework of the Nazi Party, so that economic interaction would be reduced to a branch of intraparty affairs.[45] Organizations and enterprises which either refused or opposed this dictum and those which the party regarded as "unsocial" would be destroyed.[46]

Wagener's (and Strasser's) ideas were not uncontroversial even in

42. The best account of the struggle over economic orientation after 1933 is Arthur Schweitzer, *Big Business in the Third Reich* (Bloomington, Ind., 1964). See also Ingeborg Esenwein-Rothe, *Die Wirtschaftsverbände von 1933 bis 1945* (Berlin, 1965).

43. See the caption under a group photograph of Hitler's entourage in the *Illustrierter Beobachter* (cited hereafter as *IB*), 11 Feb. 1933.

44. See Rämisch, "Berufsständische," pp. 265 ff.

45. In April, for example, Wagener began to force all German employers to take out party membership. See Bruweiler (of the Union of German Employer's Associations) to membership, 27 April 1933, HAB/77/13.

46. The practical definition of "unsocial" became apparent in the spring of 1933 when the party organizations of Thuringia and Baden began the systematic destruction of consumers' cooperatives. See Schoenbaum, *Hitler's Social Revolution*, p. 137.

the NSDAP. In the summer of 1932, Hitler had permitted Wilhelm Keppler[47] to establish an industry-oriented "Circle of Business Friends," which rapidly became a rallying ground for the party's fellow travelers among big business circles. (The group eventually developed close connections with Himmler and the SS.) Keppler's group rejected Wagener and all he stood for. "Wagener," wrote one of them, "has no knowledge whatever of economics, let alone of how to manage an economic recovery."[48]

In the first weeks of victory, however, Wagener and the Ständestaat kept the upper hand. With the enthusiastic support of the party's middle-class and lower-middle-class economic affiliates (to whose membership the NSDAP owed a great deal of its pre-1933 political influence), Wagener set out to partify the German economy. The national "office of estate development" (*Amt für Ständischen Aufbau*), aided by the active and often riotous support of such organizations as the *NS-Handels- und Gewerbeorganisation* (National Socialist Retailers' Association, NS-Hago) and the *Kampfbund für den gewerblichen Mittelstand* (Militant Association of Commercial Small Businesses, Kampfbund), attempted to establish its control organs as integral parts of the party's administrative offices in each Gau. The assault failed, revealing in its wake a major reason for the political impotence of the NSDAP in the latter half of the year. Although the party's economic associations enthusiastically tackled the problem of "controlling" economic life (that is, eliminating unwanted competitors) in the towns and cities,[49] they never showed any great interest in coordinating their resentments into overall national or even regional plans. Instead, the economic affiliates, utilizing the virtually unlimited power of the commissioners, succeeded in disrupting and unsettling day-to-day economic life to such an extent that Hitler began to fear for law and order and the beginnings of his rearmament program. The PL corps was either un-

47. On Keppler see "Cross-Examination of Keppler . . . 18 Aug. 1947," in United States military government in Germany, *Trial of War Criminals Before Nuremberg Military Tribunals: Case 5: U.S. vs. Flick* (Washington, 1952), VII, 289; and Orlow, *Nazi Party*, p. 240.

48. Kiehn (a business friend of Strasser's and Frick's) to Frick, 15 May 1933, HAB/320/35.

49. See below, pp. 41–42.

willing or unable to control the outbursts of the economic affiliates; indeed only a handful of the Gauleiters seemed to recognize the political power potential of the affiliates' activities.

One of those who did attempt systematically to put Strasser's and Wagener's ideas into practice was the Gauleiter of Silesia, Helmuth Brückner, and his eventual failure may serve to illustrate the potential significance which subjecting Germany's economy to the direct control of the NSDAP would have had for the future development of the Nazi dictatorship. Brückner had always been an avowed exponent of the party's left wing, and with Hitler's appointment as chancellor he saw an opportunity to subject the future economic development of Silesia to the immediate dictates of the NSDAP's Gau office.[50] The administrative device was simple: Brückner merely insisted that the Gau economic advisor (*Gauwirtschaftsberater*) run the affairs of the Silesian chamber of commerce, an ostensibly private organization whose membership included all major business and industrial firms in the province. The Gauleiter was willing to tolerate a figurehead president, but his sole function was to carry out the orders of the Gau economic advisor. Brückner was clearly not content with the mere *Gleichschaltung*[51] of the Silesian chamber of commerce—since the president was already a party member, this had in fact been accomplished—but desired the thoroughgoing partification of all Silesian economic life, that is, the actual administration of societal institutions by offices of the party cadre system, rather than by officials who as individuals were party members. Since the Silesian business interests also realized the importance of the distinction, a bitter feud developed between Brückner and the president of the chamber of commerce. The latter objected vigorously to the Gauleiter's plans for the party's take-over of his organization. Brückner, in turn, had the president expelled from the party for opposing his Gau-

50. The documentation for the following is in HAB/77/13.
51. Literally, "to switch equal." The term comes from the field of physics and originally denoted the coordination of different types of electrical current. The Nazis used the term in the sense of political coordination of various groups and institutions. In practice it meant that an economic, social, or professional organization accepted a Nazi party member as president and adopted the "leadership principle" as the basis of its internal administration. See Cornelia Berning, *Vom "Abstammungsnachweis" zum "Zuchtwart"* (Berlin, 1964), p. 95.

leiter's wishes. The final outcome was a defeat for the Gauleiter, but only because Brückner, for a variety of related and unrelated reasons, was dismissed as Gauleiter at the end of 1934.[52]

Silesia was, however, an exceptional case. Most of the other Gauleiters made no real effort to centralize the control of economic affairs in their Gau offices. Rather, they allowed the economic affiliates a virtually free hand to organize petty and vindictive terror campaigns which in their overall effect brought discredit both to the party's militant economic groups and to the person of Wagener himself. Instead of realizing his ambitions of remaining either Reich economic commissioner (he held that office only two months, from April to June 1933) or becoming minister of economics, he rapidly vanished from the political scene.[53] Wagener's dismissal as Reich economic commissioner coincided with Hitler's prohibition of further local activities by the middle-class economic groups.

It was indicative of the PLs' declining influence in the Third Reich that Hitler authorized not the party cadres but governmental offices to enforce the new prohibition on local actions.[54] That the Nazi revolution was not proceeding according to the wishes of the cadres was actually apparent as early as the end of February. The young Third Reich developed a marked tendency to let the new *gleichgeschaltete* (put under Nazi control) state organs handle substantive questions, while the PL cadres found themselves forced into the background, away from the real decision-making power.[55] Nevertheless, at this time the PLs had not lost hope. The party cadres expected a new forward thrust from the scheduled March elections. After all, the NSDAP was still only the senior partner in a Nazi-Nationalist coalition government, and, as Goeb-

52. The case was carried through the party courts, and the OPG in effect ruled in November 1934 that Brückner had overstepped his authority (Brückner was dismissed as GL in December).

53. He later started—and failed at—a number of business ventures and attempted to receive compensation from the NSDAP for his "sacrifices" to the party. This too was denied. The relevant documents on the demise of the office for estate development are in T-580, roll 310, folder 123; Wagener's own misfortunes are detailed in IfZ/FA 143.

54. Schoenbaum, *Hitler's Social Revolution*, p. 81; and Bracher, *Machtergreifung*, p. 190.

55. This becomes very clear when one leafs through the issues of the *VB* for February 1933.

bels said, an overwhelming Nazi victory in the March elections might well give the party a monopoly of power.[56] The Nazi Prussian minister of justice, Hans Kerrl, had only expressed in a public campaign speech what most PLs thought in private: the March election would be the last campaign.[57]

This explains in large part the extraordinary amount of energy which the NSDAP threw into the propagandistic and technical preparations for the campaign. At the beginning of February, Goebbels, as national campaign manager, discussed technical details at a meeting of the Gauleiters in Berlin. Hitler, speaking at the same conference, set the tone of the party's efforts by emphasizing the "brutality (*Härte*) with which we will expand our victory."[58] By the middle of the month regional managers, usually the various Gauleiters, had been appointed. These in turn mobilized their cadres in huge Gau congresses (in Munich 1500 PLs assembled)[59] from which the party's activists fanned out to blanket Germany with mass meetings, posters, and rallies. In contrast to the experience of November 1932, the NSDAP now had neither financial nor organizational problems. The national media were at its disposal, no community closed its halls to party meetings, campaign contributions flowed freely.[60] The catalogue of ideal conditions even included police forces who smiled benignly on the excesses of SA and SS terror squads.

Although the entire party apparatus participated vigorously in the election campaign, the economic affiliates outdid themselves in zeal and energy. Since Hitler, in his keynote address at the beginning of February, had all but encouraged their hopes for a revolutionary leap forward after the election, the NS-Hago and the Kampfbund performed almost superhuman feats of activism to bring out the vote of their members and sympathizers. In Düsseldorf alone the economic affiliates staged thirty-five mass meetings (almost one a day) during the brief cam-

---

56. Goebbels, *Kaiserhof*, entry for 4 March 1933, p. 273. See also Schwarzwälder, *Machtergreifung in Bremen*, p. 51.

57. *VB*, 7 Feb. 1933. See also Goebbels, *Kaiserhof*, entries for 31 Jan. and 5 March 1933, pp. 254 and 275.

58. Goebbels, *Kaiserhof*, entry for 2 Feb. 1933, p. 256. On the meeting see also *VB*, 2–4 Feb. 1933.

59. *VB*, 15 Feb. 1933.

60. Goebbels, *Kaiserhof*, 3 Feb. 1933, p. 256. See also Allen, *Seizure*, pp. 151–52.

paign, and there as elsewhere the election results reflected their influence and enthusiasm.[61]

Actually, Hitler, as was his frequent custom, had spoken with a forked tongue. While his words were radical for intraparty consumption,[62] the publicly presented candidate lists of the party emphasized the respectable, "right wing" of the NSDAP. The Reich list contained forty-one names, headed by Hitler, Frick, and Göring, of whom at least the last two represented in the public mind "state" rather than "party." Goebbels was listed in fourth place, but Hess did not appear until the ninth spot, and Wagener occupied number thirty-seven.[63] The list for the Prussian *Landtag* (state legislature) revealed a similar makeup, although the presence in seventh place of the ex-Kaiser's son, Prince August Wilhelm (who was also an SA leader), seemingly served to demonstrate the party's support of monarchist leanings.[64]

The results of the election and the parliamentary maneuverings that legally yielded dictatorial power into Hitler's hands seemed to confirm Goebbels' initial jubilant reaction: "There are no difficulties anywhere; what seemed impossible yesterday, solves itself of its own accord today."[65] Since there were no longer any constitutional obstacles to the Nazi revolution, the work of the NSDAP could run its course. "We [the Nazi Party] must get every available position of power into our hands," so that "the National Socialist movement [will] become the state" was the succinct description of the new goals given by Adolf Wagner, the Gauleiter of Munich.[66] A major, and psychologically gratifying, part of the intended transformation was the continuing purge of civil service personnel in government offices. PL cadres at all levels pursued these activities with renewed vigor. In part, they still carried out their anger

61. Hans-Peter Görgen, "Düsseldorf und der Nationalsozialismus" (Dissertation, Cologne, 1968), p. 35; and Schwarzwälder, *Machtergreifung in Bremen*, p. 67. For a detailed analysis of the election results see Bracher, *Machtergreifung*, pp. 95–133.

62. The portion of his 2 Feb. 1933 speech quoted above was not contained in the official account of the address.

63. *VB*, 24 Feb. 1933. For a list of those elected on the Reich list, see *ibid.*, 21 March 1933.

64. *VB*, 2 March 1933.

65. Goebbels, *Kaiserhof*, entry for 6 March 1933, p. 276.

66. Adolf Wagner (GL of Munich-Upper Bavaria), "Staat und Partei," 24 April 1933, p. 1, BGStA, MA 105475.

against erstwhile political opponents or gave vent to their primitive anti-Semitic feelings,[67] but the postelection phase of the purges had far broader overtones as well. It was as though, before the election, the NSDAP cadres could not quite believe that permanent and absolute power was theirs, but after March 5, they realized the full extent of their victory. The PLs began not only to dismiss individual civil servants, but to treat with contempt the entire system of government based upon extrapersonal law. "It is ridiculous," wrote Wilhelm Kube, "that we, the actual victors of the National Socialist revolution, should have to follow the directives of bureaucrats!"[68] In addition, the purge now included in particular erstwhile fellow travelers from the Nationalist Party whenever the PL felt that such officials lacked ruthlessness or the ability to close both eyes as the party's revolution marched forward.

In spite of the increased vigor with which the party conducted the second phase of the personnel purge, it was no more centralized or systematic than the preelection efforts. On the contrary, the political cadres of the party's Reichsleitung played no major role in the second act of the Machtergreifung; for the Reich governmental agencies the turnovers were administered almost entirely by the Reich ministry of the interior, acting under the auspices of the "Law on a Professional Civil Service."[69] Hitler was not as yet willing to revise his directives of December, and consequently at this time the NSDAP still had a very weak central executive structure. Instead, he encouraged the regional cadres to initiate "spontaneous" actions and complaints, which then enabled the national *government* organs of the Reich to eliminate the remaining obstacles to Nazi power in the name of law and order.[70]

As a result, after March 5 the two most important party officials were the Gauleiters and the *Kreisleiters.* (The German *Kreis,* or *Bezirk—* district—is comparable to a county in the United States.) In their ca-

67. The documentation for numerous cases of this sort is in HAB/77/9.

68. Kube to Kurt Daluege (at this time Göring's assistant in Prussia), 6 April 1933, BDC/Kube (PKC). For the arrogance with which party officials treated the civil service see Bernhard Lösener, "Als Rassereferent im Reichsministerium des Innern," *Vjh.f.Z.,* IX (July 1961), 267.

69. The law was passed in April 1933. For a full discussion see Mommsen, *Beamtentum,* pp. 39 ff; and Peterson, *Limits of Hitler's Power,* pp. 86–96.

70. Bracher, *Machtergreifung, pp.* 139–41. This process is particularly well documented for Hamburg in Timpke, *Dokumente,* pp. 35 and 57–59; and for Bremen in Schwarzwälder, *Machtergreifung in Bremen,* pp. 53, 59, and 69–79.

pacity as governmental commissioners for the territorial units, these
PLs were near the sources of physical or police power and had significant means of publicity at their disposal.[71] In practice, the process of
carrying out the personnel and policy wishes of the Gauleiters involved
the cooperation of a number of Gau offices, principally the intelligence
office (usually the SS's Security Service—*Sicherheitsdienst*, SD—which
before 1933 had been used to report on political opponents), the civil
service office (representing the National Socialist Association of Civil
Servants—*Nationalsozialistischer Beamtenbund*, NSBB), the political
department (*Innenpolitische Abteilung*),[72] and the legal department.
The first of these usually produced, often literally, incriminating material which gave the Gauleiters in their capacities as governmental
commissioners an excuse to dismiss or suspend accused officials.[73] In
their place moved interim appointees, selected from lists compiled
either by the NSBB or by one of the numerous Nazi professional affiliates, ranging from the National Socialist Lawyers' Association (*NS-
Rechtswahrerbund*) to Alfred Rosenberg's Militant Association for
German Culture (*Kampfbund für deutsche Kultur*).[74] Once installed
in their offices, the new incumbents began to issue decrees and directives at a feverish pace, knowing that "no action is worse than misjudgment in the means of action."[75] Simultaneously, the Nazi take-over

71. Wolfgang Schäfer, *NSDAP* (Hanover, 1956), p. 32; Mommsen, *Beamtentum*,
p. 46; and Bracher, *Machtergreifung*, pp. 491 and 584. Cf. the public pressure for
Brückner's appointment as *Oberpräsident* of Silesia in the clipping from the *Schlesi-
scher NS. Beobachter*, 18 March 1933, in HAB/77/4.

72.   For the activities of the RL's political department before 1933, see v.d.
Heydebrand u.d. Lasa (deputy chief of the department) to Lammers (at this time
state secretary at the Reich Chancellery), 29 March 1933, HAB/77/10; and
Meyer (GL of Westfalen-Nord) to Grauert, 15 March 1933, HAB/77/2.

73. The type of material sought can be illustrated by a directive of the Gau
propaganda leader in Koblenz-Trier (dated 7 June 1933) which requested the
district leaders in the Gau to compile a list of all civil servants who shopped in
Jewish stores. The document is quoted in Genschel, *Verdrängung*, pp. 70–71.

74. For the overall national picture see Bracher, *Machtergreifung*, p. 518; and
Hildegard Brenner, *Die Kunstpolitik des Nationalsozialismus* (Reinbek b. Ham-
burg, 1963), p. 37. A good account of developments at the local level is in
Görgen, "Düsseldorf," pp. 47–49.

75. Röhm, "Betrifft: Sonderkommissare in Bayern," 31 March 1933, T-580, roll
49, folder 272.

of the German police departments continued alongside the personnel purges.[76]

Paradoxically, even the appointment of most of the Gauleiters as Reich governors (*Reichsstatthalters*) and heads of the provincial government (Oberpräsident)—the former title was used in the non-Prussian states, the latter in Prussia—in May,[77] which involved their nominal subordination to the Reich minister of the interior, strengthened the Gauleiters' parochialism, since the new law again bypassed the party's Reichsleitung as an effective control organ. Their position as Reichsstatthalters quickly led most of the Gauleiters to adopt the particularist tendencies of pre-Napoleonic German princes. They even revived the outward forms. The newly appointed governor of the ministate of Brunswick, Gauleiter Wilhelm Loeper (Magdeburg-Anhalt), for example, arrived for his first official visit on May 8 by special train from Berlin, and was met by the usual honor guard and ceremonies due a head of state.[78]

The weakness of the party's Reichsleitung became particularly apparent when the party tried to deal with governmental units that covered more than one Gau. This was especially true of the huge area contained in the state of Prussia. Göring continued in his position as Reich commissioner and political strong man there, and his assistant, Kurt Daluege, after the March elections entered the Prussian civil service as *Ministerialdirigent* (roughly, deputy chief of a ministerial department). This appointment in effect regularized the Daluege's position, as he had been handling civil service personnel questions as Göring's special commissioner since the beginning of February.[79] On the party side, Kube attempted to expand his office when he appointed Gerd Rühle, a young (born in 1905) former Hitler Youth official from

---

76. In Bremen the number of "auxiliary police" increased from eight on 7 March to 100 at the end of April. See Schwarzwälder, *Machtergreifung in Bremen*, p. 104.

77. Of the Reichsstatthalters, only Epp (Bavaria) was not a GL, and of the ten Prussian Oberpräsidenten five were GL. See Gerd Rühle, *Das Dritte Reich: Das erste Jahr 1933* (Berlin, 1934), pp. 107 and 112–13; and Bracher, *Machtergreifung*, p. 465.

78. See the report in the *Braunschweigische Zeitung*, 10 May 1933. Clipping in BDC/Alpers, Friedrich (SS).

79. The relevant documents are in Daluege's SS personnel papers in the BDC.

Hessen-Nassau-Süd as his assistant.[80] In theory, close cooperation existed between the Nazis in the Prussian government (Göring and Daluege) and the Nazis in the cadres (Kube and Rühle). Kube dispatched
questionnaires to the Prussian Gauleiters asking for their suggestions
on new appointments for the various major government offices affecting
their Gaus.[81] His office would then coordinate these requests and discuss the results with Göring, Daluege, and Frick. (Frick entered into
the dealings in his capacity as Prussian minister of the interior.) In fact,
the intended procedure did not work well at all. Kube's authority as a
supra-Gau party official was never clear, either to himself[82] or to his
government partners. As late as March 28, the exact formulation of
Kube's powers was still a matter of considerable dispute in the Prussian interior ministry.[83] As a result, Kube's coordinating efforts came to
little, and his anger and frustration mounted as his ineffectiveness became increasingly more apparent.[84]

It is useful to contrast Kube's failure to impose the party's control
over the Prussian governmental appointments with the success of two
other prominent Nazis, Joseph Goebbels and R. Walther Darré, both
of whom became Reich ministers in the spring. All three had jurisdictional responsibilities extending beyond the borders of one Gau, but
there the similarity ended. Kube had been appointed by Robert Ley in
his capacity as Reich organizational leader of the NSDAP; Goebbels
and Darré owed their ministerial posts directly to Hitler. Goebbels' new
post was more or less a personal reward for the brilliance of his work
as propaganda chief and Gauleiter of Berlin in the Kampfzeit, and his
appointment as propaganda minister had been decided upon long before the election, although the formal appointment did not come until

80. The GL of Hessen-Nassau-Süd, Jacob Sprenger, was head of the NSBB.
Rühle subsequently joined Kube as *Regierungsrat* in the Oberpräsidium of Brandenburg and in 1939 entered the diplomatic service.
81. See, for example, Murr (GL of Württemberg-Hohenzollern) to Kube, 17
March 1933; and Jordan (GL of Halle-Merseburg) to Kube, 17 March 1933,
HAB/77/2.
82. Cf. Daluege's marginalia on a letter of Kube's complaining of his inability
to enforce his wishes: "After all, Kube can order compliance himself." Kube to
Daluege, 6 April 1933, BDC/Kube (PKC).
83. See the remarks and corrections by officials of the ministry in Kube to Frick,
28 March 1933, HAB/77/2.
84. Kube to Daluege, 6 April 1933, BDC/Kube (PKC).

March 13.[85] Once installed as the Reich's youngest minister, Goebbels built up his ministry along the lines of the party's Reich propaganda office, staffing it primarily with party officials,[86] but he made no attempt to partify the ministry. On the contrary, he imposed the authority of the Reich ministry on the NSDAP and allowed (at least until the war) both the RPL (Reich propaganda leadership) and his own position as Gauleiter of Berlin to recede from public view.[87]

Darré's swift rise to national honors had even more aspects of biting the hand that had fed him. When his appointment as the new Reich minister of agriculture was announced in June, Darré had achieved his ambition with the indispensable and active aid of his highly centralized cadre system in the party's agricultural apparatus (*agrarpolitischer Apparat*, a.A.).[88] This organization, which by 1933 had the support of most German farmers, was very active in organizing protest demonstrations and petitions against the incumbent minister, the nationalist Alfred Hugenberg, and there can be little doubt that Darré owed his position primarily to these outbursts of support.[89] Nevertheless, once appointed, he too prevented the party's a.A. from swallowing the ministry. The Reich food estate (*Reichsnährstand*), which became the compulsory farmers' organization, was run by the old a.A. officials, but its authority was derived from its affiliation with the ministry, rather than the party.

The party cadres established a clear position of superiority over the governmental agencies only at the local and, to a somewhat lesser extent, at the county level. By the end of the spring, virtually all mayors of sizable towns in Germany had been selected from the ranks of the party's district leaders or chairmen of the NSDAP's office of communal affairs.[90] At this level of society, a clear process of partification took place; both the political-totalitarian and the social-revolutionary aspects

85. Goebbels, *Kaiserhof*, entry for 15 Feb. 1933, p. 263.

86. Bracher, *Machtergreifung*, p. 548.

87. See Goebbels, *Kaiserhof*, entries for 6, 7, and 13 March 1933, pp. 275, 276, and 281.

88. For its organization and function before 1933 see Orlow, *Nazi Party*, pp. 194 and 231.

89. On these pressures see the *VB* for these weeks, and Anton Ritthaler, ed., "Eine Etappe auf Hitlers Weg zur ungeteilten Macht," *Vjh.f.Z.*, VIII (April 1960), 195–96.

90. Bracher, *Machtergreifung*, p. 506.

of the NSDAP assumed practical significance. The party completely politicized communal affairs. Especially in small towns and villages, where political affiliations had never been a factor in local elections, the Nazi district leader now refused to confirm nonparty members as mayors or municipal councilors. As a result, the old rural and small-town elite, consisting of independent farmers and small businessmen, was rapidly replaced by small landholders or farm laborers, who had joined the NSDAP early in order to escape their economic and social difficulties, and now possessed the requisite status of "old fighters."[91]

These developments were also the primary basis for the extraordinary increase in the power and prestige of the party's Kreisleiters. Before the Machtergreifung the districts had held an unimportant and precarious position between the established administrative levels of Gau and local party organization, but after January they were the only administrative unit of the party whose boundaries were in almost every instance the same as those of the governmental district. As a result, the Kreisleiters became natural control agents for their area of jurisdiction.[92] Their power in the first months of the Nazi dictatorship was virtually unlimited; until the end of 1934, for example, all confidential and personnel records of government agencies in the districts had to be made available (at the Kreisleiter's request) to the district leader in his office, that is, in a manner that all but encouraged pilfering of documents.[93]

Since as a group the party's Kreisleiters in 1933 were typically frustrated, lower-middle-class individuals,[94] they exhibited upon their rise to power all of the symptoms of a declining social class that suddenly sees a chance to reverse the trend of historical development. The average Kreisleiter saw himself as the representative of the "real" people and the avenger of the past. "As a National Socialist I express the feelings of the people; I am not concerned with legal niceties" was a fitting motto

91. HMB/NBO, 4 May 1933, p. 2, BGStA, MA 106672.

92. Haag (one of the auditors on the staff of the party's Reich treasurer) to Schwarz, 1 April 1938, T-580, roll 806, box 238, folder 44. See also Hermann Meyerhoff, *Herne 1933–1945* (Herne, 1963), pp. 9–10.

93. Mommsen, *Beamtentum*, p. 74.

94. On 1 January 1935 the NSDAP had 776 district leaders (there are no statistics available for 1933). Of these, 454 (58.5%) listed their occupation as white-collar worker or civil servant. See ROL, Amt für Statistik, *Partei-Statistik* ([Munich, 1935]), II, 344–45.

for their activities.[95] For himself, the Kreisleiter demanded the position of county executive or mayor, even if he was only twenty-one years old and completely unqualified or if another candidate had been unanimously elected.[96] In larger cities, the next step was to appoint members of his immediate clique[97] as commissioners of the various municipal departments. These in turn attempted to give government jobs (and the prestige that went with such positions in the German society of that time) to as many "old fighters" as possible.[98] The numbers were often staggering. In Düsseldorf, for example, 351 party comrades had found employment in the city administration by April 1935; a year later, the number had reached 676. In the small Hanoverian county seat of Thalburg the change-over involved 25 percent of the city's civil servants.[99]

Despite these upheavals, the party-sponsored revolution in the spring of 1933 was, on the whole, a failure. The NSDAP was, to be sure, able to exercise a clear veto over personnel appointments at all levels of societal and governmental decision-making. In other words, the party could force out of office or block the appointment of any candidate who did not have the "confidence of the party."[100] Yet, the party had by no means achieved the position accorded the Communist Party of the Soviet Union, which made all major decisions and had reduced the

95. Köhler (district leader of Eisenach in Thuringia) to the Gau party court of Thuringia, 19 June 1939, MiU/GAC, folder 12. A Kreisleiter's exercise of power often took grotesque forms. "Needless to say," wrote one to a newly elected village mayor in his district, "your confirmation as mayor is dependent upon your subscribing to the *Pommerische Zeitung* [the Gau's official organ]." Haut to village mayor of Zoltin (Pomerania), ca. Sept. 1933, HAB/77/3.

96. Zörner (later lord mayor of Dresden) to Buch (chief justice of the party courts), 30 June 1933, BDC/Klagges, Dietrich (OPG); and HMB/OBB, 19 May 1933, BGStA, MA 106670.

97. For the importance of cliques in the NSDAP at the Gau level see Peter Hüttenberger, *Die Gauleiter* (Stuttgart, 1969), pp. 56 ff.

98. Meyerhoff, *Herne*, p. 11; and Dr. Welpburger to Zörner, 26 June 1933, BDC/Klagges (OPG).

99. Görgen, "Düsseldorf," p. 55; and Allen, *Seizure*, p. 168. The position of the party's local leaders was less clear-cut. In the larger cities and in the villages they were clearly less powerful than the district leaders, but in smaller towns they often seized the opportunity to become local dictators. For an example see Allen, *Seizure*, pp. 159 and 169.

100. See Grauert to Pünder (Regierungspräsident of Münster), 5 May 1933, HAB/77/10, and the documentation in HAB/77/9. See also Bracher, *Machtergreifung*, p. 192.

state to the status of an administrative assistant. Apparently, Hitler had something like this in mind as the final position of the NSDAP in his Reich,[101] but for the moment, the Nazi Party had not reached a position of power remotely comparable to that of the Communist Party in the USSR. Except at the Gau and district levels, the party did not, as a rule, initiate policies; it simply reacted to the measures proposed by the state organs, although, of course, the party's reaction was decisive for the success of any project.[102] Only in the districts and localities did the party cadres enjoy what amounted to a monopoly of power. Here the Nazi revolution was more than a halfway measure.[103]

There were essentially two obstacles to the further evolution of the NSDAP's power position in the Third Reich. One, which was to plague the party throughout its existence, was the chronic lack of cadre personnel with developed technical or administrative skills.[104] The party simply did not have and could not attract to the full-time PL ranks the highly skilled technical elites that are necessary to administer a modern industrial society.[105] Most of its "old fighters" were at best political fanatics, with few technical skills,[106] and at worst human wrecks.[107] As a result, they could intuitively react, but rarely initiate. The second, and perhaps even more significant, difficulty was Hitler's reluctance to allow the recentralization of the political party cadres. For the moment, he preferred to allow the party's political focal point to be vested in

101. Bracher, *Machtergreifung*, p. 217.
102. On the general relationship between party and state see *ibid.*, pp. 219, 500, and 515; Schäfer, *NSDAP*, p. 34; and Schoenbaum, *Hitler's Social Revolution*, p. 217.
103. Bracher, *Machtergreifung*, pp. 507–08, n. 174 and p. 509; Allen, *Seizure*, pp. 167 and 259–60; Schoenbaum, *Hitler's Social Revolution*, p. 211; and Karl Schwend, "Die Bayerische Volkspartei," in Matthias and Morsey, *Ende der Parteien*, pp. 500–01.
104. Schäfer, *NSDAP*, p. 34, draws particular attention to this point.
105. This problem is still common among totalitarian political parties. For a discussion of conditions in the present-day Socialist Unity Party in the German Democratic Republic, see *Süddeutsche Zeitung*, 29 April 1970.
106. The newly appointed comrades in the Düsseldorf city administration had to receive on-the-job training before they could fulfill the rudiments of their tasks. See Görgen, "Düsseldorf," p. 55.
107. The new head of "Thalburg's" health department had just served a prison sentence for embezzlement. Allen, *Seizure*, p. 168.

him (as it always had been) and the Gauleiters, rather than in the Reichsleitung. Indeed, while refusing to strengthen the hand of the central party offices in Munich, he transferred some of his authority to the Reich ministries.[108]

Hitler soon realized that this decision had been a political mistake. The radicals of the party could develop their activism within the now virtually autonomous Gaus and districts without fear of being checked by the Reichsleitung. Although this was of little concern to the Führer as long as it involved only atrocities against Jewish citizens and political opponents,[109] such activities became a serious problem when they threatened the economic equilibrium of the country. In the spring of 1933 this danger became acute. It will be recalled that the party's economic affiliates had contributed rather massively toward the NSDAP's electoral victory in March. It was therefore understandable that the militant middle-class organizations would insist on translating their programmatic demands into policy directives.[110] As before, the Gauleiters showed little interest in this aspect of the revolution. Only four of the thirty-two provincial leaders could be listed as prominent supporters of the economic affiliates (Brückner, Wilhelm Karpenstein, Friedrich Hildebrandt, and Koch), and three of these administered areas in the primarily agricultural East.[111] Several others supported only a part of the radicals' program; Josef Bürckel (Palatinate), for example, was a particularly fierce enemy of any form of department store.[112] The Reich minister of economics, Alfred Hugenberg, was a vigorous opponent of the party's economic affiliates.[113] On the other

---

108. Hermann Mau, "Die 'Zweite Revolution'—der 30. Juni 1934," *Vjh.f.Z.,* I (April 1953), 119.

109. For examples see BA/R 43 II/1195.

110. Schumann, *Nationalsozialismus,* p. 62; Schwend, "Bayerische Volkspartei," p. 513; and Bracher, *Machtergreifung,* pp. 191–92.

111. Schoenbaum, *Hitler's Social Revolution,* p. 171. Karpenstein, born in 1903, became GL of Pomerania in 1931; he was dismissed in the wake of the Röhm affair (see below p. 123). Hildebrandt, a former agricultural laborer, was born in 1898. He was one of Hitler's earliest followers and remained GL of Mecklenburg until the end of the Nazi era. Koch was thirty-seven in 1933 and had been GL of East Prussia since 1927. He was one of the most powerful and brutal among the GL.

112. Genschel, *Verdrängung,* p. 82.

113. See "Etappe," pp. 205 and 209.

hand, the principal spokesman for the partification of economic life, Wagener, was now serving his brief term as Reich economics commissioner, and many of the party's district and local leaders showed genuine enthusiasm for an economic revolution along the lines of the Ständestaat.[114] Consequently, in cities and counties throughout Germany, the party's offices for estate development, the NS-Hago, and the Kampfbund issued decrees which curtailed, prohibited, or controlled what these elements considered to be the major competitors of small shopkeepers, principally the department stores and consumers' cooperatives. Local ordinances closed restaurants in department stores and enjoined Woolworth's from selling gardening equipment—apparently because the local commissioner of the licensing bureau happened to own a gardening equipment store.[115] Other agents attempted to enforce an NS-Hago decree against German businesses holding insurance policies with Jewish firms, and during the height of the campaign, the so-called April boycott, a number of firms dismissed their Jewish employees.[116]

The April boycott against Jewish businesses and the campaigns against consumers' cooperatives in May were both climax and turning point of the Nazi economic revolution in 1933. Both were nationally organized efforts which had Hitler's formal approval. More than that, the Führer spent three days discussing the boycott[117] with its national chairman, the notorious Jew-baiter Julius Streicher, Gauleiter of Franconia. Streicher in turn placed the implementation of the boycott in the hands of the NS-Hago. The PLs were subordinated to the directives of this affiliate for the duration of the boycott.[118] A month later, the NS-Hago pounced with similar vengeance on the consumers' cooperatives, which in the twenties had been closely linked to the Social Democratic Party and the German labor unions. This time, the middle-class organization secured the cooperation of the party's Reich organizational leader, and

114. Genschel, *Verdrängung*, p. 49; and Görgen, "Düsseldorf," pp. 66–67.

115. The example is from Meyerhoff, *Herne*, p. 35.

116. See the NS-Hago form letter in Rudolf Karl-Karlo to Reich chancellery, 15 June 1933, BA/R 43 II/1196 (the letter-writer complained to the Reich chancellery about such practices); and Genschel, *Verdrängung*, p. 73.

117. Domarus, *Hitler*, I, 247.

118. See Streicher's proclamation in *Angriff*, 31 March 1933. A full description of the boycott is in Genschel, *Verdrängung*.

Robert Ley set out to destroy the cooperatives—again with Hitler's full approval.[119]

The April boycott and the events in May were not isolated developments, but part of a larger, subdued, and bitter controversy over the future role of the party in the Third Reich. There existed a multitude of plans and theories to deal with the prevailing dualism of party and state, but as yet none had the official approval of the only man who could render such decisions, Adolf Hitler. Theories of power distribution among the Nazis ranged from a naive "believe in the Führer and all will be well"[120] to the somewhat more sophisticated but equally controversial plans of the NSBB and Helmut Nicolai. Since Nicolai and the NSBB reached exactly opposite conclusions about the future of the NSDAP, their ideas may serve to illustrate the parameters of theorizing within the party at this time. The civil service group planned to let the state (or at least its decision-making powers) wither away, while the NSBB implemented the partification of the state by vesting control of civil service affairs in the Gau and regional offices of the NSDAP's civil service affiliate. In consequence, the NSBB was to evolve from a social and economic interest group into a powerful control organization.[121]

Nicolai wanted to avoid precisely that. A trained civil servant and long-time member of the party, he had headed the Reichsleitung's political department (Innenpolitische Abteilung) under Strasser until October 1932. He enjoyed the reputation of being "an exceptionally able administrator," but always remained something of an outsider among the "old fighters." "Very much the type of dueling student with prewar mannerisms; an intellectual, whose character might not fit the NSDAP's demands," was the judgment of Gauleiter Brückner in 1931.[122] After the Machtergreifung Nicolai was appointed chief of administration (*Regierungspräsident*) in Magdeburg, but his views soon clashed with those of the local Gauleiter, Loeper (Nicolai at one point sent him a challenge for pistols), and he was forced out of office.[123] Frick then gave

119. On this episode see Kuno Bludau, *Nationalsozialismus und Genossenschaften* (Hanover, 1968), pp. 110–12, and 118.
120. This was the time in which heartburn medications called "Mein Kampf" were sold in Germany. See Brenner, *Kunstpolitik*, pp. 40–41.
121. For documentation see the correspondence in BA/R 2/22583.
122. Brückner to Strasser, 18 June 1931, BDC/Nicolai (PKC).
123. For Loeper's views on Nicolai see his letter to Ley, 14 Nov. 1933, *ibid.*

him a position in the Reich ministry of the interior, but in 1935 he was expelled from the party for homosexual offenses, and vanished into obscurity.[124] In the meantime, however, Nicolai had had ample opportunities to make his views on the future of the party known. In a series of memoranda[125] he suggested that the PLs should be subordinated to the propaganda leaders within the cadre apparatus and that no party organ should have any authority over either government offices or individual civil servants.[126] In short, Nicolai felt that after January 1933 the NSDAP had achieved its purpose and could gracefully retire to staging propaganda shows. Caution and tactfulness were never characteristics of Nicolai's personality, and he all but challenged the PLs to united action with the publication (in May 1933) of his book *Der Staat im nationalsozialistischen Weltbild* (*The State in the World View of National Socialism*). It raised a storm of protest from the Gauleiters, whose status, according to Nicolai, should be reduced to that of stage managers for Nazi rallies. After some months, Hitler prohibited both the further circulation of the book and discussion of it.[127]

As the fate of Nicolai and his ideas illustrates, Hitler himself could come to no quick decisions during the controversy over the party's future. Emotionally, his sympathies clearly lay with the proponents of the party's role as guardian of a revolutionary future; throughout his adult life Hitler hated legal restrictions on the personal exercise of his power, and his hostility toward jurists and civil servants as a group was well known.[128] There are also indications that, at least immediately after the March election, he saw a chance of realizing his nihilistic, revolutionary aims by unleashing, as it were, the party's radicals. On March 29 the triumphant Gauleiters assembled in Berlin. There is no

124. OPG, second chamber, "Beschluss," 14 March 1935, BDC/Nicolai (OPG).

125. Nicolai to Grauert, 19 May 1933, HAB/77/10; and Nicolai to Lammers, 11 Aug. 1933, BA/R 43 II/426a.

126. The latter point was a material issue during Nicolai's trial before the party courts. He denied the court's jurisdiction over a civil servant like himself, but Hitler personally decided that civil servants who were also party members were subject to the party courts. See OPG to Nicolai, 13 Sept. 1934, BDC/Nicolai (OPG).

127. Lammers to Loeper and Röver (GL of Oldenburg), 11 Dec. 1933, BA/R 43 II/495. For additional discussion of Nicolai and his ideas see Bracher, *Machtergreifung*, pp. 593–96; Mommsen, *Beamtentum*, pp. 47, 99, and 118; and Diehl-Thiele, *Partei*, pp. 57 ff.

128. Bracher, *Machtergreifung*, p. 517.

detailed record or protocol of the meeting, but even from the *Völkischer Beobachter* (*VB*) account of Hitler's major speech it appears that, aside from mouthing the usual rhetorical phrases about educating the German people in the ideology of National Socialism, Hitler expressed himself rather forcefully about the permanence of the party and the need for continuing organizational effectiveness. Indeed, his statement "that the work done outside the state organs was decisive"[129] could only suggest that the party would be put increasingly in charge of political decision-making.

A number of organizational developments within the party seemed to be practical implementations of Hitler's remarks. On April 1 the NSDAP made public the establishment of its foreign policy office (*Aussenpolitisches Amt*, APA). This organization, until recently considered one of Alfred Rosenberg's usual boondoggles, has lately been rescued from obscurity. It is now clear not only that the APA had vast ambitions, but that its activities were of considerable significance in the spring and summer of the year.[130] The ambitions of the new office were apparent from the beginning. As the *VB* made clear, the establishment of the APA showed "that as in all other areas, so in the field of foreign affairs, only the NSDAP can determine the final form of [Germany's] foreign policy."[131] This was not mere journalistic boasting. Throughout most of 1933, for example, it was the party, not the government's foreign ministry, that determined German foreign policy moves toward Austria. Here the NSDAP hoped to let history repeat itself; it attempted to topple the Dollfuss regime with the same strong-arm methods that had succeeded so well in putting the Nazis in charge of the German Länder governments.[132]

A similar outburst of party activism could be noted in the area of judicial "reform." As noted above, this was of particular concern to

129. *VB*, 22 March 1933.

130. On the APA see Hans-Adolf Jacobsen, *Nationalsozialistische Aussenpolitik 1933–1938* (Frankfurt, 1968), pp. 45 ff.

131. *VB*, 7 April 1933. The author of the article was Walther Schmitt, the foreign policy editor of the *VB* and later staff member of the APA.

132. See the report on the preparation of the July 1934 coup by SS-Standartenführer Wächter (in 1934, head of the illegal Austrian SS) to Himmler, 31 May 1938, T-175, roll 32, frames 2539841–45. On the Austro-German developments in 1933 in general, see Dieter Ross, *Hitler und Dollfuss* (Hamburg, 1966), pp. 33, 38, 47, and 67.

Hitler, and attacks upon the Weimar judicial system had been a prominent part of the party's propaganda line during the Kampfzeit. In addition, during the Strasser era, the party's Reichsleitung had done considerable proto-legislative work, drafting (under the leadership of Nicolai) a number of anti-Semitic bills and other far-reaching revisions of the Weimar constitution.[133] After the Machtergreifung the "legal group"[134] within the party—Hans Frank, Roland Freisler, Otto Thierack, Curt Rothenberger, Hellmut Nicolai, Wilhelm Stuckart, and Werner Best—sought to develop these beginnings into a full-fledged system of partification of the nation's judicial system. Their basic aim was the complete politicization of law and legal proceedings, so as to make the administration of justice an integral part of the machinery available to accomplish the political ends of the Nazi regime.[135]

In the spring of 1933 the chances for success of such a venture seemed good. The Nazi press, especially the *VB*, gave massive propagandistic backing to the activities and aims of the party's judicial affiliates,[136] and their political position seemed exceedingly strong. The most prominent member of the group, Hans Frank, a man who was already widely known as a result of his numerous court appearances as Hitler's defense attorney, became Reich commissioner of justice. He thus held a position analogous to that of Wagener in the economic field. He also headed a powerful professional affiliate of the party, the National Socialist

133. Among the measures were drafts for a new constitution, a law on citizenship (citizenship defined by race), and suggestions for purging "party-book" officials from the civil service. See v.d. Heydebrand u.d. Lasa, "Übersicht über die bei der Reichsleitung . . . vorhandenen Vorarbeiten und Unterlagen." This is an enclosure in Heydebrand to Lammers, 29 March 1933, HAB/77/10.

134. The term is that used by Weinkauff, *Deutsche Justiz*, pp. 56 ff. With the exception of Nicolai, who thought the party's role had been fulfilled in January 1933, all of these men rose to high positions in the Third Reich. Hans Frank served as Reich commissioner of justice and Bavarian minister of justice (until 1935) and during the war was governor-general of occupied Poland. Freisler became state secretary in the Reich ministry of justice and later president of the People's Court. Thierack was Reich minister of justice from 1942 to 1945, Rothenberger his state secretary during part of the tenure. Stuckart served as state secretary in the Reich interior ministry, and Best had an SS career before his appointment as Reich plenipotentiary in Denmark.

135. Bracher, *Machtergreifung*, pp. 520, 522, and 534.

136. See the *VB* for March through May 1933, particularly 30 June 1933. Cf. also Bracher, *Machtergreifung*, p. 532.

Lawyers' Association,[137] and with massive propagandistic fanfare he succeeded in establishing a pseudoscientific body, the Academy for German Law (*Akademie für deutsches Recht*), which was to serve as a forum for the extraministerial (that is, party-dominated) reform of the German law codes.[138]

Another major effort by the party to gain immediate control of a large segment of German societal life was the struggle over the reorganization of the Protestant churches. This chapter of Nazi Germany's history has already been described in some detail,[139] but one point deserves renewed emphasis in the context of analyzing the position of the NSDAP at this time. The radical *Deutsche Christen* (German Christians, DC), whose aims the party later hastened to disavow, had at this time clear and open support from several prominent leaders,[140] and consequently there can be little doubt that this group's efforts to take over the Protestant churches were a part of the campaign to partify German society.

As had often been the case in the history of the NSDAP, the organizational implementation of Hitler's earlier decision (or, perhaps, indications of a decision) was still running its course when the Führer reversed himself. Hitler soon recoiled before the practical difficulties produced by the activism of the party. (Needless to say, he did not consider that his decision to weaken the powers of the Reichsleitung might have been a major factor in these, from his point of view, negative developments.) The setbacks were real enough. The April boycott, whatever its value in satisfying the sadistic impulses of the PLs and the SA, had brought about a rapid deterioration of the German export and raw materials balance.[141] Indeed, Hitler began to develop very acute fears about the economic situation. It proved relatively easy to

137. This later became the NS-Association of Jurists (NS-*Juristenbund*).

138. For an account of the founding of the academy see *VB*, 27 June 1933.

139. See Klaus Scholder, "Die evangelische Kirche in der Sicht der nationalsozialistischen Führung bis zum Kriegsausbruch," *Vjh.f.Z.*, XVI (Jan. 1968), 15–35; Hans Buchheim, *Glaubenskrise im Dritten Reich* (Stuttgart, 1953); John S. Conway, *The Nazi Persecution of the Churches, 1933–45* (New York, 1968); and Kurt Meier, *Deutsche Christen* (Halle, 1965).

140. See, for example, Kube to Grauert, 11 April 1933, HAB/77/19. See also Scholder, "Evangelische Kirche," p. 18.

141. Sprenger to Terboven, 1 June 1933, HAB/320/52; and Bludau, *Genossenschaften*, p. 118.

convince him that the economic disadvantages of destroying the consumers' cooperatives would outweigh the ideological advantages, and,
as a result, to halt the already ordered move against the cooperatives.[142]
The campaign against the Protestant churches led to the first really
genuine mass popular sentiments against the new regime,[143] and even
the Nazi judicial reform efforts seemed to make little headway as they
bogged down in the customary lawyers' verbosity.

Yet all these factors were minor irritants compared with the basic,
overwhelming problem of the NSDAP's unsuitable cadre structure and
personnel. After two months in power, the Nazi Party was an overblown, cumbersome, disunified, and almost disorganized political organism. It had grown tremendously in membership; the *VB* claimed
one and a half million members in late March, and another one million
applications had arrived in Munich before the cutoff date of May 1.[144]
Most of the increase came from the "victims of March" (*Märzgefallene*), so dubbed by the "old fighters" because they did not discover
their enthusiasm for Nazism until after the election of March 5. Many
of these, of course, were part of the professional and managerial classes,
anxious to retain their positions and status under the new regime.[145] In
addition, large numbers of those who had left the NSDAP in late 1932
because its future seemed bleak now hastened to reverse their decision.[146] Then, too, the Reichsleitung offered membership badges virtually wholesale to members of the nationalist parties in order to destroy these erstwhile rivals from within.[147]

Like the nouveau riche it was, the NSDAP could not decide whether

142. On the negotiations see Bludau, *Genossenschaften*, pp. 111–16. See also the
statement by the former executive secretary of the cooperatives' central buying office,
Everling, in the de-Nazification folder of the Hamburg senator Ahrens, Forsch.
Hbg./PA/12/A.

143. See Buchheim, *Glaubenskrise*, pp. 86–88; and Conway, *Nazi Persecution*,
pp. 53–56.

144. *VB*, 22 March 1933; and *Verordnungsblatt der Reichsleitung der NSDAP*
(cited hereafter as *VOBl*), II (30 April 1933), 95. In some areas the percentage
increases reached 400%. See Allen, *Seizure*, pp. 233–34.

145. Weinkauff, *Deutsche Justiz*, pp. 107–08.

146. See *VB*, 26 and 27 Feb. 1933; and *VOBl*, II (28 Feb. 1933), 90. The SA and
SS too were flooded with new members. See Heinrich Bennecke, *Hitler und die SA*
(Munich, 1962), pp. 214–15; and Heinrich Himmler, "Rede vor Vertretern der
deutschen Justiz in Kochem am 25.5.44," T-175, roll 93, frame 2613785.

147. Ritthaler, "Etappe," p. 196; and Timpke, *Dokumente*, p. 43.

to be proud of its new popularity or fearful lest it lose its status as the elite of the new age. On the one hand, there were numerous complaints about the "fat bourgeois" (*Spiesser*) whose only interest in the party were the economic and social advantages they could derive from it,[148] but at the same time a publication issued by the ROL reprimanded any comrade who could not win at least three new members for the movement.[149] Himmler complained bitterly some years later that it took him two years to purge the ballast of 1933 from the SS,[150] but he was also the first one to surround himself with a "circle of friends" drawn primarily from the haute bourgeoisie.

Actually, the party had no choice but to take in a large number of Spiesser if the cadres were to play a major decision-making role in the technical and administrative aspects of German societal life. The "old fighters" simply did not have the necessary skills; as Karl-Dietrich Bracher has remarked, even most of the Gauleiters were unable to interpret the legal texts that defined their powers as Reichsstatthalters.[151] Consequently, the party made no effort to close the floodgates before May 1, though the Reich treasurer (*Reichsschatzmeister*, Rschm.) did attempt to halt the practice of forcing individuals to join the NSDAP.[152] Schwarz decreed a halt in applications on May 1 (announced April 19), but this did not include applications from members of the SS, SA, Hitler Youth (HJ), and the NSBO.[153] Since all of these affiliated organizations had by now vastly increased memberships (the relationship of "old fighters" and Märzgefallene in the SA was one to four),[154] the membership of the party proper continued to rise after the formal stoppage. Even the two-year probationary period, or candidate-membership, which all new members had to undergo, was not a meaningful distinction between the elite and the nonelite, since in practice many of the candidates were immediately assigned to cadre positions; the party simply did not have

148. Goebbels, *Kaiserhof*, entries for 17 March and 8 April 1933, pp. 283 and 296; and ROL, *Dienstvorschrift 1933*, p. 32.
149. ROL, *Dienstvorschrift 1933*, p. 30.
150. Himmler, "Rede vor Vertretern," frame 2613785.
151. Bracher, *Machtergreifung*, p. 588.
152. Reichsschatzmeister (cited hereafter as Rschm.), "Bericht über die Gauschatzmeistertagung am 25. November 1937," p. 41, T-580, roll 842, box 267, folder 348.
153. Buchheim, "Mitgliedschaft," p. 316.
154. Bennecke, *Hitler und die SA*, p. 215.

skilled personnel to fill its PL positions. By 1940 virtually none of the Reichsleitung's full-time functionaries had held their position before 1933, as table 1 reveals.

TABLE 1

Length of Service for Full-time Cadre Personnel of the Reichsleitung at the End of 1940

Percentage	Length of Service
32.87%	Up to 2 years
32.37	Up to 4 years
16.84	Up to 6 years
14.58	Up to 8 years
3.39	More than 8 years

SOURCE: Rschm., Reichsfinanzverwaltung, "Jahresbericht 1940," p. 9, T-580, roll 833, box 256, folder 267.

The indispensability of the newcomers made them no less unacceptable to the alte Kämpfer. On the contrary, the swift rise of the newcomers to cadre positions and the widespread exclusion of the "old fighters" from the material rewards of the Machtergreifung[155] embittered relations between the two groups. The new cadre personnel with its better educational background despised the pseudointellectualism of the old lower-middle-class functionary nucleus,[156] and lame statements from the Reichsleitung that not all of the Märzgefallene were opportunists did little to ease the tensions.[157] Since the "old fighters" were both pathetically anxious to see tangible rewards for their loyalty to the party[158] and unable to compete with the newcomers in the area of skills, they turned to a variety of shady self-help schemes that turned many party offices into mires of corruption. Despite the Reich treasurer's

155. Schoenbaum, *Hitler's Social Revolution*, p. 224.

156. For a particularly violent counterattack of a prominent "old fighter" see Franz Woweries, "Von Jahr zu Jahr," *Schulungsbrief*, III (Jan. 1936), 8.

157. *VB*, 11 and 12 June 1933. There is no doubt that many of the new members were indeed pure opportunists. See Bracher, *Machtergreifung*, p. 512.

158. Martin Bormann, the later head of the party chancellery, realized rather belatedly that the horizon of most "old fighters" did not extent beyond such interests. See "Aktenvermerk für Pg. Friedrichs und Pg. Dr. Klopfer 14.4.42," T-580, roll 834, box 799 B, folder 2. Friedrichs was head of the chancellery's "party division," Klopfer head of the "state" division. See also Wahl, *Deutsche Herz*, pp. 125 ff.

repeated admonishments, Gau and district offices kept unaudited accounts, used party moneys, to finance pet economic schemes, and in general developed little financial empires of their own.[159]

The funds deposited in the secret accounts of various Gauleiters and district leaders were usually obtained by a mixture of blackmail and embezzlement. In these early weeks opportunities for such activities were abundant. Business firms were forced to pay protection money to avoid visits by SA terror squads; sizable amounts were siphoned off by the often utterly incompetent Nazi *Treuhänders* (essentially receivers) who were put in charge of various gleichgeschaltete organizations. (The take-over of the labor unions was a particularly rich source for corruption.[160]) And if all else failed, there was still the provincial party press, which before 1933 had been plagued by dismal writing and worse sales. Although the party's official publishing house (which put out the *VB*) protested vigorously,[161] the Gaus and districts pushed the sale of the provincial press by a wide variety of legitimate and illegitimate practices.[162] Finally, the ingenuity of the "old fighters" reached almost unprecedented heights in the Gau Cologne-Aachen. Here the Gau office had made arrangements to be cut in on the profits from a chain of one-armed bandits to be distributed throughout the Gau.[163]

Not all of these factors had become acute dangers in late April, when Hitler again addressed the party leaders, but the general trends were sufficiently apparent to lead the Führer to all but reverse the tenor of his speech of a month before. Again, no protocol of his remarks has survived, but from a variety of sources it is possible to piece together the general emphasis of his speech. He spoke for three hours, ranging

159. See Schwarz's circular to all GL, 9 June and 3 July 1933, Rschm., *Rundschreiben des Reichsschatzmeisters* (cited hereafter as *Rdschr.*) (Munich, 1934–1942), I. The documents in these volumes are arranged chronologically; there is no pagination.

160. Schumann, *Nationalsozialismus*, pp. 88–89. See also Hermann Rauschning, *Hitler Speaks* (London, 1938), pp. 96–100.

161. Oron J. Hale, *The Captive Press in the Third Reich* (Princeton, 1964), pp. 123–24.

162. *Ibid.*, pp. 102–11 gives a vivid description of the worst offenders and their tactics. See also Allen, *Seizure*, pp. 193–95.

163. Although the Reich treasurer managed to put a halt to this scheme before it became operable, he dispatched a general order to all GL—lest they had developed plans along similar lines. Rschm. circular to all GL, 19 Oct. 1933, *Rdschr.*, I.

over such diverse subjects as the need for cooperation among the political and military cadres of the party and his own views on art. In its political part, the address now assigned the NSDAP a role as stabilizer of state and governmental authority; there was a decided de-emphasis on revolutionary initiatives. Historically, Nazism had ushered in a revolutionary epoch, but since it would last at least a thousand years, there was clearly no need for immediate action.[164] Hitler had suddenly become cautious; the "Führer is really tackling his great tasks as a statesman."[165]

As usual, the practical application of the new line had begun before its verbal formulation. With Hitler's obvious approval, the administrative offices of the government regrouped their forces and began to counterattack. They were aided by those Nazis who had obtained major government posts, and who were now anxious to guard the authority of their new position—even against the party.[166] Thus Frick issued sharp orders against the party's control of the civil service and the Nazi state secretary of the Reich finance ministry wrote Gauleiter Jacob Sprenger a sharp letter protesting the Gau office's attempt to subject the ministry's employees in field offices in Hessen-Nassau-Süd to its control.[167] The most significant attempt to reestablish the state's authority was the Law on Reich Governors (*Reichsstatthaltergesetz*), which had, as previously mentioned, made most of the Nazi provincial leaders chief of state in the German Länder, or, in Prussia, of the provinces. Although the new measure was not an effective curb on the autonomy of the Gauleiters, it did strengthen, at least for the moment, the position of the Reich

---

164. This analysis of Hitler's address of 22 April is drawn from the following sources: *VB*, 23, 24 and 25 April 1933; Goebbels, *Kaiserhof*, entry for 22 April 1933, p. 302; and Domarus, *Hitler*, I, 257.

165. Goebbels, *Kaiserhof*, entry for 22 April 1933, p. 302.

166. Thus Göring, who was never closely identified with the party cadres, was one of the first to protest the activities of the various party-appointed commissioners. See "Aufzeichnung von Straatsrat Dr. Schultz (Hamburg) . . . über die Ministerbesprechung vom 25. April 1933," in Mommsen, *Beamtentum*, p. 162. On the other hand, Max Amann, the head of the party publishing house, who did not get a government job, felt obliged to remind Darré that the latter did, after all, owe his ministerial post to the NSDAP. See Amann to Darré, 3 Oct. 1933, BDC/Amann (PKC).

167. Bracher, *Machtergreifung*, pp. 468, 496, and 593–94; Mommsen, *Beamtentum*, pp. 136 and 162; and Reinhardt to Sprenger, 13 June 1933, BA/R 2/22583.

minister of the interior, Wilhelm Frick. The minister, one of Hitler's earliest followers, had remained at heart a civil servant who abhorred wild and uncontrollable actions by undisciplined party officials.[168] Under the Reichsstatthaltergesetz he became the administrative (not political) supervisor of the Reich governors. Similarly, the Law to Restore a Professional Civil Service (passed on April 7) was an attempt to regularize the purge of the German civil service. It transferred the major role in the purging process to the interior ministry, thereby curtailing independent actions by Gauleiters and district leaders.[169]

Within the party itself, the immediate consequences of Hitler's speech were less dramatic. The radical Deutsche Christen were curbed promptly; their take-over of the Protestant church in Mecklenburg had to be rescinded four days after the April conference.[170] The NS-Hago was subjected to additional curbs by the Gau economic advisors,[171] and Hitler attempted to deal with the confused practices of the Gaus in accepting new members by strengthening the review powers of the party courts,[172] but as yet the Führer was not willing to recentralize the decision-making powers in the Reichsleitung of the NSDAP.

As a result, even after April the NSDAP remained subject to a variety of centrifugal tendencies that solidified the power of the provincial leaders and correspondingly weakened the influence of the central offices. Since Hitler did not curb the power and prestige of the Gauleiters, and Frick proved too weak to exercise political control over them, the immediate effect of the Law on Reich Governors was to create virtually autonomous provincial jurisdictions in Germany. "The [imperial] electors of old would have enjoyed our time," wrote one disgruntled Nazi

168. Lösener, "Rassereferent," p. 265.

169. See Bracher, *Machtergreifung*, p. 497; and the undated memorandum in the files of Grauert (state secretary in the Reich ministry of the interior), HAB/77/1.

170. Scholder, "Evangelische Kirche," p. 18; Friedrich Zipfel, *Kirchenkampf in Deutschland 1933–45* (Berlin, 1965), p. 266. See also Conway, *Nazi Persecution*, p. 39.

171. Schumann, *Nationalsozialismus*, p. 63. See also Brückner (GL of Silesia) "Sonderrundschreiben," 29 May 1933, BDC/Brückner (PKC); and *VB*, 30 May 1933.

172. *VOBl*, II (31 March and 30 April 1933), 93 and 96. The membership figures for the Gau Franken (GF) rose from 13,785 in April to 17,759 in May. After the new order, however, they fell to 15,833 in June and continued to fall until November. See BA/GF/20.

commentator of the rise of neo-absolutist princes.[173] The Gaus did not
even fear the financial powers of the Reichsleitung; many were by now
virtually independent as a result of massive donations (voluntary and
forced) from business and industry.[174] There were gradations of arrogance and ruthlessness among the Gauleiters, of course, but the worst
offenders[175] were numerous enough and located in regions of the Reich
important enough to make them a genuine menace to the stability of
Germany.

The new princes used a variety of means to gratify their longing for
status and power. Wilhelm Kube's directive that the ringing of church
bells had to accompany his travels around the Gau Ostmark was a ludicrous but essentially harmless demand.[176] The Gauleiters of Pom-
merania (Karpenstein), East Prussia (Koch), and Munich–Upper Bavaria (Wagner) had more extensive ambitions. Karpenstein attempted
to subject the press, all government officials, and the churches in his
Gau to the immediate control of the Gauleiter's office,[177] and Koch quite
frankly stated that he would refuse to follow any directive that did not
originate with Hitler.[178] Adolf Wagner, whose position was particularly
strong because of his membership in Hitler's Munich circle, was a genuine revolutionary for whom the Catholic Church was a particularly
hateful organization.[179] Others exercised their powers through vetoes,
as when Carl Röver (Oldenburg and Bremen) prevented the adminis-

173. Robert Ley, "Rede vor der Führerschaft Ostpreussens," *Hoheitsträger*, VII
(June 1943), 4. Significantly, the GL of East Prussia was one of the worst offenders.
See also Walter Baum, "Die 'Reichsreform' im Dritten Reich," *Vjh.f.Z.*, III (Jan.
1955), 40.

174. Goebbels reported that when he turned over the administration of Berlin
to his deputy, the Gau had a cash reserve of RM 200,000. See Goebbels, *Kaiserhof*,
entry for 10 March 1933, p. 297.

175. Bracher, *Machtergreifung*, pp. 925–26, lists the following: Koch (East Prus-
sia), Mutschmann (Saxony), Sauckel (Thuringia), Streicher (Franken), Adolf
Wagner (Munich–Upper Bavaria), Bürckel (Palatinate), Terboven (Rhineland-
Ruhr), and Kaufmann (Hamburg).

176. Zipfel, *Kirchenkampf*, p. 31.

177. The relevant documentation is in HAB/77/1 and HAB/77/26.

178. Otto Bräutigam, *So hat es sich zugetragen* (Würzburg, 1968), pp. 367–68;
and the documents in BDC/Koch (OPG).

179. Speer, *Erinnerungen*, p. 83; and Ludwig Volk, *Der bayerische Episkopat
und der Nationalsozialismus 1930–1934*, 2d ed. (Mainz, 1966), pp. 63–64, 94 ff.

tratively sensible union of the three Hanseatic cities of Hamburg, Bremen, and Lübeck into a single *Land* (federal state).[180]

Yet even the Gauleiters were not omnipotent. Although in general the Gauleiter's word was law within the borders of his own Gau, at least a few provincial leaders had virtually no influence in their area of jurisdiction. The nominal leader of Hanover, Bernhard Rust, was Reich minister of culture, but in his Gau his views counted for little. A cabal of four officials, the prime minister of Brunswick, two district leaders, and the head of the SS, divided the power between them. Of the four, the prime minister, Dietrich Klagges, an "undisciplined but clever"[181] individual, was the most important. Various efforts by the Reich governor, Gauleiter Loeper of Magdeburg-Anhalt, and the deputy Gauleiter of Hanover, Kurt Schmalz, to put the Gau in order met with little success.[182] Outside his own Gau the authority of even a prominent Gauleiter in an important state position was severely limited. As Bavarian minister of the interior, Adolf Wagner was in charge of supervising the internal administration and police forces in all of Bavaria, yet the district leader of Nuremberg successfully defied the minister because he enjoyed the active support of his own Gauleiter, Streicher of Franconia.[183] In an even more extreme case, Röver (Oldenburg) had to intrigue for some time to remove a district leader in his own Gau, simply because the Kreisleiter's area of jurisdiction, Bremen, lay in a separate *Land*.[184]

The political cadres faced even greater dangers from the affiliates than from the intrigues of their peers. By May, the NSDAP had eliminated all political opposition and gleichgeschaltet every organized form of activity in Germany with the exception of the youth groups. In a

180. Timpke, *Dokumente*, p. 149; and "Tagebuch–Aufzeichnung Dr. jr. Erwin Garrens . . . ," Forsch. Hbg./PA/12/F.

181. Christian Opdenhoff (of the staff of the deputy Führer) "Aktenvermerk für Pg. Friedrichs," 10 Nov. 1939, T-580, roll 80, folder 371. On Klagges see also Ernst-August Roloff, *Bürgertum und Nationalsozialismus* (Hanover, 1961).

182. For details of the often highly involved intrigues, see the bulky BDC/Klagges (OPG) file. For an analysis of the struggles in Brunswick see also Shlomo Aronson, "Heydrich und die Anfänge des SD und der Gestapo" (Dissertation, Free University of Berlin, 1967), pp. 224 ff.

183. Wagner to Epp, 24 March 1933, BGStA, MA 105475.

184. Schwarzwälder, *Machtergreifung in Bremen*, p. 58.

sense, the NSDAP had imposed its organizational form on the entire society,[185] but in the process the distinction between political elite and affiliated mass organizations was becoming increasingly nebulous. The fault lay in large part with the party's own propaganda, which indulged in a cult of numbers and thereby tended to negate all qualitative differences between the political cadres, the paramilitary organizations, and the socioeconomic affiliates.[186] Without that distinction, however, the core party was in danger of being inundated despite the membership stoppage of May 1. After this date, membership in the NSDAP was closed to all but certain specified categories of applicants, while the rolls of the affiliates remained open. The result, predictably, was a veritable flood of membership applications to the affiliates by those who hoped that affiliate membership would be a steppingstone to eventual full-scale party membership. The affiliates themselves, many of whom had always exhibited esprit de corps of their own, used the new popularity to increase both their organizational and their financial freedom of action within the Nazi movement.[187] With considerable understatement, even Ley admitted that there was a general "decline of comradeliness" between the various Nazi organizations.[188]

The largest and potentially most dangerous party group outside the political cadres was the SA. The oldest of the Nazi paramilitary organizations had performed invaluable services for the NSDAP as a whole, both before and after January 30. Most of the acts of violence and destruction that had frightened the conservatives into yielding power so readily to Hitler had been carried out by SA terror squads. Many of the commissioners came from its ranks. The SA established the first concentration camps, which were as yet outside the control of the SS or the Gestapo.[189] It was thus understandable that the SA regarded itself as the activist elite of the movement, in many ways superior to the bureaucrats in the political cadres. The organization's leader, Ernst Röhm,

185. Bracher, *Machtergreifung*, p. 192.
186. See the *VB* for April and May 1933.
187. See Meyerhoff, *Herne*, p. 12; and Hans-Christian Brandenburg, *HJ—Die Geschichte der HJ* (Cologne, 1968), p. 146. For the complaints made by Goebbels and Schwarz about organizational independence among the affiliates, see *VOBl*, II (31 May and 15 June 1933), 103 and 105.
188. Ley, "Rede . . . ," p. 4.
189. Aronson, "Heydrich," p. 122.

had some quite definite, though not very well-developed, ideas on the future role of his mass organization. Röhm wanted to use the SA as a huge militia base for a thoroughly rearmed Germany organized along more or less national-bolshevist lines.[190] He was willing to acknowledge Hitler as supreme political leader of the new Germany, but he had little use for the political cadres, and wanted to restrict them to propagandistic functions.[191] Their place would be taken by SA commissioners, who were to become permanent political supervisors of the governmental administration. In the course of these developments Röhm, would, of course, become the man next to Hitler in the political hierarchy of Germany.[192]

The PLs could hardly develop much enthusiasm for these musings. The Gauleiters were particularly vehement in their opposition, and countered with the demand that the SA units in their Gaus be subordinated to the control of the PLs in the *Gauleitung* (provincial leadership).[193] Among the party's prominent national leaders Röhm's foremost enemies were Hess, Goebbels, Ley, and Göring, although only the last was of immediate danger to him; as Prussian prime minister Göring was able to prevent the SA's take-over of the important police positions in Germany's largest state.[194]

With its smaller membership, Himmler's SS was not yet a serious rival for the PO, and relations between the two groups were relatively free of friction and bitterness. Nevertheless, the beginnings of a future power struggle were apparent. The SS was already exhibiting the early period of its "elite of elites" feeling, while some Gauleiters commented bitterly on the rise of erstwhile Junker types to positions of authority in Himmler's ranks.[195] The major institutional barriers to good relations between the SS and the PO were the activities of the SS's intelligence-gathering office, the Security Service (SD). For while the SD was theo-

---

190. Mau, "Zweite Revolution," p. 125. In "Thalburg" the SA and SS conducted regular military field maneuvers in March. See Allen, *Seizure*, p. 204.

191. See Ley to Hess, 14 April 1936, T-580, roll 549, folder 746.

192. Aronson, "Heydrich," pp. 101–02; and Timpke, *Dokumente*, p. 173.

193. See SA Untergruppe Hessen-Nassau-Nord to Obergruppe III, 20 Feb. 1933, BDC/Weinrich (PKC). See also Heinrich Bennecke, *Die Reichswehr und der "Röhm-Putsch"* (Munich, 1964), p. 42.

194. Mau, "Zweite Revolution," pp. 123 and 128.

195. Simon (GL of Koblenz-Trier) to Ley, 7 Sept. 1933, BDC/Waldeck (SS); and Kube (GL of Ostmark) to Himmler, 15 Nov. 1933, BDC/Kube (SS).

retically concerned only with information about the party's external enemies, it could never quite withstand the temptation of gathering material on the PO's and SA's failings as well.[196] In addition, the head of the SD, Reinhard Heydrich, essentially agreed with Röhm on the expendability of the PO after the Machtergreifung,[197] but was somewhat more tactful than Röhm in expressing such views.

Among the party's economic and social affiliates, the problem was not political elitism, but size of membership and the growing development of the various affiliates into pressure groups lobbying for the parochial interests of their membership. In the spring of 1933 the most active of the economic affiliates was the office of agricultural policy (*Amt für Agrarpolitik*, AfA) and its vertical cadres, the agricultural apparatus, a.A. Headed by R. Walther Darré, the AfA had both a fully verticalized corps of functionaries and a clear program. As a result, alone among the affiliates it was able to carry out Strasser's original Gleichschaltung plans after the Machtergreifung. The AfA could dispense with the appointment of temporary commissioners, because its provincial officials (the Gau experts on agriculture; *Landwirtschaftliche Gaufachberaters*, LGFs) already had the farmers well in hand.[198] As noted above, Darré's organization was also instrumental in forcing the nationalist Reich minister of agriculture out of office and it succeeded subsequently in merging the party and state agricultural administrations into a single mammoth institution staffed with personnel that was technically competent and politically Nazified.[199] At the same time the AfA was a typical lobbying group for a special interest; it really was able to secure genuine economic benefits for its constituency.[200]

The PLs had good reason to resent the AfA. With its centralized apparatus, subject to the orders of the Reichsleiter for agricultural policy, that is, Darré, rather than to the Gauleiters,[201] its close ties to the

196. See Aronson, "Heydrich," p. 65.

197. Heinz Höhne, *Der Orden unter dem Totenkopf* (Gütersloh, 1967), pp. 166 and 168.

198. *VB*, 6 April, 4 and 11 May, 1933; and Bracher, *Machtergreifung*, p. 188.

199. Bracher, *Machtergreifung*, p. 575.

200. Georges Castellan, "Bilan social du IIIe Reich (1933–1939)," *Revue d'histoire moderne et contemporaine*, XV (1968), 502–04.

201. See Hitler, "Verfügung," 12 April 1933, T-580, roll 12, folder 169.

SS hierarchy,[202] and its genuine popularity among the farmers, the AfA was clearly a potential threat to the predominant position of the PO in the Gaus. One of the first to realize this was the Gauleiter of East Prussia, Erich Koch. He resented the AfA's lobbying activities on behalf of the agricultural interests and noted, "The purpose of the *NS-Landvolk* [the mass organization sponsored by the AfA] is not to represent the farmers, but to make National Socialists out of them."[203] And since Koch was an impulsive man, he took immediate action: using his dual position as Gauleiter and provincial governor, he had the LGF of East Prussia arrested and expelled from the party. Darré countered by refusing to speak or write to Koch.[204]

Potentially equally dangerous was the party's Association of Civil Servants, the NSBB. Like the AfA, the NSBB had been effective in infiltrating a major professional group in the last years of the Republic. In addition, it had a highly centralized organization (modeled after that of Fascist Italy) with nineteen different branches to encompass the various types of civil servants.[205] Its leadership consisted of a highly ambitious Gauleiter, Jacob Sprenger (Hessen-Nassau-Süd), as president and the equally ruthless organizational secretary Hermann Neef, after July 1933 successor to Sprenger.[206] Their immediate aim was to partify the German civil service, but indirectly they also hoped to eclipse the political power of the PO. Their demand that the control of appointments to all civil service positions be subject to the approval of personnel officials named by the NSBB would have prevented the PO from controlling the operations of the German governmental offices.[207]

202. Bracher, *Machtergreifung*, pp. 570–71.

203. (GL of East Prussia), "Denkschrift über die Umtriebe im . . . Landvolk im Gau Ostpreussen," ca. July 1933, BDC/Koch (OPG).

204. The relevant documentation is in Koch's OPG file in the BDC.

205. See Sprenger to Grauert, 28 March 1933, HAB/77/13.

206. Sprenger, born in 1884, was a postal inspector before he became Gauleiter of Hessen-Nassau-Süd in 1927. In May 1933 he was appointed Reichsstatthalter of Hessen. He committed suicide in April 1945. Neef, born in 1904, by profession a customs official, spent his entire Nazi career in the party's civil service group, though he held simultaneous positions as a member of the Reichstag and Regierungsrat in the Reich interior ministry.

207. On the qualifications for the NSBB's personnel officials, see Neef's state-

The third of the party's prominent affiliates in the Strasser era, the National Socialist Organization of Factory Cells (NSBO), survived in the Third Reich only in diluted and changed form. The NSBO had been founded late in 1930 as a proto-union and a year later it had some eighteen thousand members.[208] But after January, the Nazi leadership had little use for a workers' interest group. Instead, Hitler and Ley decided on April 21 to seize the offices of the old unions and dissolve their organizations.[209] The action took place on May 2 (after Goebbels' staged parody of the traditional May Day parade the day before) and was carried out by the SA and NSBO.[210] In place of the free unions moved the giant German Labor Front (DAF), a compulsory organization encompassing all employees and employers in Germany, and headed by the NSDAP's Reich organizational leader, Robert Ley.[211] Ley had no more interest in genuine representation of the workers' wishes than Koch did in an organization representing the farmers; Ley wanted to transform the DAF into a vast propaganda enterprise and, more than incidentally, to use the new organization in conjunction with the PO as a power base for himself.[212] Consequently, Ley quickly reduced the NSBO to the status of a propaganda office, though a number of the old NSBO staffers retained positions in the vast DAF bureaucracy.[213]

There can be little doubt that at midyear the centrifugal forces in the NSDAP were still far more active than the institutional means at hand to coordinate the party's policies and personnel. The basic reason, as Rudolf Hess put it in a mild understatement in 1938, was that the

---

ment quoted in "Führerprinzip und Reaktion bei der Reichsbahn," *Der National-sozialistische Eisenbahner*, IV (1 Feb. 1934). Clipping in HAB/77/26.

208. Gerhard Starcke, *NSBO und Deutsche Arbeitsfront* (Berlin, 1934), pp. 34–38.

209. Timpke, *Dokumente*, p. 87, n. 1; and Goebbels, *Kaiserhof*, entry for 17 and 28 April 1933, pp. 299 and 304.

210. Bracher, *Machtergreifung*, pp. 181–82.

211. For a character sketch of Ley, see Schumann, *Nationalsozialismus*, pp. 151–55. A full-scale history of the DAF has not yet appeared; for a brief but accurate analysis, see Dieter v. Lölhöffel, "Die Umwandlung der Gewerkschaften in eine nationalsozialistische Zwangsorganisation," in Esenwein-Rothe, *Wirtschafts-verbände*, pp. 145–84.

212. Claus Selzner (in 1933, staff associate for organization), "Der Auftrag an Dr. Ley," *Hoheitsträger*, III (Feb. 1939), 10.

213. Bracher, *Machtergreifung*, p. 185. For additional discussion of the DAF and its role in the development of the party see below, pp. 69–70.

distribution of power within the party was "unclear" in 1933.[214] In less
veiled language this meant that Hitler in his fear of a restrengthened
Reichsleitung had allowed the Gauleiters to seize control of the territorial cadres, while a host of affiliates and paramilitary organizations
prospered at the expense of the political cadres as a whole. In addition,
Hitler had ignored his own introduction of yet another factor compli-
cating his traditional policy of divide and conquer. Both the Reichsleiters and Gauleiters derived their power directly from Hitler, and he
reserved the right to withdraw such grants at any time. With his appointment as chancellor, however, these derivative powers were also
transferred to the Reich ministers, who came to regard themselves as
the equals of the party leaders, with a similar right of direct access to
Hitler. And while it is true that no state leader achieved membership in
Hitler's inner circle, the constitutional changes wrought by the Nazis
gave the Reich ministries additional power positions. With the destruction of federalism in Germany, the Reich ministries in effect reduced
the former Länder to the status of field offices, controlled from Berlin.
Where a union of party organization and state offices took place, as in
the case of the Reich food estate or the Reich chamber of culture, the
result usually benefited a party affiliate rather than the PO. In the one
instance of a merger between the PO and a new mass organization, that
of the DAF, the political cadres were in danger of becoming an insignificant junior partner in the new institution.

Sometime in April, Hitler seems to have reached the conclusion that
the NSDAP would be eclipsed by its own affiliates and the gleichgeschaltete state organs unless he permitted at least a partial restoration
of the authority which had been vested in the Reichsleitung under
Strasser, thereby enabling the PO to become a significant national power factor in the Third Reich. At this time, the PO had four offices which
could claim partial jurisdictional powers over the entire PL cadre apparatus: the office of the Reich treasurer, the Reich organizational leadership, and the two control commissions, that is, the "investigation and
mediation committee" (*Untersuchungs- und Schlichtungsausschuss*,
Uschla), which by this time constituted a full-fledged intraparty court
system, and the party's Political Central Commission (Politische Zen-

214. Rudolf Hess [Rede auf Reichsparteitag 1938 vor Reichs- Gau- und Kreislei-
tern] (special printing; [Munich, 1938]), p. 3, MiU/GAC, folder 51.

tralkommission, PZK).[215] Of these, the office of the Reich treasurer and the ROL were in potentially good positions to subject the PL cadres to their influence. The treasurer's domain had not been involved in the Strasser crisis, while the ROL had inherited the bulk of Strasser's former powers.[216] In addition, both had fully verticalized staff organizations, ranging from Reich to local levels. The other two national offices faced serious barriers to their immediate effectiveness: the party courts administered by the Uschla were dependent on the cadre functionaries to initiate actions against party members or groups, and the PZK had not as yet attempted to exercise any of its control powers. Moreover, the PZK had virtually no staff organization at the Reich level, let alone below that.

The NSDAP's Reich treasurer and chief membership secretary Franz Schwarz was in many ways a curious exception to the prevailing pattern of frustrated failures among the top Nazi leaders. A man of advanced years (born in 1875), he was a model German bureaucrat. After a successful career in the municipal accounting office of Munich, he joined the NSDAP in 1925 and quickly became its national treasurer. In private life he was quiet and withdrawn; his hobbies included raising two young bucks at his summer cottage on the Tegernsee. He paralleled the emotions of other party leaders only in his blind devotion to Adolf Hitler. Although much older than his idol, he was clearly emotionally dependent upon the Führer.[217] Hitler in turn rewarded Schwarz's loyal devotion with unusually large and explicit grants of power. As early as 1926, Hitler had given the Reich treasurer blanket authority over the financial affairs of the party (except insofar as Hitler himself chose to take matters into his own hands), so that he was "completely independent of the political leadership in the party."[218] Concretely, this meant that Schwarz received a fixed percentage of the membership dues to insure the financial autonomy of his own subordinates at all levels

215. The office of national executive secretary, still headed by Phillip Bouhler, no longer exercised significant control functions.

216. Schäfer, *NSDAP*, p. 64.

217. A. Dresler, "Reichsschatzmeister F.X. Schwarz, der Mann und sein Werk," p. 2, BDC/Schwarz (PKC); and Ulf Lükemann, "Der Reichsschatzmeister der NSDAP" (Dissertation, Free University of Berlin, 1963), p. 23.

218. Franz X. Schwarz, "Ergänzung zu meiner Aufstellung über den Geschäftsbereich des Reichsschatzmeisters der NSDAP," p. 3, T-580, roll 47, folder 266.

of the party's administration, that he controlled the regular income and expenditures of all PO offices, and that he had the right to audit the books within the PO and most of the affiliate party organizations.

Throughout his party career, Schwarz pursued extremely orthodox financial policies. He attempted, not always successfully, to conduct the party's financial affairs on a cash basis. Since he feared the Gauleiters' inability to resist the temptations of contracting large debts— albeit for "worthy" political reasons—Schwarz consistently labored to make all routine expenditures subject to the approval of his staff officials at the various PO levels and to require his own prior approval for all but routine payments and investments. The latter category included in particular the granting of subsidies to the floundering Gau press.[219] As a result, Schwarz presided over a large staff of functionaries. His organization had eleven hundred full-time employees at the beginning of 1934; three hundred had their desks at party headquarters in the Brown House.[220] He also valued professional competence among his subordinates, and alone among the Reichsleitung department heads permitted discussion of technical and substantive issues in staff meetings. The treasurer's organization was the only cadre office in the NSDAP in which something akin to collegiality developed.[221]

Nevertheless, Schwarz was confronted with a number of serious problems. He saw the financial independence of the party (and his office) endangered by the careless euphoria with which Gau and district party offices suddenly ignored the pay-as-you-go regulations, contracted vast debts, and committed party funds to a number of shady business deals.[222] The Reich treasurer did not object to party-sponsored money-making schemes, nor did he oppose accepting state moneys for party purposes;[223] but he was unwilling to tolerate devices that might give

219. Schwarz, "Ergänzung," p. 3.

220. *VB*, 29 April 1934; and Dresler, "Reichsschatzmeister Schwarz," p. 2.

221. See *VB*, 5 May and 3 and 4 Sept. 1933; Rschm., "Rundschreiben" to all GL, 25 Aug. 1933, in *Rdschr.*, I.

222. *VB*, 21 March and 21 Sept. 1933; see also Goebbels to Schwarz, 21 April 1934, BDC/Schwarz (PKC).

223. Thus Schwarz announced plans for a "really large-scale" national lottery (Rschm., "Rundschreiben" to all GL, 11 May 1933, *Rdschr.*, I) and gladly accepted payment of the expenses of a GL conference by the Prussian state government. See Prussian ministry of finances to Prussian ministry of the interior, 20 July 1933, HAB/77/12.

the Gaus independent sources of income (deposited in secret bank accounts) or that would force the Reichsleitung to rescue a careless subordinate office from bankruptcy.[224] The Reich treasurer adjusted rapidly to the new situation. The most important control device available to his office was obviously the right to audit books. Before the Machtergreifung, the auditing procedures of the NSDAP had been somewhat irregular; rather perfunctory audits took place annually and special audits were ordered only when there were signs of glaring irregularities. After January, Schwarz augmented his auditing staff significantly. By October, all Gaus had to have a full-time auditor on their staffs; his sole responsibility was to check the books of all offices which reported to the Gauleiter. The auditors submitted monthly reports directly to Munich.[225] The Gau auditors were appointed by the Gauleiters after they had obtained the approval of the Reich treasurer. Since Schwarz insisted that the auditors have previous experience in money management and be trained in banking techniques, the Gauleiters were usually unable to appoint personal cronies to the post.

The Reich treasurer attempted to secure control of the party finances in a number of other ways as well. To prevent collusion between party offices and smaller private banks, he insisted that all party funds be kept in public savings banks or publicly controlled banks (for example, the postal checking system). The locals were permitted to keep only small amounts of cash in their treasuries; the remainder had to be turned over to the Gau and re-requested from the Gauleitung.[226] More significantly, Schwarz realized that the newly activated districts, particularly in urban areas, would soon become a major focal point of party activity, and eclipse the locals as the basic territorial units of the NSDAP. Consequently, he moved early to insist that the districts submit annual

224. That danger was real enough. The GL did attempt to escape from Schwarz's administrative control and tried to cover up cases of embezzlement among their staff officials. See Robert Wagner (GL of Baden) to Ley, BA/NS 22/200; and Rschm., "Rundschreiben" to all GL, 22 Dec. 1933, *Rdschr.* I.

225. Since the SA and SS jurisdictions usually covered more than one Gau, the paramilitary groups were excluded from his jurisdictional province, but their books were audited by a staff of Reich auditors operating from Munich.

226. Rschm., "Rundschreiben" to all GL, 1 July and 28 Aug. 1933, and 9 April 1934, *Rdschr.*, I. See also *VB*, 14 Oct. 1933.

budgets to the Reich office for approval.[227] Finally, Schwarz sought to establish a national salary scale for full-time party employees in order to prevent the often highly irregular reimbursement-for-expenses schemes in the Gaus as well as to facilitate the transfer of officeholders from Gau to Gau. Here, however, Schwarz failed; his hope of February 1934, that the salary scale would be issued "in the next few months"[228] could not be realized until well into World War II.

The Reich treasurer's failure to secure an amount of money sufficient to pay regular salaries to all full-time employees illustrated the limitations of his office as a central control mechanism for the entire party. Schwarz controlled the income from regular dues, but after January 1933 other sources of income, over which the Reich treasurer had no direct control, played an increasingly important role in the financing of party projects. Ley, for example, controlled the vast DAF funds (which included the treasuries of the former labor unions) and drew on these for his pet building projects "without contacting me," as Schwarz complained bitterly at the end of the war. The large business contributions flowing into the Adolf Hitler Fund from German Businessmen (*Adolf-Hitler-Spende der deutschen Wirtschaft*) were administered by Rudolf Hess and Martin Bormann. Himmler had a "circle of friends" (*Freundeskreis*) which contributed lavishly to the expansion of the SS.[229] Even the SA, though financed primarily by a portion of the membership dues, was at this time powerful enough to have its funds transferred directly to the SA's national office in Munich.

The situation in the affiliates was not much better, though the general incompetence of their staffs brought their finances into disarray and consequently enabled Schwarz to curtail their financial autonomy. Nevertheless, by the end of the year he was administering only the National Socialist Women's League (*NS-Frauenschaften*, NSF), the NSBO, the Winter Help (*Winterhilfswerk*, WHW) and the National Socialist Welfare Organization (*NS-Volkswohlfahrt*, NSV). Of these,

227. Rschm., "Rundschreiben" to all GL, 23 March 1934, *Rdschr.*, I. See also Haag to Schwarz, 1 April 1938, T-580, roll 806, box 239, folder 44.

228. Rschm. "Rundschreiben" to all GL, 28 Feb. 1934, *Rdschr.*, I.

229. Schwarz, "Ergänzung," pp. 2–3, and 12; and ROL, *Dienstvorschrift 1933*, p. 25.

only the last two were politically significant. As the only party-affiliated welfare organizations, the WHW and the NSV annually collected and administered sums that ran into millions of marks, and Schwarz clearly wanted to keep these sums out of the Gauleiters' hands.[230] The NSF, on the other hand, was a financially bankrupt, politically impotent organization, and the NSBO lived only a shadowy existence under the control of the DAF.[231]

Since Schwarz could draw moneys for his planned salary fund only from the regular membership dues, his control of the membership rolls became crucial. Technically, the matter was clear-cut: The locals received membership applications and sent them on to the Gau. Here they were compiled into Gau lists and forwarded to Munich. Only after Schwarz's office had processed the papers could the new applicant be considered a member who was liable to dues payments. Neither a local nor a Gauleiter was empowered to grant membership status.[232] In practice, the system worked considerably less well; both locals and Gaus kept back applications from unwitting applicants in order to collect their dues without transferring the Reich share to Schwarz. This practice was a major reason for the ban on new applications at the beginning of May.[233] The ban was actually at least in part ineffective, since it enabled the affiliates to expand their membership rolls dramatically, at the expense of the party, but Schwarz apparently felt the ban was necessary to prevent the accumulation of further private membership rolls in the Gaus. Even so, Schwarz had seriously underestimated the quiet defiance of his authority. He had expected the rolls to be reopened after a year,[234] but it took until 1937 to bring order into the membership chaos. At best, then, Schwarz's usefulness as a centralized control organ for the PO was severely limited; moderately effective as a guardian of financial orthodoxy in the party, he neither sought nor was able to exercise significant influence over the political dynamics of the PO.

230. Rschm., "Rundschreiben" to all GL, 24 July, 9 Oct., and 22 Dec. 1933, *Rdschr.*, I .

231. *Ibid.*, 31 Oct. 1933; and "Rundschreiben" to all NSBO-Gau treasurers, *VOBl*, III (4 Dec. 1933), 131.

232. Rschm., "Bekanntgabe," 28 Sept. 1933, *VOBl*, III (1 Oct. 1933), 119. See also Kaufmann to OPG, 3 July 1934, BDC/Böckenhauer (PKC).

233. *VB*, 22 April 1933.

234. *VOBl*, II (15 Aug. 1933), 114.

This was even more true of the Reich-Uschla. The party courts were headed by a man who, though considerably younger than Schwarz, was in many ways similar to him. Walther Buch, a retired army major, was another one of those "idealists" in the party who expected Hitler and the party to usher in an era of moral uplift. For Buch, morality consisted primarily of a series of negatives, chief among them anti-Semitism, antifreemasonry and antipornography. His relationship to Hitler, however, was, at least until 1935, essentially identical to that of Schwarz. Buch, too, stood in awe of the new Germanic duke. On the other hand, the administrative powers of the two offices showed little similarity. Unlike the Reich treasurer's, Buch's organization neither had a clear mandate from Hitler nor was staffed with technically able officials. Virtually none of the party judges (including Buch) had judicial training, and their judgments consequently showed no positive uniform line or overall concept.[235] Moreover, Buch had little control over disputes within the PO. In quarrels between Reichsleiters and Gauleiters, for example, his role was restricted to that of a mediator, and no cadre functionary could appeal to the Uschla system if his complaint involved dismissal or transfer from office.[236] In fact, the only politically significant control function which the Reich-Uschla exercised was its role in the disputes over membership status. Since the local PO leaders and the local party judges were often "old fighters" who attempted to purge many—opportunistic in their view—new party members as soon as they entered,[237] Hitler permitted Buch to make the Reich-Uschla the final court of appeal for the membership controversies.[238] It was obviously not much of a base on which to erect the exercise of authority over the PO.

On balance, it is clear that neither the Reich treasurer nor the party's chief judge had the ability or the authority to become a strong coordinator at the Reich level. The Reich organizational leader, Robert Ley, on the other hand, seemed to possess all of the necessary prerequisites for the role of strong man in the NSDAP. Hitler considered him a genuine

235. See Nicolai to Lammers, 11 Aug. 1933, BA/R 43 II/426a.
236. Buch to Hermann Czirmick (Stettin), 15 May 1933, T-580, roll 554, box 377, folder 877; OPG, "Beschluss: in Sachen . . . Heinrich Schleth [*et al.*]," n.d.; and Koch to Buch, 8 Nov. 1934, BDC/Koch (OPG).
237. See *VB*, 28 April 1934.
238. *VOBl*, II (30 June and 31 July 1933), 108 and 112 respectively.

idealist, as head of the ROL he had inherited the bulk of Strasser's jurisdictions, and he had surrounded himself with a number of able administrators.[239] In mid-1933, Ley was, in his own words, "the Reichs-leiter of the PO appointed by the Führer and solely responsible to him." Under Ley functioned a number of "staff administrators," who handled both aspects of the territorial cadre administration and a number of affiliates. For the PO these included personnel, organization, in-service training (*Schulung*), and the bulk of the inspectorate system. Among the affiliates, in addition to the DAF, Ley administered the organiza-tions for the civil servants, corporate construction (*Amt für Ständischen Aufbau*), communal affairs, physicians, veterans' affairs, the NSF, and the NSV.[240] At least on paper, a formidable empire lay at Ley's dis-posal. In the political cadres he had a fully verticalized structure; the affiliates under his control affected virtually every adult German, and their resources, headed by the DAF's vast funds, made Ley largely independent of Schwarz's organs.

Nevertheless, the giant machinery had a number of flaws—most of them reflecting weaknesses and peculiarities of its chief administrator. Quite aside from some of Ley's personal foibles, such as his alcoholism, there was size itself. Ley suffered from what his enemy Alfred Rosen-berg called "gigantomania,"[241] that is, he exhibited an uncontrollable desire constantly to organize and reorganize offices and jurisdictions, without bothering to coordinate the scheme which he had put into effect the day before with his new idea for today.[242] Organization in a political party should be the deployment of offices, uniforms, and func-tions among the cadres to enable the organization as a whole to achieve its political goals, but in the case of the ROL, organization became an end in itself. Ley was convinced that in the Kampfzeit the party had raised political organization to the level of a science, and it was his duty to see that the science was not lost. As a result, there was some-thing almost scholastic about organizational guidelines published by

239. Schumann, *Nationalsozialismus*, p. 152.

240. ROL, *Dienstvorschrift 1933*, p. 19. Ley used the term "staff administrator" (*Stabswalter*) deliberately to obscure the fact that he actually functioned as Hitler's chief of staff (*Stabsleiter*) for the PO. Technically, Hitler had taken personal charge of the PO in 1932.

241. Rosenberg, *Letzte*, p. 175.

242. Schumann, *Nationalsozialismus*, p. 153.

the ROL's office. They left nothing to chance; there were even instructions on how an "artistically talented" party member was to draw the proper organizational chart for each office and directives on the color of the heads of pins to be used in indicating the residences of party members and functionaries on a map of each local. Ley's instructions were considerably less explicit on items that really mattered for a party that claimed to provide the political elite of the Third Reich. The *Dienstvorschrift* (administrative handbook) for 1933 contained little on the inspectorate system and less on the significance of the districts in a mass party. The guidelines for cadre selection by the personnel offices were of little help in finding functionaries with technical skills. Far more important than such mundane considerations as technical competence, seemingly, were the candidates' racial ancestry and their political bills of health. But even when these had been established, personnel officials would need a good knowledge of human nature and long years of experience to find a PL who "has firmly grasped the ideas of National Socialism." Ley was only relatively clearer on the relationship of the PO, the paramilitary branches, and the affiliates in the NSDAP. He did establish that the affiliates and paramilitary groups were politically subordinate to the PO, though the statement that the cadre functionary was the "soul of everything" was not much of a practical aid.[243] Similarly, the always troublesome question of the relationship between the Gauleiters and the staff officials at the Gau level reporting to the various Reichsleiters (for example, the LGFs) found no real resolution; Ley wanted to strengthen both groups.[244]

What was unclear in theory was obscured even further in practice by Ley's relationship to the DAF. It soon became apparent that Ley increasingly neglected his role as party cadre chief, and turned toward the organizational buildup of the DAF.[245] In part, the DAF attracted Ley because it was a virgin organizational field, but Ley had far-reaching, if somewhat vague, political ambitions as well. He hoped eventually to merge the NSDAP and the DAF into a gigantic "university of the NS *Weltanschauung*," that is, a huge organism encompassing

243. This resume utilizes regulations found in the ROL, *Dienstvorschrift 1933*, pp. 18, 21, 29, 36, 71, 81, and 94–96.
244. *VOBl*, II (31 Aug. 1933), 116, and III (15 Nov. 1933), 130.
245. Schoenbaum, *Hitler's Social Revolution*, p. 84.

virtually all Germans, with a single, or at least interchangeable, system of functionary corps, training centers, and so on.[246] Here was the fundamental reason for Ley's eventual failure: he attempted to fuse two concepts that were essentially incompatible. The NSDAP could not simultaneously be an elite organization guiding policy decisions in the Nazi totalitarian society and a mass organization "taking care" (Ley's favorite word was betreuen) of all Germans, educating them in the ways of the NS Weltanschauung. The concept of "taking care" reduced the PO to the status of glorified propagandists and social workers; the idea of a political elite excluded Ley's role as chief Betreuer of the nation.

All this meant that none of the three fully verticalized offices in the party, the ROL, the party courts (Uschla), and the Reich treasurer, could effectively carry through the recentralization of the NSDAP. Hitler either had to create a new Reich-level office with clear powers or watch the party's Reichsleitung wither before the strengthened state apparatus and the Gauleitungs. Since the latter development would have spelled an end to Hitler's own "divide and conquer" policy, he chose the former course of action. On April 21, 1933, the Führer appointed Rudolf Hess, his private secretary and head of the PZK, to the position of deputy Führer (*Stellvertreter des Führers*, StdF). It was clear from the title and description of the new position that Hitler regarded the situation in the party as serious. Hess was the first and last bearer of the title; Hitler obviously felt the new office should be endowed with as much prestige as possible. Yet even now Hitler could not bring himself to establish a clear-cut division of authority between the Reichsleiters, the Gauleiters, and the new deputy Führer. Hess's power over the PO was indirect rather than immediate. At the time of Hess's appointment, Hitler reiterated the significance of the territorial cadres in the NSDAP and strengthened their position vis-à-vis the functional staffs and the affiliates. He then assigned the deputy Führer far-reaching control functions over the PL cadres, thereby indirectly placing the political control of the NSDAP in his hands.[247]

With this appointment a long-time, but relatively obscure[248] Nazi

246. See, for example, *VB*, 9 and 10 June 1933.
247. *VB*, 29 April 1933. The terms of Hess's appointment are also printed in Domarus, *Hitler*, I, 257.
248. See the comment on the appointment in *VB*, 29 April 1933.

leader moved into the political limelight. Rudolf Hess was born of German parents in Alexandria, Egypt, in 1895. He served in the flying corps during World War I, and after demobilization became a student in Munich. Here he succumbed to Hitler's spell, remaining his "apostle"[249] for the rest of the Führer's life. After the 1923 putsch, Hess stayed with Hitler during his imprisonment at Landsberg. Following Hitler's release, Hess became his private secretary. In this position he distinguished himself by utter loyalty and devotion, though not, his contemporaries thought, by a particularly strong character or sound political judgments. Instead, the dominant characteristics remembered by his peers seem to have been his rather unusual hobbies (which included astrology and magnetism) and his hypochondriac tendencies.[250] But there was clearly another side to Hess's personality. He was by no means unintelligent and his published letters, dating, to be sure, from his imprisonment in England and Spandau, show him as a man of some genuine feeling, a quality which he had communicated earlier to his fellow leaders in the party and to the public at large.[251] Similarly, his circle of personal friends contained many eccentrics, but also some genuinely interesting personalities.[252] In the twenties, the relationship between Hess and Hitler was obviously mutually warm and trusting. There are reports that their relations cooled soon after 1933,[253] but this seems to have been an oversimplified impression. At any rate, Hitler's so-called table talks reveal only positive comments about Hess even

249. Joachim C. Fest, *Das Gesicht des Dritten Reiches* (Munich, 1964), pp. 257–70, describes the relationship between Hitler and Hess as typical of an apostle and his god.

250. Hans Frank, *Im Angesicht des Galgens* (Munich-Gräfeling, 1953), pp. 165–67, and 273–74; Konstantin Hierl, *Im Dienst für Deutschland* (Heidelberg, 1954); p. 124; Rosenberg, *Tagebuch*, entry for 3 Dec. 1939, p. 108; Lutz Graf Schwerin von Krosigk, *Es geschah in Deutschland* (Tübingen, 1951), pp. 239–40; and Fritz Wiedemann, *Der Mann der Feldherr werden wollte* (Velbert, 1964), p. 197. See also Joseph Wulf, *Martin Bormann* (Gütersloh, 1962), p. 26. A description of a medical examination of Karl Haushofer (Hess's friend and well-known "geopolitician") by a "spiritual healer" in Hess's presence is given in T-253, roll R 61, frames 1517834–37.

251. See the statement by Buch, p. 3, Institut für Zeitgeschichte, Munich (cited hereafter as IfZ)/ZS 855.

252. Speer, *Erinnerungen*, p. 58.

253. Otto Dietrich, *Zwölf Jahre mit Hitler* (Cologne, 1955), p. 204; and Ernst Hanfstaengl, *Unheard Witness* (Philadelphia, 1957), p. 242.

after the StdF's flight to England,[254] and there are numerous instances
throughout the thirties in which Hitler made his approval of a course of
action contingent upon Hess's agreement with the proposal.[255] Equally
controversial are Hess's work habits and administrative talents. There
is little doubt that, like Hitler, the new deputy Führer disliked desk
work and administrative routine. Instead, he quickly developed the
habit of formulating his decisions (usually given orally) on the basis of
short excerpts from letters and memoranda prepared by his staff.[256]
This style of administration, while hardly a bureaucrat's ideal, met the
needs of the moment. At least in the early years after the Machtergreifung, Hess accompanied Hitler on the Führer's almost constant and
peripatetic travels, and this mode of life undoubtedly precluded any
regular office hours—even if Hess had been inclined to run his office in
a more conventional manner.

At the time of his appointment as deputy Führer, Hess held two
other positions in the NSDAP: he headed the PZK and an agency called
the Liaison Staff (*Verbindungsstab*). At the time neither office seemed
very significant, and the rapid growth of the StdF's staff has all but
obscured them, but they were important as the institutional bases for
Hess's expansion of power in the NSDAP. The PZK was the less important successor of Strasser's inspectorate system. While Ley had six
field inspectors at his disposal, Hess had to be content with a single
"Reich inspector for special purposes" (*Reichsinspektor zur besonderen
Verwendung*). On the other hand, the appellate, or residual, powers of
the PZK were considerable, since they included the formal right to approve appointments to all Reich-level or multi-Gau positions in the PO.
There is no record of the Liaison Staff's founding, but it was created on
Hitler's orders, and as early as March 20, it had both an office and letterhead stationery. Nominally, its primary function was to act as a sort of
national clearing-house for all requests originating with party offices
but directed toward state agencies. Apparently, it attempted to do for

254. See Henry Picker, ed., *Hitler's Tischgespräche im Führerhauptquartier
1941–1942*, ed. Percy-Ernst Schramm *et al.*, new ed. (Stuttgart, 1965), pp. 160 and
215.

255. See, for example, Lammers to Darré, 28 March 1939, BA/R 43 II/1390a.

256. See Klopfer's statement, p. 10, IfZ/ZS 352. See also *VB*, 15 April 1934; and
Das Reich, 22 Dec. 1940. For a negative appraisal of Hess's administrative habits,
see Peterson, *Limits of Hitler's Power*, p. 21.

the Reich as a whole what Kube's ineffective office tried to do for Prussia. Above all, of course, this involved dealing with the demands for dismissal of various civil servants. The Liaison Staff had some hopes that channeling the requests through its office in Berlin would prevent public disagreements among party leaders and thus strengthen the position of the party as a whole in its negotiations with governmental personnel officials.[257] In addition, as noted above, the Liaison Staff and the PZK handled the behind-the-scenes economic and social persecution of Strasser's friends and followers.[258]

The leading officials associated with the Liaison Staff are shrouded in mystery. Its director of day-to-day operations was Consul Rolf Reiner, but his name is virtually all that is known about him. He has no personnel record in the Berlin Document Center (BDC), and his only public appearance was a failure: he was on the NSDAP Reich list for the Reichstag election of 1933, but was not elected. Thereafter he vanished into obscurity. Other staff members are better known, but only because they had subsequent careers in other organizations and institutions of the Third Reich. Thus Kurt Daluege and Erbprinz von Waldeck had successful SS careers, while Hitler's favorite piano player, Putzi Hanfstaengl, eventually made his way to the Allied side.[259]

At least a partial explanation for this lack of substantial information about the staff's personnel lies in the fact that as a coordinating institution it was unsuccessful. Without a clear mandate, Reiner, despite Hess's vigorous backing, could not enforce his judgments on the unruly Gauleiters and Reichsleiters. Even the prime ministers of small states

257. On the liaison staff, see Verbindungsstab, "Anordnung," 24 March 1933; Verbindungsstab to Epp, 20 March 1933, BGStA, MA 105475; and Daluege to Staatskommissar Fuchs, 27 April 1933, BDC/Ordner, Parteikanzlei, Staatssekretär Präsidialkanzlei. For a brief Nazi discussion of the liaison staff, see Gottfried Neesse, *Partei und Staat* (Hamburg, 1936), p. 68.

258. The PZK and the liaison staff kept a special file on "Strasser-friends" and determined to what extent these men should still be subject to economic or social retaliatory measures. See Kiehn to Frick, 25 April 1936; Kiehn to Hess, 29 Nov. 1933, HAB/320/35; Grauert to Grohé, 17 June 1933; and Heinrichsbauer (another business associate) to Grauert, 16 Nov. 1935, HAB/77/6. This information was also verified by a letter written to the author by Mr. Heinrichsbauer, 23 Dec. 1962.

259. On these staff members see Höhne, *Orden*, p. 75; Waldeck to RFSS, 30 March 1933, BDC/Waldeck (SS); and Hanfstaengl to Esser, 11 May, 1933, BGStA, MA 105477.

ignored him,[260] and when Hess wrote Ley that he (Hess) had transferred his full authority to Reiner, Ley replied in all pseudoinnocence that to date Hitler had not informed him of the ROL's subordination to Reiner's dictates.[261]

The major difference between the authority of the Liaison Staff and the new office of the StdF was the nature of the Führerbefehl that created the new office: the office of StdF was directly sanctioned by Hitler, while the Liaison Staff had been only indirectly authorized. It was understandable that Hess quickly abandoned his efforts to strengthen Reiner and emphasized instead the significance of his new title and functions. The deputy Führer immediately acquired a "luxuriously furnished" office in the Brown House,[262] although such externals were hardly of decisive importance. Considerably more significant was the relatively rapid acceptance by governmental agencies of Hess's claim to be the supreme spokesman for the party; the most important manifestation was clearly the vote by the Reich cabinet to let Hess participate in all of its meetings.[263]

It proved considerably more difficult to assert central authority within the party itself, however, particularly because Hitler seemed to withdraw part of the power grant to the StdF only a few weeks after he had given it. On June 2, the Führer named sixteen Reichsleiters who together were to form the "Reichsleitung of the NSDAP." Hess was among the group, but so were such lesser notables as Wilhelm Grimm, the head of the second chamber of the OPG (*Oberstes Parteigericht*; Supreme Party Court), and Otto Dietrich, the party's Reich press chief.[264] Hitler did not formally reduce Hess's authority, but the appointment of sixteen Reichsleiters, all of whom theoretically had direct

260. See the unsigned note "Betr.: Braunschweig," 19 April 1933, BDC/ Klagges (OPG).

261. Hess to Ley, 2 June 1933; and Schmeer (of the office of the ROL) to Reiner, 17 May 1933, T-580, roll 549, folder 746.

262. Speer, *Erinnerungen*, p. 41.

263. Lammers to Hess, 27 June 1933, BA/R 43 II/1196. See also *VB*, 30 June 1933. For relations between the StdF and the Reich ministries, see Hans Buchheim, "Der 'Stellvertreter des Führers,'" in Kluke, *Gutachten*, pp. 323–24; and Neesse, *Partei und Staat*, pp. 62–63.

264. Hitler, "Verfügung," 2 June 1933, *VOBl*, II (31 May 1933), 101. The sixteen were: Hess, Röhm, Himmler, Schwarz, Bouhler, Buch, Grimm, Ley, Darré, Goebbels, Frank, Dietrich, Amann, Rosenberg, Schirach, and Fiehler.

access to Hitler (the Gauleiters maintained this right as well), certainly gives the impression that Hess had been reduced from *primus* to *pares*. A clear division of labor existed only between Hess and Schwarz. Hitler had specifically stated, and Hess equally explicitly acknowledged, that Schwarz's jurisdiction was excluded from the StdF's field of competence.[265] That left fourteen jurisdictionally unclear areas, and an equal number of potential rivalries and disputes. For the moment, then, the StdF could progress in asserting his authority within the party only indirectly, by expanding his undisputed right to represent the party vis-à-vis the state. In practice, this meant that the office of the StdF had to create a staff organization that was able to coordinate and translate the political goals of the Reichsleiters into legal bills which could be presented to governmental organs. In time, such rights of coordination might become the right to give orders. Similarly, the StdF would buy the Gauleiters' cooperation by becoming their champion in the struggles between the party chiefs and the ministerial bureaucracy.[266]

The fulcrum of the entire plan was the staff of the StdF; Hess had as yet no vertical structure, though he would soon attempt to begin building one. His administrative personnel was at first limited to a few staff officials at his Munich office, the Reich inspector for special purposes he had inherited from the PZK, and the skeleton crew at the Liaison Staff in Berlin. As his chief of staff (*Stabsleiter*), the deputy Führer chose Martin Bormann,[267] a man who was not unknown in the party, though at this time he was not yet one of its prominent leaders. The qualifications which Bormann brought to his new post were administrative skill and excellent personal relations to Hitler and other top Nazis. For some years before 1933 he had demonstrated his administrative acumen as manager of the party-owned insurance business, and he had made his influence felt on a number of political issues as well. He took part in the 1932 abortive attempt to dismiss Röhm, and in the

265. *VOBl*, II (31 May 1933), 102.

266. This strategy provided no real solution to the problem of the ROL's jurisdiction over the PO, but here only a frontal attack or a new power grant from Hitler would have been effective.

267. Soon after his initial appointment, Bormann became a Reichsleiter as well. Hess insisted on this in order to underscore that the chief of staff of the StdF's office had a position equal to that of the staff leader of the PO, Robert Ley. See Diehl-Thiele, *Partei*, p. 210.

fall of that year was a member of Hitler's Kaiserhof clique. Bormann always remained a man of the inner sanctum: he had no propagandistic skills and never administered a party territory. He made up for that failing by a good marriage. In 1929 he married Gerda Buch, the daughter of the party's chief judge. Hitler attended the ceremony, and thereafter the relations between the Führer and Bormann became increasingly close. There is some doubt about the genuineness of Bormann's feelings toward Hitler, but none about the manner in which he expressed them. Even in his private letters, Bormann worshipped his chief,[268] and he was one of the few in the Führer's entourage who openly emulated his vegetarian habits.[269] Hitler, in turn, apparently valued Bormann less as a person than as a useful instrument that had the uncanny ability to cast Hitler's oral ramblings into formulations that could be dispatched as administrative orders to party and state offices.[270] In addition, Hitler undoubtedly appreciated the efficient manner in which Bormann managed the Führer's personal affairs, particularly the expenditure of the moneys collected through the Adolf Hitler Fund from German Businessmen. Bormann financed the various building projects at Hitler's Obersalzberg mountain retreat with these sums.[271]

The relationship of Hess and Bormann has been the subject of considerable controversy. There is no doubt that at some point before May 1941 the subordinate eclipsed the superior and that Hess eventually came to hate Bormann.[272] The date of this development is less easily fixed. At least one author has placed the reversal of roles in the early thirties,[273] but there is considerable evidence that at least until the beginning of the war the two men worked quite well together: Bormann needed Hess's popularity and standing among the PLs to assert the authority of the office, and Hess could not perform without Bormann's

268. See Bormann to Gerda Bormann, 6 July 1943 in Hugh R. Trevor-Roper, ed., *The Bormann Letters*, tr. R. H. Stevens (London, 1954), p. 12.

269. Dietrich, *Zwölf Jahre*, p. 219.

270. Albert Zoller, *Hitler privat* (Düsseldorf, 1949), pp. 220–21.

271. Dietrich, *Zwölf Jahre*, pp. 188 and 211; and Wulf, *Martin Bormann*, pp. 31–33.

272. Werner Bross, "Gespräche mit Hermann Göring," (MS photocopy, Nov. 1946), p. 188.

273. Wulf, *Martin Bormann*, p. 62. See also Mommsen, *Beamtentum*, p. 118.

administrative talent and bureaucratic perseverance. In addition, both had a direct interest in actualizing the potential powers of the StdF, or, as Bormann put it, they both knew the mind of the Führer.[274]

Martin Bormann's personality was that of a typical, apersonal administrator. He was neither cultured nor educated, though in later years he liked to issue pseudophilosophical musings. For the most part, however, he was wedded to documents and competencies—so much so that his physical appearance changed with the status of the office he held. Photographs of Bormann as head of the NSDAP's party chancellery show him as a heavy-set man, whose most prominent feature is the famous bull neck; but a photograph taken in early 1933 (when Bormann still managed the insurance office) reveals an almost completely different individual: he is shown at a small desk in a minuscule room devoid of all decoration, wearing a Bavarian-type Loden jacket. His frame was narrow and his hair was brushed upward, as if to add additional height. He looked very much as Hanfstaengl remembered him: "tidy, modest, thrifty."[275]

For a time the Liaison Staff and the Munich office of the StdF developed as parallel entities. The Liaison Staff retained both its title and its office in Berlin. Not until sometime in the later thirties was it reduced to the status of the StdF's lesser branch office in the Reich capital. The StdF's staff in Munich for all practical purposes emerged from and eventually superseded the PZK. It began its work at the beginning of June with a group of "two to three," a far cry from the several hundred who worked for the StdF at the end of the decade.[276] The original staff consisted of three PLs: Martin Bormann, Alfred Leitgen, and Gustaf Adolf von Wulffen. Of these, only Bormann had previous administrative experience in the party. Leitgen, who was not even a party member before his appointment, was a journalist and an acquaintance of Otto

274. Kurt Borsdorff, "Mit Reichsleiter Martin Bormann auf dem Obersalzberg," p. 4, T-580, roll 79, folder 368. This manuscript is a highly adulatory interview with Bormann written in May 1939. It shows corrections by a member of Bormann's staff, but the article was never published.

275. Hanfstaengl, *Unheard Witness*, p. 242. For a fuller characterization of Bormann see Fest, *Gesicht*, pp. 175–89. The only book-length biography of Bormann is Wulf, *Martin Bormann*, but it is rather offhandedly written. The physical description is based on the picture in *IB*, 18 Feb. 1933.

276. Bormann's appointment was dated June 1. See *VOBl*, II (15 July 1933), 109. The figures are quoted in Borsdorff, "Reichsleiter Martin Bormann," pp. 3–4.

Dietrich. He was engaged as Hess's press secretary, presumably because the new deputy Führer felt the necessity of publicizing his office as quickly as possible.[277] Wulffen was equally far from the status of an "old fighter." He had been a professional officer in World War I, then a traveling salesman, becoming eventually business manager of an ultra-conservative businessmen's association, the *Nationalclub* in Hamburg. In between he also joined the SA. In May, Wulffen came to Munich hoping for a position in the SA Reichsleitung. Since none was available, or at any rate no one showed much interest in him, he was sent to the new StdF office. Here staffers were urgently needed and Wulffen became head of Hess's personnel office, a position which at that time involved primarily maintaining the records of the StdF's PLs and clerical employees. His tenure with the deputy Führer lasted until the late thirties, when Wulffen went on to the decoration and insignia office of the presidential chancellery.[278]

Beyond the core of these three men ranged the six *Beauftragte*, or investigators, the pitiful remnant of Strasser's territorial inspectorate system. Their status was a bit cloudy. Administratively, they were part of the ROL's staff, but their work clearly fell into Hess's province as head of the PZK. At any rate the StdF moved quickly to have the investigators identify their careers with his office, though formally they remained within the ROL's organization until 1934. The deputy Führer insisted that all six (in addition to the immediate staff members) become Reichstag deputies.[279] More important, Hess used the investigators and his own position in the PZK as the immediate jurisdictional base for activating his new office within the PO.[280] The device was simple: Hess encouraged the cadres to send complaints about excesses

277. For Leitgen's difficulties in getting into the party, see BDC/Leitgen (OPG); information about his professional journalistic activity is in BA/NS6/100.

278. This account of Wulffen's career may be somewhat unfair. It is based on Bormann's evidence, and the chief of staff came to hold a very low opinion of Wulffen. Nevertheless, it appears to be accurate in the main; Wulffen was certainly not a strong personality. See Bormann to Osaf, 29 May 1933; and Bormann to Himmler, 16 Feb. 1944, BDC/v. Wulffen (PKC).

279. See the undated listing in HAB/320/38.

280. *VB*, 20 Dec. 1933. For the handling of a specific case see "Zu den Akten Braunschweig," 27 Sept. 1933, BDC/Klagges (OPG). See also the interrogation of Karl Kaufmann (GL of Hamburg) 31 March 1948, Forsch. Hbg./PA/12/K.

and corruption to his office. The results were a veritable flood of letters and memoranda.[281] The cases became so numerous, in fact, that the six investigators had to be supplemented by Gau inspectors, who handled less difficult cases confined to a single Gau area.[282]

The growing chaos of party activism gave added impetus to the investigative and decision-making powers of the StdF,[283] but it also continued to weaken the power position of the party as a whole. Hitler was aware of these developments and, after a few half-hearted attempts to curtail the party's decentralized activism by more informal means,[284] decided sometime between the middle and end of June that the acute "revolutionary" phase of the Machtergreifung had to come to an end. The final decision came rather suddenly. As late as June 14, Hitler had told the assembled Gauleiters that the revolution had not yet run its course,[285] and a week later the presidents of the German chambers of commerce met with the clear object of planning in earnest the economic upheavals dictated by a restructuring of the German economy along "estate" lines. There was no direct connection between the two meetings, but it is significant that the Gau leaders of the Amt für Ständischen Aufbau were present at both sessions.[286] Five days later, the arrest and dispatch to a concentration camp of four second-echelon NSBO officials signaled a reversal of the policy. In widely publicized charges, the four were accused of attempting to limit Hitler's freedom of action by in-

281. See BA/GF/33.

282. *VB*, 12 May 1933.

283. Hess's first general directive to the party prohibited interference by local party organs in the economy. See Genschel, *Verdrängung*, pp. 78–79.

284. This took the form of admonitions to party officials to check a denunciation before arresting the accused and remarks to prominent leaders that the revolution had to proceed in an orderly fashion. See Hitler to Reichsstatthalter and the Prussian prime minister, 31 May 1933; enclosure in Bavarian minister of justice to district attorney, 16 June 1933, BGStA, MA 105479; Walter Buch, *Vortrag des Reichsleiters Buch über Parteigerichte und oberste Parteigerichtshoheit* (gehalten vor Offizieren des RKM am 14.10.37) [(Berlin, 1937)], T-77, roll 380, frame 1227049; and Killinger (SA leader in Saxony) to OPG, Aug. 1936, BDC/Killinger (OPG).

285. *VB*, 16 June 1933; Domarus, *Hitler*, I, 283. As late as 27 June, GL Koch announced that "the second wave of the revolution will begin its course here [East Prussia]." See Darré to OPG, 4 Oct. 1933, BDC/Koch (OPG).

286. See Pieper (president of the chamber of commerce in Küstrin) to Grauert, 20 June 1933, HAB/77/45. See also *VB*, 7 June 1933.

terfering in the economic life of the country.[287] In short, they had put into practice what the Führer had promoted in theory a week earlier. Within the next week Hitler became more direct and explicit: at a new meeting of the Gauleiters and SA leaders, he formally proclaimed the end of the Nazi revolution.[288]

There is little doubt that developments in the economic field, particularly the activism of the Amt für Ständischen Aufbau and other economic affiliates, were the primary cause of Hitler's decision to curb the radicals. He never drew a direct causal connection between the two events, but his statements at the beginning of July reveal the concern clearly enough. On July 7, he treated the Gauleiters to a lengthy discussion of the economy—immediately after he had noted that the revolution had to be "contained" (*auffangen*).[289] A few days later (July 12), he spoke again to an assemblage of Gauleiters and party economic experts. This time he specifically opposed the dynamic radicalism of the Amt, and counseled lengthy "preparations" before putting any plans into practice.[290] Nevertheless, the economy was not the only factor. The party activists had created negative reactions in a number of other areas as well. Hitler had to realize that a Machtergreifung in Austria could not be achieved with the methods which had been so successful in Germany. Although he had expected the fall of the Dollfuss regime by the end of 1933, it was clear at midyear that the NSDAP's campaign of violence had not weakened the position of the Austrian government.[291] The radical forays of the party-sponsored "German Christians" (DC) similarly alienated many Germans, and yielded no politically significant results. The NSDAP attempted to put all of its weight behind the July election campaign for synodical seats in the Protestant churches, but the results were disappointing. In consequence, Hitler rapidly severed the connection between the party and the DC and decreed a

287. Domarus, *Hitler*, I, 285.

288. Mau, "Zweite Revolution," p. 120; and Bracher, *Machtergreifung*, p. 474.

289. [Epp], "Besprechung des Reichskanzlers mit den Reichsstatthaltern in Berlin . . . 6.VII. [1933]," pp. 2–3, BGStA, Rsth. 148. See also Domarus, *Hitler*, I, 286–87.

290. Domarus, *Hitler*, I, 289; and Amt für Ständischen Aufbau to all Gaufachberater für Ständischen Aufbau, 26 July 1933, T-580, roll 310, folder 123. See also *VB*, 26 July 1933.

291. Ross, *Hitler und Dollfuss*, p. 87.

position of "neutrality" in church affairs.[292] Finally, there was the time element. Hitler disliked announcing major policy changes at party congresses, and the 1933 congress was already scheduled for early September. Either the change had to come before the congress—or he had to wait until after September. Since the latter seemed the more dangerous of the two courses, Hitler announced his decision rather abruptly at the end of June.[293]

The September congress went through the usual round of parades, speeches, and receptions without any overt disagreements over policy questions. It was remarkable primarily for Hitler's progressive dilution of the NSDAP's revolutionary image and his substitution of an aura of powerful defender of the present accomplishments. Hitler's appearances and speeches at the 1933 congress set the pattern for all of the national rallies in the thirties. He spoke or had his proclamation read on five occasions: an address at the opening reception in the city hall of Nuremberg, the proclamation formally opening the congress (always read by the Munich Gauleiter Adolf Wagner, whose accent and diction closely resembled Hitler's), an address to the special "culture" meeting of the congress, his remarks at a reception for foreign diplomats attending the congress, and his closing address.[294] In 1933, this last address was most remarkable for its emphasis on the evolutionary and long-term role of the party. Hitler spoke with considerable feeling on the need for training and attracting future party cadres. Every "genuine genius" should be encouraged to seek a career as a PL, and the party had the duty to promote promising material already in the cadres.[295] He repeated this theme on several other occasions during September. For the immediate present, the role of the NSDAP was rather minimal. Its task was the "moral and intellectual education of the German people,"[296] a commission that was strikingly vague when compared with Hitler's explicit orders to the Reichsstatthalters to uphold the authority of the

292. Scholder, "Evangelische Kirche," pp. 19–20; and Conway, *Nazi Persecution*, p. 54.

293. Perhaps to avoid such dilemmas in the future, Hitler announced on 8 August that after 1933 party congresses would be held at biannual intervals—a decision he reversed after the successful 1933 congress. See Domarus, *Hitler*, I, 292.

294. *Ibid.*, p. 297.

295. Hitler's speech of 3 Sept. 1933, quoted in Rühle, *Dritte Reich*, pp. 209–10.

296. *VB*, 30 Sept. 1933.

Reich's governmental agencies against all undermining influences, including those sponsored by the NSDAP.[297]

At least implicitly, Hitler had exempted constitutional and territorial reforms in Germany from his prohibition of further revolutionary changes. Perhaps to strengthen the position of the Gauleiters against the Reichsleiters and SA leaders, he railed against the "unnatural" boundaries of the German states, and at the party congress specifically announced (though without a timetable) the liquidation of the Länder and their replacement by Reichgaus. As if to underscore the revolutionary significance of this measure, Hitler pointedly alluded to the parallel of the Reichgaus and the creation of the French departments.[298] Hitler quickly realized, however, that he had opened another Pandora's box. There was no agreement among the Gauleiters on what constituted the definition of a Reichsgau,[299] and consequently each Gauleiter immediately set to work proving that the "natural" boundaries of his Gau were considerably larger than the present map showed. In desperation, Hitler terminated all discussion of the Reichsreform.[300] Thereafter such minuscule accomplishments as the union of the two Mecklenburgs (Strelitz and Schwerin) into a single Land had to suffice as major triumphs of the planned Nazi territorial readjustments.[301]

By the end of the summer, every promising avenue of revolutionary activity by the party had been blocked, but the sudden close of the revolutionary period of the Machtergreifung left the NSDAP as a unit (or units) of political power in the form of an overblown organism without much purpose or plan. The StdF was not yet generally recog-

297. Domarus, *Hitler*, I, 303; and Epp, "Besprechung mit den Reichsstatthaltern am 28. September 1933, p. 8, BGStA, Rsth. 148.

298. Epp, "Besprechung," 6 July 1933, p. 8; and Baum, "Reichsreform," p. 41. See also Gunter d'Alquen, "Um das Reich," *VB*, 26 and 27 Nov. 1933.

299. Thus the GL of Bayreuth, Hans Schemm, wanted his Reichsgau defined as that area of Bavaria in which he had campaigned ("won the people for national socialism") during the *Kampfzeit*. See the enclosure in Schemm to Siebert (prime minister of Bavaria until his death in 1942), 4 Nov. 1933, BGStA, MA 105284.

300. Reiner (at this time the adjutant of GL Sprenger, later deputy GL of Hessen (not to be confused with the consul), "Vorbesprechung der Reichsstatthalter anlässlich der Reichsstatthalterkonferenz am 28.9.1933 in Berlin," BA/R 43 II/1391. The prohibition appeared in print in *VOBl*, III (15 Oct. 1933), 122. For a full discussion of the entire problem, see Baum, "Reichsreform."

301. Rühle, *Dritte Reich*, p. 342.

nized as the party's political coordinator, and the end of the revolution left some elements more than a little dissatisfied.[302] The only immediate beneficiaries were the Reich ministries and the Gauleiters. The latter understandably saw their future role in rather simple and optimistic terms: the future would bring them power without responsibility. They saw the new policy as an opportunity to subject both the paramilitary organizations and the affiliates to their direct authority, thereby reducing the Reichsleiters to mere figureheads. On the other hand, they did not recognize the need to respect the authority of the governmental offices. The Gauleiter of Franconia, Julius Streicher, who was not known for the subtlety of his arguments, expressed the typical Gauleiter's position: "He did not want a state office, particularly not if it contained binding instructions. He wanted to serve the movement."[303]

There is considerable evidence that Hitler was rather uneasy about the expectations which his policy change seemed to have aroused. For the moment, he took refuge (as he always did in times of crisis) in reiterating the need for intraparty discipline and in alluding to the creation of a party senate.[304] The latter institution, which never came into being, was his favorite balm whenever he sensed that the NSDAP was in the grip of a major internal crisis. Beyond this, Hitler concerned himself with the problem of squaring the circle; that is, how to give the party a body of technically competent cadre functionaries who would have the requisite expertise to enforce the party decision-making claims in the major areas of national policy formulation (economics, foreign policy, and so on) without eclipsing the power of the Gauleiters, who, as Hitler's original derivative agents, were the most secure base of his own undisputed power in Germany and in the party.[305] However, many

302. The official termination of the revolution lead to riots by SA members in several major German cities including Berlin, Frankfurt, Dresden, Essen, Dortmund, and Königsberg; by the end of the year, 200,000 members throughout the Reich had been expelled from the SA. See Schumann, *Nationalsozialismus*, pp. 89–90.

303. See Epp, "Besprechung . . . 18.7.33," p. 7. GL Bürckel said much the same a few minutes later. *Ibid.*, p. 8. See also Siebert's remarks in "Auszug aus dem Bericht über die Ministerratssitzung v. 26.7.33," BGStA, MA 105256.

304. Epp, "Besprechung . . . 6.7.33," pp. 9–10; Domarus, *Hitler*, I, 292.

305. Epp, "Besprechung . . . 6.7.33," p. 4. See also *VB*, 18 and 19 June 1933; Bracher, *Machtergreifung*, p. 219; and Messerschmidt, *Wehrmacht*, p. 10.

of the Gauleiters had few skills beyond those of streetcorner agitators. Since Hitler had no solution to the dilemma,[306] the future of the party was again left to the informal, but nevertheless bitter, infighting of the Reichleiters and Gauleiters. The only new rule in the game was the prohibition on activities or plans for major economic and social up- heavals or threats to the authority of both the Reich government and the army.

Among the Reichsleiters, the Reich treasurer was undoubtedly least effected by the policy changes of June. Schwarz simply continued his efforts to increase the party revenues and, through his control over ex- penditure of these moneys, to control the party's cadres. Robert Ley should have been a major beneficiary of Hitler's new policy decisions. In his dual capacity as ROL and head of the DAF, his authority extended over both of the two large areas of concern which Hitler had assigned to the NSDAP: the propagandistic education of the German people and the training and deployment of cadre functionaries. Moreover, Ley was known to oppose the more radical elements in the NSBO, and he could thus be counted on as a safe "antirevolutionary." Ley clearly saw the vital connection between his two posts,[307] and seemed to move quickly to exploit his opportunities. He worked toward a fully inte- grated, completely centralized cadre organization[308] which would vest authority almost equally in the territorial cadre leaders at the Reich, Gau, district, and local level and in the functional offices of the socio- economic affiliates under Ley's control.[309] The territorial cadre chiefs (who held the title *Hoheitsträger*, literally "bearers of sovereignty") were to work themselves up through the ranks, and the entire organi- zation was to be self-rejuvenating through constant in-service train- ing: weekly local membership meetings, bimonthly district meetings,

306. In mid-June he let a major opportunity slip by to proclaim guidelines for future cadre training when he attended but did not speak at the opening of the new Reich school for NSDAP and NSBO functionaries at Bernau. Ley had ex- propriated the old school for union officials and converted it to a party training center. See *VB*, 17 June 1933.

307. ROL, *Dienstvorschrift 1933*, p. 7.

308. "[When] the [Führer] presses the button, even the last party member is set immediately into motion." *Ibid.*, p. 11.

309. *VOBl*, III (15 Oct. 1933), 124.

and semiannual Gau rallies would keep the cadres at their peak performance.[310]

For Ley the schooling or training aspects of his program were its most important parts. He regarded himself as a "teacher or gardener,"[311] and consequently felt that the training office of the ROL should be the most important in the party; indeed, it was the crystallization of all other party concerns.[312] Ley began the construction of his all-encompassing schooling system immediately after the termination of the revolutionary phase,[313] and by the end of the year every Gau had its own "training castle" (*Schulungsburg*). These attempted to channel all of the Gau's PLs through a series of two- to three-week courses, and Ley was already hard at work expanding the system to the districts— though here he was stymied for the moment because Schwarz balked at the expense involved.[314]

Although Ley talked a great deal about the elite status of the party's functionary corps, and sought to give the training centers the aura of pseudo-Teutonic castles, his entire schooling system was thoroughly unsuited to produce the technically competent political elite needed to bring about an able administration of German society. Not only was it naive to duplicate the brutality of Weimar politics with broad-jump contests and pseudophilosophical lectures about racial selection,[315] but the very attempt was counterproductive. The Nazi Party of the Kampf-zeit had essentially negative aims: it wanted to destroy the Weimar Republic. After 1933, the NSDAP had the primary task of preserving the new Third Reich. The graduates of the ROL's training institutes, however, still sought primarily negative goals.

310. ROL, *Dienstvorschrift 1933*, pp. 41–43, and 69. See also Allen, *Seizure*, p. 242.

311. Ley, "Der Weg zur Ordensburg," in Robert Ley, *Wir alle helfen dem Führer*, ed. Heinrich Simon (Munich, 1937), p. 119.

312. Otto Schmidt, "Bericht über die Tagung des Hauptschulungsamtes in Oberursel am 7. und 8. Mai 1938," 13 May 1938, T-454, roll 77, frames 133–34, 136, and 138. See also ROL, *Dienstvorschrift 1933*, p. 37.

313. See Frick to Oberste Reichsbehörden, 4 Aug. 1933, BA/R 43 II/1196; and Domarus, *Hitler*, I, 280–81.

314. ROL to Kreisleiter Straubing, 22 March 1939, T-580, roll 549, folder 730.

315. For a typical curriculum at a district school, see the article on a course for PLs at Straubing in *VB*, 6 April 1934.

Yet, in another sense; Ley's training system was not sheer folly. It was, in fact, an integral part of another approach to the problem of power in the Third Reich. The ROL aimed not at an exclusive elite of competent party functionaries, but at a large number of minimally trained, ideologically fanaticized officials subject to his immediate direction. In effect, Ley wanted to merge the NSDAP, the DAF, and Darré's Reich food estate (sans Darré) in a gigantic organization encompassing virtually every adult German. The scheme had both a political and an economic side. Through the control of the major Nazi economic and social affiliates, especially the DAF, the ROL potentially directed all human factors in the German economy. With this base Ley set to work establishing his version of the "estate principle" in German life. In midyear, he brought both the Amt für Ständischen Aufbau and the Nazi welfare system under his control,[316] and in the fall a massive propaganda campaign was launched to popularize the new Ständestaat.[317] The final result would have been a major accumulation of economic power in the form of a modified corporate system anchored in the DAF organization.[318] Understandably enough, Ley devoted most of his efforts in 1933–1934 to the organizational development of the DAF, neglecting the PL cadres by comparison.[319]

The PO's role in the scheme was limited and indirect. The major political pillar of Ley's plan was a system of state councils (*Staatsräte*). These organs were to be pseudoparliamentary assemblies of notables; their function was to advise the prime ministers of the German Länder. The most important of these was obviously the Prussian Staatsrat, which first met in September 1933. Its membership included a number of prominent representatives from a variety of occupations and interest groups, but the dominant element was the contingent of party functionaries. According to the blueprints drawn up by Ley, membership in the Prussian state council included the chief of staff of the SA, the Reich leader of the SS, the Prussian Gauleiters, SA and SS leaders, and the ROL. Significantly, the membership list did not include the deputy

316. *VB*, 8 June 1933; *VOBl*, II (15 June 1933), 106; ROL, *Dienstvorschrift 1933*, p. 98; and Bludau, *Genossenschaften*, p. 114.

317. *VB*, 13 and 14 Aug. 1933.

318. See ROL, *Dienstvorschrift 1933*, p. 98.

319. Robert Ley, "Die Ordensburg Sonthofen," *Hoheitsträger*, III (May 1939), 19.

Führer; thus Ley alone represented the political and economic side of the party's Reichsleitung.[320]

As usual, Ley's theoretical constructs created more practical problems than they solved. Quite aside from the opposition of various interest groups and prominent Nazi leaders (Darré, Göring, Hess),[321] it failed by its own standards as well. Since Ley insisted on treating the party and the DAF as interchangeable organizations,[322] it appeared to other Nazi leaders that the DAF tail increasingly wagged the NSDAP dog, which had not been the original intention when the DAF was linked with the party.[323] The DAF became the subject of increasingly vociferous criticism precisely because it was unable to accomplish its primary purpose, the Nazification of the German working masses. The DAF became the dumping ground for functionaries who were too incompetent to meet the not very high standards of the PO.[324] Nevertheless, even under these circumstances, the DAF did not have enough Nazi functionaries to fill its positions, and many of the old union secretaries kept their posts,[325] where, to their credit, they did all they could to work against the Nazis. The result was a huge organization, riddled with corruption, incompetence, and passive resistance,[326] that was rejected by most German workers. This became glaringly apparent during the elections for factory councils (*Betriebsräte*) held in April. In a number of cases the outcome was so disastrous for the Nazi candidates that Ley decided against further elections.[327] Moreover, there was little

320. See Ley's draft law in ROL, Stabsleiter to Esser (in 1933, Bavarian minister of economics), 27 June 1933, BGStA, MA 105272. See also Bracher, *Machtergreifung*, p. 513.

321. The *Staatsrat* plans quickly ran into trouble. In Hamburg the old business interests all but controlled the council (Timpke, *Dokumente*, p. 130), and in Bavaria no agreement could be reached on the membership and functions of such a body. See the excerpts from the protocol of the Bavarian cabinet meeting of 18 July 1933, BGStA, Rsth. 36/1–7.

322. See *VB*, 19 Dec. 1933.

323. Hess to Göring *et al.*, 2 Feb. 1938, BA/NS 6/448. Ley had to defend himself against this accusation as late as 1939. See Selzner, "Der Auftrag an Dr. Ley," pp. 8–10.

324. Schumann, *Nationalsozialismus*, p. 102.

325. Nagel (one of the DAF's regional commissioners) to Pohl (of the Reich ministry of labor), 7 Aug. 1933, HAB/77/16.

326. See below, pp. 126, 208–09.

327. Matthias, "Die Sozialdemokratische Partei Deutschlands," in *Ende der Parteien*, p. 195.

hope for future improvement of the conditions within the DAF, since even Ley admitted his training methods for new functionaries in 1933 were "extremely deficient."[328]

The deputy Führer began the postrevolutionary era with far less ambitious schemes. Without clear rights of command over the Gauleiters or Reichsleiters,[329] and with neither a large staff nor a vertical substructure, the StdF was for the moment content to mediate party disputes, encourage complaints, and continue his purge of Strasser's followers. Aside from these routine pursuits, Hess took care to emphasize the primary importance of the party's political cadres (rather than its affiliates) as the "backbone and steel girders of German society" and to inhibit further organizational disintegration of the NSDAP by prohibiting the creation of new party affiliates without his permission.[330] The StdF's first, albeit indirect, conflict with Ley came over the renewed activism of the party's retailers' affiliates. It was by now clear that the NSDAP's promises to the German middle classes would not be fulfilled,[331] and the NS-Hago grew understandably more frustrated and volatile. Hess had already subordinated the Gau economic advisors to his office. Their function was to control the economic Gleichschaltung actions in the Gaus,[332] but before July their effectiveness seems to have been limited. Thereafter, Hess (with Hitler's obvious approval)[333] moved quickly against the party's economic radicals. On July 7, he prohibited further demonstrations against department stores (one of the NS-Hago's favorite targets), and five days later Wagener's economic department in the party was dissolved.[334] Its successor was an economic department headed by Wilhelm Keppler, the conservative

328. Ley, "Mannestum," in *Wir alle*, p. 149.

329. Diehl-Thiele, *Partei*, p. 208.

330. *VB*, 17 and 20 June, and 7 July 1933; and *VOBl*, III (15 Dec. 1933), 133.

331. Castellan, "Bilan," p. 507.

332. *VOBl*, II (15 March and 30 April 1933), 91 and 97.

333. For Hitler's relations with the social revolutionaries in early July, see Dietrich Eichholtz, *Geschichte der deutschen Kriegswirtschaft 1939–1945*, vol. I, *1939–1941* (Berlin [East], 1969), p. 39, n. 77.

334. *VB*, 9 and 10 July 1933; see also Hess to Loeper, 13 Oct. 1933, T-580, roll 12, folder 169. *VOBl*, II (15 July 1933), 109. Wagener later claimed that this resulted from the (false) rumor that he (Wagener) opposed the appointment of Schmitt as Hugenberg's successor to the post of Reich minister of economics. See OPG, "Beschluss in Sachen Wagener," 17 Nov. 1936, IfZ/FA 143.

businessman who had been Hitler's informal advisor on economic matters since early 1932. Organizationally, Keppler became part of Hess's Liaison Staff. The transfer of titles had practical consequences in the Gaus as well. In September, Wagener's vertical substructure was dissolved. His Gau officials, the so-called Gau economic plenipotentiaries (*Gauwirtschaftsbeauftragte*), were dismissed, so that the Gau economic advisors were the only PO officials concerned with economic policies still operating in the Gaus. These Hess subordinated firmly to both Keppler's and his own authority: Keppler gave orders involving economic issues; Hess, orders on political affairs.[335] But since Keppler was, in the final analysis, a subordinate of Hess, it was clear that the control of economic decision-making in the party had been transferred to Hess's office. At the same time, the deputy Führer tied his moves in the economic area to his political investigative powers: his economic subordinates had the right to investigate complaints by business enterprises.[336] Behind these moves lay shrewd political calculations. Radical economic measures had the support of several Gauleiters, and these men had at first little intention of obeying the new directives.[337] On the other hand, both Hitler and the business community wanted, above all, law and order—Hitler for both domestic and foreign policy reasons;[338] the business circles in order to feel secure that the free enterprise system would be preserved under the Nazis. And since the latter were even willing to pay substantially for the privilege of law and order,[339] Hess's efforts were assured of Schwarz's support.

Primarily, the StdF linked his extensions of power to the solid core

335. *VOBl*, III (15 Sept. 1933), 117. See also *VB*, 15 Sept. 1933; and Genschel, *Verdrängung*, p. 115.

336. Wirtschaftspolitische Kommission (Kugler) to Siebert, 28 Sept. 1933, BGStA, MA 105256. In fact, the short-term political factors were decisive in the work of the Gau economic advisors. They never received instructions on long-term economic policies or plans. See Dr. Heffter *et al.*, "Aktennotiz über ein Gespräch mit Herrn Dr. Wolff [the Gau Economic Advisor of Hamburg] am 20.9.1950 . . . ," Forsch. Hbg./PA/12/T.

337. GL Bürckel noted as late as October 1933 that on the matter of department stores "we old fighters are not concerned a hoot about the pronouncements of some come-lately, well-known Nazi." See his "Rundschreiben," 3 Oct. 1933, quoted in Genschel, *Verdrängung*, p. 82.

338. See his speech of 18 Oct. 1933 in Domarus, *Hitler*, I, 317.

339. *VOBl*, II (31 July 1933), 111.

of his established authority as chief inspector of the NSDAP. To be sure, until the fall, neither the "Reich inspector for special purposes," Wilhelm Freiherr von Holzschuher, nor the six regional inspectors had been a very effective check on the party's disintegrative tendencies. Holzschuher complained that his mediation met with little success,[340] and the Gauleiters all but ignored the territorial inspectors, especially since the latter's administrative superior, Ley, made virtually no use of them.[341] In October, the StdF began to activate the party's inspectorate system. Each of the regional inspectors was assigned a specific number of Gaus as his jurisdictional area.[342] This move did not as yet dispose of the rank discrepancy between the inspectors and most of the PLs they would have to investigate,[343] but it was clearly a step toward the revival of Strasser's tightly centralized inspectorate system.

Yet none of these measures touched the heart of the party's dilemma in the fall of 1933: the growing restlessness of the SA cadres and the developing conflict between the storm troopers and the PO,[344] on the one hand, and the incredibly low level of competence of the average PL on the other. After seven months in office, the NSDAP was still far from united in its goals or homogeneous in its membership. It remained a vast institution with an overblown apparatus that interfered with every aspect of German societal life,[345] but there was little attempt to systematize and coordinate these efforts. The Reichsleitung was still both impotent and bitterly divided on the political and personnel goals of the movement. Indeed, even if there had been unity of concept, there was no competent cadre personnel to put the decisions into effect. At the local level the party's political leader often controlled all aspects of political

340. Holzschuher to Hess, 18 Sept. 1933; Klagges to Hitler, 18 Sept. 1933; and Holzschuher to Loeper, 23 Oct. 1933, BDC/Klagges (OPG).

341. Diehl-Thiele, *Partei*, p. 212.

342. *VOBl*, III (15 Oct. 1933), p. 124.

343. Of the six, two were district leaders (Oexle and Seidel), two were Gau staff officials (Manderbach and Bauer), one was a local leader (Brockhausen), and one, Tittmann, had no formal rank at all but owned a Nazi publishing house in Saxony.

344. Epp, "Besprechung . . . 18.7.1933," BGStA, MA 105255. For Röhm's views on the status of the SA in the NSDAP, see his interview with the *Algemeen Handelsblad*, quoted in *VB*, 5 Oct. 1933.

345. For a description of the Berlin party organization "in action," see *VB*, 14 Oct. 1933.

decision-making, though even here the renewed strength of the state bureaucracy made itself felt. One local leader noted sarcastically, "I only have to serve two masters: the governor (*Regierungspräsident*) and the district leader."[346] In the Gaus the situation varied widely. In some areas, civil servants thought the party had control over their promotion schedules, but in other areas Gauleiters complained that the governmental bureaucrats blocked their most rudimentary wishes.[347]

Since Hitler had no long-term solutions to the conditions of latent frustration and dissatisfaction in the party, he devised a short-term activity to relieve the pressure. In mid-October, he decided to throw the party's forces into something at which they excelled: an election campaign. Ostensibly the reason was to organize a national plebiscite on the government's decision to leave the League of Nations,[348] but a more pressing reason was quite frankly to give both the "old fighters" and the new members received since the Machtergreifung something to do.[349] Although the outcome was a foregone conclusion, the NSDAP staged a vigorous month-long campaign, beginning with a meeting of the leadership corps on October 17.[350] In November, Germany was blanketed with a series of largely useless rallies; the Gau Munich-Upper Bavaria alone staged 1,043 meetings in preparation for the national plebiscite.[351]

The enthusiasm of the party's campaign workers was rewarded with the predictable overall result of 92.2 percent favoring the government's decision on the League question,[352] but the outcome could not alter the NSDAP's highly amorphous position as the year ended. To be sure, the Nazi Party was surrounded with the symbols of power and respect. The Law for Unity of Party and State (December 1, 1933) made the NSDAP the sole political organization in Germany, and defined insults

346. See Orgleiter Wildpark (Potsdam) to Kreisleiter Palsch, 3 Oct. 1933, HAB/77/4.
347. See the correspondence in HAB/77/2 and 3.
348. *VB*, 15 and 16 Oct. 1933.
349. *VB*, 2 Nov 1933.
350. *VB*, 18 Oct. 1933.
351. See the report on the Gau's activities for 1933, *VB*, 24 Feb. 1934.
352. *VB*, 14 Nov. 1933. Some of the methods used by the PLs to arrive at this figure are illustrated by the Bavarian party workers who announced that only traitors would avail themselves of the secret ballot. See HMB/OBB, 4 and 17 Dec. 1933, BGStA, MA 106670.

to its symbols as crimes against the people.[353] Röhm and Hess became Reich ministers in December to bring the total number of Nazis in the cabinet to four,[354] but the addendum "without portfolio" for the new men indicated that the party continued to be an organization without much purpose.

This fact was still hidden behind a facade of flag-waving and parades. At the end of the year the Gaus put out proud statistical reports of "1201 communities gleichgeschaltet,"[355] but the disproportionate number of functionaries in comparison with the rank and file membership rendered the NSDAP top-heavy and politically ineffective. In February 1934, the functionaries of the NSDAP and its affiliates were divided as shown in table 2. The situation in the Gaus and districts was corre-

TABLE 2

Functionaries of the NSDAP and Its Affiliates, 1934

Organization	*Number of Functionaries*
PO (staffs of the RLs, GLs, Kreisleitungs, and locals)	373,000
NSBO	120,000
NS-Hago	57,000
NSKVO (Veterans' Welfare Organization)	25,300
Amt für Beamte (staff of the NSBB)	34,000
NS-Frauenschaften	53,000
a.A.	20,000
NS-Lehrerbund (Teachers' Organization)	12,700
NS Association of Physicians	1,500
NS Lawyers' Association	1,600
NS Welfare Organization	68,000
Office for communal affairs	3,600
Party courts	2,500
Propaganda offices	14,000
Press offices	7,400
Hitler Youth	205,000
Reich labor service	18,500
Total	1,017,000

SOURCE: *VB*, 25 Feb. 1934.

spondingly grotesque. The Gau Baden had 22,414 party functionaries, of whom 12,884 were in the PO. A large municipal district like Stuttgart

353. Buchheim, "Der Stellvertreter des Führers," p. 324.
354. *VB*, 3 and 4 Dec. 1933.
355. Annual Report of Munich–Upper Bavaria, *VB*, 24 Feb. 1934.

boasted 7,000, but even the small suburban district of Pasing (near Munich) kept 520 functionaries on its rolls.[356] Of particular interest is, of course, the figure for the PO. By comparison, it may be noted that, while the NSDAP with a membership of perhaps 2.5 million needed a functionary corps of 373,000, the Weimar Social Democratic Party with 1 million members needed only 10,000.[357] But the problem was more than simply excessive numbers. In many cases the party's cadres had mushroomed without any real concept or plan. The Gau Munich–Upper Bavaria, for example, did not even establish a personnel office until November,[358] while at the national level virtually no really effective control organs existed. Hitler attempted to put some order into the chaotic cultural policy field, but in appointing Alfred Rosenberg "plenipotentiary for the philosophical supervision and education of the NSDAP" he merely continued his habit of combining a grandiose title with few real powers.[359] Similarly, the Reich Uschla established a second chamber to deal with the increased load of cases,[360] but that was a reaction to the problem rather than a solution.

Somewhat more effective were the attempts to create some semblance of organizational order within the staff offices of the Reichsleitung and the Gauleitungs. At the beginning of 1934 Hitler decided that the Reichsleitung consisted of the following divisions: treasury, executive secretary, Uschla, legal department, press office, foreign press office, propaganda leadership, PO cadres (with the subdivisions: the women's group, the NSBO, the National Socialist war victims, and the National Socialist apothecaries and "healing practitioners"), commission for economic policy, Reich youth leadership, National Socialist Physicians' Association, the insurance department, and the supreme command of the SA (which still included the SS).[361] At the same time, the PO cadres were divided into seventeen rank groupings (see table 3), each, inevitably, with elaborately detailed uniforms. Other aspects of the year-end streamlining involved new rules for membership so as to re-

356. N.a., "Gau Baden" [Feb. 1934], BA/NS 22/200; and *VB*, 21 Feb. 1934.
357. The latter figure is from Sigmund Neumann, *Politische Parteien* (Stuttgart, 1965), p. 34.
358. *VB*, 24 Feb. 1934.
359. Brenner, *Kunstpolitik*, p. 72; *VB*, 1 Feb. 1934; and Domarus, *Hitler*, I, 348.
360. *VOBl*, III (15 Jan. 1934), 137.
361. *VB*, 18 Jan. 1934.

TABLE 3

Rank Groupings by Jurisdictional Level

RL	GL	District	Local
Reichsleiter	Gauleiter	District leader	Local leader
	Deputy Gauleiter		
Divisional chief	Divisional chief	Divisional chief	Outpost leader
Department head	Department head	Department head	Cell leader
Subdepartment head	Subdepartment head	Subdepartment head	Block administrator

SOURCE: *VB*, 22 Jan. 1934.

move prominent Reich and Gau functionaries from possible harassment by local leaders, some differentiation between the titles assigned functionaries in the PO and the affiliates, and the issuance of identity cards to all PLs. The latter were issued by Ley's personnel office for PO cadres and the commission on economic policy for the Gau economic advisors.[362] The entire program was capped by a massive national oath-taking ceremony on February 24; Hess administered a pledge of loyalty to Hitler over national radio to over a million party functionaries.[363] Ley was ecstatic: the reforms demonstrated "that the German people have finally obtained the political leadership for which it strove for 2,000 years."[364]

A closer look at the organizational reforms of late 1933 certainly reveals that they were neither consistent, well thought out, nor far-reaching; they were merely another stopgap solution to meet an acute problem. There was, to begin with, no clear division between the po-

362. *VOBl*, III (15 and 31 Dec. 1933 and 15 Jan. 1934), 133–34, 135, 136, and 139; StdF to all RL, 4 Dec. 1933, T-580, roll 12, folder 169.

363. Before the radio ceremony, Hess had personally inducted the RL and their division heads at the Brown House. On the various ceremonies see *VB*, 25 and 26 Feb. 1934. The program for the oath-taking ceremonies was announced in the *VB*, 6 Feb. 1934, and it is likely that it was discussed at the RL and GL meeting in early January, over which Hess presided. The February 24 rally was also the first time that Bormann was singled out for particular publicity. See *VB*, 26 Feb. 1934.

364. *VB*, 22 Jan. 1934.

litical and purely administrative aspects of the Reichsleitung. The Reich treasury was certainly a far more important office than Putzi Hanfstaengl's foreign press department. Phillip Bouhler's office as executive secretary was by now virtually moribund, and the NS healing practitioners certainly did not belong in the PO. The division of ranks and titles was similarly confused. Since the Reichsleiters, Gauleiters, and deputy Gauleiters occupied 82 of the 96 ranks, only 14 ranks were left to be divided among some 373,000 cadre functionaries—hardly a sufficient number to achieve a fully differentiated structure in the party. (When, during the war, a complete organization was devised by the StdF and the Reich treasurer, the number of PO ranks was fixed at 30.) The year-end scheme shows every characteristic of having been devised in great haste (the elaborately described uniforms were not yet available for purchase, for example) to give the appearance of finality and solidity to the party after its first year in office. The plan was intended as an additional indication that the revolution had ended and the period of internal construction begun.[365] Hitler and the PO leadership were well aware of the continued existence of groups in the NSDAP which resented Hitler's decision to end the revolution after only five months of undisputed power.

Undoubtedly, the most important of these lingering rivalries was the smoldering conflict between the SA and the PO. By the end of the year, Röhm's SA was demanding ever-increasing political rights in the Third Reich. The SA's chief of staff had already drafted a plan which would have assigned the SA political control of Reich and Länder affairs, while the PO would have had to be content with a role in communal developments.[366] In public, all party leaders counseled unity, of course,[367] but the differences were too serious to be papered over. The party press attempted to appease the SA's anger by favorable press coverage of its activities,[368] but the political leaders were not willing to grant Röhm and his organization the positions of power he demanded. Thus, although the SA was able to achieve something like

365. *VB,* 25 Feb. 1934.
366. This is based upon the bitter analysis of Röhm's ideas sent by GL Robert Wagner (Baden) to Ley, 15 Dec. 1933, BA/NS 22/300.
367. See Hess's and Sauckel's speeches to the Thuringian PLs, 4 Dec. 1933, *VB,* 5 Dec. 1933.
368. See, for example, *VB,* 9 Dec. 1933.

power-parity with the PO in some locals and even districts,[369] neither
Gauleiters nor Reichsleiters were willing to let the PO be eclipsed by
the paramilitary.[370]

These developments aided the StdF's drive for power in the party;
the PLs' and particularly the Gauleiter's fear of the SA considerably
mitigated their resentment against a more centralized structure for the
PO. Hess had never left any doubt about his clear identification with
the PO of the party. Even before the Machtergreifung he had supported
Reinhard Heydrich's Security Service (one of whose tasks was to spy
on the SA)[371] and he now underscored his close relationship to the
PO.[372] Nevertheless, the deputy Führer's moves to strengthen the central authority in the party were not as yet dramatic; rather, a series of
seemingly insignificant offices came to be part of his staff organization.
The party's *Auslandsorganisation* (AO), the organization of Nazi party
members living outside Germany and Austria, came under Hess's control, as did the architectural office of Albert Speer and the nebulous
cultural affairs department of Phillip Bouhler. A newly established
"department for cultural peace" was actually a control agency to curb
the enthusiasm of the German Christians.[373] None of these organizational additions were important in themselves; rather they were har-
bingers of a larger trend: Hess was reconstructing the conceptual and
planning aspects of Strasser's old Reich organization leadership. The
developments achieved immediate significance only in view of the

369. See Meyerhoff, *Herne*, p. 15; and Kreisleiter Göttingen, "Bericht der Kreis-
leitung der NSDAP Göttingen Stadt u[nd]. Land," 23 Feb. 1934, T-580, roll 547,
folder 651.

370. Mau, "Zweite Revolution," p. 127. See also [Stimmungsbericht GL Süd-
hannover, Feb. 1934], n.d., *ibid*; Epp, "Besprechung . . . 22. März 1934," p. 5,
BGStA, Rsth. 148. The GL of Baden suggested that the RM 200,000 subsidy asked
by the SA for its spring maneuvers might be used more effectively to buy uniforms
for the PLs. GL Baden (Stabsleiter) to Ley, 10 Feb. 1934, T-81, roll 121, frame
1417920.

371. Aronson, "Heydrich," p. 90.

372. *VB*, 5 Dec. 1933 and 27 Jan. 1934. Hess was also developing future plans.
He had asked Ley for a report on the relationship of party and state in fascist Italy.
See Ley to Hess, 25 Nov. 1933, T-580, roll 549, folder 746.

373. *VB*, 20 Feb. 1934; *VOBl*, III (15 Jan. and 15 March 1933), 92 and 137;
Speer, *Erinnerungen*, p. 69; Zipfel, *Kirchenkampf*, p. 57; Buchheim, *Glaubenskrise*,
p. 123; and StdF, "Anordnung" (not to be published), 27 Feb. 1934, T-580, roll 12,
folder 169.

simultaneous and direct political actions by the deputy Führer: his continuing efforts to rebuild the inspectorate system, his concerns with cadre recruitment,[374] and, above all, his opposition to a merger of the DAF and PO cadres.[375]

While Hess worked quietly to strengthen the PLs, Robert Ley continued his efforts to merge the PO and the DAF. Thus, Ley saw no difficulty in speaking of the PO and the administrative staffs of the affiliates as the "political general staff for thousands of years," or in defining the task of the party as "conquering the people philosophically with the help of the Strength through Joy [*Kraft durch Freude*, KdF] movement."[376] He devoted an inordinate amount of effort and time to the DAF's organization.[377] This included a massive membership drive, which, according to Schwarz, interfered with the Reich treasurer's efforts to put some order into the chaotic DAF and NSBO finances.[378]

Presented with the sharply differing plans of Röhm, Hess, and Ley, Hitler remained indecisive. The February ceremonies had, to be sure, demonstrated that he rejected the SA's goals, but beyond this, his plans for the party as a whole and his relationship to the PO in particular were highly obscure. The Führer's New Year's proclamation was of little help. He reiterated all of the Nazi's past successes and singled out the party's brutality, propaganda, and organizational skill (in that order) as contributing factors, but among the organizational groupings only the SA, SS, and the Hitler Youth seemed worthy of praise. The PO was not mentioned.[379] Somewhat more encouraging for the PO were the series of Hitlerian public thank-you notes which the *VB* published between January 1 and 10. These came in three series: Hess, Schwarz, Max Amann, Himmler, Röhm, Goebbels, and Rosenberg on January 1; Göring, Ley, Schirach, Buch, Franz Seldte (the Reich minister of labor who was a member of the Nationalist Party) on

374. *VB*, 6 and 7 July, 1933.

375. See Helmuth Friedrichs, "Rede Friedrichs auf der Tagung der Stellvertretenden Gauleiter am 11. Januar 1940 in München," p. 27, T-580, roll 843, box 268, folder 352.

376. *VB*, 5 Dec 1933 and 3 Feb. 1934. The KdF was the DAF's social service wing.

377. See, for example, *VB*, 27 Jan. and 2 March 1934.

378. Rschm., "Rundschreiben" to all Gau treasurers, 16 Dec. 1933, *Rdschr.*, I.

379. *VB*, 1 Jan. 1934.

January 3; and, apparently as an afterthought, Darré on January 10. Presumably, the order was as important as the content of the short notes, and Hess's position as the first recipient underscored his *primus inter pares* status. In his note to Hess, Hitler praised his deputy's loyalty to the party, but said nothing about his future tasks. On the other hand, the letter to Ley ignored his position as head of the ROL, and dwelt only on his leadership of the DAF. Actually, the only explicit letter was the one to Röhm, which contained a clear mandate to the SA to preserve the gains that had been made rather than propel the revolution.[380]

Nevertheless, there are a number of indications that Hitler leaned more toward Hess's than Ley's concepts for the party. At a meeting of the party's leaders at the end of January 1934, Hitler spoke with some feeling on the party's need to develop technically able cadres that would manage to fill any position in government and society. Once the NSDAP had developed this type of functionary in sufficient numbers (which would "take time"), the state, Hitler hinted, would cease to exist.[381] His Reichstag speech of January 30 emphasized the elitist character of the NSDAP. Here, the Führer issued a clear call for a purge of the party membership. The large number of "parasites" who had slipped in repelled the "honest people" and prevented them from applying for party membership. The "honest people" presumably contained large numbers of the technical experts whom Hitler hoped to attract to the PO's cadres, though he did not indicate that he favored lifting the ban on new members.[382]

For the moment, however, the "new" party was little in evidence. Despite the increasingly visible efforts of Schwarz and Ley to control the centrifugal tendencies within the party, developments in the first half of 1934 were characterized primarily by ingrowing bureaucratization[383] (what Nazi propagandists with far less justification used to call

380. He expressed the same thoughts at the meeting of SA leaders later in the month. See *VB*, 23 Jan. 1934.

381. *VB*, 3 Feb. 1934. See also Zoller, *Hitler privat*, p. 163.

382. Domarus, *Hitler*, I, 354–55. For the entire controversy, see also Mau, "Zweite Revolution," p. 128.

383. It obviously did not help that, at the end of 1933, 25% of all party members were either civil servants or teachers. See StdF to Reich ministry of interior, 26 Jan. 1938, BA/R 43 II/426a.

Verbonzung in the Social Democratic Party), and the frustrated anger of the Gauleiters, which vented itself in attacks on the restorationist-monarchist movement and in the continuing efforts to maintain private membership rolls in the Gaus.[384] All of these difficulties were, however, overshadowed by the conflicts between party and state and, even more important, the struggle with the SA.

The conflict between party and state centered on basic personnel policies. The governmental agencies interpreted Hitler's statement ending the revolution as a clear mandate to maintain control over the appointment and promotion of their administrative corps, while the PO continued to press for substantial party influence in state personnel matters. Thus, Hans von Helms, who had been the "party representative" in the Reich interior ministry, and whose ideas were characteristic of the thinking within the PO,[385] complained in a long memorandum to the StdF that the party's influence on state offices had been considerably reduced in the months since Hitler's announcement. He advocated some radical changes, culminating in the demand that all personnel directors in governmental offices be replaced by "trustees" (*Vertrauensleute*) of the party and "old fighters."[386]

The state organs were certainly able to prevent their wholesale subordination to party influences at both the Reich and Gau levels.[387] The main reason continued to be Hitler's preference of law and order to party activism, but a number of additional factors aggravated the situation from the PO's point of view. The Reichsleiters feared a further

384. Bracher, *Machtergreifung*, pp. 597 and 911; and Rschm. "Rundschreiben" to all GL, 20 Dec. 1933 and 7 Feb. 1934, *Rdschr.*, I.

385. Schomerus (OPG) to Helms, 1 Aug. 1934, BDC/Grauert (OPG); and Mommsen, *Beamtentum*, p. 66.

386. Helms, "Denkschrift . . . vom 26. Mai 1934 über Nationalsozialistische Personalpolitik," quoted in Mommsen, *Beamtentum*, pp. 171–73. A copy of the entire memorandum is in BDC/Grauert (OPG). See also Jung (of the StdF staff) to Grauert, 28 March 1934, HAB/77/2.

387. Significantly, Helms was transferred against his will from the Berlin ministry to a post in the police department at Altona. His protests against the decision were fruitless. See Helms to Hess, 31 Aug. 1934, BDC/Grauert (OPG). For an example of an unsuccessful attempt by a GL to subordinate the civil service to its control, see Gau Hessen, Gaupersonalamt B, "Rundschreiben R 2/34" to Kreisleiter, 10 May 1934, BA/R 2/22583; and Landesfinanzamt Kassel to Reich ministry of finance, 2 June 1934, *ibid.*

shift of power to the Gauleiters, and consequently supported the Reich ministries against the provincial party leaders.[388] Simultaneously, the Gauleiters had their difficulties with the district leaders. Many of the latter notables could not cope with their new duties and often became simple front men for the old conservative elite groups in their communities, particularly since the state organs in effect subsidized many of the party's activities at this level.[389]

Against this backdrop of declining party influence, the various attempts at centralization by Reich-level offices became increasingly important. Some, like the effort by Buch to assert the independence of the Gau party courts in their relations with the Gauleiters,[390] were at best feeble, since the judges on the Gau courts were usually drawn from the Gauleiters' cliques anyway. More significant were similar efforts by the Reich treasurer. In the course of the spring, Schwarz moved increasingly into the limelight. In an interview with the *VB*, he emphasized that in his jurisdiction there was no need for reform; the party's financial administration was an "exemplary" institution.[391] In practice this meant that Schwarz systematically extended and perfected the control devices he had by this time established. He was particularly eager to strengthen the bonds between his office and those of the Gau treasurers, knowing that a Gau treasurer who felt a primary loyalty to the Gauleiter would be unlikely to aid Schwarz's attempt to control the Gau finances. To hasten the identification, Schwarz drew a clear division between those organizations which were subject to regular audits by Gau auditors and those whose books were checked only at Schwarz's specific request. The first group included, in addition to the PO, the NSBO, the Women's League,[392] the NSV, the NS-Hago, and the organization of war victims.

388. See, for example, Regierungspräsident Düsseldorf to Grauert, 2 June 1934, HAB/77/2; and Simon (GL Koblenz-Trier) to Grauert, 28 March 1934, HAB/77/5. See also Bracher, *Machtergreifung*, pp. 924–25.

389. See Beauftragter IV (Martin Seidel) to ROL, 14 March 1934, T-580, roll 547, folder 651; and Rschm. enclosure to "Rundschreiben 69/34," 25 Oct. 1934, *Rdschr.*, I. For various Kreisleiter scandals in these months see HAB/77/13. See also *VOBl*, III (30 April 1934), 156.

390. *VOBl*, III (15 May 1934), 162.

391. *VB*, 29 and 30 March, 1934.

392. This was by now an all but dormant organization. Its total dues collection for 1933 was RM 385.66. See Ried (Reich auditor) "Revisionsbereich: Deutsches Frauenwerk," 9 March 1934, BDC/Hilgenfeldt (OPG).

Included in the second group were the paramilitary organizations and the Hitler Youth, and also the various professional groups, and above all, the DAF and the Reich food estate.[393] In addition, Schwarz felt strong enough to put some effective curbs on the Gauleiters. Using his right to interpret the financial provisions of the Law for the Unity of State and Party, he denied legal status to any subdivision of the PO or the paramilitary organizations, making it necessary for the Gaus to get Schwarz's (or the respective Gau treasurer's) permission before entering into financially binding contracts.[394] To control the regular Gau outlays, the Gauleiters were required to submit annual budget estimates to the Reich treasurer's office.[395] Schwarz even ventured into the delicate field of personnel policies. He severely criticized the PO offices for the practice of appointing unemployed but incompetent party members to PO positions and then paying them very small salaries or even giving them handouts in order to save money. He attempted to eliminate the private membership caches of the Gauleiters: the provincial offices had until January 15 to send to Munich those applications for membership which they had kept back since May 1933.[396]

Implicitly, many of these decrees criticized the ROL, who was, after all, responsible for the routine deployment of the party cadres. Ley's office did not even deny the validity of the charges; in a rare moment of self-criticism his staff director for organization actually admitted that the PO was riddled with PLs who were "philosophically all right," but who had no other qualifications for membership in the political elite of the Third Reich.[397] But few practical reforms followed this theoretical mea culpa. Ley did appoint some ambitious officials to head the Reich organizational office (Claus Selzner and Klaus Mehnert), and the new men attempted to put some order into the PO through the establishment of a personnel office and field inspections,[398]

393. Rschm., "Rundschreiben 9/34," 4 May 1934, *Rdschr.*, I; and *VB*, 21 April 1934.

394. *VB*, 27 March and 15 May, 1934; and Rschm., "Rundschreiben 12/34," 8 May 1934, *Rdschr.*, I.

395. Rschm., "Rundschreiben 14/34," 7 May 1934, *Rdschr.*, I.

396. Rschm., "Rundschreiben 11/34 [and] 19/34," 5 and 23 May 1934, *ibid.*

397. ROL, Organizational Office to Buch, 11 April 1934, T-580, roll 554, box 377, folder 877.

398. Reich Organizational Office, "Rundschreiben 18/34," 15 May 1934, T-580, roll 12, folder 169.

but these measures did not really touch the heart of the problem. There was, for example, a sharp division between the organizational and the schooling office on the qualifications of cadre personnel. While Selzner wanted to see dynamic young "old fighters" in the major posts, Otto Gohdes, the Reich schooling leader, insisted that only graduates of his entire training system were qualified to hold office.[399] Efforts to settle the dispute at the Gau level by the appointment of a Gau staff leader (*Gaustabsleiter*), an office on whose establishment the StdF would later insist, failed at this time because of Ley's opposition.[400] Ley had no interest in a strong PO per se, because he still persisted in his plans to treat the PO and the various affiliates under his control as equal partners.[401] Throughout the first half of the year, Ley worked systematically to raise the DAF's status. To be sure, he emphasized at times that the DAF was subordinate to the PO, but such statements stood in clear contrast to a variety of other utterances which placed the functionaries of the PO and the DAF on an equal footing[402] and which underscored Ley's insistence that the NSDAP had to be restructured as a result of the DAF's establishment.[403]

In contrast, the StdF attempted to capitalize on his public image as the foremost leader of the PO.[404] As a result of the oath-taking ceremony in February, Hess's office was described in the *VB* as the organizational right hand of Hitler, and Hess personally received a supreme compliment: he was the most creative and artistic of the Nazi leaders. The StdF's self-image was not overburdened with modesty: the jurisdictional scope of his staff's activities included all areas of "societal life."[405] Even in the propaganda-oriented Third Reich, however, public

399. *VB*, 5 April and 21 June 1934; Reich Organizational Office, "Rundschreiben 18/34," 15 May 1934; and *VB*, 20 Feb. 1934.

400. Robert Wagner to Ley, 26 Feb. 1934, BA/NS 22/200. See also Ley's formal prohibition in *VOBl*, III (31 May 1934), 166.

401. *VB*, 28 Jan. and 17 May 1934. See also Ley's scheme to have specific party offices "taking care of" (*betreuen*) the numerous affiliates. *VOBl*, II (31 May 1934), 165.

402. ROL, "Rundschreiben," 15 May 1934.

403. *VB*, 17 May 1934.

404. In its issue of 6 April 1934, the *VB* began a series of descriptions of various party offices under the general title *So arbeitet die Partei* ("this is the way the party operates"). The series continued until 2 June 1934, and the StdF's office headed the list. It was also the only agency which was featured in three articles.

405. *VB*, 6 April 1934.

image was not the equivalent of political power, and Hess's influence was by no means universally accepted,[406] but there is no doubt that the StdF's position was growing stronger. Hess for the first time indirectly limited the authority of the Reichsleiters, and, far more directly, moved against the ROL. In April, he issued a decree requiring the Reichsleiters to keep his office informed of all major decisions affecting their spheres of competence and to ask his prior permission for all "substantial (*wesentliche*) decrees."[407] The vagueness of the last phrase was undoubtedly deliberate; the StdF was not yet strong enough to risk open conflict with the Reichsleiters. Instead, he attempted to secure the support of the Gauleiters. To inhibit the growing organizational autonomy of the Reichsleiters' Gau-level subordinates, Hess insisted that all correspondence between the Gau officials and their superior Reichsleiter had to pass through the offices of the Gauleiters.[408]

Far more significant in the long run were the beginnings of the bitter conflict between Hess and Ley, a controversy which was to extend throughout most of the thirties. At issue were Ley's investigative powers and his authority over personnel policies in the party. Ley's first defeat came in January, when Hitler announced that, as leader of the party, he would personally appoint all department heads at the Reichsleitung. In practice, the decision transferred these personnel appointments to the office of the StdF, since Hitler charged his deputy with making nominations for the posts and maintaining the necessary personnel papers.[409] The decision gave Hess his first opportunity to influence personnel policy in the party,[410] and it was reflected almost immediately in the further expansion of the StdF's staff. In March the Gau organizational leader of Hessen, Helmuth Friedrichs, nicknamed "Long Friedrichs" because of his size, joined the staff as head of the "party division." Friedrichs was to become the most important staff official after Bormann and remained with the StdF and later the party

406. Hess still complained that his decrees were ignored by other party offices. See StdF, "Anordnung," 21 Feb. 1934, T-580, roll 12, folder 169.

407. StdF, "Verfügung," 9 April 1934, *ibid.*

408. StdF, "Anordnung," 27 Feb. 1934, *ibid.* The document bears the handwritten note: "important."

409. StdF to all RL, 30 Jan. 1934, T-580, roll 12, folder 169.

410. Cf. Ley's complaints against this development in Ley to Hess, 20 June 1939, T-580, roll 549, folder 546.

chancellery until the end of the war. Further blows to Ley's power and prestige followed in April and May. Hess forced the ROL to give up the designation "Political Organization" to describe the PL cadre organization. This term, Hess wrote, suggested that Ley (who used the title "Chief of staff of the PO of the NSDAP") had responsibility for political decisions, when in fact his field of competence was solely organizational and statistical.[411] It was a logical corollary of this principle that Ley also lost the administrative control over the six territorial inspectors which he had retained. In May, the StdF incorporated them into his office, after he had informed Ley of his intentions a month earlier.[412]

Once lodged within his office, the StdF did not hesitate to make full use of the inspectors. Their activities increased significantly in both volume and importance as they traveled constantly to investigate complaints brought to the StdF. A typical inspector's itinerary for this time read as follows:

May 2–3	meetings with GL in Halle and Weimar
May 7–9	meetings with Hess
May 10	meetings with district leader Chemnitz
May 12	meetings with district leader Leipzig
May 14	meetings with [SS] Oberführer Bautzen
May 15–16	working session in Berlin
May 23–26	Gau congress in Zippendorf
May 29–31	meetings with GL Sauckel, work on twelve cases of complaints, the same with GL Jordan.[413]

At the same time, the StdF sought to verticalize his staff by creating a network of Gau-level officials who looked upon themselves primarily as the representatives of the deputy Führer in the Gaus. He showed a particular interest in the deputy Gauleiters and the Gau inspectors. The

411. Hess to Ley, 19 April 1934, in T-580, roll 549, folder 746.
412. StdF to all RL and GL, 11 May 1934, T-580, roll 12, folder 169. The order was published in *VOBl*, III (31 May 1934), 164; and *VB*, 19 May 1934. See also Hess to Ley, 8 April 1934, T-580, roll 549, folder 746.
413. Bauer, "Spesenaufstellung der Gebietsinspektion III [Robert Bauer] für den Monat Mai 1934," enclosure in Bauer to Schwarz, 2 June 1934, T-580, roll 803, box 237, folder 15. Additional reports on the inspectors' activities are in the same folder.

deputy Gauleiters were for the most part simply personal friends of the Gauleiters, but Hess realized their potential significance for the future. Since many of the Gauleiters had to divide their time between state and party positions, the deputies were often the highest full-time party functionaries in the provinces. Hess consequently insisted that these cadre functionaries identify completely with the party. They had to have been party members since before September 30, 1930, and they could hold no party office beyond that of deputy Gauleiter.[414] The StdF built up the corps of Gau and district inspectors to supervise and report day-to-day party activities in their territories. In addition to investigating and settling complaints of local or provincial impact, these officials became the StdF's private reporting service. Part of their function was to send monthly reports to Munich describing the mood and rumors of the party in their areas. In this way, the StdF was able to establish at least a partial counterbalance to the SD's reports, which also reached his office.[415]

The StdF increased the activism of his office in a number of other areas as well. There are some indications that Hess was the principal conductor of the Nazi foreign policy toward Austria in the summer of 1934.[416] He also integrated the Gau economic advisors increasingly into the PO structure,[417] and used them, albeit indirectly, to check the power of the DAF. Their work was supplemented by the creation of a "department of business ethics" (Abteilung für betriebliche Moral) within the StdF's staff, which investigated primarily cases of bribery and corruption,[418] and by the planning activities of the commission for economic policy. But the expansion of the StdF's field of activity was not all directed toward asserting his power over the party: the deputy Führer also took care to emphasize his service function to the party in its relationship to the state. The Berlin Liaison Staff received a new head,

414. StdF, "Anordnung," 26 June 1934, T-580, roll 12, folder 169.
415. Ibid. The reports were also the basis for some propagandistic and legislative initiatives by the StdF. Thus the deputy Führer's office at one point showed a particular interest in reports of scandals involving members of the clergy. See Gau inspector München-Oberbayern to Kreisleiter Eichstätt, 16 March 1934, BA/GF/33.
416. Ross, Hitler und Dollfus, p. 216.
417. Schwarz had by now approved that they were to receive regular salaries from party funds. See Rschm. "Rundschreiben" to all GL, 26 Feb. 1934, Rdschr., I.
418. StdF, "Anordnung" (not to be published), 8 March 1934, T-580, roll 12, folder 169.

Herbert Stenger, and with the change in leadership came a spurt of new energy. The Liaison Staff described itself as the agency through which "the pulse beat of the party constantly and unceasingly flows into the [government] offices of the Wilhelmsstrasse."[419]

Hess was not willing to allow other pulse beats to be felt in the same governmental offices. He defended his right as sole representative of the NSDAP's voice in the councils of the Reich-level agencies both as a general principle against the claims of other Reichsleiters,[420] and in his decisions on individual political issues. Among the latter, the continuing agitation over the Reichsreform was a particular danger. Hess had again prohibited (with "severest penalties" for violations[421]) the discussion of the subject among the party's leaders; but both discussion and planning were hard to suppress—particularly since the state agencies were clearly going ahead with their own plans,[422]—and Hitler's well-known dislike of the present situation all but encouraged further work by the party's leaders. Since the subject could not be closed, the StdF decided to concentrate the party's side of the planned Reichsreform within his staff organization. In May, Hess appointed the Gauleiter of Munich, Adolf Wagner, to head a new section of the staff, the *Referat Reichsreform*. Wagner's task was very broadly defined to encompass "all questions that concern the reconstruction of the Reich."[423] With this appointment, Hess had selected one of the most radical centralists to head the NSDAP's planning efforts. Wagner was a vehement opponent of any form of federalism and proposed the abolition of the Länder and their governments. In their place would move field offices of the Reich ministries and the party's Reichsleitung.[424]

For the moment, however, the controversy over the Reichsreform was suppressed by the growing difficulties between the PO and the SA. The NSDAP's largest paramilitary organization had become a

419. *VB*, 15 April 1934.

420. See Bormann to Lammers, 24 Nov. 1939, BA/R 43 II/1200.

421. *VB*, 10 Jan. 1934.

422. See Siebert's report on a meeting with Frick, 26 March 1934, BGStA, MA 105285; and Frick's interview with the *Königsberger Allgemeine Zeitung*, quoted in *VB*, 3 June 1934. A copy of the complete interview is in HAB/320/1.

423. See Wagner to Siebert, 18 May 1934, BGStA, MA 105285; and *VOBl*, III (31 May 1934), 163.

424. Wagner to Frick, 23 June 1934, BGStA, MA 105285.

formidable, confident, and well-financed power in the Third Reich.[425] The SA's problem was essentially unused energy; it spent itself in largely useless propaganda marches, but also in a great deal of public grumbling, local violence and—more important—increasing resentment by the SA's leadership corps against the PO and even Hitler himself.[426] Substantively, the SA resented above all the end of the revolution, and here it had at least the sympathy of many "old fighters," especially in the economic affiliates, and even some of the Gauleiters.[427] Hitler, on the other hand, continued to be apprehensive about the economic situation. In March he issued another sharp warning against party interference in the economic life of the nation because he feared a national bank crisis.[428] The SA, for its part, made plans for a huge national spring meeting in Berlin. It was to be financed by the Gauleiters, although, as Schwarz reminded the party, the debts for the maneuvers of autumn 1933 were still not paid.[429] Clearly, a triangular confrontation was developing between the PO, the SA, and, less visibly, the SS. As yet, it expressed itself only in mutual slights among the various leaders (especially in Bavaria and the Rhine-Ruhr area) and in attempts by both the SA and the SS to secure the aid of leading PO officials for their "service,"[430] but these problems obviously portended sharper conflicts in the future.

425. See Bennecke, *Reichswehr*, p. 28; Rschm., "Tätigkeitsbericht des Haushaltsamtes für das Jahr 1935," 13 March 1936, T-580, roll 833, box 256, folder 270.

426. Bennecke, *Hitler und die SA*, p. 218. It is significant in this context that only a minority of the SA members also held party membership. In Hamburg fully two-thirds of the SA were not members of the party. See Timpke, *Dokumente*, p. 296, n. 1.

427. See the report of the Regierungspräsident, Aachen, 5 March 1934, quoted in Bernhard Vollmer, ed., *Volksopposition im Polizeistaat* (Stuttgart, 1957), p. 38; Domarus, *Hitler*, I, 371; and the report on a speech by GL Brückner, *VB*, 15 Feb. 1934.

428. Epp, "Besprechung mit den Reichsstatthaltern 5. März 1934," p. 2, BGStA, Rsth. 148; and Bracher, *Machtergreifung*, p. 924.

429. Rschm., "Rundschreiben" to all GL, 3 March 1934, *Rdschr.*, I. The spring maneuvers were canceled on 4 April. See *ibid.*, 4 April 1934.

430. The roles in all this of the SA's chief of training, F. W. Krüger, and the GL Adolph Wagner were particularly unclear. The former apparently provoked the Reichswehr, whereas Wagner may have deliberately fomented the SA's dissatisfaction in Bavaria. See Bennecke, *Reichswehr*, pp. 30, 47, and 75; and the report of the *VB*, 9 and 10 May 1934, on Wagner's address to the SA-Leibstandarte. See also Joseph Wagner (GL Westfalen-Nord) to Röhm, 24 and 30 May 1934,

From the beginning, both the StdF's office and Hess personally played a major role in the crisis. Apparently apprised of the growing dissatisfaction among the SA's leadership corps by Röhm's eventual successor, Victor Lutze (at this time SA leader and Oberpräsident of Hanover), early in 1934, Hess simultaneously labored to defuse the conflict and prepare the PO for an open clash with the SA. While Hitler remained indecisive and unwilling to take action,[431] the StdF sought indirectly to warn the SA leaders,[432] but he also attempted to obtain some personnel changes in the SA's territorial commanders in order to strengthen the position of the PO's territorial cadres.[433] Moreover, he apparently encouraged the anti-SA intelligence activities of the SS, and was undoubtedly privy to Schwarz's decision in April that rescinded the treasurer's previous willingness to exempt SA members from the general ban on new applications for party membership.[434]

By May, Hitler was becoming convinced that the SA situation could no longer be ignored. He approved Goebbels' controversial[435] campaign against "critics and spoilers" of the regime.[436] In the massive propaganda effort that followed Hitler's May 1 speech in Berlin,[437] the SA was never mentioned by name, but the Führer's open threat to "hit hard" at the slightest sign of opposition was obviously directed at the paramilitary group.[438] The conflict headed toward open confrontation. Nevertheless,

BDC/Wagner (OPG); Joseph Wagner to Hess, 10 July 1934, BDC/Giesler (SA); Röhm to Hitler, 3 May 1934, BDC/Wächtler (PKC); SA-Oberführer Lohbeck to OPG, ca. May 1934, BDC/Florian (OPG); Murr to Himmler, 14 Sept. 1934, BDC/Murr (SS); and RFSS to Eberstein, 8 Oct. 1934, BDC/Wächtler (SS).

431. Höhne, *Orden*, p. 83.

432. Helmut Sündermann, ". . . Eine Unterredung mit dem Stellvertreter des Führers," *VB*, 7 July 1934.

433. Bennecke, *Reichswehr*, p. 59.

434. Zipfel, *Kirchenkampf*, p. 146; and Rschm., "Rundschreiben 5/34," 19 April 1934, *Rdschr.*, I. As of 15 February the SA's share of the membership dues no longer went directly to the SA's Reich office. See Rschm. to all GL, 29 Jan. 1934, *Rdschr.*, I.

435. Adolf Wagner thought it was a pretty useless exercise. See Wagner to Frick, 23 June 1934, BGStA, MA 105285.

436. The German words *Kritikaster* and *Miesmacher* imply a type of criticism which attacks a positive accomplishment without basis in fact and for the sheer joy of destruction.

437. Domarus, *Hitler*, I, 379; and *VB*, 12 May 1934.

438. Speech given at the Gau congress of Thuringia, 17 June 1934, in Domarus, *Hitler*, I, 390.

the Führer still hesitated to unleash the now thoroughly aroused PO. Hess again took the initiative. Between May 23 and 26, a conference of all Gauleiters (the regional inspectors also attended) was arranged at Bad Zippendorf in Mecklenberg. Hitler was not present, and Hess presided in his absence. Attendance was mandatory for the Gauleiters,[439] an indication that the primary subject of discussion was the SA-PO conflict. The meetings were disguised as routine working sessions (with addresses by Schwarz, Amann, Schirach, and others), but the heart of the conference was obviously something described vaguely as the "personal exchange of views between the deputy Führer and the Gauleiters" that followed the formal speeches.[440] Apparently, Hess counseled a disengagement. At least one high SA leader reported a more conciliatory attitude on the part of the PO immediately after the conference,[441] and Röhm, too, did his best to lessen the tension. After a discussion with Hitler early in June, Röhm pretended illness and furloughed the entire SA for the following month.[442]

An uneasy calm prevailed throughout most of June. Hess seemed to make a last effort to prevent the situation from exploding, with a speech in Cologne on June 25. Speaking as a "Nationalist Socialist, not a Reich minister," he issued a clear warning to the SA, yet also suggested that Hitler was as much interested in furthering the revolution as ever—one only had to trust the Führer.[443] Other PO leaders were equally conciliatory. Gauleiter Kube, for example, published an article at this time (which was to cause him considerable embarrassment a few days later) that praised Röhm as one of Hitler's most loyal paladins.[444] But it was too late. On June 28, perhaps provoked by reports from the SS and the SA's double-dealing training chief, F. W. Krüger, the Army Officers' Association expelled Röhm from its ranks. At almost precisely the same time, Hitler finally made up his mind to stage a bloody coup against

439. StdF to all GL, 7 May 1934, T-580, roll 12, folder 169.
440. On the Zippendorf meeting see *VB*, 26 and 28 May 1934.
441. Giesler (SA leader in Westphalia) to Groeben, 28 May 1934, HAB/77/22.
442. *VB*, 8 and 9 June 1934. According to Hitler's Reichstag speech of 13 July 1934 he had a five-hour talk with Röhm at the beginning of June. See Domarus, *Hitler*, I, 384.
443. The speech was printed in its entirety in *VB*, 26 June 1934; Domarus, *Hitler*, I, 392 gives some excerpts.
444. See the report by the Gestapo office at Aachen, 6 Aug. 1934, quoted in Vollmer, *Volksopposition*, p. 68.

the SA.[445] Until then, as was usual with him when he could not reach a decision, he had traveled. In mid-June he was in Italy; at the end of the month he visited the Rhineland with Hess. There the Gauleiters, especially Josef Terboven, who was a bitter enemy of the SA and identified closely with the SS, apparently related their difficulties with the SA in vivid colors. Hitler came away convinced that the SA represented a threat to his own power and that only a bloodbath could eliminate the danger.

In one sense, the decision meant that Hitler had failed in his first eighteen months in office. Emotionally, Hitler was much more sympathetic to Röhm's ideas of far-reaching revolutionary changes and the violent destruction of the old value system than he was to the bureaucratized terror of the SS and the cold-blooded planners on the staff of the StdF. The Führer had given every indication since January 1933 that fundamentally he defended the unsubtle social revolutionaries in the party who sought to destroy cooperatives and department stores, who wanted to eliminate the norms of the Rechtsstaat by force, and who were about to murder Engelbert Dollfuss as the prelude to the Austrian Machtergreifung.[446] It was only a question of timing that led Hitler to destroy Röhm and, for the moment, energize the conservative elements in the armed forces.[447] Yet that very time element was also of immense importance for the further development of the power relationships within the NSDAP. The Röhm decision assured that the real winner of the first eighteen months in office was Rudolf Hess,[448] since only the office of the deputy Führer had both a concept of power and the necessary personnel to establish its authority in the post-Röhm NSDAP.

445. Domarus, *Hitler*, I, 393; and Höhne, *Orden*, pp. 104–05.
446. For an excellent analysis of Hitler's concepts of party and power see Ross, *Hitler und Dollfuss*, esp. p. 257.
447. See Robert J. O'Neill, *The German Army and the Nazi Party 1933–39* (London, 1968), pp. 95–123, for a brief but useful account of the major highlights in the relationship of party to army in Nazi Germany from 1933 to 1938.
448. Schäfer, *NSDAP*, p. 78; Schoenbaum, *Hitler's Social Revolution*, p. 22; and Frank, *Im Angesicht*, p. 167.

Purges, Struggles, and Crises

What became known as the Röhm affair or the Röhm putsch was actually neither an affair nor a putsch, but a purge. Between June 30 and the end of the year Hitler, Schwarz, the office of the deputy Führer, and the SS destroyed the political power potential of the SA and the conservative-monarchist movement, physically exterminated a sizable number of storm troop leaders as well as other political enemies, and significantly altered the personnel composition of the PO. Basically, the "new" Nazis, the advocates of bureaucratic power management in the offices of the StdF and the SS, used the myth of a planned putsch by the SA to eliminate the power potential and influence of the remaining pockets of doctrinaire leftist revolutionaries in the paramilitary groups and the PO.

Although friction between the SA and the PO had been part of the political landscape in Germany since January 1933 (and before), the conflict came to a bloody climax only in the last days of June 1934. Three days after Hess's threatening speech on June 25, Hitler held "last consultations" with his closest advisors in the party. This group now included Robert Ley for the first time.[1] (The PO's chief of staff was notorious for his inability to keep official confidences, and his involvement undoubtedly meant Hitler had decided on a swift course of action.) The only major officials accompanying Hitler to his confrontation with Röhm and the SA's leadership, however, were Hess and Goebbels. The deputy Führer had of course taken a leading part in the develop-

---

1. Alfred Rosenberg, *Das politische Tagebuch Alfred Rosenbergs 1934/35 und 1939/40*, ed. Hans-Günther Seraphim (Munich, 1964), entry for 7 July 1934, p. 45.

111

ing crisis, and Goebbels came along either at his own request[2] or because Hitler did not trust him and wanted the propaganda chief at his side.[3] The next day (June 29) Hitler resumed the seemingly leisurely pace of his inspection tour of the western Gaus; he spent the day reviewing PO personnel in Cologne and Aachen.[4]

In retrospect it is obvious that Hitler's activities on June 29 were a deliberate deception, though it is less clear what precisely happened in the twenty-two hours betwen midnight on June 29 and 10:00 P.M. the next day. The official version, first elaborated by Hess to an assembly of East Prussian PLs several days after the events,[5] presented a determined Hitler calmly and methodically keeping a rendezvous with history. According to Hess, Hitler's party—including his adjutant, Brückner, his chauffeurs Julius Schaub and Julius Schreck, as well as Goebbels, Dietrich (Hitler's press chief), and Hess—arrived at Munich from Bad Godesberg by air at 2:00 A.M. on June 30. They proceeded immediately to the Bavarian interior ministry, where the minister, Gauleiter Wagner, gave them a short report of the SA's plottings. (Wagner, on his own, had relieved the two Bavarian SA leaders of their command.[6]) From the ministry Hitler proceeded to Bad Wiessee, where the major SA leaders had been asked to assemble for a conference, and there he arrested the SA chieftains. He then returned to Munich, spoke to the party leaders at the Brown House, drafted his orders appointing Lutze as successor to Röhm and the twelve-point reform program for the SA, and returned to Berlin, to be met by Göring at Tempelhof Airport.

This picture of an omniscient and prescient Hitler was retouched at a number of points. To begin with, it did not do justice to the independent actions of either the SS or Gauleiter Wagner. Lutze, who in later years grew increasingly bitter about the SS's role in the party, blamed Himmler's organization for enlarging the number of deaths from the planned seven to the official eighty-two (though the latter figure, too,

2. *Ibid.* Rosenberg claimed that Goebbels literally begged Hitler to be permitted to join the expedition.

3. Max Domarus, ed., *Hitler, Reden und Proklamationen 1932–45* (Munich, 1965), I, 395, n. 125.

4. *Ibid.*, I, 394.

5. *Völkischer Beobachter* (cited hereafter as *VB*), 9 July 1934.

6. Domarus, *Hitler*, I, 399.

was below the actual number murdered between June 30 and July 2).[7] Wagner not only was responsible for the orders executing the Munich SA leader, August Schneidhuber, without specific authority from Hitler, but he also set up SS patrols at the Munich railway station to check the papers of arriving SA leaders.[8] In addition, Wagner saw to it that a trusted PL of his own staff, Hausböck, then adjutant of the deputy Gauleiter of Munich-Upper Bavaria and later chief of staff of the Gau, went to the confrontation at Bad Wiessee.[9]

Hess's report also minimized the role played by the deputy Führer himself during the drama. Hitler's party made its way to Bad Wiessee in three cars: Hitler, his driver, Lutze, and Hess in the first, followed by the SS squad car, and finally a third automobile carrying Goebbels and Hausböck. After the arrests in Bad Wiessee, Hess took charge of informing the party leaders of Hitler's actions. He called the SA leaders (that is, those not yet shot or arrested), the Reichsleiters, and several, but not all, Gauleiters together for a conference at noon in the Brown House. Hess also told Schwarz and, somewhat later, Buch of the morning's events.[10]

Hitler's noon address to the party leadership was a largely disjointed catalogue of complaints against the SA climaxed by the demand that the sharp division between the tasks of the SA and the Reichswehr be preserved. Perhaps to underscore the guilt feelings of his audience, Hitler forced the party leaders to stand throughout the hour-long speech.[11] In the afternoon Hitler drafted his telegram of appointment to Lutze, challenging the new chief of staff to fashion from the SA "the

7. Alcohol tended to release Lutze's bitterness rather frequently. These remarks were made during a *Bierabend* attended by Lutze, the Pomeranian Gauleiter Schwede-Coburg, and the latter's staff. An SS officer present reported Lutze's views to Himmler. See SS-Standartenführer Schulze, "Bericht," 21 Aug. 1935, Berlin Document Center (cited hereafter as BDC)/Lutze (Sturmabteilung [SA]), II.

8. Domarus, *Hitler*, I, 399; Heinrich Bennecke, *Die Reichswehr und der "Röhm-Putsch"* (Munich, 1964), p. 57.

9. See Hausböck's report in *Mitteilungsblatt Kreis München der NSDAP* (cited hereafter as *Mittbl. Kr. Mü.*), no. 25 (31 Aug. 1936). This publication is not always paginated.

10. Bennecke, *Reichswehr*, p. 57; and Walter Buch, "Vernehmung," p. 8, Institut für Zeitgeschichte, Munich (cited hereafter as IfZ)/ZS 855.

11. Bennecke, *Reichswehr*, p. 58.

instrument which the nation needs and which I envision."[12] He also jotted down the twelve principles which were to be the basis of the party purge. Hitler's final task came late in the afternoon. Bormann had arrived at the Brown House about 5:00 P.M. and proceeded to select for immediate execution some of the SA leaders, including Röhm, held at Stadelheim Prison. Just before returning to Berlin, Hitler approved the selections, and the executions were given legal authority by Wagner in his capacity as Bavarian minister of the interior.[13] On the Führer's arrival in the Reich capital the Prussian prime minister, Hermann Göring, presented Hitler with a report of the executions initiated by Göring and his henchmen in Prussia. By now, Hitler was understandably exhausted, and shortly after his return he joined the Goebbels family for an extended vacation, first at Heiligendamm on the Baltic and later at Berchtesgaden.[14]

The immediate Röhm crisis was solely an intraparty affair; the larger German public knew nothing of the bloody events until July 2. The *VB*'s July 1 issue (printed, since the *VB* was a morning paper, during the evening of June 30) devoted its headline to the fact that the *Graf Spee* would be Germany's third battle cruiser. A special issue appeared later that day, but it carried only news of Röhm's arrest and Lutze's appointment. Not until the following day did the *VB* announce Röhm's execution.[15] Even within the party, Hitler and Hess took considerable pains to prevent the formation of a crisis atmosphere. A Reichsleiters and Gauleiters meeting at Flensburg (on the Danish border, as far removed from Munich as possible) called for July 4 and 5 was characterized by a rather forced aura of "normalcy." The delegates did offer a telegram and a "Sieg Heil" for Lutze and Hitler to celebrate

12. Hitler to Lutze, 30 June 1934, BDC/Lutze (SA), II.

13. Domarus, *Hitler*, I, 402 and 402, n. 140. An official (i.e., incomplete) list of those executed is in the National Archives, Microcopy No. T- (cited hereafter as T-) 81, roll 90, frames 103458–64. The executions in Munich were carried out by the SS and members of the "Austrian Legion" (i.e., Austrian Nazis who had fled to Germany in order to escape prosecution for acts of terror against the Dollfuss government). See Hermann Mau, " 'Die Zweite Revolution,'—der 30, Juni 1934," *Vierteljahrshefte für Zeitgeschichte* (cited hereafter as *Vjh.f.Z.*), I (April 1953), 134.

14. Ernst Hanfstaengl, *Unheard Witness* (Philadelphia, 1957), pp. 262 and 271.

15. *VB*, 1 July (special ed.) and 2 July 1934.

the "victories" of June 30, and Hess, who chaired the meeting, emphasized the "disciplined attitude" of the PO, but most of the sessions were devoted to such routine matters as rural resettlement problems, organizational problems of the DAF, and a variety of economic issues.[16]

Hess offered a somewhat fuller account of the Röhm affair when he spoke to the East Prussian PLs three days later, but Hitler did not appear in public again until July 13, when he addressed a special session of the Reichstag. Indeed, Hitler seems to have been genuinely shaken by the bloodbath of June 30. Not only was the entire political situation in Germany—in view of President Hindenburg's imminent death—extremely delicate, but Hitler's own attitude toward Röhm and his ideas was strangely ambivalent. At heart, Hitler hated bourgeois morality and capitalistic striving as much as Röhm; the Führer merely had a greater sense of political realities. Nevertheless, Hitler in later years referred to his moves against the SA as a bitter necessity, and he attempted to assuage his conscience by granting large pensions to the widows and children of the executed SA leaders.[17]

For the moment, however, Hitler was an omniscient savior of the nation, a man who had acted at the last minute to prevent a large-scale putsch attempt to overthrow the government. The special session of the legislature on July 13 met solely to give approval to a government bill retroactively legalizing the murders between June 30 and July 2 as "emergency defense measures of the state" (*Staatsnotwehr*). Hitler, in introducing the bill, gave a lengthy account of the entire affair,[18] portraying himself as a long-suffering moderate who moved only when no other course of action was possible. For good measure, he pretended to have been shocked to learn of Röhm's homosexuality. The Reichstag, needless to say, gave unanimous approval to the government's bill, and, with that Hitler apparently hoped the matter was closed. A Reichsleiters and Gauleiters meeting after the Reichstag session, which Hitler attended, seems to have been devoted entirely to agricultural questions.[19]

Actually, the month of July was memorable primarily for setbacks to the Nazi cause. The Röhm murders shocked many of the "old fight-

16. *VB*, 5 and 6 July 1934.
17. Domarus, *Hitler*, I, 458, n. 252.
18. *Ibid.*, pp. 410–24.
19. *VB*, 15 July 1934.

ers" in the party and helped to produce a feeling of alienation between them and their Führer. A large proportion of the old party membership clearly sympathized with Röhm's revolutionary ideas, if not with his sexual mores.[20] At the end of the month the abortive coup by Austrian Nazis added to the regime's difficulties. Although this putsch attempt had been planned in Vienna, high German party officials (including Hess) were kept abreast of the plans, and the German chargé d'affaires in Vienna gave shelter to several Austrian fugitives from justice.[21] Hitler must have been relieved when Hindenburg finally died on August 2, enabling Hitler to portray himself as the man who would carry on the torch of national greatness left by the fallen leader.[22] Politically, the significance of the president's death and Hitler's assumption of the powers of his office lay in the fact that there now remained not even a theoretical alternative to the omnipotence of the Nazi leader, and, by extension, his institutionalization in the Nazi Party.[23]

These considerations in turn increased the importance and bitterness of the purge within the party; after August 2 the amount of potential power at stake was vastly greater than before. As a result, the purge was characterized not only by anxious demonstrations of surface conformity,[24] but by multifaceted intraparty warfare that included attempts by the SS to gain power at the expense of both the SA and the PO.[25] During the purge Hitler kept in the background, leaving the power struggle in the hands of those leaders who had been actively involved in planning the moves against Röhm: Himmler, Schwarz,

20. Domarus, *Hitler*, I, 425.

21. Dieter Ross, *Hitler und Dollfuss* (Hamburg, 1966). In a subsequent OPG (Oberstes Parteigericht) trial, the head of the Austrian SS claimed that his orders right up to the Putsch came directly from Munich. See SS-Standartenführer Wächter to Himmler, 31 May 1938, T-175, roll 32, frames 2539839–45.

22. *VB*, 3 Aug. 1934.

23. William S. Allen, *The Nazi Seizure of Power* (Chicago, 1965), p. 235.

24. The office of the StdF denounced such local practices as forced attendance at party rallies. See StdF, "Rundschreiben," 19 July 1934, T-580, roll 12, folder 169.

25. On the SD's surveillance of the PO during this time see Shlomo Aronson, "Heydrich und die Anfänge des SD und der Gestapo" (Dissertation, Free University of Berlin, 1967), p. 326. Both v. Helms and Otto Wagener had been arrested during the "Putsch" as a result of local denunciations. See v. Helms to Hess, 31 Aug. 1934, IfZ/FA 113; and Bormann to Lutze, 28 Feb. 1936, IfZ/FA 143.

Buch, and Hess. For reasons which will become clear in a moment, neither Ley nor the Gauleiters as a group benefited from the purge.

The most immediate beneficiary was, of course, the SS. Himmler's elite guard was removed from nominal subordination to the SA's chief of staff and placed directly under Hitler. Even more significant, the SD of the SS received virtually blanket permission to set up an espionage system covering the SA and the PO. Finally, Hitler appointed one of Himmler's closest subordinates, Kurt Daluege, to purge the SA groups in Berlin, Pomerania, East Germany (*Ostmark*), Silesia, and Central Saxony (*Mitte*)—the territorial heart of the leftist sentiments in the SA.[26]

Indirectly, the SS also influenced Schwarz's measures against the SA. With his customary vigor, the Reich treasurer used the opportunity of the "putsch" to expand his control of the party's finances. In "consultation with Lutze," Schwarz appointed Willy Damson, in later years one of Himmler's informants in the Reich treasurer's office,[27] as national treasurer of the SA.[28] Simultaneously, all of the Reich auditors (by now numbering seventeen) were dispatched to subject the SA's books to close scrutiny. The work was to have been completed by August 28, but actually it took most of 1935 to obtain an accurate account of the SA's finances.[29] The SA's debts turned out to be sizable, but the party suffered no financial loss: the bulk was paid with state moneys, specifically a RM 45 million grant from the Reich ministry of the interior.[30] Simultaneously, Gau and district auditors examined the books of the SA units in their areas, though their thoroughness was apparently not exemplary.[31]

26. Adolf Hitler, "Verfügung," 2 July 1934, BDC/Daluege (SS).

27. See below, p. 343.

28. *VB*, 6 July 1934; *Verordnungsblatt der Reichsleitung der NSDAP* (cited hereafter as *VOBl*), IV (15 July 1934), 177. See also Reichsschatzmeister (cited hereafter as Rschm.), "Tätigkeitsbericht des Haushaltsamtes für das Jahr 1935," 13 March 1936, p. 1, T-580, roll 833, box 256, folder 270.

29. Rschm., "Rundschreiben," 9 July and 8 Aug. 1934, in *Rundschreiben des Reichsschatzmeisters* (cited hereafter as *Rdschr.*) (Munich, 1934–1942), I; and Rschm., "Tätigkeitsbericht 1935," p. 1. In the spring of 1935 Schwarz added the HJ, BDM, SS, and NSKK to the list of audited organizations.

30. Rschm., "Tätigkeitsbericht 1935," appendix 1.

31. Rschm., "Rundschreiben 61/34," 9 Oct. 1934, *Rdschr.*, I.

Schwarz cast his net far wider than the SA's finances. He used the crisis atmosphere to move against secret accounts in the Gaus and districts and to obtain financial accounting from all party units by mid-October.[32] The Reich treasurer also hastened to order audits of several left-leaning Gaus.[33] And his statement advocating a general purge of those party members "who had come in with the big push in 1933"[34] laid the basis for an alliance with Hess and Buch.

On June 30, the deputy Führer and Buch, the head of the party courts (along with Amann, the head of the party publishing house), had distinguished themselves by a particularly bloodthirsty attitude toward the SA. Buch and Hess competed with each other in the number of SA leaders each wanted shot, and Hess offered to execute Röhm personally.[35] Hitler, as usual, rewarded such loyalty with additional power grants. To Buch fell the delicate task of supervising the PLs' elimination of their SA rivals throughout Germany. Hitler obviously wanted the PLs to have the opportunity for a widespread purge, but he was unwilling to countenance a PO run amok. The head of the party courts attempted to meet his and Hitler's political goals by, on the one hand, ordering the party courts to act in close cooperation with Hess's Reich inspector for special purposes, Holzschuher, and by reminding the tribunals of their duty to serve the party, not objective truth,[36] while, on the other hand, fashioning a semiautonomous position for the party courts as a result of their usefulness to the leadership during the purge.[37] In order to handle the expected load of appeal cases, the OPG

32. Rschm., "Rundschreiben 58/34 [and] 75/34," 26 Sept. and 20 Nov. 1934, *Rdschr.*, I. Almost half of the GL had not submitted their reports by the deadline.

33. Hermann Haag, "Inspektionsbericht Gauleitung Pommern-Stettin," 4 Aug. 1936, T-580, roll 842, box 267, folder 348. The books of the Gau were not found in good order.

34. Rschm., "Bericht über die Gauschatzmeistertagung am 25. November 1937," n.d., p. 40, *ibid.*

35. Heinz Höhne, *Der Orden unter dem Totenkopf* (Gütersloh, 1967), pp. 111–12.

36. Buch, "Anordung," 28 Sept. 1934, *Parteirichter*, I (10 Oct. 1934), 29; and n.a., "Die Stellung des Politischen Leiters in parteigerichtlichen Verfahren," *ibid.*, I (10 July 1934), 4.

37. "Stellung," p. 2; and Buch, "Stellung des Parteirichters in der Organisation," *ibid.*, I (10 Aug. 1934), 13.

at the end of September created two chambers of final appeal.[38] Eventually, Buch hoped to raise the corps of party judges to the status of moral arbiters of the movement.[39]

Buch failed long before he came close to realizing his final ambitions. Though no less totalitarian in his mind-set than Hitler, he tended to be far less agile in changing his black and white categories than the Führer. While Hitler was primarily concerned with leftist influences in the party, Buch in the summer of 1934 continued to see the devil in the subtle influence of freemasons in the party,[40] a political and social connection which involved far more prominent members of the right wing than the left. Because Hitler soon tired of Buch's politically inopportune moral fervor, the party's judicial system was never a serious rival to the office of the StdF in the race for political benefits from the Röhm purge.

Personally and institutionally Rudolf Hess was closest to Hitler in the days and months after the "affair." In the first few days immediately following June 30 (before the Führer left for his vacation with Goebbels' family), Hitler was extremely nervous and seemed to tolerate only Hess's company.[41] The deputy Führer also relieved Hitler of such tasks as facing the widow of an SA leader shot "by mistake,"[42] and it was Hess, of course, who first explained to the nation (his July 8 speech was broadcast over all radio stations) the necessity for executing Röhm. Like Buch, Hess was not selfless. While he gave generous thanks to the SS in his utterances, he also emphasized, both on July 8 and earlier at the meeting of Gauleiters and Reichsleiters, that the PO's position in the party had been significantly altered by the Röhm "affair": the political cadres were now the most important formation in the party.[43]

38. *VOBl*, IV (30 Sept. 1934), 195; and *Parteirichter*, I (10 Oct. 1934), 28.

39. See the excerpt from Buch's speech at the 1934 party congress in *Parteirichter*, I (20 Sept. 1934), 17.

40. See, for example, "NSDAP und Freimaurer," *Parteirichter*, I (10 Aug. 1934), 9–10; and *VB*, 1 Sept. 1934.

41. Hermann Rauschning, *Hitler Speaks* (London, 1938), p. 171.

42. Bennecke, *Reichswehr*, p. 72.

43. *VB*, 5 and 9 July 1934. The second part of Hess's speech of 8 July reflected Hitler's foreign policy fears; it was an appeal for peace and mutual understanding among all veterans of World War I.

The office of the StdF wanted to utilize the purge authority both to increase the PO's independence of state officials[44] and other party formations and to expand the control functions of the deputy Führer within the PO. The StdF hoped to accomplish his goal by an intricate carrot-and-stick policy. He encouraged the PLs to vent their anger against the SA and conservative state officials,[45] though the StdF also asked the PO to report false denunciations to his six Beauftragte, whose scope of activity and budgets increased vastly in the months after June 30.[46] Hess had no lack of information with which to fill his personnel folders; in fact, less than three weeks after encouraging the reporting of denunciations to his Beauftragte, he had to caution the PLs against "professional denouncers."[47]

Compared with the spectacular trials that marked the Stalinist purges at about the same time, the Nazi Party purge was a quietly desperate behind-the-scenes struggle, punctuated only by noisy unity demonstrations. The first of these came in mid-August, when the Nazis staged a plebiscite to show the nation's approval of Hitler's step to combine in his person the powers of the presidency and the chancellorship. All factions of the NSDAP had a vital interest in a smooth transition from Hindenburg to Hitler, since only Hitler's assumption of total power meant that "all positions of power were now in the hands of the party."[48] Despite strong nationalist appeals,[49] and lavish use of money,[50] the results were disappointing by totalitarian standards. In the Reich as a whole 89.9 percent voted for the proposition, but in some areas (for example, Aachen), as many as 27.4 percent cast negative votes.

The party hastened to explain such lack of popularity as the result

44. Hess announced that the penalty for communicating party matters to state officials would in the future be "ruthless expulsion." StdF, "Verfügung," 16 Aug. 1934, T-580, roll 12, folder 169.

45. See the report of the provincial governor of Aachen, 10 Oct. 1934, quoted in Bernhard Vollmer, *Volksopposition im Polizeistaat* (Stuttgart, 1957), pp. 105–06.

46. Friedrichs to Schwarz, 23 Oct. 1934, T-580, roll 802, box 237, folder 15.

47. StdF, "Bekanntgabe," 19 July 1934, T-580, roll 12, folder 169.

48. *VB*, 21 Aug. 1934.

49. The *VB* headlined the announcement of the plebiscite as follows: "A joyful 'yes' for the Führer as the last thanks to Hindenburg." *VB*, 11 Aug. 1934.

50. Each GL received between RM 25,000 and RM 30,000 for campaign expenses. Rschm., "Rundschreiben 50/34," 28 Aug. 1934, *Rdschr.*, I.

of "rootless proletarians" and "clerical influences,"[51] but the poor showing remained. Consequently, the 1934 party congress assumed even
greater significance as a demonstration of unified party strength than
was usually the case. Schwarz authorized massive money collections,[52]
the pace of the purge seems to have been slowed down in preparation
for the congress,[53] and even Hitler acknowledged it as a watershed in
the party's history. His opening statement emphasized that "the National Socialist revolution as a revolutionary, power-oriented development had reached its conclusion."[54] The remainder of the congress was
a studied attempt to demonstrate a party unity and continuity that
had little basis in political reality.[55] And hardly had the delegates returned home when they devoted their energies to the next demonstration of party-nation unity, the Saar plebiscite scheduled for January
1935.[56]

The party purge was conducted beneath and behind the facade of
martial parades and election campaigns. Its most numerous category
of victims was of course SA leaders and members. There are no absolute
figures on the actual number of those expelled from the party and the
SA,[57] but there is little doubt that the PO offices from the Reich to the
local level relentlessly pursued their erstwhile rivals in the paramilitary

51. See the report of the provincial governor of Aachen, 7 Sept. 1934 quoted in
Vollmer, *Volksopposition*, p. 87; and the report of the election bureau in the
electoral district Köln–Aachen, "Bericht über das Wahlergebnis am 19. August
1934," 21 Aug. 1934, Hauptarchiv Berlin (cited hereafter as HAB)/77/32.
52. Rschm., "Rundschreiben 33/34," 3 July 1934, *Rdschr.*, I. See also the report
of the Gestapo office in Aachen, 4 Sept. 1934, quoted in Vollmer, *Volksopposition*,
p. 31.
53. At least the number of court cases reported increased significantly after 15
September. See *VOBl*, IV (15 Sept. 1934), 193–94 and 197–98.
54. Domarus, *Hitler*, I, 447.
55. The best propagandistic record of the 1934 congress is Leni Riefenstahl's
film *Triumph of the Will*. The various speeches are reprinted in NSDAP, *Der
Kongress zu Nürnberg vom 5. bis 10. September 1934* (Munich, 1934).
56. On the importance of the Saar plebiscite for Hitler, see Otto Dietrich,
Zwölf Jahre mit Hitler (Cologne, 1955), p. 43.
57. The extent of the purge may be indicated by the fact that in Düsseldorf alone
1,126 individual SA men were dismissed and two entire local units dissolved. See
Hans-Peter Görgen, "Düsseldorf und der Nationalsozialismus" (Dissertation, University of Cologne, 1968), p. 119.

organization.[58] The provincial SA leaders aroused the particular ire of the Gau and district leaders. The vehemence of the PO leaders' pursuit may be illustrated[59] by the fate of two major SA leaders who later rose to high positions in the Third Reich, that is, two officials who were obviously free from the taint of association with Röhm. Wilhelm Schepmann became Lutze's successor as the SA's chief of staff in 1943, and Paul Giesler was appointed Gauleiter of Munich–Upper Bavaria after Adolf Wagner's death in 1942. Both Schepmann and Giesler had served in the politically volatile Ruhr area, and now encountered the wrath of the Gauleiter of South Westphalia, Josef Wagner. The Gauleiter accused the two, and particularly Schepmann, of preparing an armed SA uprising on June 30 and resisting the authority of the SS and the Gauleiter.[60] The OPG cleared both SA leaders, but Wagner was not content. He charged Schepmann and Giesler in a second trial, and the OPG again cleared both.[61] Nevertheless, as late as June 1935, Wagner protested to Schwarz against a plan to give Giesler a badge of honor.[62] While not every SA leader was as hated by his Gauleiter as Schepmann and Giesler were, the immediate result of the purge for the SA was a position of political impotence and virtual subordination to the PO. At the Reich level Lutze did not inherit Röhm's cabinet seat, so that Hess alone now represented the party in this body.[63] In the states and localities, with virtually every SA leader facing charges in the party courts, the SA lost what influence it had had over personnel and policy decisions. In Bavaria, for example, Röhm's commissioner system disappeared "without a whimper."[64]

The purge also included the PO itself, though its basis here was

58. Mau, "Zweite Revolution," p. 136. See also the report of the Gestapo office Aachen, 6 Aug. 1934, quoted in Vollmer, *Volksopposition*, p. 64.

59. On 27 August 1934 the SA special court wrote Giesler: "Your case is by no means unusual. A large number of high SA leaders find themselves in the *same* [*sic*] situation. See BDC/Giesler (SA).

60. OPG to Schepmann, 24 Oct. 1934, BDC/Schepmann (SA).

61. OPG, second chamber, "Beschluss," 10 April 1935, *ibid.*

62. Wagner to Schwarz, 25 June 1935, BDC/Giesler (SA).

63. The cabinet decision of 3 July 1934 is quoted in Domarus, *Hitler*, I, 406.

64. Halbmonatsberichte des Regierungspräsidiums von Oberbayern (cited hereafter as HMB/OBB), 8 Aug. 1934, p. 1, Bayerisches Geheimes Staatsarchiv (cited hereafter as BGStA)/MA 106670.

less concrete and its extent more circumscribed than in the SA. Hitler had already indicated one ground for accusations when he specifically included the PLs in his denunciation of luxurious living habits and public drunkenness among party officials.[65] There was no doubt that such practices were as widespread among the PL as in the SA,[66] but in fact Hitler was little concerned with their elimination. His attack was primarily a public relations gesture; the list of officials purged from the PO makes it clear that ideological deviation was far more often the basis for dismissal than loose living. The Reichsleiter group was least affected by the purge. Only Gottfried Feder, the oldest Reichsleiter in terms of party membership and a prominent exponent of leftist economic ideas, was dismissed from his position as state secretary in the Reich economics ministry, and vanished into obscurity.[67]

The toll of Gauleiters and district leaders was considerably larger. Two of the Gauleiters were dismissed outright: Helmuth Brückner in Silesia and Wilhelm Karpenstein in Pomerania. Brückner had long sympathized with Röhm's ideas,[68] and obviously tolerated the machinations of the Silesian SA leader, Edmund Heines. Brückner was officially accused of "Byzantine habits" and homosexuality,[69] but the actual reasons for his downfall were clearly political. His successor was Josef Wagner (who added Silesia to his own Gau of Westphalia), one of the SA's bitterest enemies. Karpenstein was a less prominent leftist, but he had been too weak to control the SA organization in his Gau. His successor Franz Schwede-Coburg, an old-time party member from Bavaria, was appointed on July 22 and given special authority to

65. See Lutze's Order of the Day, 30 June 1934, quoted in Domarus, *Hitler*, I, 401.

66. See the report of the Hamburg senator (minister) of the interior, July 1934, in Henning Timpke, ed., *Dokumente zur Gleichschaltung des Landes Hamburg 1933* (Frankfurt, 1964), pp. 286–87.

67. Domarus, *Hitler*, I, 462. See also SdtF, "Verfügung," 11 Nov. 1934, T-580, roll 12, folder 169.

68. Hans-Gerd Schumann, *Nationalsozialismus und Gewerkschaftsbewegung* (Hanover, 1958), p. 106.

69. StdF to all GL and RL, 4 Dec. 1934, T-580, roll 12, folder 169; and RFSS, "Vortrag" (Nov. 1935), BDC/Brückner (SS). See also *VOBl*, no. 109 (31 Nov. 1935), p. 348. That the SS leader in Silesia, v. Woyrsch, had a particular dislike for Brückner no doubt hastened the Gauleiter's fall. See Brückner to Darré, 10 Oct. 1934, BDC/Woyrsch (SS).

"strengthen the political unity of the Gau as a whole."[70] Three other Gauleiters came under suspicion at least temporarily. In East Prussia, Erich Koch's numerous cases of corruption were under investigation by the SS, but the Gauleiter survived; the territorial SS leader later regretted that he had "pardoned" him.[71] Friedrich Hildebrandt (Mecklenburg), like Koch a sometime sympathizer of the "socialist" wing in the NSDAP, was investigated by both Frick and Hess,[72] though eventually he, too, stayed at his post. Finally, the notorious Julius Streicher (Franconia) was, according to rumors, near dismissal,[73] but he stayed on for another six years. Streicher's case is a blatant example of Hitler's minimal interest in the corruption issue. The Franconian Gauleiter had committed no political offenses, though his Gau and his own living habits were, in fact, cesspools of corruption.

Understandably enough, the largest numbers involved in the purge were among the lower PL ranks (district leader and below). Almost one fifth (19.8 percent) of those holding PL posts at the time of the Machtergreifung were no longer in office at the beginning of 1935 (40,153 out of 203,304). To be sure, not all of these officials were purged, but of the total number leaving the PO, 67.7 percent had either been dismissed (26.4 percent) or left for "other reasons" (41.3 percent). (The remaining departures were attributed to "professional reasons.")[74] There is a clear correlation between the personnel changes in the Gaus exhibiting the largest percentage of dismissals (see table 4) and the anti-SA purge. In Swabia the Gauleiter, Karl Wahl, had had numerous difficulties with the SA; East Hanover was Lutze's home Gau; Westphalia-North, Hessen, and Kurhessen included the Rhine-Ruhr territories of Schepmann and Giesler; and, as noted above, the Gauleiters of East Prussia and Pomerania were subject to investigation and dismissal respectively. In general, it can be noted that the purge in the

70. PK, "Lebenslauf des Gauleiters Schwede-Coburg," 24 May 1943, BDC/ Schwede-Coburg (PKC). See also GL Pomerania, *Gau Pommern im Aufbau* ([Stettin, 1934]).

71. Wachlin (Reich auditor) to Schwarz, 6 Dec. 1935, BDC/v.d. Bach (SS).

72. Frick to Hess, 13 July 1934, HAB/320/77.

73. See the documentation in the Bundesarchiv (cited hereafter as BA)/NS 22/201.

74. Reichsorganisationsleiter, Amt für Statistik, *Partei-Statistik* ([Munich, 1935]), II, 278. See also Wolfgang Schäfer, *NSDAP* (Hanover, 1956), p. 42.

PO affected primarily those PLs who had cooperated with rather than opposed the SA leaders in their area of jurisdiction.[75]

TABLE 4

The PO Purge, 1934–1935

Gau	Percentage of PLs Dismissed
Schwaben	35.1%
Osthannover	24.0
Westfalen-Nord	35.1
Hessen-Nord	32.8
Köln-Aachen	32.4
Ostpreussen	32.1
Pommern	31.6
Kurhessen	30.0

SOURCE: Wolfgang Schäfer, *Die NSDAP* (Hanover, 1956), p. 43.

Robert Ley, already indirectly affected by the large-scale purge of the PO (after all, he had been responsible for personnel policy since December 1932), suffered additional loss of prestige when the purge reached the ranks of the affiliates. In many affiliates the purge was not extensive, if only because some of them were still in a rudimentary organizational state.[76] Several, however, had their powers severely circumscribed. The National Socialist Association of Civil Servants, for example, while still claiming to control personnel policy in state offices,[77] was reduced to the level of a social club for the government employees among the party membership.[78] The NS-Hago was similarly confronted with cold reality. At the same time that its Gau officials were planning the most effective means of influencing the party's economic policies,[79]

75. The absence of Silesia from the list in the table is explained by the relative ineffectiveness of Josef Wagner as the new GL. He was sharply opposed on a number of issues by his deputy and eventual successor (in 1941), Fritz Bracht. See below, p. 270.

76. Gottfried Neesse, *Partei und Staat* (Hamburg, 1936), p. 241.

77. See GL Gross-Berlin of the Civil Servants' Organization to Maas and Grauert, 25 Aug. and 25 Oct. 1935, respectively, HAB/77/9 and 13.

78. See the directive of the Reich minister of the interior, 27 Dec. 1934, quoted in Hans Mommsen, *Beamtentum im Dritten Reich* (Stuttgart, 1966), p. 145.

79. See Gau official for estate development in München-Oberbayern to Reich office . . . , 4 Oct. 1934, BDC/Hayler (PKC).

Schwarz was confiscating the organization's liquid assets.[80] The National Socialist Student Association (NSDStB), which had often harbored particularly radical elements, was directly taken over by the StdF; Hess appointed his close associate Gerhard Wagner as the NSDStB's interim leader.[81] Above all, Ley's own DAF was subject to suspicion. Its core, and the only genuinely leftist Nazi element in the labor organization, the NSBO, had continued to support many of Strasser's pseudosocialist ideas, and was for this reason strongly influenced by the SA's views. Three of the leading NSBO officials were almost immediately dismissed from their positions because they had "sabotaged Ley's constructive work."[82] Ley attempted to erase this black mark against him by all but dissolving the NSBO[83] and by trying to associate the DAF even more closely with the PO. At the end of July all DAF offices became subdepartments of established PO offices.[84] The ROL also requested that Schwarz supervise the activities of the DAF's treasury.[85] Nevertheless, Ley's problems did not cease. A full-scale purge of the DAF Gau offices was underway, as SS-affiliated police officials sought to comb out what they regarded as entrenched bastions of homosexuality in the DAF;[86] and as late as August, the ROL felt obliged to point out that a number of persons had been arrested for spreading rumors against him.[87] Alone among the affiliates, the agricultural apparatus gained rather than lost power and stature. This was undoubtedly in large part because the a.A., with its emphasis on independent ownership of farms, had successfully avoided identification with leftist ideas.[88] As a result, the agricultural affiliates increased their

80. Rschm., "Rundschreiben 81/34," 1 Dec. 1934, *Rdschr.*, I.

81. *VB*, 20 July 1934. This did not, however, end either the group's activism or its organizational difficulties. See below, pp. 148–49.

82. ROL to OPG, 8 Aug. 1935, T-580, roll 554, box 377, folder 877. See also Schumann, *Nationalsozialismus*, pp. 104–05.

83. As early as 28 June, Ley had eliminated the budgetary autonomy of the NSBO. *VB*, 28 June 1934.

84. See *VB*, 25 July and 15 Aug. 1934.

85. *VOBl*, IV (1 Aug. 1934), 179; and *VB*, 25 July 1934.

86. See Gerum (the police chief of Würzburg) to the Bavarian minister of the interior, "Vorgänge bei der Gauleitung Mainfranken," 5 May 1935, BDC/Gerum (PKC).

87. *VB*, 10 Aug. 1934.

88. Hess's specific directive ("Verfügung," 9 Jan. 1935, *VOBl*, V [31 Jan. 1935],

independence from the PO, and Darré, the minister of agriculture, could with impunity in late 1934 attack a PL who was both a Gauleiter and a provincial governor.[89]

Darré's audacity can also be explained in large part by his close relationship to the SS, but to argue that the 1934 purge meant the takeover of most party functions by the SS[90] misses the essence of the juxtaposition of power groups after Röhm's death. The symbiotic relationship that emerged between Himmler, Hess, and Schwarz benefited the SS in immediate power and independence, but for the long-range future, the cadres, too, fashioned for themselves a stronger basis of influence. This was true, above all, in the field of finances. From the available figures it is clear that Schwarz diverted most of the large sums used by the SA before June 1934 to the cadre administration or to permanent reserves. Table 5 shows the increase in financial resources

TABLE 5

NSDAP Income, 1933–1937

Year	Amount (Millions of RM)
1933	15.4
1934	35.6
1935	49.8
1936	67.6
1937	100.8

SOURCE: Rschm., "Bilanz und Finanzbericht der Reichsleitung der NSDAP 1937," p. 3, T-580, roll 833, box 256, folder 268.

of the NSDAP between 1933 and 1937. As a result, the lower party organs were largely freed from financial problems. At the end of 1934, for example, a typical district in the Gau Kurmark (the province of Brandenburg surrounding Berlin) had a cash balance of RM 10,000, while each district leader personally received between RM 100 and 150 in subsidies from the Gau per month.[91]

---

235), that officials of the agricultural organization did not have to be members of the DAF made it clear that Hitler wanted to keep it that way.

89. The official involved was Hinrich Lohse, the GL of Schleswig-Holstein. See Buch to Lohse, 12 Nov. 1934, BDC/Darré (PKC).

90. This view is put forth by Joseph Nyomarkay, *Charisma and Factionalism in the Nazi Party* (Minneapolis, 1967), p. 139.

91. See Tittmann to Kube, 25 Jan. 1935, BDC/Tittmann (OPG).

The Reich treasurer saw to it that financial bounty did not result in administrative independence. He utilized the bad example of the SA to place all of the paramilitary formations and affiliates as well as the OPG under his financial supervision.[92] The only major exception was the DAF, which operated largely with the seized assets of the old socialist labor unions, and thus maintained its day-to-day financial independence.[93] Schwarz reserved his strongest financial ties for the PO itself, however. Here his administrative trump card was his absolute control of the entire treasurers' personnel in the party. The Gau treasurers were appointed by the Reich treasurer "in agreement" with the Gauleiters and were "politically" subordinate to the Gau chief, but in "substantive" matters (*sachlich*) they obeyed only Schwarz. The Gau treasurers in turn controlled the Gau auditing staff and the district and local treasurers in the Gaus.[94] Somewhat later, a new directive regularized the Gau finances. The essentially political offices of the Gau were financed entirely from regular Gau funds, subject to a budget approved by Schwarz's office and routinely supervised by the Gau treasurer.[95] Finally, Schwarz found a miser's ideal solution to the continuing[96] problems of the Gauleiters' secret accounts: he allotted each Gauleiter a sizable expense account, or "disposition fund." The money came from the Gaus themselves, specifically from sums collected by the Gau in excess of regular dues and fees through such devices as "voluntary" contributions from firms and individuals. Schwarz, however, determined the amount of each expense account, and he had the right to refuse one altogether if he felt the Gau's financial condition did not warrant a special grant.[97] For the Gauleiters the major advantage of the scheme

92. Rschm., "Tätigkeitsbericht 1935," pp. 1–2; and *Parteirichter*, I (10 Nov. 1934), 34.

93. See Rschm., "Rundschreiben 76/34," 22 Nov. 1934, *Rdschr.*, I.

94. Rschm., "Rundschreiben 34/34," 5 July 1934, *Rdschr.*, I.

95. Rschm., "Rundschreiben 31/35," 22 Feb. 1935, *Rdschr.*, II The offices involved were the following: treasurer, executive secretary (staff office), personnel 1 (PO), organization, propaganda, party court, training, inspectorate, press, communal affairs, and the student organization.

96. *Ibid*, "Rundschreiben 43/35," 29 March 1935; and Ulf Lükemann, "Der Reichsschatzmeister der NSDAP" (Dissertation, Free University of Berlin, 1963), pp. 57–59.

97. Schwarz to Bürckel, 18 Dec. 1934, BDC/Bürckel (PKC); and Schwarz to Jordan, 18 Dec. 1934, BDC/Jordan (PKC). The leaders of well-endowed Gaus,

lay in their absolute right to dispose of the sums as they wished; even the Gau treasurer was permitted only to check the mathematical accuracy of the expense account books.[98]

A logical corollary to control of the Gau finances was supervision of the district budgets. After 1933 the districts became the most important lower party jurisdictions and the most difficult to control financially. Since the overlapping of party and state affairs was particularly pronounced at this level, many of the party activities were, in fact, at least partially financed with municipal or county funds. Schwarz had no objection to the principle of state subsidies, but he did object to the direct flow of moneys to lower party organs. Instead, he preferred to request the funds from the Reich ministry of finance. The party treasurer's office would then channel them to the districts.[99] The Gauleiters, of course, were less than enthusiastic about Schwarz's plan,[100] and this time the Reich treasurer had to compromise. Since he was unable to force through the centralized allocation of state funds, he decided to do without such funds altogether: the districts' activities were to be financed by the Gaus, using 75 percent of the additional income generated by the new (and increased) dues schedule to be published on January 1, 1935.[101]

The difficulties between Schwarz and the Gauleiters were minor skirmishes compared with the life-and-death battle raging between the StdF and the ROL in the latter half of 1934. Despite his tarnished reputation, Ley had not essentially changed his concept of the party. He still hoped to develop the DAF "from a pillar into a pyramid,"[102] that is, to construct a superaffiliate that would dwarf all other affiliates and the PO itself. This trend was clearly indicated by an in-service training system which continued to make no distinction between PO and DAF officials and a salary scale that paid DAF officials far more than their

---

on the other hand, emerged with monthly checks reaching RM 5,000 or 10,000. See Schwarz to Murr, 18 Dec. 1934, BDC/Murr (PKC) and Schwarz to Mutschmann, 18 Dec. 1934, BDC/Mutschman (PKC).

98. Rschm., "Rundschreiben 87/34," 14 Dec. 1934, *Rdschr.*, I.

99. Rschm., "Rundschreiben 37/34," 2 July 1934, *Rdschr.*, I.

100. *Ibid.*, "Rundschreiben 53/34," 14 Sept. 1934.

101. *Ibid.*, "Rundschreiben 89/34," 19 Dec. 1934.

102. Claus Selzner, "Rede vor dem Sonderkursus des NSDStB," July 1935, T-81, roll 75, frames 86902–06.

counterparts in the PO.[103] The predictable result of this emphasis on the DAF's Betreuung concept was inadequately trained PO personnel who were unable to deal appropriately with substantive questions of leadership and control.[104]

In contrast, the StdF's office systematically used the purge to develop an elitist concept of the party cadres and to prevent the identification of the PO with any affiliate, including the DAF.[105] In practice, however, Hess's and Bormann's plans were impeded by the indirectness of their control over the PO; as yet Hitler had not altered his December 1932 directive giving Ley charge of the vertical cadre organization, including such basic matters as most personnel appointments, deployment, and in-service training. The StdF, however, used his office's exclusive right to represent the party in all dealings with the state as an indirect but effective base to expand his influence over the PO. After Röhm's death Hess alone represented the NSDAP in the Reich cabinet, and after July 27 his office obtained the right to participate at all stages of the ministerial bill-drafting process.[106] Within the StdF's office this phase of the deputy Führer's activities was handled by the "division of state affairs" (*Staatsrechtliche Abteilung*), headed after September 1934 by Walter Sommer. As far as the party was concerned, this department handled all legislative affairs, all personnel appointments for Reich and Länder positions, and all "other basic issues." The StdF noted in these matters that "only my view is binding for the party [as a whole]."[107] For the Gauleiters and Reichsleiters in the NSDAP this concentrated power of the StdF had a number of far-reaching effects: it made their theoretical right of immediate access to Hitler largely illusory, it all

103. See *VB*, 8 Aug. 1934; *VOBl*, IV (31 Nov. 1934), 214 and 223–24; and Robert Wagner to Hess, 2 Oct. 1934, BA/NS 22/200.

104. See the report of the Gestapo office in Aachen, 6 Oct. 1934, quoted in Vollmer, *Volksopposition*, p. 101.

105. See Bormann to Reich ministries of finance, justice, and labor, 7 Jan. 1935, BA/R 43 II/1198.

106. Hitler to Reich ministers, 27 July 1934, BA/R 43 II/141. Hess later argued that Hitler's letter was a direct result of the Röhm affair (Hess to Göring *et al.*, 18 Feb. 1938, BA/NS 6/448), but at least a draft of the decree existed earlier. See Frick's draft of 8 and 14 June 1934, BA/R 43 II/1197.

107. Hess to Reich ministers *et al.*, 13 Feb. 1937, BA/R 43 II/1199.

but excluded the RLs from making programmatic or national policy decisions on their own, and, perhaps most important, it established control over state personnel and policy decisions in the same office in the party.[108] For all practical purposes, the status of derivative agents[109] accorded the Reichsleiters in the course of 1932 was being weakened.[110]

Hess lost little time in bringing his programmatic powers into play. In a series of meetings[111] and directives in the latter half of 1934, he prohibited intraparty discussions of programmatic issues, and at the same time expanded his office's right to make binding pronouncements in a number of areas. The StdF reaffirmed his ambition to concentrate all activities connected with the planned constitutional and territorial reform of Germany within his *Referat* (task force) Reichsreform,[112] and somewhat later he intervened in the ecclesiastical battles raging within the party by curtailing the activities of the party radicals against the established churches.[113] Similarly, the StdF took an active part in the foreign policy of the Third Reich after the failure of the Austrian putsch.[114] At the same time, almost unnoticed, Hess had expanded his influence over personnel appointments in the Reichsleiters' offices. Wulffen's hitherto insignificant personnel office suddenly rose to prominence as Hess claimed a voice in all major personnel appointments.[115]

All of these measures affected primarily the Reichsleiters, although some of them suffered no great setbacks. As yet, the StdF had disturbed

108. Mommsen, *Beamtentum*, pp. 76–78 and 182. Officials with the StdF's office were well aware of the potential significance of this connection. See v. Helms to Schomerus (OPG), 28 July 1934, BDC/Grauert (OPG).

109. For a description of this concept see Dietrich Orlow, *The History of the Nazi Party: 1919–1933* (Pittsburgh, 1969) pp. 81 ff.

110. Hans Frank, *Im Angesicht des Galgens* (Munich, 1953), p. 168.

111. E.g., on 8 November 1934, StdF to RL, 31 Oct. 1934, T-580, roll 12, folder 169. See also StdF, "Anordnung," 23 Nov. 1934, *ibid.*

112. Haushofer to Staatsrat Dr. Kollmann, 29 Sept. 1934, T-580, roll 77, folder 362.

113. Klaus Scholder, "Die evangelische Kirche in der Sicht der nationalsozialistischen Führung bis zum Kriegsausbruch," *Vierteljahrshefte für Zeitgeschichte* (cited hereafter as *Vjh.f.Z.*), XVI (Jan. 1968), 25.

114. Ross, *Hitler und Dollfuss*, pp. 238 and 242–43.

115. Bormann to all RL, 7 May 1934, HAB/320/22; and StdF to all RL, 16 July 1934, T-580, roll 12, folder 169.

neither the entrenched position of the Gauleiters nor Ley's specific powers as head of the ROL. Here the key to the deputy Führer's strategy lay in the concept of the Hoheitsträger (the territorial cadre chief). It will be recalled that part of Hitler's divide-and-conquer policy had been to give both the Reichsleiters (responsible for a policy area) and the Gauleiters (responsible for a geographic area) the status of derivative agents. The resulting conflicts had already permeated the entire administrative structure of the NSDAP, but the StdF had discovered an effective means of utilizing the conflicting positions for his own purposes: Hess alone was both Reichsleiter and Hoheitsträger. As a result, he could expand his control over the Reichsleiters through his powers over policy decisions, while subordinating the Gauleiters with the established practice whereby each Hoheitsträger exercised vertical control over the next smaller territorial units in his area of jurisdiction. Hess was more than willing to increase the authority of all Hoheitsträgers because it strengthened his own position as "Reichshoheitsträger." Thus he noted that political leadership within the entire party could be exercised only by the Hoheitsträgers, that is, "by me, the Gauleiters, district leaders, and local leaders."[116] Consequently, the StdF consistently supported the Gauleiters' and district leaders' claim of personnel control not only against the SA, but against state and communal agencies as well.[117]

This policy brought with it the danger that the Gauleiters and perhaps even the district leaders might become too powerful to control, but for the moment Hess needed them both as a counterweight to the ROL[118] and to establish his influence over the state administration. The monthly Gauleiters' reports provided the basic source of informa-

116. StdF to all RL, GL, and *Beauftragte*, 25 Oct. 1935, T-580, roll 12, folder 169.

117. For documentation of GL-state conflict over personnel appointments, see HAB/77/3 and 4; the relevant documents on the district leaders are in BGStA, Rsth. 291. For the latter see also the chapters by Hermann Weinkauff, "Die deutsche Justiz und der Nationalsozialismus," pp. 70 and 120; and Albrecht Wagner, "Die Umgestaltung der Gerichtsverfassung und des Verfahrens- und Richterrechts in nationalsozialistischen Staat," p. 233, in Hermann Weinkauff *et al.*, *Die deutsche Justiz und der Nationalsozialismus* (Stuttgart, 1968).

118. In addition, ambitious district leaders tended to counterbalance the Gauleiters. See, for example, the complaints of GL Loeper to Grauert, 1 Nov. 1934, HAB/77/2.

tion on state personnel matters and legislative affairs, without which the StdF could not effectively exercise his influence in the Reich ministries.[119] At the same time, Hess's inspectors provided an implicit check on the autonomy of the Hoheitsträgers: they had the authority to investigate all matters brought to their attention, and their reports went only to the office of the StdF.[120] Moreover, self-interest dictated that the territorial cadres cooperate with Hess. The success of Ley's efforts to merge the PO and the DAF would destroy the concept of the PO as an elite decision-making body in the party.

After he had prepared the ground through his de facto alliance with the Gauleiters and district leaders, Hess launched a major attack on Ley in the late fall. In October he issued a directive "clarifying" the jurisdiction of various Reichsleiters. Significantly, Ley was authorized to give binding orders only in the area of organizational deployment in the PO, not in the realm of personnel appointments.[121] Almost simultaneously, Hess charged Ley with violations of the party statutes, though this seems to have been a bluff or diversionary move.[122] Far more important were two pieces of correspondence reaching Ley during the month of November. On the tenth, Hess informed Ley that the PO was not an autonomous division of the party, like the paramilitary organizations, but included all of the party's cadres. As a result, its political leadership and supervision came under Hess's, not Ley's auspices. In addition, the deputy Führer emphasized that the ROL had not inherited Strasser's powers and that Ley was merely the technical supervisor of the PO's organizational deployment, with primary responsibility for providing statistical information on the PL cadres of the party.[123] Ley attempted to salvage what could be saved. He yielded on the title question, and agreed not to style himself "Reichsleiter for

119. Peter Diehl-Thiele, *Partei und Staat im Dritten Reich* (Munich, 1969), pp. 230–31, gives a list of the areas covered in the monthly reports.

120. Hess to Ley, 12 Nov. 1934, T-580, roll 549, folder 746.

121. *VOBl*, IV (31 Oct. 1934), 203.

122. See Buch, "Verfügung," 23 Oct. 1934, BDC/Ley (PKC). This is the only document on the matter in the ROL's personnel file, and no disposition of the case is indicated. See also Diehl-Thiele, *Partei*, p. 211.

123. Hess to Ley, 11 Nov. 1934, T-580, roll 549, folder 746; and StdF, "Verfügung," 10 Nov. 1934, T-580, roll 12, folder 169.

the PO," but on the larger issue he was determined to resist Hess. Ley's counterattack was rather oblique, although clear enough: the PO cadres would be led as they had been in the past, that is, by Ley.[124] But Ley stood on sinking ground; Hess had obviously coordinated his moves with Hitler before he began his battle with Ley. At the end of the month, Ley received a letter from Hitler, in effect supporting Hess's position in the dispute. Ley's tasks in the PO, wrote Hitler, were the deployment, supervision, and training of the cadre personnel and the keeping of statistical records. His authority over the Gauleiters was limited to purely organizational questions. The political leadership of the PO, as well as all personnel appointments down to and including district leaders, Hitler reserved to himself.[125] Now Ley gave in. At the end of the year he issued yet another "clarifying" directive acknowledging that in his capacity as head of the ROL he was "responsible in every sense to the Führer or, as the case may be, to the deputy Führer, party member Rudolf Hess."[126]

The StdF had clearly defeated Ley. As far as the long-term future was concerned, the most important shift resulting from the Ley-Hess dispute was the concentration of all major cadre personnel appointments in the hands of Hitler, or, in actuality, in the office of the StdF. Here lay the all-important springboard for transforming the PO from a Betreuungs-organization to an elitist control group. Hess set to work immediately,[127] although by late 1934 the cadres as a whole were beset by a variety of problems. The PO personnel were still permeated with corruption,[128] and a general lack of enthusiasm among the mass of party members led to large-scale dues arrears.[129] In addition, Hitler's

---

124. ROL, "Anordnung," 16 Nov. 1934, *VOBl*, IV (31 Nov. 1934).

125. Hitler to Ley, 29 Nov. 1934, T-580, roll 77, folder 363.

126. ROL, "Anordnung," 28 Dec. 1934, *VOBl*, V (15 Jan. 1935), 229.

127. To take stock of the present cadre personnel, he issued a directive which required that by 1 January 1935 all PLs had to have an identification pass signed by the StdF in order to be confirmed in office. See StdF, "Anordnung," 14 Nov. 1934, *VOBl*, IV (31 Nov. 1934), 213.

128. StdF, "Anordnung," 23 Nov. 1934, T-580, roll 12, folder 169. See also the reports of the Gestapo office and the provincial governor in Aachen, 4 Nov. 1934 and 2 Feb. 1935, quoted in Vollmer, *Volksopposition*, pp. 113 and 178, respectively.

129. Rschm., "Rundschreiben 90/34," 28 Dec. 1934, *Rdschr.*, I. Schwarz tried to

decision in the Ley-Hess dispute had been more chaos-producing than
Solomonic: Ley had lost control over appointments, but his continuing enthusiasm for overorganization and excessive bureaucratization made the PO apparatus cumbersome and paralyzed it.[130] The
party's lack of forward momentum as the purge neared its end was a
factor in Hitler's strange silence in the last month of 1934. He was
increasingly becoming an institutionalized superperson,[131] but between
November 23 and December 18 he did not appear at all in public.
Rosenberg suggested the reason was illness,[132] but it is equally likely
that Hitler was in one of those despondent moods that frequently over-
came him when he was forced to make unpleasant decisions. At the
end of 1934 this involved nothing less basic than the future of the party
and the nature of the Nazi regime. Germany now stood at a crossroad.
Hitler personally and the party as his institutionalized will[133] had
achieved total negative control over all phases of public life in Germany;
it was virtually impossible to accomplish anything against the will of
the party. On the other hand, the much-heralded Nazi revolution had
made little headway. The NSDAP still largely reacted, rather than
initiated. Indeed, as Hitler moved against the left in the party the
more conservative "state" power group (that is, the permanent bureaucracy) viewed itself as a vindicated element in Nazi Germany.[134]
Cowed before the initial onslaught of the party, the civil servants now
came to regard the NSDAP as a rival, but not necessarily superior

---

compensate for this situation at least in part by a new dues schedule. The schedule,
which provided for monthly dues adjusted to the members' monthly income, is in
"Rundscreiben 78/34," 30 Nov. 1934, *ibid.*

130. For complaints on this score see the reports of the Gestapo office in Aachen,
5 Dec. 1934 and 7 Jan. 1935, quoted in Vollmer, *Volksopposition*, pp. 132 and 146.

131. One of his last links with bourgeois existence had just been cut. At the end
of the year Hitler was declared exempt from all personal taxes; a tax bill of RM
405,494 which he had accumulated at the time was never paid. See Oron J. Hale,
"Adolf Hitler as Taxpayer," *American Historical Review*, LX (July 1955), 830.

132. Rosenberg, *Tagebuch*, entry for 26 Dec. 1934, p. 61.

133. On 1 December 1934 the NSDAP became a corporation in public law, i.e.,
it was legally raised above the status of a private political organization to become
a quasi-public body.

134. Joseph Goebbels, "Reichsminister Dr. Goebbels auf der Gauleiter-Tagung
am 3. August 1944 in Posen," p. 22, IfZ/276/52/ED 8.

group.[135] Similarly, the public at large lost interest in party activities,[136] and the NSDAP grew almost defensive about its role in the Third Reich. It anxiously avoided unpopular measures like wage reductions, and worried about food supply problems.[137]

Two years in office had not diminished the party's appetite for more and more power, but neither had it increased its realistic appraisal of how effectively to exercise such absolute power in German society. To be sure, there were some party agencies who did indeed propose to allow the party to establish entirely new norms of behavior. A series of National Socialist principles (*NS-Leitsätze*) issued by the party's legal office in 1935 declared that as the "innermost life nucleus" (*innerster Lebenskern*) of the nation the party had the right to judge the seriousness of all political crimes, while PLs who committed deeds defined as crimes by the established legal codes should be free from prosecution if they acted in the line of duty.[138] On the other hand, party officials who also held state positions saw the relationship between party and state in less simplistic, although no more clear terms. A major constitutional reform plan drafted by H. J. Hofmann, the state secretary of the Bavarian Reich plenipotentiary, Franz von Epp, was typical of the confusion rampant among many PLs. The plan called for placing "the primacy of political decision-making" in the hands of the party, while state offices would be reduced to the role of "technical executors." Yet Hofmann insisted that the lower party jurisdictions (districts and locals) should not interfere with the work of state offices. Similarly, the party should be in charge of in-service schooling for civil servants, but should not control their appointment.[139]

Confusion over the future of the party was also reflected in the membership situation. At the beginning of 1935 the NSDAP had per-

135. See, for example, Oberpräsident West (i.e., Rhine-Ruhr area) to Grauert, 21 Feb. 1935, HAB/77/2. See also the report of the Gestapo office in Aachen, 7 Jan. 1935, quoted in Vollmer, *Volksopposition*, p. 150.

136. See the Gestapo reports, 5 Dec. 1934 and 6 Feb. 1935, in Vollmer, *Volksopposition*, pp. 132 and 162.

137. StdF, "Anordnung 102/35," 22 May 1935, T-580, roll 12, folder 170; and Grohé's "Stimmungsberichte" for these months, T-580, roll 546, folder 616.

138. Reich legal office, *NS-Leitsätze*, pp. 2/48–52 and 90–92 (*sic*).

139. H. J. Hofmann, "Begründung [zum Entwurf der Änderung des Gesetzes vom 1.12.1934]" (ca. 1935), T-81, roll 185, frames 335560–75.

haps 2.5 million members (card numbers reached up to four million),[140] and while some Gaus showed noticeable increases in 1935,[141] membership for the Reich as a whole stagnated; that is, relatively few members of the affiliates joined the party. The national correlation of party members to population was 1:24.4 (3.78 percent of the population), and in North Westphalia the ratio was 1:38.[142] Moreover, the membership patterns at the beginning of 1935 showed a number of statistical imbalances. The proportion of civil servants and teachers among the members remained considerably higher than in the German population as a whole. Most of the increase had come after January 30, 1933—for nonideological reasons, as the ROL's statistical office readily admitted.[143] Opportunism was also a factor in the age distribution. Both before and after the seizure of power, the largest number of party members (40.4 percent and 31 percent respectively) had come from the twenty-one to thirty age group,[144] that is, those who saw the party as a means of rapid advancement but who had relatively few specialized skills with which to aid the advance of the party.

The result was, from the party's point of view, a vicious circle. As the NSDAP's future in the Third Reich continued to be unclear, fewer Germans joined its ranks,[145] and those who were already members showed little interest in participating actively in party life, becoming instead mere dues-payers.[146] This development, of course, had far-reaching consequences for the growth of the party's PL corps, the actual basis for realizing any of the NSDAP's ambitions. Even Ley's statistical office, no enemy of pencil-pushing politics, saw a danger of

140. Hans Buchheim, "Mitgliedschaft bei der NSDAP," in *Gutachten des Instituts für Zeitgeschichte*, ed. Paul Kluke (Munich, 1958), p. 316.
141. Membership in the Gau Franken, for example, increased from 37,887 in January 1935 to 43,284 at the end of the year. See "Entwicklung des Mitglieder-
142. ROL, *Statistik 1935*, I, 34.
143. *Ibid.*, pp. 65 and 75. As a solution the ROL's officials played around with *numeri clausi*: 40,000 agricultural workers and 15,000 miners should be co-opted into the party to balance the white-collar elements.
144. *Ibid.*, p. 166.
145. Report of the Gestapo office in Aachen, 7 Jan. 1935, quoted in Vollmer, *Volksopposition*, p. 146.
146. ROL, *Statistik 1935*, I, 212. See also David Schoenbaum, *Hitler's Social Revolution* (New York, 1966), p. 225.

bureaucratization (Verbonzung) when 17.6 percent of the party's PLs were civil servants and 80 percent of these had joined the NSDAP after January 1933, that is, were at least theoretically tainted with opportunism.[147] But was there an alternative? The "old fighters," whose lack of suitable skills and behavior had to be constantly excused by the fact that they were "old fighters,"[148] were hardly suitable technicians of power in a modern society. And now, after two years of power, even the opportunists bypassed careers as PLs in the NSDAP. It was little wonder that several highly placed leaders in the party had neglected to pay their dues for periods of up to a year.[149] Indeed, for a moment Hitler was apparently desperate enough to consider basing his world-power ambitions on an institutional basis other than the NSDAP.[150]

It goes almost without saying that Hitler could not seriously consider jettisoning the party—it was, after all, the institutional foundation of his own dictatorship—and thus he had to continue to square the circle.[151] As always, Hitler's solution to essentially insoluble problems was to put the issues solely in personal terms. His own person formed a living synthesis of seemingly irreconcilable, antithetical issues. At a hastily called conference[152] of the Gauleiters and Reichsleiters on January 3, 1935, Hitler revealed his rearmament plans,[153] and presumably some of his foreign policy ambitions, and having impressed his audience with the scope of his vision, he staged another December 1932 crisis. He wept openly, imploring the party's leadership to recognize that his plans for the rebirth of Germany's power could be realized only if they "formed a single community, loyal (*ergeben*) to him." Without such utter devotion his striving would be fruitless. He underscored the point by threatening to commit suicide. The conference was once again

147. ROL, *Statistik 1935*, I, 155.
standes des Gaues Franken der NSDAP von 1935 bis 1940," BA/Gau Franken/20.
148. See Rschm., "Rundschreiben 5/35," 12 Jan. 1935, *Rdschr.*, I; and Buch, "Rechtsfindung innerhalb der Parteigerichte," *Parteirichter*, I (10 March 1935), 43.
149. Rschm., "Rundschreiben 75/35," 27 June 1935, *Rdschr.*, II.
150. Friedrich Hossbach, *Zwischen Wehrmacht und Hitler*, 2d ed. (Göttingen, 1965), p. 41.
151. On this issue see Karl-Dietrich Bracher *et al.*, *Die nationalsozialistische Machtergreifung* (Cologne, 1960), p. 586.
152. See the StdF's invitation to Epp, 1 Jan. 1935, BGStA, Rsth. 48/1–7.
153. This can, at least, be deduced from the fact that Gen. Milch spoke about the buildup of the air force. See Rosenberg, *Tagebuch*, entry for 24 Feb. 1935, p. 70.

suitably stunned, and under Hess's chairmanship hastened to assure the Führer of its unquestioned loyalty to his plans and person.[154]

Apparently the major purpose of Hitler's emotional outburst was to gain time, although the divisions among the various power segments subordinate to his direct control were real enough; he merely neglected to say that he had deliberately created them. Indirectly, however, his plea for unity aided the efforts of the StdF to centralize the PO under his own leadership. Hess's office was well prepared to take advantage of the opportunity presented by Hitler's speech. Hitler's personal relationship with both Hess and his chief of staff continued, from all appearances, to be excellent. Hitler paid Hess the singular honor of visiting him at Hohenlychen Sanatorium when Hess was ill in mid-1935,[155] and Bormann had by now taken control of the administration of most of Hitler's personal affairs, including management of the Obersalzberg building activities.[156] It has been argued that Bormann had in fact eclipsed his nominal superior in actual importance by the middle of 1935,[157] but a more accurate description of their relationship would appear to be "symbiotic interdependence." Hess permitted his chief of staff (as well as the other leading staffers) a great deal of autonomy and decision-making power in their negotiations with other party and state offices,[158] while they, in turn, made no effort to develop a public image of their own. Even Bormann, who accompanied Hess on most of his public appearances, stayed consistently in the background.[159]

The organizational growth of the StdF's office at this time seemed to exhibit the characteristics of an amorphous, polyp-like development, but behind the seemingly unplanned growth lay a single-minded pur-

154. See the report on the conference in Domarus, *Hitler*, I, 468.

155. *Ibid.*, p. 518.

156. Joseph Wulf, *Martin Bormann* (Gütersloh, 1962), pp. 34–35 and 39; and Fritz Wiedemann, *Der Mann der Feldherr werden wollte* (Velbert, 1964), p. 72.

157. Mommsen, *Beamtentum*, p. 35; and Friedrich Zipfel, *Kirchenkampf in Deutschland 1933–45* (Berlin, 1965), p. 16.

158. StdF, "Rundschreiben 60/30," 22 March 1935, T-580, roll 12, folder 170.

159. For documentation see the private snapshots taken by the district leader of Eisenach during a visit made by Hess and Bormann to Thuringia, in the University of Michigan German Archival Collection (cited hereafter as MiU/GAC), folder 73; and [Gau Thüringen, Propagandaamt, ed.], *Fahrt der 300 dienstältesten Politischen Leiter der NSDAP . . . durch den Gau Thüringen vom 9. bis 12. Oktober 1935* (Munich, 1936).

pose. Each new tentacle of the staff organization was in fact a cancerous cell invading the jurisdiction of an already established party office.[160] And the spreading cancer grew rapidly; a comparison of the organizational charts at the beginning of 1935 and at the end of the year shows the picture in figures 1 and 2. This was not, to be sure, a fully

FIGURE 1

The StdF's Office in Early 1935

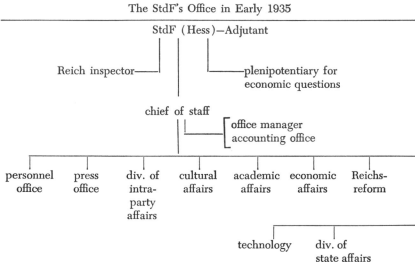

SOURCE: Gau Hamburg, *Gaunachrichten* (Alstadt ed.), I (Feb. 1935), 4.

centralized and integrated structure. Several of the staffers obviously had career ambitions far beyond holding a subordinate position in the office of the StdF. Joachim von Ribbentrop, for example, although listed as head of the foreign policy office, was in fact busy building his own Bureau Ribbentrop as a rival of the German foreign office. Other staff members, like the folkish art historian Schulte-Strathaus (scientific affairs) were political has-beens, serving out honorable sinecures. In addition, the division of labor within the staff was not nearly as complete as the organizational chart might indicate.[161] Indeed, not until the end of the year did the business manager get around to issuing de-

160. See Ley's complaints on this score in his letter to Hess, 20 June 1939, T-580, roll 549, folder 746.
161. Interrogation of Klopfer, 14 Nov. 1947, p. 8, IfZ/ZS 352.

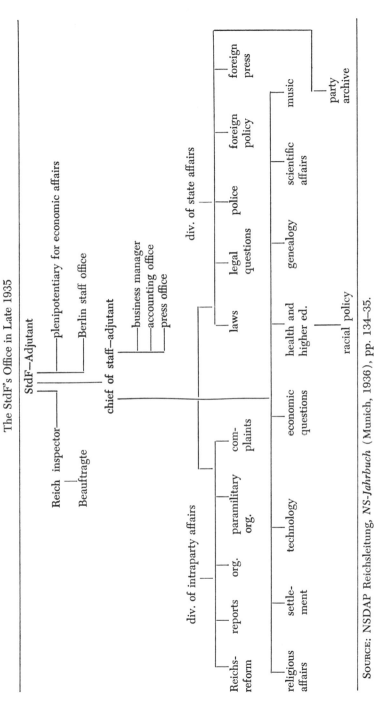

FIGURE 2

The StdF's Office in Late 1935

StdF—Adjutant

Reich inspector——plenipotentiary for economic affairs
Beauftragte ——Berlin staff office

chief of staff—adjutant
——business manager
——accounting office
——press office

div. of intraparty affairs

Reichs-reform ——reports ——org. ——paramilitary org. ——com-plaints

religious affairs ——settle-ment ——technology ——economic questions ——health and higher ed. ——laws ——legal questions ——police questions ——foreign policy ——foreign press

racial policy ——genealogy ——scientific affairs ——music

div. of state affairs

party archive

Source: NSDAP Reichsleitung, *NS-Jahrbuch* (Munich, 1936), pp. 134–35.

tailed guidelines on the preparation of reports, the correct use of steno-
graphic personnel, and so on.[162] The central importance of the rapid
growth of the staff organization lay in the fact that each office represented a jurisdictional foothold on the part of the StdF in a policy field
also covered by either a Reichsleiter's office or a ministerial agency.

The two divisions for intraparty and state affairs represented the
actual core of the StdF's staff organization. Coordinated by Bormann,[163]
their activities covered the most important power segments in Nazi
Germany. Their personnel were also largely indigenous to the StdF,
that is, they had no career alternatives but the office of the StdF. The
division of state affairs was formally created in April 1935, although its
duties had actually been performed for some months prior to that date.
Its essential function was to formulate the StdF's position on all state
legislation and personnel appointments. The division issued its opinions
on the basis of the reviews and reports which the Reichsleiters and
Gauleiters submitted to the StdF's office.[164] This provision, in fact, represented less consultation than exclusion. It meant that neither the
Gauleiters nor the Reichsleiters could communicate directly with Reich
ministers, or with Hitler himself, for that matter.[165] The StdF had always claimed such dual exclusive jurisdiction—the right to act as spokesman for the party in negotiations with state offices and to address the
party as Hitler's deputy[166]—but the claim did not become accepted
practice until 1935.[167] The reason was partially Hitler's pathetic emphasis on unity, but also the realization, particularly among the Reichsleiters, that the sharp division among party leaders did indeed hinder

162. Copies of his various "Rundschreiben" are in T-580, roll 12, folder 170.
163. Kurt Borsdorff, "Mit Reichsleiter Martin Bormann auf dem Obersalzberg,"
(ca. spring 1939), p. 5, T-580, roll 79, folder 368; and Hans Buchheim, "Der 'Stellvertreter des Führers,'" in Kluke, *Gutachten,* p. 325.
164. Klopfer, pp. 3, 4, and 8–9, IfZ/ZS 352. Klopfer became head of the division in May 1941; in 1935 he was chief of the office of police affairs within the
division.
165. In June 1935, for example, Hitler noted that before the Bill on Local Government (*Deutsche Gemeindeordnung;* DGO) was discussed by the cabinet, he
wanted to consult personally with Hess. See Lammers to Frick, 25 June 1935,
quoted in Mommsen, *Beamtentum,* p. 212. On the DGO, see below pp. 145–46.
166. See Bormann to all RLs and GLs, 15 May 1941, HAB/320/22; and Mommsen, *Beamtentum,* p. 78.
167. For documentation see BA/R 43 II/1198.

the party's drive for superiority over the reinvigorated state agencies. There was, for example, the issue of church-party relations. The radicals wanted agitprop campaigns against the churches,[168] the moderates saw in the appointment of Hans Kerrl (the former head of the Nazi party delegation in the Prussian Landtag) as Reich minister of church affairs a step toward the utilization of the churches for party purposes.[169] Hess adjudicated the dispute by decreeing absolute "neutrality" of the party in ecclesiastical matters and by centralizing church-party relations in the office of religious affairs within his own staff organization.[170]

The StdF's ambitions met with more effective resistance among his fellow Hoheitsträgers, especially the Gauleiters. As a group the provincial chiefs thought very little of centralization. They obviously preferred a situation in which they could, for example, try to build informal Nazi party cells in the army or to interfere directly in the judicial processes.[171] Above all, the Gauleiters had an overriding interest in the territorial reorganization of the Reich; in 1935 the Reichsreform was the most "in" subject of discussion and planning. Virtually every Gauleiter (and even district leader) either drafted plans for his new position as head of an autonomous Reichsgau[172] or blithely instituted organizational reforms that anticipated boundary and jurisdictional changes.[173] Some Gauleiters had drafted regular multiyear development plans for

168. Rosenberg, *Tagebuch*, entry for 24 Feb. 1935, p. 71; Hannes Schneider, "Vortrag auf [dem] Sonderkursus [des] NSDStB Juli 1935 in der Reichsschule Bernau," n.d., T-81, roll 75, frames 86534–35; and Kurt Meier, *Die Deutschen Christen* (Halle/Saale, 1965), p. 74. The appointment of GL Terboven as provincial governor of the Prussian *Rheinprovinz* was widely interpreted as an attack upon the Catholic Church. See the report of the Gestapo office in Aachen, 5 April 1935, quoted in Vollmer, *Volksopposition*, p. 182.

169. John S. Conway, *The Nazi Persecution of the Churches, 1933–45* (New York, 1968), p. 131.

170. The office operated under the rather misleading title of "Department for Cultural Peace" (*Abteilung für kulturellen Frieden*).

171. Manfred Messerschmidt, *Die Wehrmacht im NS-Staat* (Hamburg, 1969), p. 101; and StdF, "Rundschreiben 91/35," 22 May 1935, T-580, roll 12, folder 170.

172. District leader Niedersonthofen to Reich chancellery, 30 April 1936, BA/R 43 II/494.

173. See state commissioner of Berlin to Grauert, HAB/77/10; GL Telschow to Hess, 12 March 1935, HAB/77/9; and district diet of Swabia, *Neugliederung des Reiches; hier der Gau Schwaben* ([Augsburg, 1935]). The last publication was intended "only for the relevant offices."

their anticipated Reichsgaus, only to find their colleagues openly ridiculing such foresight.[174]

From Hess's viewpoint, only the activation of the Referat Reichsreform in his staff organization could prevent the de facto declarations of independence by the thirty Gauleiters, particularly since the Reich ministry of the interior was also still working on reform plans.[175] It will be recalled that Adolf Wagner, the Gauleiter of Munich, had been appointed to head the Referat in May 1934, but the purge activities had prevented the office from doing positive work until 1935. Wagner and his superior agreed that neither other party agencies nor state offices should have a major role in the Reichsreform.[176] "The ministerial bureaucracy," wrote Wagner, "can give advice when they are asked for it."[177] The party side of the controversy was rather easily disposed of when the StdF obtained a new directive from Hitler prohibiting all discussion of the Reichsreform within the party.[178] In the meantime, Wagner moved quickly; on February 6 he was able to submit a lengthy (twenty-nine pages) secret staff paper entitled "The Reconstruction of the Reich" ("Der Neubau des Reiches"), embodying the outline of the new territorial divisions and constitutional principles in Germany. The boundaries of the planned Reichsgaus derived directly from the ideas of the well-known Munich geopolitician Karl Haushofer. (Hess had close personal ties both to Haushofer and to his son, Albrecht). They involved essentially a series of concentric economic-strategic[179] circles grouped

174. GL Hellmuth to OPG, 14 March 1935, BDC/Hellmuth (OPG).

175. Mommsen, *Beamtentum*, p. 107.

176. Bracher, *Machtergreifung*, p. 611.

177. Adolf Wagner, "Der Neubau des Reiches," 6 Feb. 1935, pp. 5–6, T-580, roll 77, folder 363.

178. StdF, "Anordnung 46/35," 14 March 1935, T-580, roll 12, folder 170. The Gauleiters (many of whom were Reichsstatthalter as well) also complained that full-scale conferences of the Reich governors had been systematically prevented. See Fritz Sauckel, "Denkschrift über die Verlagerung der Zuständigkeiten . . . von den bisherigen Ländern . . . nach den Berliner Ministerialverwaltungen sowie deren politische und verwaltungsmässige Auswirkung," p. 13, 27 Jan. 1936, BA/R 43 II/494.

179. Wagner noted that the Reich planning office of the NSDAP (presumably his own *Referat*) was already at work developing a "science of economics and strategy." Wagner, "Neubau," p. 15.

around the "heartland of central Germany." The study also suggested both names for the new Gaus and the specific areas to be included. They were constructed so as to cut across the traditional federal boundaries and to avoid the existing religious groupings.[180] Constitutionally, the Wagner-Hess plan would have formalized the preponderance of the party. The StdF's reform plan called for the concentration of all legislative and executive decision-making powers in the hands of the party; the state organs would have been reduced to the status of administrative handmaidens. As could be expected, the plan envisioned an inordinate strengthening of the role of the Hoheitsträgers. (After all, both Wagner and his superior fell into this category.) The heads of the new Reichgaus (Wagner called them *Gaugrafen*—Gau earls, or counts—citing an expression of Hitler's) would have been undisputed viceroys of their territory, though presumably subject to the directives of the Reichshoheitsträger. Wagner saw no need for the present heads of provincial governments to report to the Reich minister of the interior.[181]

The "great" Reichsreform never reached beyond the paper-planning stage; there were too many conflicting views,[182] and Hitler lost interest.[183] The StdF was able, however, to achieve a major voice for the party in communal affairs when the *Deutsche Gemeindeordnung* (Law on Local Government, DGO) went into effect in April 1935. The need for a basic reform act was urgent, because many of the German municipalities were virtually bankrupt owing to the tax squeeze brought on by the depression. The StdF, however, also recognized the political importance of the DGO, and his staff engaged actively in the bill-drafting process from the very beginning.[184] Hess's aim was to provide a decisive influence on the decision-making process at the local level for the lower Hoheitsträgers. The state officials objected, with the argument that few

180. *Ibid.*, pp. 2, 10, 11, 14, and 17–18.
181. *Ibid.*, pp. 2 and 16. Needless to say, Frick's plans called for a strengthening of precisely these institutions. See Mommsen, *Beamtentum*, p. 109.
182. Cf. Sauckel's "Denkschrift" with Wagner's "Neubau."
183. Walter Baum, "Die 'Reichsreform' im Dritten Reich," *Vjh.f.Z.*, III (Jan. 1955), 36–56.
184. Much of this work was done in close cooperation with the party's office for communal affairs, headed by the Nazi lord mayor of Munich, Karl Fiehler. The relevant documents are in T-580, rolls 884–88.

of the PLs at this level had any expertise in communal affairs, but Hess naively countered that their quality would improve.[185] In the end, the StdF won on most essential points, although the state's officials did not yield gracefully.[186] The DGO provided that communal officials, particularly the mayors, were now subject to a dual system of supervision: on the one hand, the Reich ministry of the interior, on the other, the local party leader or, in the case of county seats, the district leader.[187] The DGO demonstrated above all the close, if informal, cooperation between the StdF and the Reich treasurer. With a veto right over communal expenditures, the party could (and did) receive substantial subsidies in the form of tax moneys without encountering the danger of being accountable to state auditors for the use of these funds.[188] At the same time, the DGO embodied Hess's concept of an elitist, controlling role for the NSDAP. The local leader did not "betreuen"; he exercised political judgments and, significantly, he did not have to justify his decisions except to his superiors in the party.

Similar considerations guided the policy of the StdF's office with regard to the party's role in the appointment and promotion process of high-level civil servants. Here its legal base for influence was far more circumscribed. The law of December 1, 1934, specifically prohibited direct interference by party offices, and as Reich minister of the interior Frick was determined to preserve the status quo.[189] As a result, Hess had to utilize his powers as political consultant. In March 1935, Walter Som-

185. Hess to Grauert, 8 Nov. 1934, HAB/77/10. The StdF was also unwilling to wait for qualitative improvements; Hess originally insisted that the law go into effect on 1 January 1935.

186. Ludwig Grauert, the state secretary in the Reich ministry of the interior concerned with the DGO negotiations, suggested early in 1935 that the party ought to play a minor role as a control mechanism in communal affairs. The StdF brought charges against him before the OPG, and in June 1936 Grauert "retired" as state secretary. The documents on Grauert's OPG trial are in BDC/Grauert (OPG); his retirement was announced by the press office of the ministry. A copy of the notice is in HAB/97/3.

187. Bracher, *Machtergreifung*, p. 620. For a contemporary analysis see, Neesse, *Partei und Staat*, pp. 70–71.

188. Edward N. Peterson, *The Limits of Hitler's Power* (Princeton, 1969), pp. 308–09 and 361.

189. Mommsen, *Beamtentum*, pp. 33–35.

mer, head of the StdF's division of state affairs sent Heinrich Lammers, state secretary of the Reich chancellery, a list of officials whom the StdF wanted to "evaluate politically" prior to their appointment or promotion. The ranks involved included practically all civil servants above the level of clerk-typist (in the Reich ministries, Section chief and above), as well as major police officials and county executives.[190] Moreover, the StdF left no doubt that consultation was intended as a euphemism for control. As Bormann put it, "It is the function of the party to create the will of the state."[191] The role of the Gauleiters in the "consulting" process was not entirely clear. The StdF intended that they submit political evaluations to his office, but leave the final judgments to his staff, particularly since the StdF's Beauftragte submitted parallel reports on the various nominees.[192] The Gauleiters wanted at least to have the final word on officials in their area of jurisdiction, but Hitler sided with Hess.[193] In actual practice, the StdF's role in the appointment process was largely negative. True, Bormann kept a card file on the various civil servants,[194] but the number of qualified PLs was too small to permit the large-scale "Nazification" of the German civil service. For most state officials, then, the StdF's power remained a permanent sword of Damocles; a negative political judgment could ruin a promising professional career.[195]

A year after the Röhm "affair," Hess issued a proud review of his service to the party: "In the last eleven months . . . I have been able to restore the influence of the party, which had been almost eliminated before, on the details of the legislative process." The reason for his success, in the eyes of the StdF, was the ability of his staff members to represent the party in their numerous dealings with other

190. Sommers to Lammers, 4 March 1935, BA/R 43 II/421. In practice, the StdF had a particular interest in politically sensitive posts. Nominees to the People's Court, for example, which handled political offenses against the regime, received particularly close and rapid scrutiny. See the documents in BA/R 43 II/1517c.
191. Bormann to Frick, 26 April 1935, quoted in Mommsen, *Beamtentum*, p. 35.
192. Hess to Frick, 14 March 1935, BA/R 43 II/1199.
193. Bormann to Lammers, 12 July 1935, BA/R 43 II/421. The final decree was published in the *Reichsgesetzblatt*, I (1935), 1203.
194. Walter Schellenberg, *Memoiren* (Cologne, 1956), p. 285.
195. See Grauert to Schwede-Coburg, 12 March 1935, HAB/77/5.

power segments.[196] Other party leaders were less convinced of Hess's beneficence for the party,[197] but Hitler's silence rendered their protests futile, particularly since the Hess-Schwarz alliance continued to form a solid barrier against decentralizing tendencies. At the end of March, an "administrative interpretation" was issued over the signature of Hitler, Hess, and Frick, on the relationship between the affiliates and the "core party" (*Kernpartei*). It acknowledged that the affiliates could be legal entities in their own right, but insisted that they were subject to Schwarz's financial and Hitler's (that is, Hess's) political supervision.[198]

The StdF was not slow in using his new authority. With Schwarz willingly acknowledging Hess's political superiority (and being assured in turn of his administrative and financial autonomy),[199] the deputy Führer turned the tables on Ley. Taking Ley at his word, he in effect acknowledged the close relationship between PO and DAF and, as a consequence, demanded to be fully involved in DAF affairs. Within the staff organization, Hess assigned the DAF to his division of intraparty affairs.[200] The most celebrated affiliate case in 1935, however, was the status and future of the National Socialist Student Association (NSDStB). The NSDStB had had a rather checkered career since the Machtergreifung. It became a haven for radicals (from the Nazi point of view) of all sorts: in Berlin it harbored progressive artists and intellectuals, while other groups stood in the forefront of the attack on

196. StdF, "Verfügung 141/35," 10 July 1935, T-580, roll 12, folder 170.

197. See [office of RL Rosenberg], "Denkschrift" (ca. 1941), T-81, roll 23, frames 20545–47. Rosenberg, naive as usual, suggested a sort of collegial *Reichsleitung* with himself as *primus inter pares* in his capacity as "Reichsleiter for the Security of the NS-*Weltanschauung*." *Ibid.*, frames 20551–73.

198. *VOBl*, V (15 April 1935), 259–60. For a contemporary interpretation see Neesse, *Partei und Staat*, pp. 41–42. Hess was the final court of appeal for all cases in which the OPG had original jurisdiction, i.e., cases involving Reichsleiters and Gauleiters. See OPG, "Anordnung 12/35," 1 Feb. 1935, *Parteirichter*, I (10 March 1935), 48.

199. Anton Lingg, *Die Verwaltung der Nationalsozialistischen Deutschen Arbeiterpartei*, 2d ed. (Munich, 1940), pp. 26 and 52.

200. Hess to Ley, 16 Jan. 1935, T-580, roll 549, folder 746; StdF, "Anordnung 88/35," 7 May 1935, T-580, roll 12, folder 170. One practical result was that when the NS-Hago became involved in a controversy with the NSBO in Schleswig-Holstein, the StdF assigned his Beauftragter Oexle to deal with the difficulty. See the documents in BA/NS 22/612.

the churches.[201] The situation grew even more complicated when the NSDStB, supported by a number of Gauleiters (for example, Streicher, Adolf Wagner, and Kube), attacked the dueling fraternities and their alumni president, the old-time Nazi Heinrich Lammers.[202] In the end, Hitler had to intervene, but, as was to be expected, he simply confirmed Hess's personal friend Gerhard Wagner as head of the student organization.[203]

Aside from Hess, the Reich treasurer was most successful in dealing with the problems of his jurisdiction in 1935. The new dues schedule[204] brought in substantially larger sums, and while the debts of some party organizations still plagued Schwarz's office,[205] the overall financial picture continued to improve.[206] Schwarz could therefore concentrate on a series of administrative reforms. Almost alone among the RL offices, the Reich treasurer worked to improve the technical competence of the PLs under his supervision. Working sessions of the Gau treasurers, for example, seem to have involved instruction and discussion of actual problems encountered in the day-to-day operations of these offices, rather than meaningless addresses on grand political lines.[207] Schwarz's

201. See Hildegard Brenner, *Die Kunstpolitik des Nationalsozialismus* (Reinbek b. Hamburg, 1963), p. 66; and Hannes Schneider, "Vortrag auf [dem] Sonderkursus für [den] NSDStB," July 1935, T-81, roll 75, frame 86527.

202. Streicher wired Lammers on 15 July, "You are a saboteur of NS-principles." BDC/Lammers (PKC). Other relevant documents on the controversy are in BA/R 128/39.

203. See the speeches made by Ley and Derichsweiler before the *Sonderkursus* 16 and 17 July 1935, T-81, roll 75, frames 86582–87 and 86590–91, respectively.

204. Monthly party dues now ranged from RM 1.00 to RM 5.00. Employed party members had to pay at least RM 2.00, and even unemployed persons paid RM 1.00. See *VOBl*, IV (15 Dec. 1935), 219.

205. See, for example [office of the Reich treasurer], "Rechenschaftsbericht des Reichskassenverwalters Pg. Berger . . . über . . . HJ in den Jahren 1935–39," 27 April 1939, T-580, roll 806, box 239, folder 42.

206. Schwarz claimed that the party operated in the red until 1940 (Rschm., "Tätigkeitsbericht 1935," pp. 7–8; and "Jahresbericht 1940" [25 Oct. 1940], pp. 3–5, T-580, roll 833, box 256, folder 267), but this did not include the steadily rising state subsidies (RM 5.96 million in 1935; RM 88.56 million in 1940), which made up an increasingly large percentage of the party's annual budget (17.8% in 1935; 32.3% in 1940). See Rschm., "Jahresbericht 1940," p. 21.

207. See Rschm., "Rundschreiben 35/35 [and] 89/39," 23 Feb. and 22 July 1935, *Rdschr.*, II.

basic purpose was to build a basis of both competence and esprit de corps throughout the vertical lines of his organization so as to counter the clique tendencies of the Hoheitsträger staffs and to expand Schwarz's control over the party's finances. Throughout the year, the Reich treasurer was particularly concerned with the buildup of his auditing staff. The number of auditors increased from forty-eight (January 1, 1935) to seventy-six at the end of the year. In addition, Schwarz created sixteen "Reich auditing districts" and established the post of "plenipotentiary of the Reich treasurer for auditing purposes" within his own office.[208] The auditors had detailed instructions to get tough with uncooperative offices if necessary,[209] and although their primary field of activity was the PO itself, they could also pounce on the affiliates' books without waiting for Schwarz's specific permission.[210] In addition, the Reich treasurer moved to put teeth into his prohibition of the practice of issuing membership cards without reporting the new members to Munich. He reaffirmed his earlier decree that only membership books issued by his office had official validity,[211] and, in order to pressure the Gauleiters into final conformity, obtained an agreement from the OPG that after April 1 it would no longer deal with cases of doubtful membership.[212]

The development of the paramilitary organizations in 1935 was largely a story of SS successes and SA reverses. Himmler's guards continued to benefit from the bandwagon effect of their actions in June 1934. Former SA officials flooded to their ranks; civil servants sought their blessing.[213] Buch regarded Himmler as the true ideological spokes-

208. Rschm., "Jahresbericht 1935," pp. 4 and 7 .

209. The duty of tactfulness incumbent upon an auditor should "not preclude energetic behavior which might be necessary in certain cases." Schwarz to all auditors, 9 Feb. 1935, *Rdschr.*, II.

210. Rschm., "Rundschreiben 25/35 [and] 109/35," 16 Feb. and 27 Aug. 1935, *ibid.*

211. Rschm., "Rundschreiben 20/35," 12 Feb. 1935, *ibid.* Printed forms for tabulating new members at the Gau offices appeared in a number of issues of the *Rdschr.* II and III.

212. *VOBl*, V (15 Jan. 1935), 227.

213. See Hergenröder (LGF of Franconia and an SA member since 1928) to Himmler, 21 Oct. 1935, BDC/Hergenröder (SS); and SS-Abschnitt XIII to SS-Oberabschnitt Nord, 28 May 1935, BDC/Bismarck-Schönhausen (SS). The particular civil servant involved, the *Regierungspräsident* of Stettin, Count Bismarck, was later executed for his involvement in the July 1944 plot.

man of the Nazi movement,[214] and the agricultural organizations became in effect SS affiliates.[215] The SD (with Hess's approval) further centralized its spy network in the PO, although here the outlines of the bitter animosity between the PO and the SS that lay ahead were becoming apparent. The Gauleiters had regained their self-confidence, and sought to curtail the SD's invasion of their jurisdictions.[216] In contrast, the SA continued its political decline. Schwarz's severe budget cuts forced a number of SA leaders to try their luck in private business,[217] and this trend was furthered by Hitler's insistence that police posts should not be regarded as a private reserve of the SA.[218] Attempts by the SA to rise above its present level of political impotence met with little success. Lutze tried to launch his own investigation of the events of June 30, but the SS was on guard.[219] How little the SA's judgments counted can be surmised from Hitler's directive that members of the veterans' organization, *Stahlhelm* (which had been incorporated into the SA in 1933 and was now dissolved), needed to obtain the approval of their Hoheitsträger and Schwarz's office in order to become party members. The evaluation of their SA leaders was of no consequence.[220]

Toward the end of the year the always smoldering conflict between the StdF and Ley flared up again. Despite the various setbacks to his plans of merging the DAF and the PO, Ley remained a formidable foe. He was still one of Hitler's personal favorites,[221] and the bulk of the PLs continued to regard him as their direct superior.[222] On the

214. Buch to Himmler, 9 Aug. 1935, BDC/Buch (SS).

215. The conclusion is based upon an examination of the SS personnel records in the BDC, particularly those of SS officials with low membership numbers.

216. See, for example, the SD's Hamburg office to Heydrich, 28 Dec. 1935, BDC/Falkenberg (SS); v.d. Bach to Himmler, 8 April 1935 and 2 Feb. 1936, BDC/v.d. Bach (SS).

217. See the reports of the Gestapo office in Aachen and the Regierungspräsident in Aachen, 7 Jan. and 13 June 1935, quoted in Vollmer, *Volksopposition*, pp. 148 and 231; and "Stimmungs-und Lagebericht des Gauleiters Grohé, Gau Köln-Aachen," 8 June 1935, T-580, roll 546, folder 616.

218. Himmler to Daluege, 29 Nov. 1935, BDC/Pflomm (SS).

219. Gestapo office in Hamburg to Heydrich, 29 July 1935, BDC/Lutze (SA), III.

220. Hitler to Seldte, 7 Nov. 1935, quoted in Domarus, *Hitler*, I, 550; and Rschm., "Rundschreiben 147/35," 15 Nov. 1935, *Rdschr.*, II.

221. Wiedemann, *Der Mann*, p. 194.

222. Hess complained that not all party members directed their complaints exclusively to his office. StdF to all RL, 27 April 1935, T-580, roll 12, folder 170.

other hand, Ley's concept of the future of the party was no more work-able in 1935 than it had been before. The PO was a large, cumbersome, inexperienced, and unstable group. To begin with, it was top-heavy: almost half (44.1 percent) of all PLs were Hoheitsträgers.[223] Personnel stability was noticeable only among the Gauleiters and their staff cliques, as table 6 shows. The age grouping among the PLs demon-

TABLE 6

Personnel Stability of PLs

Level of Jurisdiction	Percentage of Party Members before Jan. 30, 1933	Percentage of Party Members after Jan. 30, 1933
Gaus	84.0%	16.0%
Districts	62.3	37.7
Locals	41.9	58.1
Lesser jurisdictions	31.1	68.9

SOURCE: ROL, *Statistik 1935*, II, 86, 90, 98, and 104.

strated that the cadres were still primarily composed of men who had failed in other occupations: the largest contingent (27.0 percent) was made up of the thirty-one to forty age group, followed by the fifty-one to sixty group (17.9 percent) and the group over sixty-one (10.4 per-cent). After three years in power, the vision of a party career had not captured the youth of the nation. The age groups eighteen to twenty and twenty-one to thirty made up only a fraction (6.0 percent and 14.7 percent respectively) of the PL cadres.[224] In other words, younger Ger-mans sought the security of party membership, but few were interested in a PL career. These difficulties were compounded by Ley's organi-zational mania, which led him to create organizational entities without PLs, let alone qualified PLs, to fill them. The theory of Betreuung ran well ahead of the available personnel.[225] The result was that who could

223. ROL, *Statistik 1935*, II, 7.
224. *Ibid.*, p. 213. The most complete analysis of the 1935 statistical data is in Schäfer, *NSDAP*, pp. 27–55.
225. See the report of the Gestapo office in Aachen, 2 Feb. 1935, quoted in Voll-mer, *Volksopposition*, pp. 161–62. For a quite interesting comparison of the situa-

sought a state position,[226] and those who remained, especially at the lower level, had no real long-range conception of their position in the power structure of the Third Reich. They either tried to do everything (for example, settle disputes between tenants and landlords) or did nothing substantive and passed all responsibility on to higher offices.[227] Their remaining time was spent in such vital pursuits as investigating which PL might have purchased a cake at a Jewish bakery.[228]

Almost inevitably, the ill-defined but potentially vast powers of the PLs encouraged corruption. In 1935 alone, the office of the Reich treasurer uncovered 2,350 cases of embezzlement or other financial misdeeds involving a total of RM 1,114,799.98. Of the PLs involved, twenty-nine committed suicide, and the remainder were sentenced to 573 years in jail. Schwarz noted publicly that these figures were small in view of the total sums and number of PLs involved in the party's administration,[229] but the fact that these statistics were undoubtedly only the tip of the iceberg[230] made it clear that the party's administrative corps hardly approached the ideals of the Prussian civil service. Moreover, many of the PLs who were not actually guilty of embezzling party funds used their party position to gain personal advantages. Count Wolf Heinrich von Helldorf, the police president of Berlin and later member of the resistance, received a loan of RM 80,000 from the Gau Berlin to pay his personal debts.[231] That his was not an isolated case is indicated by Hess's directive to the PL corps as a whole to be honest

---

tion in the East German SED, see Joachim Schultz, *Der Funktionär in der Einheitspartei* (Stuttgart, 1956), pp. 194 and 256.

226. ROL, *Statistik 1935*, I, 285; and Mommsen, *Beamtentum*, p. 108.

227. StdF, "Anordnung 173/35," 26 Aug. 1935, T-580, roll 12, folder 170; and the report of the Gestapo office in Aachen, 6 Feb. 1935, quoted in Vollmer, *Volksopposition*, p. 162.

228. See the cases discussed in the *Parteirichter* for 1935 and Buch, *Vortrag des Reichsleiters Buch über Parteigerichte und oberste Parteigerichtsbarkeit . . . 14.10.1937* ([Berlin, 1937]), T-77, roll 380, frame 1227048.

229. Rschm., "Jahresbericht 1935," pp. 3–4 and appendix 1.

230. The Hoheitsträgers tended to aid in covering up cases of corruption among their staffs (see Hubert Schorn, *Der Richter im Dritten Reich* [Frankfurt, 1959], p. 254). This was an understandable reaction, since they preferred relatives or personal acquaintances as their associates. See StdF, "Anordnung 62/35," 10 April 1935, T-580, roll 12, folder 170.

231. T[heodor] E[schenburg], ed., "Die Rede Himmlers vor den Gauleitern am 3.8.44," *Vjh.f.Z.*, I (Oct. 1953), 380.

and prompt in the payment of their taxes.[232] Finally, the PLs underwent physical changes: they literally grew fat and self-satisfied, a fact that evoked caustic comments from both Hess and Hitler.[233]

Actual remedies, however, were not forthcoming. Hitler himself had little interest in eliminating corruption per se,[234] and without Hitler's backing Schwarz and Hess, who were genuinely concerned about the problem,[235] could do little against the prevailing attitude of "growth-at-any-price" in the NSDAP. Robert Ley was the foremost advocate of this policy. His Betreuungs ideal for the party meant an ever increasing number of staff positions at the lower ranks, and in 1935, 93.6 percent of all PLs held positions at the local and sublocal level.[236] Ley was not yet satisfied. He apparently still had plans to incorporate the Reich food estate into the DAF-KdF complex[237] and then to merge their officials, most of whom were not even party members, with the PLs. The result would have been an administrative monster with about one PL for every one and a half party members.[238] Among the number of PLs were very few technical experts. Ley claimed the party needed "politically thinking . . . men, not experts (*Fachmänner*)."[239] In practice, this dictum meant that Ley wanted fanatical believers, and that his system of training centers and schools studiously avoided presenting the mass of lower-rank PLs with anything that might be of practical use in their jurisdictions. The result was a continuation of an already prevalent paradox. The block leader could bask in the knowledge that he was a "fighting instrument" of the party,[240] but his *Dienstbuch des Block-*

232. *VOBl*, V (15 Jan. 1935), 227. Hitler, of course, could hardly serve as a shining example. See above, p. 135, n. 131.

233. StdF, "Rundschreiben," 26 March 1935, T-580, roll 12, folder 170; and Karl Wahl, *Es ist das deutsche Herz* (Augsburg, 1954), p. 127.

234. Wiedemann, *Der Mann*, pp. 71–72.

235. Yet even the StdF held fast to a sort of esprit-de-corps ideal in the party. In May 1935 he reprimanded the PL corps for turning over their comrades to the regular courts without sufficient evidence. See *VOBl*, V (15 June 1935), 281.

236. ROL, *Statistik 1935*, II, 4.

237. Hannes Schneider, "Vortrag . . . ," July 1935, T-81, roll 75, frame 86531; and Messerschmidt, *Wehrmacht*, pp. 108–10.

238. ROL, *Statistik 1935*, I, 160 and 218; Simon to Hess, 25 July 1935, BDC/Simon (PKC).

239. Schneider, "Vortrag . . . ," frame 86532.

240. ROL, *Statistik 1935*, II, 476.

leiters (*Official Handbook of the Block Leader*), issued by the Gau Berlin in 1935, should have quickly disillusioned him. It contained detailed instructions on the collection of dues and on proper uniforms and a firm admonition to express no opinions on foreign policy questions. There was nothing whatever about his role as political leader in the Nazi society.

This excessive concern with the minutiae of administration also dominated party life at the Gau and district level in the spring and summer of 1935 and made it correspondingly dull, vexing, and listless. On paper, the party's administrative hierarchy was logic itself; the third volume of Ley's statistical analysis is studded with neat organizational charts demonstrating an optimum of jurisdictional clarity.[241] Actually, even a cursory glance at the charts reveals their political innocence: for example, to list the NSBO as the politically superior office of the DAF simply meant that Ley had blithely ignored the political developments of the last two years. Actually, the Gauleiters themselves complained of their impotence in dealing with the DAF.[242] And the provincial leaders had other problems as well. Ley systematically prevented them from creating clearly defined jurisdictional boundaries in their staff organizations, and specifically prohibited the establishment of a Gau staff office to coordinate the rapidly expanding maze of offices at the Gau level.[243]

The excessive administrative growth also led to numerous financial problems. The Gau income tended to vary rather widely with the prevailing political climate. There was no possibility of political opposition in Nazi Germany, but there were means of expressing degrees of political enthusiasm. The Gaus had a steady source of income from a percentage of the regular dues, but the financial gravy came in the form of 25 percent of the income from the sale of buttons, pamphlets, and various other forms of semivoluntary contributions.[244] In 1935, both types of income fluctuated from Gau to Gau and from month to

241. *Ibid.*, III, 126–27.
242. Hellmuth, "Stellungnahme zum Bericht des Pg. Gerum vom 10. Mai 1935 . . . ," 27 June 1935, BDC/Gerum (PKC).
243. Schäfer, *NSDAP*, p. 74; and Hellmuth Friedrichs, "Rede des Hauptamtsleiters Friedrichs auf der Tagung der Stellvertretenden Gauleiter am 11. Januar 1940 . . . ," p. 29, T-580, roll 843, box 268, folder 352.
244. Rschm., "Rundschreiben 36/35 [and] 87/35," 26 Feb. and 20 July 1935, *Rdschr.*, II.

month.[245] In general, the membership dues flowed very sluggishly; in some Gaus there was a decline in the membership figures, and about 10 percent of the members paid no dues at all.[246] Since the Gau costs, particularly the expenses for administration and salaries, climbed relentlessly,[247] the Gaus were forced to pay for current expenses out of their irregular and fluctuating contributions.[248]

Although it is understandable that many Gauleiters were opposed to Ley's plans for constant expansion, the employment of large numbers of ill-trained and often incapable PLs did in fact strengthen the position of the provincial chiefs, particularly in the large Gaus, insofar as it aided their construction of homogeneous cliques.[249] Perhaps the three most powerful Gauleiters in the mid-thirties were Martin Mutschmann, Josef Wagner, and Erich Koch. Each was representative of a particular "Gauleiter style," and for that reason illustrates the difficulties which the Reich leadership faced in dealing with the provincial chiefs. Mutschmann, a former lace manufacturer and one of Hitler's earliest supporters, was the most parochial of the three. He administered his large Gau of Saxony much in the style of an early nineteenth-century factory owner, treating his district leaders as employees. He presented no danger to the Reichsleitung because he had no interest in matters that extended beyond his Gau. On the other hand, he saw no need to acknowledge the superiority of the party's Reich offices. Hitler's decision of November 1934 reserving to himself the right to appoint all district leaders was not published in Saxony, since, according to an official of the StdF's office, for Mutschmann "the Reich leadership does not exist."[250]

245. Cf. Gau treasurer Koblenz-Trier to GL Koblenz-Trier, 3 June 1935, and GL Hildebrandt to Ley, 2 April 1935, T-580, roll 547, folder 626.

246. In Koblenz-Trier the membership declined from 53,000 (1 May 1933) to 51,000 (3 June 1935). See Gau treasurer Koblenz-Trier to GL, 3 June 1935), *ibid.*

247. *Ibid.*; and Haag, "Inspektionsbericht Gauleitung Hamburg," 24 July 1936, T-580, roll 806, box 239, folder 44. In Hamburg the salary expenses rose from RM 97,250.61 in the first half of 1935 to RM 133,392.02 a year later.

248. Gau treasurer Koblenz-Trier to GL Koblenz-Trier, 3 June 1935, T-580, roll 547, folder 626.

249. Peter Hüttenberger, *Die Gauleiter* (Stuttgart, 1969), pp. 56 ff. See also H. P. Ipsen, "Niederschrift der Mitteilungen von . . . Prof. Ipsen . . . 19.8.1950," p. 10, n.d., Forschungsstelle für die Geschichte des Nationalsozialismus in Hamburg (cited hereafter as Forsch. Hbg.)/PA/12/H.

250. This appraisal of the Saxon Gauleiter is based upon a long and "strictly

While the Gauleiter of Saxony acted with Hitler's unspoken toleration, Josef Wagner became dictator of Silesia with the Führer's expressed approval. Wagner's power was based entirely upon Hitler's mandate to purge the party organization of Silesia after the Röhm affair. In his dual capacity as Gauleiter and provincial governor (Oberpräsident) he dismissed PLs outright, appointed district leaders without consulting the Reich leadership, and forced the Reich minister of the interior to appoint county executives "without bureaucratic inhibitions."[251] In view of his plenitude of "authorized" power, it is hardly surprising that Wagner also attempted to make his influence felt in jurisdictional areas that remained outside his sphere, for example, the party courts.[252] Erich Koch, the long-time (since 1928) Gauleiter of East Prussia, one of Germany's more backward areas, was the prototype of a colonial viceroy. He claimed absolute powers in East Prussia as Hitler's derivative agent: "Since I am politically responsible to the Führer for the province of East Prussia, I must insist that the political guidelines be determined by me, insofar as this is not done by the central offices in Berlin."[253] Koch's remark not very subtly expressed his intention to ignore the party's central offices, in Munich, and in this he was remarkably successful. To be sure, his reign was marked by running feuds with various party offices ranging from the SS[254] to the Reich food estate, but neither Hitler nor Hess (who was aware of Hitler's feelings) endangered Koch's position.[255] On the contrary, the Gauleiter was able to secure for his Gau economic aid in the form of subsidies and privileges that aroused nothing but envy in a visiting Bavarian dignitary.[256]

Since Hitler refused to curb the excesses of his "Gau counts" (in-

---

secret" report by Buer (of Hess's staff) to Hess, 18 March 1935, BDC/Mutschmann (PKC).

251. Bormann to Wagner, 25 Feb. 1935, T-580, roll 554, box 377, folder 877; Wagner to Grauert, 2 June 1935, and Grauert to Mrs. v. Dirksen, 1 Aug. 1935, HAB/77/4 and 5, respectively.

252. Buch to Wagner, 28 March 1935, T-580, roll 554, box 377, folder 877.

253. Koch to Himmler, 12 Aug. 1935, BDC/v.d. Bach (PKC).

254. Himmler to Buch, 1 Sept. 1935, BDC/Buch (SS).

255. Bach to Best (deputy head and inspector of the Prussian Gestapo), 1 Aug. 1935, BDC/Bach (SS), II.

256. See the report of the Bavarian representative in Berlin, 26 Aug. 1936, BGStA, MA 105271.

deed, he took a certain pride in their independence and lawlessness[257]),
and Ley encouraged such tendencies among the Gauleiters in order to
win their support against Hess and Schwarz,[258] for the moment there
was little the two "centralizers" could do against the self-willed provincial chiefs. By mid-1935, however, the districts were well on their
way to becoming yet another focal point of semi-independent power,
and here the two Reich offices did move decisively to inhibit further
developments along the same lines. As a result of the DGO, which was
of particular significance in urban areas,[259] and the powers given the
districts to curb the economic excesses of the affiliates, the split personality of the NSDAP merged briefly at the district level. The DGO
assigned the district leader, as "representative of the party," far-
reaching powers over the civil administration of the German counties
and municipalities. District leaders virtually controlled the appointment
of mayors, and Hess pursuaded Frick that the district leaders should be
present at all discussions "of general importance" among civil servants
in their areas.[260] In the field of economics, the district leader, acting
through the district economic advisor, who was his direct subordinate,
had substantial means of influencing the economic life of his territory;
the activities of the economic advisor ranged from reporting economic
trends to the supervision of the laws on price controls.[261] Finally, the
office of the StdF encouraged a certain amount of independence on the
part of the district leaders. It attempted to create a corps of well-paid,
full-time district leaders[262] who would identify their interests with those
of the office of the deputy Führer.[263] The motive was only partly one of
providing the district leaders with a position of financial security and

257. See Hugh R. Trevor-Roper, ed., *Hitler's Secret Conversations 1941–44*,
(New York, 1953), entry for 24 June 1942, pp. 499–502.

258. Diehl-Thiele, *Partei*, p. 213.

259. In rural areas the DGO effected no great changes. See Peterson, *Limits of
Hitler's Power*, p. 419.

260. Gau München-Oberbayern to Reich office for communal affairs, 30 Jan. 1934,
BDC/Fiehler (SS); Groeben to D., 13 June 1935, HAB/77/4; and Frick to head of
provincial administration, 18 June 1935, BGStA, MA 145252.

261. Gau Hamburg, *Gaunachrichten* (Altstadt edition), I (1 Feb. 1935), 12
and 18.

262. GL Hildebrandt to Ley, 2 May 1935, T-580, roll 547, folder 626.

263. See the proceedings of the de-Nazification court at Bielefeld, "Öffentliche
Sitzung gegen [Kreisleiter] Brandt," 17 Nov. 1947, Forsch. Hbg./PA/12/B.

official prestige in order to strengthen the party's position in its dealings with the state;[264] the StdF was also grooming a corps of loyal subordinates who would be potential allies against the often recalcitrant Gauleiters.[265]

In effect, the StdF concentrated his major efforts in the field of personnel policy on the deputy Gauleiters and the district leaders. Both were long-range projects: the incumbents of the two offices were "old fighters" (all of the deputy Gauleiters and 99.7 percent of the district leaders had joined the NSDAP before the Machtergreifung),[266] secure in their posts as a result of good personal relations with the Gauleiters or in entrenched positions in their districts. Still, in 1935 the deputy Führer had laid the foundation for an effort to control personnel policy in the party. Hess and his successor continued their quest doggedly throughout the remaining years of the Third Reich.

For the moment, Hess had a primary interest in a steady flow of detailed information. The Gauleiters' reports had by now reached substantial proportions, and while much of the materials formed the basis of the staff work in the StdF's "division of state affairs,"[267] Hess also emphasized the importance of personnel information by noting that Hitler himself read the reports.[268] More directly concerned with active personnel policy were the activities of Hess's six territorial investigators (Beauftragte) and, in the Gaus themselves, those of the deputy Gauleiters and Gau inspectors. Theoretically, the investigators worked closely with the Gau officials to carry out purges and investigate complaints,[269] and Hess claimed that the Gauleiters appreciated the efforts

264. Schäfer, *NSDAP*, p. 75. The district leaders spent about 40–70% of their time and 50% of their budgets on "communal affairs." Haag to Schwarz, 1 April 1938, T-580, roll 806, box 239, folder 44.

265. Schwarz was less sanguine about developments at the district level. He complained about the incompetence of the district auditors and attempted to prevent the financial subordination of the locals to the districts. See Rschm., "Rundschreiben 84/35 [and] 85/35," 12 and 17 July 1935, *Rdschr.*, II.

266. ROL, *Statistik 1935*, II, 50.

267. StdF, "Rundschreiben 64/35 [and] 139/35," 11 April and 9 July 1935, T-580, roll 12, folder 170.

268. StdF to all GL and deputy GL, 7 May 1935, *ibid.*

269. The purge of Silesia was in fact a common effort of Josef Wagner and the territorial investigator, Tittmann. See Tittmann to Bormann, 31 Jan. 1935, BDC/Tittmann (OPG).

of his trouble-shooters, but the deputy Führer's unwillingness to permit discussion of the investigators at Gauleiter meetings casts considerable doubt on the popularity of the institution.[270]

The information flowing into Munich from the Gauleiters' and investigators' reports in turn served as the raw material upon which the StdF's personnel office based its judgment on the various PLs who might be candidates for one of the offices which Hitler filled personally. In addition, the personnel office was primarily responsible for transferrals within the party. Hitler had given Hess the power to transfer or suspend all PLs with the exception of Gauleiters and Reichsleiters.[271] The personnel office was nominally still under Gustaf von Wulffen, but actually a new functionary had already pushed the weak Wulffen into the background. Christian Opdenhoff[272] confronted the massive task of confirming a staggering number of incumbent PLs and of finding suitable candidates for new appointments. From the information sought it was clear that Hess's office was determined to seek men who were both competent technicians and fanatical Nazis. Aside from such nebulous categories as "character" and "attitude toward superiors and subordinates" the StdF's personnel files also contained concrete information about each PL's schooling, job experience, and "special accomplishments." "Evaluation of his competence" formed a special section of the personnel forms.[273] The mass of replacement personnel in future years was expected to come from the ranks of the Hitler Youth leaders,[274] although this plan proved to be much more impracticable than antici-

270. StdF to all GL, 9 July 1935, T-580, roll 12, folder 170.

271. Hitler, "Verfügung 79/35," 18 April 1935, *ibid.*

272. Christian Opdenhoff was born on 2 October 1902 and joined the NSDAP in 1925 (membership no. 19633). By profession he was a locksmith and sometime farmer. Despite his status as an "old fighter," his career as a party functionary did not really begin until late 1932 when he became district leader of Werningerode (Gau Oldenburg). In September 1933 he was appointed head of the Gau training school in Dessau and Gau personnel leader in Magdeburg-Anhalt. He joined Hess's staff sometime in 1935 and became a member of the Reichstag in 1936. His later career included terms as the StdF's representative in occupied Poland and, after May 1940, deputy Gauleiter of Oberdonau.

273. *VOBl*, V (15 May 1935), 272.

274. StdF, "Anordnung 193/35," 8 Oct. 1935, T-580, roll 12, folder 170. See also Friedrichs, "Rede 1940," pp. 33–34. The last phases of the Hitler-Jugend's *Gleichschaltung* were completed by the end of 1935. See Hans-Christian Brandenburg, *HJ—Die Geschichte der HJ* (Cologne, 1968), p. 178.

pated. For the present incumbents, the office of the StdF devised a small-scale but effective system of in-service training. In April Hess asked the Gauleiters to send specially selected younger PLs to the office of the StdF for four-week training courses. Two months later, the deputy Führer also instructed the Gau inspectors and the Beauftragte to nominate suitable cadre personnel as part of their inspection tours, and in October the StdF singled out deputy Gauleiters and Gau staff leaders for a tour of duty in Munich.[275] Hess insisted that the primary reason for the program was to provide the Gaus with better-trained administrators, though in fact the later appointment patterns in the party demonstrated that the StdF's personnel office was collecting a core of reliable PLs who could be appointed to particularly important or sensitive posts.

In the meantime, Hess continued his attacks on Ley. He complained publicly and privately that the ROL organized for the sake of organizing,[276] and seized every opportunity to inform Hitler of Ley's political[277] and financial difficulties.[278] Hitler reacted by empowering Schwarz to supervise the finances of the affiliates more closely and by prohibiting the ROL from appointing the same official to the posts of PO district leader and DAF district functionary.[279] These directives were symptomatic of a series of defeats suffered by Ley in 1935. Little by little, obviously with Hitler's approval, Hess narrowed Ley's field of competence as head of the PO. Hess and Hitler rejected Ley's candidate (Karl Wahl) for successor to the Bayreuth Gauleiter Hans Schemm, who died

275. StdF, "Rundschreiben 74/35, 105/35 [and] 174/35," 26 April, 5 June, and 26 Aug. 1935, T-580, roll 12, folder 170. Significantly, the monthly budgets of the Beauftragte were increased considerably in early August. See office of the Reich treasurer, dept. VII to Schwarz, 8 Aug. 1935, T-580, roll 802, box 237, folder 15.

276. Hess, "Rundschreiben," 19 Feb. 1935, HAB/320/36; and Hess to Ley, 25 Feb. 1935, T-580, roll 549, folder 746.

277. Despite the earlier disaster, in April 1935 Ley organized elections for factory councils. The vote cast for the Nazi candidates was again so dismal that Ley attempted to keep the results from Hitler. See T[heodor] E[schenburg], ed., "Streiflichter zur Geschichte der Wahlen im Dritten Reich," *Vjh.f.Z.*, III (July 1955), 314–16.

278. Schuhmann, "Bericht für den Stellvertreter des Führers—betr.: Die Finanzlage der DAF," 27 March 1935, BA/NS 20/20 BD 3; and Wiedemann, *Der Mann*, pp. 194–96.

279. Bormann to Ley, 25 Feb. 1935, T-580, roll 549, folder 746; and Hess to Lammers, 22 Feb. 1935, BA/R 43 II/1198.

in an airplane accident in the spring of 1935.[280] Ley was similarly unsuccessful in regaining control of Hess's investigators.[281] Above all,
however, the StdF in July removed the last remaining base for Ley's
claim that he was Strasser's successor. Noting that the term "PO" had
been specifically created for a "transition period," Hess prohibited its
further use as illogical: since the entire NSDAP was a political organization (that is, not a Betreuungs agency), a part of the whole could
not be the "political organization."[282]

Ley's counterattacks were feeble in the extreme. He did reorganize
his vertical office scheme, and attempted to appoint particularly reliable
functionaries as organizational leaders at the Gau and district levels,[283]
but his major effort to reverse the trend of power accumulation in the
hands of the StdF was a complete failure. Ley proposed a new and inclusive *Disziplinarordnung* (rules of conduct) which was to delineate
precisely the jurisdiction of each Reichsleiter, including the StdF. The
administrator of the new order would presumably be Ley. Since jurisdictional definitions were synonymous with restrictions, the Reichsleiters
enthusiasm was limited. Hess laid the project to rest through the simple
device of asking the other Reichsleiters if they had any interest in the
proposed document. They did not.[284]

Toward the end of the summer, a variety of factors seemed to
permit the NSDAP to face the upcoming party congress with greater
confidence. The calm international scene (none of the big powers seriously protested Hitler's unilateral violation of the Treaty of Versailles
when he reintroduced compulsory conscription in Germany), the declining jobless rate, and the phasing-out of the purge led the Gauleiters to
report a much improved relationship between party and people.[285] Ac-

280. Ley to Hess, 6 March 1935, T-580, roll 549, folder 746.

281. Bormann to Schwarz, 13 June 1935, and Schwarz to Bormann, 19 June
1935, T-580, roll 802, box 237, folder 15.

282. *VOBl*, V (15 Aug. 1935), 304. As a descriptive term for the cadre organization of the party the abbreviation PO will continue to be used in this study.

283. *VOBl*, V (15 Jan. 1935), 230.

284. StdF, "Rundschreiben 44/35," 16 March 1935, T-580, roll 12, folder 170.

285. See GL Grohé, "Stimmungs- und Lagebericht . . . ," 8 June 1935, T-580,
roll 546, folder 616. A later report from Bavaria did note that in view of the fear
of denunciations and concentration camps it was rather difficult to gauge the true
state of public opinion. See HMB/OBB, pp. 2–3, 11 Nov. 1935, BGStA, MA 106670.

tually, the smoldering dissatisfactions of the "old fighters" had not been extinguished, but merely banked for the party congress—the traditional annual climax of the party's political life. Before[286] and after[287] the congress the PLs' dissatisfactions flared up anew. The reasons for continued grumbling were both psychological and material. There is no doubt that as a professional political elite the PLs felt insecure. Despite Schwarz's best efforts, the often promised salary scale (in effect giving the PO the same salary security as the civil service) was still not published; the fact that lower party organs kept millions of marks from reaching Munich was a symptom and an explanation, but not a cure.[288] For most PLs, not even their position was secure: at the end of the year only a minute number of PLs had been confirmed in their posts.[289] To these disappointments must be added the frustrations felt by many "old fighters" among the PLs when they saw certain segments of society specifically excluded from the party's control,[290] and seemingly defeated political groupings find a new haven in party organizations.[291]

Unable to confront the causes of their dissatisfaction directly, the PLs gave vent to their feelings in a series of renewed anti-Semitic outbursts. Unlike the later pogrom of November 1938, these excesses were not centrally initiated; on the contrary, the Reich leadership had no interest in direct actions at this time.[292] In April and May "spontaneous" actions (that is, actions organized by lower party organs on their own initiative) against Jewish shops and department stores erupted in several areas of western and southern Germany, the traditional regions of

286. For a description of the generally revolutionary mood of the "old fighters" during the 1935 congress, see Albert Speer, *Erinnerungen* (Berlin, 1969), p. 174.

287. Goebbels was roundly booed when he attempted to appear before the district leaders of Berlin in November 1935. The scene is variously described in Boris v. Borresholm and Karena Niehoff, eds., *Dr. Goebbels* (Berlin, 1949), p. 139, and Alfred Rosenberg, *Letzte Aufzeichnungen* (Göttingen, 1955), p. 195.

288. Schwarz to Hess, 15 Oct. 1935, BDC/Mutschmann (PKC).

289. See the accumulated totals for the years in *VOBl*, no. 111 (31 Dec. 1935).

290. Hess had no influence over the appointment of civilian officials in the armed forces, much less the officers themselves. See Hossbach to Blomberg, 25 Oct. 1935, BA/R 43 II/426.

291. GL Koch, for example, genuinely hated the old East Prussian conservatives and accused the SS of giving them a political refuge. The relevant documents are in the BDC/Bach (SS) file.

292. Heinrich Uhlig, *Die Warenhäuser im Dritten Reich* (Cologne-Opladen, 1956), p. 155.

pioneer anti-Semitism.[293] By July and August the movement had spread to all parts of the Reich except Berlin,[294] and a number of offices sought to utilize the popularity of these actions for their own purposes. The DAF organ, *Der Angriff*, had commented favorably on the attacks as early as April 26, and somewhat later Goebbels' propaganda ministry became actively involved.[295] An even greater danger lay in the fact that such "informal" pogroms enabled every Gauleiter and district leader to give the force of law to his personal definition of "Jew" and "Jewish."[296] It did not take Hitler and Hess long to recognize the potentially disintegrative force of such a development.

The result was the infamous set of decrees known as the Nuremberg laws. This legislation, passed by a special session of the Reichstag held in Nuremberg during the 1935 party congress, deprived the German Jews of their citizenship and provided for their virtual elimination from German societal life. As such, the Nuremberg laws were a definite step on the road to Auschwitz, but their more immediate purpose was to appease the grumbling "old fighters"[297] and to centralize the handling of anti-Jewish actions within the party. With the decrees, the state accepted the party's "racial" definition of a Jew, but that victory brought with it two corollary acceptances: the party had to view the state as ally, rather than enemy,[298] and the party's enforcement and interpretation desires in the area of anti-Semitic legislation had to be channeled through the office of the StdF.

293. Among the GLs the most active anti-Semites were Sprenger (Kurhessen) and Streicher (Franconia). See Bernhard Lösener, "Als Rassereferent im Reichsministerium des Innern," *Vjh.f.Z.*, IX (July 1961), 282.

294. HMB/OBB, pp. 6–10, 9 Sept. 1936, BGStA, MA 106670; Helmut Genschel, *Die Verdrängung der Juden aus der Wirtschaft im Dritten Reich* (Göttingen, 1966), pp. 108–12; and Uhlig, *Warenhäuser*, pp. 155–57.

295. Genschel, *Verdrängung*, pp. 111–12.

296. Lösener, "Rassereferent," p. 278.

297. The provisions of the Nuremberg Laws were actually old pioneer demands: they can be found in the appendix to Dietrich Eckart's article, "Die Midgardschlange," *Auf gut deutsch*, I (20 Dec. 1919), 694–98. Significantly, Hitler wanted no discussion of the other favorite topic of the party, the *Reichsreform*, at the party congress. See Bormann to Frick, 2 Sept. 1935, HAB/320/29.

298. Hess put particular emphasis on this point in his speech to the PLs at the party congress. Because of the significance of the StdF's remarks, Bormann later sent a copy of the salient points in the address to every GL and district leader. See StdF, "Rundschreiben," 12 Oct. 1935, T-580, roll 12, folder 170.

The office of the StdF therefore had an immediate interest in the drafting and enforcement of the laws. The actual initiative came directly from Hitler, and although the technical work was performed by civil servants in the Reich interior ministry, two of the leading staffers in Hess's office, Gerhard Wagner and Walter Sommer, were involved in the negotiations.[299] Significantly, the StdF was the only party office consulted; Darré, for example, head of the SS's main office for race and settlement, had no part in the drafting process.[300] Actually, the StdF was less concerned with the wording of the laws than with their subsequent interpretation and enforcement. Here Hitler had already underscored the importance of the party as the ideal of anti-Semitic thought and action: in his address proclaiming the new laws, the Führer not only thanked the NSDAP for its anti-Semitic deeds, but also announced that the Nuremberg laws were the last effort to solve the "Jewish problem" by state action; if this failed, the entire problem would be turned over to the party.[301]

Once the Nuremberg decrees had the force of law, the StdF moved quickly to seize the initiative in their interpretation. While the Gauleiters were kept in the background,[302] Hess's office attempted to force the Reich interior ministry to accept the categorical definitions put forth by the deputy Führer and to persuade the ministry's expert on racial questions to join the staff of the StdF.[303] Hess failed in the latter effort, but on most other substantial points he won. His office had to be consulted in all cases involving exceptions from the ban on "Aryan-Jewish" marriages—and the StdF consistently refused to permit exceptions.[304] The fact that Hitler did not express himself on the subject of the Nuremberg laws during the conference of Reichsleiters and Gau-

---

299. Lösener, "Rassereferent," pp. 273–74.

300. Interrogation of R. Walther Darré, p. 51, IfZ/ZS 863.

301. Domarus, *Hitler*, I, 525 and 537. Contemporary Nazi authors immediately grasped the implication of this threat. See Neesse, *Partei und Staat*, p. 47; and Walter Sommer, "Die NSDAP als Verwaltungsträger," in Hans Frank, ed., *Verwaltungsrecht* (Munich, 1937), pp. 169–71 and 174.

302. StdF, "Anordnung 190/35," 27 Sept. 1935, T-580, roll 12, folder 170. See also Hess, *Rede auf dem Reichsparteitag 1938 vor Reichs- Gau- und Kreisleitern* ([Munich, 1938]), pp. 7–8.

303. Lösener, "Rassereferent," pp. 280–82.

304. *Ibid.*, p. 284.

leiters in late September[305] in effect strengthened the hand of the StdF. Hitler's silence merely confirmed the leading role of the StdF.

The administrative history of the Nuremberg laws was only part of a general pattern that emerged in the last months of 1935. Aided by the mistakes of his potential rivals among the Reichsleiters, Hess was increasingly able to strengthen his *primus inter pares* status in his dealings with state and party organs.[306] The Reich ministry of justice accepted the StdF's right of judicial review.[307] Hess was able to dissolve his "office for cultural peace," ostensibly because the question of church-state relations was now handled by the Reich ministry for ecclesiastical affairs, but actually because the NSDAP as a whole had accepted the StdF's basic opposition to the Christian churches as such.[308] Hess's rivals, in the meantime, aided his advance by a series of blunders. Ley affronted his erstwhile allies, the Gauleiters, by opposing inter-Gau arrangements of any sort,[309] and aroused the ire of Schwarz when he attempted to obtain more money for his schooling system.[310] Above all, Ley made the mistake of directly offending Hitler. Anxious to possess a paramilitary force of his own, Ley established *Werksscharen* (industrial brigades) just in time to have them march past Hitler at the September party congress. The Führer took one look and that was the end of Ley's army—the Werkscharen reminded Hitler too much of Communist shop steward brigades.[311]

Buch, too, faced the frowns of his idol. In the course of the year the party's chief judge discovered the importance of the family. In a series of articles he proclaimed the stability of the family and matrimonial faithfulness to be the cornerstones of Nazism.[312] As always, Buch

305. *Ibid.*, p. 281. See also Domarus, *Hitler*, I, 542. Domarus incorrectly gives the date of the conference as September 24.
306. StdF, "Anordnung 223/35," 29 Nov. 1935, T-580, roll 12, folder 170.
307. StdF, "Rundschreiben 180/35," 3 Sept. 1935, *ibid.*; and Reich ministry of justice, "Hausverfügung," 30 Nov. 1935, BA/R 22/21.
308. Hitler, "Verfügung," 14 Nov. 1935, T-580, roll 12, folder 170; and Conway, *Nazi Persecution*, p. 160.
309. *VOBl*, no. 110 (15 Dec 1935), p. 354.
310. Rschm., "Rundschreiben 127/35," 12 Oct. 1935, *Rdschr.*, II.
311. See below, pp. 256–57.
312. See *Parteirichter*, I (10 April and 10 June 1935), 51–53 and 57–58; and II (10 Aug. and 10 Oct. 1935, and 10 Jan. and 10 June 1936), 2–5, 9–14, 26–29, and 40–44.

was in dead earnest, and even tried to enlist Himmler's aid in his campaign.[313] All might have been well if Buch had not included two practical consequences in his program of "moral cleanliness" in the NSDAP: he specifically demanded that the moral offenses of party leaders be treated with the same severity as those of lesser comrades, and he planned to transfer that part of the Hoheitsträgers' disciplinary supervision (*Dienstaufsicht*) dealing with the moral conduct of the PLs to the party courts.[314] Buch had obviously touched a raw nerve.[315] It was an open secret that at least one Reichsleiter (Goebbels) and two Gauleiters (Streicher and Kube), as well as numerous lesser PLs, were anything but faithful to their wives. The party's moral adjudicator therefore soon faced a formidable phalanx of enemies, including Hitler, who had no objection to love affairs among his PLs as long as such lapses were not coupled with political opposition.

Buch retreated. He resigned as head of the OPG's first chamber. His successor, Johannes Schneider, had a better grasp of political realities. He promptly announced that the party judges could not act without instructions from the Hoheitsträgers, and, as head of a newly created central office in the OPG, he presumably applied these principles in the selection and schooling of court personnel.[316] Buch, however, was determined to prolong his crusade. (His articles continued to appear regularly in the publication *Parteirichter*.) As a result, he was ordered to appear before Hitler on November 14. When he arrived back in Munich, the chief judge of the party was no longer an important figure in the NSDAP.[317]

Schwarz, on the other hand, continued undeterred in his ways. He

313. Buch to Himmler, 13 Dec. 1935, and 6 Jan. 1936, BDC/Buch (SS).
314. *Parteirichter*, II (10 Oct. 1935), 10–14.
315. Ulrich (Oberpräsident of Kassel) to Grauert, 25 Feb. 1936, and Grauert to Ulrich, 29 Feb. 1936, HAB/77/1.
316. *Parteirichter*, II (10 Oct. 1935 and 10 Jan. 1936), 8–9 and 24.
317. See the office of the chancellor to Buch, 12 Nov. 1935, BA/R 43 II/1198. Hitler's criticism came as a complete shock to Buch. Until his meeting with Hitler he had apparently believed that only Bormann opposed his "save the family" plans. On the confrontation see Buch to Himmler, 23 Dec. 1935, BDC/Buch (SS); Interrogation of Buch, p. 5, IfZ/ZS 855; and Bormann to Gerda Bormann, 28 Nov. 1943, in Martin and Gerda Bormann, *The Bormann Letters*, ed. Hugh R. Trevor-Roper, tr. R. H. Stevens (London, 1954), p. 34.

expanded his auditing staff,[318] resisted another attempt by Ley to equate DAF and party membership,[319] and obtained Hess's agreement that the Beauftragte were not authorized to make decisions involving the treasurer's vertical or horizontal staff.[320] Finally, in yet another attempt to force the Gauleiters to register their "hidden" members in Munich,[321] the Reich treasurer introduced a system of dues payment based upon prepaid stamps: each month the Gauleiters received only a sufficient number of stamps to cover those members registered with the Reichsleitung. All others could obtain no stamps and hence were unable to show proof of membership.[322]

At the end of the year, then, the StdF and the Reich treasurer had made considerable headway in recentralizing the party's administration, although the outlook for the NSDAP's future as a political elite continued to be bleak. The personnel problems alone were formidable. As a group the Hoheitsträgers were at the chronological extremes of the party membership: most local leaders were over forty-one and many were more than fifty-nine; the majority of the sublocal leaders were less than thirty. Professionally, the PO continued to be dominated by middle-class groups. Most of the district leaders had either been civil servants or white-collar employees before joining the PL corps. With few exceptions, the much celebrated worker and farmer element in the party did not rise to Hoheitsträger positions above the sublocal level.[323] Even so, the NSDAP continued to experience difficulty in replacing its purged district leaders. At the beginning of 1935, the party had 827 Hoheitsträgers in the districts; ten months later the number had

318. "Experience has shown," noted the Reich treasurer caustically, "that offices of the party and the affiliates call upon the Reich treasurer only when they are threatened with immediate financial collapse." See Schwarz to Hess, 15 Oct. 1935, BDC/Mutschmann (PKC). See Rschm., "Rundschreiben 116/35 [and] 151/35," 21 Sept. and 5 Dec. 1935, *Rdschr.*, II.

319. See the report of the Bavarian state police on the meeting of the GL München-Oberbayern, 29 Oct. 1935, BGStA, MA 145252; and Rschm., "Rundschreiben 141/35," 31 Oct. 1935, *Rdschr.*, II.

320. Schwarz to Bormann, 10 Sept. 1935, T-580, roll 802, box 237, folder 15.

321. Schwarz estimated the number of unreported members at 600,000. See Schwarz to Hess, 15 Oct. 1935, BDC/Mutschmann (PKC).

322. Rschm., "Rundschreiben 144/35," 25 Oct. 1935, *Rdschr.*, II.

323. ROL, *Statistik 1935*, II, 445.

dropped to 776, even though the number of local leaders rose from 13,733 to 14,111 in the same time span.[324] The StdF's influence in the area of personnel appointments was as yet more theoretical than actual. Hess was able to exercise absolute control over the confirmation process for PLs in the party: after January 1 only a card issued by the office of the StdF empowered a PL to hold office.[325] The system of in-service training, on the other hand, made little headway. In November, only three provincial functionaries were actually in residence at the Brown House.[326]

Perhaps more significant, the party's future role among the power blocs of the Third Reich was no nearer to a clear definition than it had been three years before. The Reichsreform, no less urgent or popular than before, had been laid to rest on Hitler's orders. The Führer himself was increasingly involved with foreign policy decisions; the reoccupation of the Rhineland was in the air. As a consequence, Nazi political science engaged in increasingly tortuous circumlocutions to avoid stating the obvious: as presently constituted, the NSDAP was a largely superfluous element in the Nazi power constellation. Nazi theorists in 1936 were particularly fond of the "mosaic" as a metaphor. Upon closer examination, however, the mosaic bore a close resemblance to other vague causal agents, such as Adam Smith's invisible hand. Walter Sommer, the head of the StdF's division of state affairs, wrote: "Only one person, the Führer, knows what the new state will look like after ten years, and his certainty will not be shaken by other writings—no matter how knowledgeable."[327] Needless to say, the "knowledgeable" writings did appear in abundance. A trained civil servant and deputy leader of the Nazi Association of Civil Servants, Gottfried Neesse, tried valiantly to show the complementary character of state and party, but he too fled quickly to the mosaic. "The mosaic [of the relationship of state and party] is not yet complete, but the observer feels intuitively that a planned concept will be realized in the future." Unfortunately, the

324. *Ibid.*, p. 322.
325. *VOBl*, no. 110 (15 Dec. 1935), p. 353.
326. Mackensen (business manager of the office of the StdF), "Anordnung 206/35," 5 Nov. 1935, T-580, roll 12, folder 170.
327. Sommer, "NSDAP," p. 175.

Nazi ideology was not much of a guide; it was only a "pale indicator into the unknown land of the intellect."[328] Hitler himself made no positive contribution at all. His 1936 New Year's proclamation admonished the NSDAP to be a "fanatically sworn community,"[329] but he assigned the party no specific tasks. Nine months later the Führer advised the PLs to be standards of optimism for the people[330]—which meant that the PLs were to supply joyful explanations for the fact that the rearmament program led to a shortage of consumer goods.[331]

The practical results of the continuing state of flux were not far different from those observed in earlier months, but their very continuance aggravated the seriousness and ridiculousness of the situation. At the top, the NSDAP had enough Reichsleiters to supply a cabinet list, but most of them were by now empty titles; their functions had long since been taken over by other state and party offices.[332] In the lower PL ranks the effects of what Goebbels used to call "sour pickle times" were listlessness and general purposelessness among the functionaries,[333] sluggish dues payments, and nonattendance at meetings for the membership.[334] Corruption and pettiness continued to be rampant throughout the organization.[335]

All territorial levels from the Gau on down wallowed in organizational routine. The number of Gau offices (*Gauämter*)—that is, organi-

328. Neesse, *Partei und Staat*, pp. 12, 28, 30 and 45. The quotations are from pp. 30 and 45.

329. Domarus, *Hitler*, I, 562.

330. *Ibid.*, I, 647.

331. See GL Grohé, "Stimmungsbericht," 12 Aug. 1936, T-580, roll 546, folder 616.

332. Schwarz to Bormann, 22 Feb. 1936, BDC/Ordner PK, Staats- und Präsidialkanzlei.

333. Most of the PLs in Saxony, when questioned about their party functions in late 1935, answered, "collection of dues, sale of pamphlets, periodicals and tickets [to party-sponsored events]." See Kadatz, *Block und Zelle in der NSDAP* (Dresden, 1936), p. 7; and Rschm., "Anordnung 36/39," 22 June 1936, *Rdschr.*, II.

334. See the situation report of the county executive in Kreuznach, January 1936, quoted in Franz-Joseph Heyen, *Nationalsozialismus im Alltag* (Boppard am Rhein, 1968), p. 314; the report of the Gestapo office in Aachen, 10 Feb. 1936, quoted in Vollmer, *Volksopposition*, p. 241; and GL Berlin, *Gau*, nos. 1, 4, 9, and 16 (1 Jan. —15 Feb., 1 May, and 15 Aug. 1936), pp. 5, 90, 169, and 274.

335. Rschm., "Verfügung 1/36," 2 Jan. 1936, *Rdschr.*, II; and GL Berlin, *Gau*, no. 5 (1 March 1936), p. 99.

zations reporting to the Gauleiter (who was often also Reich governor)—was staggering: twenty-one in Berlin, twenty-nine in Thuringia, thirty-six in Hessen.[336] Understandably, the rapid buildup of offices and office buildings (construction was the ROL's second great mania) was reflected in the financial situation of the Gaus. Salaries were the largest budget item in the Gaus. The Gauleitung Essen, for example, had seventy-eight full-time employees in mid-1936. Their total monthly salary was RM 19,995, or an average of RM 244 per functionary.[337] With stagnating membership lists and correspondingly inadequate dues income, the Gaus relied increasingly on contributions and ever more frequent collections to maintain their solvency. In the short run, this was effective; the Gaus reported significantly increased amounts from "voluntary" contributions, particularly from industrial sources.[338] But the Gaus also recognized the long-range dangers of continuing these practices. The constant collections repelled the population at large,[339] and reliance on moneys "begged" (*geschnurrt*) from industry led to the danger of political dependence on such sources as well.[340]

From all appearances neither the interests of the party nor those of its industrial benefactors were appreciably furthered by the large expenditures. In January 1936 the Gau Berlin began publishing a biweekly information sheet for its PLs, and the first issue contained some revealing items on the routine duties of a typical head of a Gau office (*Gauamtsleiter*). Their banality was complete. The list began with the correct use of address and title among PLs, described the NSBO uniform

336. GL Berlin, *Gau*, no. 1 (1 Jan. 1936), p. 5; GL Hessen-Nassau, *Gautag Hessen-Nassau 8.-12. July 1936* ([Frankfurt, 1936]), p. 13; and GL Thuringia, *Organisations- und Geschäftsverteilungsplan der Gauleitung Thüringen der NSDAP* ([Weimar, June 1936]). A copy of the latter document is in MiU/GAC, folder 39.

337. Haag, "Inspektionsbericht Gauleitung Essen der NSDAP," 6 July 1937, T-580, roll 806, box 239, folder 44. In Düsseldorf salaries represented 22% of the Gau's total income. See Haag, "Inspektionsbericht Gauleitung Düsseldorf," 23 June 1936, *ibid.*

338. See Haag, "Inspektionsbericht Düsseldorf," *ibid.*; and Reich auditor in Silesia (Krüger) to Reich auditing office, 15 Jan. 1941, T-580, roll 813, box 242, folder 84.

339. Grohé, "Stimmungsbericht," 17 June 1936, T-580, roll 546, folder 616; and Kratzer (Reich auditor) to Schwarz, 24 June 1936, T-580, roll 813, box 242, folder 84.

340. GL Röwer to Schwarz, 20 Jan. 1936, BDC/Röwer (PKC).

in detail, lingered lovingly on the purchase of uniforms and the repair of the PLs' official pistols, and ended with a description of the duties of the Gau's liaison official in the propaganda ministry.[341] To be sure, there were other items,[342] but the overall impression of the Gau administration in 1936 is that of offices exhausting their energies and funds in routine and politically insignificant pursuits. The more perceptive Gauleiters had no great difficulty recognizing this state of affairs. Fritz Sauckel complained bitterly that the transfer of the *Führerprinzip* (leadership principle) to the Reich ministries had in effect reduced the provincial leaders to the status of second-class officials, unable to exercise any real power.[343] He was not alone. Others focused on the uselessness of national meetings of Gauleiters and Reichsleiters for the political leadership role of the party or noted that the StdF and the Reich interior ministry discussed issues concerning their Gaus without consulting the provincial leaders.[344]

By contrast, the districts stood on somewhat firmer jurisdictional ground. They too were top-heavy and overbureaucratized, but at this level there was a more direct relationship between the party activities and the concerns of the population at large, and unlike the Gaus, the districts exercised far more clearly defined powers in their dealings with the state administrations.[345] In a sense, even their financial situation was simpler. Since the districts had no income of their own, it fell to the Gaus and the Reich treasurer to finance their operations.[346] Most

341. Gau Berlin, *Gau*, no. 1 (1 Jan. 1936), p. 5.

342. Thus the PLs were to a large extent involved in the implementation of the Nuremberg laws. See *ibid.*, no. 7 (1 Sept. 1936), p. 287; and the remaining issues of the *Gau* for 1936.

343. Sauckel, "Denkschrift," pp. 1 and 7–11.

344. GL Grohé, "Stimmungsbericht," 13 May 1936, T-580, roll 546, folder 616; and GL Eggeling (Halle-Merseburg) to Grauert, 25 Feb. 1936, HAB/77/3.

345. Schäfer, *NSDAP*, pp. 75/78 [*sic*]. This applied primarily to provincial towns; in a city-state like Hamburg the Gauleiter was in fact a superdistrict leader and hence more directly involved in the administration of the territory. See GL Kaufmann, "Vernehmung," 22 April 1947, Forsch. Hbg./PA/12/B.

346. A typical district in the Gau Bayreuth had a monthly budget of RM 15,000; district leaders in Düsseldorf received a salary of between RM 500 and RM 600 per month. See Saupert to Gau treasurer Bayreuth, 16 May 1935, T-580, roll 842, box 267, folder 348; and Haag, "Inspektionsbericht Düsseldorf," 23 June 1936, T-580, roll 806, box 239, folder 44.

of the PLs' activities at the district level ranged around the broad categories of socioeconomic measures and the manufacture of a favorable
climate of public opinion. Both these categories came under the official
euphemism of "living organization."[347] The socioeconomic activities
were very heavily dominated by the DAF's modified estate concept,[348]
and, with only an occasional acknowledgment of the goal of free enterprise and the need for competition,[349] these activities continued to
emphasize the party's role as Betreuer of small and middle-sized businesses.[350] The propaganda themes popular at district meetings ranged
very widely from attacks on modern dances to sympathetic ("we agree,
but there are practical difficulties") efforts to calm the members' desires for more active social revolutionary measures. There is no clearly
apparent propaganda line; the district propaganda leader floundered
from one topic to another. The party had an answer or opinion for
every subject: art, peace, equality, churches, Sunday walks, farming,
and, of course, Jews.[351]

The NSDAP locals, once the most important part of the party's
organizational hierarchy, had reached a low point of political importance. Although their organizational charts looked impressive,[352] their
primary function was to correlate the activities of the party's sublocal
organizations, the block and cell. The block was the lowest territorial
organization, usually encompassing four to eight apartment house complexes. The block leader's purpose was simultaneously to betreuen,
control, and fleece the inhabitants of his neighborhood. (The establishment of party blocks was determined by the population figures,
not the number of party members.) In public, the block leader made
his rounds of apartment houses primarily to collect dues, sell buttons,
tickets, and so forth, and, in theory, to serve as a general ombudsman

347. *Mittbl. Kr. Mü.*, no. 21 (28 May 1936).
348. See the topics of discussion (i.e., speeches) and the organizations involved
in the various district congresses in the Gau München-Oberbayern throughout
1936, in BGStA, Rsth. 444.
349. *Mittbl. Kr. Mü.*, no. 9 (5 March 1936).
350. *Ibid.*, nos. 2–7 (Jan.–Feb. 1936).
351. This analysis is based on the propaganda themes presented in the issues of
the *Mittbl. Kr. Mü.* published in 1936.
352. Kadatz, *Block*, pp. 13 and 34; and *Mittbl. Kr. Mü.*, no. 17 (30 April 1936).

for his charges.[353] But he was also the party's spy. In his rounds he attempted to sound out the "mood of the people," reporting "chronic" oppositional voices orally to his superior cell leader. The latter in turn, also orally, turned the names over to the local leader. Only at this level did the information become bureaucratized: the local leader sent written reports to the district.[354] Neither the block nor the cell PLs were at liberty to develop much initiative in their work. The block leader was admonished never to agree with views critical of the regime, and a propaganda rally sponsored by a cell leader was bound to put the listeners to sleep: even an "experienced" cell leader should refrain from making an extemporaneous speech on such occasions, and should read instead—preferably a chapter from *Mein Kampf*.[355]

Party life in early 1936 was, in a word, boring. Again something had to be done to rekindle the PLs' enthusiasm and sense of mission. Hitler decided on a two-pronged remedy: the Rhineland coup and national elections. This is not to ignore the importance of the reoccupation of the Rhineland in Hitler's program of achieving European hegemony for the Reich; nevertheless, the German foreign minister was entirely correct when he interpreted the causes of the Rhineland coup to be more domestic than foreign.[356] National elections had always been one of Hitler's favorite political weathervanes. He regarded them as genuine indicators of popular feelings toward himself and his policies[357] and as proof of the effectiveness of the party's organization. In addition, elections served as a test of the popularity of individual Gauleiters.[358] It was more than a propagandistic trick, then, when Hess and Goebbels both emphasized that the Reichstag election campaign had to take precedence over all other party activities.[359]

353. Kadatz, *Block*, pp. 14–18, and 23–27; and Wahl, *Deutsche Herz*, p. 186.
354. Kadatz, *Block*, p. 29.
355. *Ibid.*, pp. 18–19, and 30.
356. Manfred Funke, "7. März 1936," *Aus Politik und Zeitgeschichte/Parlament* (3 Oct. 1970), p. 6. For the Rhineland crisis itself see Gerhard L. Weinberg, *The Foreign Policy of Hitler's Germany* (Chicago, 1970), pp. 239–263.
357. Wiedemann, *Der Mann*, p. 74.
358. Manfred Killinger, the SA leader in Saxony, reported that on 50% of the ballots in 1936 Mutschmann's name had been crossed out as a candidate for the Reichstag. Killinger to OPG, Aug. 1936, BDC/Killinger (OPG).
359. Friedrichs to Ley, 19 March 1936, and Hess to Ley, 31 March 1936, T-580,

Quite aside from its propagandistic aspects, the 1936 election was also an important battleground in the continuing intraparty power struggles. The voters, of course, had no choice among the candidates, but within the party the process of selecting the final candidate lists involved a considerable number of conflicts. There was no shortage of nominees, partly because the post of Reichstag deputy involved no onerous duties and a salary of RM 600 per month, but also because the relative importance of a party office could be measured by the number of Reichstag deputies affiliated with the organization. And a comparison of the composition of successive Reichstags provided at least one indicator of the rise and fall of the party's power components. It was by no means insignificant that in 1936 the SS received eight new seats, while the Reich propaganda office and the main office for technology fought over one deputy.[360]

The nominating process was a complicated procedure involving virtually every party office. All of the Reichsleiters and Gauleiters received automatic places on the list, but after that the law of the jungle took over. Some of the Gauleiters seem to have had considerable influence over the entire list, others virtually none.[361] After each office had pleaded its cause for weeks, a marathon meeting of all Reichsleiters and Gauleiters and Hess, Frick, and Bormann took place on March 9.[362] Whatever disagreements remained after that had to await Hitler's definitive decision. This last phase of the procedure was firmly in the hands of the StdF. Bormann prepared the final candidate lists for presentation to Hitler.[363] As a result, the 1936 list showed a heavy preponderance of functionaries associated with offices that could be con-

---

roll 549, folder 746; Reichs-Wahlkampfleitung, *Richtlinien für den Reichswahlkampf zum 29. März 1936* ([Berlin, 1936]). A copy of this confidential publication is in HAB/320/38. See also Rschm., "Anordnung 9/36," 10 March 1936, *Rdschr.,* III.

360. Himmler to Frick, 3 March 1936, BDC/Körner (SS); and Hans Fabricius, "Vermerk f. Herrn Minister [Frick]," 21 March 1936, HAB/320/88.

361. Schwede-Coburg to Lutze, 30 March 1936, HAB/77/7; Wächtler to Frick, 9 April 1936, and Frick to Wächtler, 14 May 1936, BA/NS 20/20/Bd 1; and Fabricius to Rosenberg *et al.,* 7 March 1936, HAB/320/38.

362. See Frick's drafts and working papers in HAB/320/38.

363. *Ibid.* See also the documents at the end of HAB/77/13.

sidered allies of the StdF: the SS and the PO at the Gau and district levels. There were relatively few PLs from Reichsleiter offices, and no cadre personnel from a territorial jurisdiction below the district.[364]

After Hitler had issued general guidelines on March 8,[365] the actual campaign lay in the hands of Goebbels as Reich propaganda leader. He ran a very centralized campaign. All speeches had to be based on materials issued by the RPL, and all official speakers had to tune in to Goebbels' nationally broadcast keynote address on March 10.[366] As always, the entire party participated vigorously in the election preparations,[367] and the results brought forth the usual lopsided figures. All of the Nazi candidates were elected, and Hitler could bask in the knowledge that, on paper at least, 99 percent of the German voters approved of him and his system.[368]

The 1936 election campaign had momentarily relieved much of the listlessness among the PL corps, but it provided no lasting answer to the dilemma of the future of the NSDAP in the Third Reich. Hitler, glorying in the public relations success of the Olympic Games and burying himself in foreign policy plans and economic preparations for war,[369] gave little attention to the party. The Reich treasurer's office was among those that were least affected by Hitler's neglect of party affairs. Schwarz continued to centralize his entire jurisdiction, not only reorganizing the central office in the summer of 1936,[370] but also expanding his control over the Gau and district treasurers.[371] Simultaneously, the Reich treasurer demanded clear acknowledgment of his

364. This analysis is based upon the official compendium [Bureau des Reichstags, ed.] *Verzeichnis der Mitglieder . . . 1936* (Berlin, 1936).

365. Domarus, *Hitler*, I, 597.

366. Reichs-Wahlkampfleitung, *Richtlinien . . . 1936*.

367. See the report of the Gestapo office in Aachen, 6 April 1936, quoted in Vollmer, *Volksopposition*, p. 384; and *Mittbl. Kr. Mü.*, nos. 12–14 (19 March–3 April 1936).

368. Domarus, *Hitler*, I, 617.

369. For the latter aspects see Wilhelm Treue, ed., "Hitlers Denkschrift zum Vierjahresplan 1936," *Vjh.f.Z.*, III (April 1955), 184–203. For a discussion of the significance of the memorandum see Weinberg, *Foreign Policy*, pp. 353–56.

370. See Rschm., "Rundschreiben" to all department heads, 30 May 1936, T-580, roll 47, folder 266; and the organizational chart in Lükemann, "Reichsschatzmeister," pp. 27–29.

371. Rschm., "Anordnung 21/36," 9 April 1936, *Rdschr.*, III; and *Mittlb. Kr. Mü.*, no. 29 (23 July 1936).

authority over the party's financial administration from the Gaus, the affiliates, and even the office of the StdF.[372] The difficulties that remained were not primarily of Schwarz's making. Foremost among them continued to be the missing salary scale, without which a party career held few attractions for young party members.[373] At the moment, the NSDAP did not even have a regular emergency fund for destitute "old fighters."[374] Since Schwarz was unable to issue the salary scale with the party's present financial resources, he proposed a two-pronged plan to remedy the situation: on the one hand, a reopening of the membership rolls to increase the income from dues[375] and, on the other, the elimination of several Reichsleiters' offices, so as to reduce the top-heavy PL cadres. The first phase of the plan was a little like driving out the devil with Beelzebub. After all, there was something illogical in diluting the ranks of an elitist organization in order to strengthen the elitist role of that same organization, but in view of the constantly expanding number of offices in the PO, neither Schwarz nor Hess saw a viable alternative. The Reich treasurer had broached the subject of reducing the number of Reichsleiter offices as early as February. He specifically singled out Hans Frank, Karl Fiehler, Epp, and Darré as expendable, and voiced the opinion that Goebbels' positions as Reich minister and Gauleiter were really incompatible.[376] Schwartz even ventured to add that some of the PLs in the office of the StdF might be superfluous, but here a tour of the establishment, conducted personally by Bormann, convinced him that this view was incorrect.[377]

Once Schwarz had withdrawn the last part of his streamlining plan, the StdF was in full agreement. The elimination of several Reichsleiters fit in rather well with the continuing centralizing effort of the deputy

372. Schwarz to Hess, 5 Aug. 1936, T-580, roll 833, box 256, folder 271; Schwarz to Pohl (Reich treasurer of the SS), 7 Jan. 1936, BDC/Pohl (SS)/ II, 2; Schwarz to GL Forster, 7 May 1936, BDC/Forster (PKC); Gau treasurer Hamburg to Schwarz, 16 May 1936, and Saupert to Gau treasurer Hamburg, 26 May 1936, BDC/Kaufmann (PKC).

373. GL Grohé, "Stimmungsbericht" 12 Dec. 1936, T-580, roll 546, folder 616.

374. Rschm., "Anordnung 13/36," 27 March 1936, *Rdschr.*, III.

375. Rschm., "Bekanntgabe 13/36," 28 May 1936, *ibid.*; and StdF, "Verfügung 95/36," 2 Aug. 1936, T-580, roll 12, folder 171.

376. Schwarz to Bormann, 22 Feb. 1936, BDC/Ordner, PK, Staats- und Präsidialkanzlei.

377. Schwarz to Hess, 25 Sept. 1936, T-580, roll 833, box 256, folder 271.

Führer.[378] Much of his work now took place behind closed doors and in secret planning sessions.[379] There was no longer any realistic hope of a large-scale Nazi Reichsreform,[380] and thus the StdF had to continue his subterranean efforts to increase his influence in party and state. Generally speaking, the deputy Führer's aim in his relations with non-party segments of German society was to establish that the NSDAP was formally equal[381] and actually superior to the state's and the army's decision-making apparatus. Hess attempted to establish a party bridge-head in the army when he requested that soldiers be permitted to register complaints of a "political" nature with his office, but here the high command resisted successfully.[382] As far as the state administration was concerned, the StdF hoped to "reconstruct" the civil service in the image of the party.[383] In practice, this involved not only a new generation of Nazified civil servants, but also the assertion that the NSDAP had the right to supervise the state's decision-making apparatus.[384]

Formally, the StdF's largest advance came in the area of national civil service appointments. The German Civil Service Law (*Deutsches Beamtengesetz*, DBG), passed in 1937, made the appointment of civil servants dependent upon party approval, and within the party the evaluation pyramid placed final responsibility in the hands of the StdF. Although all of the Hoheitsträgers supplied detailed information on civil servants seeking appointment or promotion,[385] the chain effectively

378. Like most national reform plans in the Nazi party, Schwarz's scheme had no practical consequences. Hitler refused to eliminate any Reichsleiter titles or their offices until well into World War II.

379. See Eftger to Elberding, 13 May 1941, Rijksinstituut voor Oorlogsdokumentatie, Telex-Berichte of the RK for the occupied Netherlands, XV. The letter refers to a projected huge party affiliate, encompassing civil servants, farmers, as well as industrial and agricultural laborers, for which both Eftger and Elberding drew up plans in the staff of the StdF in the thirties. See also Helmut Heiber, *Walter Frank und sein Reichsinstitut für die Geschichte des neuen Deutschlands* (Stuttgart, 1966), pp. 836–37.

380. Baum, "Reichsreform," p. 45. See also Mommsen, *Beamtentum*, p. 91.

381. Thus Bormann insisted that Hitler wanted Reich ministers and the party's Reichsleiters to be treated as equal in rank. See Bormann to Frick, 17 Feb. 1936, BDC/Ordner, PK, Staats- und Präsidialkanzlei.

382. Hossbach, *Zwischen*, pp. 45–46.

383. Sommer, "NSDAP," pp. 169–71.

384. See Frick to Lammers, 30 April 1936; and Hess to Frick, 3 July 1936, BA/R 43 II/426.

385. StdF, "Anordnung 52/36," 30 March 1936, T-580, roll 12, folder 171.

bypassed the Gauleiters. Even high civil servants were not permitted to correspond directly (that is, without informing the StdF) with the provincial leaders.[386] The StdF also attempted to expand his system of training camps for younger civil servants. Separate camps existed at Jüterbog (Mecklenburg) for judicial personnel and at Tutzing (Bavaria) for ministerial civil servants. Both establishments attempted to partify their students though with mixed success. At Tutzing, the quality of lecturers left much to be desired, and future district attorneys at Jüterbog complained of an excessive emphasis on sport and paramilitary training.[387]

The StdF expanded his influence in a number of other programmatic areas as well. His office was involved in the renewed flare-up of antichurch attacks in 1936,[388] he continued his cooperation with the SS,[389] and his agency acquired a reputation of increasing importance in the field of relations between the NSDAP and foreign proto-Nazi parties.[390] Hess's claim to programmatic and administrative superiority was perhaps most completely realized in the area of economics. After the office for estate development had been dissolved,[391] all of the party's economic policy organizations found their administrative home within the StdF's office. The more anticapitalistic and middle-class-oriented commission for economic policy, a body headed by Bernhard Köhler, was primarily active in the area of long-range planning, while Wilhelm Keppler's economic-political commission[392] supervised the day-to-day work of the Gau economic advisors.[393] The Reich minister of economics, Hjalmar Schacht, had virtually no influence over the party's economic

386. Grauert to Simon, 11 Feb. 1936, HAB/77/2.

387. Werner Johe, *Die gleichgeschaltete Justiz* (Frankfurt, 1967), pp. 222–24; and StdF, "Rundschreiben," 28 Sept. 1936, T-580, roll 13, folder 171.

388. Conway, *Nazi Persecution*, p. 158.

389. In 1936 Hess acquired control of the liaison office for ethnic Germans (*Volksdeutsche Mittelstelle*; *Vomi*), but permitted Himmler to appoint one of his Obergruppenführer, Werner Lorenz, as new head. Höhne, *Orden*, p. 255.

390. Rost to Mussert, 14 Sept. 1936, in Minoud Marinus Rost van Tonningen, *Correspondentie van Mr. M.M. Rost van Tonningen*, ed. A. J. van der Leeuw (The Hague, 1967), I, 333.

391. *VOBl*, no. 115 (28 Feb. 1936), p. 385.

392. This is not a misprint; the German titles were *Kommission für Wirtschaftspolitik* (Köhler) and *Wirtschaftspolitische Kommission* (Keppler).

393. *VOBl*, no. 116 (15 March 1936), 390; and Hess to highest Reich offices, 13 Aug. 1936, T-580, roll 12, folder 171.

views; Hitler even refused to let him address the Reichsleiters and Gauleiters.[394]

Within the PO, developments proceeded less smoothly. To be sure, the purge of 1934–1935 had run its course. The number of denunciations (the StdF preferred the more neutral term "complaints") had been reduced to a trickle, and Hess dismissed all but one of his *Beauftragte*. Gustav Oexle, with the title Beauftragter for special purposes, alone continued the work of the earlier group of six. He was empowered to investigate all complaints emanating from any Gau in the Reich and also to call national meetings of the Gau inspectors. In effect, the Gau inspectors became his direct subordinates.[395] The other five investigators found new positions in the offices of the StdF and the ROL. Richard Manderbach, Robert Bauer, and Fritz Tittmann joined Ley's organization,[396] while Martin Seidel and Ralf Brockhausen stayed with Hess. Brockhausen in particular continued to be active as one of Hess's agents outside the home office. At first he handled censorship affairs (in effect invading the jurisdiction of Phillip Bouhler), and later he took over leadership of the ostensibly private Association for Germans Abroad (*Volksbund für das Deutschtum im Ausland*, VDA).[397]

Despite the end of the active purge, the process of confirming the incumbent PLs made very slow progress. Functionaries in the offices of the Reich treasurer and the StdF had no difficulties, but for others confirmation was by no means automatic.[398] Some of the difficulties were mechanical (the comrades had considerable problem complying with

394. StdF, "Verfügung 73/36," 22 May 1936, T-580, roll 12, folder 171.

395. StdF, "Anordnung 97/36," 1 Aug. 1936, T-580, roll 12, folder 171; and Friedrichs to Saupert, 22 May 1936, T-580, roll 802, box 237, folder 15. For an example of a case handled by Oexle, see district economic advisor in Bremen to Hoffmann (office of the StdF), 1 Sept. 1936, T-81, roll 641, frame 5444080.

396. Manderbach later served as commandant of the Ordensburg Vogelsang. Bauer had a similar position at Sonthofen and after the German attack on Russia became a minor territorial administrator in the Baltic area. Tittmann divided his time between sulking on his estate in Saxony and functioning as Ley's liaison official for racial affairs to the SS.

397. Bormann to Schwarz, 29 Sept. 1936, T-580, roll 802, box 237, folder 15; and the documents in BA/NS 6/180.

398. For the StdF and the Reich treasurer's office, see *VOBl*, no. 122 (31 May 1936), pp. 1, and 3–4. In contrast, by the same date only Koch had been confirmed in East Prussia; Wagner, two Gau officials, and three district leaders, in Silesia. *Ibid.*, pp. 3–4, and 8.

the requirement that they trace their ancestries back to 1801), but the PO was also racked by some major scandals. The scandal involving Gauleiter Wilhelm Kube (Kurmark) had the most far-reaching political consequence. Late in 1935 Kube, already married, fell in love with his secretary. The secretary became pregnant, and the Gauleiter instituted divorce proceedings against his wife, in the course of which he persuaded his grown son to testify against his own mother. Buch was understandably furious at such moral decadence, although Hitler could see nothing particularly wrong in this part of the affair. Kube, however, was determined to have revenge against the party's chief judge and distributed an anonymous broadsheet accusing Mrs. Buch of Jewish ancestry. This was too much even for Hitler. Kube had to resign as Gauleiter, although, remarkably, nothing more serious happened to him.[399] He was replaced by Emil Stürtz, and the new deputy Gauleiter of Kurmark was Paul Wegener, a staff member of the StdF, who now began his rapid rise as Bormann's golden boy.[400]

Simultaneously, the outlines of the later rivalry between the SS and the PO were becoming apparent.[401] The SS was increasingly staffed with a new generation of officers, drawn from the ranks of the HJ and the NSDStB. Far less identified with the party than the old *Freikorps* (anticommunist vigilante groups active just after World War I) mercenaries,[402] the new element saw in the SS the true elite organization of the Nazi regime, and did not hesitate to attempt Gleichschaltungs within the Gleichschaltung, that is, to have the SS take over already Nazified organizations.[403]

These developments led the staff of the StdF to intensify its efforts

399. The relevant documents on the Kube scandal are in BDC/Kube (SS) and BDC/Buch (SS). See also Helmut Heiber, ed., "Aus den Akten des Gauleiters Kube," *Vjh.f.Z.*, IV (Jan. 1956), 77–78.

400. *VB*, 18 Aug. 1936.

401. See, for example, Gau Berlin, district leader IV to Gau organizational leader, 2 July 1936, BA/NS 22/538; Wolff to Heissmeyer, 24 Dec. 1936, BDC/Schmauser (SS).

402. A good example was Gunter d'Alquen, born on 24 Oct. 1910. He was the new editor of the SS weekly, *Das Schwarze Korps*. See Shlomo Aronson, "Heydrich," p. 184.

403. This was, for example, the case with the veterans club, Kyffhäuser-Bund. See SS Abschnitt XII to Oberabschnitt Ost, 5 Feb. 1936; and Oberabschnitt Ost to RFSS, 10 Feb. 1936, BDC/Lange (SS).

to strengthen the PO. The staff members were aware that any major reform was futile without Schwarz's salary scale,[404] but Hess and his associates did their best within the available possibilities. At the beginning of 1936, Hess had issued a lengthy and critical analysis of the PO's personnel status. He was particularly concerned with the need for competent PLs at the district and higher levels. In view of the dual state-party capacity of most Gauleiters, the StdF emphasized the supreme importance of the deputy Gauleiters. In the future, his office would recommend no PL for a position as deputy Gauleiter who had not served as district or local leader and as Gau staff official, preferably as head of one of the "political" departments, that is, executive secretary (staff leader), organization, propaganda, in-service training, personnel, or inspectorate. Simultaneously, the StdF insisted that the "political" Gau staff divisions be headed by full-time salaried PLs and that each Gau have at least two full-time inspectors.[405] To implement this ambitious program, Hess expanded his training courses at the Brown House to include district leaders,[406] increased his direct control over the transfer of even lower PO staff officials,[407] and, more indirectly, placed his hopes in the Hitler Youth. Long-time (four-year) members of the HJ could take out party membership even before the general reopening of the rolls in 1937,[408] and Hess may have been instrumental in the appointment of Baldur von Schirach as Reich youth leader late in 1936. The consequent expansion of the HJ certainly fit in well with the StdF's plan to create a large reservoir of potential PLs.[409]

Chronologically parallel to Hess's efforts, but far different in aim and scope, was Robert Ley's last major attempt to retain control of the PO—his organizational reforms of 1936. Although the published plans

---

404. In the Reich treasurer's office reports circulated that StdF staffers were severely critical of Schwarz for his failure to issue a salary scale. See Wachlin, "Akten-Vermerk," 3 April 1937, T-580, roll 813, box 242, folder 84.

405. StdF, "Verfügung 22/36," 17 Feb. 1936, T-580, roll 12, folder 171.

406. StdF, "Anordnung 3/36," 7 Jan. 1936, *ibid.*

407. StdF, "Anordnung 11/36," 20 Jan. 1936, *ibid.*

408. *VOBl*, no. 112 (15 Jan. 1936), 365; and Rschm., "Anordnung 7/36," 3 March 1936, *Rdschr.*, III.

409. Schirach's appointment marked the actual culmination of the Nazification of the German youth. See Brandenburg, *HJ*, pp. 200–01.

came to be known as "Robert Ley's fairy tales,"[410] because of their lack of relationship to administrative reality, even Hitler regarded the effort itself as an important undertaking.[411] In the latter half of 1936, Ley gathered up the powers that remained to him as head of the PO's offices for organizational deployment and in-service training and issued over his signature a massive scheme reorganizing and streamlining the various jurisdictional levels of the party organization. The preparations had been apparent for some time. Throughout the year, the various Gaus and districts began publication of printed information sheets to regularize the flow of orders to their subordinate offices. Special training sessions acquainted virtually every Gau staff official with his duties and responsibilities.[412] Ley shared Hitler's enthusiasm for uniform and title design, and issued extremely detailed instructions on such matters throughout the year.[413]

Although Ley claimed to be hard at work codifying his various reform proposals throughout 1935, and promised to issue his *Organisationsbuch* (*Organizational Handbook*) in November of that year,[414] the massive work did not in fact appear until late in 1936. Then, however, Ley announced it modestly as the book that would answer all questions.[415] In its published form the *Organisationsbuch* was less a new departure than a reworking of Ley's numerous "suggestions," which had appeared throughout all the volumes of the 1935 *Statistik* (*Statistics*). Insofar as Ley's effort was organizational and definitional, it clearly served the position of the party as a whole, but as before, his primary goal was not service-oriented but power-oriented. Seemingly, the heart

410. Cf. GL Kaufmann's "Erklärung," 13 Feb. 1948, Forsch. Hbg./PA/12/L.

411. Harold Scholtz, "Die 'NS-Ordensburgen,'" *Vjh.f.Z.*, XV (July 1967), 280.

412. The scheduled meetings are listed in various issues of *Rdschr.*, III.

413. See *Schulungsbrief*, III (Sept. 1936); and Gau Berlin, *Gau*, no. 1 (1 Jan. 1936).

414. Ley to Hess, 31 Oct. 1935, T-580, roll 549, folder 746.

415. ROL, "Rundschreiben," 26 Oct. 1936, T-580, roll 521, folder 37; ROL, *Organisationsbuch der NSDAP*, 2d ed. (Munich, 1936), p. 487. The various editions of the *Organisationsbuch* will be cited hereafter as *Organisationsbuch*, 2 (1936), etc. The 1936 edition of the *Organisationsbuch* had been planned as a definitive publication, requiring only minor changes in the years to come. See *Organisationsbuch*, 2 (1936), p. xviii; *VOBl*, no. 167 (30 April 1938); and Gau Berlin, *Gau*, nos. 22 and 36 (15 Nov. 1936 and 1 June 1937), pp. 340 and 110 respectively.

of the *Organisationsbuch* was an endless series of job descriptions and jurisdictional delineations which, in their totality, established three basic principles: the verticalization of the PO,[416] the superiority of the party in its relationship to state offices,[417] and the stipulation that there should be two vertical lines of authority in the NSDAP: the affiliates' functionary corps, headed by the Reichsleiters, and the PO with the deputy Führer at the apex. The last feature of the work was the most explosive politically, because with it Ley attempted to have the ROL replace the StdF's office as the most important Reich party office. The basis of Ley's claim was his dual position as Reich organizational leader and head of the DAF. In this capacity, Robert Ley was the only Reichsleiter who both had a PO cadre position and controlled a major affiliate. As a result, the dual line of PO officials and affiliate functionaries came to a single apex (aside from Hitler himself)[418] in the person of Ley as head of the DAF and the PO. To be sure, a proposed institution, the party senate, would stand above even Robert Ley,[419] but he knew as well as every other party leader that Hitler would never appoint that body for fear of endangering his own absolute control.

Ley's method became very apparent in his "descriptions" of the roles played by the offices of the Reich treasurer, the plenipotentiary for Nazi philosophy (the catchall office of Alfred Rosenberg, BÜE), and the StdF in the NSDAP. Schwarz's formal authority was described accurately enough, including his extensive auditing rights over all party organizations, but the *Organisationsbuch* nevertheless managed to convey the impression that the Reich treasurer had solely administrative powers, a description that all but denied Schwarz's successful efforts to gain absolute control over the vertical cadre personnel of his office.[420] Ley accorded an even more cavalier treatment to the office of his archenemy Alfred Rosenberg. Although Hitler's 1934 directive had

---

416. Even top civil servants were, as party members, subordinate to the local leader in charge of their area of residence. The latter was, however, asked not to "abuse" his position of authority. *Organisationsbuch*, 2 (1936), p. 12. See also *ibid.*, pp. 486–551.

417. Schäfer, *NSDAP*, p. 72; and Helmut Mehringer, *Die NSDAP als politische Ausleseorganisation* (Munich, 1938), p. 104.

418. *Organisationsbuch*, 2 (1936), p. 148.

419. *Ibid.*, pp. 487–88.

420. *Ibid.*, pp. 286–94.

assigned the BÜE supervisory functions in the area of curriculum development for the party's training system, the *Organisationsbuch* contained no mention of it. The *Organizational Handbook* reduced Rosenberg's complex of offices to the publication of the periodical *NS-Monatshefte*.[421] Above all, the handbook was a major attempt to shunt the StdF into the politically dead-end area of party-state liaison, rather than party coordination and control, and to deny his supervisory powers over the DAF.[422]

In the handbook, Hess's loss was Ley's gain. The Queen of Hearts would have been proud of Ley's ability to let the title "organizational leader" mean precisely what he wanted it to mean—certainly nothing less. The ROL did acknowledge Hess's political control of the entire party, but in practical terms Hess's powers seemed to matter very little. Ley described the ROL's jurisdictional sphere as "administration, organization, personnel decisions, and discipline." And, lest the impact of that statement not be clear, he added that in-service training, personnel policy, and organization formed a single unit of party activity; so that cadre selection fell definitely within Ley's sphere.[423] Obviously, the realization of Ley's claims depended upon the Hoheitsträgers' willingness to accept his office as the apex of their vertical structure, and upon his ability to retain control of personnel policy in the NSDAP.

The organizational leader's primary method of working with the territorial cadre leaders was bribery. Generally, the *Organisationsbuch* acknowledged the Hoheitsträgers' authority over all PO personnel in their area of jurisdiction and at least their disciplinary control over the functionaries of the affiliates as well.[424] Ley was particularly concerned about the Gauleiters. Formally, he assigned them total control over their immediate staffs; the handbook made no mention of the special relationship which the StdF's office was attempting to establish with the deputy Gauleiters and inspectors.[425] In addition, Ley attempted to expand the Gauleiters' appointment powers by decreeing the rapid growth

421. *Ibid.*, p. 312.

422. The *Organisationsbuch* described the Gau economic advisors, who were Hess's direct subordinates and overseers of the DAF in their areas, as "honorary advisors." *Ibid.*, p. 336.

423. *Ibid.*, pp. 78–81, and 154.

424. *Ibid.*, pp. 157–61.

425. *Ibid.*, p. 140.

of the horizontal offices at the district level—these functionaries were subject to appointment by the Gauleiters.[426] Far more important, however, Ley became the provincial leaders' champion against the oppression of the Reich treasurer. In a letter to the StdF, Ley wrote that twenty Gauleiters had complained that "the party exists for the Reich treasurer." He demanded a restoration of the Gauleiters' financial sovereignty.[427] Ley also generously offered to help finance the Gauleitungs with DAF funds.[428]

Ley realized, of course, that Hitler had already expressed himself on the matter of personnel policy in the party, and he made no attempt to alter the terms of Hitler's April 1935 decree; the *Organisationsbuch* merely reprinted the provisions of Hitler's directive.[429] But Ley treated nomination and promotion as entirely separate issues. Here a detailed description of the ROL's main personnel office revealed that it intended to do far more than perform mechanical handmaiden services for the StdF's personnel office.[430] Ley put particular emphasis on the authority of his office for personnel in the PO and the affiliates and on the need for PO cadres to have experience in the affiliates, particularly the DAF. Indeed, for the lower levels the handbook all but decreed a merger of the PO and the labor organization.[431]

Despite the readily apparent value for the party's administration of many of Ley's proposals, in its totality the *Organisationsbuch* was a challenge to at least three Reichsleiters: Hess, Rosenberg, and Schwarz. There came about a complete break between Ley and Rosenberg,[432] and while this alone was of no great import, Schwarz and Hess had more powerful weapons at their disposal. The Reich treasurer concen-

426. *Ibid.*, pp. 10 and 79–80.
427. Hess to Ley, 14 April 1936, T-580, roll 549, folder 746.
428. Diehl-Thiele, *Partei*, p. 213.
429. *Organisationsbuch*, 2 (1936), p. 19.
430. *Ibid.*, p. 173.
431. *Ibid.*, pp. xxiv, 13, and 156.
432. Ley accused Rosenberg of violations of their previous working agreement. At the same time the controversy revealed the potential danger of accepting funds from Ley: as a consequence of the break the ROL cut off all DAF subsidies to Rosenberg's office. See Ley to Rosenberg, 6 May 1936, in the Centre Documentation Juive Contemporaine/CXLII–375.

trated his attacks on the instability of Ley's organizational reforms[433] and on the judicial difficulties of the DAF,[434] which were usually the result of financial mismanagement.[435] Moreover, even the Gauleiters saw Ley's support as a Trojan horse. Ley's organizational mania had created many of the Gaus' financial problems, and in some respects the remedy seemed worse than the disease: the Gauleiters already resented Ley's favoritism toward the DAF.[436]

In the area of personnel training and cadre selection the ROL faced the combined opposition of Schwarz and Hess.[437] This was understandable, since here, in essence, lay the heart of Ley's future plans. Ley was an ideological fanatic. He sincerely wanted to convert all Germans to his version of the Nazi Weltanschauung,[438] and, since "educating" an entire nation was a stupendous undertaking, he saw his training system and its product, the "political soldier," as the foundation of all NSDAP activities. Accordingly, Ley had established or planned to build schools and training centers for every conceivable type of functionary in the PO and the affiliates. Gau and district training "castles" were already in operation. These were used primarily to train incumbent PLs in a series of weekend and two-week courses. In addition, the Gau schools selected particularly promising cadre material for special sessions at the Reich schools.[439] In most of the "Gau training castles," the course content consisted primarily of instruction in the proper application of the prevailing Nazi propaganda line to the PLs' routine administrative tasks.[440] Only a few of the Gau schools attempted to prepare young

433. See Rschm., "Bekanntgabe 16/36," 29 June 1936, *Rdschr.*, III; and Lükemann, "Reichsschatzmeister," p. 106.

434. Schwarz to Ley, 25 May 1936, BDC/Ley (PKC).

435. For the problems of the DAF in the courts, see the documentation in T-580, roll 834, box 257, folder 278.

436. GL Röwer to Schwarz, 20 Jan. 1936, BDC/Röwer (PKC); and the auditor for Süd-Hannover-Braunschweig, 20 May 1936, T-580, roll 817, box 244, folder 98.

437. Schwarz to Bormann, 23 Sept. 1941, T-580, roll 77, folder 363.

438. Volker R. Berghahn, "NSDAP und 'Geistige Führung' der Wehrmacht 1939–1943," *Vjh.f.Z.*, VII (Jan. 1969), 18, n. 3. See also Ley, "Der Aufbau des Hauptschulungsamtes," in Robert Ley, *Wir alle helfen dem Führer*, ed. Heinrich Simon (Munich, 1937), pp. 143–47.

439. "Vernehmung [Amandus] Brandts," 3 May 1947, Forsch. HBG./PA/12/B.

440. Scholtz, "NS-Ordensburgen," p. 283.

political leaders for decision-making roles within the PO.[441] As a result, the curricula were heavily permeated with Ley's pedagogical ideas, and the PLs sank into their beds at night exhausted from their daily athletic contests and paramilitary games.[442] If intellectual topics were touched upon at all, they came in the form of lectures devoted to a glorified history of the Nazi movement and other themes designed to reinforce already prevalent prejudices against the Treaty of Versailles, communism, Soviet Russia, and so on. The aim was to create a political leader who was above all a convinced propagandist. The entire system emphasized the ideological Betreuungs-fanatic that remained Ley's goal, rather than the decision-making role stressed in the StdF's office.[443] The district-level schooling was essentially similar to that at the Gau level, except in Berlin, where a so-called flying Gau school moved from district to district with a team of instructors to bring the training center to the political leaders on the spot, rather than concentrating them in a particular locale surrounded by the accouterments of Teutonic castles.[444] (The affiliates, of course, ran their own institutions.)[445] For the future, Ley's plans were even more ambitious. At the center of each local would be a proud "local castle" (*Ortsburg*) as the symbol of the party's ongoing educational efforts. The local leader would become commissioner of education, charged among his other duties, with selecting promising HJ members for further training at the *Napolas*,[446] one of the party's systems of elite schools for boys between twelve and eighteen. Since there were as yet few Napolas, Ley planned to construct one in each district, appointing the district leader school supervisor.[447] For the graduates of the Napolas, Ley built the crowning achievement of his pedagogical system, the *Ordensburgen* (literally "order castles";

441. Gau Hamburg, *Gaunachrichten*, Barmbeck-Nord edition, III (1 June 1937), 17.

442. *Ibid.* (15 June 1937), p. 7; Gau Berlin, *Gau*, no. 55 (1 March 1938), p. 54.

443. GL Grohé, "Stimmungs- und Lagebericht . . . vom 19. März 1937," T-580, roll 546, folder 616.

444. Gau Berlin, *Gau*, no. 22 (15 Nov. 1936), p. 345.

445. For concrete examples see *ibid.*, no. 10 (15 May 1936), p. 190; and *Mittbl. Kr. Mü.*, no. 25 (25 June 1936).

446. On the development of the Napolas see Horst Ueberhorst, *Elite für die Diktatur* (Düsseldorf, 1968).

447. Ley, "Die Gemeinschaftshäuser der Partei und die Erziehung des Führernachwuchses," in Ley, *Wir alle*, pp. 138–39.

training institutes for the party's cadres). On April 24, 1936, Hitler formally accepted the Ordensburgen as the DAF's gift to the party, though at the time he was careful not to endorse Ley's educational philosophy in public.[448]

The practical and philosophical objections to various aspects of Ley's plans were numerous. To begin with, the curricula were virtually undifferentiated among the various types of functionaries; even mayors spent their training weekends doing physical exercises and listening to pseudophilosophical lectures on German prehistory. As a result, many PLs attempted to avoid the training sessions, and those who were unable to do so complained that they derived little benefit from them.[449] And, having returned home with sore muscles, the functionaries got no more practical advice from Ley's basic training paper, the *Schulungsbrief*, a sort of political weekly reader. Throughout the year no articles appeared on practical political issues; instead, the editors ranged over such varied topics as medieval history, "racial science," German colonialism, and Richard Wagner. An analysis of the question and answer column for the same time period shows a preponderance of items dealing with the DAF and with proper appearance in public (uniforms, insignia, and so on); a total of only seven items was devoted to judicial, insurance, training, propaganda, and administrative affairs of the party.

In the long run, the most disastrous of Ley's measures from the StdF's point of view was the training system for PL replacements. The one thing it could not produce was a PL corps suitable for a leadership role throughout the German industrialized society. The best evidence is a sort of involuntary self-indictment published in a series of articles in the DAF daily, *Der Angriff*.[450] The pieces emphasized as particular virtues what were in fact the most serious defects of the system: the lack of separate curricula for those wishing to become officials in the PO, the paramilitary organizations, the affiliates, or, for that matter, the governmental civil service; and the anti-intellectualism of the order castles. Examinations at the Ordensburgen tested rote memory; one of the *Der Angriff* articles used this phrase: the answers "came off like

448. Scholtz, "NS-Ordensburgen," pp. 276–77.
449. See *Mittbl. Kr. Mü.*, no. 25 (25 June 1936).
450. See van Berk, "Die härteste Schule." The series appeared in the issues of 26, 28, and 31 March, and 1 and 2 April 1937.

arrows from above." Given the resources available to the *Ordensjunker*, the official title for students at the training institutes, little else could be demanded. A typical Ordensburg had a library of three hundred volumes; that is, one book for every four students. But this number seems to have sufficed, since the trainees were not avid readers. They read even fewer newspapers than the average German. Ley substituted faith for method ("a Führer is born, not made," was his philosophy),[451] but this hardly produced promising PL material.

The number of applicants and the quality of the candidates was extremely low; and thus the bulk of the trainees at the Ordensburgen were in fact not an elite, but simply an opportunistic group for whom the Ordensburgen and a party career represented a marked improvement over their present, mediocre jobs. In 1936–37 those applying for acceptance to the order castles were not graduates of the Napolas, but "old fighters" without a job. A year later, the candidates came primarily from the working classes. In fact, those who were on the job market before they became Ordensburg candidates seldom earned more than RM 200 per month, a figure well below the national average.[452] Although this development may have been ideologically gratifying, most of these future PLs had only a grade school education and were therefore ill-prepared for higher leadership positions. As a result, the Ordensburgen gained a reputation as a career dead end, and in 1938–39 Ley had to accept DAF members because not enough party members applied for admission.[453] Since a substantial number of the candidates found the curriculum and atmosphere highly tedious and left the schools at the end of two years, rather than staying the normal three years, the actual graduates were a group of ill-trained, physically perfect specimens with low intelligence and high expectations. Indeed, most of them felt entitled to become at least a district leader after their Ordensburg sojourn. As a matter of fact, they faced severe disappointments. Schwarz, who had no great opinion of Ley's products, seldom allocated funds which

451. See the directive of the organizational and personnel leaders of the Gau München-Oberbayern in *Mittbl. Kr. Mü.*, no. 24 (18 June 1936).

452. Otto Schmidt, "Bericht über die Tagung des Hauptschulungsamtes in Oberursel am 7. and 8. Mai 1938," 13 May 1938. T-454, roll 77, frames 135–36.

453. Scholtz, "NS-Ordensburgen," p. 287; and Schoenbaum, *Hitler's Social Revolution*, pp. 270–72. See also the list of successful candidates for the Munich district in *Mittbl. Kr. Mü.*, no. 20 (20 May 1936).

were commensurate with the job expectations of these freshly spawned PLs.[454] Late in 1936 Schirach and Ley agreed to establish yet another school system, the Adolf Hitler Schools (AHS) for twelve-to-eighteen-year-olds, but since neither the standards of selection nor the curricula differed essentially from those of the order castles, the new creation merely compounded the already existing problems.[455]

In terms of its practical results, Ley's grandiose educational system, like his reform efforts, was a stillborn concept. In particular, the elite schools graduated men who were the opposite of sophisticated. Rather, they arrogantly worshiped themselves and the present; their concern for the future was minimal. As a result, neither the Gauleiters nor, at this time, Hitler seems to have thought much of the schools or their products.[456] In this sense, Ley's reforms had primarily a negative result. They demonstrated rather forcefully that Ley's concepts were thoroughly unsuitable as the basis for the development of an effective power position for the NSDAP in the Third Reich.

Ley's failure was not unique. The NSDAP as a whole at the end of 1936 could also be described as a failure. Shortly after Hitler assumed the chancellorship, he had boasted that he would ask the German people to judge his record at the end of four years,[457] and while much had changed in Germany since the beginning of 1933, neither Hitler nor the party could be wholly satisfied with the results of their efforts at this point.

Ironically, the Nazi Party had succeeded to a far greater extent in limiting the freedom of action of the other power segments in German society than it had in solving its own internal problems. Hitler's take-over of the powers of the presidency, the DGO, the law on the civil service, the Nuremberg laws were all milestones in the continuing pattern of legalized Nazi Party interference in all aspects of German societal relations. Still, they were reactions; the NSDAP remained too paralyzed with internal conflicts to develop a unified grand design of partification.

454. Scholtz, "NS-Ordensburgen," pp. 278, n. 26, 285, 288, and 288, n. 46.
455. On the Adolf-Hitler-Schools see Dietrich Orlow, "Die Adolf-Hitler-Schulen," *Vjh.f.Z.*, XIII (July 1965), 272–84; and for a somewhat different and more recent interpretation, Scholtz, "NS-Ordensburgen."
456. Scholtz, "NS-Ordensburgen," p. 277; Speer, *Erinnerungen*, p. 532, n. 2; and GL Grohé, "Stimmungsbericht," 13 May 1936, T-580, roll 546, folder 616.
457. Domarus, *Hitler*, I, 207.

True, the purges of 1934 had confirmed the PO's position as a major power grouping in the party, but within the cadres themselves bitter conflicts between Hess, Schwarz, and Ley continued unabated. Ley was steadily losing ground, yet as long as Hitler refused to denounce the Betreuung concept as unworkable, Hess could not apply his plans for the reorganization of the PO on a large scale. Hitler refused to solve the dilemma. He preferred to think that territorial expansion would not only bring him closer to his goal of European hegemony, but render the party's internal problems insignificant as well.

Stalemate at Home, Expansion Abroad

The years 1936 and 1937 represent a watershed for the history of the
Nazi Party in a number of respects. Beginning, really, with the Rhineland crisis, Hitler turned increasingly from domestic concerns to the
pursuit of an aggressive foreign policy.[1] The Reichsreform ceased to be
an acute political issue, and such territorial changes as were approved
by Hitler found his favor precisely because they were not part of an
overall Reichsreform.[2] Ley's administrative reforms, which found their
culmination with the publication of the *Organisationsbuch* late in 1936,
were the closing of an era in party-state and intraparty relations rather
than a new beginning. In the *Altreich* (the territory of the Reich prior
to the annexation of Austria) party and state settled down to an uneasy
coexistence. The state accepted defeat in the personnel affairs of the
civil service[3] (although the shortage of trained party-oriented personnel allowed the defeat to appear rather undramatic) and, as the numerous awards of golden party badges to high civil and military officials
at the beginning of 1937 showed, the conservatives who dominated the

1. A. J. P. Taylor, *The Origins of the Second World War*, 2d ed. (New York,
1961), p. 287.
2. The most important territorial change was the creation of the Greater Hamburg administrative district in the fall of 1937. (For details, see pp. 224–25.)
Hitler, however, specifically prohibited efforts by Berlin and Munich in the same
direction, although Hess approved of these efforts. See Lammers to Regierungspräsident Potsdam, 12 Dec. 1936; Tempel (city councillor, Munich), to Lammers,
11 Feb. 1937; and Lammers to Tempel, 22 Feb. 1937, Bundesarchiv (cited hereafter as BA)/R 43 II/572 b.
3. For a fuller discussion see below, pp. 226–28.

civil service recognized the ideological supremacy of the party.[4] The old battles over the partification of German society were by no means concluded. On the contrary, the disputes continued; their scenes were merely transferred from the Altreich to the territories annexed by Germany between the spring of 1938 and the summer of 1943.

In this sense it was no more than fitting that Hitler's personal life began about 1937 to follow the patterns that characterized his daily routine during the war years. The familiar picture of nocturnal work sessions (necessitated by a Führer who seldom rose before noon) and endless monologues over empty tea cups emerged next to the already present highly irregular work habits in the last two years before the outbreak of the war. In these years, too, Hitler increased his withdrawal from his old contacts and his flights to the Obersalzberg sanctuary.[5] The Führer's numerous retreats to the "mountain," as the Obersalzberg was called in party circles, increased the importance of Martin Bormann. Hitler did not—yet—become disenchanted with Hess,[6] but as the man in charge of the administration and construction of the Obersalzberg complex,[7] the StdF's chief of staff became Hitler's almost constant companion,[8] while Hess and other party leaders remained in Munich or Berlin. As a result, Bormann in practice assumed more and more the duties of an official whose title he would not bear for another five years, that of Hitler's private secretary. Bormann increasingly controlled access and proximity to Hitler; for the 1937 party congress he was in charge of room assignments for party leaders in Hitler's hotel. The Führer, in turn, placed explicit trust in Martin Bormann. When Hitler

4. Max Domarus, ed., *Hitler, Reden und Proklamationen 1932–1945* (Munich, 1965), I, 678–79. These awards were more than a formality; recognizing this, the Reich minister for postal services, v. Rübenach, refused to accept his golden badge. *Ibid.*, p. 679.

5. This picture of Hitler's changing life patterns is drawn from Albert Speer, *Erinnerungen* (Berlin, 1969), p. 97; Otto Dietrich, *Zwölf Jahre mit Hitler* (Cologne, 1955), pp. 198–201; and Albert Zoller, *Hitler privat* (Düsseldorf, 1949), p. 21.

6. Speer, *Erinnerungen*, p. 93.

7. See Bormann (writing on stationery with the letterhead "Administration of the Obersalzberg"), "Rundschreiben," 5 Oct. 1938, BA/NS6/231. On the Obersalzberg project see also Speer, *Erinnerungen*, pp. 98 and 100–01; and Kurt Borsdorff, "Mit Reichsleiter Martin Bormann auf dem Obersalzberg," p. 8, National Archives, Microcopy No. T- (cited hereafter as T-) 580, roll 79, folder 368.

8. Borsdorff, "Reichsleiter Martin Bormann," pp. 6, 8, and 9; and Joseph Wulf, *Martin Bormann* (Gütersloh, 1962), p. 27.

made a new will in 1938, he named Bormann deputy executor (Schwarz remained chief executor).[9]

Hess's deputy became an integral member of Hitler's innermost circle, but the party as a whole took little part in the issues that were foremost in Hitler's mind during these years. With the appointment of Hermann Göring as administrator of the Four Year Plan, Hitler had all but excluded the NSDAP from the decision-making process in German economic life. Göring had never been a "party man," and his close ties to heavy industry circles could only be interpreted as an affront to the small business interests represented by Bernhard Köhler. Indeed, in a number of instances the old economic interests had absorbed whole cliques in the party.[10] The formerly powerful NS-Hago (as well as the rabidly anti-Semitic *Stürmer* magazine)[11] attempted to continue the battle against Jewish retailers and all department stores,[12] but the party as a whole had no interest in reviving the controversies of 1933.[13] The NSDAP's direct concern with the Four Year Plan was restricted to reporting the public's reaction to the resulting shortages,[14] and, of course, to serving as the plan's propagandistic handmaiden. Göring had hoped that the party would contribute financially to his business enterprises, but Schwarz, in whose office the party's handling of the Four Year Plan was concentrated,[15] refused.[16]

9. Gerhard L. Weinberg, "Hitler's Private Testament, May 2, 1938," *Journal of Modern History*, XXVII (Dec. 1955), 419.

10. See the documents in the Berlin Document Center (cited hereafter as BDC)/ Nathusius (SS). Nathusius was a high SS official in Hamburg who was involved in a series of political and business scandals.

11. Heinrich Uhlig, *Die Warenhäuser im Dritten Reich* (Cologne-Opladen, 1956), p. 169.

12. See "Niederschrift über eine Besprechung zwischen Eiffe und Dr. Heffter," 24 Feb. 1950, Forschungsstelle für die Geschichte des Nationalsozialismus in Hamburg (cited hereafter as Forsch. Hbg.)/PA/12/E. Eiffe was the representative of the city-state of Hamburg in Berlin. See also the issues of Gau Berlin, *Gau*, for 1936 and 1937.

13. The StdF issued a directive noting that department stores were contrary to the principles of national socialism ("Anordnung 134/37," 23 Oct. 1937, T-580, roll 346, folder 1), but the order carried with it no permission to resume nationwide attacks on these stores.

14. StdF, "Rundschreiben 142/36," 10 Nov. 1936, T-580, roll 13, folder 171.

15. Anton Lingg, *Die Verwaltung der Nationalsozialistischen Deutschen Arbeiterpartei*, 2d ed. (Munich, 1940), p. 221.

16. Ruoff to Saupert, 15 Nov. 1937, T-580, roll 813, box 242, folder 84. Indi-

The impact of Ley's reforms on the daily routine of the PO also forced the party to forego a forceful role in the political decisions of 1937. Ley was unable to prevail in his attempt to upset the balance of power in the NSDAP, but there is no doubt that his more mechanical reforms effected a number of changes, especially at the lower territorial level. The publication of the *Organisationsbuch* did lead to a more effective verticalization and bureaucratization of the PO offices from block to local.[17] The ROL worked hard at this task. Pedantic as usual, Ley's office requested the Gaus to send in copies of their official information sheets (*Mitteilungsblätter* or *Nachrichtenblätter*). These were then returned with long-winded comments on layout, content, and so on.[18] Special articles in the *Mitteilungsblätter* detailed the functions of various cadre positions for the PLs.[19] Within the locals, familiarizing the PLs with the new regulations even took precedence over such vital matters as pistol-shooting practice.[20] The local party organizations really strove to translate Ley's Betreuungs theories into actual practice; they attempted to become the focal point of all public activities within the community.[21]

In the steps above the local in the party's territorial hierarchy, the district and Gau levels, the Achilles heel of Ley's reforms was already glaringly apparent. As before, the ROL stumbled over the practical impossibility of combining power and Betreuung into a workable concept for the entire NSDAP. The statement that "the district leader is directly subordinate to the Gauleiter; functional (*fachliche*) directives

---

rectly, NSDAP officials did participate prominently in the administration of the Four Year Plan. GL Joseph Wagner, for example, became the new Reich price commissioner.

17. See Gau Berlin, *Gau*, no. 21 (1 Nov. 1936), p. 326; Gau organizational leader Magdeburg-Anhalt to ROL, 9 April 1937, BA/NS 22/577; and the documents in BA/NS 22/580.

18. See ROL to Gau organization leader of Danzig, 5 May 1937, BA/NS 22/540.

19. See Gau Berlin, *Gau*, no. 21 (1 Nov. 1936), pp. 324 and 326; and Gau München-Oberbayern, *Mitteilungsblatt des Kreises München der NSDAP* (cited hereafter as *Mittbl. Kr. Mü.*), nos. 41, 49, 50, and 51/52 (15 Oct., 10, 17, and 31 Dec. 1936), pp. 4–5, 3–4, 2–3, and 2–3 respectively.

20. Gau organizational leader Magdeburg-Anhalt to ROL, 9 April 1937, BA/NS 22/577. See also *Mittbl. Kr. Mü.*, nos. 41–46 (15 Oct.–19 Nov. 1936).

21. See the lists of projects in *Mittbl. Kr. Mü.* (nos. for Nov. and Dec. 1936), and the remarks of Nippold (deputy GL of München-Oberbayern) on the image of the party at a district congress, *ibid.*, no. 41 (15 Oct. 1936), p. 2.

by the relevant Gau office heads are binding upon the district leader"[22] clarified the authority of neither the Gauleiter nor the district leader. Similarly, the seemingly clear statement that the National Socialist Association of Civil Servants, the NSBB, was responsible for assuring that the personnel in state offices was "in line with" (*ausgerichtet*) Nazi ideas[23] in effect muddied the equally clear directive that only a Hoheitsträger could give political evaluations. At the Gau level, Ley's inability to differentiate between the significant and the formally routine had the most serious consequences for the success of his reforms. The Gauleiters, usually no outstanding administrators to begin with, already overburdened (by their own choice) with a variety of state and party jobs, became inundated with routine paper work demanded by the ROL's central offices.[24] As a consequence, most Gauleiters simply ignored the detailed directives of the *Organizational Handbook*.[25] Ley did not seem to mind:[26] as was often the case with him, he lost interest in the reform project after it had achieved concrete form on paper. There was more than a grain of truth in Rosenberg's accusation that Ley's primary motive in launching the 1936 reforms was to satisfy his personal vanity.[27]

While Ley kept virtually every PL busy trying to recognize the rank of a functionary by the color of his uniform decorations, parallel developments in the office of the StdF went practically unnoticed by the propagandistic organs of the Third Reich. Hess's staff did pursue a few favorite projects in the larger political sphere—notably the continuing efforts to reduce the influence of the churches[28] and to install counter-

22. ROL, *Organisationsbuch der NSDAP*, 2 (Munich, 1936), p. 131.

23. *Ibid.*, p. 247.

24. For documentation see T-580, rolls 346 and 347.

25. Karl Wahl, *Es ist das deutsche Herz* (Augsburg, 1954), p. 185. For additional criticism see also Gau Berlin, organization office to Ley, 28 July 1939, BA/NS 22/638.

26. By early 1937 a number of Gaus had stopped sending in monthly activity reports, but the ROL's office seemed to make no effort to revive the practice. See Gau training leader Weser-Ems, "Tätigkeitsbericht für den Monat Dezember 1936," 9 Jan. 1937; and Gau Hamburg, "Tätigkeitsbericht . . . März 1937," 20 April 1937, BA/NS 22/577.

27. [Rosenberg's office], "Bericht," ca. 1941, T-81, roll 23, frame 20548.

28. See Rolf Eilers, *Die nationalsozialistische Schulpolitik* (Cologne, 1963), pp. 91 and 108–09; and Klaus Scholder, "Die evangelische Kirche in der Sicht der na-

parts of Soviet-style commissars in the Reichswehr[29]—but on the whole
the energies of the StdF were directed toward the internal strengthening of the staff structure. The process could be most effectively described
by the terms "routinization," "personnel expansion," and "task differentiation." In October 1936 the StdF had a staff of fifty full-time functionaries. As a group, the staffers exhibited a number of interesting characteristics. It was top-heavy with high-ranking functionaries. Of the
fifty, more than half (twenty-seven) were confirmed in the rank of
department head (*Amtsleiter*) or higher, that is, they held what were
then the three highest ranks in the PL corps.[30] New additions to the
staff were typically men who were relatively young and who also had
good connections with other party organizations. Wilhelm Zander, for
example, who joined the staff early in 1937, was born in 1911. He joined
the NSDAP in 1931, receiving the membership number 552,659. Somewhat later, he became a member of the SS as well. His superior in the
SS described his as "especially valuable, constantly ready to make
sacrifices for the movement, a fanatical, experienced National Socialist."
On the staff of the StdF and the party chancellery, he became one of
Bormann's trouble-shooters.[31] The functionaries also formed a highly
homogeneous social unit. Since virtually all of the staff's activities were
concentrated in Munich (Hess's liaison office in Berlin simply arranged
appointments for visiting party leaders and handled the deputy Führer's and Bormann's social obligations in Berlin),[32] all major staff officials worked in the Brown House. And they even lived together. At
Pullach, just outside Munich, a special settlement, consisting of twenty

tionalsozialistischen Führung bis zum Kriegsausbruch," *Vierteljahrshefte für Zeitgeschichte* (cited hereafter as *Vjh.f.Z.*, XVI (Jan. 1968), 28 and 30–32. Even in
this campaign individual initiative was uncalled for. GL Röver had to rescind an
order removing crucifixes from the schools of his Gau. See Austrian embassy to
Austrian foreign ministry, 16 Dec. 1936, BA/R 43 II/178.

29. Volker R. Berghahn, "NSDAP und 'Geistige Führung' der Wehrmacht 1939–
1943," *Vjh.f.Z.*, XVII (Jan. 1969), 19. See also Robert J. O'Neill, *The German
Army and the Nazi Party 1933–39* (London, 1968), p. 121.

30. *The Verordnungsblatt der Reichsleitung der NSDAP* (cited hereafter as
VOBl) published confirmation lists throughout 1936.

31. The quotation is drawn from an evaluation of Zander dated 16 Jan. 1937 in
the BDC/Zander (SS).

32. StdF, "Anordnung 107/39," 9 May 1939, T-580, roll 549, folder 746.

one- and two-story houses surrounded by a five-foot-high wall, was constructed to house the staff and their families.[33] The key to a smooth and efficient running of the staff machinery was, of course, Martin Bormann. Hess's chief of staff had no doubts about his importance and capabilities,[34] but on the whole the staff of 1937 was only inching its way toward the legendary omnipotent status of the later party chancellery. To begin with, Bormann was never an easy man to work for; he bullied and mistreated his subordinates mercilessly.[35] Perhaps as a result, he had continuing personnel problems. With the number of high-ranking functionaries on the staff, it was not surprising that some developed primadonna attitudes.[36] Bormann himself recognized a chronic shortage of "really able" PLs, especially in the division for internal party affairs.[37] Finally, Bormann's own peripatetic ways seem to have been contagious for some of his subordinates; the business manager complained that he often had to hunt down staff personnel in the *Osteria Bavaria*, a favorite party hangout in Munich.[38]

Nevertheless, the StdF's organization made considerable headway in its efforts to restructure the PL corps. Ley clung to the myth that the root of the problem lay in the party's "giving" a large number of PLs to the state,[39] but within the office of the StdF the cause had long been recognized as the "old fighters" themselves. Or, to put it even more brutally, the NSDAP did not give away an able PL corps because it never had one suitable for exercising power in an advanced society.

33. After the war the compound served as the headquarters of the West German Intelligence Agency. This description is drawn from the series "Pullach intern," in *Der Spiegel*, XXV (5 April 1971), 172.

34. Bormann to all GL, RL, affiliate, and paramilitary heads (personal and strictly confidential), 15 May 1941, Rijksinstituut voor Oorlogsdokumentatie, Amsterdam (cited hereafter as RvO)/BDC/H 1164. The BDC documents in the RvO are photocopies of records made by the RvO at the Berlin Document Center.

35. Speer, *Erinnerungen*, p. 101, reports that Bormann treated his subordinates "as though they were cows and oxen."

36. StdF, office of the business manager, "Vorlage an Stabsleiter," pp. 12–13, 21 June 1937, BA/NS 6/384.

37. Bormann wrote in 1943 that he had "screamed for years" about this state of affairs. See Bormann to Friedrichs, 11 May 1943, T-580, roll 80, folder 371.

38. StdF business manager "Vorlage," p. 12.

39. *Organisationsbuch*, 2 (1936), p. 152.

The "old fighters" were, by and large, "wild men," incompetent and vain, who looked upon the party as a refuge from the consequences of their own failures and whose rule had been a "nightmare" for the German people.[40] How, then, could a new PO be created? Further training by the ROL's organs was obviously useless. Relying on the existing Hoheitsträgers was similarly a dead end, since the clique conditions at the district and Gau levels made these territorial chiefs very unreliable judges of meritorious PLs.[41]

Instead, the StdF inaugurated a multistep plan. The first phase was to create a clear differentiation between full-time and part-time functionaries in the PO. The latter would be restricted to positions at the block and cell level, while the higher-ranking positions would be reserved for PLs who identified solely with the party. There is no doubt that a large number of PO functionaries had attempted to keep a foot in both the party and the state camp. Throughout the year the number of confirmations in office and dismissals among PLs were about the same. There were a variety of reasons involved,[42] but more often than not, a dismissal was the result of "transfer to a state office."[43] Table 7 reveals the extent of the problem at the Gau and district levels. Clearly, the most glaring anomaly in this tabulation was the status of the deputy Gauleiters. Only one of the five Gaus had a full-time deputy Gauleiter, even though this official was in most Gaus the highest PL concerned with the day-to-day administration of the PO. It was therefore more than understandable that the StdF's office became particularly concerned about the quality and full-time status of the deputy Gauleiters. Not only did the StdF demand an extensive evaluation of all present

40. Heinrich Heim, "Vorlage an Pg. Friedrichs," 12 April 1944, BA/NS 30/51.

41. For the districts see the issues of *Parteirichter*, IV (1937); and *Mittbl. Kr. Mü.*, no. 44 (5 Nov. 1936), p. 7. At the Gau level Hess noted that all too many complaints made by the Gauleiters proved, after investigation by his organs, to be groundless. See StdF, "Rundschreiben 138/36," 4 Nov. 1936, T-580, roll 13, folder 171.

42. Ley to GL Lohse, 25 March 1937, BA/NS 22/612.

43. This analysis is based upon the list of PL changes printed regularly in the *VOBl*. In October the StdF reinforced this divisional process by ruling that all full-time PLs had to resign from any additional state positions they held. See Hans Mommsen, *Beamtentum im Dritten Reich* (Stuttgart, 1966), p. 109.

TABLE 7

Division of Personnel at Gau and District Levels

	Offices							
		Political		Gau				
	Deputy GL	Dept. Heads[a]		Inspectors		Kreisleiters		
Gau	Full-Time	Part-Time	Full-Time	Part-Time	Full-Time	Part-Time	Full-Time	Part-Time
Hessen-Nassau	0	1	6	0	3	n.i.	6	30
Hamburg	0	1	4	2	0	3	3	12
Madgeburg-Anhalt	0	1	5	1	0	1	12	3
Bayrische-Ostmark	1	0	5	1	2	0	17	16
Danzig	0	1	4	2	n.i.	n.i.	0	9

Source: Compilation of Gau lists dated Feb. 1937 in BA/NS 22/536, 540, 579, 580, 590.

a. Personnel, organization, training.

n.i. = no information.

incumbents,[44] but he attempted to break up the prevailing Gau cliques whenever possible. The new men selected were at times StdF staffers (for example, Wegener in the Gau Ostmark), but more often old deputy Gauleiters transferred to a new Gau. In either case, the danger of a cliquish relationship between the "old fighters" in the Gau and the deputy Gauleiter was considerably lessened, and thus the new deputy had to rely on the backing of the StdF's office to establish his authority.[45]

The deputy Gauleiters undoubtedly occupied key positions in the PO personnel structure, but quantitatively their appointment was of little import in restructuring the cadre functionaries. From the StdF's viewpoint, little could be done for the moment. The training program at the Brown House was "very useful,"[46] but numerically its effect was negligible. The StdF did manage to exclude the ROL's office from the

44. For examples see Grohé's evaluation of his deputy GL in BDC/Schaller (PKC); and J. Wagner's judgment of his associate Bracht in BDC/Bracht (SS).

45. For an example of the struggles between the "old fighters" of a Gau and a new deputy GL, see the documents in BDC/Peper (PKC). See also Telschow's (GL Osthannover) evaluation of Peper, 8 Aug. 1936, *ibid.*; and n.a., "Aktennotiz: . . . Personalien im Gau Sudetenland und im Gau Osthannover," 10 Feb. 1940, BDC/Donnevert (PKC), part II.

46. StdF, "Anordnung 141/36," 7 Nov. 1936, T-580, roll 13, folder 171.

confirmation process for PLs,[47] and he realized that Ley's Ordensburg graduates were largely unsuitable for major PO positions,[48] but these, too, were negative, not positive decisions. Somewhat more promising, to carry the developments ahead a bit, were Hitler's renewed interest in the training of younger PLs[49] and the formal appointment of Christian Opdenhoff as head of the StdF's personnel office in November 1937.[50] The new man formulated his concepts very succinctly: the party needed a far more homogeneous, full-time PL staff, with a clear division between "total leadership personalities" (for example, the Gauleiters) and technical-political specialists, such as propaganda leaders, treasurers, and so on.[51] But precisely here lay the crux of the by no means new problem: to create a full-time PO corps, staffed with technically competent experts, the party, quite aside from any competency wrangles over personnel questions, needed sufficient sums of money to make a cadre career attractive for the ambitious, young, and opportunistic elements in German society.

The need for money was really the key reason for the reopening of the membership rolls in May 1937. The expected personnel expenses of the future added to the financial problems of the NSDAP in 1937, but they did not create them. To be sure, the number of full-time functionaries at the various Reichsleitung offices in Munich had already increased from 2,546 at the end of 1936 to 3,172 a year later.[52] There were other contributing factors as well. Ley kept establishing new offices, which, even when staffed with volunteer or part-time PLs, required certain budgetary expenses.[53] Many of the Gaus were still either in debt or mismanaged, or both.[54] Since, in addition, the provincial leaders

47. See the documentation in BA/NS 22/568.

48. Joachim Ruoff, "Besuchs-Vermerk . . . Amtsleiter Opdenhoff," 12 Nov. 1937, T-580, roll 81, folder 393.

49. See Hitler's speech on September 6, 1937 in Nuremberg. Domarus, *Hitler*, I, 716.

50. StdF, "Rundschreiben," Nov. 17, 1937, BA/ NS 6/ 227.

51. Ruoff, "Besuchs-Vermerk . . . Amtsleiter Opdenhoff."

52. Reichsschatzmeister (cited hereafter as Rschm.), "Bilanz- und Finanzbericht der Reichsleitung der NSDAP 1937," 1 April 1938, p. 20, T-580, roll 833, box 256, folder 268.

53. [Rschm.], "Auszug aus der Niederschrift über die Gauschatzmeistertagung am 16./17.11.1936," T-580, roll 81, folder 393.

54. See the series of Gau audits in T-580, roll 806, box 239, folders 44 and 45.

kept demanding status symbols in accordance with their ambitions, rather than with the resources of their Gaus,[55] the results were massive subsidies to the Gaus by the Reich treasurer's office: RM 656,000 in 1936, RM 281,000 in 1937.[56] There was no decisive improvement in the districts. The Hoheitsträgers demanded high salaries,[57] but the funds were not forthcoming from the locals, many of which continued to be plagued with the nonpayment of dues by party members.[58] Paradoxically, the financial costs of the local and sublocal level had increased particularly dramatically since 1933.[59] Schwarz's somber description of the NSDAP's financial situation as "tense, though not dangerous,"[60] was quite correct.

There were other considerations involved in reopening the membership rolls, but they were clearly less vital. With this device the party hoped to force members of important socioeconomic groups still outside the NSDAP to join the party and thereby submit more directly to its political control processes.[61] Moreover, reopening the membership rolls was expected to help alleviate the shortage of PL cadres. It was already a widespread custom within the party to give low-level PL posts to individuals who were not members of the party,[62] but this pro-

---

The audits include the Gaus Bayerische Ostmark, Halle-Merseburg, Danzig, and Köln-Aachen.

55. Thus GL Hellmuth (Mainfranken) requested permission to purchase a Mercedes for RM 22,246, but Schwarz limited him to an expenditure of RM 15,000. See Schwarz to Hellmuth, 19 Jan. 1937, BDC/Hellmuth (PKC).

56. Rschm., "Bilanz 1937," p. 25.

57. Rschm., "Bericht über die Gauschatzmeistertagung am 25. November 1937," p. 9, T-580, roll 842, box 267, folder 348. Schwarz insisted that the heads of Gau staff offices should receive the same compensation as district leaders. *Ibid.*, p. 10.

58. Gau Berlin, *Gau*, no. 33 (15 April 1937), p. 83; and Hermann Haag, "Inspektionsbericht der Gauleitung Köln-Aachen der NSDAP," 23 Feb. 1937, T-580, roll 806, box 239, folder 45.

59. See the excerpts from Schwarz's speech to the GLs and Kreisleiters at the Ordensburg Sonthofen, 18 Nov. 1937, T-580, roll 829, folder 197; and Rschm., "Bericht, Nov. 1937."

60. [Rschm.], "Ressortbesprechung 1/37," 5 April 1937, T-580, roll 81, folder 393.

61. This was particularly true of judicial personnel. See Hermann Weinkauff, "Die deutsche Justiz und der Nationalsozialismus—Ein Überblick," in Weinkauff *et al., Die Deutsche Justiz und der Nationalsozialismus* (Stuttgart, 1968), I, 122; and Walter Buhl, "Eidesstattliche Erklärung," 7 Aug. 1947, Forsch. Hbg./PA/Rothenberger.

62. See "I. Gaulehrabteilung Barmbeck-Nord," Gau Hamburg, *Gaunachrichten*

cedure was obviously not suitable for district and Gau level positions. Rather, the influx of new members into low-level positions would free the present incumbents for promotion to middle- and upper-echelon posts.[63]

When the formal announcement of the reopening came it was almost an anticlimax. The move had been rumored and discussed since early 1936, but Schwarz had held back. He waited until every aspect of the new membership drive had been approved by Hitler[64] and until the Führer had confirmed all of the Gau treasurers in office.[65] The negotiations over the administration of the drive were marked by an informal but not entirely friendly rivalry between the offices of the StdF and the Reich treasurer.[66] Yet even after this conflict was resolved, with Schwarz getting his way,[67] the reopening involved a number of uncertainties and controversies. On paper, the list of those eligible for party membership seemed clear enough. At the end of April the Reich treasurer issued a sizable list of groups whose application for membership would be welcome. These included persons who had held continuous membership in the paramilitary organizations, the National Socialist Women's League, and the functionary corps of the DAF since October 1, 1934 (that is, since the first wave of the post-Röhm purge had been concluded). In addition, all cell and block leaders who had held office since October 1936, leading Hitler Youth officials (with no prescribed length of service), and individuals who had performed special services for the party were eligible.[68] The 1937 drive was, then, in no sense a full-scale opening of the party to all who wanted to join. Instead, Schwarz's cate-

---

(edition Barmbeck-Nord), III (1 July 1937), 7; and Gau Berlin, *Gau*, no. 54 (15 Feb. 1938), p. 41.

63. Gau Berlin, *Gau*, no. 54 (15 Feb. 1938), p. 41; and Rschm., "Anordnung," 11 May 1937, T-81, roll 91, frame 104033.

64. Schwarz to Himmler, 8 Oct. 1936, BDC/Himmler (PKC); and Schwarz to Hilgenfeldt, 12 Oct. 1936, BDC/Hilgenfeldt (PKC).

65. [Rschm.], "Ressortbesprechung 5/37 . . . 10.5.1937," 11 May 1937, T-580, roll 81, folder 393.

66. Hans Saupert (Schwarz's deputy), "Besprechungs-Vermerk," 3 March 1937, T-580, roll 81, folder 393.

67. Rschm., "Ressortbesprechung 5/ 37 . . . 10.5.1937," 11 May 1937, *ibid.*

68. Rschm., "Bekanntgabe," 20 April 1937, *VOBl*, no. 143 (30 April 1937), p. 486. See also Hans Buchheim, "Mitgliedschaft bei der NSDAP," in Paul Kluke, ed., *Gutachten des Instituts für Zeitgeschichte* (Munich, 1958), p. 316.

gories contained clear-cut political guidelines for the future development of the NSDAP. The last category, special services, was vague and was obviously a device to co-opt the conservative social and economic elite into the party. In effect, Schwarz, Hess, and Hitler wanted the NSDAP to receive as members the lower PLs, the purged SA and SS, the Hitler Youth leadership corps, and the functionaries of the DAF. Significantly, the political leadership had no interest in the mass of DAF members. As with most Nazi projects, what was clear on paper became muddled in practice. In the membership drive, the major difficulty lay in the multiplicity of offices involved in screening the new candidates. In February, Hess had issued a lengthy directive describing the evaluation process. Each prospective member had to be judged by the various personnel offices for political attitudes and by the party courts for moral character. In addition, the organizational leaders were to ascertain that the new members as a group represented a socioeconomic balance, while the party treasurers were to administer Schwarz's detailed technical directives. The evaluation of the candidates also included a very specific application of the 1935 Nuremberg laws.[69] Continuing the cooperation of the two offices, Schwarz repeated Hess's directives and added some regulations of his own relating to technical questions in a new directive dated June 1, 1937.[70]

The inability or unwillingness of the various offices to work together was undoubtedly a contributing factor to the disappointing financial and numerical result of the drive. The evaluation by officials at the local and county levels turned out to be considerably more careful, perhaps a better word is vindictive, than was originally expected. As a result, the party courts had to be involved in a far larger number of cases than anticipated.[71] There seems to have been a widespread, although uncoordinated, effort by the "old fighters" to sabotage the membership drive. At times they hid behind the technical directives. The Gau Berlin,

---

69. StdF, "Anordnung 24/37," 9 Feb. 1937, *Verfügungen, Anordnungen, Bekanntgaben* of the PK, I, 552–56.

70. Rschm., "Lockerung der Mitgliedersperre," Gau Berlin, *Gau*, no. 35 (15 May 1937), pp. 26–28; and Gauschatzmeister Berlin, "Aufnahmeverfahren," *ibid.*, no. 32 (1 June 1937), pp. 32–33.

71. Trautmann (deputy GL of Magdeburg-Anhalt) to the staff of the StdF, 30 May 1938, BDC/Jordan (PKC).

for example, went so far as to issue a forty-two page booklet giving in incredible detail the various technical requirements necessary to receive a new member.[72] At the local level, things were at times even more chaotic. The defensive measures reported in Gau journals were reminiscent of practices used to exclude black voters in the U.S. South: it appeared that many candidates failed the test of membership simply because they were unable to answer correctly the questions put to them by their local leader. Unfortunately, there is no record of what these difficult queries might have been.[73] Needless to add, these practices discouraged many prospective candidates from applying, particularly since refusal of an application could bring with it serious professional and economic consequences. Many of those eligible felt, according to an official in Schwarz's office, that it was safer to join one of the affiliates instead.[74] Consequently, applications flowed into Munich at a trickle. The Reich treasurer noted that by August several Gaus had still not submitted any candidate lists to the Munich office.[75] In the overall tabulations, the membership figures in individual localities and Gaus increased dramatically, at times as much as 100 or even 200 percent,[76] but the Reich increase from 2.4 million members at the beginning of May to 3.9 million at the end of 1938,[77] though significant, was not as large as might be anticipated in view of the number of persons eligible for membership. Accordingly, the financial rewards were equally dis-

72. *Richtlinien für das Mitgliedschaftwesen im Gau Berlin der NSDAP* ([Berlin, 1937]).

73. "O[rts]-G[ruppen] Versammlung in Lohbrügge," Gau Hamburg, *Gaunachrichten* (edition Hamburg-Land), III (15 July 1937), 7. See also the address by the deputy Gauleiter of Hamburg on the—obviously middle class—types not wanted in the party, "Nicht Spiessbürger, sondern Kämpfer sein," *ibid.* (edition district 3), V (1 Feb. 1939), 5.

74. Cottes [?] (auditor for the Gaus Westfalen-Nord and Hanover), "Stimmungsbericht," 31 Aug. 1937, T-580, roll 817, box 244, folder 98.

75. Rschm., "Bericht, Nov. 1937," p. 38.

76. The membership figures for the local Eisenach-Nord (Gau Thuringia) rose from 408 at the end of February 1938 to 1024 at the end of January 1939. See the undated tabulations in the University of Michigan German Archival Collection (cited hereafter as MiU/GAC), folder 1. The membership of the Gau Mainfranken climbed from about 35,000 to 67,000 in the same period. Gauschatzmeister Mainfranken to Reichsschatzmeister, "Stimmungsbericht 1938," 1 Feb. 1939, p. 5, T-580, roll 804, box 239, folder 40.

77. Rschm., "Bilanz 1937," p. 27.

appointing. To be sure, the party's income from dues was RM 23,616,-000 in 1937 as contrasted with RM 17,815,000 a year earlier. There was a sizable jump in application fees (RM 407,000 in 1936, RM 3,526,000 in 1937) but these were a direct result of the 1937 drive and could not be budgeted as an annual source of income.[78]

Despite its partially disappointing result, the 1937 membership drive was a major factor in clarifying the relationships between various power blocs in the NSDAP. As noted above, preparations for the membership reopening had led to at least a momentary lapse in the cordial relations between the StdF and the Reich treasurer. It was not a serious quarrel, since the two offices continued to pursue essentially similar political objectives,[79] and by the end of the year relations between Schwarz and Hess had improved to such an extent that for the first time members of Hess's staff attended working sessions and briefings conducted by the Reich treasurer.[80] Precisely that element of cooperation was missing from the relationship between Hess and Ley. In 1937, Ley launched further large-scale initiatives against the StdF. Early in the year, he attempted to obtain access to all of the information contained in the monthly Gauleiter reports sent to the office of the StdF, but Hess quickly rebuffed him.[81] The ROL then tried another approach. After much infighting among prominent DAF leaders,[82] Ley late in 1937 submitted a draft law to Hitler which provided, in essence, for the virtual dissolution of all formal ties between the DAF and the NSDAP. The heart of the new draft was contained in paragraph 3, which stated that the head of the DAF was to be subordinate not to the StdF, but solely to the Führer.[83] At the same time Ley insisted on retaining his post as head of the ROL,[84] which in view of the interconnected finances of the

---

78. *Ibid.*, table 7.

79. Hess to Göring *et al.*, 18 Feb. 1938, BA/NS 6/448.

80. Rschm., "Bericht, Nov. 1937," p. 1.

81. Hess to Ley, 8 Feb. 1937, T-580, roll 549, folder 746.

82. Saupert, "Besuchs-Vermerk . . . Hoffmann, 9.2.38," 9 Feb. 1938, T-580, roll 81, folder 393.

83. The text, a memorandum from the DAF supporting the draft law, and a variety of documents showing the opposition of various Reich ministries is in BA/NS 6/448. The text of the draft has also been published in Peter Diehl-Thiele, *Partei und Staat im Dritten Reich* (Munich, 1969), pp. 214–15.

84. See Robert Ley, "Rechenschaftsbericht des . . . Dr. Ley auf der 5. Jahrestagung der Deutschen Arbeitsfront zu Nürnberg vom 11. September 1937," in Paul

DAF and the PO,[85] could only mean that Ley was using the DAF as a lever to eliminate the StdF's control over his offices.

Both Hess and Schwarz recognized the danger of Ley's challenge. Indeed, the staff of the StdF was at work developing plans that were headed in the opposite direction, that is, they envisioned an increase of the PO's control over the party's economic affiliates.[86] Bormann and Hess, then, immediately launched a full-scale counterattack appealing for support not only from the Gauleiters,[87] but from Hermann Göring and other Reich leaders as well.[88] Hess even voiced a threat to deprive Ley of his dual positions as head of the DAF and the PO by noting that the "present *Personalunion* of the two offices was a momentary coincidence."[89]

Schwarz combated Ley on the other flank. Working closely with the staff of the StdF in the course of 1937 he progressively narrowed Ley's financial authority over the DAF and other affiliates, until, by the end of the year, the DAF was no longer financially autonomous.[90] As before, the struggle involved far more than financial independence per se. Schwarz, like Hess, contested Ley's basic political direction in the NSDAP. Thus, in a major decision of August 1938, Schwarz insisted that contrary to Ley's view a PL need not be a member of the DAF.[91] Since Hitler preferred stalemates in the political rivalries of his Reichsleiters, Ley could undoubtedly have stood his ground on the power issue had he not weakened his defenses through a series of financial scandals in the DAF. Until 1937 the DAF was for all practical purposes independent of Schwarz's financial controls. It was subject to Schwarz

Meier-Benneckenstein, ed., *Dokumente der Deutschen Politik* (Berlin, 1938), V, 371–72.

85. At this time the publication of the PO organ *Hoheitsträger* was financed entirely by the DAF. See Schwarz to Ley, 3 Nov. 1941, BA/NS 22/12.

86. See Pannenborg to Hoffmann (both of the StdF's staff), 27 July 1938, T-81, roll 641, frame 5444195.

87. See Bormann to Lohse (GL of Schleswig-Holstein) (marked secret, personal), 22 Feb. 1938, BA/NS 6/448.

88. Hess to Göring *et al.*, 18 Feb. 1938, *ibid.* See also Hoffmann to Friedrichs, 18 June 1938, T-81, roll 641, frames 5444117–18.

89. Hess to Göring, 18 Feb. 1938, BA/NS 6/448.

90. Ulf Lükemann, "Der Reichsschatzmeister der NSDAP" (Dissertation, Free University of Berlin, 1968), pp. 111–13, and 126–31.

91. *Ibid.*, p. 126.

only for occasional audits, so that a DAF reasonably free of corruption could well have maintained its status. Ley, however, had not learned the lessons of 1934. In the fall, it was discovered that a real estate enterprise had paid substantial amounts of money in the form of bribes to several of Ley's close associates. Schwarz saw his chance. He insisted on a full-scale audit of the DAF by his officials, and demanded for the future that the financial administration of the DAF be placed under the regular control or at least the regular supervision of the Reich treasurer's office. Ley, to whom the entire affair seems to have come as a complete surprise, gave in immediately.[92] Schwarz savored his triumph, as well he might. "I have been overjoyed that the moment has finally come," he told a gathering of Gau treasurers, "I have immense patience, but now we have arrived at the point where Dr. Ley has come to me and has agreed to cooperate with me. Ley has become convinced that he, too, cannot solve his problems without the help of the Reich treasurer."[93] Schwarz had broken the DAF's financial stranglehold over the PO. In January of 1938, the Reich treasurer assumed responsibility for financing the three major political offices of the ROL, that is, organization, personnel, and schooling, and this maneuver gave Schwarz an indirect veto over all the activities of these offices.[94]

While the conflicts within the Schwarz-Ley-Hess triangle were approaching something of a conclusion in 1937, the PO as a whole was facing a more serious, albeit still indirect, challenge from the SS. There had always been a number of potential and at times actualized points of friction between the SS and the PO, but until this time the SS had not made any systematic effort to challenge the dominant position of the PO in the Nazi movement. By 1937, however, the SS had undergone a number of internal changes which resulted in a greatly augmented sense of confidence. It had succeeded in getting the support of a large number of members of the pre-1933 conservative elite and in restructuring these elements into an organization with an equally elitist but now Nazified claim to superiority within the Third Reich.[95] The new power

92. Saupert, "Ausserordentliche Ressortbesprechung 16/37 . . . 24. Sept. 1937," T-580, roll 81, folder 393. See also Lükemann, "Reichsschatzmeister," pp. 116–19.
93. Rschm., "Bericht, Nov. 1937," p. 37.
94. Lükemann, "Reichsschatzmeister," p. 120.
95. David Schoenbaum, *Hitler's Social Revolution* (New York, 1966), p. 277.

grouping seemed to feel little need to associate itself with the parent NSDAP: until April 1938, when the elite formation of the military SS, the *Leibstandarte Adolf Hitler*, was received almost bodily into the party, only 21 of the 1,450 members of the regiment were members of the party.[96] At the same time, the SS itself was growing rapidly—so much so that by the beginning of 1938 a large number of administrative posts were not filled within the SS; that is, the membership had grown faster than the functionary corps available to administer it.[97]

The SS's attempt to expand its influence within the PO involved both programs[98] and personnel, but the latter effort was far more significant and more effective. In this area its object was to gain the allegiance of as many key PLs as possible and, conversely, to destroy those who refused to cooperate. Himmler's organization had no lack of incriminating material, since the SD continued its intelligence-gathering activities within the PO.[99] At times, the SS leader confronted the StdF with the personnel problems of the PO.[100] The SS weekly paper, *Das Schwarze Korps*, publicly attacked the PO's practice of not prosecuting corruption cases when they involved "old fighters" and, conversely, praised particular Gauleiters for their social attitudes.[101] Actually, the SS had no great interest in eliminating corrupt and incompetent PLs; such conditions created a welcome element of fear and lack of confidence that led several high-ranking PO leaders to seek a closer relationship with the SS. Thus Gauleiter Kaufmann in Hamburg was under something of a shadow because Himmler suspected him of having been a homosexual in the past.[102] The Gauleiter, perhaps to wipe out this

96. Schwarz to Gau treasurer of Berlin, 4 April 1938, BDC/Dietrich (SS).

97. Pohl (chief of administration for the SS) to Saupert 18 Feb. 1938, T-580, roll 817, box 244, folder 104.

98. Himmler's successful attempt to establish the expertise of the SS in the administration of all anti-Semitic measures in effect deprived the StdF's office of a major power level. See Bernhard Lösener, "Als Rassereferent in Reichsministerium des Innern," *Vjh.f.Z.*, IX (July 1961), 288.

99. See Hugo Jury (staff of the StdF), "Vermerk," 21 April 1938, T-580, roll 79, folder 368.

100. Helmuth Friedrichs, "Notiz für den Stabsleiter," 16 Dec. 1938, *ibid.*

101. *Das Schwarze Korps*, 3 and 10 Feb. 1938.

102. [v. Woyrsch] (HSSPF Nord) ["Aktenvermerk,"] ca. Aug. 1938, BDC/Nathusius (SS), folder II/3.

stigma, encouraged his PLs to join the SS.[103] When a provincial leader proved less tractable, the SS wooed and won the deputy Gauleiter. In Silesia, the higher SS and police leader (HSSPF), von Woyrsch, openly intrigued against Gauleiter Joseph Wagner (an activity of which even Himmler disapproved),[104] but the deputy Gauleiter, Fritz Bracht, had a very close relationship with Himmler and obviously regarded himself as a man of the SS.[105] Deputy Gauleiter Heinrich Peper in Hanover was deemed "worthy" to join the SS.[106] In Bavaria, a deputy Gauleiter and the SS leader worked together to solve difficulties which were really internal problems of the PO rather than matters between the SS and the PO.[107] In some areas Himmler felt strong enough to make personnel appointments within the Gaus' SS units even when the Gauleiter disapproved of the particular individual.[108] On the other hand, the SS could bestow tangible advantages on Gauleiters. Those who served as Oberpräsidents had as much interest as the SS in attempting to weaken the control functions of the Reich interior ministry.[109]

The SS also extended its burrowing activities to the affiliates. These are the years, 1937 and 1938, when the formerly very close relationship between the SS and Darré became one of marked tension. The conflict became particularly venomous, insofar as Herbert Backe, Darré's deputy who headed both the *Reichsnährstand* (Reich food estate) and the Reich ministry of agriculture, was singled out by the SS to replace Darré. The minister was understandably unwilling to acquiesce in

103. "Sitzung des Grossen Schiedhofes beim Reichsführer-SS," 17 Nov. 1938, *ibid.*, folder II; and "Eingabe v. Bocks," 7 June 1949, Forsch. Hbg./PA/12/B.

104. August Heissmeyer (head of the SS training office), "Niederschrift," 1 Dec. 1936, BDC/v. Woyrsch (SS).

105. Bracht to Himmler, 22 Dec. 1938, BDC/Bracht (SS).

106. SS-OA Mitte to SS-Brif. Pancke (Hamburg), 27 May 1937, BDC/Peper (SS).

107. See Gau personnel office (München-Oberbayern) to SS-Brif. Diehn, 3 March 1938, BDC/Högner (SS).

108. Brandt (of Himmler's personal staff) to Schmitt (SS leader in Mecklenburg), 12 Dec. 1938; and Schmitt to Hildebrandt, 5 Dec. 1938, BDC/Hildebrandt (SS). All this is not to suggest that the SS actually controlled the Gauleiters; particularly when members of their cliques were involved, the territorial chiefs were well able to protect them even against SS attacks. See the voluminous documentation on the Nathusius affair in Hamburg. BDC/Nathusius (SS).

109. Daluege to J. Wagner, 5 July 1939, BDC/Wagner (PKC).

his own eclipse, and the immediate result of the bitter struggle was not only a personal animosity between Himmler and Darré, but, for a moment at least, the physical collapse of Backe.[110] This was apparently the result of a genuine personal conflict: Backe was being courted by the SS against Darré at the same time as he was attempting to remain loyal to his superior. Darré was fond of his subordinate and had done his very best to get a number of honors and decorations for him.[111] The SS was unable to force Darré out of office, but in April 1938 the Reich agricultural leader was, at his own request, relieved as head of the SS main office for race and settlement. Darré obviously wanted nothing further to do with the SS. He asked Himmler to give him no further appointments, and retained only the vague position of an advisor to the SS.[112]

Relations between the SS and the offices of the Reich treasurer and the StdF were less one-sided. There were no points of friction between Schwarz and Himmler as yet; on the contrary, the Reich treasurer, parsimonious as ever, eagerly supported Himmler's efforts to curb the expansionist designs of Darré's agricultural apparatus.[113] There was also a very close personal bond between Schwarz and the SS's chief of administration, Oswald Pohl. Schwarz apparently acted as something of a father confessor to Pohl, and guided him through a severe personal crisis.[114] At the same time, Schwarz was by no means a pawn of the SS. He certainly drew the line when he felt that the SS was exceeding its financial resources.[115] The StdF was also cautious. In some policy

110. See n.a., "Notiz über die Besprechung mit Staatssekretär Backe am 6.3.37," n.d., BDC/Backe (SS); and the documents on the so-called Westphalian Peasants' War in BDC/Kost (SS).

111. Backe to Darré, 31 July 1937; and Schwarz to Bouhler, 18 Jan. 1938, BDC/Backe (PKC).

112. Himmler to Darré, 26 April 1938; Himmler, "Aktennotiz," 5 March 1938; and Darré to Himmler, 6 July 1938, BDC/Darré (SS). Himmler may have been gathering evidence to have Darré declared insane. On a paper signed "30.10.36 R. Walther Darré" tracing the linguistic origin of the German word *wahnsinnig* ("insane") Himmler wrote the marginalia: "To be filed with Darré's personnel papers. According to a psychiatrist, evidence of schizophrenia. 5.VII.42 HH."

113. Schwarz to Darré, 20 Sept. 1937, BDC/Darré (PKC).

114. Pohl to Schwarz, 24 Jan. 1938, BDC/Pohl (SS) vol. II/2.

115. Schwarz to Pohl, 17 April 1937, *ibid.*

areas the SS and the deputy Führer's organizations worked in complete agreement. Both Hess and Himmler had an immediate interest in depriving the semiprivate VDA (Association for Germans Abroad) of its monopoly position in the realm of *Volkstumsarbeit* (the concern for ethnic Germans beyond the borders of the Reich) and securing this jurisdiction for the party. When the StdF obtained control of all Volkstumsarbeit within the party in the fall of 1937, he transferred his powers to the SS's *Volksdeutsche Mittelstelle* (Liaison Office for Ethnic Germans, Vomi), headed by SS *Obergruppenführer* (Lieutenant General) Werner Lorenz. Lorenz was only nominally Hess's subordinate; actually he carried out Himmler's orders.[116] So did the SD, and that was less pleasing to the StdF. Hess certainly recognized the SD and the Gestapo as the only internal investigating organizations within the Third Reich, but he was very careful to distinguish the gathering of what he termed "facts" from the preparation of so-called critical evaluations. In practice, Hess wanted the SD to submit its intelligence reports to the political offices of the party and then leave the drawing of political or personnel conclusions from the gathered material to the Hoheitsträgers, that is, to the office of the StdF and whatever other levels he chose to involve.[117] Hess also opposed putting the SD under the control of Himmler as Reich chief of police and thereby letting it escape the political supervision of the office of the StdF.[118] Similar ambivalence characterized the membership of StdF staffers in the SS. Toward late 1936, a number of key staff officials became members of the SS,[119] but a year later Hess asked Himmler to remove him from the list of SS officers.[120] The deputy Füh-

---

116. StdF, "Rundschreiben," 5 Oct. 1937 and 13 Nov. 1937 (secret), BA/NS 6/227. For the development of the Vomi see Robert Koehl, *RKFDV—German Resettlement Policy 1939–1945* (Cambridge, Mass., 1957), pp. 37 ff.; and Hans-Adolf Jacobsen, *Nationalsozialistische Aussenpolitik 1933–1938* (Frankfurt, 1968), pp. 234–46.

117. StdF, "Anordnung," 20 Nov. 1937 and 14 Dec. 1938, BA/NS 6/227 and 331.

118. Walter Schellenberg, *Memoiren* (Cologne, 1956), p. 34.

119. Bormann to Himmler, 20 Oct. 1936, BDC/Friedrichs (SS). The form of address in the letter is the familiar *du*. The officials involved were Müller, Friedrichs, Heim, Sommer, Wemmer, Hoffmann, and Schweter. Bormann noted that further applications would follow.

120. Knoblauch (staff of the StdF) to SS personnel office, 26 Oct. 1937, BDC/

rer obviously wished to avoid the impression that he was in any way a subordinate of the *Reichsführer* SS (RFSS).

While his immediate subordinates fought over the future direction and control of the NSDAP, Hitler himself intervened only rather obliquely in the struggle. On April 29, 1937, he gave one of his semi-secret (that is, unpublished) speeches before a large corps of party workers, in this case the district leaders. Speaking at one of the Ordens-burgen, the Führer ranged widely and rather incoherently over a number of topics, but the substance of his remarks expressed what amounted to guidelines for the role and tactics of the NSDAP in the second half of the thirties. He clearly wanted a party that controlled the German people, instead of one that acted as their Betreuer. The relationship between a political leader (it should be remembered that he was addressing middle-echelon Hoheitsträgers) and the people in his jurisdiction should be one of master and slave. The drift of public opinion was not a valid ground for political decisions; these had to be based on "that which must be done." He reiterated that the goals of the party must never be discussed openly, and that once a decision had been made, all discussion had to cease even within the confines of the party itself. To illustrate his point, Hitler cited the example of his own decision to re-occupy the Rhineland a year earlier. He noted that if there had been the slightest doubt about the popular appeal of this venture, he would nevertheless have ordered troops into the demilitarized zone, but would not have permitted the subsequent plebiscite. Hitler also seemed to support the StdF's concept with regard to trained, competent PLs. Political leaders of the future had to "know" the people in the sense that they had to be expert factory workers, farmers, and so on. The reason, however, was not technical competence, but propagandistic effectiveness. He emphasized the critical importance of the Hoheits-trägers. Each territorial leader was to be virtually autonomous (though he did not use that word) within his area of jurisdiction. Above all, the NSDAP must never tolerate pressure by an inferior PL upon a superior. With these maxims in mind, the Hoheitsträgers could dispense with outstanding administrative talents. Hitler did. He noted that he had no

---

Hess (SS). At the same time Hess gave up his title of Reichsleiter in order to emphasize his unique position in the party. See *VOBl*, III (1 Oct. 1937), 119.

interest whatever in receiving regular reports on the party's activities and that the best method of dealing with difficult matters was to ignore them. He suggested that the district leaders emulate his own practice of asking that all items requiring a difficult or controversial decision be resubmitted after two months. Within that time, Hitler said, nine tenths of the matters would have settled themselves of their own accord.[121]

Despite Hitler's anti-intellectual remarks in the passages dealing with the training of future party cadres, on the whole the address was more "Hessish" than "Leyish." Also, true to his own precept, Hitler had ignored the difficult question of how to finance the desired centralized and competent Hoheitsträger corps. Schwarz and Hess, however, had not yet discovered a convenient means of escaping these difficulties. Resubmitting them in two months proved to be useless; they were still there at the end of the year. In 1937, the party had a surplus of RM 28,500,000,[122] but the rapidly rising costs rendered this amount a mere pittance. The 1937 party congress alone cost RM 9,000,000, and increases in personnel costs for 1937 were "staggering."[123] As a result, Schwarz was unable to carry through some of his major plans. He could announce neither a national budget for the entire party[124] nor the long-expected salary scale, although in November Ley announced that the latter would be forthcoming soon.[125] And in 1937, for the first time, the customary Christmas bonus for PLs was not paid.[126] Schwarz's solutions to the problems had not really changed, although there was increasing doubt about their usefulness. The Reich treasurer continued to remold his staff, both at the Reich office and among the Gau treasurers, into a highly competent body of officials with a well-developed esprit de corps. Their meetings were characterized by a marked degree of civility and openness; officials at the Reich office apparently felt free

121. The speech is printed along with several other addresses in Hildegard v. Kotze and Helmut Krausnick, eds., *Es spricht der Führer!* (Gütersloh, 1966). Specific reference is here made to pp. 132–35, 140–43, 147–49, 152–55, 157, and 149.

122. Rschm., "Bilanz 1937."

123. *Ibid.*, p. 1; and Rschm., "Bericht," p. 22.

124. Rschm., "Bericht, Nov. 1937," p. 19.

125. See Ley's final remarks at a party leader conference on 18 Nov. 1937, T-580, roll 829, folder 197.

126. Rschm., "Vertrauliche Mitteilung," 7 Dec. 1937, *Rundschreiben des Reichsschatzmeisters* (cited hereafter as *Rdschr.*), V.

to bring to the attention of their chief virtually any technical problem that required attention.[127] But the political and financial effects of these measures were dubious. Schwarz still issued a steady stream of directives dealing with the nonpayment of dues.[128] Respect for the accounting competency of the treasurer's vertical staff apparently did not go far beyond the staff members themselves. Many a Hoheitsträger, particularly at the district level, for all practical purposes used his treasurer as a financial advisor whose advice he could either take or ignore as he chose.[129] A Gau treasurer felt obliged to point out that condescension by the PLs toward the administrative personnel was out of place, and to remind the Hoheitsträgers that they really were subordinate to their treasurers in the matter of finances.[130]

The alliance of Hess and Schwarz was particularly stable (as working agreements among Nazi leaders went), because the two men shared a common goal: the professionalization of the PO. For his part, Schwarz had made considerable headway in his own jurisdiction, and in October Hess announced a major reform for the PO as a whole. In an important directive, the StdF prohibited the district leaders from holding salaried state or communal posts in addition to their party offices.[131] There is no doubt that the decree touched a rather raw nerve in the PO. The routine duties of the district leaders, particularly in the urban areas, by now required a full-time functionary,[132] and there were subtler social con-

127. See Saupert to department heads at the Reich treasurer's office, 3 April 1937, and additional documents in T-580, roll 808, box 240, folder 58. See also Rschm., "Bericht, Nov. 1937," pp. 4–5.

128. Rschm., "Anordnung 32/37," 18 June 1937, *Rdschr.*, V.

129. See, for example, Walther Lage-Schulte (district treasurer of Harburg) to the de-Nazification tribunal at Hiddesen, 19 May 1947, Forsch. Hbg./PA/12/K.

130. See Schwarz's remarks printed in the *Hoheitsträger*, II (Jan. 1938), 6–8; and the draft article (intended for publication in the *Hoheitsträger*) by the Gau treasurer of Köln-Aachen, "Ordnung und Sauberkeit in der Verwaltung . . . Das Aufgabengebiet des Gauschatzmeisters," T-580, roll 829, folder 197. Schwarz refused permission to have the piece published because it dealt with "basic" questions of policy.

131. StdF, "Rundschreiben," 25 Oct. 1937, BA/NS 6/227. The decree involved a number of other PLs as well. The Gau treasurer of Silesia, for example, had to decide between the party and his civil service position in the post office department. See [staff office of the Reich treasurer], "Aktennotiz," Jan. 1938, BDC/Bracht (SS).

132. See the job description of Amandus Brandt, at this time the district leader of Harvestehude (Gau Hamburg) in Forsch. Hbg./PA/12/B.

siderations underlying the directive as well. Since the bulk of the district leaders were of lower-middle-class origins, they had eagerly seized the opportunity to upgrade their professional status when higher-level positions became available to those with party connections. Thus on a list of twenty-six Thuringian district leaders, two trained lock-smiths styled themselves "tax inspector" and "Thuringian state coun-cilor," respectively, while a store clerk and a post office clerk became "county executive" and "mayor," respectively.[133] Professionally, then, the important party officials identified not with their PL status, but with the old occupational hierarchies of German society at large.

Since the district leaders (and other PLs) were not eager to cut their ties with their prestigious titles,[134] Hess and Schwarz had to dem-onstrate the concrete advantages of identifying wholly with the PO. To this end, Hess strengthened the position of the Hoheitsträgers as terri-torial party chiefs and gave them more power in their relations with the affiliates. The StdF had already dismissed his regional inspectors and transferred most of their functions to the Gau inspectors. The Hoheits-trägers, however, gained a great deal of additional authority because most of the routine complaints that came from the membership were now brought to the attention of the territorial chiefs themselves, rather than handled by the inspectors and the StdF's office.[135] The Gau inspectors handled primarily disputes involving charges brought by one PL against another.[136] Hess also attempted to guard against the tactics of the affiliates in placing themselves above the party. He de-creed that an affiliate court had the right to expel a member of an affiliate or paramilitary group, but the decision had no influence upon the indi-vidual's party membership.[137] Deprivation of party membership could only be determined by the regular party courts, which, as Hess un-

133. Gau organizational office Thuringia, *Organisations- und Geschäftsvertei-lungsplan der Gauleitung Thüringen der NSDAP* ([Weimar], June 1936), MiU/ GAC, folder 39.
134. The district leaders of Franconia "breathed a sigh of relief" when Hitler agreed to postpone enforcement of Hess's directive in their Gau. Haag, "Inspektions-Bericht Gauleitung Franken der NSDAP," 14 May 1937," BDC/Streicher (PKC).
135. StdF, "Anordnung," 8 Oct. 1937, BA/NS 6/227.
136. De-Nazification court at Bielefeld, "Becker Urteil," n.d., Forsch. Hbg./PA/ 12/B.
137. StdF, "Anordnung," 22 Dec. 1937, BA/NS 6/227.

doubtedly knew, except for the OPG, were still pretty much courts of private vengeance in the hands of the Hoheitsträgers.[138] Hess and Schwarz almost pushed the affiliates away from the party. The StdF permitted them to absorb new occupational groups, but the Reich treasurer also assigned them a legal status below that of the PO.[139]

Schwarz attempted to add more than a modicum of financial security to Hess's gift of stabilized power for the PLs. Although the Reich treasurer was still unable to issue a salary scale for the entire party, he did attempt to replace the widespread practice of expense account payments with salary figures for the major full-time functionaries.[140] Once issued, the salaries were well above comparable renumeration in private business or the German civil service (see table 8). Salaries for the higher party leaders were even more substantial. A Reichsleiter, like Buch, received a monthly salary of RM 1200; a deputy Gauleiter of a prosperous Gau, RM 1500. District leaders began at RM 400 and peaked at age fifty at RM 800.[141] In comparison, salaries for comparable non-party positions in Germany at this time were much lower; see table 9. Despite Schwarz's efforts, many of the figures still existed only on paper. There were as yet no detailed national budgets, and salaries differed widely according to the liquid assets of the various Gaus.[142] In the future, Schwarz hoped to avoid this through an equalization scheme,[143] but the disappointing results of the 1937 membership drive had rendered this plan illusory for the moment.

In the meantime, the party's administration did become subject to a variety of rationalization schemes. At the beginning of the year Schwarz had imposed new and very detailed budgetary forms on the

138. This is a collective judgment based upon the compilation of OPG cases for these years in the BDC.

139. StdF, "Rundschreiben," 26 Oct. 1937, BA/NS 6/227; and Rschm., "Anordnung 59/37," 23 Sept. 1937, quoted in Schwarz to Bruckbauer (representative of the Reich treasurer in the Netherlands), 27 Oct. 1942, Rv0/BDC/H 1143.

140. Rschm., "Anordnung 2/38," 7 Jan. 1938, *Rdschr.*, V.

141. Schwarz to GL Kaufmann, 23 Aug. 1937, BDC/Kaufmann (PKC). Other totalitarian parties also realized the importance of high salaries for full-time party functionaries. For an analysis of salaries in the East German Socialist Unity Party, see Joachim Schultz, *Der Funktionär in der Einheitspartei* (Stuttgart, 1956), p. 96.

142. Schwarz to Ley, 18 March 1937, BDC/Ley (PKC).

143. Rschm., "Bericht, Nov. 1937," p. 11.

TABLE 8

Monthly Salaries for Major Full-Time Functionaries, 1937 (in RM)

Salary Group	Job Description	Starting Salary	After 2 Yrs.	After 4 Yrs.	After 6 Yrs.	After 8 Yrs.	After 10 Yrs.	After 12 Yrs.	After 14 Yrs.	After 16 Yrs.	After 18 Yrs.	After 20 Yrs.
AIa	Head Gau division	450	495	540	585	630	675	720	765	810	855	900
AIb	Head Gau office	350	385	420	455	490	525	560	595	630	665	700
AIc	Performs work equivalent to head Gau office	300	330	360	390	420	450	480	510	540	570	600
AId[a]	Head Gau sub-office	275	303	330	358	385	413	440	468	495	523	550
AIe	Gau-level PL	200	220	240	260	280	300	320	340	360	380	400
AIIa	District leader	400	440	480	520	560	600	640	680	720	760	800
AIIb	Head district division	250	275	300	325	350	375	400	425	450	475	500

Source: Appendix to Rschm., "Verfügung," 3 Sept. 1937, T-580, roll 47, folder 266.
a. AId figures are rounded to the nearest RM.

TABLE 9

Salaries for Nonparty Positions, April–May 1938 (in RM)

Position	Monthly Beginning Salary	Top Salary
Banking employees[a]	127.21	216.47
Public service employees[b]	556.28	745.86
Ministerial-level civil servants[c]	852.00	978.00

SOURCE: Statistisches Reichsamt, *Statistisches Jahrbuch für das Deutsche Reich 1938* (Berlin, 1938), pp. 352, 354, 355.
  a. Grade school education, married.
  b. College degree, married.
  c. College degree, department head (*Ministerialrat*), married.

Gaus,[144] and throughout the year the party's official publication, the *Verordnungsblatt*, listed territorial changes, particularly the merger of two or more districts. These changes were made partly because of low population or party membership figures[145] and partly because a substantial number of district leaders resigned their party posts after Hess's decree prohibiting dual state-party positions.[146] The lost Kreisleiters would obviously have to be replaced from within the party, which in turn brought the further professionalization of the PL corps face to face with the ever vexing issue of the discovery and training of PL replacements. As before, Ley and Hess-Schwarz held almost diametrically opposed views, but in November 1937, Hitler seemed to cut the Gordian knot. If he had been ambivalent in April, he now seemed to agree entirely with Ley's pedagogical ideas. In a speech before the district leaders and Gauleiters in the Ordensburg Sonthofen, the Führer listed as indispensable qualities in a political leader blind obedience toward his superior and physical bravery.[147] This was grist for Ley's mill, and the time from the beginning of 1938 until the outbreak of the war was

144. For a sample see Rschm., "Anlage zur Anweisung 21/36," 22 Dec. 1936, *Rdschr.*, III.

145. Rschm., "Bilanz 1937," p. 28; and Wolfgang Schäfer, *NSDAP* (Hanover, 1956), p. 74. The *VOBl* published a list of territorial changes involving various *Kreises* in almost every issue published in 1937 and 1938.

146. Of the twenty-six Thuringian district leaders referred to above, seven were no longer in office at the end of 1937. See Gau personnel office Thuringia, *Dienstrangliste der Politischen Leiter des Gaus Thüringen der NSDAP: Stand vom 31. Dezember 1937* [Weimar, 1938], MiU/GAC, folder 40.

147. Domarus, *Hitler*, I, 762–63.

about the only time span in which party agencies outside the ROL's office took his training system at all seriously. Ley obviously interpreted the fact that Hitler had made his remarks at one of Ley's Ordensburgen as an endorsement of these political boarding schools.

To be sure, although Ley claimed that his Ordensburgen combined the best features of the training institutes of the Roman Catholic priesthood, the diplomatic service of Great Britain, and the Prussian officers corps,[148] the castles had not yet produced effective political leaders.[149] In fact, the only noticeable change or addition to Ley's intricate pedagogical system in the months between Hitler's April and November speeches was the publication of the *Hoheitsträger* in October. The *Schulungsbrief* continued as a totally open publication, that is, it could be subscribed to by anyone, although Ley's schooling office considered it particularly important for the political leaders of the PO and the DAF.[150] Its contents remained almost entirely propagandistic; during the entire run of 1937 not one article appeared which concerned itself with the practical problems facing a full-time party functionary. Even so, the publication ran afoul of Hitler and Hess. Its issue of April 1938 (just after the annexation of Austria) made the mistake of reproducing a map showing the Alto Adige section of Italy as German in ethnic composition. The result was the arrest of the editor (who was also head of the ROL's main schooling office), Franz-Hermann Woweries, and the destruction of the issue.[151] In October 1937, Ley placed the *Hoheitsträger* alongside the *Schulungsbrief*. As the title of the former indicates, its circulation was restricted to the territorial chiefs of the PO, down to the local leader. Ley intended the publication to provide propaganda at a somewhat higher level than the *Schulungsbrief* and to give some practical guidelines for the Hoheitsträgers. In fact, the basic difference between the two periodicals was the quality of the paper on which they were printed and the greater brazenness of the *Hoheits-*

---

148. Helmuth Stellrecht, "Drei Beispiele für die Bedeutung des Führerkorps," *Hoheitsträger,* I (Oct. 1937), 8–9.

149. As late as March 1937 only eight of the thirty-two Gaus had asked to add *Ordensburg* graduates to their PL staffs. See Hans Schwarz van Berk, "Die härteste Schule," *Angriff,* 31 March 1937.

150. Gau Berlin, *Gau,* no. 29 (15 Feb. 1937), p. 52.

151. The relevant documentation is in BA/NS 22/830.

träger in pursuing the Nazi propaganda line. Concern with practical problems was little in evidence. Instead, the readers received a steady diet of pseudometaphysical and self-congratulatory articles on the excellence of the party's training system. Ley did not have to wait long for criticism of his new effort. In December Hess wrote him that the publication contained far too many theoretical articles and not enough information on practical problems. In addition, he reminded Ley that the *Hoheitsträger* could not be used to discuss political problems which were in fact not yet ripe for discussion,[152] a guarded reference to the lack of subtlety in Ley's publication. Hess's complaints did not result in a noticeable change of editorial policy.

With at least two clear concepts of the future of the party at hand and with Hitler's seeming endorsement of the demonstrably less workable one of the two, the NSDAP had obviously reached a dead end at the close of the year 1937. It may be useful to stop here, before going on to the role of the party in the conquest of Austria and Czechoslovakia, and analyze the PO's role in the day-to-day life of Nazi Germany. At the end of 1937 the party had reached the pinnacle of its organizational and personnel expansion for its self-proclaimed dual role as controlling force and Betreuer in the territorial limits of the Altreich. The organizational charts of the party were by now incredibly complex, the number of officials seemingly limitless. The Gau-level administrative offices of a large, urban Gau like Berlin consisted of 102 separate offices and suboffices, staffed by 140 full- and part-time functionaries. They covered all manner of societal groups, from teachers to physicians, but a disproportionately large number were essentially internal in character. Fully half (51) of the offices and almost the same proportion (68) of the functionaries were concerned with the administration of the PO itself.[153] The emphasis on self-administration was also apparent from the activity reports of the Gaus for 1937. Although it is true that problems connected with the membership drive dominated some of the party activity during the year, it is equally apparent that the reporters regarded such peripheral items as pistol practice, gymnastics, and uniform inspections

---

152. Hess to Ley, Dec. 1937, T-580, roll 829, folder 197.
153. This information is compiled from Gau Berlin, *Gau*, no. 40 (1 Aug. 1937), pp. 56–61.

as no less important than meetings of the Gaus' Hoheitsträgers.[154] Above all, the Gau-level party organization did not initiate actions that indicated a larger political purpose. At most it reacted to prevailing conditions, as did the Gau Berlin in publishing a running list of restaurants that were off limits to party personnel.

The districts showed a more consistent pattern of activities. Their chief job was to keep their populations quiet at all cost, and joyous if possible. Party journalists developed neat theories of "internal" and "external" work for the party, but in essence the districts were expected to control dissatisfaction ("ideological guardianship") and propagandize the party's services to the people.[155] The party's personnel and the extent of its horizontal organization, especially in the urban districts, was little short of that found in the Gaus.[156] In the rural areas, the party's district organization tried desperately to replace the church as the focal point of cultural and social life. The district congress was to become "the undisputed high point in the life of the population." There were suggestions that the annual party congress be combined with the district *Kirmes*, or various meetings of social and professional organizations, so that it might become a sort of substitute county fair.[157] In consequence, the party at the district level spent a great deal of time simply celebrating something or other in the course of the year. One author has tabulated that 55 of the 365 days of the year 1937 were devoted to a mass meeting, a public money collection, or a similarly stirring event staged by the party or its affiliates. In other words, every seventh day called for a celebration.[158] The function of the NSDAP as an instrument of terror or at least surveillance was further perfected in the local and sublocal organizations. Vast hordes of party officials[159] were both in-

154. This is based upon the excerpts from a number of Gau reports submitted to the StdF's office between February and November 1937 in BA/NS 22/577.

155. F. H. Woveries, "Der Hoheitsträger," *Hoheitsträger*, I (Oct. 1937), 12–15.

156. Gau Hamburg, *Gaunachrichten* (edition Barmbeck-Süd), III (1 June 1937), 7. A Hamburg district leader reported after the war that his office had a PL staff of sixty with a district population of 220,000. See Forsch. Hbg./PA/12/B.

157. StdF, "Rundschreiben," 26 Oct. 1937, BA/NS 6/227. See also the clippings from the *Thüringer Gauzeitung* of June 1937 in MiU/GAC, folder 54.

158. Hermann Meyerhoff, *Herne 1933–45* (Herne, 1963), pp. 98–99.

159. Of the 11,104 PLs in Gau Thuringia, 9,687 held positions at the local and sublocal level. See *Dienstrangliste der Politischen Leiter . . . 31. Dezember 1937*, MiU/GAC, folder 39.

structed and rather specifically trained to maintain a political watch over every single individual living within their territorial jurisdiction. The block leaders in particular developed ever more elaborate household files containing entries for every utterance or other sign of potential resistance to the Nazi regime by their friends and neighbors.[160]

The lack of an accepted, systematic conceptualization of the party's control role obviously had a fundamental bearing upon the future relationship of party and state in the Third Reich. This was recognized both by commentators within the party and by the Reich ministers directly concerned.[161] Even Hitler himself seemed vaguely troubled. He devoted a considerable portion of his April speech to the district leaders to the relationship between the party, the state, and the army. In contrast to some earlier remarks, he seemed to envision a rather positive role for the state in the Third Reich, but a closer reading of the text reveals that Hitler had a unique concept of the state. For him the state was not the totality of legal and governmental institutions, but something much more nebulous, called the "organic, folkish state." In concrete terms there was little substance to this state; in the same speech Hitler noted that the two pillars supporting the Third Reich were the party and the army.[162] Given this cue, other party leaders vied with one another denying the state legitimate fields of authority. Robert Ley in his speech before the party congress in 1937 reiterated that the party decided while the state administered.[163] The Gauleiters continued to attack the territorial integrity of the German federal states,[164] although only one of them met with significant success; after November, Gauleiter Kaufmann was able to preside over "Greater Hamburg." The creation of the Hamburg city-state was one of the few administratively sensible acts in the

160. De-Nazification Court at Bergedorf, Öffentliche Sitzung gegen . . . [Amandus] Brandt," 17 Nov. 1947, Forsch. Hbg./PA/12/B. See also Fritz Mehnert, "Menschenführung durch die NSDAP," *Hoheitsträger*, I (Oct. 1937), 24–25; and Gau Berlin, *Gau*, no. 51 (1 Jan. 1938), p. 1.

161. See Frick's remarks quoted in the *Völkischer Beobachter* (cited hereafter as *VB*), 20 Oct. 1937. See also Reichspropagandaleitung, "Anordnung 3/38," quoted in Gau Berlin, *Gau*, no. 56 (15 March 1938), p. 70.

162. Hitler's address to the district leaders, 29 April 1937, in Kotze and Krausnick, *Es spricht der Führer*, pp. 126–27.

163. Ley, "Rechenschaftsbericht . . . 1937," p. 375.

164. Frick to Lammers, 26 Feb. 1938; and Lammers, "Vermerk," 5 March 1938, BA/R 43 II/494.

Nazi era, and one of a handful to survive after 1945. The problem of the small city-states had plagued the Weimar Republic long before the Nazis came to power. Reduced to its essentials, the problem was that these federal units had too small a tax base to operate effectively as states. Ancient rivalries, however, prevented mergers. Only when the Nazi Machtergreifung removed parliamentary sensibilities could the reorganization of northern Germany make headway. Appealing to Göring (significantly not to the party's Reichsleitung), Kaufmann was able to obtain Hitler's approval to annex portions of Schleswig-Holstein and Oldenburg. Göring also agreed to smooth the ruffled feathers of Hinrich Lohse and Carl Röver, the Gauleiters of these adjacent territories. Lohse had a street named after him in Hamburg, and Röver was permitted to annex Wilhelmshaven and add it to the city-state of Bremen.[165]

At the Reich level, the party-state relationship was a struggle over legislation, the administration of justice, and personnel appointments. Among this list the first, because of the paucity of legislative plans and initiatives on the part of the NSDAP, remained the least significant. The party never did develop a full-scale alternative to the bulk of the social and economic values prevailing in post-1918 Germany. The party had an immediate and passionate interest only in the application of the Nuremberg laws.[166] The administration of justice was an entirely different matter. The various Hoheitsträgers had, of course, long interfered in the working of the courts, but not until late 1938 did the StdF attempt to formulate such informal practices into a formal right. On September 30, 1938, the StdF sent to the head of the Reich chancellery, Lammers, a long memorandum concerning a new draft of the German code of criminal law. Hess objected less to specific provisions than to the general tenor of the draft; it failed to provide for the special role of the party. The StdF insisted that the NSDAP could not be bound by the present legal norms in judging an individual who had offended against the principles of National Socialism. The key sentence in the memorandum read, "The area of its [the party's] activity is limitless and it is not possible to foresee how the party may be forced to pass judgment

165. "Niederschrift . . . Eiffe . . . Dr. Heffter," 24 Feb. 1950, Forsch. Hbg./PA/ 12/E; and H. P. Ipsen, "Niederschrift der Mitteilungen von . . . Prof. Ipsen . . . 19.8.1950," n.d., Forsch. Hbg./PA/12/H.
166. Lösener, "Rassereferent," p. 286.

on an individual." In other words, the StdF demanded an extralegal, purely self-judged status for the NSDAP under the judicial laws of the Third Reich.[167] Hess's ideas were put into limited practice in Hamburg. Here the senator (minister) of justice, Curt Rothenberger, who during the war became the state secretary in the Reich ministry of justice, insisted that judges be "100 percent National Socialists" and that they enjoy the trust and confidence of the political leadership of the party in order to remain in office. Hitler's words were the judges' most important source of legal interpretation, though even Rothenberger came to the conclusion that the Führer's utterances could not have the force of law except in very unusual circumstances.[168]

Formally, the party's most significant victory came in the area of personnel appointments to the German civil service. The German Civil Service Law (DBG), passed on January 26, 1937, was essentially an attempt by the party, with initiative provided by the StdF, to control the German civil service. The law made promotions dependent upon a political bill of health and sanctioned the massive spoils system which had been in effect since 1933. For the future the party hoped to guard against the intolerable presence of "politically neutral"[169] officials in the civil service by insisting that only party members should be promoted to significant civil service positions.[170] In addition, from the standpoint of the StdF, the DGB had the salutary effect of preventing independent actions by local and affiliate officials in the area of civil service appointments.[171]

The field of application for the new law in the area of party-state relations was wide enough. Only five of the thirty-eight Ministerialräte (department heads) holding office in the Reich ministries at the beginning of 1938 were party members and all of these had joined the party

167. Hess to Lammers, 30 Sept. 1938, BA/R 22/20681.

168. See Rothenberger's speech "Nationalsozialistische Rechtssprechung," 5 Oct. 1936, Forsch. Hbg./PA/12/(R) Rothenberger. See also August Schuberth (former district attorney in Hamburg), "Eidesstattliche Erklärung," 7 Aug. 1947, *ibid.*; and Werner Johe, *Die gleichgeschaltete Justiz* (Frankfurt, 1967), p. 161.

169. See GL Kaufmann's remarks in "Unser Appell vor dem Gauleiter," Gau Hamburg, *Gaunachrichten* (edition Altona), III (1 June 1937), 11.

170. The most complete discussion of the DBG is in Mommsen, *Beamtentum*, pp. 37–39, and 213–14.

171. *Ibid.*, p. 74; and Schoenbaum, *Hitler's Social Revolution*, p. 196.

after 1933.[172] And there was still a sizable reservoir of party members wanting civil service positions. For this reason the StdF was particularly opposed to the reinstitution of civil servants dismissed as a result of the 1933 purge law. In addition, Hess insisted on more than pro forma identification with the party by civil servants who were party members.[173] These state employees had the right and indeed the duty to report to the party any significant developments occurring in their offices. Conversely, they had no authority to report internal party items to sources outside the party, including their civil service superiors. They were also fully subject to the authority of the party courts; conviction by a party tribunal almost invariably resulted in dismissal from the civil service.[174]

Within the party, the most important effect of the DBG was to give the force of law to political evaluations by the Hoheitsträgers. This meant a further concentration of power in the hands of the territorial chiefs.[175] In accordance with the vertical structure of the PO, the StdF's office became the major coordinating agency for the entire evaluation process and in addition had the right of initial and final evaluation in the case of all Reich-level civil servants.[176] In order to prevent the growth of Gau and district civil service cliques paralleling the already existing PO groupings, Hoheitsträgers below the StdF were not empowered to recommend candidates, but were merely allowed to evaluate those who had been proposed by the regular ministries.[177] The Hoheitsträgers was also not authorized to give orders directly to state agencies.[178]

172. StdF to Lammers, 1 Feb. 1938, BA/R 43 II/1138b.

173. Wachlin, "Besuchs-Vermerk," 27 July 1937, BDC/Opdenhoff (PKC). This attitude persisted. See Reich ministry of the interior to highest Reich offices *et al.*, 20 June 1939, BA/R 43 II/455. The reopening of the membership rolls had provided this opportunity, of course. See Mommsen, *Beamtentum*, p. 88.

174. StdF to Reich ministry of the interior, 26 Jan. 1938, BA/R 43 II/426a; and StdF, "Rundschreiben," n.d., *VOBl*, no. 163 (28 Feb. 1938); and *Mittbl. Kr. Mü.*, no. 49 (10 Dec. 1936).

175. *Organisationsbuch*, 2 (1936), p. 246 still assigned the power to give political evaluations of civil servants to the "main office for civil servants" of the ROL "by order of the Hoheitsträgers."

176. Mommsen, *Beamtentum*, p. 75.

177. StdF, "Anordnung," n.d., *VOBl*, no. 189 (30 March 1939).

178. De-Nazification Court at Bergedorf, "Öffentliche Sitzung gegen . . . Brandt."

The practical effect of the DBG is difficult to estimate. There is no doubt that the German civil service as a whole was not "Nazified" in the sense that its members became avid party stalwarts. Indeed, in the more technical ministries, the proportion of party members remained small throughout the Nazi era.[179] Yet mere statistics do not tell the whole story.[180] It was obvious that the party was particularly eager to infiltrate the "political" ministries, and here its success was more evident. The Reich ministry of justice, for example, undertook a fairly major reevaluation of its entire appointment and judicial process after the DBG was passed.[181] As a result, at the end of 1938 almost half (257 out of 530) of the corps of civil servants were party members and 20 percent (106) held a PL rank.[182]

The DBG was intended as the second (the DGO had been the first) of a set of three laws designed legally to establish the control function of the NSDAP over the state administration. The third, the Law on the Reorganization of the German Districts (*Deutsche Kreisordnung*, DKO) was planned, but never put into effect. At the end of 1937 the StdF's office began to work on drafting the DKO.[183] The basic impetus for the law was a situation in the districts which both the party and the state found unsatisfactory. Since the Machtergreifung, a large number of PLs had served simultaneously as party district leaders and governmental county executives. Both sides saw disadvantages in this arrangement: the state because the Kreisleiters tended, by and large, to be incompetent;[184] and the party because its districts were at least partially subject to the authority of the governmental agencies. In accordance with his November directive Hess ordered an end to all such Personalunionen as of January 1, 1938, in the obvious hope that by then the DKO would have clarified the status of the district leaders.[185] Under the

179. Mommsen, *Beamtentum*, p. 57–59.

180. Schoenbaum, *Hitler's Social Revolution*, p. 197, argues that the entire effect of the DBG was minimal.

181. See the documentation in BA/R 22/20681.

182. See the untitled tabulations by the business office of the ministry, 17 Dec. 1938, BA/R 22/21.

183. StdF, "Rundschreiben," 23 Nov. 1937, BA/NS 6/227.

184. Mommsen, *Beamtentum*, pp. 62–63.

185. Gau Berlin, *Gau*, no. 51 (1 Jan. 1938), p. 2.

planned legislation, these party officials were to be in effective control of major governmental functions within the counties, specifically personnel appointments and budgets. At the same time, they would be accountable only to their party superiors, not the Reich interior ministry.[186] In the end, the DKO fell victim to the party's chronic personnel problems. The law was never passed because the party did not have a sufficient number of full-time district leaders who were administratively competent to act as political decision-makers at the county level.[187] As a result, relations between party and state remained ambiguous. The district leaders' influence obviously grew as the party expanded its program of activities.[188] The party financed many of its projects with state appropriations at the county level,[189] but the NSDAP never achieved the formal subordination of the county government to the party's political control.

Like so much else begun by the party in the Third Reich, the legal framework for party-state relations remained an incomplete patchwork. In fact, at the end of 1937 the NSDAP was further than ever from a systematic remaking of German society. The grandiosely planned Reichsreform remained tabled on Hitler's orders.[190] Economic affairs were in the greedily grasping hands of Hermann Göring. The party had been unable to infiltrate the Reichswehr officer corps to any marked degree. No wonder the party was in an ugly mood, seeking an outlet for its frustrations. Hitler, cheered wildly by the PLs,[191] lashed out at opponents of his regime who had no concrete means of defending themselves. The churches, conceded the Führer in a speech to the PLs in November, could take charge of "the German people in the hereafter," but the

186. These are the suggestions of GL Grohé to Bormann, 9 Dec. 1937, T-580, roll 546, folder 616.

187. Diehl-Thiele, *Partei*, p. 175.

188. Meyerhoff, *Herne*, p. 11.

189. District leader of Eisenbach to mayor of Eisenach, 30 May 1938, MiU/GAC, folder 4.

190. Walter Baum, "Die 'Reichsreform' im Dritten Reich," *Vjh.f.Z.*, III (Jan. 1955), 51. As usual, such blanket prohibitions did not entirely settle the matter: the Oberpräsident of Hanover was permitted to "defend himself" against the unjustified expansion attempts of his neighbors. See Lammers to Frick, 17 March 1938, BA/R 43 II/494.

191. Kotze and Krausnick, *Es spricht der Führer*, p. 171.

party demanded total control while these human beings were still living on earth.[192] Simultaneously, Alfred Rosenberg was unleashed and attacked the fellow-traveling Deutsche Christen, not so much because they opposed the party line (which they did not), but because they insisted upon remaining ideologically within the Christian framework.[193] One of the less subtle Gauleiters, Karl Florian in Düsseldorf, put the issue a bit more crassly: "Either you kneel before God or you are loyal to the Führer."[194]

Hitler's well-developed political instincts prevented him from launching a frontal attack on such established social institutions as the churches, but there were other outlets for the pent-up dynamism of the party. Beginning in the spring of 1938, the Austrian Anschluss, the Munich crisis, and the subsequent annexation of the Sudetenland revealed in stark austerity the policy of territorial conquest of the Nazi regime. There is no direct and obvious connection between the radical ferment of the Nazi Party and the foreign policy initiatives of the German government, but it is certainly clear from the speeches and addresses which Hitler made in the course of 1937 that the events of 1938 should have come as no great surprise to observant PLs. To a remarkable extent, the party was indirectly privy to Hitler's plans. In early June Hitler gave a major "secret" address in which he discussed foreign policy and economic problems within the context of his *Grossraum* (territorial conquest) and *Lebensraum* (living space) theories.[195] Shortly before the Hossbach conference on November 5, Hitler, in remarks to the Gau propaganda chiefs, anticipated essentially what he would say to the military leaders a week later. He emphasized that he did not expect to live long and that therefore the problems of the German Lebensraum would have to be settled by the present generation of leaders. Unwittingly, Hitler demonstrated in the speech the underlying connection between his attacks on the churches and his foreign policy activism: both represented a deliberate turning away from the moral

192. Hitler's speech to the GL and district leaders, 23 Nov. 1937, in Domarus, *Hitler*, I, 762.

193. Kurt Meier, *Die Deutschen Christen* (Halle/Saale, 1965), p. 294.

194. Statement made by Florian to visiting district leaders. See "Niederschrift . . . Eiffe . . . Dr. Heffter," 24 Feb. 1950, Forsch. Hbg./PA/12/E.

195. Hitler's speech of 2 June 1937, in Domarus, *Hitler*, I, 697.

value system of his nineteenth-century background.[196] The NSDAP would resume its revolutionary course; having failed to eliminate the values of Wilhelminian Germany, it turned its attention to the destruction of the balance of power in Europe.

The party was by no means a neglected factor in Hitler's forthcoming attempt to attain a position of European hegemony for the Reich. In a sense, the NSDAP was to make plausible what logic held to be impossible: the reversal of the military defeat in World War I. The Third Reich may have rested on two pillars, but they were of unequal strength. Hitler made it very clear that he regarded the party as the more reliable of the two. The party would remain fanatically loyal to him no matter what the outcome, and the party was to transfer this feeling of utter devotion to the armed forces and thereby give it strength beyond its numbers and equipment.[197] The movement eagerly welcomed its coming challenge. Something like the euphoria of 1933 began to seize hold of the party again as the conflict with Germany's neighbors took on definite form.[198] And although no party office was directly involved in the conduct of German diplomacy, a number of party agencies made active preparations for the future expansion of the NSDAP into as yet unconquered territories. At the beginning of 1938 the StdF established the "office of the special assistant for foreign policy questions in the staff of the deputy Führer," which appears to have had primary responsibility for insuring that speeches by lesser party leaders did not endanger Hitler's timetable of crises.[199] Both Bormann and Hess

196. As to his relations with the church, Hitler remarked that after he had liberated himself from the ideas of his childhood he felt "happy as a colt in the pasture." See *ibid.*, II, 745.

197. Wilhelm Treue, ed., "Rede Hitlers vor der deutschen Presse (10. November 1938)," *Vjh.f.Z.*, VI (April 1958), 189; and Manfred Messerschmidt, *Die Wehrmacht im NS-Staat* (Hamburg, 1969), pp. 232 ff.

198. Cf. Speer's description of the reaction of the party's GLs and district leaders to Hitler's pronouncement, "Our enemy no. 1 is England" in a speech on 23 November 1937. Speer, *Erinnerungen*, p. 539, n. 5. See also n.a., "Meine Herren, zur Besprechung," *Hoheitsträger*, II (Oct. 1938), 16 and 50.

199. Hitler, "Verfügung," 25 July 1938; StdF, "Anordnung," 2 Dec. 1937, BA/NS 6/230 and 227; and Langsdorff (head of the new *Dienststelle*) to Brockhausen, 25 May 1938, BA/NS 6/185. Langsdorff (born in 1898) was closely connected to the SS and had been head of Ribbentrop's Eastern desk since the summer of 1937. See Jacobsen *Aussenpolitik*, pp. 278, 300, and 702.

were in attendance and participated behind the scenes at the Munich conference of September 1938.[200] The Ordensburgen, as always educational pioneers, sought instructors for various East European languages including one, Baltic, which was no doubt spoken only at the order castles.[201] Within the party's agricultural office a special department was at work planning German settlements in southeastern Europe and the Ukraine.[202]

The major offices of the PO prepared for the coming era of territorial expansion by, momentarily at least, curtailing their desperate infighting. At the beginning of 1938 the StdF, Ley, and the Reich treasurer had achieved what amounted to an informal modus vivendi. Schwarz had pretty much won his battles with the Gauleiters. About the same time each of the Gaus accepted a special auditing representative of the Reich treasurer, and a new set of national accounting guidelines went into effect.[203] In addition, the provincial chiefs acknowledged the Gau treasurers as independent heads of the entire financial and business side of the Gaus.[204] With a view toward his future personnel needs, Schwarz established an elaborate file system of possible replacements for the present officials working in the offices of the Reich, Gau, and affiliate treasurers.[205] There remained a number of problems, of course. Although the party as a whole had a budgetary surplus of RM 100 million in 1938,[206] the situation in individual Gaus was far from satisfactory.[207] And Schwarz continued to accuse the paramilitary organizations of

200. See the documentation in BA/NS 6/166.

201. Schmidt, "Bericht," frame 135.

202. Hermann Reischle, *Rede des Reichshauptamtsleiters Dr. Reischle in Vogelsang* [(Munich, 1939)], part 2, pp. 5–6.

203. [Rschm.] "Dienstanweisung für den Beauftragten des Reichsschatzmeisters in Revisions-Angelegenheiten," Nov. 1937, T-580, roll 48, folder 266; and *Reichsverwaltungsordnung der Nationalsozialistischen DAP [sic]—Reichskassenordnung 1.1.1938* (Munich, 1938). See also Rschm., "Anordnung 11/38 [and] 21/38," 8 March and 13 July 1938, *Rdschr.*, V.

204. See Gau treasurer Hamburg, "Stimmungsbericht 1938," 17 Jan. 1939, appendix 3, T-580, roll 804, box 239, folder 39.

205. Schwarz, "Anordnung 6/38," 12 Feb. 1938, *Rdschr.*, V.

206. Rschm., "Jahresbericht 1940," [25 Oct. 1940], p. 3, T-580, roll 833, box 256, folder 267.

207. In East Prussia only seven of thirty-eight district leaders regarded their budgets as "satisfactory," twenty-eight as "unsatisfactory," and three as "conditionally satisfactory." See special representative of the Reich treasurer, "Geheim-

financial mismanagement. He commented to the Gau treasurers, in a rare moment of utter candor, "If you knew what the paramilitary organizations cost me in the way of money . . . you are embarrassing me—if the brigades would only manage correctly, then . . . [*sic*]."[208] Even Ley rested briefly on the laurels of his organizational efforts. The vertical and territorial reorganization of the PO was more or less complete.[209] The ROL proudly published a definitive list of the Gaus and districts.[210] Other aspects of Ley's jurisdiction were developing along less satisfactory lines. The StdF complained of excessive paperwork in the party and of the corruption rampant among the "old fighters."[211] Schwarz criticized Ley's tendencies toward overorganization, and refused to honor Ley's requests for training funds,[212] because he felt there was an inadequate amount of coordination among the various offices.[213] The StdF's problems were of a different nature. The office had no financial worries. Bormann's and Hess's expenses were paid from moneys appropriated in the regular Reich budget.[214] This arrangement seemed justified since Hitler agreed that Hess performed valuable services as Reich minister for party affairs, although technically his title remained "without portfolio."[215] Like the other units of the PO, the office of the StdF started no new departures at the beginning of the year, but continued

Bericht—Inspektion der Gauleitung Ostpreussen," 8 Feb. 1938, T-580, roll 842, box 267, folder 347.

208. Rschm., "Bericht, Nov. 1937," p. 23.

209. See Hans Fabricius, "Organisatorischer Aufbau der NSDAP," *Verwaltungs-Akademie*, I, Gruppe 1, Beitrag 6a (Feb. 1938); and the indexing arrangement of the *VOBl* which was put into use at the end of January 1938.

210. ROL, *Gau- und Kreisverzeichnis der NSDAP—1. Ausgabe, January 1938* [(Munich, 1938)].

211. StdF, "Anordnung," 11 Jan. 1938, and 9 Feb. 1938; and "Rundschreiben," 24 March 1938, BA/NS 6/228. See also Saupert, "Gedächtnisprotokoll . . . 27. Juni 1938," 4 July 1938, T-580, roll 82, folder 393.

212. Schwarz to Ley, 3 Jan. 1938, BDC/Ley (PKC); and Eilers, *Schulpolitik*, p. 119. In the affiliates, where Schwarz had only indirect control over the budgets, vast sums were spent on so-called training programs. The Nazi Teachers' Organization managed to spend RM 1,000,000 in 1938 alone for something called "the march of young teachers." See ROL, Hauptschulungsamt to Simon, 16 Aug. 1938, BA/NS 22/701.

213. Rschm., "Bericht, Nov. 1937," p. 16.

214. Diehl-Thiele, *Partei*, p. 221, n. 51.

215. Lammers to Reich ministers, 4 Feb. 1938, BA/R 43 II/139.

to strengthen already established policy lines. The StdF in particular carried on his efforts to secure permanent StdF-approved deputy Gauleiters for the Gaus of the Altreich.[216]

The ides of March 1938 brought Hitler one of his most sought-after triumphs, and opened a new era in the history of the NSDAP as a power component in the Third Reich. That the annexation of Austria was the beginning of a chain rather than an isolated incident was clear not only to the party leaders,[217] but to the party's potential rivals as well. The army, especially, accepted the Anschluss as a major crack in the solidity of its position as pillar of equal strength with the party. The so-called *Soldatenbund* (Soldiers' Association), a loose organization of professional officers formed in 1935 in order, among other things, to ward off infiltration of the party into the Reichswehr, was dissolved after the Anschluss.[218] The party, of course, saw the annexation of Germany's southeastern neighbor as a convincing demonstration of its thesis that "the party creates, the state administers."[219]

The NSDAP had made careful preparations to remove the stain of the 1934 putsch attempt from its record. As early as April 1937 the StdF had begun to organize the Nazi refugees from Austria so that they might be available as a shock-force when the Austrian question became acute again.[220] As the crisis neared, the StdF increasingly took charge of the party's role in the coming drama. In September Hess entrusted the entire political preparation of the Anschluss to Wilhelm Keppler, who was eventually to become the Nazis' man on the spot in Vienna.[221]

216. See Langendörfer (office of Reich treasurer), "Aktenvermerk—Telefongespräch mit . . . Personalamt des [StdF], 28.1.38," 17 Feb. 1938, T-580, roll 81, folder 393.

217. Fritz Wiedemann, *Der Mann der Feldherr werden wollte* (Velbert, 1964), p. 125. See also the excerpt from a speech of GL Hellmuth (Mainfranken) on 4 March 1938, in Domarus, *Hitler*, I, 756.

218. Domarus, *Hitler*, I, 808 and 826.

219. This phrase is the leitmotif of a speech made by Friedrichs to the newly-installed PLs in Austria. See Eft[ger] (staff of the StdF), "Stichworte für eine Rede . . . Friedrichs vor den Gauleitern, Gauamtsleitern und Kreisleitern in Österreich," 12 July 1938, T-580, roll 79, folder 368.

220. Rschm., Reichsrevisionsamt, "Revisionsbericht vom 11.11.1938 über das illegale Hilfswerk für Österreich des NSDAP Flüchtlingshilfswerkes Berlin," 22 Nov. 1938, pp. 1–17, RvO/BDC/PlD. Additional documents are in BDC/Rodenbücher (SS) and RvO/BDC/PlA. Rodenbücher headed the illegal operation.

221. StdF, "Anordnung," 19 Sept. 1937, BA/NS 6/227.

Five months later Hess prohibited further propagandistic and organizational directives by Reich party agencies to the Austrian Nazis, and at the beginning of March he extended the prohibition to travel by German party leaders in Austria.[222] The annexation also cost the party a great deal of money. On March 10, Odilo Globocnik, then Gauleiter of Vienna, received 417,000 Austrian schillings. The moneys were specifically earmarked for political purposes and were not subject to normal audits.[223] Similarly, large funds were required to send various Reich party officials into Austria in order to instruct the Austrians on how to run their own affairs. This was true both of the district leaders who came as "advisors" from the Altreich and of a variety of other PLs, particularly financial administrators, who were necessary to accomplish the party's side of the Anschluss.[224] There are no specific figures on the amounts, but they appear to have been sizable. The expenditures were apparently so large that Schwarz once again had to delay publication of the planned salary scale.[225]

From the beginning, the NSDAP leaders were determined to restructure Austria along the lines of the party's concept of the relationship between state and party. The *Wehrmacht* (armed forces) may have tramped across the borders, but its force was exerted for the benefit of the party.[226] The German party leaders were also the first to arrive in their new fief. Josef Bürckel, the Gauleiter of the Palatinate and the newly appointed "commissioner for reunification of Austria with the German Reich," arrived in Vienna before noon on March 11; Hess followed at 5:00 P.M., some twelve hours before Hitler's caravan acknowledged the ecstatic cheers of the Austrian masses.[227] Bürckel occupied a peculiarly dual state and party position. Although appointed by Hitler in his capacity as head of the Reich government to supervise the work-

222. StdF, "Anordnung," 17 Feb. and 12 March, 1938, BA/NS 6/228.

223. Rschm., "Revisionsbericht . . . Hilfswerk Österreich," pp. 11–12.

224. [Saupert?] to Gau auditor Sudetenland, 2 Feb. 1939, T-580, roll 809, box 240, folder 60. See also Saupert, "Vermerk . . . 19.3.1938," 21 March 1938, T-580, roll 81, folder 393.

225. Schieder (office of the Reich treasurer), "Bericht über die Tagung der Gauinspekteure . . . vom 8.-23. Juni 1939," T-580, roll 817, box 244, folder 106.

226. Karl Stadler, ed., *Österreich 1938–1945 im Spiegel der NS-Akten* (Vienna, 1966), pp. 22–24.

227. Domarus, *Hitler,* I, 810 and 817.

ings of the fellow-traveling Austrian government headed by Arthur Seyss-Inquart,[228] the commissioner was also authorized to control all negotiations between German and Austrian party agencies.[229] Hess stated that Bürckel's office was subject to Schwarz's audits, but not accountable to the German governmental auditors. The StdF justified his unusual pronouncement by the revealing statement that Bürckel received his orders from the party, not the government.[230] Hess, for his part, was not similarly modest in his dealings with state affairs in Austria. Only a month after the Anschluss, Hitler decreed that the Austrian government had to consult the StdF before issuing decrees or passing legislation.[231]

Bürckel's relationship with both Schwarz's and Hess's offices was excellent—far better in fact that his relations with the Austrian governmental organs. He established an office of "membership affairs" to regularize the intake of Austrian Nazis into the NSDAP, and generally cooperated in a thoroughly satisfactory manner with Schwarz's representative in Vienna.[232] In a similar manner Bürckel supported the activities of the StdF's office in Austria. The "native" Austrian Gauleiters Globocnik (Vienna), Friedrich Rainer (Salzburg), and Hubert Klausner (Tyrol) regarded Hess as their immediate superior within the party. Shortly after the Anschluss, the three went to Berlin to consult with the StdF on their progress and complaints.[233] Hess's representative in Bürckel's office was Albert Hoffmann, a long-time staffer in the office of the deputy Führer and one of its brightest prospects.[234] As *Stillhaltekommissar* (literally, stoppage commissioner) he was in charge of the political, organizational, and to a lesser extent the economic Gleichschaltung of Austria. The take-over of the Austrian Nazi Party organiza-

228. Hitler to Seyss-Inquart, 23 April 1938, BA/R 43 II/131a.
229. StdF, "Anordnung," 14 March 1938, BA/NS 6/228.
230. Hess to Frick, 29 March 1939, T-580, roll 842, box 267, folder 347.
231. Lammers to the Reich ministers, 12 April 1938, BA/R 43 II/139a.
232. Saupert, "Besuchs-Vermerk . . . ," 4 June 1938, T-580, roll 81, folder 393. To be sure, like most Nazi political leaders he was a bit too much of a spendthrift for Schwarz's taste. See Willy Schieffer (Schwarz's auditor for Upper Austria) to Schwarz, 13 April 1938, T-580, roll 813, box 242, folder 84.
233. Rainer to Himmler, 6 July 1939, in Stadler, *Österreich*, p. 42.
234. Born in 1907, Hoffmann joined the NSDAP in 1926 (membership no. 41,165). By profession he was a traveling salesman, and he came to the staff of the StdF in August 1934.

tion by its parent institution in Germany took place via Hoffmann's office. He had the power, for example, to halt or intervene in any negotiations between a party office in the Altreich and an Austrian party group.[235]

Bürckel and his superiors in the Reich were determined to achieve in Austria what they had been unable to accomplish in the Altreich: the thoroughgoing partification and Nazification of the society. As a result, Bürckel soon pushed aside the more conservative "native" Austrian Nazis. At the beginning of 1939 Globocnik resigned (technically at his own request) as Gauleiter of Vienna, and Bürckel took his place.[236] The actual reasons for the change seem to have been some financial irregularities and, more important, Globocnik's effort to work for something akin to Austrian autonomy.[237] The latter desire was also the underlying cause of the bitter feud between Bürckel and Seyss-Inquart. This struggle, which reached such proportions that both men corresponded only through mediators, lasted well into the war; even Himmler was not able to mediate between these two SS comrades (both Bürckel and Seyss-Inquart held high honorary SS ranks).[238] The Austrian prime minister, for all of his fellow-traveling habits, was essentially a conservative in that he favored the preservation of much of the old order, and merely wanted to use the Nazis' power position to retain the essence of Austrian authoritarianism. As Bürckel put it succinctly, "You are for conserving; by order of the Führer, my function is to liquidate."[239]

Above all, the Nazis wanted to liquidate the remnants of the values and traditions of the old imperial Austria which Hitler had come to hate in his youth. Consequently, they attempted in every sense of the word to create in Austria a new political and territorial organism which, even formally, was to have as little as possible to do with the old Austria. The Austrian provinces were not only dissolved as federal states, but were

235. StdF, "Anordnung 31/38," 24 March 1938; and Bürckel, "Anordnung," 11 April 1938, BA/NS 22/626.

236. Hitler, "Anordnung 36/39," 30 Jan. 1939, T-580, roll 548, folder 659, part 2. Globocnik later served as SS leader in Poland.

237. Schieder, "Telefonische Unterredung 22. September 1938," 23 Sept. 1938; and Saupert, "Besuchs-Vermerk . . . Saupert, Wachlin . . . Hoffmann," 29 Aug. 1938, T-580, roll 82, folder 393.

238. The relevant correspondence is in the BDC/Bürckel (SS) file.

239. Bürckel to Seyss-Inquart, 8 Aug. 1939, *ibid.*

renamed so that the word Austria no longer appeared in any provincial designation. The Reichsreform, dead in the Altreich, came to sudden life in Austria. The Nazis created seven Reichsgaus, headed by Gauleiters who, as chiefs of the governmental administration in their areas, had considerably greater powers than their counterparts in the Altreich.[240] The model for the Austrian Reichsgaus was the "Greater Hamburg" law of 1937,[241] not the Reichsstatthalter law of 1933. As in Germany, the governmental and party districts had the same borders; there were eighty-two districts in Austria.[242]

Since the Nazis came to power in Austria by conquest from without, rather than erosion from within, as was the case in Germany in 1933, the establishment of party-state and intraparty relationships in Austria was subject to far fewer pressures and counterpressures from already established societal power factors than had been the case in the Altreich. In practice, the party's institutions, and in particular the office of the StdF and his Stillhaltekommissar, proceeded with a singular lack of tact and subtlety. The NSDAP in Austria was organized essentially according to blueprints worked out within the office of the StdF. Money, for example, was no object. In the brief year of its existence, about RM 14 million were handled by Hoffmann's office.[243] The integration of the Austrian party structure into what was now called the Greater German Reich was accomplished primarily with Reich German personnel. Ley sent Gau organization leaders to Austria, relieving the Austrians of the chance to make their own mistakes.[244] In addition, every district leader in Austria received a Reich German "advisor."[245] There was apparently no lack of candidates for these positions in Austria, a development which is not surprising in view of the fact that the district leaders' salaries for the duration of their service in Austria were considerably higher

240. Lammers to the Reichsstatthalters (with the exception of Austria and the Sudeten areas), 24 April 1939, BA/R 43 II/1390d.

241. Ipsen, "Niederschrift," p. 7.

242. ROL, *Gau- Kreis- und Ortsgruppenverzeichnis . . . Österreich.*

243. Schuh (auditor in the Reich treasurer's office) and Schieder, "Telefon-Notiz," 5 Dec. 1939, BDC/Bürckel (SS).

244. Ley to Bürckel, 10 May 1938, BA/NS 22/626.

245. See Hermann Dröge, "Drei Wochen Dienstleistung in Österreich," *Hoheitsträger*, II (June 1938), 18–19.

than they were in the Altreich.[246] Throughout the Austrian Gleichschaltung, the party leaders in Munich were visibly determined to apply
the lessons of five frustrating years of semitotal power in Germany.[247]
The head of the StdF's personnel office conducted a thorough investigation of the Austrian PL folders from the beginning,[248] rather than
waiting until the men had proved disastrous as full-time cadre functionaries before attempting to replace them. His superior, Helmuth
Friedrichs, required the clear subordination of the affiliates to the Hoheitsträgers.[249] On the other hand, the party was lavish with economic
gifts to the "old fighters." The Viennese Gau economic advisor, Walter
Rafelsberger, attempted to secure expropriated Jewish shops for as
many "old fighters" as possible.[250] For that matter, the motto "enrichez-
vous" had a definite meaning for the party organization itself. Almost
RM 700,000 of the funds deposited in the account of the Stillhaltekommissar came from seized Jewish assets.[251]

The party's take-over in Austria took place behind the scenes, but
Hitler and the NSDAP were determined to demonstrate public approval
of the Auschluss by staging a prebiscite and Reichstag election. The
annexation of Austria brought the party and the Third Reich close to
a foreign policy revolution. Germany had finally annexed a territory
in Europe which had not been a part of the Wilhelminian Reich, and
whose seizure therefore could not be justified under the guise of revis-

246. Office of the financial and party administrator in the Sudetenland to Schieder, 31 March 1939, T-580, roll 809, box 240, folder 60.
247. With the benefit of hindsight, even staffers in the office of the StdF felt
there had been an excessive amount of Reich German interference in the Gleichschaltung of Austria. See Eftger, "Vorlage für Pg. Schmidt," 7 Oct. 1942, RvO/
Generalkommissar zur besonderen Verwendung in den Niederlanden/1c. Fritz
Schmidt, another StdF staffer, became head of the NSDAP organization in the
Netherlands after the German invasion of Holland.
248. Great Britain, Ministry of Economic Warfare, *Who's Who in Germany and
Austria* (London, 1945), II, 116.
249. Friedrichs to Bürckel, 30 July 1938, T-81, roll 641, frame 5444198.
250. Helmut Genschel, *Die Verdrängung der Juden aus der Wirtschaft im Dritten Reich* (Göttingen, 1966), pp. 162 and 165–66.
251. Schuh and Schieder, "Telefon-Notiz," 5 Dec. 1939, BDC/Bürckel (PKC).
See also Genschel, *Verdrängung*, pp. 165–66. Simultaneously, the DAF attempted
to seize control of the funds held by the Austrian insurance companies. See Hupf-
auer to Simon, 12 May 1938, BA/NS 22/626.

ing the Treaty of Versailles. Hitler was fully aware of the importance of this departure and, as was his custom, concretized his further ambitions in architectural terms. In the euphoric mood of early 1938 he declared that the new Reich chancellery (which was still under construction) was already to small. He told his adjutant that it would be turned over to Hess as the official residence of the deputy Führer, while Hitler would move into yet another building, presumably larger and more commensurate with his increased status in the world.[252] Directed as always by Goebbels[253] and backed by a lavish use of money,[254] the NSDAP's campaign was also the baptism of fire for the German district leader-advisors in Austria.[255] The result of the plebiscite and election was a predictable 99.0827 percent for the Anschluss[256] and a new Greater German Reichstag—the last to be seated during the Third Reich. Its membership, suitably augmented by a number of prominent Austrian "old fighters" and fellow travelers, consisted mostly of full-time PLs.[257]

There is no doubt that the annexation of Austria signaled a major shift in the power relationships of the various components in the NSDAP. Above all, it bolstered the position of the StdF's office, both in its own eyes and in those of Hitler. The Führer even suggested that Hess needed a more precise title. "Deputy Führer" implied too much, since Hess was not Hitler's deputy for the army and the government, but "deputy Führer of the NSDAP" suggested too little, because Hess was obviously far more than merely Hitler's deputy chief for the party.[258] Hess's staff could not have agreed more. The head of the di-

252. Wiedemann, *Der Mann*, p. 203.

253. Winfried B. Lerg, "Die Ansprache von Joseph Goebbels am 19. März 1938," *Publizistik*, VII (May/June 1962), 171–73.

254. All campaign expenses in Austria were paid with Reich government funds. See Saupert, "[Telefon] -Vermerk . . . Schwarz . . . Bormann, 16.3.1938," T-580, roll 81, folder 393. For the financial aspects in the *Altreich* see Rschm., "Anordnung 22/38," 25 March 1938, *Rdschr.*, V.

255. Ley to Bürckel, 6 May 1938, BA/NS 22/626.

256. *VB*, 11 April 1938.

257. A number of incumbents were apparently not renominated because they did not hold a full-time cadre position. See DAF to Frick, 12 April 1938, Hauptarchiv Berlin (cited hereafter as HAB)/320/39. For the makeup of the candidate lists see Fabricius, "Vermerk," 1 Feb. 1938, *ibid.*

258. Lammers to Hess, and Bormann to Lammers, 7 and 14 June 1938, BA/R 43 II/139a.

vision of state affairs was convinced that a low-level civil servant was able to handle work within the staff of the StdF for which a ministry required at least an assistant secretary, a view that Bormann regarded as tactless, but not necessarily untrue.[259] There is no indication that Hess disagreed with his chief of staff; on the contrary, the relationship between the two men was still quite cordial. Their division of labor seems to have been well established and mutually respected. At this time (1938) Hess was still very much in the thick of the party administration; his appointment calendar for October of 1938, for example, lists a series of conferences with Gauleiters and other party leaders. It is true that the two officials saw each other infrequently in person, since Bormann was in constant attendance upon Hitler, but Helmuth Friedrichs, the head of the party division, served as liaison officer. In weekly meetings with the deputy Führer, lasting up to three hours, he obtained Hess's basic policy decisions. He then communicated these to Bormann, who cast them into orders, directives, and binding opinions of the office of the StdF.[260]

The StdF used the increased stature of his office after the Anschluss to reclaim the party's influence in a number of policy areas which had seemingly been closed to the party before 1938. Notable among these were church affairs, judicial reform, and economics. As far as the churches were concerned, the StdF sabotaged plans of the Reich minister for church affairs, Kerrl, to achieve a modus vivendi between church and state in Nazi Germany. Since Hess had to approve all ministerial acts touching on ideological questions, his consistent refusal to voice an opinion on Kerrl's projects permanently tabled the initiatives of the ministry for church affairs.[261] There could be no question, of course, of genuine neutrality for the party. Internally, the NSDAP continued

259. Heinrich Hanssen, "Vermerk für den Reichsleiter," 17 Oct. 1938; and Bormann's marginalia dated the same day, T-580, roll 79, folder 368. Staffers in the division of state affairs were automatically promoted along the civil service ladder in addition to their PL career.

260. A series of documents relating to Hess's appointments and decisions in the fall of 1938 are in T-580, roll 79, folder 368.

261. Hess was extremely candid about his obstructive tactics in *Rede auf dem Reichsparteitag 1938*, special ed. ([Munich], 1938), p. 5. Bormann had the speech printed and sent to all district leaders. A copy is in MiU/GAC, folder 51. See also Kerrl to Lammers, 22 Nov. 1938, BA/R 43 II/178.

to subject its PLs to vigorous antichurch propaganda.[262] In the area of penal reform, the StdF was looking ahead to the party's legal role in wartime Germany. Hess wanted a provision put in the German penal code giving the party the right to define a person as asocial (and hence subject to incarceration in a concentration camp), and generally demanded greater powers for the NSDAP during times of declared states of war and national emergency.[263] In the field of economic policy, the Anschluss inaugurated a more active phase of the economic persecution of the German Jews. "Aryanizations," that is, the forcible expropriation of Jewish business properties at a fraction of their actual worth and their reassignment to Reich Germans, enabled the party to interfere directly in the economic life of the country. Since most of the expropriated properties were small businesses, the StdF and the Gau economic advisors had a unique opportunity to revive the 1933 policies favoring small businesses: at least indirectly the party was to determine who could obtain one of the expropriated businesses.[264] Technically, this power was placed with the various chambers of industry and commerce, which operated under the control of the Reich economics ministry, but the party made very sure that the Gauleiters and Hess had a veto over appointments in the chambers. In addition, the Gau economic advisors were placed on an equal footing with the chief of civil administration and the police chief as far as the chambers of industry were concerned.[265] Needless to say, the StdF insisted upon political guidelines to determine the economic suitability of the waiting vultures. Anyone who had been found guilty by a party court could not operate an "Aryanized" business.[266]

The policy initiatives also had an intraparty effect. Among the PLs a sort of minor purge took place in mid-1938. The result was, at least on paper, a more streamlined and homogeneous PL corps. The ROL eliminated such vestigial offices of the Kampfzeit as that of business

262. See, for example, Rschm., "Anweisung 38/38," 30 Nov. 1938, *Rdschr.*, V.
263. Hess to Lammers, 30 Sept. 1938, BA/R 22/20681. See also Hess, *Rede 1938*, p. 10.
264. See StdF, "Anordnung," 31 Oct. 1938, BA/NS 6/vorl. 232.
265. Gau economic advisor Berlin, "Bekanntmachung 5/38," *Gau*, no. 62 (15 June 1938), p. 138.
266. StdF, "Anordnung," 30 Sept. 1938, BA/NS 6/231; and Rschm., "Anordnung 57/38," 2 Sept. 1938, *Rdschr.*, V.

manager, whose functions had long been divided among the various "political" offices of the PO.[267] These minor reforms also provided the ROL with yet another—no doubt welcome—opportunity to launch a special training program for the remaining PLs.[268] The StdF's office was more concerned with the position of the Hoheitsträgers and the social homogeneity of the PL corps. Its personnel measures were directed primarily against church membership and church affiliation among PLs. In a series of directives issued in the summer of 1938, the PLs were prohibited from holding any major church office, and ordained ministers and priests were simply forbidden to hold party membership. The StdF at first merely prohibited lay church officials from being Hoheitsträgers, but he added that they should be excluded as political leaders as soon as replacements could be found.[269] At the same time, the StdF's office was again working on a more sophisticated ranking scale within the party, a bureaucratic feature that was as much a prerequisite for a highly mobile and sharply differentiated party bureaucracy as Schwarz's salary scale.[270]

The status of the Hoheitsträgers was less subject to simple solutions. The aim of the StdF's office was clear enough: to establish the Hoheitsträgers as definitely superior to the horizontal offices in their staffs[271] and clearly inferior to the Hoheitsträgers of the next larger territorial unit. This meant, of course, that Hess as the sole Reichshoheitsträger of the NSDAP had authority over both the Reichsleiters[272] and the

267. See *VOBl*, nos. 174, 175, 176, and 186 (15 and 31 Aug., 15 Sept. 1938 and 15 Feb. 1939). The office of the Reich business manager had long since been abolished and its incumbent, Philipp Bouhler, relegated to an obscure basement office in the Brown House.

268. The various training courses were announced in the issues of *Rdschr.*, V.

269. StdF, "Anordnung," 1 June and 27 July 1938, BA/NS 6/229 and 230. By mid-1938 the party was making efforts to convert the local leaders into full-time PO functionaries. See Gumpert, "Die Arbeit des Ortsgruppenleiters," *Hoheitsträger*, II (June 1938), 22.

270. Saupert, "Besuchs-Vermerk . . . Saupert . . . Friedrichs . . . 9.6.38," 10 June 1938, T-580, roll 82, folder 393.

271. Lange (of the staff of the StdF), "Stichworte für eine Rede . . . Friedrichs vor den Gauleitern, Gauamtsleitern und Kreisleitern der NSDAP im Lande Österreich," 11 July 1938, T-580, roll 79, folder 368.

272. Hoffmann to Pannenborg (both of the StdF's staff), 31 Aug. 1938, T-81, roll 641, frame 5444193. See also the new "Beschwerdeordnung" published in *VOBl*, no. 172 (15 July 1938).

Gauleiters.[273] The latter, in turn, would control the district leaders. None of these ideas were new, but the StdF obviously hoped that in the atmosphere of the post-Anschluss months his plans would make greater headway. On the whole, this was not the case. For all its commonsense logic, the vigorous verticalization of the party was no more pleasing to Hitler now than it had been before. Formally, the appointment procedure in the party continued to stand in its way. Hess appointed neither the Reichsleiters nor the Gauleiters; Hitler did. And the Gauleiters did not name their district leaders; Hitler did. The Führer, moreover, had no intention of endowing his deputy with formal control powers over the Gauleiters. As a result, these continued to act much as they had before, ignoring to a large extent their superior Reichshoheitsträger. On the other hand, in view of the Gauleiters' special relationship to Hitler, it is doubtful that formal powers would have been of much use to Hess. His colleague in the Reich treasurer's office, who had been given plenipotentiary powers in 1926, still found some Gauleiters incurring debts without approval and attempting to use the Gau treasurer to rubber-stamp rather than control expenses.[274]

The party congress of 1938, held at Nuremberg, was one of the most important after the Machtergreifung. It was also the last party congress ever to be held, but the marchers could hardly foresee that. The participants were aware, however, that it was the first party congress since the meetings of 1934 in which a major political issue dominated the proceedings. In 1934, the congress was under the shadow of the Röhm affair; in 1938 the party congress served as a climactic prelude to the Munich crisis. The NSDAP was determined to spare no expense or effort to make the congress a grandiose show of Nazi power, discipline, and determination. Schwarz had labored for most of the year to keep the deficit as small as possible.[275] Even so, the anticipated revenues fell far short of the expected expenses. The Reich treasurer hoped that the various special collections and other sources of income would bring in

273. StdF, "Anordnung," 3 Aug. 1938, BA/NS 6/230.
274. Such was the case in Koblenz. See "Bericht der Gaurevisionshauptstelle [Koblenz] nach dem Stand v. 1.7.38," n.d.; and Lambert (Gau treasurer of Koblenz), "Vertraulicher Bericht," 27 May 1938, T-580, rolls 48 and 82, folders 266 and 393.
275. Documentation on the organization of the 1938 party congress is in HAB/320/29 and 31. See also Rschm., "Anordnung 39/38," 2 June 1938, *Rdschr.*, V.

RM 11.8 million, but the total expenses of the Congress were projected as RM 19.8 million, leaving a deficit of roughly RM 8 million.[276] Other party offices were equally eager to do their best to assure a magnificent show. The ROL staged a beauty contest in which points were awarded to the Gau groups on the basis of their appearance during the various martial parades. The total number of points to be earned was 500 and since the discipline of the Munich-Upper Bavarian Gau, to choose an example, left a great deal to be desired, it only managed sixteenth place. Alas, no prize.[277]

It is difficult to assess the role of the 1938 party congress as a final causal factor in the outcome of the Munich conference. Did the power and discipline demonstrated at Nuremberg confirm the British and French leaders in their appeasement policy, or had the surrender of Czechoslovakia already been determined?[278] There was no doubt, however, that the cession of the Sudetenland to Germany shortly after the congress confirmed the NSDAP's view that the Nazi territorial revolution was irresistible. In the eyes of the party, the result of the Munich conference provided the NSDAP with another area that could be organized according to the party's prescriptions. To be sure, there were a few political "givens" which even the Reich Nazi leadership could not ignore. The appointment of Konrad Henlein as Sudetenland Gauleiter was a foregone conclusion, although his subsequent purge of the older wing of the Sudeten Nazi movement was by no means pleasing to the Reich leadership.[279] Nevertheless, even Henlein was not an independent agent. Hitler's proclamation of the Sudetengau on October 15 included a number of powers reserved to the StdF. Henlein had to organize his Gau according to Hess's directives. In addition, Hitler authorized a number of surrounding Gaus to annex parts of the Sudetenland, and, again, it fell to Hess to determine the time of transfer. As had been the case in Austria, hordes of Reich German advisors descended upon Henlein's new Gau. Indeed, many were already in Austria, and simply traveled further southeast.

276. Saupert, "Aktenvermerk," 7 June 1938, T-580, roll 82, folder 393.
277. ROL to GL München-Oberbayern, 21 Nov. 1938, BA/NS 22/133.
278. For a full discussion of the congress and its relation to the Munich crisis see Boris Celovsky, *Das Münchener Abkommen* (Stuttgart, 1958), pp. 331–40.
279. See the complaints of Heydrich to Bormann, 18 Oct. 1938, BA/R 43 II/1199a.

Schwarz sent as his special representative a man who had been the Gau auditor of Bürckel's Gau Palatinate. He remained in the Sudetenland until the end of May 1940 and spent sizable sums for "pure party purposes."[280] Hess's man in Reichenberg, the capital of the Sudetengau, was Albert Hoffmann. His title was again Stillhaltekommissar, but his powers were considerably greater than they had been in Austria. In Austria, Hoffmann, had been Bürckel's subordinate, but in the Sudetenland he became for all practical purposes Henlein's equal. All directives from Altreich party agencies had to be countersigned by both Henlein and Hoffmann before they could be enforced within the Sudetengau.[281] The ROL also sent three of his major officials,[282] and in the end Henlein had to accept forty-five Reich German "district leader–advisors" for his Gau as well. It may be assumed that the Gauleiter was not particularly anxious to play host to these PLs. They were not sent until December, but then they had to leave their Reich posts on twenty-four hours' notice.[283]

It is indicative of the next target of the party's renewed activism that the StdF showed particular interest in the rapid establishment and verticalization of the office of Gau economic advisor in the Sudetenland.[284] Indeed, there is a remarkable telescoping of the time span between successive Nazi aggressions after the Anschluss. Seven months elapsed between Austria and the Munich crisis; it took only another month to stage the *Kristallnacht* (Night of Crystal, from the amount of broken glass) and an additional three months before Hitler moved into the remainder of Czechoslovakia. At first glance the Kristallnacht, the series of riots and pogroms against the German Jews from November 8 to 10, 1938, does not seem to belong in this series of international crises, but actually it was part of the renewed pattern of extralegal violence

280. Rschm. to Gau treasurer Saarpfalz, 31 May 1940, T-580, roll 809, box 240, folder 60; and Baum (the official in question) to Saupert, 4 Nov. 1938, *ibid.*

281. StdF, "Verfügung 148/38," 11 Oct. 1938, BA/NS 22/616. See also Hoffmann, "Lebenslauf," n.d., BDC/Hoffmann (SS).

282. ROL, "Bestätigung," 5 Oct. 1938, BA/NS 22/616.

283. Saupert, "[Telefon]-Vermerk, 3.12.38," 6 Dec. 1938, T-580, roll 82, folder 393.

284. Gau Sudetenland, "Weisung des Gauorganisationsleiters," 22 Nov. 1938, T-580, roll 547, folder 650.

by the NSDAP. In fact, while the Night of Crystal in one sense was the culmination of a whole set of legal and semilegal moves against the Jews of Germany,[285] in another it was a radical departure: not since the early days of the Machtergreifung had the party as a whole been engaged in a nationwide, centrally directed, violent wave of anti-Semitism. After almost six years of frustration, direct action was "in" again. The riots were precipitated by the dramatic assassination of the German diplomat Ernst von Rath by a Polish Jew, Herschel Grünspann, on November 7.[286] The same day riots broke out in Hessen and Magdeburg-Anhalt, areas which had always been particularly strong anti-Semitic focal points.[287] Hitler was informed by the Gauleiter of Hessen, and specifically ordered that the disturbances not be halted.[288] In this explosive atmosphere most party leaders gathered in Munich for the traditional anniversary celebration of the November 9 Putsch. That evening Goebbels made a speech so inflammatory that it sent the Gauleiters rushing to the telephones to arrange for riots in their Gaus.[289] Hitler was not present for Goebbels' address, but he approved fully of the subsequent actions. The day after the riots, in a speech to the German editors, he was obviously proud of the push-button type of obedience with which he was able to move the party.[290]

Essentially, the events of the Kristallnacht involved the murder of several persons and an orgy of violence against Jewish persons and property. The activities involved, particularly, the plundering of small retail and department stores and setting fire to numerous synagogues throughout Germany, but there also took place, to the party's chagrin,

285. Gau Hamburg, *Gaunachrichten*, (edition district 3 [Borgfelde]), IV (1 Sept. 1938), 7.

286. For the background of the 1938 pogrom see the introduction in Treue, "Rede Hitlers . . . 1938," pp. 175 ff.

287. Heinrich Uhlig, "9. November 1938," *Aus Politik und Zeitgeschichte–Das Parlament*, B 45/63 (6 Nov. 1963), p. 4; and Hermann Graml, *Der 9. November* (Bonn, 1953), p. 7.

288. Wiedemann, *Der Mann*, p. 189.

289. *Ibid.*, p. 190; Uhlig, "9. November 1938," pp. 4–5; Graml, *Der 9. November*, pp. 8–9.

290. The atmosphere is described in the autobiographical novel by Bruno E. Werner, *Die Galeere* (Frankfurt, 1949), pp. 149–54. The speech itself has been published in Treue, "Rede Hitlers . . . 1938."

a number of cases of "racial shame," that is, rapes by party officials and SA bullies of young Jewish girls.[291] It would appear that the SS had no part in the excesses. Neither Heydrich nor Himmler was present for Goebbels' speech and both were thoroughly surprised when the riots broke out.[292] Goebbels had intended to place the actual direction of the pogroms in the hands of his propaganda officials in order to recoup his standing with Hitler,[293] but actually the riots were managed in most localities by the PO and the SA.

At the district and local level the party's district leaders for all practical purposes ordered riots to take place,[294] while in the larger cities the SA took over, pushing the PLs pretty much into the background.[295] In some of the largest cities, notably in Hamburg, rioting took place only on a very limited scale. Here, the disturbances were staged almost entirely by agents provocateurs from the neighboring Gaus of East Hanover and Schleswig-Holstein. Kaufmann was not in Munich for Goebbels' speech, and issued strict orders against any riot organization by his own PLs.[296] In contrast, Berlin felt the full fury of the Nazis' unleashed passions. As Gauleiter, Goebbels was determined to set a particularly bad example.

The riots were terminated as quickly as they had begun, and about as spontaneously. On November 10 the StdF sent a telegram to the Gauleiters ordering a cessation of all further arson and destruction of Jewish property.[297] However, actions of mass violence, while easily unleashed, are difficult to stop. The Reich leadership was obviously afraid that the Kristallnacht would lead to radical actions in other areas and eventually to uncontrollable anarchy. The signs of the future were already there. Gauleiter Fritz Wächtler of Bayreuth used the opportuni-

291. A series of such cases which were tried by the OPG is in T-81, roll 57, frames 59972 ff.

292. Graml, *Der 9. November*, p. 9.

293. *Ibid.* This was the time of Goebbels' liaison with the Czech actress Lida Baarova, an affair of which Hitler heartily disapproved.

294. Köhler to Sauckel, 21 Aug. 1939, MiU/GAC, folder 4; Graml, *Der 9. November*, p. 10; and Lionel Kochan, *Pogrom: 10 November 1938* (London, 1957), pp. 64 ff.

295. Graml, *Der 9. November*, pp. 11–12.

296. *Ibid.*, p. 11.

297. StdF, "Anordnung," 10 Nov. 1938, BA/NS 6/231.

ty to force public school teachers in his Gau to sign a pledge that they would no longer teach religion within the public schools.[298] The numerous cases of individual, as opposed to institutionalized, sadism by the rioters demonstrated a progressive lack of control by the staging authorities once the action had begun. Finally, the deliberate abandonment of the normal rules of commercial intercourse in the "transfer" of Jewish businesses to "Aryan" owners led, predictably, to a sharp increase in cases of financial corruption in the various Gaus. Gauleiters and other party officials did indeed get considerable sums with which they started independent business ventures and resurrected their secret accounts.[299] Göring, blunt as always, complained, "I have seen horrible things: chauffeurs and Gauleiters amassed fortunes worth millions."[300] Since further developments along these lines would have negated the centralizing efforts of six years by Schwarz and Hess, the offices of the Reich treasurer and the StdF sharply opposed such practices.[301]

The inherent inability of the party to know when to stop deprived it of most of the anticipated benefits from the Kristallnacht. The NSDAP had expected not only a direct transfer of the Jewish assets to the party, but a series of further legal moves against the Jews as well. There was certainly ample precedent for the first phase of the pogrom. In Austria, the district leaders had financed the buildup of the party simply by seizing the property of Jews residing in the district.[302] Nor was Hitler opposed to this in principle; he had indicated to Goebbels that he favored initiatives by the Gaus in "Aryanizing" Jewish shops.[303] The Reich propaganda minister also felt that the party was entitled to the penalty which was to be levied on the German Jewish community

298. John S. Conway, *The Nazi Persecution of the Churches 1938–1945* (New York, 1968), p. 188. Hess ordered Wächtler's directive to be rescinded.

299. Lükemann, "Reichsschatzmeister," p. 147.

300. Lösener, "Rassereferent," p. 289. In the Gau Franken the Gauleiter received 25% of the value of all "Aryanized" property as a commission. Genschel, *Verdrängung,* p. 242.

301. See StdF, "Anordnung 65/39," 30 March 1939, *Anordnungen, Rundschreiben, Verfügungen* (cited hereafter as *ARV*) (Munich, 1939). This is an unpaginated compendium of directives, circulars, etc. issued by the office of the StdF. It was superceded in 1940 by the publication of the *Reichsverfügungsblatt.*

302. Dröge, "Drei Wochen," p. 18.

303. Uhlig, "9. November 1938," pp. 8–9.

for "precipitating" the riots, but then the party's handling of the riots gave Göring ample opportunity to protest.[304] Thereafter Göring seized the initiative.[305] Under the circumstances not even Hess protested. In a mammoth conference of state, party, and SS officials on November 12, Göring, supported by the SS, was able to wrench many of the Aryanization procedures and most of the economic benefits out of the hands of the NSDAP and have them transferred to the state and to private industry.[306] To the party were left only indirect crumbs; the primary beneficiaries of the "Aryanizations" were the large German industrial concerns. Nevertheless, the party was not left without influence, particularly at the Gau and district levels. Here the Hoheitsträgers had been given orders to screen the applicants for "Aryanized" properties and hence favor members of their cliques.[307] Anyone who was a remote friend of a party leader suddenly obtained Jewish-owned real estate or business enterprises—especially the "old fighters," who, having failed in every other way, received yet another chance to prove that political stalwartness sufficed for effective economic management.[308]

The rise of the *Mittelstands* (middle-class) elements in the party was not only short-lived but counterproductive. Unable to make good the financial losses incurred in the annexation of Austria and the Sudetenland by robbing the Jews, Schwarz was forced not only to delay—again—the often promised salary scale,[309] but to initiate a number of budget cuts for fiscal 1939.[310] At the same time, Hess decreed a further separation of party and communal finances.[311] Even the anti-Semitic campaign came to an abrupt halt: Hitler made the announcement that

304. Graml, *Der 9. November*, p. 17.

305. Genschel, *Verdrängung*, p. 172, n. 143b.

306. Graml, *Der 9. November*, pp. 17–18; Lösener, "Rassereferent," p. 289; and Göring to highest Reich offices *et al.*, Dec. 1938, BA/NS 6/231. Göring's order was issued "in agreement" with Hess. See StdF, "Rundschreiben," 16 Dec. 1938, *ibid.*

307. A good example of the infighting involved in Aryanization cases is in the BDC/Nathusius (SS), folder III. See also Köhler to Schieber (Gau economic advisor of Thuringia), 30 June 1939, MiU/GAC, folder 4; and "Die Praxis der Arisierung," *Hoheitsträger*, III (July 1939), 14–15.

308. Genschel, *Verdrängung*, pp. 160 and 192–94.

309. It had been planned for the end of the year. See Schwarz, "Bericht," Nov. 1937," p. 7; Rschm., "Vertrauliche Mitteilung," 18 Nov. 1938, *Rdschr.*, V.

310. Rschm., "Anordnung 81/38," 19 Dec. 1938, *Rdschr.*, V.

311. StdF, "Anordnung," 27 Oct. 1938, BA/NS 6/231. Schwarz did not, of course, object to the steadily mounting subsidies from the Reich government to

there would be no public identification badge for Jews,[312] so that the radicals did not even have the satisfaction of that achievement. After the emotional release of the Kristallnacht, the PO woke up to find itself confronted with much the same internal problems. The party's administration was growing by leaps and bounds,[313] but there was neither money nor personnel to staff the new positions. Ley continued to oppose a transfer of his personnel office to the staff of the StdF,[314] and Hess's program of in-service training, though expanded to a year's service at the Brown House for each selected PL,[315] still included only a small number of PLs. The ROL, while wanting to retain the personnel office, seemed to have lost all interest in pursuing a systematic personnel policy. The documents processed by Ley's office for this period reveal an incredible number of routine concerns and show absolutely no overall concept or long-range planning. The officials were obviously kept extremely busy giving away prizes for march-pasts, organizing pistol-shooting matches, and the like.[316] No wonder that the Hitler Youth leaders had little interest in a PL career or even in party membership.[317] In 1938 and 1939 Ley appeared to have time only for his training system. He was concerned with channeling all PLs through his various schooling offices, and he took very personal charge of the various marching exercises, which he regarded as the foundation of the next successful party congress.[318] The amount of money needed to carry on the schooling was reaching staggering proportions. The ordinary budget proposed by Ley's office for 1939 came to a grand total of RM 22 million of which roughly RM 16 million was to be paid by the affili-

---

the party. These amounted to RM 32,000,000 in 1938, RM 54,000,000 in 1939 and RM 79,500,000 in 1940. See Rschm., "Jahresbericht 1940," p. 27.

312. Lösener, "Rassereferent," p. 302.

313. Rschm., "Anordnung 81/38."

314. Friedrichs, "Notiz für den Stabsleiter," 17 Nov. 1938, T-580, roll 79, folder 368.

315. Rschm., "Anweisung 7/39," 26 Jan. 1939, *Rdschr.*, VI.

316. The relevant documentation is in BA/NS 22/133 ff.

317. Gau treasurer Thuringia, "Stimmungsbericht 1938," 21 Jan. 1939, p. 7, T-580, roll 804, box 239, folder 39; and Hermann Köhler, "Rundschreiben 37/39," 11 May 1939, MiU/GAC, folder 26.

318. The dates and officials of the numerous training courses are listed in *Rdschr.*, V and VI. Before the 1939 party congress the ROL planned to inspect personally at least one district in each Gau. See Rschm., "Anweisung 8/39," 28 Feb. 1939, *ibid.*, VI.

ates.[319] This meant that in effect the affiliates would have at least a financial hold over the training programs and that, as a result, the Betreuungs image would continue to be the focal point of the entire effort. Ley's sangfroid was all the more remarkable in the face of persistent reports that matters at the Ordensburgen were going from bad to worse. In 1939 Ley's personnel office directed that members of the defunct Werkscharen could become Ordensjunkers even if they were not members of the party.[320] In very crass terms, Ley had been unable to accept Hitler's indirect mandate of November 1937; the ROL's training institutions had proved incapable of producing an efficient PL corps.[321]

Was the Führer now willing, perhaps equally indirectly, to reverse himself and endorse the concepts of the StdF? This would no doubt depend primarily on Hitler's judgment of the party's role in his past and future expansionist plans. Apparently, the party had successfully passed the test. There are a number of indications that Hitler did regard the party as a positive asset in the revolution of German foreign policy. His New Year's proclamation spoke of the accomplishments of the last twelve months as primarily the result of the party's efforts: "The whole movement has brought about this miracle; when the Lord (*der Herrgott*) allowed this work to be accomplished, then the party was His instrument."[322] Two weeks later, Hess assembled the Reichsleiters, Gauleiters, and, significantly, the deputy Gauleiters, in the new Reich chancellery to hear addresses by Hitler and his deputy. The Führer again thanked the party leaders for their aid during the past year,[323] and Hess touched on a number of substantive issues for the future as well. Indeed, the conference dealt with the gamut of public issues, and demonstrated the party's claim to participate in their determination.[324] At the same time, a number of Gauleiters placed a renewed emphasis upon the

319. ROL, main training office, "Der ordentliche Haushaltsvoranschlag," ca. Dec. 1938, BA/NS 22/701.

320. "Bericht des Gauschulungsleiters Kölker im Gau Köln-Aachen," 1 July 1939, BA/NS 8/231.

321. Schwarz regarded Ley's training institutions as so useless that he all but prohibited his staff officials from attending the sessions. See [Rschm.], "Ressortbesprechung 7/39," 8 March 1939, T-580, roll 842, box 267, folder 347.

322. Domarus, *Hitler*, II, 1025.

323. *Ibid.*, pp. 1037–38.

324. See "Aktenvermerk über die Reichs- und Gauleitertagung am 13. und 14. Januar 1939 in Berlin," T-580, roll 833, box 256, folder 271.

leadership and control function of the NSDAP.[325] Hitler availed himself of the advice and talents of individual party leaders on a number of occasions during the year. Gauleiter Streicher was present when Hitler attempted to convince the Italian minister Roberto Farinacci to inaugurate anti-Semitic policies,[326] while Keppler and Bürckel, the old dynamic Austrian team, managed yet another semiannexation, the proclamation of autonomy by Slovakia in March of 1939.[327] And when Germany annexed the rest of Czechoslovakia and proclaimed it the "protectorate" of Bohemia-Moravia, the management of the Reich Germans living within this area was again given to the party.[328]

All these developments brought the StdF and the party as a whole face to face with persistent personnel problems. In this area the spring and summer saw some remarkable developments; it is only a slight exaggeration to state that the PO personnel policy was the focal point of party activity in the months before the outbreak of the war.[329] As a first step in the direction of an effective elite party, the membership rolls were reopened on May 1, 1939. They remained open until February 2, 1942.[330] The aim of the new drive was not to blur the status of party and affiliate member, but, on the contrary, to receive into the party about 10 percent of the population.[331] Thereafter the rolls would be closed permanently and members would be received only as replacements for losses by attrition or through co-option. From the beginning, the new membership drive was coupled with a final effort to launch the national salary scale. The reason was obviously to reduce the excessive heterogeneity in the social composition of the PL corps. Except for age, the PO was less a corps of functionaries than an array of sometime bureaucrats thrown together by happenstance.[332] In what

325. Gau Hamburg, *Gaunachrichten*, (edition district 8) IV (1 Feb. 1939), 10; and Gustav Simon, "Verwaltungsreform im Bereich der westdeutschen Gaue," 10 Jan. 1939, BA/NS 22/581.

326. Domarus, *Hitler*, II, 1045.

327. *Ibid.*, pp. 1090–91.

328. Hitler, "Anordnung," 21 March 1939, *VOBl*, no. 190 (15 April 1939).

329. See the speech of GL Jordan (Magdeburg-Anhalt), 3 June 1939, as quoted in *Der Mitteldeutsche*, 4 June 1939, BDC/Jordan (PKC).

330. Buchheim, "Mitgliedschaft," p. 316.

331. Rschm., "Anordnung 34/39," 10 May 1939, *Rdschr.*, VI.

332. Schoenbaum, *Hitler's Social Revolution*, pp. 256–57. See also Fritz Mehnert, "Die Statistik der NSDAP," *Hoheitsträger*, III (Aug. 1939), 10–11.

were to be the final preparations for the salary scale, the StdF at the beginning of March decreed a complete freeze on all promotions,[333] and Ley worked out an intricate system of service points to determine seniority positions among the PL.[334] The ROL also put the final touches on a list of all PL positions in the party, a project that had been under way since early 1938.[335]

These developments formed the prelude to what turned out to be a fairly massive reorganization of the entire party structure in April and May of 1939, and this elicited a new blast from Ley's office. His house organ, the *Hoheitsträger*, had already announced that in 1939 Ley would "focus his untiring work" on the party organization,[336] which apparently meant yet another effort to halt the steady accumulation of power by the office of the StdF. There was no doubt, of course, that the deputy Führer's office had continued to grow at the expense of other party offices. In particular, the staff's horizontal organization had expanded and with it the self-esteem of Martin Bormann.[337] In May 1939, Hess's chief of staff for the first time allowed himself to be the subject of a word-portrait which gave him the aura of a charismatic leader with which Nazi greats liked to surround themselves.[338] Accordingly, Ley laid his plans rather carefully. He offered the SS an alliance in the form of letting the SD have access to the detailed *Haushaltskarteien* (family data cards) kept by the block leaders.[339] Similarly, Ley made overtures to secure the goodwill of the Reich minister of economics, Walther Funk. Funk, who had succeeded the staunchly conservative (and by this time antiparty) Hjalmar Schacht in February 1938, pursued a policy of appeasement toward the party.[340] The StdF

333. StdF, "Anordnung 54/39," 4 March 1939, *ARV*.

334. ROL, "Anordnung," 1 Aug. 1939, T-175, roll 26, frames 2532371–76.

335. Bormann to Ley, 3 April 1939; and Simon to Bormann, 15 May 1939, T-580, roll 549, folder 746.

336. [F.H.] Woweries, "Fackelträger nicht nur in Nürnberg," *Hoheitsträger*, III (Feb. 1939), 16.

337. Bormann to Ley, 21 July 1939, T-580, roll 549, folder 746, and other documents in this folder. See also Friedrichs, "Rede . . . auf der Tagung der Stellvertretenden Gauleiter am 11. Januar 1940 . . . ," 9 Jan. 1940 [*sic*] pp. 13–14, T-580, roll 843, box 368, folder 352.

338. Borsdorff, "Reichsleiter Martin Borman."

339. Schellenberg, "Vermerk," 11 Aug. 1939, T-175, roll 233, frames 2728150–51.

340. See Funk's speech at the January 1939 GLs and RLs conference, in n.a.,

in turn used Funk's weakness to strengthen the position of the Gau economic advisors (Bernhard Köhler had just died) and to weaken the influence of the economics ministry. Funk objected, and Ley took the minister's side in the dispute.[341]

With this background of negotiations Ley, sometime between April and August 1939, approached Hitler with an ingenious plan. He asked the Führer to appoint him Reich minister of labor and to give formal approval to Ley's 1936 proposal for specific jurisdictional definitions of the Reichsleiters' duties. Since this meant in practice a reduction of the StdF's power, Hitler saw himself confronted with a direct conflict between two Reichsleiters. As was his custom in such situations, he made no decision, or rather, suddenly discovered procedural difficulties. Hitler is reported to have replied (there is no record of what he actually said, but the answer rings true) that while he agreed with Ley's plans, he could not formally endorse them because Ley had drawn them up without consulting the StdF.[342] Ley apparently interpreted this Delphic pronouncement as a sign of approval—and, again, overplayed his hand. In order to obtain the aid of the Gauleiters for his attack on the StdF, he had proposed the revival of something like Gregor Strasser's regional Gau conferences. This was too much for Hitler. He had already prohibited all discussion at Gauleiter conferences,[343] and in Ley's proposal he detected a potential united front against him. In consequence he decreed that the Gauleiters would report to him only as individuals, never as a group. Bormann managed to add a personal sting in conveying Hitler's decision to Ley: "Insofar as necessary the Führer will hold . . . individual conferences [with the Gauleiters], because he can use the occasion to reach decisions which you are in no position to make."[344]

After this rebuff the StdF had no great difficulty in warding off Ley's initiative against the deputy Führer's office itself. At the end of June

---

"Aktenvermerk über die Reichs- und Gauleitertagung am 13. und 14. Januar 1939 . . . ," 16 Jan. 1939, T-580, roll 833, box 256, folder 271.

341. See the relevant correspondence in Bormann to Funk, 8 May; Ley to Funk, 9 May; and Funk to Ley, 17 May 1939, BA/NS 22/561.

342. Schellenberg, "Vermerk," T-175, roll 233, frame 2728150; and SD, staff office, "Vermerk," 21 April 1939, frames 2728144–45.

343. Friedrichs, "Notiz für den Stabsleiter," 6 Jan. 1939, T-580, roll 79, folder 368.

344. Bormann to Ley, 20 May 1939, T-580, roll 549, folder 746.

Ley wrote Hess a long letter complaining essentially about the usurpation of power by the StdF's staff. What he said was true enough. Since 1934 the staff's horizontal organization had more or less duplicated all offices of the Reichsleitung within the bureau of the StdF, while independent control commissions outside the StdF's organization tended to disappear.[345] This meant that the control functions of the StdF were in fact exercised by a series of party bureaucrats of lesser rank than the Reichsleiters and Gauleiters they were supervising. Ley demanded a return to the letter of Hitler's 1933 directive, that is, the "restoration" of Hess's personal control functions and the abolition of the staff organization.[346] Hess and Bormann obviously failed to heed Ley's advice, and two months later Ley tried again. This time he was considerably more modest; he asked merely that the present staff positions be frozen by surrounding them with firm descriptions of their functions.[347] The StdF, rather haughtily, refused. There could, he said, be no specific definition of the deputy Führer's functions, because his field of activity, like that of the Führer himself, was limitless. As to a firm staff organization, this, too, was unnecessary because the Reich treasurer had not indicated a need for such a listing. Finally, if a staff official seemed to make decisions in the name of the StdF, it was only because "as a result of their long experience, these officials are often able to predict the judgment of the deputy Führer with absolute certainty."[348]

What remained of Ley's reorganization scheme was not a redistribution of the power at the top, but a further clarification of the positions at the bottom. The attempt to upgrade the controversial Werkscharen was a complete failure; they were firmly subordinated to the local leader of the party.[349] Whatever large-scale functions Ley had intended for them certainly did not materialize. Their sole remaining project was a campaign to persuade factory workers that they really ought to eat

345. In July Keppler's commission on economic policy was dissolved, but there was no change in the position of the Gau economic advisors or their monthly reports to the StdF's office. StdF, "Anordnung 150/39 [and] 162/39," 31 July and 24 Aug. 1939, *ARV*.

346. Ley to Hess, 20 June 1939, T-580, roll 549, folder 746.

347. Ley to Hess, 17 Aug. 1939, *ibid.*

348. Bormann to Ley, 31 Aug. 1939, *ibid.*

349. *VOBl*, nos. 194 and 196 (15 June and 15 July 1939).

warm lunches rather than bring sandwiches.[350] For the PO as a whole, Ley was able to continue his efforts to develop more precise job descriptions for the PLs at the lower levels[351] and to undertake a project that must have been more than ample compensation for his inability to defeat the StdF: a whole new series of uniforms and insignia designed to upgrade the public image of the PLs.[352]

The StdF was particularly concerned in the last months before the outbreak of the war with the development of a comprehensive personnel policy. The need for some major initiatives in this area was ever more glaringly apparent. Particularly at the Gau and district levels, the PL corps lacked most of the qualities necessary for a group of dynamic political leaders. The average age of the 26,516 PLs active in the Gau Thuringia in April 1939 was 41.5 years, and the group as a whole was solidly white collar: 43.99 percent of the Thuringian PLs were either trained civil servants or office workers, but of these people only 2.2 percent had ever held high-level civil service positions; 97.8 percent had either been teachers or low-ranking civil servants. In addition, fully half of the office workers had been employed by the state in non–civil service positions before they came to their party positions.[353] In effect, the PLs of Thuringia were by profession bureaucrats in subordinate positions with no special talents or training. One district leader described his PLs in these discouraging terms: "Our PLs today are to a large extent overaged, physically handicapped, mentally very slow, and generally inactive people . . . our human material is really the behind-the-lines formation (*Etappenformation*) in the party."[354] The StdF was fully aware of these difficulties, but as yet his remedies had little effect. The in-service training program was still conducted on too small a scale,[355] and such other devices as asking the Gau inspectors to find suitable

350. Ley, "Der Weg der Werkschar," *Hoheitsträger*, III (July 1939), 7–8.

351. See, for example, P. Müller, "Zentralisation oder Dezentralisation," *Hoheitsträger*, III (May 1939), 27–28.

352. ROL, "Anordnung," 9 June 1939, T-175, roll 26, frames 2532386–97. See also *VOBl*, nos. 193 and 194 (31 May and 15 June 1939).

353. Karl Astel and Erna Weber, *Die Kinderzahl der 29000 politischen Leiter des Gaues Thüringen* (Berlin, 1943), pp. 13–16.

354. District leader Rheingau-St. Goarshausen (Gau Koblenz-Trier), "Stimmungsbericht," May/June 1939, p. 5, T-81, roll 119, frame 139812.

355. StdF, "Anordnung 11/39," 10 Jan. 1939, *ARV*.

younger PLs[356] were not systematic enough to yield quick results.

Instead, there was a shift of emphasis. The StdF began to attack those values in German society which, from the party's point of view, prevented the emergence of a properly motivated PL corps. In particular he singled out the Christian churches. As indicated earlier, the StdF excluded all party members with strong church ties from the PL corps.[357] In addition, the party moved against such officials as army chaplains because the NSDAP regarded them as an unhealthy influence in the lives of the soldiers.[358] The Hoheitsträgers quickly joined in. The Gauleiter of Baden, Robert Wagner, was the first within the Altreich to attempt a complete separation of church and state. He insisted that the church was a private club and not entitled to tax moneys.[359] Considerably more dramatic were the moves within the party. In cooperation with the Reich treasurer, the StdF attempted to set up a small-scale alternative to the massive failure of the Adolf Hitler Schools and the order castles. The "Reich School" at Feldafing on the Starnberger Lake (Bavaria) was a boarding school of twelve grades. Its students were thoroughly segregated from the rest of society and it was anticipated that the graduates would be exclusively available for the PL corps of the party. A number of sons of prominent party leaders, including Martin Bormann's eldest son, attended the school. The curriculum of the school was apparently considerably more intellectually oriented than that offered at the Adolf Hitler Schools, and all Feldafing's graduates gained practical experience in party offices.[360] There is little doubt that the StdF hoped to draw replacements for the most important PO positions from the graduates of the school at Feldafing.[361]

356. From 19–23 June the Gau inspectors held a national convention. See Rschm., "Anweisung 38/39," 15 June 1939, *Rdschr.*, VI.

357. StdF, "Rundschreiben 23/29," 23 Jan. 1939, BA/NS 6/201; and "Anordnung 140/39," 14 July 1939, *ARV*. On church-regime relations in general see Speer, *Erinnerungen*, p. 137; Scholder, "Evangelische Kirche," p. 33; and Conway, *Nazi Persecution*, p. 228.

358. See the documents in T-79, roll 83, frames 578–89.

359. Köhler to local leader Eisenach-Süd, 22 Feb. 1939, MiU/GAC, folder 12; and Scholder, "Evangelische Kirche," p. 34.

360. Rschm., "Anweisung 10/37," 14 April 1937, and "Anordnung 49/39," 18 Sept. 1939, *Rdschr.*, VI; and Gau Berlin, *Gau*, no. 34 (1 May 1937), p. 90.

361. StdF, "Anordnung 156/39," 8 Aug. 1939, *ARV*.

For the more immediate future the personnel office of the StdF for the first time was quietly at work—for the moment on paper—reshuffling Gauleiters. This was obviously dangerous ground; the Gauleiters were Hitler's derivative agents and their position, as Opdenhoff admitted, was in principle "untouchable."[362] But, he added, the dismissal of Globocnik had already rendered untouchability a relative concept.[363] The StdF's office was particularly eager to relieve three Gauleiters of their posts: Joseph Wagner (Westphalia and Silesia); Bernhard Rust (Hanover), and, surprisingly, Joseph Bürckel (Palatinate and Vienna). The first two held multiple positions which made them ineffective as party leaders. Wagner was Gauleiter of Westphalia and Silesia as well as Reich price commissioner. In addition, his close relationship to the Catholic Church obviously did not endear him to the officials of the StdF. Rust was a weak leader who had taken no active part in the administration of his Gau since his appointment as Reich minister of culture in 1933. Bürckel's deficiencies were an entirely different matter. Although he, too, held two Gauleiter posts, he was obviously a strong Gauleiter who had served Hitler well in a number of sensitive jobs. But precisely because of his dominant personality, he was particularly adept at clique building. Both in the Palatinate and in Vienna, Bürckel had surrounded himself with his own crowd, making centralized control of his Gaus difficult. In the end, none of the three officials were dismissed. There were simply no suitable replacements. The StdF hesitated to turn to individuals outside the PO (one of those under consideration was August Heissmeyer, the head of the SS's training office), and among the PLs "no one had been tested (*erprobt*) to the extent that one could unhesitatingly entrust a Gau to him."[364]

That judgment included the deputy Gauleiters, presumably the logical reservoir of Gauleiter replacements. To increase the feeling of security among the territorial leaders, Hitler had already decreed that no deputy Gauleiter would ever become Gauleiter in the area in which he had served as second in command,[365] but perhaps deputy Gauleiters

362. Opdenhoff to Hess, 20 Feb. 1939, quoted in Stadler, *Österreich*, p. **44.**
363. [Opdenhoff], "Niederschrift," 23 Feb. 1939, T-580, roll 80, folder 371.
364. T-580, roll 80, folder 371 is devoted entirely to the 1939 search for new GLs. The quotation is from Opdenhoff's "Niederschrift," *ibid.*
365. Bormann to Lammers, 23 Aug. 1939, BA/R 43 II/1390b.

could be reassigned to other Gaus. The personnel office of the StdF accordingly took stock of the deputy Gauleiter corps. As a first step, the Gauleiters were asked to evaluate their chief assistants. The predictable results were uniform paeans—either because the deputies were personal friends of the Gauleiters or because a Gauleiter hoped to have his deputy transferred.[366] Typical was the judgment of deputy Gauleiter Harry Henningsen in Hamburg, whom Kaufmann described as extremely able. Opdenhoff knew better. "The Gauleiter would like to get rid of him, but I don't think there is much use for him elsewhere."[367] After compiling massive lists of candidates, Opdenhoff could develop no great enthusiasm for the possibilities among most of the incumbents.[368] Instead, the StdF's office set out to groom the younger PLs who were either already on the staff of the StdF or who had looked particularly impressive during their year in the Brown House.[369]

There remained a third route to influence the personnel of the PO. In July, 1937 the StdF had established a section on mobilization within his staff organization, and appointed the SS Colonel Knoblauch to head the new office.[370] Knoblauch worked quietly but effectively to prepare the party for war, and by the time of the Munich crisis the necessary directives lay ready to be issued.[371] The StdF's "assistant for mobilization" (*M-Beauftragter*) had functions ranging far beyond the drafting of an administrative preparedness program for the party. With the appointment of M-assistants in all Gaus and districts (this was completed in July 1938), the StdF created a fully verticalized line of officials sub-

366. See the evaluation of deputy GL Holz (Franken) and Henningsen (Hamburg) by their respective GL in BDC/Holz (PKC) and BDC/Henningsen (PKC).

367. Opdenhoff, "Niederschrift," 23 Feb. 1939. Kaufmann had been attempting to have his deputy transferred since 1937. See Friedrichs to Ley, 16 March 1937, BA/NS 22/578.

368. Opdenhoff, "Niederschrift," 23 Feb. 1939.

369. See Friedrichs, "Vorlage an den Stabsleiter," 20 Nov. 1939, BDC/Giesler (SA); and Hanssen to Bormann, 12 April 1939, BDC/Heim (PKC).

370. See Robert Ley, "Die innere Front tut ihre Pflicht," *Schulungsbrief*, VI (Sept. 1939), 330.

371. Schneider (office of the Reich treasurer), "Denkschrift über Einsatz und Arbeitsgebiet des Ressorts Reichsschatzmeister im Kriegsfalle," 9 Aug. 1937, T-580, roll 842, box 267, folder 347. See also Rschm., "Bericht, Nov. 1937," p. 45; and Saupert, *Vortrag des Beauftragten des Reichsschatzmeisters . . . VI. Arbeitstagung der Gauschatzmeister am 17. März 1939* ([Munich, 1939]), pp. 4 and 6–30.

ject only to his directives. Since the StdF was the only Reichsleiter of the party to hold membership in the Reich-level "ministerial council for the defense of the Reich,"[372] his authority in the area of mobilization was exclusive within the party, and his M-assistants, consequently, were responsible only to the deputy Führer. As a result, Hess selected as his M-assistants in the Gaus the deputy Gauleiters or Gau staff leaders, the two most important party officials other than the Hoheitsträgers.[373]

With the outbreak of World War II the NSDAP faced the supreme test of its existence. It failed, of course. But had it made realistic preparations for a battle waged to the death? By and large, no. As before, the NSDAP could not decide between its roles as political decision-maker and popular ombudsman. The party was still torn between its love for power and its desire to be loved.[374] The same PLs who were exercising control functions[375] still devoted inordinate amounts of time to the execution of propagandistic routines and the sale of brochures to boost the party's finances.[376] In most party offices popularity was an indication of political effectiveness. Yet there was within the PO a sizable residue of that old revolutionary fervor which had characterized elements of the party during the Kampfzeit. Some Gauleiters[377] and district leaders clearly looked upon themselves as social revolutionaries (one district leader openly spoke of the "pigs on the south side" of his town, the south side being the more wealthy residential section).[378] The "peaceful" ex-

372. Domarus, *Hitler*, I, 1240.

373. StdF, "Abwehrmassnahmen der NSDAP, ihrer Gliederungen und angeschlossenen Verbände," 1 July 1938, T-580, roll 43, folder 253. See also StdF, "Anordnung," 2 July 1938, BA/NS 6/230.

374. This judgment is based upon the "Tätigkeitsberichte" of the district leadership of Eisenach for 1939, in MiU/GAC, folders 1, 26, 27, and 28.

375. ". . . und alles ehrenamtlich," Gau Hamburg, *Gaunachrichten*, (edition district 4) IV (1 Feb. 1939), 9; and "'Leitender Ingenieur' des Kreises," *ibid.* (15 Feb. 1939), 6. See also district organizational leader of Eisenach, "Rundschreiben 22/39," 17 March 1939, MiU/GAC, folder 26.

376. Cf. the list of songs each PL had to know by heart. Köhler, "Rundschreiben 25/39," 24 March 1939, MiU/GAC, folder 26; cell leader 9 local Eisenach-Ost, "Bericht über die Tätigkeit eines Blockleiters . . . April . . . Mai 1939" [June 1939], *ibid.*, folder 11.

377. "Die Rede des Gauleiters," Gau Hamburg, *Gaunachrichten* (edition district 4), IV (15 Feb. 1939), 2–6.

378. See the documents on the daily activities of the district leader in Eisenach, MiU/GAC, folders 20–23. See also local leader Eisenach-Ost to district leader Eisenach, 27 Jan. 1939, *ibid.*, folder 11.

pansion of the Reich's borders in 1937 and 1938 had already given the radicals new grounds for their activities. With the outbreak of war, with the beginning of what quickly became a struggle for the existence of the regime itself, these tendencies not only received an additional lease on life, but in fact were able increasingly to control the party and the Third Reich as the fortunes of war turned against both. In that sense, the declaration of World War II was a confirmation of the radicalism that had characterized the NSDAP in the first months of the Machter-greifung.

Dizzy with Success

The decision to send tanks and Stukas across the Polish frontiers at dawn on September 1, 1939, was Hitler's own. As an institution, the party was not consulted about the steps that led to the outbreak of World War II. Indeed, the commencement of actual hostilities caught many PLs by surprise. When Hitler addressed the Reichstag in a special session later that morning, more than a hundred of the members were not in Berlin. Göring hastily rounded up local party functionaries to fill the gaping holes in the audience.[1]

The party's passivity in the decision-making process contrasted with the active role which Hitler assigned it in the war effort. While the Führer shut himself off from all spontaneous and most large-scale contact with the German people,[2] he gave the party the responsibility of maintaining morale among the civilian population—an exceedingly ungratifying task since the news of war was received by most Germans with sullen stoicism. For Hitler, the party was to guarantee that there would not be another November 1918; throughout the war, the Nazi leader lived in fear of a revolution at home. It was also something of a triumph for the StdF's office that Hitler placed most of the responsibility (and hence power) for carrying out the wartime role of the NSDAP in the hands of the Hoheitsträgers. "Let no one report that morale might be low in his Gau, district, local group or cell," Hitler declared on September 1. "You are responsible for morale in your Gau

1. Max Domarus, ed., *Hitler, Reden und Proklamationen 1932–1945*, 2d ed. (Munich, 1965), II, 1311.
2. *Ibid.*, p. 1005. See also, StdF, "Anordnung," 14 Nov. 1939, Bayerisches Geheimes Staatsarchiv (cited hereafter as BGStA), Reichstatthalter 48/1–7.

or district."[3] As a reward for its difficult labors, the Führer publicly raised the status of the party in the succession lineup: although Göring remained his immediate successor, he was now followed by Hess, and, should both be unavailable, the decision would be made by the phantom party senate.[4]

The PLs' reaction to the outbreak of World War II was a combination of exhilaration and fear. There is no doubt, and this would become increasingly apparent as the war effort intensified, that many of the PLs welcomed the opportunities for career advancement and the possible resumption of social dynamics that could be pursued under the guise of wartime sacrifices. The actual outbreak of hostilities brought new tasks in both the control and Betreuung areas. In one sphere, the party was entrusted with aiding the population in dealing with the new rationing system and the myriad problems that arose when the husband and provider was drafted into the army.[5] At the same time, the war brought opportunities for political denunciations, intraparty purges,[6] and increased influence over other institutional components in the Third Reich.[7] Yet the party was also apprehensive about popular reaction to the war. Especially in the early days and weeks of the war, it had

3. Domarus, *Hitler*, II, 1317.

4. *Ibid.*, p. 1316.

5. See StdF, "Anordnung 173/39," 18 Sept. 1939, *Anordnungen, Rundschreiben, Verfügungen* of the deputy Führer (cited hereafter as *ARV*); Hellmuth Friedrichs, "Rede . . . Friedrichs auf der Tagung der Stellvertretenden Gauleiter am 11. Januar 1940 in München . . . ," 9 Jan. 1940 [*sic*], pp. 1 4, and 7, T-580, roll 843, box 268, folder 352; Alfred Rosenberg, *Das politische Tagebuch Alfred Rosenbergs 1934/35 und 1939/40*, ed. Hans-Günther Seraphim (Munich, 1964), entry for 24 Sept. 1939, pp. 95–96; and Wolfgang Schäfer, *NSDAP* (Hanover, 1956), p. 50. For a district leader's impression of his wartime role see Johannes Lange, "Eingabe Langes," 28 May 1947, Forschungsstelle für die Geschichte des Nationalsozialismus in Hamburg (cited hereafter as Forsch. Hbg.)/PA/12/L.

6. Reichsschatzmeister (cited hereafter as Rschm.), "Anordnung 60/39," 5 Sept. 1939, *Rundschreiben des Reichsschatzmeisters* (cited hereafter as *Rdschr.*), VI. See also the documents in the Hauptarchiv Berlin (cited hereafter as HAB)/320/40–44, relating to the purges of Nazi Reichstag members for a variety of nonpolitical reasons, ranging from alcoholism to forgeries.

7. In November 1939 the district leaders (or their representatives) received permission to be present at the physical examination of draftees. See StdF, "Rundschreiben 23/42 [*sic*]," 30 Nov. 1939, *Verfügungen, Anordnungen, Bekanntgaben* of the PK (cited hereafter as *VAB*), III, 274.

genuine fears, if not of a popular revolt, at least of widespread tendencies toward disengagement or passive resistance.[8]

Since the party's fears proved to be groundless, the various wings of the PO began to include the opportunities inherent in the new situation as part of their strategy for power accumulation. The office of the deputy Führer found itself in a particularly advantageous position. Following Hitler's emphasis on the importance of the Hoheitsträgers, Hess underscored his own position as Reichshoheitsträger while simultaneously reducing both the power and the importance of other Reichsleiters' offices.[9] The StdF classified his peers' authority as subordinate to his own; all decisions of the Reichsleiters had to be cleared by the StdF's office before being enforced or made public.[10] Hess claimed these additional shackles were necessary because martial situations called for increased unity of purpose within the party. Under no circumstances could criticism from below be tolerated; such attitudes were "always the first step toward mutiny." In contrast, "positive criticism" from higher offices was a healthy sign of vigilance.[11] Hess also took care to reiterate that his office alone could speak for the NSDAP in all party-state negotiations.[12]

The StdF realized that to a very large extent the effectiveness of the PO's function as controller and Betreuer of the German population de-

---

8. See Domarus, *Hitler*, II, 1072; StdF, "Anordnung 175/39 [and] 176/39," 20 and 25 Sept. 1939, *ARV*; and head of provincial government in Aurich to Reich Defense Commissioner X, 12 Aug. 1940, Bundesarchiv (cited hereafter as BA)/NS 6/417. In order to prevent even the opportunity for massed action, the StdF specifically prohibited a repetition of the 1938 pogrom after an attempt on Hitler's life in November, 1939. See StdF, "Anordnung 217/39," 9 Nov. 1939, *ARV*. For a discussion of the attempt itself see Anton Hoch, "Das Attentat auf Hitler im Münchner Bürgerbräukeller 1939," *Vierteljahrshefte für Zeitgeschichte* (cited hereafter as *Vjh.f.Z.*), XVII (Oct. 1969), 383–413.

9. StdF, "Anordnung 170/39," 15 Sept. 1939, *ARV*. See also Friedrich Wilhelm Lampe, *Die Amtsträger der Partei* (Stuttgart, 1941), p. 98.

10. StdF, "Anordnung 182/39 [and] 215/39," 1 and 17 Oct. 1939, *ARV*; and "Bekanntgabe 24/40," 11 May 1940, *Reichsverfügungsblatt* (cited hereafter as *RVBl*). Hitler indirectly supported Hess's decree by all but denying the Reichsleiters immediate access to his person. See StdF, "Anordnung 215/39," 17 Oct. 1939, *VAB*, I, 11.

11. Friedrichs, "Rede Stellv. GL 1940," p. 11.

12. StdF, "Anordnung 182/39," 1 Oct. 1939, *ARV*.

pended upon an accurate flow of information from the lower levels of the Hoheitsträgers to his office. As a result, very shortly after the outbreak of the war Hess inaugurated a system of weekly reports from the Gau and district Hoheitsträgers. Each Saturday every Gauleiter and district leader sent to Munich a lengthy analysis of morale conditions. At the Brown House the reports were collated, digested, and, if necessary, followed up by the staff of the StdF. At Hitler's headquarters, Bormann regularly received a Telexed summary.[13] The mechanics of assembling and preparing the reports at the Gau and district level were assigned to a newly established office, staffed by a full-time PL.[14] Even so, Hess distrusted the honesty of the PLs. Lest the reports contain only desk-bound banalities, the Hoheitsträgers were reminded that their tasks took them to the streets and towns of their jurisdictional areas, rather than offices and conference rooms.[15] And, in obvious contradiction to the previously announced policy on criticism within the PO, the StdF encouraged direct denunciations to his office. Individuals reporting to the StdF were not traitors, but informants.[16]

This last aspect of the reporting procedures was actually an integral part of the StdF's personnel policy after September 1. With the beginning of the war, the already apparent concentration of personnel decisions in the hands of the StdF was markedly accelerated.[17] Since the StdF's office controlled the fate of applications for draft exemptions among the PLs, its arsenal of punishments for unsatisfactory PO functionaries was enlarged by a simple but effective device: release of a PL for service in the armed forces. The man in charge of this sensitive area at the StdF's office was Wilhelm Zander, a particular favorite of Bormann's, and a PL with both close ties to the SS and considerable prewar

13. Bormann to Lammers, 31 Aug. 1939, BA/R 43 II/139a.

14. StdF, "Anordnung 177/39," 1 Oct. 1939; and PK to Fritz Schmidt (see below, pp. 304 ff.), 15 Dec. 1942, Rijksinstituut voor Oorlogsdokumentatie, Amsterdam (cited hereafter as RvO)/Arbeitsbereich der NSDAP (cited hereafter as Arb. NSDAP) Ni/3 A I.

15. See Friedrichs, "Rede Stellv. GL 1940," pp. 9–10; and StdF, "Anordnung 181/39," 1 Oct. 1939, ARV.

16. StdF, "Rundschreiben," 20 Feb. 1941, VAB, I, 60. In addition, Hess, Himmler, and Goebbels continued to receive the SD's reports.

17. StdF, "Verfügung," n.d., Verordnungsblatt der Reichsleitung der NSDAP (cited hereafter as VOBl), no. 206 (March 1940).

experience in dealing with the interaction of political and military affairs.[18] To be sure, in general the StdF used his control of draft exemptions primarily to preserve intact the PO corps, rather than to purge individual PLs. The Reich's overall policy of draft exemptions deliberately favored the party over the civil service. Most state officials were not draft-exempt, but the Hoheitsträgers were automatically freed from military service. In addition, all PLs in offices at the local level and higher were to stay on the job until further notice.[19] For all practical purposes, only PLs who were younger than twenty-nine could even be considered for the draft, and if a functionary volunteered for service in what would become the occupied Polish territory, the draft-exempt age was as low as twenty-seven.[20] In addition, the party was even entitled to a replacement whenever a full-time PL volunteered for military service.[21] Since the PO corps continued to expand in the first years of the war, it is not surprising that the number of draft-exempt PLs increased rapidly. In September 1940 (unfortunately no statistics are available for 1939) the figure was 9,000, by the end of the year it had reached 16,800, and twelve months later the figure had more or less stabilized at roughly 20,500 full-time draft-exempt PLs.[22]

Although the PO's propaganda stressed the supreme sacrifice made by the political wing of the NSDAP in the war effort,[23] other components of the party were less appreciative of the StdF's generous draft

18. See [Wilhelm Zander], "Entwurf-Anordnung," ca. Dec. 1939; "Vorlage," 9 Dec. 1939; and the massive folder "Notizen und Aktenvermerke des Mob.-Bearbeiters Pg. Zander . . . ," 7 Dec. 1939–15 May 1944, National Archives, Microcopy No. T- (cited hereafter as T-) 580, roll 874, box 799b, folder 3.

19. Hans Mommsen, *Beamtentum im Dritten Reich* (Stuttgart, 1966), p. 89. For criticism of this practice from within the Nazi establishment see Bach to Wolff (head of Himmler's personal chancellery), 23 Oct. 1939, Berlin Document Center (cited hereafter as BDC)/Bach (SS), I.

20. StdF, Mob. Department to Mob. Department of RL, 3 June 1940, T-580, roll 843, box 268, folder 354.

21. GL München-Oberbayern, Mob. Office, "Austausch der hauptberuflichen . . . NSDAP . . . Männer zwischen Wehrmacht und Partei . . . ," 16 Oct. 1939 (secret), T-580, roll 44, folder 253.

22. See undated (ca. Feb. 1942) PK chart entitled, "UK-Stellungen für die Partei," T-580, roll 873, box 799, folder 2.

23. Robert Ley, "Die innere Front tut ihre Pflicht," *Schulungsbrief*, VI (Sept. 1939), 330–32.

exemption policies for the PO.[24] Indeed, Hess's mobilization efforts were part of the continuing power play to raise the status of the PO within the party as a whole and, simultaneously, to inaugurate significant personnel changes within the PO's ranks. These efforts were beset by an increasing number of difficulties. The StdF's program of in-service training at the Brown House for promising PLs received renewed emphasis after the November 1939 attempt to assassinate Hitler,[25] but the theoretically large-scale reservoir of future PLs, the Hitler Youth, lay virtually dormant because most HJ leaders were of prime draft age.[26] In view of such obvious obstacles to a broadly based policy of personnel replacements from below, the StdF's office again considered cutting the Gordian knot with a large-scale program of Gauleiter and deputy Gauleiter appointments. There was a sense of urgency permeating the effort; in late fall of 1939 the end of the war seemed to be very near at hand. The view of the PO's top ranks from the vantage point of the StdF's office was not very encouraging: by now at least five Gauleiters (Wagner in Westphalia and Silesia, Rust in Hanover, Franz Kutschera in Carinthia, Streicher in Franconia, and Bürckel in Vienna) and three deputy Gauleiters (Saxony, Württemberg-Hohenzollern, and Warthegau) needed immediate replacements.[27] In addition, ten other deputy Gauleiters should have been transferred to other Gaus.[28] On the other side of the ledger, Hitler was pathologically reluctant to dismiss his old derivative agents, and even had he shown greater willingness to do so, Hellmuth Friedrichs could point to only eight PLs at ranks below deputy Gauleiter "who could be appointed to any office."[29] Opdenhoff, the head of the StdF's personnel office, did no better. He proposed solving the dilemma by moving a number of Gauleiters around and appointing some major leaders of the paramilitary organizations

24. Bach to Wolff, 23 Oct. 1939, BDC/Bach (SS), I.

25. [Opdenhoff], "Aktenvermerk für Pg. Friedrichs," 10 Nov. 1939, T-580, roll 80, folder 371.

26. StdF, "Vertrauliche Information 3/16," 9 Oct. 1940, *VAB*, I, 617.

27. Bormann to Hess, 1 Dec. 1939, T-580, roll 80, folder 371.

28. Friedrichs, "Nachstehend die Liste der einsatzfähigen Parteigenossen eingeteilt in verschiedene Gruppen," 17 Sept. 1939, T-580, roll 80, folder 371.

29. *Ibid.* At least four of these had subsequent careers in the offices of the StdF and the later PK.

to provincial leadership positions, but Bormann was unenthusiastic. A cross-fertilization of the PO corps with paramilitary leaders like Giesler of the SA (who eventually, in 1942, did become Gauleiter) or the SS leader Joachim Meyer-Quade would not only discourage ambitious PLs, but defeat the very purpose of the search: to strengthen the PO against the other components of the party. In the end, the 1939 talent search produced little more than myriad sheets of paper filled with the same names. Bormann noted in exasperation on one of the documents "that to submit the same proposal ten times after it has been rejected really does seem pointless."[30]

After all the memoranda had been drawn up, only Julius Streicher and Joseph Wagner had actually been caught in the dragnet, and even in these two cases it took the StdF's office the better part of 1940 to effect the final ousters.[31] This is all the more remarkable since the case of Julius Streicher involved years of flagrant corruption and sexual misconduct as well as more harmless eccentricities, such as walking to his office in bathing trunks.[32] Mindful of the adverse effect of Streicher's behavior on public opinion throughout Germany, Hitler did finally force Streicher to retire in May 1940. His replacement, however, was not an ideal choice from the StdF's point of view. He was Karl Holz, the district leader of Nuremberg and the only strong party personality in Franconia—aside from Streicher himself. But Holz had also been closely associated with many of Streicher's financial scandals (although sexually he appears to have been irreproachable) and was regarded as a man only slightly less unbalanced than his predecessor. The StdF's office placed its hopes for a permanent solution to the Franconian problem in

30. The various documents are in T-580, roll 80, folder 371. Bormann's marginalia is on a "Vorlage" by Friedrichs, 2 Dec. 1939.

31. In addition, Baldur von Schirach replaced Bürckel as Gauleiter of Vienna in August 1940, but since Bürckel added Lorraine to his home Gau of the Palatinate (see below, p. 318) this transfer involved a loss neither of power nor status for Bürckel.

32. For the Streicher affair see Martin (police chief of Nuremberg) to Wolff, and Himmler to Bormann, 28 and 27 April 1940, respectively, T-175, roll 123, frames 2648437–41, and 2648443. The infighting is also described at some length in Edward N. Peterson, *The Limits of Hitler's Power* (Princeton, N.J., 1969), pp. 275–85. For a good character analysis of Streicher see Eugene Davidson, *The Trial of the Germans* (New York, 1966), pp. 39–57.

the appointment of a strong deputy Gauleiter[33] and in Hitler's permission to have the StdF conduct a purge of the PO in Franconia.[34]

The cause of Joseph Wagner's downfall was not corruption, but ideological deviation. Wagner, who was generally regarded as one of the more able and sensible among the Gauleiters, had added Silesia to his own Gau of Westphalia-South in the aftermath of the Röhm affair. At that time he had been a protégé of Göring, who in 1936 appointed him Reich price commissioner as well, but by 1939 the power constellation in the Third Reich had changed greatly, and Göring's star had sunk while Bormann's and Himmler's had risen. The last two were particularly resentful of Wagner's and his family's close ties to the Catholic Church.[35] In addition, the deputy Gauleiter of Silesia, Fritz Bracht, had ambitions to succeed Wagner, and intrigued against his chief.[36] As usual, Hitler hesitated to dismiss a prominent old comrade, but when Mrs. Wagner, apparently with her husband's approval, flatly forbade their daughter to marry an SS officer because he was not a Christian, Himmler and Bormann had an issue which would persuade even Hitler. By September 1940 Wagner had all but handed the administration of Silesia over to Bracht.[37] It was, however, a rather short-lived triumph. In the end none of the three—Himmler, Bormann, and Bracht—were entirely content with the settlement of Silesia. Hitler refused to appoint Bracht Gauleiter of all of Silesia (which had been enlarged by part of the Polish territorial booty), but instead divided the Gau into two parts, Upper and Lower Silesia, and left Bracht in charge of Upper Silesia.[38] (Since the SS territorial district did not change, the division meant that in the future the HSSPF for Silesia would have to deal with two Gauleiters.) The new Gauleiter of the other half, Karl Hanke, was obviously Hitler's personal choice; his name is not prominent among the 1939 list

33. See Friedrich's and Bormann's "Vermerk," 5 Nov. 1939, and 2 Jan. 1940, T-580, roll 80, folder 371. The man Bormann had in mind was Witt, one of Bormann's chief assistants.

34. See *VOBl*, no. 208 (May 1940).

35. For the affair see Alfred Rosenberg, *Letzte Aufzeichnungen* (Göttingen, 1955), p. 169; Otto Dietrich, *Zwölf Jahre mit Hitler* (Cologne, 1955), p. 171; and Martin Broszat, *Nationalsozialistische Polenpolitik* (Stuttgart, 1961), p. 36.

36. Saupert, "Besuchs-Vermerk [Scholz, Gau treasurer of Silesia]," 24 April 1940; BDC/Bracht (SS).

37. Wagner to Schwarz, 6 Sept. 1940, T-580, roll 813, box 242, folder 84.

38. Hitler's decree is in Domarus, *Hitler*, II, 1656.

of names shuffled from desk to desk at the StdF's office. Indeed, Bormann regarded him as lacking in oratorical talents and, "in addition [as] very weak."[39] Albert Speer, Alfred Rosenberg, and Goebbels' later press chief, Wilfried von Oven, on the other hand, were impressed with Hanke's energy and native intelligence.[40] In the final analysis, Hanke owed his promotion to his role in Goebbels' amorous adventures of 1938 and 1939. Until his appointment as Gauleiter, Hanke had been state secretary at the propaganda ministry. In this capacity he had championed Mrs. Goebbels' cause (and perhaps had a mild affair of his own with Magda Goebbels) against his minister's infatuous desire to marry the Czech actress Lida Baarova. Hitler in turn regarded Hanke as something of a knightly champion and rewarded his romantic services with a Gauleiter position.[41]

The uncertain success of proposals for dismissal and appointment of Gauleiters gave added significance to the role of the deputy Gauleiters in the personnel calculations of the StdF. The deputy Führer attempted to mold these functionaries into something approaching a territorial staff of his office. The group was assembled about once a month in early 1940 for national conferences (for example, January 11, February 10, and March 5, 1940), which in fact became planning sessions with members of the StdF's staff.[42] As a result, the conventions of deputy Gauleiters were far more than the usual pro forma assemblies of party leaders. The StdF's staff officials rather openly alluded to sensitive areas of party concerns and anticipated upcoming policy thrusts. Thus Friedrichs' speech to the deputy Gauleiters in March of 1940 emphasized that the party was opposed both to the churches themselves and to an alliance of army and church. He raised at this early date the problem of teacher training, a matter that did not become acute until 1942. Friedrichs also spoke frankly of the difficulties with the Hitler Youth. There was even some discussion of the last point among the functionaries, but

39. Bormann, "Vorlage," 4 Dec. 1939, T-580, roll 80, folder 371.

40. Albert Speer, *Erinnerungen* (Berlin, 1969), p. 35; Rosenberg, *Tagebuch*, entry for 6 Feb. 1939, pp. 81–82; and Wilfred von Oven, *Mit Goebbels bis zum Ende*, 2d ed. (Buenos Aires, 1949), II, entry for 9 July 1944, pp. 46–47.

41. Hitler had mentioned to Himmler as early as December 1939 that he intended to appoint Hanke as Wagner's successor. See Oven, *Mit Goebbels*, II, entry for 9 July 1944, pp. 46–47.

42. Schieder, "Besuchs-Vermerk," 12 Jan. 1940, BDC/Greiser (PKC).

this was apparently too much of a deviation from the Führerprinzip: Friedrichs expressed the hope that the April meeting would dispense with discussions.[43] In between national meetings, the StdF's staffers maintained constant liaison with individual deputy Gauleiters.[44]

Hess and Bormann tried hard to place staff officials into key deputy Gauleiter positions and to upgrade the power and prestige of the group as a whole. In neither aspect were they wholly successful. The Gauleiters resented the StdF's agents in their offices, and it is noteworthy that two of the three new Gauleiters named in 1940–1941 were able to prevent the appointment of an StdF staffer to their Gaus. Only Bracht had to accept one of Bormann's prominent trouble-shooters, Albert Hoffmann, as his deputy Gauleiter.[45] The only other major staff official appointed to a deputy Gauleiter post at this time was Richard Donnewert, who was sent to Reichenberg specifically to control the Gauleiter of the Sudetenland, Konrad Henlein.[46] The appointments of Ludwig Ruckdeschel (Bayreuth) and Fritz Schlessman (Kurhessen)[47] were moves by the StdF to reward an old fighter and a rehabilitated SA leader rather than to increase the influence of the StdF's element among the deputy Gauleiters. There remained, then, the less tangible, prestige-oriented benefits for these important functionaries in the provinces. In this area the StdF attempted in particular to place a disproportionately large number of the deputy Gauleiters as members of the Reichstag.[48]

In contrast to the StdF's purposeful, if not wholly successful, attempt to advance his means of control and power over the PO, Ley for the moment glorified in the increased Betreuung tasks that could be handled by the PO after September 1. The opportunities seemed boundless: from rationing cards and "psychological Betreuung of the sick and wounded" to chitchat letters to home-town soldiers at the front—the

43. Friedrichs, "Schlussrede . . . Tagung . . . 5.3.40," 11 March 1940, T-580, roll 79, folder 368.

44. This information is based upon the appointment book of Fritz Schmidt, at this time a special assistant to Bormann and the StdF's liaison official to the propaganda ministry. The original calendar is in the RvO/Reichskommissar zur besonderen Verwendung in den Niederlanden/1a.

45. See Hoffmann, "Lebenslauf," n.d., BDC/Hoffmann (SS).

46. The relevant documentation is in BDC/Donnewert (SS), II.

47. *VOBl*, no. 203 (Dec. 1939).

48. [Opdenhoff], "Aktenvermerk für Pg. Friedrichs," 10 Nov. 1939, T-580, roll 80, folder 371; and the documents in HAB/320/49.

PLs had a part in every aspect of civilian wartime activities.[49] At the same time, the outbreak of the war did not cure Ley's organizational schizophrenia. On the one hand, he sensibly ceased publication of the *Hoheitsträger* and the *Schulungsbrief* and eliminated closed in-service training sessions,[50] but on the other, he insisted that the letter of the *Organisationsbuch*'s regulations be carried out.[51] At any rate, Ley's self-imposed sacrifices were not of long duration. After a few weeks, Ley's journals began to reappear, and the usual round of training congresses involving PLs from agencies ranging from the press office to that of the Gau training leaders continued unabated until the military setbacks of 1943.[52] After the first shock of wartime conditions, things returned to business as usual at the ROL's office.

Since Ley did not use the outbreak of hostilities to reopen his feud with the StdF, relations between the two offices became relatively frictionless. The German army and the StdF solved one of Ley's more vexing problems: in the fall of 1939 he finally found a use for the unemployed graduates of his order castles as well as for the half-empty building complexes themselves. With the swift defeat of Poland, Hitler annexed vast new areas to the Reich and, in effect, assigned the party the task of establishing a civilian government. The largest supply of available PLs was Ley's Ordensjunkers—those ill-trained but arrogant young men whose services the party offices in the Altreich had rather unanimously rejected. Suddenly, these supernumeraries were in short supply, and the StdF requested that Ley use the training facilities at the Ordensburgen to school still more PLs for service in the East. Beginning in 1940 the ROL trained between one hundred and one hundred and ten functionaries in a series of ten-day courses at the order castle Sonthofen.[53] The quality of the curriculum had neither changed nor im-

49. Ley, "Innere Front," pp. 330–31.
50. Ley to Hess [draft], 30 Sept. 1939, BA/NS 22/134; and district training leader Eisenach, "Rundschreiben 39/40," 31 July 1940, University of Michigan German Archival Collection (cited hereafter as MiU/GAC), folder 27.
51. See the mass of material in BA/NS 22/188–198.
52. Rschm., "Anordnung 58/39 [and] 5/40," 13 Nov. 1939, and 2 Feb. 1940, *Rdschr.*, VI and VII. The various meetings were announced in *Rdschr.*, VI and VII.
53. Harold Scholtz, "Die 'NS-Ordensburgen," *Vjh.f.Z.*, XV (July 1967), 275 and 288, n. 46; and Rschm., "Anweisung 19/40 [and] 43/40," 25 July and 23 Nov. 1940, *Rdschr.*, VII. Once encouraged, Ley developed his usual excessive ambitions. At the beginning of 1941 he requested Hess to turn the Reich school at

proved: the order castles were still "a university in the morning and a barracks in the afternoon," a combination "that could never produce the desired type of National Socialist leadership corps."[54]

In addition to training PO functionaries for Poland at Hess's request, the ROL also cooperated with the StdF's personnel policy drive in the Altreich. Ley had apparently given up any hope of halting the transfer of his influence over personnel policies to Hess's agencies. Instead, he was content to work on routine tasks, such as compiling the papers and evaluations needed for promotion decisions in the PO. Ley's office performed only clerk or cypher duties and did not attempt to interfere in the actual personnel decisions.[55] Ley was even permitted to resume work on the jurisdictional definition of the Reichsleiters' offices, but this time the party's compulsive organizer made no efforts to delineate the power of the StdF.[56]

The best one-word description of the prevailing mood among the PLs at the third major Reichsleiter's office in the PO, that of the Reich treasurer, was pride. Schwarz and his associates were convinced (and had apparently persuaded Hitler as well) that the NSDAP's finances and internal administration not only were fully prepared for the wartime situation, but had reached a state of near perfection.[57] Schwarz based this conclusion on the technical competence of his staffs at the Reich and Gau level[58] and on the monetary riches of the NSDAP. The war was a tremendous financial boon for the party. The interest on the party's cash deposits alone increased from RM 196,959 in 1938 to RM 1,247,998 in 1939 and RM 4,534,752 a year later.[59] The increased funds were the result not of a sudden influx of dues, but of massively augmented sub-

---

Feldafing over to him. The StdF refused. See StdF office [the official's name is illegible] to ROL, 28 Jan. 1941, T-580, roll 549, folder 747.

54. ROL, main training office, "Bericht über die Arbeitstagung des Hauptschulungsamtes . . . 16.–23.6.1941," n.d., p. 8, BA/NS 22/29.

55. See Selzner's report on a telephone conversation between Ley and Friedrichs, 30 Jan. 1941, T-580, roll 549, folder 747.

56. See the documentation in T-580, roll 535, folders 312 and 314.

57. Rschm., "Bekanntgabe 6/40," 3 April 1940, *Rdschr.*, VII; and Domarus, *Hitler*, II, 1427 and 1625.

58. See the various "Stimmungsberichte" in T-580, roll 804, box 239, folders 39–40.

59. Rschm., "Jahresbericht 1940," 25 Oct. 1941, T-580, roll 833, box 256, folder 267.

sidies from the Reich government. The moneys were transferred directly to Schwarz's office, so that the Reich treasurer could use the funds both to subsidize and to control the Gaus, whose deficits reflected the vastly increased expenses brought on by the war. The Reich treasurer, of course, exacted a price for his financial aid; he added to the web of controls that restricted the financial autonomy of the Gaus and the districts.[60] Above all, Schwarz perfected his budgeting procedures for the Gaus. In October of 1939, he ordered each Gau to submit a detailed budget for the coming year, and then throughout 1940 followed up this proposal by painstaking accounting of individual budget items.[61] In addition, at the beginning of the war (literally, on September 1) Schwarz ordered all liquid assets transferred to the party's Reich account, so that party agencies had to request funds from Schwarz's office even for their routine expenses. By the twenty-fifth of each month, every party office had to ask for a specific sum for its jurisdiction for the following month. Schwarz was extremely proud that he managed to maintain this system until the end of the war.[62]

Schwarz also moved against the remaining rights of financial autonomy of Reichsleiters' offices, particularly the DAF. Until the beginning of 1940, the DAF had been paying rather sizable subsidies to various offices of the ROL. In addition to financing the entire cost of the so-called personnel office II of the Reich organizational leader (that is, the personnel department responsible for the appointment of DAF functionaries), the German Labor Front also gave sizable amounts to actual PO offices, including a monthly grant of RM 5,000 to the ROL's main personnel office and RM 30,000 toward the publication of the *Schulungsbrief*. By March Schwarz had successfully eliminated these DAF payments, preventing the Labor Front from exercising an effective control device over some major PO offices.[63] The Reich treasurer also managed to obtain an order from the StdF sharply curtailing the DAF's frequent "voluntary" collections from German business firms. The financial sums involved were sizable. Goebbels estimated that the

60. *Ibid.*, p. 4.

61. *Ibid.*, p. 15; and Rschm., "Anordnung 83/39," 31 Oct. 1939, *Rdschr.*, VI.

62. Franz X. Schwarz, "Ergänzung zu meiner Aufstellung über den Geschäftsbereich des Reichsschatzmeisters . . . ," pp. 3–4, T-580, roll 47, folder 266.

63. DAF to ROL, 26 Jan. 1940, BA/NS 22/701; and Rschm., "Anordnung 16/40," 27 March 1940, *Rdschr.*, VII.

absence of these collections would mean a loss to the DAF in the Gau Berlin alone of at least RM 1,000,000.[64]

All of Schwarz's efforts were not negative, however. He used the improved financial state of the party to increase the material benefits of its major functionaries. In line with the efforts of the StdF's office, Schwarz singled out the deputy Gauleiters for particularly favorable treatment. Fritz Bracht, the deputy of (undivided) Silesia, for example, at the age of forty received a base salary of RM 1,500 per month, while the highest rank of the permanent civil service in a Reich ministry received a monthly compensation of RM 1,051 just before retirement.[65]

Aside from the big Three—Hess-Bormann, Schwarz, and Ley—the array of Reichsleiters was pretty much left to wither on the vine. The wartime tasks and powers of such agencies as the office for communal affairs and even the OPG were minimal to begin with, and declined steadily as the hostilities dragged on. There was only one major exception to this rule: the political resurrection of Joseph Goebbels. The Reich propaganda minister and Gauleiter of Berlin had sunk rather low in the eyes of both Hitler and the Berlin PLs. The Lida Baarova scandal offended Hitler's political sensitivities and aroused his Victorian sympathies for the wronged wife.[66] The "old fighters" of Berlin regarded Goebbels as a man who had turned his back on them, and they apparently utilized a number of opportunities to express openly their feelings of disgust.[67] But Goebbels' situation changed radically with the outbreak of the war. With his constant fear of declining morale among the civilian population, Hitler needed his master propagandist no less than in the frantic Kampfzeit days. Goebbels, of course, seized the opportunity to return to the Führer's favor. His basic propaganda leitmotif from the beginning of the war was to compare the victories and crises of the conflict with crucial developments in Prussian-German history

64. Willi Boelcke, ed., *Kriegspropaganda 1939–1941* (Stuttgart, 1966), entry for 9 Oct. 1940, p. 544.

65. See, for example, Schwarz to Bracht, 21 June 1940, BDC/Bracht (SS); and Reich Statistical Office, *Statistisches Jahrbuch für das Deutsche Reich 1939/40* (Berlin, 1940), p. 370.

66. Boelcke, *Kriegspropaganda*, pp. 28–30; Albert Zoller, *Hitler privat* (Düsseldorf, 1949), pp. 212–13.

67. Rosenberg, *Tagebuch*, entry for 6 Feb. 1939, pp. 81–82.

and in the party struggles.[68] The propaganda minister did not, however, involve the party's propaganda apparatus in the decision-making process to any marked degree, so that his return to power meant a simultaneous weakening of the PO in an area that had at one point been the key element in its activities. Aware of his unpopularity with many PLs, Goebbels used the Reich propaganda office of the NSDAP only as an organ of policy execution; decisions on propaganda lines were made at the ministry in Berlin.[69]

Below the Reich level the Gauleiters and district leaders were the immediate beneficiaries not only of Hitler's emphasis on the wartime role of the Hoheitsträgers, but of his previously expressed view that the territorial chiefs should solve difficulties in their jurisdictions with whatever power resources were at their own disposal.[70] Even when the bombing war began to assume major proportions in Germany, Hitler had little interest in the extent of the damage; his estimation of a Gauleiter's ability corresponded directly to the speed with which the provincial chief could restore production and morale in his Gau to pre-raid levels.[71] In the first months of the war the damage from enemy bombing was minimal, but the Gauleiters themselves all but wreaked havoc on the Reich as a whole. In their anxiety over their personal popularity, they blithely ignored national directives,[72] interfered in individual court cases,[73] and stopped supply trains headed for other areas of the Reich, distributing the goods in their own Gaus instead.[74] The last-named practice reached such proportions that Hess issued a specific order not only prohibiting it, but stating that in the future he would not protect Hoheitsträgers who engaged in this sort of activity from criminal prosecution.[75]

68. See Boelcke, *Kriegspropaganda*, entry for 16 Jan. 1940, p. 267.
69. *Ibid.*, pp. 96–97.
70. See Hitler's speech to the district leaders, 29 April 1937, in Domarus, *Hitler*, II, 1713, n. 214.
71. Speer, *Erinnerungen*, p. 311.
72. Rschm., "Anordnung 20/40," 18 April 1940, *Rdschr.*, VII; and Boelcke, *Kriegspropaganda*, p. 129.
73. See the documents on Streicher's interference with the judicial process, BA/R 22/20291.
74. Boelcke, *Kriegspropaganda*, entries for 23 Jan. and 5 Feb. 1940, pp. 272 and 281. See also Eberhard Jäckel, *Frankreich in Hitler's Europa* (Stuttgart, 1966), p. 82.
75. StdF, "Anordnung 19/40," 17 Feb. 1940, *ARV*.

Several Gauleiters used their mandate for greater autonomy to curtail or eliminate what they considered to be peripheral aspects of the PO's activities. In Hamburg, for example, Gauleiter Kaufmann closed down the Gau training school from 1939 to 1943, eliminated all ideological training, and sent his Gau training staff to the food rationing office to gain experience in handling the coupon system.[76]

There was little Robert Ley could do about the recalcitrant Gauleiters, but both Schwarz and Hess moved vigorously to assert the authority of the Reichsleitung offices. As noted above, the Reich treasurer established a rigid framework of control to prevent any financial freedom of movement in the Gaus. The StdF, for his part, attempted to strengthen the position of the deputy Gauleiters and the district leaders as counterweights to the provincial lords. The districts were well on their way to becoming direct subordinate offices of the deputy Führer. For the most part, the StdF communicated his orders directly to the districts, rather than permitting an informational screening by the Gauleiters.[77] Similarly, the district leaders had a direct part in the administration of highly sensitive political programs. The district leader, for example, was fully consulted in the planning of the killings in his district carried out under the Nazi euthanasia program.[78]

To be sure, the bulk of the district leaders' time was occupied with Betreuung functions. At the end of 1939 the StdF reiterated the party's "sole responsibility for human relations (*Menschenführung*) functions." A contemporary commentator found Hess's decree a particularly "clear formulation,"[79] but in essence it meant that there was literally no societal function in which the district leader could not "legally" make his influence felt. A listing of routine activities handled by the district leader of Eisenach in the first year of the war may illustrate the decree's application in practice. The tasks included: liaison with drafted party

76. "Eingabe [Albert] Henze," 29 May 1947, Forsch. Hbg./PA/12/H. Henze was the Gau training leader from 1936 to 1945.

77. "Erklärung Friedrich Schusters," n.d. (1947), Forsch. Hbg./PA/12/S. See also a comparison of the relevant issues of the *RVBl*, editions A and B. The A edition went to the Gauleiters, B to the district leaders.

78. Hermann Langbein, . . . *wir haben es getan* (Vienna, 1964), pp. 20–21.

79. Lampe, *Amtsträger*, p. 17. The decree itself is in *RVBl* (edition A), I (Jan. 1940), 45.

members, membership, road construction, formation of new party bloc organizations, mediation among party members, political evaluation of nominees for the Mother's Cross decoration, follow-up on denunciations, mediation of businessmen's disputes, and so on. Indeed a particularly fanatical PL like the district leader of Eisenach regarded himself as the dictator of the home front in his territorial jurisdiction.[80] It must be underscored that by no means all of this activity was benevolent or rational. The district leader's private snapshot collection also reveals that he organized pseudomedieval punishments in Eisenach. In March 1941 a citizen of Eisenach flanked by two SS guards, was forced to exhibit himself in the central square of the town, wearing around his neck a placard reading, "I have had relations with a Polish girl," while a crowd of three to four hundred persons milled around the grim scene.[81]

Obviously inherent in all of these activities were potentialities for power aggrandizement that might transform the districts into as much of a centrifugal threat to the central offices as the Gaus. There is considerable evidence that the districts both were aware of their new status and had begun to take practical advantage of it. Schwarz complained of the reestablishment of secret accounts and blackmailing of communal officials by district party offices,[82] while the StdF discovered that some districts were defying directives of six years' standing and negotiating directly with Reich ministries.[83]

Since it was clearly impractical to check the district leaders by activating the local Hoheitsträgers below them, the Reich offices contented themselves with issuing vigorous decrees and adopting a policy of divide and conquer toward the Gaus and districts. At the local level, the wartime tasks in the early months of the conflict were primarily propagandistic and denunciatory. The local leader, "the guarantee of a desire for victory in the German people,"[84] had the specific tasks of preventing panic among the population as a result of air raids and of checking the

---

80. The listing is a resume of the information in MiU/GAC, folders 1 and 11 ff.
81. *Ibid.*, folder 76.
82. Rschm., "Bekanntgabe 6/40 [and] Anordnung 8/41," 3 April 1940, and 12 March 1941, *Rdschr.*, VII and VIII.
83. StdF, "Anordnung 40/40," 3 April 1940, *ARV.*
84. District leader Eisenach, "Rundschreiben 67," 3 Sept. 1939, MiU/GAC, folder 26.

origin and spread of rumors and jokes directed against the regime.[85] The block and cell leaders in turn fed such information to the local chieftain. On their own, the sublocal PLs were apparently kept busy mediating disputes among apartment dwellers whose nerves had been rubbed raw by the shortages and anxieties of the war.[86]

With the unexpectedly swift victory over Poland, the party's original feeling of apprehension faded, giving way to a pervading sense of euphoria. The war had brought not only vast territorial expansion, but opportunities for rekindling ideological confrontation with antiparty forces in Germany. This was particularly true of the NSDAP's relationship with the churches. Friedrichs keynoted the party efforts in a speech to the deputy Gauleiters with the words: "Our educational work must be so intensified that each German of his own accord obeys only the Führer and not an ecclesiastical organization."[87] Although the party moved quickly to dissolve a number of monasteries (under the guise of needing space to care for the war wounded) and prohibited the attendance of PLs at church-related functions,[88] the drive was not a marked success. The youth of the nation in particular seemed to gravitate to what the party labeled "politicizing priests."[89] The reason was of course at hand: the party had no ideology worthy of the name that could replace the traditional Christian doctrine. This basic truth was even admitted by the Nazi minister of church affairs,[90] although both Rosenberg and Bormann bristled with indignation at the statement.[91] The party's ideological chief had fought a running feud with the churches since 1930, and now even Bormann tried his hand at religious reforming.

85. Boelcke, *Kriegspropaganda*, entries for 25 May, 28 and 30 Aug. 1940, pp. 364 and 480–81, respectively.

86. See, for example, cell leader 03 (Eisenach) to district leader Eisenach, 30 Aug. 1940, MiU/GAC, folder 11.

87. "Auszüge aus einem Bericht des Gauorganisationsleiters [Berlin] über die Tagung der stellvertretenden Gauleiter und Gauinspekteure ... 5. März 1940 ... ," BA/NS 8/231.

88. Bormann to Lammers, 1 March 1941, BA/R 43 II/455; StdF, "Anordnung 46/40," 18 April 1940, ARV. See also Martin Broszat, "Verfolgung polnischer Geistlicher," (Munich, 1959), pp. 29–30. This is an unpublished staff paper, Institut für Zeitgeschichte, Munich (cited hereafter as IfZ)/Oqk/7 (a).

89. StdF, "Anordnung 30/40," 12 March 1940, ARV.

90. Kerrl to Stapel, 6 Sept. 1939, quoted in Rosenberg, *Tagebuch*, p. 181.

91. Rosenberg to Hess, 29 Sept. 1939, *ibid.*, p. 178. For Rosenberg's overall opinion of Kerrl see *ibid.*, entry for 1 Nov. 1939, p. 105.

He drafted guidelines for Hitler Youth activities that included—aside from the usual pantheistic gobbledygook and racial purity admonitions —"useful precepts from the [Ten] Commandments."[92] At the same time, Hitler gave Rosenberg formal permission to begin setting up the Advanced Institute (*Hohe Schule*) of the NSDAP.[93] With the leadership of the fanatically anti-Christian Alfred Rosenberg at its head, the establishment of this institution could only signal further attacks on the churches by the party. The Führer also pushed ahead with his plans for the reconstruction of the Linz waterfront, the building complex which Hitler regarded as his chief architectural legacy to the world.[94] Concrete anti-Semitic acts flared up again as well. Gauleiter Mutschmann's suggestion to force all Jews to wear an identifying Star of David was some two years ahead of its time,[95] but it certainly reflected the ebullient mood of the party after the Reich's first victories.

As the war raised the stature and significance of the army to unparalleled heights, the party sought simultaneously to ride the coattails of the soldiers' popularity in order to increase its influence over intra-army affairs and yet to prevent complete identification of army and party. The NSDAP insisted on placing itself between the people and the armed forces,[96] and the Gauleiters won the right to participate in courts-martial if they felt their presence was necessary from the party's point of view.[97] At the same time, the Reich labor service refused to adopt the army's code of conduct because "our mother [is] the party and . . . nothing can prevent us from remaining true to the time of our birth [the National Socialist revolution]."[98]

The most dramatic initiative by a party leader in the field of party-army relations was Alfred Rosenberg's attempt, at the beginning of 1940, to extend his functions as "ideological supervisor" of the Nazi

92. Bormann to Rosenberg, 24 Feb. 1940, *ibid.*, p. 207.

93. Domarus, *Hitler*, II, 1447.

94. Hildegard Brenner, *Die Kunstpolitik des Nationalsozialismus* (Reinbek b. Hamburg, 1963), pp. 156–59.

95. Bernhard Lösener, "Als Rassereferent im Reichsministerium des Innern," *Vjh.f.Z.*, IX (July 1961), 302.

96. Boelcke, *Kriegspropaganda*, entries for 8 and 12 Feb. 1940, pp. 283–84.

97. StdF, "Anordnung 74/40," 17 July 1940, *RVBl* (A), no. 16 (18 July 1940), pp. 110–11.

98. Hierl to all labor service Gau leaders *et al.*, 2 March 1940, *ARV*. The StdF prohibited publication of Hierl's decree.

Weltanschauung to include military indoctrination programs. Specifically, Rosenberg offered to supply the high command of the armed forces
(OKW) with a supply of fanatic agitprop officers. Since the weak and
thoroughly Nazified head of the OKW, General Wilhelm Keitel, raised
no serious objections to the plan, the OKW and Rosenberg's office signed
a draft agreement and submitted it for Hitler's approval. Like so many
of Rosenberg's projects, this one was stillborn. In a dramatic, high-level
meeting of party, government, and military leaders on February 9, 1940,
Rosenberg was unable to win approval for his plan. Objections were
forthcoming not only from the individual armed services, but also from
Heinrich Himmler and Martin Bormann. Only Hess supported Rosenberg, and the deputy Führer's position was no longer strong enough to
save the day for Rosenberg.[99]

The party's ideological chief must have been particularly surprised
and hurt by the attitude of Bormann, but the StdF's chief of staff had
far-reaching plans of his own. They certainly included the training of
agitprop officers (though under the auspices of the StdF's office, rather
than Rosenberg's agencies), but they went far beyond this. There was,
for example, Bormann's institution of the "comrades' services" (*Kameradschaftsdienst*) in the early weeks of the war. In effect, Bormann proposed that in noncombat situations the party was to be the partner of
the army in dealing with the day-to-day problems of the soldiers. Officers were encouraged to correspond with their men's district leaders
and involve them in whatever problems individual enlisted men within
their units might have.[100] On paper, these measures were designed to
relieve the anxiety of the individual soldier about his loved ones at home,
but actually the Kameradschaftsdienst was intended and would later
turn out to be an effective means of controlling the German soldiers
through the Hoheitsträgers.

The NSDAP also looked upon the war as a major opportunity to
inaugurate a new phase in its continuing attacks upon the integrity and

99. For this episode see Volker R. Berghahn, "NSDAP und 'geistige Führung'
der Wehrmacht 1939–1943," *Vjh.f.Z.*, XVII (Jan. 1969), 20–30. For an analysis
of the decline of Hess's influence, see below, p. 328.

100. StdF., "Rundschreiben 221/39," 18 Nov. 1939, *VAB*, I, 67–68. See also
Manfred Messerschmidt, *Die Wehrmacht im NS-Staat* (Hamburg, 1969), p. 245.
The obvious next step in this process, granting a soldier the right to complain to
the party about his superior officer, was not instituted until 1944.

power of the civil service. There is no doubt that the prewar program of forcing high civil servants to join the NSDAP and placing fanatical party members in influential civil service positions had largely been a failure.[101] As a result, the party shifted emphasis.[102] Instead of destroying the civil service from within, the new program called for rendering it impotent from without. Concretely, the party wanted information and control. Citing its monopoly position in the area of human relations, the party insisted that it be fully informed of internal morale factors in the government bureaus. (A reciprocal arrangement would be "unthinkable in view of the party's superior position.")[103] Controls came in a number of forms. The PO continued its efforts to destroy the spirit and prestige of the civil service corps, using such devices as planting party cells within government offices;[104] supervising the training of civil servants and teachers; and, in line with the upgrading of the district leader's position, granting to this level of Hoheitsträger further rights of interfering in county government.[105] In connection with the last-mentioned goal, the StdF had now reached a firm decision against a Personalunion of district leaders and county executives, so that the party's chief would be free to criticize and control without the encumbrances of responsibility.[106]

Despite its revived ambitions, the party's efforts to subordinate the civil service to its direct control were not significantly more successful than its earlier endeavors. In large part this was the result of the continuing, fierce intraparty struggles. Hitler's refusal to permit any manner of Reichsreform in the Altreich left the party and governmental jurisdictions hopelessly jumbled, and a government office could usually

101. Mommsen, *Beamtentum*, pp. 85 and 196.
102. The StdF did insist, however, that among the civil servants purged in 1933 only those who had been particularly active in the party since their dismissal could be reinstated in their positions. See StdF, "Anordnung 211/39," 26 Oct. 1939, ARV.
103. Lampe, *Amtsträger*, p. 113.
104. "Konzentration der politischen Kräfte der NSDAP in den Betrieben und Verwaltung des öffentlichen Dienstes," 16 May 1940, BA/R 22/21.
105. See Bormann to all GLs (outside of Austria), 2 Feb. 1941, RvO/Telex-Berichte of the RK for the occupied Netherlands (cited hereafter as TB)/folder IX. The Telex-Berichte is a collection of copies of telex messages sent and received by Schmidt's office. See also Mommsen, *Beamtentum*, p. 233.
106. Friedrichs, "Niederschift . . . Friedrichs . . . zur Frage der Personalunion von Kreisleiter und Landrat," early 1940, quoted in Mommsen, *Beamtentum*, pp. 228–33.

be confident that two or more party jurisdictions would find it impossible to agree on a joint plan of attack.[107]

The NSDAP's far-reaching plans for securing a controlling influence in the German economy failed primarily because they rested upon two fundamentally incorrect assumptions: the problem of wartime inflation would be immaterial because of the war's short duration;[108] and, again because of the limited time of the acute emergency, the party could inaugurate a program of direct interference in the economy without materially affecting the production needs of the war effort. In terms of officials and institutions, initiatives during the first several months of the war originated in the economic policy office of the StdF, while their execution rested with the Gau economic advisors. For both, the new plans meant a decided upturn in their institutional fortunes. The party's economic offices had since 1936 been overshadowed by Göring's office of the Four Year Plan; and with the death in 1938 of the party's radical "expert" in this area, Bernhard Köhler, the StdF's office for economic policy had become all but insignificant. A major change came in mid-1940 when Hans Bärmann, an ambitious and dynamic StdF staffer, became head of department B (economics) of the division for state affairs in the deputy Führer's office.[109]

In the first months of the war, the party's long-range planning activities remained hidden by the frenetic energy expended on a seemingly endless series of party-sponsored collection and recycling projects,[110] but the officials at the StdF's office were also thinking far into the future. At the end of the war (which was always expected to be near at hand), the economic policy division planned to have a direct voice in the appointment of major executives in German businesses plus a position as equal partner with the economics ministry in the Aryanization process. Friedrichs was very candid in his March 1940 address to the deputy Gauleiters: in the [victorious] peacetime Reich, . . . company,

107. See GL Baden, office for communal affairs to Reich office for communal affairs, 13 Jan. 1940, BDC/Murr (PKC).
108. PK, "Rundschreiben 25/41," 15 Oct. 1941 (top secret), IfZ/PK/Rdschr. geh.
109. The activities of this office are documented in BA/NS 6/103.
110. StdF, "Anordnung 18/40," 15 Feb. 1940, *ARV*. See also *VOBl*, no. 207 (April 1940); and Köhler, "Rundschreiben 14/40," 1 April 1940, MiU/GAC, folder 27.

managers (*Betriebsführer*) could be appointed only if they could demonstrate active participation in party projects and if their talents as *Menschenführer* (leaders of men) were confirmed by a party evaluation.[111] Bärmann wanted the decision-making power concerning Aryanizations firmly anchored in the Gau authorities, that is, the Gau economic advisors and, formally, the Gauleiters.[112] Both of these projected economic controls would in effect have reversed the economic balance of power between party and state; the NSDAP would have regained the territory lost by its undisciplined behavior after the Kristallnacht.

A final initiative of the party in the area of socioeconomic control was the appointment in November 1940 of Robert Ley as Reich building commissioner (*Reichswohnungskommissar*). The military realities rendered the office largely stillborn,[113] but its planned role as social control mechanism illustrated the party's self-image, in the heady atmosphere of 1940, as an institution of social revolution. Ley's primary function (with active participation by the StdF's office)[114] was not so much to build homes as to correlate types of families and housing. In essence, the party reserved to itself the right to determine the living conditions of the German people by applying its standards of relative racial valuation to individual families.[115] Ley seemed particularly suited to this role because he already had at hand vast sources of information about the

111. "Auszüge aus einem Bericht . . . ," BA/NS 8/231. See also Dr. H. Hassbargen, "Der ehemalige Gauleiter Kaufmann im Spiegel seiner eignen Worte," 13 Aug. 1951, Forsch. Hbg/PA/12/K (Kaufmann).

112. StdF, "Bekanntgabe 59/40," 20 Aug. 1940, *RVBl* (A), no. 21 (22 Aug. 1940).

113. Ley soon fell victim to his usual gigantomania. Goebbels took care to keep from the German press Ley's completely unrealistic projections (5 million new apartments, 100 KdF steamers, and ten new hotels with 20,000 beds each by the end of 1941); see Ley, "Das grosse Geschenk," *Hoheitsträger*, IV (Dec. 1940), 11. See also Boelcke, *Kriegspropaganda*, entry for 16 Sept. 1940, p. 570.

114. Domarus, *Hitler*, II, 1617–18. The StdF's file on housing construction (BA/NS 6/253) is one of the most extensive of its documentary legacies, and Bormann continued to show a keen interest in the development of the office. See Adolf Wagner, "Vermerk über eine Besprechung bei . . . Ley . . . 11. Februar 1941," 11 Feb. 1941, BGStA, MA 105418. Ley even published his own journal, *Der Wohnungsbau in Deutschland* (1940–1944).

115. Muth, "Vermerk für Pg. Dr. Beyer," 31 March 1942, BA/NS6/253. For the party's planned central role in all communal affairs, see H. Steinwarz, "Gemeinschaftshäuser in der Ortsgruppe," *Hoheitsträger*, V (Jan.-Feb. 1941), 25.

German citizenry through the DAF organization and his additional office as Reich social security commissioner (the latter appointment dated from February 1940[116]).

The areas that were potentially most important for future power aggrandizement of the party were policy planning and administration in the conquered areas. By October 1939 the German armies had conquered Poland, in the spring of the following year the Reich was in control of Norway, Denmark, and the Netherlands, and by midsummer Belgium and northwestern France had been added to the list. There was no doubt in the mind of either Adolf Hitler or other party leaders that Nazi control of the areas would be a permanent feature of the European political landscape. Indeed, Hitler was so convinced of the permanence of his conquests that he even permitted a partial reopening of the Reichsreform question. In March 1940 the Führer agreed to the establishment of "Reichsgaus" in the former Austrian provinces. The Reichsgaus were administrative constructs in which the duality of state and party was all but eliminated. These administrative units placed both the party's monopoly of political decision-making and the state's duty to administer in the hands of the Gauleiters as viceroys. The new Gaus differed fundamentally from their counterparts in the Altreich in that they were not subject to the de jure supervisory powers of the Reich ministries.[117] In theory at least, the head of the Reichsgau was responsible only to Hitler.

It was significant that Hitler did not immediately extend the Reichsgau principle to the Altreich, where a veritable thicket of traditional and legal considerations stood in his way. This was not true, of course, of the vast areas of non-German territory that had to be organized and set up; between Minsk and Calais lay an immense administrative and political tabula rasa.[118] As a result, the first six or seven months of the

116. Domarus, *Hitler*, II, 1462.
117. Lammers to Frick, 19 March 1940, BA/R 43 II/1390b; Werner Best, *Die deutschen Aufsichtsverwaltungen* ([Berlin, 1941]), p. 83; and Henry Picker, ed., *Hitlers Tischgespräche im Führerhauptquartier 1941–1942*, new ed. by Percy-Ernst Schramm *et al.* (Stuttgart, 1965), entry for 5 April 1942, p. 254.
118. Bormann to Lammers, 2 Nov. 1940 (transmitting a letter of Greiser's), BA/R 43 II/455; and Lammers, "Vermerk," 26 Nov. 1940, International Military Tribunal, *Trial of Major War Criminals* (Nuremberg, 1947–49) (cited hereafter as *IMT*), document no. NG-227.

war were distinguished by widespread and bitter disputes over political strategy and tactics. The brutal, inhuman exploitation which came to characterize Nazi policies in all of the occupied European countries were not predetermined (in 1939 the Nazis had no set occupation policies); they were the result of intense intrasystem maneuvering. Proposals for the establishment of German control ranged from behind-the-scenes manipulation (while preserving the autonomy of the various areas) and schemes of pure economic exploitation to all but undisguised plans to formally annex large areas of foreign territory to Germany itself.[119] The arguments concerned power, policy,[120] and personnel, but in accordance with Hitler's style of rule, the primary question was that of personnel. In effect, Hitler made policy decisions by deciding personnel appointments.

The Führer personalized his rule in the occupied areas by organizing them either as Reichsgaus, if the territories then became incorporated into the Reich, or as Reich commissariats (*Reichkommissariate*) where the territories remained outside the Reich's borders. In the former case the status of the chief of administration was relatively clear: as Gauleiter of a Reichsgau he was Hitler's derivative agent for the area. The role of the Reich commissioners was considerably more complicated. Formally, the commissioners were state officials responsible to Hitler as head of the German government. Yet since almost all commissioners were drawn from the ranks of prominent party leaders, and most held Gauleiter positions in the Altreich, their status as Reich commissioners became intertwined with the role of the party in the occupied areas and their own personal relationship to Hitler.[121] The first and largest amount of territory to come under the sway of the conquering Third Reich was Poland. In the fourth division of Poland, the Nazis relinquished the eastern parts of the country (temporarily) to the Soviet Union; combined

119. Konrad Kwiet, *Das Reichskommissariat Niederlande* (Stuttgart, 1968), pp. 131, n. 73, and 153; and Best, *Aufsichtverwaltungen*, p. 82.

120. For some weeks after the outbreak of the war it was still official policy to repatriate ethnic Germans within the borders of the Altreich. See chief of Winter Help Organization, Rotterdam to Auslandsorganisation office in Den Haag, 29 Nov. 1938; and Winter Help Office in Holland to J., 6 Feb. 1939, RvO/Arb. NSDAP (Ni)/13.

121. Broszat, *Polenpolitik*, pp. 49–50; and Hans-Dietrich Loock, *Quisling, Rosenberg und Terboven* (Stuttgart, 1970), p. 343.

the western areas into two new Gaus, Warthegau and Danzig–West Prussia, and one existing Gau, Silesia; and renamed the rest, for want of a better term, the government-general (*Generalgouvernement*). The territorial dispositions were a clear demonstration that the party (in the wider sense, including both the PO and the SS) rather than the state or the army would play a dominant political role in the East. The party became Hitler's institutional voice in the conquered areas, and the party determined the standards of behavior for the new Eastern administrators.[122] As a general rule, Hitler insisted that the men sent to the East be "strong personalities," that is, fanatic and ruthless Nazis.[123] As a result, as noted earlier, Ley was finally able to find gainful employment for his idle Ordensburg graduates.[124]

In view of the central importance of the chiefs of administration in the East, it comes as no surprise to find the StdF's office primarily concerned with the PLs whom Hitler would appoint as Gauleiters, deputy Gauleiters, and Reich commissioners. Hess's personnel office began its traditional name-dropping procedures in early October, at a time when the thunder of battle had hardly died down. Specifically, Friedrichs threw out for consideration as Gauleiters: Albert Forster (the Gauleiter of Danzig), Arthur Greiser (the president of the Danzig senate), and Peter Stangier, Heinrich Peper, Paul Wegener, Ferdinand Grossherr, and Karl Gerland (the deputy Gauleiters of Hessen-North, Hanover, Brandenburg, East Prussia, and Lower Danube, respectively). Among the possibilities for deputy Gauleiters there ranked Opdenhoff, Walter Tiessler (the StdF's liaison official to the propaganda ministry), and Neuburg, Hoffmann's successor as Stillhaltekommissar for the Sudetenland.[125]

The names fell into two quite distinct categories of functionaries: the "Easterners," that is, PLs who had served in the eastern Gaus for some years or were native to the area (Forster, Greiser, Grossherr), and

122. Broszat, *Polenpolitik*, p. 118; and Robert Koehl, *RKFDV—German Resettlement Policy 1939–1945* (Cambridge, Mass., 1957), p. 65.

123. [Opdenhoff], "Vorlage" (ca. 1941), T-580, roll 80, folder 371.

124. For Ley's further plans in the East see Brixner (an official in the ROL's main training office), "Entwurf über die Bildung von Einsatztäben der NSDAP für besetzte Gebiete," 21 Feb. 1940, BA/NS 22/29.

125. [Friedrichs], "Notiz für den Stabsleiter," 4 Oct. 1939, T-580, roll 80, folder 371.

a numerically larger group of former and present StdF staffers. With the exception of Stangier and Peper the remaining men on the list had served in responsible positions in the StdF's office. And even Stangier was close to the staff, since he was a *Duzfreund* (close friend) of Fritz Schmidt, the man whom Hess and Bormann would send as the party's representative to Holland.

The actual preferences of the StdF's office are not indicated on Friedrichs' tabulations, but there is no reason to feel that the deputy Führer was dissatisfied with Hitler's choice in the Warthegau. The new Gauleiter was Arthur Greiser, an ideal choice from a number of viewpoints. He was a fanatical Nazi with driving ambition and a particular hatred for Christian churches. He was a bitter enemy of his neighboring Gauleiter, Forster, but his relationships to the SS, the deputy Führer, and Göring were excellent. There was even a personal failing which could be used against him if necessary: his wife had obtained a divorce from him early in 1934 because of his adultery.[126]

With fanatical ambition, undeterred by practical considerations, Greiser set to work making the Warthegau a vast field of experimentation for the institutional realization of the Nazi Weltanschauung. His ambition was to set his Gau up as a pioneer area, which would then serve as a model for the future of the Reich as a whole.[127] The first goal was to eliminate (or, rather, not introduce) the vestiges of the Rechtsstaat that still prevailed in the old Gaus. He insisted upon the establishment of courts-martial headed by the party Hoheitsträgers, with associated judges supplied by the police. These courts could give only one of two sentences: death or imprisonment in a concentration camp. Similarly, Greiser demanded that the right of pardon for his area be transferred from the Reich chancellery to his office. Hitler acceded to both requests.[128] Finally, the Gauleiter objected to the appointment of two separate officials in the county administrations: a head of the county government responsible to the Reich ministry of the interior and a party

126. On Greiser see Herbert S. Levine, "Local Authority and the SS State: The Conflict over Population in Danzig–West Prussia 1939–1945," *Central European History*, II (Dec. 1969), 336; and Greiser's BDC/SS folder.

127. Paul Gürtler, *Nationalsozialismus und evangelische Kirchen im Warthegau* (Göttingen, 1958), pp. 39 and 55.

128. Broszat, *Polenpolitik*, pp. 150–51.

district leader responsible to the Gauleiter. For the moment, and for at least five years after the war, Greiser wanted his district leaders to exercise the powers of both offices. Greiser saw no need for even the physical presence of a man responsible to the Reich interior ministry.[129]

The reason was clearly Greiser's determination to settle the population and church "problems" of his Gau in the shortest time and by the most ruthless means possible. The Gauleiter insisted on expelling all Poles into the Generalgouvernement and resettling his Gau with ethnic Germans within ten years after the peace treaties had been signed. Simultaneously, he hoped to prevent the establishment of a church organization for either the Polish or the German population of his territory. While the resettlement plans were never fully carried out, the Gauleiter took vigorous steps to realize his church policy goals. In this area, the Warthegau was indeed a pioneer; it is quite possible to deduce the Nazis' eventual aims from what happened here.[130] Greiser's key assistant in the antichurch drive was August Jäger, a veteran of the 1933–1934 German Christian offensives, and he was in turn systematically guided and encouraged by both Bormann and Heydrich.[131] In contrast, the Warthegau and the Reich ministry for church affairs barely maintained civil relations. Indeed, state officials consistently lost their influence in the formulation of church policies until, in the fall of 1940, all official contacts between the Reich ministry and Greiser ceased and the Gauleiter, with the deputy Führer's approval, prohibited any further activity by the Reich ministry of church affairs within his Gau.[132] Substantively, the specific aim of the Warthegau administration was first to reduce the churches to the level of private clubs and then to destroy their moral and ethical influence.[133] There were to be no full-time clerics in the Warthegau, and Greiser prohibited the maintenance of all monasteries, convents, and seminaries. All charitable activities handled by

129. Schieder, "Besuchs-Vermerk [Greiser]," 12 Jan. 1940, BDC/Greiser (PKC).
130. Broszat, *Polenpolitik*, p. 167; John S. Conway, *The Nazi Persecution of the Churches 1933–1945* (New York, 1968), chap. II; and Friedrich Zipfel, *Kirchenkampf in Deutschland 1933–1945* (Berlin, 1965), p. 257.
131. Conway, *Nazi Persecution*, p. 314; Broszat, *Polenpolitik*, pp. 165–67; and Gürtler, *Warthegau*, pp. 18, 31–32, and 190–91.
132. Broszat, *Polenpolitik*, p. 168.
133. Broszat, "Verfolgung," p. 44; and Gürtler, *Warthegau*, pp. 48–50, and 118 ff.

the churches were to be transferred to the Nazi welfare office (the NSV), a step which clearly followed along the path of social control measures (for example, the Reichswohnungskommissar's appointment) inaugurated in the Altreich.

The monopoly of power and responsibility assigned the party in the Warthegau required a correspondingly massive party organization. By September of 1940, the Warthegau had been divided into 41 districts, 501 locals, 2,425 cells, and 10,380 blocks—all this in an area with an ethnic German population of not more than 330,000.[134] Most of the PLs came from the Altreich, since there were obviously not enough native activists to fill the vacant positions. There was, however, no shortage of money. Greiser financed the party primarily from the valuables stolen from the expelled Poles and Jews who were sent to the Generalgouvernement. In effect, the Gauleiter achieved what the party had intended to do after the pogrom of 1938, that is, to derive direct economic benefits for the party from the exploitation of the Jews.[135] The sums realized from expropriation of Jewish assets were immense: the Warthegau spent RM 64.35 per month per party member in 1940; since of this amount only RM 2.30 could be expected in the form of regular membership dues, much of the remainder represented seized assets.[136]

One of the first Reich ministries to feel the impact of Greiser's goals for the PO's position in the Warthegau was Frick's interior ministry. Frick, for all his long-time Nazi affiliations, remained a bureaucrat who believed in the need for trained and competent administrators, especially at the county level. Accordingly, he nominated and actually dispatched a large number of county executives from the Altreich to the Warthegau.[137] The Gauleiter ignored all but a few of Frick's appointees, and preferred instead to name the district leaders recommended by the

134. Helbing, "Die Partei im Gau Wartheland steht," *Schulungsbrief*, VIII (May–June 1941), 74; and Rschm., "Anordnung 61/39," 24 Nov. 1939, *Rdschr.*, VI.

135. Schieder, "Besuchs-Vermerk [Greiser]," 12 Jan. 1940, BDC/Greiser (PKC).

136. Rschm., "Jahresbericht 1940," p. 17.

137. This was hardly a choice assignment; the officials were often sent there as punishment for lack of proregime activism in their old locations. The best account of the life and functions of such a transferred county executive is Alexander Hohenstein (pseud.), *Warthelӓndisches Tagebuch aus den Jahren 1941/42* (Stuttgart, 1961). The latter also contains a wealth of information on party-state relations in the Warthegau.

StdF's office for their "Eastern" suitability as county administrators. The results were a predictable preponderance of PLs over civil service officials in responsible positions in the Warthegau. In the province of Posen (Požnan) there were only three trained county commissioners, but eight district leaders of the NSDAP; and similar figures can be cited for other Warthegau areas. In effect, the Gauleiter and the StdF's office cooperated to usurp the state's traditional role in regional administration.[138] The immediate results were administrative chaos and political catastrophe. As a group, the new PL–county executives constituted a very unqualified administrative team that had little experience in governing large-scale territorial units and even less inclination to acquire such knowledge. Rather, the party functionaries regarded themselves as pioneer *Herrenmenschen* (members of the master race) whose behavior and success could not be judged by the normal standards of efficient administration.

The Warthegau's northern neighbor, Danzig–West Prussia, was not a new creation, but the expansion of the old Gau Danzig, which until September 1939 had included the free city of Danzig. Moreover, there was no real question about the person of the Gauleiter, since Hitler had promised the post to the incumbent, Albert Forster, in early October.[139] Despite the bitter personal animosities between Forster and Greiser, the policies they followed were quite similar in a number of areas: both sought to maximize the role and power of the PO in their area of jurisdiction. As in the Warthegau, the party's operations in Danzig–West Prussia were financed primarily through the expropriation of Polish property. (This led to widespread corruption and graft in the Gau, with the Gau treasurer one of the leading officials implicated in the scandal.[140]) Similarly, Foster insisted that his district leaders also serve as county commissioners, so that the influence of the Reich ministry of the interior was severely limited in this Gau as well.[141] The party's

138. Broszat, *Polenpolitik*, pp. 51, 55–56, and 57, n. 3; and Mommsen, *Beamtentum*, pp. 111 and 223–27.

139. Brozat, *Polenpolitik*, pp. 29–30.

140. *Ibid.*, p. 29; and Hoepfner (provisional Gau treasurer of Danzig–West Prussia), "Bericht über die bei der Übernahme der Geschäfte . . . vorgefundenen Zustände," 23 Feb. 1942, T-580, roll 817, box 244, folder 107.

141. Wilhelm Löbsach, "Gründung und Aufbau der NSDAP im Gau Danzig-Westpreussen," *Schulungsbrief*, VIII (March–April 1941), 44–45. See also Freisler

organization, however, prospered. Between September of 1939 and the beginning of 1941, 20,000 ethnic Germans had become members of the party and the relatively small Gau boasted 31 districts, 503 locals, 2,938 cells, and 9,660 blocks.[142] The large number of new party members was the result of the one major policy difference between Greiser and Forster. While Greiser sought to make his Gau *polenrein* (free of Poles), Forster proceeded to "Germanize" most of his ethnic Poles. Since the population of Danzig–West Prussia was primarily German, Forster set out to remove his minority by the simple device of ethnic redefinition. Those concerned had little choice in the matter. Each district leader had a quota of Germanized Poles he had to meet, and the results were population figures which had no basis in either national origin or patriotic feelings.[143] Such sloppiness in racial selection in turn earned Forster the undying hatred of Heinrich Himmler and the SS. This had little effect on Forster's policies, but produced a running feud between the Gauleiter and the HSSPF in Danzig.

The Gaus of East Prussia and Silesia were enriched with relatively small amounts of Polish territory. East Prussia received the province of Zichenau, and here too the pattern of party machinery overriding state authority prevailed. The new chief of the provincial administration was Paul Dargel, the Gau organization leader of East Prussia, and throughout the new area East Prussian district leaders became county commissioners. Indeed, the Gauleiter of East Prussia, the ambitious Erich Koch, had far-reaching plans for the permanent establishment of party rule in his new fief. These involved, among other changes, the conversion of the normal villages into something grandiosely called locales of sovereignty (Hoheitsorte).[144] Silesia formed something of an exception to the usual developments in the East. Largely as a result of Wagner's moderating influence, the party did not attempt to establish a power monopoly in annexed areas. On the contrary, until November 1939, the party was not at all established in the former Polish

(undersecretary in the Reich ministry of justice) to Himmler, 13 Jan. 1941, BA/R22 /4466, fol. 1.

142. Albert Forster, "Bewährung bestanden—Ein Jahr Danzig-Westpreussen," *Schulungsbrief*, VIII (March–April 1941), 50.

143. Broszat, *Polenpolitik*, p. 128.

144. Erich Koch, "Aufbau im neuen Osten," and Alfred Karrasch, "Im neuen Osten," *Schulungsbrief*, VIII (March–April 1941), 41 and 35–36, respectively.

counties, and even after that the Gau instituted only a rudimentary PO; neither the affiliates nor the paramilitary organizations were permitted to organize.[145] In addition, Wagner pretty much permitted the Reich interior ministry to appoint qualified and trained personnel to positions as county executives, rather than attempting to install his own district leaders.[146]

The government-general, which encompassed the largest segment of prewar Poland, was an administrative cross between an annexed territory and a colony. The Reich commissioner, who held the title governor-general, was Hans Frank, Hitler's old defense lawyer and sometime Bavarian minister of justice. Seldom was an official more singularly unqualified.[147] In addition, his deputy, Arthur Seyss-Inquart, had played a prominent part in the intrigues that led to the annexation of Austria, but had had no other extensive administrative experience. At any rate, he soon became a Reich commissioner in his own right when Hitler moved him to Holland in May 1940. From the beginning, Frank's position appeared to be so uncertain that persistent rumors of his immediate dismissal accompanied his entire tenure in office—which actually lasted throughout the war.[148] Still, Frank's position in the government-general was never very strong. He had no part in the determination of the original policy guidelines for the government-general, and his subsequent rule was marked by fierce infighting between his own staff, the SS, and the PO. There appears to have been a brief period in which the Nazi leadership was actually considering establishing something of an autonomous Polish protectorate, but by the middle of October that idea had been dropped completely.[149] Instead, it was decided to transform the Generalgouvernement into a vast slave labor camp suitable primarily for resettling and exterminating Jews and for forcing the Polish population to work for its German masters. The Poles were to be treated in the manner of nineteenth-century African

145. Fritz Bracht, "In unerschütterlicher Schlagkraft," and Paul Roden, "Werk und Ziel—Aufbauarbeit der NSDAP im neuen Oberschlesien," *ibid.*, pp. 99–100, and 112, respectively.

146. Broszat, *Polenpolitik*, p. 53.

147. On Frank see Christoph Klessmann, "Der Generalgouverneur Hans Frank," *Vjh.f.Z.*, IXX (July 1971), 245–60.

148. Broszat, *Polenpolitik*, p. 83, n. 3.

149. *Ibid.*, p. 17.

natives; they were to have no rights, only duties.[150] In consequence, the party's ideal of an administrative tabula rasa was about to be realized. The government-general would become an area of no *rechtsstaatliche* (legal and governmental) norms, and the limits of oppression would be set only by the self-imposed restraints of the oppressors.[151]

To be sure, most of the actual terror power would be concentrated in the hands of the HSSPF, but the PO was not without plans for its role in occupied Poland. The PO's institutional arm in the government-general (and later in Czechoslovakia, Norway, the Netherlands, and occupied Russia as well), was an organization with the deliberately vague title "area of work activity (Arbeitsbereich) of the NSDAP." The Arbeitsbereichs were a creation of the StdF's office, and were designed specifically to meet the PO's needs in occupied areas which had been placed under civilian administration but which had either not yet been or would not be formally annexed to the Reich. The head of an Arbeitsbereich was the party's Hoheitsträger for the territory, while the Reich commissioner represented the state. The essential purpose of the Arbeitsbereichs was thus to establish a party organism in which the authority of the StdF could be vertically transmitted through the Hoheitsträgers from Munich to the district leaders in the government-general and the other occupied areas.[152] Substantively, the Arbeitsbereichs had both a control and a Betreuung function, though the first was considerably more important. With the establishment of party Hoheitsträgers, the StdF hoped to subordinate both the party segments outside the PO (notably the SS) and the civil servants assigned to conquered areas to his control.[153]

The nominal leadership of the Arbeitsbereich government-general was in the hands of Hans Frank, but the dominant personality in the organization was Schalk, the StdF's liaison official in the government-

150. Heydrich to Daluege, 29 Sept. 1939, BDC/Daluege (PKC); and *IMT*, doc. USSR-172, quoted in Domarus, *Hitler*, II, 1591.

151. Broszat, *Polenpolitik*, p. 147.

152. "Stellungsnahme Fritz Schmidts" in Seekamp (PK staff official) to Hauptamt für Volkstumsfragen, 23 Feb. 1943, T-175, roll 72, frames 2589345–47; and Schwarz to Frank, 20 Aug. 1940, IfZ/Fb. 50. See also Kwiet, *Reichskommissariat*, p. 90.

153. Max Freiherr du Prel, ed., *Das Generalgouvernement*, 2d ed. (Würzburg, 1942), pp. 56–57.

general. Under his vigorous initiative the Arbeitsbereich soon stood as an organizational entity.[154] By the fall of 1940 it had a membership of about 16,000. Of these, 15,000 were Reich Germans assigned to the government general in some capacity or other, and 1,000 were ethnic Germans; unlike Forster, Schalk and his superior did not believe in widespread Germanization.[155] In comparison with the party organization in the Altreich, the Arbeitsbereich was considerably more centralized and rationalized. To begin with, since the party and governmental territorial jurisdictions had the same boundaries, the difficulties of control caused by the differences in the Gau and Länder borders in the Reich were eliminated. In addition, Hess and Bormann sought from the beginning to prevent the autonomous development of the paramilitary organizations and the affiliates by decreeing that both had to operate within the Arbeitsbereich framework under the direct control of the Hoheitsträger.[156] The SA accepted the ruling (and until 1943 no SA organization was established in any of the occupied territories), but the SS felt strong enough to contest it vigorously.[157] As a result, the occupied areas became one of the main battle grounds in the developing rivalry of the PO and the SS. The affiliates were effectively stunted in their growth. The NSV, DAF, and the other organizations operated, if at all, only as subordinate offices of the PO. In consequence, the StdF's planned streamlining of the party, still a matter of considerable dispute in the Altreich, had achieved practical realization to a considerable degree in the Arbeitsbereichs.

The StdF and the Reich treasurer cooperated closely in alternately encouraging and restraining the Arbeitsbereichs. Schwarz's major concern was to maintain financial control over the party organizations, which in the heady atmosphere of the wild East were almost predestined to be centers of graft and corruption. The Reich treasurer insisted that PLs temporarily assigned to the East receive the salary and fringe bene-

154. *Ibid.*, p. 57; and *VOBl*, no. 210 (July 1940).

155. Schwarz to Frank, 4 Oct. 1939; and Hänssgen (office of the Reich treasurer), Schalk, and Thüringer (Gau treasurer in the GG), "Aktenvermerk über die Besprechung in Krakau am 25.9.40 . . . ," IfZ/Fb 50.

156. "Stellungnahme Fritz Schmidts," frames 2589345–47; and Schalk to Krüger (HSSPF in the government general), 8 April 1941, T-175, roll 201, frame 2742353.

157. See the various letters exchanged on the subject of the SS Sturmbann Ost between Schalk, Krüger, and Himmler, T-175, roll 201, frames 2742351–91.

fits allotted to their permanent positions in the Reich, rather than compensation figures resulting from private deals with the Hoheitsträgers in the East. In addition, Schwarz attempted (without a great deal of success) to prevent the wholesale expropriation of private property for the purposes of the party. He was not opposed to expropriation as such, merely apprehensive about the financial and political results of placing such windfalls in the hands of the Eastern party functionaries.[158]

Hitler was well pleased with his party's activities in the East. He noted with particular pride "that immense areas are administered here by a handful of born district and local leaders."[159] This was racial wishful thinking at its most blatant. Actually, the German government in occupied Poland was from the beginning ineffective, both politically and administratively. The Eastern territories not only were rampant with corruption, but quickly lost their political glamor as well. Instead, they achieved the reputation of being areas to which one sent PLs who could not be used anywhere else. The Nazi administration in the East very rapidly became the byword of a colonial regime run amok.

The Arbeitsbereich Protectorate, the party organization for occupied Czechoslovakia, was the weakest of the new creations, primarily, it would appear, because Hitler could not make up his mind about the final disposition of the country.[160] As a result, the party's conception of its future role there was ambiguous. In May 1939, just after the German take-over, Hess ordered the PO not to interfere in Aryanization proceedings in the Protectorate, but a year later the party openly solicited applications from Reich Germans to take over Jewish businesses.[161] The Arbeitsbereich itself was the result of similarly confused origins. It even had a separate title—liaison office Bohemia-Moravia—and owed its original founding not to the StdF, as was the case with the other Arbeitsbereichs, but to a suggestion of the Gauleiter of Lower Danube, Hugo Jury. Sometime in 1939 Jury wrote Ley requesting that the ROL

158. Rschm., "Anordnung 14/41," 29 March 1941, *Rdschr.*, VIII; and StdF, "Anordnung 23/40," 21 Feb. 1940, *ARV*.

159. Hitler's speech of 8 Nov. 1942, in Domarus, *Hitler*, II, 1942.

160. The best accounts of Czechoslovakia during the war years is Detlev Brandes, *Die Tschechen unter deutschem Protektorat* (Munich, 1969); and Vojtech Mastny, *The Czechs under Nazi Rule* (New York, 1970).

161. StdF, "Anordnung 98/39," 4 May 1939, BA/R 43 II/1201; and district leader Eisenach, "Rundschreiben 2/41," 10 Jan. 1941, MiU/GAC, folder 28.

set up a central agency through which the party could channel its control functions over the Reich Germans in Czechoslovakia. Ley did not
reply, and Jury in turn wrote to Schwarz repeating the suggestion.[162]
The Reich treasurer, of course, had no authority to establish such an
office, and it was not until January 1940 that the StdF became interested. In its final form, the liaison office was headed by Gauleiter Jury,
but it had relatively ill-defined functions and lines of authority. Jury
was very much a coordinator, rather than a commander. He shared
power with the other Gauleiters whose Gaus had contiguous borders
with the Protectorate. (After the March occupation, the Protectorate
had been divided into a series of territorial districts and the Betreuung
of the Germans in each area was assigned to the neighboring Gauleiter.)
Jury's major task was to assure, insofar as he was able, that none of the
other Gauleiters conducted direct negotiations with the Reich Protector's office without the approval of the StdF.[163]

Throughout the winter and spring of 1940 a series of weather
mishaps, Hitler's own indecision, and the opposition of the German
generals delayed the long-awaited offensive in the West, but with the
blitzkrieg attacks on Norway, Denmark, Holland, Belgium, and France
in April, May, and June the party turned its eyes covetously to the opportunities that awaited in the West. Clearly, the countries in the West
were not comparable to the relatively underdeveloped areas in Poland.
The Western countries were highly sophisticated, often industrialized
societies that had been in the mainstream of European development for
centuries. In addition, there were institutional channels for the transfer
of German control available to the Nazis: all of the invaded lands had
at least rudimentary fascist organizations with which a variety of party
offices had been in more or less regular contact. Furthermore, there
was the racial aspect. According to the Nazis, the Scandinavians and the
Dutch were racially related, Germanic peoples (the German word was
artverwandt, literally "related to the species") with whom the utopian
Germanic Reich could be constructed—under German leadership, of
course; this idea was to become a particular favorite of Heinrich

162. Jury to Schwarz, 14 Sept. 1939, BA/NS 19/597.
163. Brandes, *Tschechen*, p. 33; StdF, "Verfügung 3/40," 30 Jan. 1940, *VOBl*,
no. 210 (July 1940).

Himmler and his assistant for Germanic affairs, Gottlob Berger. In general, then, the occupation of Western Europe left the normal governmental organs in these nations intact, since the Nazis, even with the help of their indigenous fascist allies, had neither the manpower nor the conceptualization to do anything but channel their policies largely through these existing institutions. The often very naive PLs who were sent to "guide" the administration of the occupied territories in the West recognized at least that fundamental fact.[164] The Rechtsstaat might be perverted, but it could not be abolished.

The first of the Western countries to come under direct German control was Norway. Although the reasons for the occupation were primarily military ones, Nazi party officials had long shown considerable interest in this peculiarly "Aryan" land. Alfred Rosenberg in particular maintained close relations with the leader of the Norwegian fascists, Vidkun Quisling, and the minuscule Nasjonal Samling Party through his, Rosenberg's, influence in the Northern Society (*Nordische Gesellschaft*) and the NSDAP's foreign policy office. There was thus some basis for Rosenberg's belief that he would be the main architect of German policy in Norway. Alas, Norway was only the next in Rosenberg's seemingly endless list of disappointments. He quickly found himself outmaneuvered both by the foreign ministry and by the new Reich commissioner, Josef Terboven.[165] Like Frank, Terboven owed his appointment to one of Hitler's personal whims. Nothing in his previous career as Gauleiter of Essen qualified him for his Norwegian post. At the same time, he was the first of the new Western Reich commissioners, and his conception of the office was bound to set precedents for his later colleagues.[166]

Terboven regarded himself as a virtually autonomous viceroy, with what he called "limitless powers of command (*schrankenlose Befehlsgewalt*)." In his capacity as Reich commissioner he was responsible to no one but Adolf Hitler, and within the German governmental structure his office stood on the same level as the Reich ministries and the Four Year Plan. In practice, Terboven's conception of his office meant that

164. Loock, *Quisling*, pp. 509 and 548.

165. See Hess to Rosenberg, 8 Aug. 1940, T-580, roll 27, folder 211.

166. Domarus, *Hitler*, II, 1494; Boelcke, *Kriegspropaganda*, entries for 23 June and 26 Sept. 1940, pp. 402–03, and 527, respectively.

he would attempt to ignore all directives that were not issued by Hitler himself, including the StdF's admonitions to send frequent reports to the deputy Führer's office.[167]

The Reich commissioner's plans for the future of his fief were a mixture of utopia and naiveté. To begin with, he wanted to rule through Quisling's Nasjonal Samling, the small fascist party that had openly welcomed the Nazi invasion and that, as a result, had become a synonym for treason for all but a handful of Norwegians. Terboven convinced himself by October 1940 that there had been a complete change of public opinion.[168] Other German leaders knew better, but there was little they could do. Goebbels, far more realistically, thought Quisling ought to be retired to the background. But Hitler by and large agreed with Terboven, so that even Goebbels had to admit that while one could be of divided opinion about Quisling's suitability prior to April, thereafter the Führer's word would have to be law.[169] Gazing further into the future, Terboven could see far beyond Quisling to the eventual absorption of Norway into the great Germanic Reich in the sky. The commissioner thought this might be some time away, but it was certainly his goal from the outset of his rule.[170]

The party's role in Norway was less visible, but no less significant than in the government-general. The actual number of PLs serving in Norway was relatively small; the Norwegian internal administration remained intact and the Nazis contented themselves with the establishment of a central controlling office and a few supervisory provincial officials. Originally, Rosenberg's chief of staff, Arno Schickedanz, had hoped to head the party operations, but Terboven quickly shunted him aside and instead made him his representative in Berlin, which meant Schickedanz was allowed to take letters to Lammers and carry back the

167. See Killy (an official of the Reich chancellery), "Besprechung mit Delbrügge" (Terboven's chief of administration), 28 May 1940; the correspondence Lammers to Terboven, 29 March 1942; Terboven to Lammers, 3 May 1942; and Lammers, "Aktenvermerk," 21 Aug. 1942, BA/R 43 II/674 and 674b.

168. Even Lammers felt obliged to comment with a skeptical explanation point on Terboven's remark that Norwegians no longer regarded the activities of the Nasjonal Samling as treason ("Monatsbericht," Oct. 1940, BA/R 43 II/674b).

169. Boelcke, *Kriegspropaganda*, entry for 24 April 1940, pp. 329–30.

170. Loock, *Quisling*, pp. 447–450.

answers.[171] In Norway itself, the Arbeitsbereich was under the leadership of Paul Wegener and Richard Schaller. Wegener was a particular favorite of Martin Bormann, had served in the office of the StdF, and was deputy Gauleiter of Brandenburg when he was sent to Norway. Schaller held a similar position in Cologne-Aachen.[172] Of the two, Wegener was much the more important; indeed, the whole Norwegian party operation had the name of *Einsatzstab* Wegener, that is, task force Wegener. The former district leader of Bremen started his Norwegian career as district commissioner in Trondheim, and in August 1940 he headed the NSDAP's staff in Norway. By this time, Quisling had taken nominal control of the Norwegian government, and it fell to Wegener and his staff to "advise" the Nasjonal Samling and "supervise the orderly development of its administration."[173] With a staff of Reich PLs numbering seventy at one point,[174] Wegener infiltrated every office of the Nasjonal Samling and the mass societal organizations of Norway. His work was aided significantly by the virtually unlimited financial resources at his disposal. In both Norway and Holland the Germans forced the national banks to grant the occupation administration unlimited credits,[175] and a large percentage of the Norwegian moneys flowed into Wegener's coffers. In 1941 he was given a total of RM 2,000,000 simply to spend on "political purposes." Significantly, this money was not subject to regular audits. By 1941 the amount had risen to over RM 4,000,-000, and this, too, could not be audited by governmental examiners. It is difficult to escape the conclusion that Wegener worked largely with bribes in order to maintain his influence over Quisling's party and the governmental administration of Norway.[176]

171. Terboven to Daitz (head of the Nordische Gesellschaft), 30 April 1940, BA/R 43 II/674.

172. "Lebenslauf des Gauleiters Paul Wegener," 11 June 1943, BDC/Wegener (PKC); and Richard Schaller, "Anlage zum Personalbogen," 31 May 1940, BDC/Schaller (PKC).

173. "Lebenslauf . . . Wegener." See also Loock, *Quisling*, p. 362.

174. Best, *Aufsichtsverwaltungen*, p. 52. As in the government general, Schwarz insisted that they be paid according to their Reich positions. See Rschm., "Anordnung 59/40," 26 Nov. 1940, *Rdschr.*, VII.

175. See the documentation in BA/R 2/4501.

176. Reich ministry of finance, "[Vermerk]," 15 Oct. 1941, BA/R 2/11470b. Additional budget figures for the years 1941 and 1942 are in this same folder.

A month after defeating Norway the German armies conquered Holland. The Norwegian pattern repeated itself: a lightning-swift attack, this time accompanied by the bombardment of Rotterdam, quick Dutch capitulation, very brief period of military rule, and then the appointment of a Reich commissioner. The Nazis saw a close connection between the developments in Norway and those in the Netherlands. Hitler showed a particular interest in rebuilding Rotterdam according to his own plans, frequent meetings were held to coordinate the policies of the two Arbeitsbereichs, and Terboven visited Holland to study the policies of his counterpart. Similar visits by Arbeitsbereich officials from the government-general underscored the similarity of tasks in all of the Arbeitsbereichs.[177] Within the party, Schwarz and the StdF looked upon Norway and Holland as similar assignments for Reich PLs. In every sense, then, it is clear that Holland and Norway were treated as parts of the developing Germanic empire.[178]

Hitler's choice for Reich commissioner in Holland was Seyss-Inquart. This time the appointment came as no great surprise. Seyss-Inquart had served Hitler well as his puppet in Austria, had then been gracefully retired as Reich minister without portfolio, and was now serving as Frank's deputy in Poland. He was exceedingly unhappy in the government-general, and had already written Himmler requesting service at the front. In addition, Hitler felt that as a result of their multinational heritage, Austrians were particularly well suited to administer foreign territories. Seyss-Inquart also had the strong support of Heinrich Himmler.[179] On May 15, the new commissioner assumed the post he was to fill with little strength and a great deal of ineptitude for almost four years. As a man without a power base of his own in either the party or the state, he was in a very weak position from the outset of his administration.[180] Throughout his tenure Seyss-Inquart referred items for de-

177. See Schalk to Schmidt, 26 March 1941, RvO/TB/folder XII.

178. Sommer (of Schmidt's staff) to Reich propaganda leadership, 14 Oct. 1940; Bormann to Schmidt, 12 Nov. 1940; and Neuburg (staff of the StdF) to Schmidt, 24 Jan. 1941, *ibid.*, folders I, IV, and VIII.

179. Kwiet, *Reichskommissariat*, pp 46–49. See also Werner Warmbrunn, *The Dutch under German Occupation 1940–1945* (Stanford, 1963), p. 29. For the relations between Seyss-Inquart and Himmler at this time, see Seyss-Inquart to Kaltenbrunner, 13 Jan. 1940, RvO/BDC/H 204; Himmler to Seyss-Inquart, 4 June 1940; and Seyss-Inquart to Himmler, 27 Nov. 1940, RvO/BDC/H 99.

180. Interrogation of Klopfer, 14 Nov. 1947, p. 6, IfZ/ZS 352.

cision to Munich or Hitler's headquarters, while Terboven issued decrees in similar situations without bothering to consult anyone.[181] As a result, Seyss-Inquart became the relatively impotent object of a power play between his two chief assistants, Fritz Schmidt, the head of the Arbeitsbereich and Hanns Rauter, the HSSPF for Holland.[182]

Rosenberg had developed no particular interests in the Netherlands, but the party organization for Germans abroad (*Auslandsorganisation,* AO) had ambitions of becoming the chief party control agency after the establishment of the civilian administration. There had always been a large number of Reich Germans living in Holland, but the AO's effectiveness in controlling or speaking for this group was not particularly impressive. In 1937 the leader of the AO in Holland, Butting, had become involved in a major espionage affair which resulted in the dissolution of the AO by Dutch authorities and Butting's own expulsion to Germany.[183] Nevertheless, Ernst-Wilhelm Bohle, the head of the AO and Hess's brother-in-law, had every intention of reconstituting the AO in Holland, although he recognized that Butting could not return to the scene of his crimes. To prepare for the organizational revival of the AO, Bohle ordered all Reich Germans to stay in Holland and dispatched one hundred copies of Ley's fairy tales (the intraparty term for the *Organisationbuch*) to Holland.[184] There is no doubt that he envisioned the AO in Holland as the watchdog and controller of the civilian administration. Bohle demanded, for example, that his AO officials be accorded the status of Hoheitsträgers, with the right to approve German civil servants assigned to Holland. He also wanted to align the party district boundaries as rapidly as possible with the borders of the Dutch provinces as a step toward the creation of a potential Reichsgau arrangement.[185]

181. Schmidt to Bormann, 13 March 1941, RvO/TB/folder XI.

182. Kwiet, *Reichskommissariat*, p. 57.

183. *Ibid.*, p. 87, n. 88; Louis de Jong, "E. W. Bohle en Nederland," p. 1, Notities voor de hoofdwerk, no. 9; and J. C. H. de Pater, "De organisatorische en culturelle werkzaamheid van de Landesgruppe Niederlande van mei tot november 1940," pp. 3–4, Notities voor de hoofdwerk, no. 103. The Notities are unpublished internal staff studies of the RvO.

184. AO (Netherlands), "Rundschreiben Nr. 5 [and] 4/40 [sic]," 15 June and 19 Sept. 1940, RvO/Arb. NSDAP (Ni)/3 II A and 29 II.

185. AO (Netherlands), "Anweisung 8/40 [and] 17/40," 1 July and 10 Aug. 1940, *ibid.*

Bohle moved quickly to take advantage of the German victory. Five days after the invasion he named Bernhard Ruberg, an old hand in the AO, as the new head of operations in the Netherlands. That, however, was his last dramatic move. Ruberg did not appear in Den Haag (The Hague), the administrative capital of Holland, until two weeks later, and even then seemed to concern himself primarily with the petty financial claims of individual Reich Germans, rather than with establishing his overall political authority.[186] Actually, such attempts would have been futile in any case. The AO was simply no match for the resolute staffs of Martin Bormann and Heinrich Himmler.

The StdF's chief of staff wanted to establish an Arbeitsbereich as the party's organization in Holland, staffed with PLs subject to the deputy Führer's direct control.[187] Seyss-Inquart, the new Reich commissioner for Holland, readily agreed to shut out the AO, although for different reasons. Like most old Austrians, he had been imbued with a heavy dose of Austrian cultural missionary zeal, and saw as one of his main tasks in Holland the purveying of "cultural policy" to the largely "materialistic" Dutch. "Kulturpolitik" was an umbrella under which traveled any number of cultural propagandistic endeavors, from exhibitions of photographs of "The Führer's Home Town" to tours of the Viennese Burgtheater. The AO had always done some of this, but its focal point was the German minority; for Seyss-Inquart's grander missionary plans the AO proved too small an organizational base.[188]

The StdF's man in Holland was Fritz Schmidt, an "old fighter," longtime staff member of the StdF, and prior to his Dutch assignment the deputy Führer's liaison man to the propaganda ministry. Schmidt's selection came almost simultaneously with that of Seyss-Inquart; by late May, Schmidt was already negotiating with numerous German and Dutch government and party officials.[189] In June he had become a regular commuter, and his talks with Seyss-Inquart and the Dutch fascist leader Adriaan Mussert indicate that at this time the StdF's office leaned

186. Pater, "Organisatorische," pp. 3 and 6.

187. A. E. Cohen, "Ontstaan en betekenis van 'Der Arbeitsbereich der NSDAP in den Niederlanden," p. 3, Notities, no. 26; and Schmidt to Bormann, 7 June 1940, *IMT*, doc. no. NG 4313.

188. Pater, "Organisatorische," pp. 17 and 25–26.

189. Schmidt, "Vorlage für den Stabsleiter," 24 May 1940, *IMT*, doc. no. NG-4314; and Schmidt, "Vormerkbuch."

toward a Quisling type of solution for the Netherlands.[190] The organizational demise of the AO in Holland came as a result of a series of steps between July and September 1940. In late July, the StdF prohibited the AO from establishing further affiliates within Holland, thereby crippling its organizational expansion.[191] The AO attempted, briefly, to fight back with renewed propagandistic activism, but Hess countered with a decree that withdrew permission for any further AO activities.[192] When the StdF followed this on October 7 with the formal establishment of the "Arbeitsbereich Netherlands," even Ruberg realized that the AO had no future in Holland.[193] He tried to make the best of a hopeless situation, and gamely issued a farewell proclamation noting that his task had been accomplished,[194] but Bormann would not even allow the memory of the AO to be perpetuated in the Arbeitsbereich. He refused a request by Bohle that the various Nazi locals retain their old AO flags.[195]

Hess's formal proclamation establishing the Arbeitsbereich was a model of vagueness. The creation of the Arbeitsbereich became necessary as a result of the peculiar circumstances of the Dutch situation and of "the special tasks which result for the Reich Germans living in Holland and particularly the party members."[196] In less guarded language this meant that "our political orders" emanated solely from the StdF's office, and that the Arbeitsbereich's basic goal was to Nazify Holland and negate the effects of the Treaty of Westphalia of 1648. In Schmidt's blunt words, "we have to see to it that everything here becomes National Socialist."[197] From the outset of German rule in Holland, the party

190. Cohen, "Ontstaan," p. 3; and Schmidt, "Vormerkbuch."

191. StdF, "Anordnung 75/40," 23 July 1940. *VOBl*, no. 211 (Aug. 1940).

192. HSSPF (Netherlands), "Bericht Nr. 33," 26 Sept. 1940, RvO/HSSPF 54a.

193. Pater, "Organisatorische," p. 14. See also AO (Netherlands), "Anweisung 25/40," 9 Sept. 1940, RvO/Arb. NSDAP (Ni)/3 II A.

194. Bernhard Ruberg, "Tagesbefehl," 15 Oct. 1940, RvO/Arb. NSDAP (Ni)/3 II A.

195. Sommer to Bühler (staff of the StdF), 17 Oct. 1940, RvO/TB/folder I.

196. Arb. NSDAP (Netherlands), "Anweisung 1/40," 22 Oct. 1940, RvO/Arb. NSDAP (Ni)/3C. StdF, "Verfügung 9/40," 7 Oct. 1940, *VOBl*, no. 213 (Oct. 1940).

197. See Schmidt's address at the "Arbeitsbereichstagung in s'Hertogenbosch am 26.1.1941," n.d., RvO/Arb. NSDAP (Ni)/3A V. See also Sommer to Walter (staff of the PK), 19 May 1941 (draft), RvO/TB/XV; and B. Casselmann, "Aufgaben und Pflichten des Orts- und Betriebsobmannes der DAF in den Niederlanden," 16 Oct. 1940, RvO/Arb. NSDAP (Ni)/29 III.

organization worked through and with the StdF's office, leaving Seyss-Inquart, the nominal head of the Arbeitsbereich, in honorable limbo. All assignments and promotions in the Arbeitsbereich Netherlands were handled entirely by the personnel office of the StdF. Schwarz cooperated fully by refusing to pay the salary of any PL who had not been approved by the StdF's personnel office. (This ruling became necessary because the Gauleiters of neighboring areas tried to place their PLs in Dutch positions as a step toward de facto annexation.)[198]

The StdF's personnel policy pursued two interconnected objectives: to eliminate the remaining PLs of the AO from responsible positions in the Arbeitsbereich,[199] and to staff the new party organization in Holland with both long- and short-term appointees approved by the deputy Führer's office. The distinction between the chronological span of the assignments corresponded to the planned long- and short-term political future of the Netherlands. A temporary appointment of two to three years corresponded more or less to the Nasjonal Samling era envisioned in Norway. During this time relatively large numbers of Reich PLs would supervise, that is, gleichschalten, every aspect of Dutch society and staff all major governmental positions with reliable collaborators. Then, after the establishment of the peacetime Germanic Reich, a skeleton crew would suffice to control the affairs of the Reich's Western outpost. PLs in the second group, among whom Schmidt considered himself, could plan on a tenure in Holland ranging anywhere from a dozen years to an entire career.[200] After a brief and unsuccessful attempt to locate jobs for various prominent cast-off PLs, for example, the notorious Gauleiter Kube, the StdF concentrated on middle-echelon officials, both from the staff itself and from the Gaus, particularly Weser-Ems. There was a logic in the choice of Weser-Ems, not only because of the close geographic proximity of the Gau to Holland, but also because Heinrich Walkenhorst, Friedrich's deputy, had originally served there and its Gauleiter, Röver, was a particular favorite of Bormann. The specific appointments to the Arbeitsbereich Netherlands under-

198. Schmidt to personnel office of the StdF, 18 Oct. 1940; Eftger to Hesseldieck of the StdF's personnel office), 23 April 1941, and Hesseldieck to Schmidt, 14 Jan. 1941, RvO/TB/I, XIII, and VIII respectively.

199. Jong, "Bohle," p. 2.

200. Bormann to Schwarz, and Walter to Eftger, 15 Feb. and 9 July 1941, RvO/TB/XX.

scored the significance of the StdF's in-service training program. Although almost all of the leading PLs in the central office of the Arbeitsbereich were transferred directly from the staff's offices in Munich,[201] the appointments of provincial representatives were for the most part (seven of nine) district leaders and Gau staff PLs who had previously had a tour of duty at the Brown House. A major difficulty arose, however, in prying these people loose from their home Gaus for service in occupied Holland.[202]

In accordance with the elite role envisioned for the Reich Germans in Holland, the Arbeitsbereich began to co-opt members of the German minority into the Arbeitsbereich (in contrast to the NSDAP in the Reich, the Arbeitsbereichs were not subject to a closing of the membership rolls), although, on Schwarz's orders, Schmidt avoided wholesale forced inductions.[203] In this respect, the Arbeitsbereich followed a policy that diverged sharply from the AO's approach. The AO had prepared long lists of potential fifth columnists among the Reich Germans prior to the invasion, but Bormann and Schmidt realized that the German community as a whole was not a politically activist Nazi group. By no means all Reich Germans living in Holland before the war had been enthusiastic supporters of the AO; on the contrary, most of them were very lukewarm toward the AO.[204] The organizational makeup of the Arbeitsbereich Netherlands was a conscious copy of the organism created earlier in the government-general,[205] which heavily emphasized control functions and paid little attention to the party's Betreuung role. Similarly, the Arbeitsbereich Netherlands never permitted the establishment of autonomous affiliates, and among the paramilitary organizations, only the SS established a powerful Dutch branch. The StdF turned down requests by the SA and the National Socialist Motor Corps

201. Hoffmann to Schmidt, 19 Nov. 1940, RvO/TB/IV; and Rosenberg, "Aktennotiz über die Unterredung mit . . . Friedrichs am 18.8.44," n.d., T-454, roll 7, frame 4913161.

202. See Schmidt to personnel office of the StdF, 31 Oct. 1940, *ibid.*, I. This was true of other Arbeitsbereichs as well. See Rschm., "Bekanntgabe 6/41," 15 March 1941, *Rdschr.*, VIII.

203. Schwarz to Schmidt, 6 Dec. 1940, RvO/TB/XV.

204. Cohen, "Ontstaan," p. 6; Arb. NSDAP (Netherlands), "Anweisung 2/40," 19 Nov. 1940, RvO/Arb. NSDAP (Ni)/3 C; and Schwarz to Schmidt, 6 Dec. 1940, RvO/TB/XV.

205. Cohen, "Ontstaan," p. 6.

(NSKK) to organize their followers in Holland.[206] Only the finances of
the party organization in the Netherlands were subject to some limitations not found in the East. To be sure, the PO hardly suffered from
cash shortages, but particularly in 1940 and 1941 there were no large-
scale expropriations of Dutch private property, and some of the PLs in
the Arbeitsbereich complained of financial strictures on their organizational expansion.[207]

The organizational chart of the Arbeitsbereich Netherlands demonstrates the party's primary concern with organs of social and political
control. The major divisions of the Arbeitsbereich were the offices of
propaganda and training, economic advisors, Hitler Youth, NSV, DAF,
and the Nazi Women's League.[208] (The Reich counterpart of the Wom-
en's League had all but ceased to exist, but since the Germans were a
minority in Holland, the party obviously wanted to politicize even the
normally despised female element.) Among the organs of social control
the DAF and NSV were the most important. Since most Reich Germans
were of working age, compulsory membership in the DAF gave the
party a ready avenue of control over them. In addition, through its supervision of all Dutch labor organizations, the DAF could indirectly
extend such control to the bulk of the Dutch population as well. Schmidt
lost no time setting to work establishing the necessary organizational
forms. As early as August 1940, he was at work drafting plans for both a
DAF organization in Holland and an NAF (*Nederlandse Arbeidsfront*)
as its Dutch counterpart after the DAF had been set up.[209] The political
impact of this arrangement was of course dependent upon the DAF's
clear subordination to the Hoheitsträgers in the Arbeitsbereich, and that
was by no means a foregone conclusion. In Germany itself the PO did

206. Arb. NSDAP (Netherlands), "Anweisung 6/41," 18 April 1941, RvO/Arb.
NSDAP (Ni)/3 c.

207. For the financial difficulties see, for example, Keil (deputy head of the DAF's
office in the Netherlands) to Schmidt, 5 Feb. 1941, RvO/Arb. NSDAP (Ni)/23.

208. See the list of planned sessions for the Arbeitsbereich conference, 25–26 Jan.
1941, RvO/Arb. NSDAP (Ni)/4A. See also "Geschäftsverteilungsplan der Dienststelle des Generalkommissars zur besonderen Verwendung," n.d., RvO/GKzbV
(Ni)/1a; and Max Freiherr du Prel and Willi Janke, eds., *Die Niederlande im Um-
bruch der Zeiten* (Würzburg, 1941), pp. 124–28.

209. Rost, "Sozialistische Arbeitsgemeinschaft," ca. Aug. 1940, quoted in Minoud
Marinus Rost van Tonningen, *Correspondentie van Mr. M. M. Rost van Tonningen,*
ed. E. Fraenkel-Verkade and A. J. van der Leeuw (Den Haag, 1967), I, 397, n. 74.

not control the DAF completely, and Ley was attempting to transfer something of the DAF's independence to Holland, while Schmidt wanted to put into effect the concept of a centralized Arbeitsbereich with complete subordination of the affiliates to the PO.[210] By February, Schmidt had pretty much won. The DAF's representative in Holland put little emphasis on his social service role, and instead regarded himself as an indoctrination arm of the NSDAP.[211] Under these circumstances the Arbeitsbereich encouraged the rapid growth of the DAF, and by the end of April, the labor front had two central offices (Den Haag and Amsterdam), seventy-four locals, and some twelve thousand members.[212]

The functions and organization of the NSV were corollaries of the DAF's role among the Reich Germans. In the Altreich, the NSV acted primarily as an inflation-combating device through its huge annual "Winter Help" collections, but, as noted before, the StdF's office also planned a major role for the NSV as a racial control mechanism. During the war, the occupied Netherlands became a testing ground for such ideas. The NSV had the power to give financial aid to those economically disadvantaged families whom the party regarded as politically and racially reliable, while refusing to aid families whose political attitude was suspect. NSV investigators were specifically instructed to give particular weight to political attitudes and "racial pride" in rating the families they visited.[213] Late in 1940, the Arbeitsbereich began to establish the Dutch NSV offices. One of the StdF's younger staffers, Robert Thiel, was assigned to head the buildup. He stayed until the end of the war (eventually holding, in addition to his NSV position, the office of provincial commissioner in Nord-Brabant) and blanketed the country with NSV offices.[214]

The Nazis looked upon the Hitler Youth as the guarantee of long-

210. Wilhelm Keil, "Situationsbericht über die Deutsche Arbeitsfront in den Niederlanden," 19 Nov. 1940, RvO/Arb. NSDAP (Ni)/25 II.

211. DAF (Netherlands), "Arbeitsanweisung 1/41," 24 Feb. 1941, *ibid.*, 29 I; and Keil, "Bericht über die Arbeit der DAF im Arbeitsbereich der NSDAP in den Niederlanden," 17 Sept. 1941, p. 2, *ibid.*, 23.

212. Keil to Eftger, 3 April 1941, *ibid.*, 23.

213. See the documentation in RvO/Arb. NSDAP (Ni)/13.

214. Arb. NSDAP (Netherlands), NSV to all NSV district offices, 29 Nov. 1940 and 24 Feb. 1941, *ibid.*, 16 II.

term German rule in the occupied areas. Accordingly, Schmidt imported yet another Reich official, Hermann Lindenburger, to lead the HJ organization in Holland. Lindenburger had been a full-time HJ functionary since May 1933, serving in a series of Gaus and in the national office of the Reich youth leadership. Although Schmidt had no complaint about Lindenburger's Nazi fanaticism or zeal in building up the HJ organization, he was less satisfied with Lindenburger's ambitions for autonomy. Since the HJ held an organizational status in the Reich largely independent of the PO, Lindenburger brazenly styled his Dutch headquarters "field office of the HJ in the Netherlands" until forced by Schmidt to acknowledge that his office in Holland was an integral subunit of the PO.[215]

All of these organizational moves were designed to strengthen the party's political impact in its relations with the German and Dutch governmental authorities and with the Dutch fascist movement. As far as Seyss-Inquart's office and the Dutch caretaker government were concerned, the Arbeitsbereich was for the moment content to emphasize that party and state had parallel tasks and that neither was subordinate to the other.[216] The matter of the Dutch fascists was considerably more delicate. Here the Arbeitsbereich had to pursue two not very compatible goals simultaneously. The party organization wanted to secure a dominant position for the German minority in the country.[217] At the same time, the Germans' control should be hidden as much as possible so that a collaborationist Dutch regime could relieve the Germans of much of the odium of the occupation policies and more indirectly, put the Reich in charge of the Dutch colonies.[218]

At the time of the invasion, the spectrum of Dutch parties included two fascist groups, neither of which was politically significant. The National Socialist Movement (*Nationaalsocialistische Bewegening*, NSB)

215. The HJ office in the Netherlands was established late in 1940. See Seyss-Inquart to Axmann (Reich youth leader), 27 Nov. 1940; Schmidt to GL Hessen, 13 Feb. 1941; and Schmidt to Axmann, 4 April 1941, RvO/BDC/H 1140.

216. Eftger, "Notiz für Pg. Schmidt," 5 May and 25 July 1941, RvO/GKzbV (Ni)/1d.

217. Arb. NSDAP (Netherlands), training office, "Redner-Information 2 [Jan. 1941]," RvO/Arb. NSDAP (Ni)/8 A.

218. Cohen, "Ontstaan," p. 5; and W. Goedhuys to Rost van Tonningen, 17 Dec. 1940, in Rost, *Correspondentie*, I, 545.

was a chauvinistic party that had been founded in the twenties by a nondescript engineer, Adriaan Mussert, during a dispute between Holland and Belgium over a canal project. Its platform was authoritarian and expansionist, calling for the union of Holland and Belgium and for a strong colonial emphasis. The NSB was not an openly anti-Semitic and racist party, and it was not originally a particularly pro-German group.[219] By the end of the thirties, the NSB had sunk to a level of political impotence, so that even the Germans did not regard Mussert's creation as a serious partner in Dutch-Nazi cooperation.[220] After the conquest of Holland, however, both parties had second thoughts about each other. The Nazis needed a collaborationist base of at least some size, and Mussert knew that the key to his only road to power lay with the Germans. He was willing to become the Dutch Quisling.[221]

The Nazis' decision to select Mussert as their partner in Holland was made considerably easier by the utter insignificance of the other fascist movement, the National Socialist Dutch Workers' Party (*Nationaalsociaalistische nederlandse arbeider partij*, NSNAP). On the surface, this group seemed ideal: it was openly pro-Nazi and racist, and advocated the annexation of Holland to Germany. The attitude of its members during the brief war was such that even Mussert termed them "traitors."[222] Unfortunately, from the German point of view, the following of the NSNAP was so infinitesimal (intelligence reports put it at one hundred for all Holland)[223] that even Schmidt had to acknowledge the NSNAP would not become a viable political group.

Torn between the political uselessness of the genuine Nazis in Holland and the less than fervent pro-German sentiments of the NSB, Schmidt's policies in the first months of the occupation were characterized by vacillation and indecision.[224] The Nazis generally acknowledged that only the NSB had a national following worth speaking of,[225] but for a time at least there were attempts to artificially build up the NSNAP.

219. Kwiet, *Reichskommissariat*, pp. 72 ff.
220. Boelcke, *Kriegspropaganda*, entries for 14 and 22 May 1940, pp. 350 and 360.
221. Warmbrunn, *Dutch under German Occupation*, pp. 85 and 92.
222. Pater, "Organisatorische," p. 4.
223. HSSPF (Netherlands), "Bericht 6a," 25 July 1940, RvO/HSSPF/54a.
224. See Bormann to Schmidt, 31 Oct. 1940, RvO/TB/IV.
225. Arb. NSDAP (Ni), "Redner-Information Nr. 2 [Jan. 1941]," RvO/Arb. NSDAP (Ni)/8A.

The party received widespread press coverage, and its organizational expansion included the much-heralded establishment of a Dutch HJ.[226] At the same time the Arbeitsbereich was engaged in a completely abortive attempt to increase the popularity of Adolf Hitler among the Dutch people.[227] Indeed, the deputy leader of the NSB (and bitter enemy of Schmidt) claimed at the end of the war that Schmidt had made tentative promises to the NSNAP that its goal of annexation would eventually be carried out.[228]

A significant shift in policy can be detected by September,[229] and by January of the following year Schmidt had given up his attempts to bolster the NSNAP. The turning point came with Mussert's visit to Hitler in the fall of 1940. Hitler never gave specific assurances of power to Mussert and the other satellite leaders during these sessions, but the visits per se raised the stature of those favored to such an extent that German support for them and their movements became axiomatic. The NSNAP sank quickly into oblivion. The Germans first stopped the press coverage of its activities and then pressured the party into dissolution and merger with the NSB.[230] Simultaneously, all criticism of the NSB was prohibited.[231] Moreover, the NSB and the Arbeitsbereich began to stage joint public functions in order to demonstrate that "the Netherlands can be free [from occupation troops] only when they have taken on National Socialism (*nationalsozialistisch ausgerichtet*) and adopted its way of life" as part of the greater Germanic Reich.[232]

226. In issuing a chronological overview of Holland after two years of occupation, the German press censor ordered the Dutch press not to mention this item. See GKzbV, press office, "Zwei Jahre Reichskommissariat in den Niederlanden . . . [May, 1942]," RvO/GKzbV (Ni)/22c.

227. Arb. NSDAP (Netherlands), propaganda office, "Mitteilung 12/40," 6 Nov. 1940, RvO/Arb. NSDAP (Ni)/4 B I.

228. Rost to Seyss-Inquart, 27 and 30 Dec. 1944, RvO/BDC/H 13.

229. Schmidt to Bormann ("to be put on the Reichsleiter's desk immediately"), 21 Oct. 1940, RvO/TB/folder I.

230. A[lgemeen] N[ederlandse] P[ersagentuur], "Noot 126," 30 Nov. [1940], RvO/DVK (Ni)/84a. The "noots" were daily instructions by the German censorship office to the Dutch press.

231. "Noot 209," 18 Jan. 1941, *ibid.*, 84b; and Schmidt to Friedrichs, 16 Jan. 1941, RvO/TB/VII.

232. Report on a speech by Schmidt to an Arbeitsbereich training session in Sittand (South Limburg), 18 May 1941, RvO/Arb. NSDAP (Ni)/73.

Nevertheless, the Nazis had learned one lesson from Norway: yielding governmental power to the Quislings should come after they had built a political stature among the population, not before. As a result, despite Mussert's repeated urgings, the Nazis refused to make him prime minister until the NSB had become a political power with more than token support. Understandably enough, Mussert never reached his goal.[233] Of course, the German aims and policies were not really of great help. Quite aside from the overriding fact of the invasion itself, there were the policy fluctuations,[234] attacks on the churches,[235] and, perhaps most important, the undeniable evidence of naked exploitation measures. Here the economic policy division of the StdF's office was particularly active. Under the guidance of the ambitious Bärmann, the Arbeitsbereich flew in the face of virtually all segments of Dutch public opinion by drafting plans for the German control of the Dutch economy and subsequently, removing German-owned enterprises from the supervision of the Dutch governmental authorities.[236] The first stage of the plans involved essentially an expropriation of all Jewish-owned businesses in Holland and their transfer under party auspices to Reich German owners, selected by the Gau economic advisors.[237] By early spring of 1941 preparations for the "Germanization" campaign were under way with meetings of the Gau economic advisors in Berlin, when, at the last moment, Seyss-Inquart developed serious doubts about the political results

233. HSSPF, "Bericht Nr. 32," 25 Sept. 1940, RvO/HSSPF/54a; Neuburg (staff of the PK) to Cassel (chief of staff of the office for racial affairs), 7 April 1943, T-175, roll 32, frame 2589342.

234. In December 1940 Rost wrote Schmidt in exasperation, "I am not clear about the policy line that you do want at this time." "Nota van M. M. Rost van Tonningen voor F. Schmidt [Dec. 1940], in Rost, *Correspondentie*, I, 559–60. See also "Fragmenten van een Rapport van M. M. Rost van Tonningen" [Dec. 1940], *ibid.*, p. 563.

235. In March 1941 the StdF's office and the SD jointly dispatched an expert on church affairs to Holland (Klopfer to RK, 8 March 1941, RvO/TB/XII). A month later a prohibition of all church-related periodicals was in the offing. GKzbV, main office for propaganda and training, "Monatsbericht für März 1941," 9 April 1941, RvO/GKzbV (Ni)/15f.

236. See Sommer to Bärmann, 8 Oct. 1940, RvO/TB/I; and Arb. NSDAP (Netherlands), "Rundschreiben 1/41," 8 Feb. 1941, RvO/Arb. NSDAP (Ni)3 C.

237. Cohen, "Ontstaan," p. 5; Arb. NSDAP (Netherlands), office of economic advisor, "[Rundschreiben]," 15 Nov. 1940 (strictly confidential), RvO/Arb. NSDAP (Ni)/9 C; and Disselberg (staff of the StdF) to Bärmann, 12 Nov. 1940, RvO/TB/III.

of the project.[238] He worried about the effect on Dutch morale created
by the wholesale transfer of Dutch businesses to German owners. Consequently, he ordered a change of tactics: there would be Aryanizations,
that is, reassignments to Dutch (pro-fascist) owners, but at least for the
moment no "Germanizations."[239] Needless to say, these subtle distinc-
tions were not reflected in a rising popularity curve in any of the public
opinion polls.

There was never much doubt about the German ability to achieve
military victories over Norway and Holland, but Hitler and the party
were considerably less sanguine about the conflict in France. Throughout the spring of 1940 Hitler made no public appearances (Hess substituted for him at his traditional May Day speech[240]) and the party's propaganda was decidedly low-key. The NSDAP was particularly eager to
avoid public pronouncements of German war aims which might be un-
realizable. Instead, Hess instructed the party to stress a single goal: "the
securing of sufficient Lebensraum, as well as work and bread."[241] Caution vanished with the defeat of France; the mood changed abruptly,
and the party now rushed forward proclaiming its contributions to the
victory. In the dramatic revenge ceremony in the railroad car at Compiègne, Hitler was accompanied by several high party leaders, notably
Hess, Bormann, Himmler, and Leitgen. Similarly, for the Führer's return from France to Berlin all Reich ministers, Reichsleiters, Gauleiters,
state secretaries, and available generals had orders to meet him at the
train.[242] For the moment, the subsequent defeat of Great Britain seemed
a mere afterthought; Goebbels noted that Hitler's July 19 Reichstag
speech "would decide the fate of England."[243] The Reich propaganda
minister was so confident of an early end to the war that he suspended
regular vacations for his employees; they were to wait until after the

238. Eftger to Disselberg, 7 Feb. 1941, RvO/TB/IX; and Schmidt, "Vorlage an
Reichsleiter Bormann," 18 Aug. 1941, RvO/GKzbV (Ni)/1d.
239. Eftger to Disselberg, 16 April 1941, RvO/TB/XIII.
240. Domarus, *Hitler*, II, 1497.
241. StdF, "Anordnung 58/40," 14 May 1940, *RVBl* (A), no. 6 (15 May 1940),
p. 77.
242. Hitler's Wehrmacht adjutant, "Einteilung für Flug und Fahrt zum Wald zu
Compiègne . . . ," 20 June 1940, T-78, roll 351, frames 6310657–60; Domarus,
Hitler, II, 1520; and Goebbels to Reich propaganda office, Munich, 5 July 1940,
BGStA, Rsth. 48/1–7.
243. Boelcke, *Kriegspropaganda*, entry for 19 July 1940, p. 430.

war. In addition, his undersecretary was asked to assemble the necessary propaganda staff for the Nazi occupation of London.[244] The peace treaty loomed large in the concerns of various party offices. The StdF's division of state affairs became the party's "general consultant for the peace treaty" with the object of coordinating the NSDAP's demands for final territorial and political adjustments.[245] Goebbels even founded a new weekly journal, *Das Reich*, as the voice of intellectual leadership for German-dominated Europe.[246]

Hitler himself made some efforts to dampen these excessive visions of early victory,[247] but the party was more concerned with the "key position" which he had assigned to the NSDAP in his July Reichstag speech.[248] A wave of virtually peacetime propaganda and party activity blanketed Germany in the latter half of 1940. But the party was not content merely to emphasize its past services; it also sought to exploit the new situation to expand its control powers at all levels of operation. The StdF's office renewed its efforts to gain increased control over the promotion of officers in the armed forces and over the awarding of decorations among both the soldiers and the civilian population.[249] The Gaus and districts moved with far greater impunity against both the state and the churches. There was a nationwide discouragement of applications for monastic orders, and at least one party office went considerably beyond this: a propaganda program in Hessen with the title

244. *Ibid.*, entries for 17 July and 3 Sept. 1940, pp. 428 and 488.

245. StdF, "Anordnung 78/40," 2 Aug. 1940, *RVBl* (A), no. 20 (15 Aug. 1940), p. 125.

246. *Das Reich* began publication in May 1940. For a description of its style and content see Oron J. Hale, *The Captive Press in the Third Reich* (Princeton, N.J., 1964), p. 278. See also Max Amann (head of the NSDAP's publishing house) to Mrs. Troost (widow of one of Hitler's favorite architects), 30 June 1940, BDC/ Amann (PKC).

247. Lammers to Heydrich, 15 June 1940, BA/R 43 II/178a (a copy of the letter was sent to all state and provincial governors); and Reich chancellery, "Vermerk," 8 Aug. 1940, BA/R 43 II/494a.

248. SD report no. 107, 22 July, quoted in Heinz Boberach, ed., *Meldungen aus dem Reich—Auswahl aus den geheimen Lageberichten des Sicherheitsdienstes der SS 1939–1944* (Neuwied, 1965), p. 90.

249. Bormann to Meissner, 14 Oct. 1940; Meissner to Lammers, 18 Oct. 1940, BA/R 43 II/421; and Hess to Keitel, 28 Feb. 1941, quoted in Klaus-Jürgen Müller, ed., "Zur Vorgeschichte und Inhalt der Rede Himmlers vor der höheren Generalität am 13. März 1940 in Koblenz," *Vjh.f.Z.*, XVIII (Jan. 1970), 119. See also *ibid.*, p. 119, n. 153.

"What Will Germany Look Like after the War?" noted that with the conclusion of hostilities, church property would be expropriated and the churches in general reduced to playing a very small role in German public life.[250] District leaders exercised their political power with considerably more openness and brazenness. Documents from these months speak of district leaders giving direct orders to mayors, commanding individual citizens to their offices for personal reprimands, and giving orders to cut off welfare payments to politically undesirable families.[251]

As always in times of power expansion, the party's efforts were directed not only against the power segments outside the NSDAP, but against rival factions within the organization. The StdF used the new thrust primarily to clarify and solidify his role as central controller and coordinator of the entire party. Just prior to the German attack on France, the StdF once again emphasized that his office was the office of the Führer, that is, it acted in the name of Hitler.[252] To avoid possible accommodations among the Reichsleiters without the knowledge of the StdF, Bormann early in 1941 insisted that agreements between Reichsleiters could not be concluded orally, but had to be formulated in written form. All such agreements were invalid until all of the Reichsleiters concerned had expressed their written assent to the StdF.[253] In June 1940 the deputy Führer began publication of his own journal of decrees and information, the *Reichsverfügungsblatt*. Issued in three separate series, A, B, and C (for Gauleiters, district leaders, and local leaders, respectively), it was distributed by a system of couriers so as to prevent possible tampering by postal employees. The *Reichsverfügungsblatt* contained three categories of items: *Verfügungen* (decrees), involving basic policy decisions; *Anordnungen* (orders), essentially implementations of the decrees; and *Bekanntgaben* (notices), which were items of information. The first two categories required immediate

250. v. Limburg (Catholic bishop of Wiesbaden) to Kerrl, 12 Dec. 1940, BA/R 43 II/178a.

251. See n.a., "Organisatorischer Aufbau und Einsatz im Kriege," *Hoheitsträger*, V (Feb. 1941), 23–24; StdF, "Bekanntgabe 7/41," *VOBl*, no. 218 (March 1941); and the relevant papers in MiU/GAC, folders 1 and 3.

252. StdF, "Bekanntgabe 24/40g," 9 May 1940, *RVBl* (A), no. 4 (11 May 1940).

253. Bormann, "Aktenvermerk für Pg. Friedrichs," 18 March 1941, T-580, roll 79, folder 368; and StdF, "Anordnung 43/40," n.d., *VOBl*, no. 209 (June 1940).

action by the Hoheitsträgers, while in the case of the third, follow-up was left to their discretion.

The victory over France also reopened the personnel question in the PO, this time with somewhat more success than in the fall of 1939. The StdF's office continued its campaign to remove PLs with church ties from the PO and again emphasized the HJ's importance as a reservoir of future political leaders.[254] Potentially far more significant, however, was the campaign to renovate the Gauleiter corps. By the end of 1940 the StdF had succeeded in replacing five Gauleiters and had failed to remove one. In addition to the cases of Streicher, Wagner, and Hanke discussed before, Hartmann Lauterbacher moved into the Gauleiter position in Hanover (replacing Rust), and Baldur von Schirach succeeded Bürckel in Vienna. Both Lauterbacher's personality and his position predestined him as the ideal prototype of the new Gauleiter. As deputy Reich youth leader he served as a concrete example of the HJ's role in supplying new PLs. As a fanatic opponent of the churches and an equally enthusiastic proponent of the party's dominant influence in national affairs, he was a particular favorite of Bormann.[255] Schirach's appointment as Gauleiter of Vienna in August 1940, on the other hand, proved to be an unmitigated disaster.[256] At the age of forty, Schirach was clearly a bit old to continue to head the Hitler Youth, and since he had ambitions in the realm of cultural policy (his father had been a theater director), Hitler thought him perfect for Vienna. The StdF's office was not successful in dismissing Kaufmann in Hamburg, although Bormann apparently launched rumors that Hitler was displeased with the Gauleiter's pragmatic administration.[257]

Josef Bürckel left Vienna with few regrets because he could look forward to heading an even bigger Gau in the West. After the defeat of France, Hitler, breaking two or three solemn promises on the way, im-

254. StdF, "Anordnung 52/40," n.d., *VOBl*, no. 210 (July 1940); StdF, "Verfügung 11/40," 30 Nov. 1940, *VOBl*, no. 215 (Dec. 1940); and district leader Eisenach to all local leaders, 28 May 1941, MiU/GAC, folder 2.

255. For a report on Lauterbacher's inauguration (with Hess present), see *Bremer Zeitung*, 20 Jan. 1941. A clipping from the paper is in BDC/Lauterbacher (PKC).

256. See below, p. 425.

257. Lindemann (at this time legal advisor to the Hamburg senate) to criminal police of Hamburg, 8 Jan. 1948, Forsch Hbg./PA/12/K (Kaufmann).

mediately severed Alsace and Lorraine from the country and destroyed
the independence of Luxembourg; Belgium and occupied northern
France remained under military administration, but there was little
doubt that their planned long-term fate was to become some sort of
Reichsgau Burgundy-Flanders.[258] Indeed, Belgium stayed under military tutelage for most of the war by default; Hitler could not find a suitable Reich commissioner. Kaufmann was under consideration, and was
apparently interested, but Bormann expressed strong opposition.[259]
Fritz Schmidt was more than willing to accept the appointment[260] but
he was persona non grata with the SS. So Hitler simply left the military
in charge and ordered the party not to discuss the Belgians' fate at all.[261]

The Führer did not hesitate to assign Alsace, Lorraine, and Luxembourg to the neighboring Gauleiters, Robert Wagner (Baden), Josef
Bürckel (Lorraine), and Gustav Simon (Koblenz-Trier). Their appointment did not constitute formal annexation of the areas, but this was
little more than a legal nicety. The Gauleiters were made Reich commissioners to enable them to Germanize and partify the semiannexed
territories with as little interference as possible from the Reich ministries in Berlin.[262] Such restraint was not placed upon the office of the
StdF, which appointed Franz Schmidt, a high-ranking staff official, as
Stillhaltekommissar. His functions were analogous to those exercised
by Albert Hoffmann earlier in Austria and the Sudetenland.[263]

The party's specific aims in Alsace were typically schizophrenic; the
NSDAP wanted both to be loved and to demonstrate its power to
ignore lack of popular affection. Hitler was convinced that the wishes
of the Alsatian people should not be a major factor in German policy
decisions,[264] yet instructed his Gauleiter, Robert Wagner, "that it was

258. See Picker, *Tischgespräche*, entry for 5 May 1942, p. 425; and Müller,
"Vorgeschichte," p. 108.
259. H. P. Ipsen, "Niederschrift der Mitteilungen von . . . Prof. Ipsen . . . ," 19
Aug. 1950, p. 13, Forsch. Hbg./Pa/12/H; and Kwiet, *Reichskommissariat*, pp. 63
and 63, n. 93.
260. See Schmidt to Friedrichs, 22 Nov. 1940, RvO/TB/III.
261. Boelcke, *Kriegspropaganda*, p. 442 (31 July 1940); and Schmidt to Tiessler
(for Goebbels) [14 Feb. 1941], RvO/TB/IX.
262. Jäckel, *Frankreich*, pp. 76–83.
263. StdF, "Anordnung 88/40," 12 Oct. 1940, *VOBl*, no. 213 (Oct. 1940).
264. Robert Ernst, *Rechenschaftsbericht eines Elsässers* (Berlin, 1954), p. 146.

his duty to win the population of Alsace . . . to the ideas of National Socialism within ten years after June 1940."[265] Wagner, who had been Gauleiter of Baden since the mid-twenties, was one of Hitler's earliest followers, and exhibited the paladin complex so typical of ex-officers who rose to leadership position in the NSDAP. He was convinced that Hitler was right even when all logic and reason indicated that he must be wrong. In addition, he was imbued with a passionate hatred of the Catholic Church, a character trait which rendered him particularly ill-suited to deal with the sensibilities of the rural population in Baden and Alsace. As a result, in spite of greater intelligence and some attempt at subtlety, his rule was as much of a political disaster as that of the blustering Bürckel in Lorraine.[266] Like other Gauleiters, Wagner had established his own clique of PLs in Baden, and chose the new masters of Alsace from this group. To be sure, most of the local leaders and even seven (of twelve) of the district leaders in Alsace came from the minute faction of native German collaborators, but the Gau staff officials and the more influential district leaders were appointees from the Gau Baden. As in the case of the other occupied and annexed areas, the transfers had the specific approval of the personnel office of the StdF.[267]

The new Reich commissioner in Lorraine, Josef Bürckel, had had considerable experience in administering annexed areas. After his conspicuous successes in the Saar and Austria, Bürckel had no hesitation in fitting his new fief into the Reichsgau mold. He immediately began to align the district boundaries with those of the counties in Lorraine so as to facilitate party control, and to demand a budget for Lorraine that was not subject to governmental audits.[268] In December 1940 the annexation of Lorraine was all but formalized when the old Gau Saar-Palatinate was renamed Gau Westmark.

The annexation of the Grand Duchy of Luxembourg to the Gau

---

265. Pierre Crénesse, *Le Procès de Wagner bourreau de l'Alsace* (Paris, 1946), p. 13.

266. Jäckel, *Frankreich*, p. 77.

267. R. Wagner to Bormann, 10 Feb. 1941, BDC/Wagner (PKC). See also Ernst, *Rechenschaftsbericht*, p. 269.

268. Jäckel, *Frankreich*, p. 82; Schieder (office of the Reich treasurer), "Vortrags-Notiz," 29 June 1940, T-580, roll 82, folder 394; and Bürckel to Siebert, 8 May 1941, BGStA, MA 105286.

Koblenz-Trier under Gustav Simon was in many ways Hitler's most ill-advised decision in the West. Koblenz-Trier, which encompassed the desolate hills of the Eiffel, was one of Germany's poorest areas, and its Gauleiter—known with little affection as the "poisonous mushroom of Hermeskeil,"—was one of the least able and most arrogant among the provincial leaders. His Gau was riddled with corruption and nepotism. One of his brothers became deputy Gauleiter and another was sent to Luxembourg to be in charge of press censorship.[269] In addition, Simon had a traditional rivalry with Bürckel (he resented that Bürckel had been appointed Saar commissioner), and sought to prove his worth to Hitler by outdoing Bürckel in the speed and ideological fervor with which he partified Luxembourg.[270]

The territorial conquests had increased both the power and the stature of the PO in the Altreich and the occupied areas, but, relatively speaking, the early wartime developments benefited the SS even more. Particularly in the occupied areas, the SS's dual power position as head of the police apparatus and of population policy gave the HSSPFs a position of near-equality with the governmental and PO authorities. In the Altreich the SS had not yet begun to challenge the prerogatives of the Gauleiters,[271] but even here its prestige and influence were growing. The younger Gauleiters and deputy Gauleiters who tended to be particularly fanatic racists were especially drawn to Himmler's emphasis on ideological and racial exclusiveness for the SS.[272] The first major institutional victim of the SS's growing position as elite within the elite was the SA. While Lutze watched in impotent and increasingly alcoholic rage, two deputy Gauleiters (Wegener and Schaller) conspicuously resigned their SA ranks and joined the SS.[273] Himmler's forces maintained a tap on Lutze's telephone, and the Reich leader SS himself agitated vigorously for Lutze's dismissal as the SA's chief of staff.[274]

269. Paul Weber, *Geschichte Luxemburgs im zweiten Weltkrieg* (Luxemburg, 1946), pp. 28–29.

270. *Ibid.*, pp. 35–36, 94, and 101.

271. See "Die Partei ist immer zuständig," *Schwarzes Korps*, 15 Aug. 1940. See also Levine, "Local Authority and the SS State," p. 339.

272. Lauterbacher to Bormann, 20 May 1942, BDC/Klagges (SS).

273. Lutze to Schaller, 10 July 1940, BDC/Schaller (PKC); and Wegener to Hess, 29 July 1940, BDC/Wegener (PKC).

274. See the special BDC/Lutze file; Berger to Brandt, 12 March 1940, quoted

But the real base of the future power position of the SS lay in the occupied areas. In his dual capacity as head of the German police and Reich commissioner for the strengthening of Germandom (*Reichskommissar für die Festigung des deutschen Volkstums*, RKFDV), Himmler significantly changed the position of the HSSPFs. Under the guise of insuring a better adminstration of law and order, Himmler strengthened his direct control of the HSSPFs. In the Altreich, the HSSPFs as heads of police were essentially subject to governmental authorities in the form of the Oberpräsidents or Reichsstatthalters, that is, the Gauleiters, but in the occupied areas, they served as Himmler's personal representatives charged with the safeguarding of security. Consequently, they had the power to overrule the PO authorities if the need for law and order dictated such action.[275] The office of the RKFDV was set up in the fall of 1939 to counter the wholesale Germanizations in Danzig, and apply instead throughout the East the rigid, four-class "German people's list" (*Deutsche Volksliste*, DVL) used in the Warthegau.[276] The more radical population policy had the support of the StdF and the party's main office for racial affairs, as well as of the SS. The racial policy office, of course, saw some logic in assigning the administration of the DVL to itself, but Himmler persuaded Hitler that racial affairs in the occupied areas were best left to the strong hands of the black guards. By late 1939, then, the SS had been catapulted to a position of at least equality with the PO in the East. Representatives of the SD sat alongside PLs on all selection committees, determining the fate of millions: Himmler's standards categorized who would be part of the Germanic in-group and who would die—whether through labor or outright execution.[277] In addition, the SS gained an exclusive right to provide ideological indoctrination to the ethnic Germans shipped from all parts of Europe for resettlement in the Germanized East. Indirectly, the

in Helmut Heiber, ed., *Reichsführer!* . . . *Briefe an und von Himmler* (Stuttgart, 1968), pp. 72–73; and Heinz Höhne, *Der Orden unter dem Totenkopf* (Gütersloh, 1967), pp. 383–84.

275. Levine, "Local Authority and the SS State," p. 339; and Cohen, "Ontstaan," p. 1.

276. On the founding of the DVL, the RKFDV, and their policies see Koehl, *RKFDV*, pp. 50 and 247–51; and Broszat, *Polenpolitik*, pp. 123 and 125.

277. Koehl, *RKFDV*, pp. 65 and 120–21; and Broszat, *Polenpolitik*, pp. 120 and 126.

RKFDV even controlled the rules for party membership, because the StdF decreed that only classes I and II of the DVL could make application for NSDAP membership.[278] In the West, the SS's power base was not the DVL, but the "guidance office for Germanic volunteers" (*Germanische Freiwilligen Leitstelle*), headed by the obsequious and ambitious Gottlob Berger.[279] He tended to lose sight of the original purposes of the agency, which was to attract volunteers for the armed SS, and remembered instead that the title of his office could be changed into "guidance office for Germanic affairs" (*Germanische Leitstelle*) without a great deal of effort.

Bormann was one of the first to recognize that the SS's powers in the occupied areas would generate additional friction between the PO and the SS, both in the Altreich and in the conquered nations.[280] Indeed, in Poland and Western Europe fierce infighting quickly became the order of the day. In the Generalgouvernement, for example, the HSSPF Krüger (the same man who had played such a crucial role in the Röhm putsch) was sent to Poland with direct orders to "finish off Frank."[281] In Danzig, Forster and Himmler were barely on writing, let alone speaking terms, and the Gauleiter angrily refused to become the RKFDV's representative in Danzig.[282] In contrast, Greiser was virtually a client of the SS, so that the Warthegau threatened to become an autonomous area of SS administration.[283] In the north, only Norway was free of friction—for the moment. In 1940 Bormann and Wegener cooperated wholeheartedly with the SS's aims, while Terboven's support for Himmler's organization had long been matched by his hatred of the SA.[284] In Holland, however, the PO-SS tensions reached a level of bitterness that easily compared with the open political warfare between Krüger and Frank in the government-general. The HSSPF, Hanns Rauter, was an Austrian Nazi

278. Broszat, *Polenpolitik*, p. 125, n. 1; and StdF, "Anordnung 7/41," 26 Feb. 1941, *RVBl* (A), no. 10 (8 March 1941).

279. Berger to Himmler, 15 May 1940, RvO/BDC/H 447.

280. StdF, "Bekanntgabe 48/40," 16 July 1940, *RVBl* (A) no. 18 (26 July 1940).

281. Höhne, *Orden*, p. 293.

282. Koehl, *RKFDV*, pp. 62–73. Bracht and Wagner also had reservations about the administration of the DVL. *Ibid.*, p. 140, n. 21.

283. Ley suggested that the StdF participate personally in Greiser's inauguration, "otherwise the SS's influence will be excessive." See Friedrichs, "Notiz für den Stabsleiter," 17 Nov. 1939, T-580, roll 79, folder 368.

284. Rosenberg, *Tagebuch*, entry for 13 Sept. 1940, p. 145.

like Seyss-Inquart, but a far stronger and more ruthless personality than the Reich commissioner. His previous career included stints in Austria and Silesia and an active role in the 1938 pogroms.[285] Rauter's relationship with the party representative in Holland, Schmidt, was one of barely disguised hostility; both of these men pursued goals that were unattainable without the political destruction of the rival. The HSSPF, obviously following the Berger line, wanted to place Belgium and Holland under SS control, while Schmidt hoped eventually to become Gauleiter of one of the Reichsgaus to be created from Holland or Belgium. To this end, the head of the Arbeitsbereich groomed the NSB in its Quisling role, and Rauter, who despised the NSB as a self-serving petty bourgeois club, sought to build up a Dutch SS organization instead. In terms of personalities, Schmidt backed Mussert, and Rauter attached himself to the fanatical Rost van Tonningen[286] and the head of the Dutch SS, H. J. Feldmeijer.[287] In addition, the SS used its control of the pseudo-cadet schools, the Napolas, to train a group of young Dutch SS leaders.[288]

In contrast to the bitterness of the struggles raging in Poland and Holland, the Reich treasurer's empire after one year of war was a haven of orderly administration. For the moment, the conflict brought only financial benefits, and the Reich treasurer's report for 1940 reflects Schwarz's gleeful rubbing of hands on every page. There had been a considerable influx of new party members in 1940, and the total membership now stood at about six and a half million.[289] As a result of the increased membership dues and vastly augmented subsidies from the Reich, in fiscal 1940 the party took in far more money than it spent (see tables 10 and 11). (The NSDAP's fiscal year ran from January 1 to December 31.) Schwarz proudly noted that the 1940 surplus was the largest in the history of the party, almost 40 percent above the figure for 1939. Despite the huge sums at his disposal, the Reich treasurer remained a conserva-

285. SS main district southeast (Breslau), "Anlage zu Beförderungsvorschlag," 15 March 1939, RvO/BDC/P1B.

286. For Rost's particular brand of "Austro-Nazism" see the introduction to Rost, *Correspondentie*, pp. 37–38.

287. See the letters for this time period in *ibid.*

288. Himmler had exclusive control over the Napolas. See Himmler to Heissmeyer (inspector of the Napolas), 7 May 1940, in Heiber, *Reichsführer*, p. 80; and Horst Ueberhorst, *Elite für die Diktatur* (Düsseldorf, 1968), pp. 103–04.

289. Rschm., "Jahresbericht 1940," p. 24.

TABLE 10

Party Income for 1940

Source	Amount (thousands of RM)
Gau transfers (membership dues, insurance premiums, income from sale of tickets, brochures, etc.)	133,199
RL income (subsidies, lottery, etc.)	141,112
Total	274,311

SOURCE: Rschm., "Jahresbericht 1940," pp. 2 and 15.

TABLE 11

Party Disbursements for 1940 (thousands of RM)

Item	Gaus	Districts	Locals	Total
Salary and personal expenses	29,615	25,219	1,547	56,381
Supplies and maintenance	15,207	13,099	21,189	49,495
Special budget	3,346	899	345	4,590
Subtotal				110,466
RL budget (not differentiated)				57,161
Total				167,627
Total income				274,311
Surplus				106,684

SOURCE: Rschm., "Jahresbericht 1940," pp. 2 and 15.

tive, even miserly banker. He let the surplus accumulate interest in a variety of savings accounts (mostly in the DAF-owned bank for German Labor in order to prevent state bank examiners from auditing the party's accounts[290]) in the sure knowledge that eventually the famous rainy day would come and he would need the reserve. The only additional outlays budgeted in 1940 were for some fifty-four hundred new PLs, for activated party training programs, and for the Gauleiters' expense accounts.[291]

Nevertheless, even Schwarz lamented his continuing problems. Some Gaus had still carried candidate members from 1937 on their books, and thereby deprived the Reichsleitung of the dues income. As a result, Schwarz eagerly looked forward to the day after the war when member-

290. [Lingg], "Verteilung der Geldgeschäfte der Reichsleitung auf verschiedene Banken," 2 Nov. 1940, T-580, roll 813, box 242, folder 84.

291. For the latter, typical sums involved were RM 4–5,000 (instead of RM 2,000). The increases are documented in the BDC personnel files for the various GLs. The new PLs are discussed in Rschm., "Jahresbericht 1940," p. 8.

ship dues would be paid by payroll deduction.[292] In addition, there was the perennial problem of retaining a number of Gaus which were really too small to maintain full Gau administrations, but which for political reasons (that is, Hitler's insistence) could not be merged with larger Gaus and therefore remained a constant drain on the Reichsleitung's reserves.[293]

The interlaced problems of corruption and financial independence created even larger headaches. A number of feuds between the Reich treasurer and Gauleiters' and Reichsleiters' offices continued into the war,[294] and the rampant corruption in the East created additional problems. The Eastern Gauleiters used the moneys expropriated from expelled and murdered Poles and Jews to start business ventures that would provide them with independent sources of income. Schwarz proceeded against these practices by a variety of methods ranging from a declaration that he would hold the PLs personally responsible for the financial liabilities of such business deals to further systematization of the budget processes. By the end of 1940 he had successfully imposed definite and detailed budgets upon every phase of the party's jurisdiction, including the previously autonomous DAF and NSV affiliates.[295] Undoubtedly, Schwarz's greatest and almost anticlimactic triumph for 1940 was the final institution of the long-awaited salary scale. In view of the accumulated surplus, the Reich treasurer now implemented the complicated system of service points and salary steps that was to streamline the POs personnel policies and further the professionalization of the PLs.[296] The actual impact of the salary scale was minimal. By the time it was finally implemented, the NSDAP's Führer was about to make a

292. Rschm., "Anweisung 38/40 [and] 41/40," 1 and 19 Nov. 1940, *Rdschr.*, VII.

293. Rschm., "Jahresbericht 1940," pp. 17–18.

294. Ulf Lükemann, "Der Reichsschatzmeister der NSDAP" (Dissertation, Free University of Berlin, 1968), pp. 81–85; and Saupert, "Besuchs-Vermerk," 27 Sept. 1940, BDC/Hilgenfeldt (PKC).

295. Lükemann, "Reichsschatzmeister," p. 125; Rschm., "Jahresbericht 1940," p. 1; Rschm., "Anordnung 62/40," 10 Dec. 1940, *Rdschr.*, VII; and Gau treasurer Hamburg to Reich treasurer, "Stimmungsbericht 1940," 8 Feb. 1941, T-580, roll 804, box 239, folder 39.

296. For an example of the tabulations by which the party arrived at a salary figure, see "Antrag auf Besoldungsfestsetzung" [1941], BDC/Gloy (PKC). Gloy was a district leader in Hamburg at the time. For objections to the new salary scale see Witt (office of the StdF), "Vorlage," 13 March 1941, T-580, roll 79, folder 368.

decision that would soon eliminate the need for any long-range peace-time personnel policies.

Despite his swift victories in the West, Hitler was uneasy about turning from his long-time *idée fixe* of winning Lebensraum in the East. As early as June 1940 the party's propaganda offices reopened the Eastern question,[297] and at the end of July 1940 Hitler decided to abandon the half-hearted attempt to invade England and attack the Soviet Union instead.[298] As usual, the party was not included in the decision-making process; moreover, the NSDAP's enthusiasm for the new venture was decidedly lukewarm. The party as a whole would undoubtedly have preferred to exploit the fruits of the German victories to date.[299] Nevertheless, once Hitler gave the order that there would be no demobilization,[300] the party reluctantly rekindled its fervor for continuing warfare. Hess reminded the party that Hitler relied as much upon it as he did upon the Wehrmacht for final victory in the war.[301] By the spring of 1941, the NSDAP approached at least theoretical wartime postures: the PLs were asked not to use their official cars more often than necessary.[302] Simultaneously, although there is no evidence of a direct causal connection, the StdF gave final form to his staff organization,[303] and in December of 1940 Heinrich Walkenhorst, who was to remain Friedrich's right-hand man until the end of the war, moved to the Brown House.[304]

As before, wartime hardships and risks also brought opportunities for power aggrandizement and territorial annexation to the PLs. In May,

297. Rosenberg's *Europa und der Osten* could not be published in 1939, but on 10 June 1940 the district leader of Eisenach ordered every party office to purchase a copy. See district propaganda office, "Rundschreiben 29/40 Prop.," 10 June 1940, MiU/GAC, folder 27.

298. Gerhard L. Weinberg, *Germany and the Soviet Union 1939–1941* (Leiden, 1954), p. 151.

299. Domarus, *Hitler*, II, 1601 and 1646.

300. Rschm., "[Ressortbesprechung]," 4 Oct. 1940 (top secret), T-580, roll 82, folder 394.

301. Hess's speech at the inauguration of Lauterbacher as GL of Hanover, *Bremer Zeitung*, 20 Jan. 1941.

302. StdF, "Anordnung 1/41g [and] 10/41," 3 and 16 March 1941, ARV, and *VOBL*, no. 218 (March 1941), respectively.

303. StdF to Schmidt, 19 March 1941,, RvO/TB/XI.

304. Walkenhorst to F. W. Meyer (on the staff of Fritz Schmidt), 20 Dec. 1940, *ibid.*, VI. Walkenhorst spent his entire previous PO career in the Gau Weser Ems, becoming Gau staff leader in October 1940.

Gauleiter Siegfried Uiberreither (Styria) and deputy Gauleiter Kutschera (Carinthia) moved quickly to establish the NSDAP's organization in the newly conquered Yugoslavian territories of Lower Styria, Carinthia, and Krain.[305] Far larger were the vistas presented to the luckless Alfred Rosenberg. On April 2, Hitler entrusted him with the formation of the "political bureau on the East," the forerunner of what was in effect to become the ministry for occupied Eastern territories. Rosenberg's energy and enthusiasm were boundless. A week later he submitted a list of suggested appointments for Reich commissioner positions in the East (including Gauleiter Koch for Moscow).[306] By early May, Rosenberg had gathered a staff around him, consisting for the most part of close personal cronies, some Russian émigrés, and, as his chief of staff, his old friend, the Westphalian Gauleiter Alfred Meyer.[307] Yet, even at this stage, much of his effort was in vain. Rosenberg had no control over police and terror appointments or policies since Himmler quite simply refused to subordinate the SS and police administration to Rosenberg's control.[308]

Hitler was not the only Nazi leader to reach decisions without consulting anyone. Sometime in the late summer or early fall of 1940, probably immediately after Hitler's decision to wage war against the Soviet Union,[309] Rudolf Hess came to the conclusion that he personally would fly to England and attempt to negotiate peace between Britain and Germany. The reasons for Hess's dramatic flight in May of 1941 are complex and by no means entirely clear. There does not seem to have been any dramatic personal estrangement between Hess and Adolf Hitler. Indeed, the Führer personally visited Hess in April of 1940 to congratulate him on his forty-sixth birthday, and in his July 19 Reichstag speech singled out the deputy Führer for particular praise. Moreover, Hitler also asked Hess in 1941 to give the traditional May Day address in his stead, since Hitler preferred to announce victories and at this moment

305. StdF, "Anordnung 22/41," 29 April 1941, *VOBl*, no. 220 (May, 1941).
306. See Nuremberg document PS-1019, *IMT*, XXVI, 555–59.
307. Alexander Dallin, *German Rule in Russia 1941–1945* (New York, 1957), p. 24.
308. Himmler to Bormann, 25 May 1941, (top secret), T-175, roll 123, frame 2648742.
309. See Hess's interrogation of 9 June 1941, in Robert M. W. Kempner, *Das Dritte Reich im Kreuzverhör* (Munich, 1969), p. 101.

there were no particular victories to announce. It may be significant that Hess did not personally congratulate Hitler on his fifty-second birthday, in 1941, but he did deliver a nationwide radio address.[310]

Nevertheless, it is clear that Hess's stature and influence were slipping.[311] Although the StdF retained the power to protect even his most controversial protégés until literally, he left Germany,[312] his chief of staff moved increasingly into the limelight. The "Great German Art Show" for 1940 was the first of these annual events to exhibit a full-length portrait of Bormann.[313] More significant, Bormann seemed to build up a personal following among the PLs in the staff and especially among those assigned to the occupied territories. Schmidt in Holland, for example, seems to have all but ignored Hess. His appointment calendar for 1940 includes an entry underlined in red for Bormann's birthday, indicating that congratulations would have to be sent, while there is no such entry for Hess. Similarly, when Mussert wrote a memorandum to be submitted to Hess, Schmidt saw to it that it went to Bormann before the StdF received it.[314] So it may well be possible that Hess saw himself outmaneuvered by Bormann, and attempted to recoup his fortunes through the dramatic peace mission. And, perhaps, the StdF was simply mentally unbalanced. At Spandau he insisted that extraterrestrial powers had suggested the trip to him.[315] Actually, his motivation might have been far more rational. Hess was one of the less bellicose among the Nazi leaders,[316] a fanatic Nazi who actually looked upon the party

310. Domarus, *Hitler*, II, 1496, 1551, 1692, and 1697.

311. For example, Hitler had apparently been shocked by Hess's taste in interior decoration during a 1938 visit to his home and pronounced him "totally unartistic." See Speer, *Erinnerungen*, p. 152.

312. Helmut Heiber, *Walter Frank und sein Reichsinstitut für die Geschichte des neuen Deutschland* (Stuttgart, 1966), pp. 1085 ff.

313. "Gesichter zur Zeitgeschichte auf der Grossen Deutschen Kunstausstellung 1940," *Hoheitsträger*, IV (March 1940), 4–9.

314. Schmidt, "Vormerkbuch"; and Schmidt to Bormann, 7 Jan. 1941, RvO/TB/VII. Schmidt was also supplying Dutch craftsmen for Bormann's building projects. See Eftger, "Vorlage an den Stabsleiter," 25 Feb. 1941, RvO/GKzbV (Ni)/1d.

315. Speer, *Erinnerungen*, p. 190.

316. According to the editor of the *Hoheitsträger*, Woweries, Hess rejected the proposed first issue of 1941 because the deputy Führer objected to its excessive glorification of war, among other items. See Woweries to Simon, 17 Jan. 1941, BA/NS 22/833.

as a dynamic force that would inaugurate something of a millennial world through a massive reform of Germany society. When Hitler decided to attack the Soviet Union, Hess saw the dream of a peacetime Nazi revolution endangered, and made up his mind to salvage it. Throughout the fall of 1940 he grew increasingly morose, and shut himself up in his house near Munich drafting peace proposals and negotiation plans.[317] Then, after two false starts, Hess in the early evening of May 10 took off from Augsburg airfield in a converted Messerschmidt airplane, landing safely in Scotland some ten hours later.

A tantalizing footnote to Hess's flight is the question of how much Bormann knew about the preparations of his superior. To be sure, the new head of the party chancellery claimed he knew as little as anyone else, but this may not be the entire story. Beginning in the fall of 1940 Hess received daily weather maps of the North Sea from Schmidt's office in The Hague. They were Telexed to Hess's home in Harlaching,[318] and there is no doubt that Schmidt informed Bormann of these dispatches.[319] On the other hand, there is no evidence that Bormann drew the correct conclusions. But it is of course quite possible that the Machiavellian chief of staff anticipated events clearly and simply kept quiet because he saw an opportunity to rid himself of a superior whose protection he no longer needed and whose office stood in the way of his own ambitions. It is certainly suggestive that Schmidt suffered no ill effects from Hess's flight, while the two equally innocent (or implicated) adjutants of the StdF were immediately dismissed and imprisoned.

To most observers in the party Hess's defection must have seemed sheer folly. One the eve of the German attack on the Soviet Union the NSDAP stood at a pinnacle of success with unprecedented vistas opening before it. The outbreak of World War II had put in motion much that had seemed stalemated before. Opportunities for Betreuung abounded, but so did the possibilities of social control and social dynamics. It is true that Hitler's fear of morale problems contained the PLs' enthusiasm for social revolutionary changes in the Altreich, but even here the war

317. These are detailed in the only full-length study of the Hess flight, James Douglas-Hamilton, *Motive for a Mission* (London, 1971). See also the interrogation of Bohle in Kempner, *Drittes Reich im Kreuzverhör*, pp. 103–06.
318. For an example see Eftger to Hess, 11 April 1941, RvO/TB/XIV.
319. Schmidt to Bormann, 30 Nov. 1940, RvO/TB/III.

brought new attacks on the churches and renewed efforts to partify the armed forces and the civil service. Moreover, both the StdF and the Reich treasurer's office used the military emergency to advance their centralization plans in the areas of personnel policy and internal party administration.

The muted developments in Germany contrasted with the uninhibited rule of the party in the occupied areas of Eastern and Western Europe. There the German conquest ushered in a period of terror and exploitation for the subject peoples, but to the PO and the SS the conquest offered the opportunity to put into effect those revolutionary theories of racial subjugation and economic oppression which political expediency kept half-hidden in Germany. Needless to say, the differing occupation policies of the various power segments in the party also led to new levels of bitterness in the intraparty power struggles. For the NSDAP the primary appeal of the attack on the Soviet Union lay in the continuation of these developments: the prospect of German rule in the Soviet Union meant virtually limitless opportunities to put into practice theories of racial oppression, and, simultaneously, to defeat rival factions within the party.

"Working like a Horse"*

While Hess enjoyed the hospitality of a Scottish farmer, his two adjutants, Karl-Heinz Pintsch and Leitgen, made their way to the Berghof with the deputy Führer's farewell message to Hitler. The two were left waiting until about noon (it was a Sunday) before they could deliver their message to the Nazi dictator. Hitler took one look at the letter, let out a gasp, followed by "an almost animal-like scream," and shouted for Bormann.[1] Hitler's first fear seems to have been that Hess might disclose the forthcoming attack on Russia during his interrogation by the British. Nevertheless, his immediate reprisals against Hess's closest associates were surprisingly mild. He did insist upon the expulsion from the party and arrest of Hess's adjutants, and refused to release them for the rest of the war, but he took no measures against Hess's wife and family. On the contrary, Mrs. Hess received a dislocation allowance and a pension.[2]

Needless to say, the political and propagandistic implications of the Hess case could not be as easily and quietly settled. There was the undeniable fact that the number two man in the Nazi hierarchy had flown off to negotiate with the enemy. For the moment, Hitler and his press

* "Working like a horse" is Bormann's description of his activities in a confidential circular letter to all RLs and GLs, 15 May 1941, Hauptarchiv Berlin (cited hereafter as HAB)/320/22.

1. Albert Speer, *Erinnerungen* (Berlin, 1969), p. 190.

2. Otto Dietrich, *Zwölf Jahre mit Hitler* (Cologne, 1955), pp. 76 and 78; and Henry Picker, ed., *Hitlers Tischgespräche im Führerhauptquartier 1941–1942*, new ed. by Percy-Ernst Schramm *et al.* (Stuttgart, 1965), entry for 27 March 1942, p. 215. The correspondence regarding Mrs. Hess's personal affairs after the flight of her husband is in the Bundesarchiv (cited hereafter as BA)/R 43 II/139a. The expulsion notices are in Pintsch's and Leitgen's SS files in the Berlin Document Center (cited hereafter as BDC).

chief, Dr. Dietrich, had no better thoughts than to publicize the solution suggested by Hess himself, that is, that the deputy Führer was mentally unbalanced.[3] It seems to have occurred to none of the three that this announcement contained the corollary admission than an insane official had been the Führer's deputy for eight years, but the implication was not lost on either the party membership or the population at large. Hess's flight created a mood of widespread depression within the party and led immediately to a rather large credibility gap; the first official explanation put out by the Berghof met with widespread skeptical cynicism.[4] Goebbels complained that the announcement merely sent the Germans to their radios to listen to British broadcasts about the Hess affair.[5]

The Reich propaganda minister was convinced that the whole episode had been completely mishandled. Characteristically, Hitler had not consulted him, but relied instead on the advice of the Reich press chief. After the fact, Goebbels strongly opposed the "insane" story, and expressed his utter disgust with the propagandistic amateurs operating from the Bavarian mountains.[6] His solution would have been to say nothing, in the hope that Hess had crashed on the way, and when that proved impracticable, to compare his flight with Strasser's resignation in December of 1932. Like the Reich organization leader, the deputy Führer was a man who "had lost his nerve at the last moment." Hence his flight was the result of a human failing rather than the action of a mentally unbalanced man—undoubtedly a propagandistically more effective version.[7]

3. Cf. Henry Picker, ed., *Hitlers Tischgespräche im Führerhauptquartier 1941–1942*, ed. Gerhard Ritter (Bonn, 1959), entry for 19 and 20 April 1942, p. 282. Picker noted that Hess's letters showed no sign of mental imbalance. *Ibid.*, p. 137.

4. Heinz Boberach, *Meldungen aus dem Reich—Auswahl aus den geheimen Lageberichten des Sicherheitsdienstes der SS 1939–1944* (Neuwied, 1965), pp.145–46 and 146, n. 2; and the monthly reports of the chief of administration for Niederbayern-Oberfranken and Oberbayern, 8 and 10 June, respectively, Bayerisches Geheimes Staatsarchiv (cited hereafter as BGStA), MA 106674 and 106671, respectively.

5. Willi A. Boelcke, ed., *Kriegspropaganda 1939–1941* (Stuttgart, 1966), entry for 21 May 1941, p. 747; and Boelcke, ed., *Wollt Ihr den totalen Krieg?—Die geheimen Goebbels-Konferenzen 1939–1943* (Stuttgart, 1967), entry for 21 May 1941, p. 173.

6. Rudolf Semmler [sic], *Goebbels—the Man next to Hitler*, ed. G. S. Wagner (London, 1947), entry for 14 May 1941, pp. 32–33.

7. Boelcke, *Kriegspropaganda*, entry for 13, 14, and 15 May 1941, pp. 728–36.

Since Goebbels' musings were a bit late for practical application, the Nazi regime did its best to hide the original mistake by declaring Hess an unperson. His pictures and words, even memories of him, were systematically erased from the record of Nazi Germany. Even group pictures including the former deputy Führer could not be re-released.[8] To counteract the depression within the party membership, the PO staged a massive series of rallies to close ranks behind the Führer.[9] Privately, the Nazi leadership undertook a widespread campaign of mudslinging against Hess. Goebbels noted that he had always known of Hess's imbalance and that, in addition, the deputy Führer was impotent. And if all this were not enough, social gatherings at his house were so incredibly boring that no one would accept the invitations.[10] Simultaneously, the party moved to curtail the practice of Hess's preferred extracurricular activities—such as astrology and faith-healing—in Germany, and reduced the stature of some of the StdF's more controversial protégés.[11]

The political power vacuum caused by Hess's flight was of very short duration: even more rapidly than the StdF could be expurgated from the pictorial record of the Third Reich, Martin Bormann assumed the powers left by his former superior. On May 12, Hitler appointed Bormann Hess's successor, in a resolution that also embodied the later-discarded insanity version of Hess's flight. In addition, Hitler set a meeting of all Reichsleiters and Gauleiters for May 13.[12] With Bormann's

---

The publication of the *Deutsche Zeitung in den Niederlanden* was prohibited for four weeks because the paper ran a story commenting on Hess's flight. See *ibid.*, entry for 17 May 1941, p. 738; and Schmidt to Goebbels, 30 June 1941, Rijksinstituut voor Oorlogsdokumentatie, Amsterdam (cited hereafter as RvO)/Telex-Berichte of the RK for the occupied Netherlands (cited hereafter as TB)/XVII.

8. RPL to RLs, GLs, Gau propaganda leaders, and leaders of affiliates, 13 June 1941, BA/R 43 II/133a. See also RPL to Heinrich Hoffmann Verlag, 13 Nov. 1941, National Archives, Microcopy No. T- (cited hereafter as T-) 81, roll 675, frames 5484213 ff.

9. See the documentation in the University of Michigan German Archival Collection (cited hereafter as MiU/GAC), folder 28.

10. Semmler, *Goebbels*, entry for 21 May 1941, pp. 35–36.

11. Boelcke, *Kriegspropaganda*, entries for 17 and 19 May 1941, pp. 739 and 741; "V.I. 1605/42," 4 Dec. 1942, *Verfügungen, Anordnungen, Bekanntgaben* of the PK (cited hereafter as *VAB*), II; and Bormann to Tiessler, 29 June 1941, T-81, roll 675, frame 5483328.

12. Bormann to all RL and GL, 12 May 1941, HAB/320/22. The decree is published in *VAB*, I, and Max Domarus, ed., *Hitler, Reden und Proklamationen 1932–1945* (Munich, 1965), II, 1716.

appointment Hitler deliberately evoked memories of the December 1932 crisis: the Führer announced that once again he would be the one to take personal charge of the PO. Ostensibly, Bormann did not become a new deputy Führer, but merely chief of a new office, the party chancellery, which served as a staff organization under Hitler's direct control.[13] In addition, Hitler avoided even the appearance of consulting the Nazi leadership corps in seeking a solution to the Hess crisis; Bormann's appointment was a fait accompli when the Reichsleiters and Gauleiters arrived at Berchtesgaden. The May 13 meeting was the usual cross between rationalization and homage to the chief which Hitler had staged repeatedly in the course of the NSDAP's development. The Führer had by now discovered a history of insanity in Hess's family, and blamed his deputy for deserting the ship in its hour of peril. The Nazi leaders responded by pledging their undying loyalty,[14] but the atmosphere remained depressed. After Hitler's speech the assembled leaders stood silently in a semicircle facing Hitler.[15]

Whatever thoughts Bormann may have had about his old chief, he hardly shared his peers' depression.[16] For Martin Bormann, May 12 represented the climax of a long road to power. To be sure, he was fully aware that he could not fill many of Hess's roles as deputy Führer. Bormann wistfully acknowledged that he had no real ability to reach people, that his talents were pretty well confined to a desk and pencil and paper. Accordingly, he did not even try to keep up Hess's more charismatic activities. He discontinued, for example, the StdF's practice of serving as guardian of children whose PL fathers had died during the Kampfzeit or at the front in World War II.[17] Hitler, too, sensed some of Bormann's limitations. He pointedly did not include the new chief of the party chancellery among his revised list of successors. Hess was,

13. Bormann to all RL and GL, 15 May 1941, HAB/320/22; and the interrogation of Klopfer, 14 Nov. 1947, Institut für Zeitgeschichte, Munich (cited hereafter as IfZ)/ZS 352.

14. Domarus, *Hitler*, II, 1717; and Dietrich, *Zwölf Jahre*, pp. 78–79.

15. See the interrogation of E. W. Bohle, in Robert M. W. Kempner, ed., *Das Dritte Reich im Kreuzverhör* (Munich, 1969), pp. 108–09.

16. One report has it that he gave a huge banquet on the night of Hess's flight. See Albert Zoller, *Hitler privat* (Düsseldorf, 1949), p. 222.

17. Martin Bormann to Gerda Bormann, 10 Sept. 1943, in Martin and Gerda Bormann, *The Bormann Letters*, ed. Hugh R. Trevor-Roper, tr. R. H. Stevens (London, 1954), p. 25; and "V.I.," 19 July 1941, *VAB*, I.

understandably, dropped, but Bormann did not move into his place.[18] Yet Bormann had other gifts. And foremost among these was his indispensability to Hitler. The Führer was particularly appreciative of Bormann's loyalty to his person,[19] and his ability (which he shared with Lammers) to cast Hitler's ramblings into what the Nazi leader, at least, felt were clear directives to the party.[20]

As before, Hitler's authority in the Third Reich rested upon his undisputed claim to omnipotence and omniscience.[21] Bormann did not challenge the first, but sought to control the second. That feat alone required immense energy and perseverance. Daily life with Adolf Hitler even in the years of military success was mentally and physically taxing. Hitler had already settled into his routine of turning night into day. He remained awake until three or four in the morning, and then rose again the next morning at eleven or twelve. Rambling lunchtime sessions lasted from two to four in the afternoon.[22] For Bormann the half hour or so immediately after lunch was the most crucial time of the day. In these thirty minutes, the Führer "administered" the party. In response to various items brought to his attention by Bormann, Hitler gave vague oral instructions which the chief of the party chancellery along with his staff then reworded into administrative directives.[23] Clearly, the key to Bormann's power lay in preventing other party leaders from having access to Hitler, and in the manner (if at all) in which he brought various issues and disputes to Hitler's attention. Martin Bormann shed copious crocodile tears over the increasing inaccessibility of Hitler for the Reichsleiters and Gauleiters, but he felt sure that the party's

18. Domarus, *Hitler*, II, 1741.

19. Several contemporaries attest that Hitler used such terms as "my most loyal comrade" and "my loyal Eckehard" in referring to Bormann. Dietrich, *Zwölf Jahre*, p. 259. The use of these terms was confirmed by the former Gauleiter of Hamburg, Karl Kaufmann, in an interview with the author on 22 August 1968.

20. Picker, *Tischgespräche*, entry for 5 May 1942, pp. 240–41.

21. Peter Diehl-Thiele, *Partei und Staat im Dritten Reich* (Munich, 1969), p. 247.

22. This description is based upon a letter written by one of Hitler's secretaries, Gerda Daranowski, to Heinz Horn (a member of the SS-Leibstandarte Adolf Hitler), 13 July 1941, Forschungsstelle für die Geschichte des Nationalsozialismus in Hamburg (citer hereafter as Forsch. Hbg.)/PA/12/H.

23. Joseph Wulf, *Martin Bormann* (Gütersloh, 1962), p. 27. See also Picker, *Tischgespräche*, p. 131.

leaders would understand the situation and trust the party chancellery to represent their interests.[24]

Bormann underscored the routine nature of the transfer of power in the StdF's office, and in a sense it is true that little had changed. Certainly, Hess had not personally administered his office for some time before his flight, so that the physical separation between the staff and its director was nothing new to the officials of the party chancellery (*Partei-Kanzlei*, PK). Moreover, since at least 1937, Bormann had had very little direct contact with his subordinates. While the new head of the party chancellery remained in close attendance upon Adolf Hitler, the several hundred staffers worked in the mazes of the Brown House. Bormann saw very few of his staff personally, but kept up a voluminous correspondence, at times reaching up to a hundred dictated memos and letters per day. There were no major personnel changes in the office. Friedrichs remained head of the political department at the PK, and Gerhard Klopfer headed the department of state affairs. The latter was technically a new appointment,[25] but Klopfer had in fact been in charge of the division while Sommer searched for greener fields. Hitler also specifically assigned to Bormann Hess's rights as the party's spokesman in dealings with state offices. Like Hess, Bormann had the powers (though not the title) of Reich minister.[26]

Despite these gratifying signs of Hitler's immediate trust, Bormann was fully aware that the removal or resignation of a major figure in the NSDAP had always resulted in challenges to the power position of that party office by rival leaders.[27] There was no real reason to regard the PK as an exception to the rule. Indeed, opportunistic academics were already hedging their bets: a study of the PO published in 1941 concluded rather cautiously that while Bormann had inherited Hess's position "at least for the time being," it was too early to say anything definite about the future evolution of the PK.[28] The first Reichsleiter to offer a direct challenge to Bormann was Alfred Rosenberg. The attempt was

24. Bormann to all RL and GL, 15 May 1941, HAB/320/22.
25. Diehl-Thiele, *Partei*, p. 220.
26. Hitler, "Erlass," 29 May 1941, *VAB*, I, 4–5.
27. Bormann to Friedrichs, 3 June 1941, BA/NS 6/126; and Bormann, "Aktenvermerk für Pgg. Klopfer und Friedrichs," 4 June 1941, T-580, roll 79, folder 368.
28. Friedrich Wilhelm Lampe, *Die Amtsträger der Partei* (Stuttgart, 1941), p. 165.

unsuccessful and rather pitiful, but it is significant that even the weak Rosenberg thought the moment was opportune to reverse the trend toward centralization of power at the StdF's office. Rosenberg submitted a major reorganization plan to Hitler which, if implemented, would have reduced the PK to a liaison office for party-state relations, given the Reichsleiters a great deal of autonomy, and, most important, elevated Rosenberg himself to a position of first among the Reichsleiters as the NSDAP's ideological oracle on "all of life's problems."[29]

As always, Rosenberg's proposals were stillborn from the moment they left the typewriter, and there is no indication that Bormann took the challenge very seriously. A similar attempt by Robert Ley, on the other hand, was a different matter. There was something inevitable about the clash of the two Reichsleiters:[30] the ROL had suffered more power reverses at the hand of the StdF's office than any other party office, and Bormann's and Ley's conception of the NSDAP's role in the Third Reich continued to be almost diametrically opposed. Bormann looked upon Ley as a man who still combined far too many positions in his hands; in particular Bormann favored a separation of the DAF and the PO.[31] Ley, on the other hand, saw the DAF-PO union in his own person as the cornerstone of the party's role in society.[32] In addition, Ley hoped to exploit the momentary weakness of the PK's authority to restore to the ROL the jurisdictional powers which had been lost to Hess during the thirties. Like Rosenberg, Ley seriously underestimated Bormann's initial strength. On May 12, that is, on the day Hitler established the PK, Ley asked the Führer for a direct transfer of powers back to the ROL, but Hitler refused.[33] Ley would have been naive to think his ploy would succeed, and he quickly turned to other tactics. In June, Ley unilaterally assigned all political training in the PO to his

29. [Dienststelle Rosenberg], "Denkschrift," ca. 1941, T-81, roll 23, frames 20549–50, and 20574–78.

30. The SS expected the struggle between the two RLs to be "tremendous." See Brandt to Berger, 16 Aug. 1941, T-175, roll 123, frame 2648461.

31. Friedrichs to Bormann, 4 June 1941, BA/NS 6/126; and Bormann, "Aktenvermerk für Pg. Friedrichs and Pg. Klopfer," 6 June 1941, T-580, roll 79, folder 368.

32. The editor of the *Schulungsbrief*, for example, had "to take into consideration [the journal's] close relationship to the DAF." See Woweries to Ley, 30 June 1941, BA/NS 22/630.

33. Speer, *Erinnerungen*, p. 190.

main schooling office, obviously in the hope that this would undercut the PK's personnel evaluations and Bormann's own training program at the Brown House.[34] The PK quickly defeated this scheme by reminding Ley that he would have to submit all curriculum plans to Rosenberg for approval. Since Ley and Rosenberg were not on speaking or writing terms at this time, Ley refused and accepted instead Bormann's compromise solution that the plans be approved by the PK instead. The compromise saved Robert Ley's face, but also destroyed the substance of his proposal.[35] In a similar manner, Bormann exploited the rivalries of Goebbels, Rosenberg, and Ley in the area of "programming National Socialist festivals" (*NS-Feiergestaltung*). All three Reichsleiters claimed jurisdiction over these pseudoreligious services, and the resulting deadlock was resolved when the rivals accepted Bormann as mediator.[36]

Since indirect challenges produced no results, Ley made one last effort to confront the PK's authority directly. On July 1, he sent Bormann a letter embodying his ideas on the responsibility for personnel policies in the PO. It was undisputed, so reasoned Ley, that Hitler had assigned to his office the task of maintaining the statistical information on the PLs, and consequently, he said, "While it is entirely clear that the appointment and removal of PLs down to the level of district leader can only be the sole preserve of the Führer, it is equally obvious that the preparation of the nominations [for these positions] and the subsequent keeping of personnel records must be done in my main personnel office."[37] Ley was apparently so certain of his case that he had already begun a reorganization of his personnel office in line with its proposed status.[38] Bormann, of course, failed to appreciate the clarity of Ley's

34. For the plan itself see ROL, main schooling office, "Bericht über die Arbeitstagung des Hauptschulungsamtes . . . 16.–23.6.1941," n.d., pp. 3–4 and 10–11, BA/NS 22/29. The implications for personnel policies are spelled out in Claus Selzner, "Die Arbeit der NSDAP im Kriege" [2 Sept. 1941], p. 3, T-580, roll 549, folder 747.

35. Dietsch (of the ROL's office for the *Schulungsbrief*) to Simon, 1 Aug. 1941, BA/NS 22/830.

36. For Ley's claims in this area see Ley to Bormann, 2 Sept. 1941, T-81, roll 674, frames 5482668–71. Bormann's decision is embodied in Bormann to Goebbels, 23 Oct. 1941, *ibid.*, frames 5482660–62.

37. Ley to Bormann, 1 July 1941, BA/NS 22/816. See also Diehl-Thiele, *Partei*, pp. 253–54.

38. The relevant documentation is in BA/NS 22/116.

argument and responded two weeks later with a clear statement that Hitler had decided statistics meant just that—statistics—there was no implication of a right to submit nominations.[39] When Ley renewed his challenge in November, Bormann, now the veteran of several successful battles, felt strong enough to admonish the ROL that he was not responsible even for PL deployment, much less nominations.[40]

Bormann's successful counterattacks against Ley and Rosenberg contain all of the elements which enabled the chief of the PK to preserve intact and even enlarge the authority of the StdF's office: hiding behind the authority of Hitler, controlling the information available to Hitler, and exploiting the rivalries of his challengers. Of these the first was undoubtedly the most significant. From the beginning Bormann insisted that the PK was not "an entity (*Gebilde*) more or less set apart from the Führer, but a direct office of the Führer."[41] Throughout these early battles Bormann never ventured beyond Hitler's established policies and phobias. He exploited the Führer's reluctance to make decisions on jurisdictional parameters among his chief lieutenants,[42] and announced that Hitler was too busy to concern himself with the Reichsleiters' squabbles.[43] In the dispute with Ley, the head of the PK defended the status quo, while Ley attempted to give a new interpretation to Hitler's words of eight years before. For reasons of his own, Bormann disliked group discussions among the Reichsleiters and Gauleiters, but the refusal to permit all but a few of this group to hold meetings or listen to foreign broadcasts[44] also reflected Hitler's constant fear of potential group criticism.[45] In addition, Bormann reinforced his position by forming alliances with the enemies of his enemies. In Ley's case, Bormann's ally

39. Bormann to Ley, 15 July 1941, T-580, roll 77, folder 363.
40. This is derived from Ley's response to Bormann, 9 Nov. 1941, T-580, roll 549, folder 747. Bormann's original letter is not available.
41. Bormann to Friedrichs, 4 June 1941, BA/NS 6/126.
42. Friedrichs to Bormann, 4 June 1941, BA/NS 6/126. See also Hans Frank, *Im Angesicht des Galgens* (Munich- Gräfeling, 1953), p. 414.
43. See, for example, Bormann to Ley, 27 June 1941, T-580, roll 549, folder 747.
44. PK, "Rundschreiben 112/41," 28 Sept. 1941, *VAB*, I, 410; Reichsschatzmeister (cited hereafter as Rschm.), "Anordnung 30/41," 25 June 1941, *Rundschreiben des Reichsschatzmeisters* (cited hereafter as *Rdschr.*), VIII; and Wulf, *Bormann*, p. 141.
45. Adolf Wagner admitted that Hitler could not consult the people before the attack on the Soviet Union because the people would have rejected the venture. See "Rede des Gauleiters Wagner," 22 Oct. 1941, BDC/Wagner (PKC).

was Schwarz, who welcomed any opportunity to curtail further Ley's financial and administrative autonomy. Thus, while Bormann dealt with Ley's PL training plans, Schwarz challenged Ley's control over the Ordensburgen and his use of DAF funds for PO purposes.[46] Bormann, in turn, sent copies of his correspondence with Ley to the Reich treasurer. Nevertheless, the chief of the PK never formed more than tactical alliances; at the end of the war Schwarz complained no less bitterly than other party leaders that he had been unable to see Hitler.[47]

By the end of the year Bormann had successfully resisted the various challenges to his fledgling office; at the beginning of 1942 its status as a successor organization to the StdF was secure and the PK could take the offensive in its dealings with the party and particularly the PO. Even so, the first task was to shore up the sagging morale and influence of the PO. While the PK fought its battles with Ley and Rosenberg, the German army had been defeated before Moscow, so that Hitler's continued admonition to the PO to produce a favorable public opinion and to prevent a new 1918[48] had become a demand for execution of a very onerous and difficult task. There was evidence that the territorial organization of the PO in particular was cracking under the strain. At least some Gauleiters had lost whatever genuine contact with their population they might previously have had; Adolf Wagner, for example, was rapidly drinking himself to death. And he was by no means alone in this category; Schwarz drew up lists of potentially suitable (and sober) candidates for a number of Gauleiter posts.[49] At the lower levels, Bormann had to admonish the Hoheitsträgers against the all too facile short-term solution to the dilemma of unpopularity: it would not do to make rash promises to the grumbling population since failure to deliver would simply result in ever greater animosity toward the party.[50]

It goes almost without saying that the struggles between the Reichs-

46. Harold Scholtz, "Die 'NS-Ordensburgen,'" *Vierteljahrshefte für Zeitgeschichte* (cited hereafter as Vjh.f.Z.), XV (July 1967), 276; and Schwarz to Ley, 7 July 1941, BA/NS 22/14.

47. Karl Koller, *Der letzte Monat* (Mannheim, 1949), entry for 9 May 1945, p. 113.

48. Fritz Sauckel, "[Rede] . . . zur Arbeitstagung der NSDAP . . . 23. November 1941 . . . zu Eisenach," n.d., pp. 18–20, MiU/GAC, folder 53.

49. Berger to Himmler, 27 Nov. 1941, T-175, roll 123, frame 2648517.

50. PK, "V.I. 395/41," 26 Aug. 1941, *VAB*, I.

leiters in 1941 encouraged the always latent centrifugal tendencies among the Gauleiters. Gauleiter Wagner in Upper Bavaria boasted quite openly that he ignored central directives from the Reich ministries. If they wanted to consult him, they would have to schedule a visit to Munich.[51] To be sure, he was referring to state agencies, but the central offices of the party fared no better. Ley noted that the Gauleiters showed no hesitation in creating new PL positions, despite an absolute prohibition on establishing offices not specifically listed in the *Organisationsbuch*.[52] Moreover, there remained the danger of alliances between some of the Gauleiters and the Reichsleiters. As usual, Rosenberg failed, but he did attempt to enlist Mutschmann's aid in his anti-Bormann drive.[53] It is difficult to surmise which possibility exasperated the PK more: the danger of Reichsleiter-Gauleiter cooperation, or the naiveté of Gauleiter Wahl. The latter suggested that the NSDAP's contribution to the war effort was so minimal that the PO should close its offices and release the PLs for fighting at the Russian front—at least for the two or three months needed to defeat the Soviet Union.[54]

Indeed, as the war entered its third year, the entire PO personnel structure staggered under an accumulation of problems. The NSDAP, largely as a result of Ley's organizational manias, had always had a vast array of unimportant offices and functionaries, yet it lacked competent PLs to staff the Gau- and district-level political offices. The war had aggravated rather than diminished the difficulties. The geographic area of administration was expanded, and the party had no large reservoir of replacements. Not only was the number of draft-exempt PLs decreasing in the first ten months of 1942 (from 20,319 to 15,458),[55] but since there was a partial halt on membership from 1942 until the end of the war,[56] the PO was forced to rely primarily upon the graduates of the order castles and the HJ to fill its thin PL ranks. The former source was

51. Wagner, "Rede . . . ," 22 Oct. 1941," BDC/Wagner (PKC).

52. *VOBl Gau Franken*, no. 23 (15 Dec. 1941), p. 11.

53. Alfred Rosenberg, *Letzte Aufzeichnungen* (Göttingen, 1955), p. 152.

54. Wahl to Hitler, 25 June 1941, T-81, roll 179, frame 328811.

55. These figures are part of a series of detailed compilations on the draft exemption of the party in T-580, roll 873, box 799A, folder 7; and roll 874, box 799B, folders 2 and 3.

56. Hans Buchheim, "Mitgliedschaft bei der NSDAP," in *Gutachten des Instituts für Zeitgeschichte*, ed. Paul Kluke (Munich, 1958), pp. 316–17.

all but useless; district leaders in the Altreich simply refused to accept Ordensburg graduates.[57] (They served in the occupied East, of course, but only because the conquered peoples there could not protest.) The administration of the HJ was plainly chaotic and corrupt in many areas. The youths' own reaction was passive resistance and large-scale indifference toward the functions and activities of the NSDAP.[58] Among the eighteen-year-old HJ boys of the Gau Mecklenburg in the years 1941, 1942, and 1943, not one planned a career as a PL. In fact, of a total of approximately one thousand only twenty-seven wanted to become associated with the party in their vocational choice at all, and among this minute minority, most planned to be officers in the armed SS.[59] In Eisenach, a large percentage of HJ and BDM (Bund deutscher Mädel, League of German Girls) members did not even plan to take out party membership, much less become PLs.[60]

The PK was fully aware of the problems and, once firmly established, took vigorous action to remedy them after its own fashion. Bormann did not share Gauleiter Wahl's low estimate of the PO's contribution to the war effort; he regarded the PLs as equal in significance to the munitions workers.[61] The PK chief's plan of action was essentially threefold: rejuvenation of the Gauleiter corps, increased authority for the Gauleiters in their dealings with every Reichsleiter except the chief of the PK, and more direct communication between the PK and the district leaders, so as to offset the augmented power of the Gauleiters.[62] The first phase of the program was merely a continuation of the StdF's earlier efforts;[63] its success was not markedly greater than before. The reduction of the Reichsleiter's power came largely as a result of cut-

57. Köhler (district leader of Eisenach) to Gau personnel office of Thuringia, 10 Sept. 1942, MiU/GAC, folder 14.

58. See Schneider, "5. Jahresbericht des Hauptmitgliedsschaftswesens für das Jahr 1941," T-580, roll 834, box 257, folder 274.

59. Enclosure to the report of the SD's Schwerin office, 29 May 1943, BA/NS 6/407.

60. See "Listenmässige Erfassung der Parteieinstellung der HJ und BDM Mitglieder des Jahrganges 1923–Angeordnet v. Kreisl. Eisenach," June 1941, MiU/GAC, folder 2.

61. PK, "Rundschreiben 13/41," 27 July 1941, IfZ/PK Rdschr. geh.

62. Diehl-Thiele, *Partei*, p. 246, n. 111.

63. Bormann to Kaufmann and Forster, 26 May 1941 and 14 Sept. 1941, respectively, BA/NS 6/166.

backs in their activities under the guise of wartime mobilization efforts, while the Gauleiters benefited from the increased decentralization of administrative power in the Third Reich after 1941. Bormann's most immediate innovation came in the area of relations between the PK and the district leaders. The PK's particular device for direct communication with the district leaders was the so-called *Vertrauliche Informationen* (*VI*), a compendium of circular letters and directives compiled by the PK's staff and sent directly to the districts. The *VI* started with a semi-weekly publication schedule, but soon appeared almost daily, and in the later war years reached such volume that the district leaders read little beyond the headings.[64] The *VI*'s major purpose was to enable the district leaders to settle morale and propaganda problems "before [they] led to legal or administrative actions [by the state organs]."[65] In effect, the PK wanted the district leaders to handle matters related to the civilian war effort before the state had an opportunity to reach a decision. As a result, the *VI*s were a miscellany of directives, long-winded explanations of upcoming and current shortages, and pseudophilosophical musings on better public relations techniques. Most of the information in the *VI* was a digest of reports sent to the PK from the districts, in response to a steady stream of questionnaires sent out by Bormann's staff.[66] In addition, the PK instituted something like the in-service training program in reverse: PK staff officials were sent directly to selected districts to improve the party's control in these areas.[67]

The PK's efforts to solve the PO's internal difficulties were in no way facilitated by the simultaneous attempts of the SS to gain control of a large share of the political decision-making process in both Germany and the occupied areas. In both the Reich treasurer's office and the PK, agents of the SS reported internal matters to Himmler and Berger, and, at least in the case of the SS's man in Schwarz's office, acted directly to

---

64. "Eingabe Langes," n.d. (1947); and "Erklärung Schusters," n.d. (1947), Forsch. Hbg/PA/12/L and S, respectively. Both Lange and Schuster had been district leaders in Hamburg.

65. *Vertrauliche Informationen* of the PK (cited hereafter as *VI*), no. 1 (3 Jan. 1942).

66. See "V.I. 737/41," 6 Dec, 1941, *VAB*, I, 96; Gau staff office of Thuringia to district leader of Eisenach, 20 April 1942, and district leader to Gau staff office, 28 April 1942, MiU/GAC, folder 14.

67. Friedrichs, "Notiz für den Reichsleiter," 17 June 1941, T-580, roll 80, folder 371.

serve the SS interests.[68] A number of Gauleiters similarly continued to identify with the SS rather than with the PO. One Gauleiter ordered his PLs to wear SS rather than PO uniforms until forbidden to do so by Himmler; another corresponded regularly with Himmler, and emphasized his rank as SS lieutenant general rather than his Gauleiter title.[69] Significantly, the Gauleiters who resisted the siren call of the SS and identified more with the PO represented almost ideal types from Bormann's point of view. Berger described them as "very young, very active, and very self-confident."[70]

At the same time it must be noted that at another, parallel level relations between the SS and the PK as well as those between Himmler and Bormann personally were characterized by cooperation and even cordiality. There was nothing contradictory in such situations in the Third Reich; both the SS and the PK-PO were power components whose individual drives for power included the other organization both as ally and object. The alliances, too, took place on several levels. There was, for example, the simple fact that Bormann had loaned Himmler money so that he could build a suitable house for his mistress.[71] This was hardly a decisive factor in their relationship, but it no doubt aided Bormann's self-esteem. On the other side of the ledger, the PK still regarded SS membership for its staff officials as a valuable status symbol,[72] thereby accepting at least in a social sense Himmler's image of the SS's role as an elite within the elite. Then there were alliances against third parties.

68. Berger to Himmler, 20 March 1941 and 7 June 1941, T-175, roll 123, frames 2648823 and 2648749, respectively. When Schwarz discovered the agent, Damson, he dismissed him summarily. See Schwarz to Himmler, 22 Sept. 1943, and Berger to Schwarz, 1 Oct. 1943, T-175, roll 128, frames 2653716 and 2653722, respectively.

69. PK, "V.I. 308/41," 26 July 1941, *VAB*, I, 23; and Lammers to Bormann, 1 Dec. 1941, BA/R 43 II/455a. The first Gauleiter was unnamed; the second was GL Scheel of Salzburg.

70. Berger was referring to the three Austrian GLs Hofer (Oberdonau), Uiberreuther (Steiermark), and Rainer (Salzburg until 27 Nov. 1941). See Berger to Himmler, 30 Aug. 1941, in Helmut Heiber, ed., *Reichsführer! . . . Briefe an und von Himmler* (Stuttgart, 1968), p. 93.

71. Wulf, *Martin Bormann*, p. 163; and Heinz Höhne, *Der Orden unter dem Totenkopf* (Gütersloh, 1967), p. 388.

72. Both Klopfer and Friedrichs received ranks of SS-Brigadeführer (lieutenant-general) in early 1942. See RFSS to SS personnel office, 26 Jan. 1942, BDC/Friedrichs (SS); and interrogation of Klopfer, p. 5, IfZ/ZS 352.

Bormann and Himmler cooperated in stripping R. Walther Darré of his powers as Reich minister of agriculture,[73] and the PK and SS formed the nucleus of a multilateral alliance system within the NSDAP against the SA and its chief of staff.[74] Finally, the SS and the PK supported more vigorous anti-Semitic measures,[75] as well as an intensification of the harsh policies Himmler pursued as RKFDV in Poland.[76]

The firm agreement of Himmler and Bormann on the need for further partification of population policies in turn strengthened Bormann's position in his relations with the state administration during his first few months in office. Although Hitler had confirmed Bormann in all of Hess's powers, such formal announcements had little meaning in the Third Reich until they were tested in specific power clashes. Like the party, the civil service challenged Bormann's mandate to continue the centralization drive of the StdF. The counterthrust was particularly strong in the area of personnel policy. Even before Hess had left Germany, the Reich ministries of interior and justice attempted to weaken the NSDAP's voice in the promotion process of civil servants. Both ministries announced that they would equate military and party service in evaluating candidates for promotion. Bormann, needless to say, objected vigorously, stressing that party service was a unique contribution to German life and could not be equated with any other form of public service.[77] The state organs were no more successful in granting automatic party membership to the higher-ranking civil servants.[78] For the same reason, Bor-

---

73. See below, pp. 391–92.

74. Schwarz, Bormann, the HJ, and the SS all opposed Lutze as a defeatist. See Berger to Himmler, 27 Nov. 1941; the SS's report on the "Gebietsführertagung der Hitlerjugend . . . 5. bis 7.12.1941," 10 Dec. 1941, T-175, roll 123, frames 2648517 and 2648497–98, respectively; and Heinrich Bennecke, *Die Reichswehr und der "Röhm-Putsch"* (Munich, 1964), p. 75.

75. Bernhard Lösener, "Als Rassereferent im Reichministerium des Innern," *Vjh.f.Z.*, IX (July 1961), 304.

76. The agreement between the PK and the RKFDV is reprinted in Robert Koehl, *RFKDV—German Resettlement Policy 1939–1945* (Cambridge, Mass., 1957), pp. 251–53. In this case the SS-PK alliance was facilitated by Bormann's less than cordial relationship with Gross, the head of the rival office for racial policy; Gross had been one of Hess's particular favorites. See *ibid.*, p. 143.

77. Bormann to Reich ministry of justice, 9 May 1941, BA/R 22/4466 fol. 1.

78. PK, "Anordnung 25/41," *Reichsverfügungsblatt* (cited hereafter as RVBl) (A), no. 24 (24 May 1941). See also Bormann to Reich ministry of the interior, 20 June 1941, BA/R 43 II/421a.

mann staunchly opposed personnel unions between state and party offices,[79] although he encouraged temporary personnel transfers between the PK and a variety of state offices, so that the PK's staffers could gain experience in a number of administrative tasks.[80] At least partially as a result of these moves, by early fall the PK was able to take the initiative in party-state relations and interfere in a large number of what had hitherto been regarded as primarily concerns of the state.[81]

The PK and the PO moved vigorously to assist the SS in preparing and implementing the "final solution of the Jewish question," that is, the extermination of the European Jews. Klopfer attended the Wannsee conference (where the extermination policy was announced) as the PK's representative,[82] and the PLs in the Arbeitsbereichs were active in classifying and rounding up Jews for shipment to collection points.[83] In the Altreich, Bormann ordered the PO to help enforce the regulations forcing Jews to wear Star of David identification badges.[84] While the PK served as Heydrich's eager associate in the anti-Semitic measures, Bormann on his own initiative intensified the battle between party and church. He had been in office less than three weeks when he issued his first major directive on church-state relations. It came in the form of a letter to Gauleiter Meyer. The Westphalian party leader had requested some broad policy guidelines, and Bormann was more than happy to comply with a lengthy epistle. His response made it clear that after the war there would be no place for the churches in Germany. As a thoroughly scientific doctrine, National Socialism would replace Christianity in all of its roles.[85] Bormann undoubtedly had Hitler's support,[86] but for tactical reasons the Führer was still reluctant to launch a full-scale at-

79. Mommsen, *Beamtentum*, p. 115.

80. Bormann to Müller (president of the Reich auditing office), 15 Jan. 1942, BA/R 43 II/705b.

81. Epp to Lammers, ca. Aug. 1941 (draft), BGStA, Rsth. 157.

82. Wulf, *Martin Bormann*, p. 85. The best and most extensive analysis of the entire extermination process is, of course, Raul Hilberg, *The Destruction of the European Jews* (Chicago, 1961).

83. Munster, "Aktennotiz," RvO/Generalkommissar zur besonderen Verwendung in den Niederlanden (cited hereafter as GKzbV [Ni])/1b.

84. See *VI*, nos. 52 and 58 (29 Oct. and 22 Nov. 1941).

85. Bormann, "Verhältnis von Nationalsozialismus und Christentum," 6 June 1941, *IMT*, XXXV, doc. D–075. See also Friedrich Zipfel, *Kirchenkampf in Deutschland 1933–45* (Berlin, 1965), pp. 511–15.

86. PK, "Rundschreiben 22/43g," 26 April 1943, IfZ/PK Rdschr. geh.

tack on the churches.[87] As a result, Bormann could vent his fanaticism only on the party. The PK sought systematically to eliminate from the ranks of the PO PLs who maintained an ideological connection other than to Adolf Hitler.[88] A number of Gauleiters shared Bormann's hatred of the churches, and enthusiastically followed his lead. Adolf Wagner in Bavaria even reopened the crucifix controversy that had led to massive unrest in Oldenburg in the mid-thirties. Throughout the summer, Bavaria was rocked by Wagner's persistent attempts to remove all crucifixes from classrooms in public schools, leaving behind (or, if necessary, replacing them with) pictures of Adolf Hitler.[89]

The Nazi dictator dragged his feet on the church issue, but he found a pet project of his own in the reform of the training system for elementary school teachers. The subject became acute in 1941 for both ideological and administrative reasons. Hitler had long felt that as a group German teachers lacked the Nazi fanaticism required to mold the younger generation, and he attributed this to their excessively intellectualized training. Moreover, educational policy was rapidly becoming a power vacuum in the Third Reich. The Reich minister of culture, Bernhard Rust, was increasingly ineffective, and a number of rivals, including Ley and Bormann, formulated plans to take over segments of Rust's jurisdiction.[90] Then, too, the reforms were part of the antichurch attack, since they were designed to eliminate the churches' influence over German public schools.[91]

Traditionally, certification as elementary school teacher in the Altreich had required graduation from a German high school (*Gymnasi-*

---

87. For example, Hitler specifically prohibited the DAF from seizing the property of church-affiliated organizations. Bormann to Ley, 3 Sept. 1941, T-580, roll 549, folder 747.

88. *VI*, no. 10 (4 Feb. 1942); GL Thuringia, "Rundschreiben" to all Thuringian Hoheitsträgers, July 1941; MiU/GAC, folder 51. See also the account of the antireligious curriculum at the Reichsschule Feldafing by a former student at the school after 1940, in IfZ/ZS 1701, pp. 2–3.

89. For the crucifix affair see Epp to Lammers (draft), ca. Aug. 1941; and the monthly reports of the governmental administrator for Niederbayern of 8 June, 8 July, 8 Aug., and 7 Sept. 1941, BGStA, Rsth. 157 and MA 106674, respectively.

90. Rolf Eilers, *Die nationalsozialistische Schulpolitik* (Cologne, 1963), p. 111; and Scholtz, "NS-Ordensburgen," p. 293. See also Helmut Heiber, *Walter Frank und sein Reichsinstitut für die Geschichte des neuen Deutschland* (Stuttgart, 1966), p. 1131.

91. Eilers, *Schulpolitik*, p. 91.

um) and, subsequently, a teachers college. The result, according to Hitler, was teachers who taught with their heads instead of their hearts. He much preferred the practice in the former Austro-Hungarian Empire which had allowed grade school graduates and retired noncommissioned officers to receive minimal postgraduate training before being assigned to teach in the elementary schools. Accordingly, Bormann issued a directive in September 1941 that introduced a modification of the Austrian system into the Altreich and, far more significantly, partified the public school policies as a whole. The entrance requirements of teachers colleges no longer included a high school diploma, but instead a political bill of health from the prospective candidate's district leader and HJ group leader. In addition, the party's approval was required before a newly certified teacher could be given a classroom assignment.[92] Since Rust was in no position to protest, Bormann pressed ahead with a reform of the public school system itself. Instead of the two-strand grade school and high school system with its rigid barrier to upward educational mobility for most students, the PK's reforms called for the establishment of a ten-grade main school (*Hauptschule*), accessible in principle to all students. In one sense, this reform was overdue, and it is one of the few Nazi policies which survived the Third Reich. Its merits during the Nazi regime, however, were all but obscured by the partification clause: only students whose applications had been approved by the district leaders could attend the new schools, and preference was given to applicants who had distinguished themselves in the HJ.[93]

Aggressiveness and self-confidence permeated the entire staff of the PK after the first six months of its existence. The total number of staff officials at the Brown House probably numbered around two hundred now; it had been one hundred in May 1939 and reached four hundred by 1944.[94] The officials worked together effectively not only because many had considerable expertise in various policy areas and shared

92. PK, "Rundschreiben 111/41," 19 Sept. 1941, *VAB*, II, 314–25. See also Eilers, *Schulpolitik*, p. 108, n. 15; PK, "Rundschreiben 87/42," 26 June 1942; and "V.I. 1/5," 3 Jan. 1942, *VAB*, II, 325–28 and 331, respectively.

93. PK, "Rundschreiben 105/41," 27 Aug. 1941, *VAB*, II, 343–52. It should be pointed out that in most areas the *Hauptschulen* existed only on paper before 1945. A ministerial directive postponed their establishment until after the war. See Hermann Meyerhoff, *Herne 1933–1945* (Herne, 1963), p. 60.

94. Diehl-Thiele, *Partei*, p. 218, n. 47.

Bormann's vision of the PK as a superministry,[95] but also because Bormann's office was characterized by a remarkable continuity among the higher ranks of officials. All of the major division and department heads had served in the office of the StdF for most of the Third Reich. As a result, they enjoyed the advantage of relatively long-term experience in their negotiations with other party and state offices. It is indicative of Bormann's confidence after six months in office that he attempted to expand and solidify the PK's role in the area of party personnel policy. In June, he had resisted Ley's request for a clearer definition of jurisdictional spheres; in November, the PK itself suggested a far-reaching delineation of its role. Bormann drafted a decree, to be issued over Hitler's signature, which embodied in very clear formulations the PK's extremely broad personnel policy goals. Bormann styled himself "area expert (*Sachbearbeiter*) for personnel questions in the party" and had Hitler note that "the head of my party chancellery issues the necessary directives in the area of personnel policy." In this capacity, he was responsible for all Hoheitsträger positions as well as the appointments, transfers, and deployment of all PLs if they involved more than one Gau or more than one Reichsleiter's office. And even for intrajurisdictional appointments the proposed decree contained the telltale loophole "insofar as I [Hitler] do not assign the handling of specific cases or general policy to my Sachbearbeiter."[96]

This time Bormann had overreached himself. Hitler then forced him to submit the draft decree to the Gauleiters and Reichsleiters for their comments before publication, and there, predictably, the grand plan met with stiff opposition and quick burial. It was undoubtedly a major factor in the rapidly thickening atmosphere of hostility that faced Bormann from within the higher party ranks after the beginning of 1942.[97] Concretely, the failure of his draft decree forced Bormann to return to more

95. Hans Mommsen, *Beamtentum im Dritten Reich* (Stuttgart, 1966), p. 115. Klopfer even briefly attempted to hold something like general staff meetings for the major officials in division III, but after two sessions this attempt at proto-collegiality was abandoned. See the reports on the two sessions in T-580, roll 82, folder 394.

96. Bormann, "Verfügung," (draft), 12 Nov. 1941, BDC/file PK, StS. Präs. Kanzlei. Another copy of the draft decree is in the Centre Documentation Juive Contemporaine (cited hereafter as CDJC)/CXLII–233. The BDC copy had gone to GL Scheel, the CDJC copy to Rosenberg.

97. Wulf, *Martin Bormann*, p. 134.

indirect means of expanding his influence over personnel policy. Since the StdF's earlier attempt to rejuvenate the Gauleiter corps as a whole had met with only modest success, the PK moved instead to push the Gauleiters into the background and make more powerful the position of the Gau staff offices and the district leaders. This is not to say that the Gauleiters became figureheads. Far from that, their powers increased significantly in the remaining years of the regime; but they did so primarily at the expense of the Reich ministries, while the routine party work (and influence) fell more and more to the Gau staff offices and the district leaders.[98] These offices became the nerve center of the administrative hierarchy in the Gau, all but eclipsing the Gau organizational offices.[99] They handled day-to-day routines and organized training sessions and collections.[100] The Gau staff offices were also in charge of feedback activity; as noted above, once a week (on Friday) each office sent a report on the mood of the Gau to the party chancellery in Munich. The PK reached into the districts primarily with the expanded *Vertrauliche Informationen,* which began publication at the beginning of 1942,[101] but there were more subtle changes as well. Despite the wartime stringencies of the bitter fall and winter of 1941, district congresses were elaborate affairs, clearly designed to emphasize the party district's central importance to the entire societal life in the county.[102] Although the evidence is far from conclusive, there are even indications of major changes in the curricula of the in-service training programs for PLs. Greater emphasis upon ideological fanaticism (against Jews, Marxists, and "plutocrats") replaced Ley's excessive concern with proper uniforms and letter-perfect obedience to the *Organisationsbuch* regulations.[103]

The two-year span encompassed by 1942 and 1943 undoubtedly was the most important time segment in the wartime history of the PK as

98. This is based upon the following sources: *VOBl Gau Franken,* nos. 2, 10, 15, and 16 (1 Feb., 1 June, 15 Aug., and 1 Sept. 1941, resp.); and *VOBl Gau Baden,* nos. 4–9 (1 Sept. to 15 Nov. 1941).

99. See Hitler, "Verfügung 4/41," 1 Nov. 1941, *VOBl,* no. 226 (Nov. 1941); and *VOBl Gau Franken,* no. 22 (1 Dec. 1941).

100. See *VOBl Gau Franken,* nos. 18, 21, and 23 (1 Oct., 15 Nov., and 15 Dec. 1941, resp.).

101. See "V.I. 1/1," 3 Jan. 1942, *VAB,* I, 102–03.

102. See *VOBl Gau Baden,* no. 6 (1 Oct. 1941).

103. *Ibid.,* no. 7 (15 Oct. 1941).

well as of the NSDAP itself. The regime had weathered the defeat of the German armies before Moscow, and easily given itself up to the renewed euphoria of the advances on Stalingrad and Egypt, before the simultaneous reverses on the Volga and in Africa brought the realization that from now on the war would be a defensive rather than an offensive enterprise. At the beginning of 1942 the mood of the country and the party was subdued; in February, Hitler pointedly refused to attend the annual celebrations marking the anniversary of the publication of the party's program.[104] In April and May the party's (and Hitler's) confidence picked up.[105] Hitler was convinced that, as in the Kampfzeit, victory had to follow a period of reverses.[106] He felt increasingly comfortable in his role as all-seeing warlord. Moscow was now termed a victory, although the Führer modestly agreed that Ley should have mentioned other factors in addition to Hitler as the cause of the victorious battle. Promises of revenge on England made the rounds again.[107] Indeed, the Gauleiters all but resumed their peacetime operations,[108] so that Bormann had to warn against the illusion of early victory, and Hitler—once again—explicitly prohibited any discussion of war aims among the party leaders.[109]

The NSDAP had no hesitation in accepting the credit for what appeared to be a new era of victories, and Bormann, in turn, used the seeming upswing in the fortunes of war to push even further both his control of the party and the PO's influence in determining decisions in all facets of public policy.[110] To be sure, the PO remained an imperfect instrument; numerous complaints about the nouveau riche airs of the PLs and the still rampant corruption were voiced even by elements

104. Domarus, *Hitler*, II, 1823 and 1843; and Boelcke, *Wollt Ihr*, entry for 29 Jan. 1942, p. 210.

105. The change of mood is particularly detectable in the editorials of *Das Reich*.

106. Picker, *Tischgespräche*, entry for 22 July 1942, p. 187.

107. Willi A. Boelcke, ed., *Deutschlands Rüstung im Zweiten Weltkrieg—Hitlers Konferenzen mit Albert Speer 1942–1945* (Frankfurt, 1969), entry for 6/7 May 1942, p. 111; and VI, no. 38 (29 May 1942).

108. Speer, *Erinnerungen*, pp. 230–31. See also VI, no. 25 (28 March 1942); and VI, no. 71 (30 Oct. 1942).

109. VI, no. 43 (19 June 1942); and Bormann to Rosenberg, 9 Sept. 1942, CDJC/CXLII–214.

110. PK, "Rundschreiben 49/42," 2 April 1942, *VAB*, I, 6.

within the party.[111] But the PO was the only institution at Bormann's immediate disposal. Systematically flattering Hitler and hiding behind his personal authority,[112] the chief of the PK worked tirelessly to subordinate the PO more directly to his own direct influence. His activities extended to virtually all areas of life (in many ways Bormann was as much of a frustrated pedagogue as Ley; the PK chief grew positively transcendental over such subjects as "cultural life in the village"[113]), but the focal point of the PK's activities had to be the personnel changes and deployment of the PLs.

An unfortunately only partially extant 267-page document of the summer or fall of 1942 (internal evidence shows that it must have been written before the reverses in Russia and Africa) from the files of the PK provides a fascinating glimpse of the agency's long-range plans for the party. The authorship of the memo is in doubt, although it is clear that it originated in the office of the Gauleiter of Weser-Ems. Edward N. Peterson attributed it to Gauleiter Röver,[114] but a more likely author is Bormann's old protégé and Röver's successor, Paul Wegener. Röver died in May 1942—apparently as a result of a stroke and paralysis—and a few weeks later Wegener took his place.[115] The arrangement of the memorandum and its style follows that common among PK staffers, so that the author's familiarity with these matters may be assumed. Moreover, the author had access to one of the "Führer-typewriters" (machines equipped with extra-large type to facilitate reading by the shortsighted Hitler), and it is certain that Wegener had such access.[116] The authorship of the document is of considerable importance, not only be-

111. PK, "Rundschreiben 17/42 [and] 152/42," 29 Jan. and 30 Sept. 1942, *VAB*, I, 35–37 and 21–22, respectively [*sic*]; PK, "Anordnung 48/42," 8 Aug. 1942, *RVBl* (A), no. 33 (8 Aug. 1942), p. 94; and Boelcke, *Wollt Ihr*, entry for 11 April 1942, p. 227.

112. Hitler was most pleased that Bormann offered to pay for the Linz project out of party funds. See Picker, *Tischgespräche*, entry for 26 April 1942, p. 393.

113. See especially Bormann's letter on cultural activities at the local level, 24 Dec. 1942, which was reprinted twice in the *VAB*, I, 190–97, and 498–505.

114. Edward N. Peterson, *The Limits of Hitler's Power* (Princeton, N.J., 1969), pp. 181–83, and 181, n. 29.

115. Heydrich to Himmler, 13 May 1942, quoted in Heiber, *Reichsführer*, pp. 119–20. Domarus, *Hitler*, II, 1881, relates Röver's death indirectly to the judicial crisis of April 1942 (on this see below, pp. 368 ff.).

116. Wegener's BDC/PKC personnel record contains letters written by him on a Führer-typewriter.

cause it helps to date the memorandum more precisely, but also because if Wegener was indeed the author, it may be assumed with reasonable assurance that the proposals and analysis reflect not only Wegener's, but Bormann's thinking as well.[117]

The "Wegener memorandum" ranges over virtually every aspect of party policy, and suggests far-reaching changes in most areas. (The second half of the voluminous document dealt with party-state relations, but it has been lost.) The basic goal of the party, according to Wegener, should be the creation of a tough, ideologically fanaticized control group with limited, co-opted membership that would provide a permanent decision-making elite for all of German society. One of the first peacetime activities should be a purge of the membership and a toughening of the party courts.[118] Subsequently, the membership flow should come almost entirely from the Hitler Youth, and in this connection Wegener proposed a major reorganization of the HJ. Instead of operating as a state enterprise, as had been the case since December 1936, the HJ would come entirely under the control of the PO, with the territorial HJ leaders serving on the staff of the various Hoheitsträgers. Similarly, the district leaders would be given a major voice in determining which HJ graduates should be co-opted into party membership.[119] As a logical corollary to the process of tightening the membership, Wegener demanded the reabsorption of the propaganda machinery by the party. Propaganda lay at the heart of the party's activities and Wegener regarded the 1933 decision to create a Reich ministry of propaganda as a mistake.[120] Even more than the propaganda operations, the paramilitary organizations were children "who had left their mother, the party."[121] The inevitable result was eventual decline and decay, which Wegener saw exemplified in the course followed by the SA since 1934. He

117. As early as 1936 Bormann described Wegener as "reliable . . . hardworking, absolutely loyal, pronounced leadership type (*Führernatur*), who is able to win over people. . . . Has a good knowledge of the party's organization and internal conditions. . . . Possesses all prerequisites for high party office." See "Beurteilungsschrift ausgestellt durch Reichsleiter Martin Bormann am 20.8. 1936," 20 Aug. 1936, BDC/Wegener (PKC).

118. [Paul Wegener?] ["Memorandum,"] n.d. (ca. summer 1942) (cited hereafter as Wegener-memo), T-81, roll 7, frames 14529–35.

119. *Ibid.*, frames 14690, 14695–703, and 14708.

120. *Ibid.*, frames 14621–26.

121. *Ibid.*, frame 14662.

admitted that the SA had no real purpose in Nazi Germany at present, and proposed that it absorb the veterans' organization (the National Socialist Reich Warriors' Association was an affiliate, not a paramilitary organization) and thereby place the veterans under direct party control.[122] On the SS, Wegener was remarkably silent. He did suggest that all of the paramilitary organizations should align their territorial units with those of the PO, but he was obviously not willing to tackle the powerful black guards directly. Instead, he obliquely suggested that the SS should really specialize in "police and security matters"—leaving political decisions to the PO.[123]

Understandably enough, Wegener devoted particular attention in his analysis to the PO's administration at the Gau level. He left no doubt that he favored an extremely strong Gau, with Gauleiters who could exercise considerable power over the party and, through the device of the Reichsgau, over state offices.[124] There should be a firm emphasis upon the PO as the nucleus of the political decision-making apparatus in the Gau.[125] Wegener was particularly opposed to the centralized operations of the Reich treasurer's office; Wegener's proposals did envision considerably more freedom for the provincial chiefs. After Schwarz had approved a budget figure for the Gau, the Gauleiter should be free to spend the money as he saw fit. Moreover, Wegener wanted both Gau treasurers and auditors subject to the Hoheitsträgers rather than to the Reich treasurer.[126] The memorandum said little about the party's administration in the districts and locals because Wegener found little to criticize at these levels. He merely favored the abolition of the DAF's local organizations and the addition of more full-time PLs to the locals.[127]

Actually, a concern with personnel problems permeated the entire

122. *Ibid.*, frames 14655–58.
123. *Ibid.*, frames 14667–68.
124. *Ibid.*, frames 14516 and 14594–96.
125. Wegener noted that in the Gaus only the staff office, organizational office, personnel office, training office, and propaganda office did "the actual direct work of the party." *Ibid.*, frame 14602.
126. *Ibid.*, frame 14633–36, and 14650. Wegener noted pointedly that the Gau treasurer's office should not be an agency exercising powers of political decision-making; it was merely an administrative office—like the press bureau. *Ibid.*, frame 14605.
127. *Ibid.*, frames 14521, 14584–89, and 14594.

memorandum. Wegener admitted that the era of the NSDAP's "growth through Darwinism" (*Wachstum durch das Recht des Stärkeren*) was past,[128] and that clearly established personnel policy guidelines and jurisdictional parameters would have to be established. He was undoubtedly aware that the PK had serious reservations about jurisdictional definitions, but he took pains to point out that such a step was necessary if the PK's in-service training program, which he wholeheartedly endorsed, was to be successful.[129] And its increased scope and success were indispensable to the future of the movement, since it was a "question of life and death" for the party that full-time PLs not be selected from the ranks of the Ordensburg graduates.[130] Its author also envisioned a massive relocation of PLs from the Reichsleiters' offices to the territorial units of the party. Wegener wanted the Reichsleiters clearly subordinated to the PK, and their staffs significantly reduced.[131] As a result, the present "unsystematic centralization," in which several Reich offices dealt with personnel policy,[132] would be replaced by clear directions from the PK leading to a large production of ideal PLs: men who possessed the characteristics of "ideological clarity, unblemished personality, above average education, exact knowledge of the party, [and] leadership qualities."[133]

The listing of ideal PL characteristics had an element of frustrated déjà vu in it, but by no means all of Wegener's proposals were equally unrealistic. On the contrary, in a number of respects the PK was able to move considerably closer to a formal realization of the centralized control position envisioned by Wegener. In a directive issued at the beginning of April, Bormann reemphasized the PK's role as advisor to Hitler on all party affairs "affecting the existence of the German people." Hitler alone decided basic policy, but only Bormann could supply the facts which formed the basis of the Führer's decisions. In consequence, the chief of the PK had to be kept abreast "from the beginning" of all plans and proposals envisioned by the Reichsleiters and Gauleiters.[134] Toward

128. *Ibid.*, frames 14517–18.
129. *Ibid.*, frames 14552–55.
130. *Ibid.*, frames 14537–39.
131. *Ibid.*, frames 14589–97.
132. *Ibid.*, frames 14579 and 14609–610.
133. *Ibid.*, frame 14542.
134. PK, "Rundschreiben 49/42," 2 April 1942, RvO/BDC/H 1164.

the end of the summer, the NSDAP witnessed some practical applications of this doctrine. In mid-July Hitler issued a decree of his own, advising the party that Bormann was to be informed of all developments which put close associates or relatives of any major party leader in a bad light.[135] A month later, Bormann demonstrated to Ley that the Reichsleiters could indeed communicate with Hitler only through the good offices of the PK. Ley, in the course of a dispute with the acting Reich minister of agriculture, Herbert Backe, had sent copies of his correspondence with Backe to Hitler's personal adjutant. Bormann sent off a sharp reprimand: Hitler had decreed that all matters affecting the party should come to him only through Bormann.[136] In addition, the Führer was so overworked that as a general principle he could not concern himself with disputes among his paladins; if they could not agree, Bormann would mediate. Bormann closed with involuntary irony. Hitler did not want to receive one-sided information; the PK's chief would bring the matter to Hitler's attention only after he had heard from all sides in a dispute.[137]

Bormann and his associates had been in the party long enough, of course, to realize that a policy guideline—even when issued over Hitler's signature—was no guarantee of practical application. In the first months of Bormann's tenure as chief of the PK, his power was still primarily negative; he could prevent the Reichsleiters and Gauleiters from increasing their might, and by manipulating the draft exemptions for PLs he was able to exercise some influence over the composition of the PO as a whole,[138] but none of the measures added up to any large-scale revamping of the PL corps. As before, the key to the restructuring of the PO along Bormann's and Wegener's lines lay with the by now sizable list of forty-two Gauleiters.[139] Bormann might have been rather discouraged by the futile search for Gauleiter material which his office

135. Hitler, "Verfügung," 14 July 1942, T-175, roll 59, frame 2574898.
136. As a result of Ley's mistake, Bormann was able to establish this as a general rule for the entire party. See PK, "V.I. 57/763," 18 Aug. 1942, *VAB*, I, 2.
137. Bormann to Ley, 2 Aug. 1942, T-580, roll 549, folder 747.
138. Compare the fate of two PLs in Holland: one had quarreled with the head of the Arbeitsbereich and was drafted; the other was regarded as indispensable and stayed at his post throughout the war. See RvO/BDC/H 1140 and H 1142.
139. Speer, *Erinnerungen*, p. 230.

conducted in 1939 and 1940, but after he became head of the PK he was determined to try again. In terms of formal powers, the PK's hand was considerably strengthened. Hitler decreed not only that all future Gauleiters should be young men (thereby eliminating disgruntled "old fighters" from consideration), but also that their appointments could be channeled only through the PK's personnel office.[140] There remained only the problems of dismissing the unsatisfactory incumbents and finding suitable replacements.

Both problems proved to be largely impossible of solution. In July 1941, Opdenhoff, the head of the PK's personnel department, submitted a draft list containing twenty-four names of PLs he regarded as possible future Gauleiters. He had been overly optimistic. Even before the list reached Bormann, Opdenhoff's superior, Friedrichs, had crossed out nine of the names, though it is not clear whether he regarded them as unsuitable or simply as unavailable. In any case, only fifteen names remained after the list had gone through a staff screening.[141] Bormann, in turn, was severely disappointed in these meager results. A backup list of fifteen replacements within the PO corps for forty-two indispensable positions was hardly encouraging. The outlook was no brighter in the paramilitary organizations. Here, too, none of the leading officials was capable of serving as either Gauleiter or, with an obvious glance in the direction of Lutze's dismissal, as chief of staff of the SA.[142] All this was no doubt particularly galling because there was no shortage of candidates for dismissal. In addition to some familiar names among Bormann's enemies—Kaufmann, Streicher, Sprenger—the list of unsatisfactory Gauleiters grew longer as the war went on. Mutschmann, although on good terms with Bormann, increasingly alienated the Saxons by his arbitrary and irrational administration.[143] Franz Schwede-Coburg was yet another provincial leader who preferred the charms of his

140. PK, "Verfügung 14/42," 24 Aug. 1942, *VAB*, I, 284–85.

141. The documentation is in T-580, roll 80, folder 371.

142. Bormann to Opdenhoff, 26 May [1941], *ibid*. See also Picker, *Tischgespräche*, entry for 5 May 1942, p. 238. Actually this could not have been Bormann's final judgment; see below for the career of the SA leader Paul Giesler.

143. See the numerous documents relating to Mutschmann's feuds in BDC/Mutschmann (PKC); and Gimbel (an anti-Sprenger *alte Kämpfer* in the Gau) to Frick, 17 June 1942, HAB/320/40.

secretary to those of his wife.[144] Gustav Scheel had only recently been appointed as Gauleiter of the micro-Gau Salzburg,[145] but Bormann was already quarreling with his church policy. There was even a vexing aftermath to the Streicher affair. The "leader of Franconia" had been suspended as Gauleiter, but he continued to treat the Gau administration building as his private property, and Hitler still refused to dismiss and censure the man who had saved his political career in 1923.[146] Hitler was similarly unwilling to touch Kaufmann's position.[147]

Despite the large number of disappointments, the successes on the other side of the ledger were not negligible. In November 1941 Bormann was able to install one of his few favorites in the SA, Paul Giesler, as Josef Wagner's successor in Westphalia-South. Half a year later Giesler also became acting Gauleiter of Munich–Upper Bavaria,[148] tactfully waiting in the wings while Wagner killed himself with cirrhosis of the liver. After a lavish funeral for Röver, attended by Hitler, and a eulogy by Rosenberg,[149] Wegener began a vigorous restructuring of the PO in Weser-Ems—starting with a RM 16,000 redecorating job for his own office.[150] In Hanover, Hartmann Lauterbacher used a momentary lapse of the prime minister of Brunswick, Dietrich Klagges (he had attended his daughter's Lutheran confirmation), to deprive a close friend of the SS of much of his authority.[151]

It is not surprising, in view of these relatively minor successes at the top, that the PK made hardly a dent on the "replacement problem" for the lesser ranks of the PO. The PK repeatedly emphasized the need for

144. Eftger, "Vorlage für Pg. Schmidt," 16 June 1942, RvO/GKzbV (Ni)/1e.
145. See Bormann to Lammers, 18 Nov. 1941, BA/R 43 II/1390c.
146. See Bormann to Zimmermann (the GL protem in Franken), 31 Oct. 1940, BDC/Streicher (PKC).
147. Interrogation of Kaufmann, 26 April 1947, Forsch. Hbg./PA/12/B; and declaration of Klopfer, 26 Nov. 1947, IfZ/ZS 352.
148. Domarus, *Hitler*, II, 1892.
149. *Ibid.*, II, 1883. Rosenberg and Röver were on *du* terms. See Rosenberg, *Letzte*, p. 144.
150. Strankmeyer to GL Weser-Ems, 29 May 1942, RvO/TB/XXXVIII; and Ruoff, "Aktenvermerk," 10 Sept. 1942.
151. Hitler was very pleased with Lauterbacher's performance as Gauleiter. See Picker, *Tischgespräche*, entry for 5 May 1942, p. 239. The documents on the Klagges affair are in BDC/Klagges (SS).

a solution,[152] but aside from gaining control of all draft-exemption cases in the party (with the exception of those in the SS)[153] and implementing some of Wegener's membership proposals,[154] there were no major initiatives. Bormann still hoped to use superannuated HJ officials as PLs,[155] but the quality of the HJ leadership corps did not hold out much promise for improvement.[156] In the end, the PK was reduced to a device that had not been particularly successful since its introduction in the early thirties: a request to all party offices to bring names of promising young PLs to the attention of the PK.[157] No wonder the PL corps was increasingly dominated by older functionaries.[158]

Although the PK made little headway in its overall effort to restructure the PO, it was a hotbed of activism compared to most other major party offices, which appeared to hibernate. Schwarz, it is true, continued in his quiet way to add further auditing powers to his jurisdiction and, in cooperation with the PK, administered the salary scale. The Reich treasurer had no financial concerns whatever,[159] and capped his achievements in October 1942 by subjecting both the NSV and the vast Winter Help welfare programs to his regular auditing authority.[160] At the same time, Ley yielded in principle on the DAF's funds, although

152. See Lingg, "Ämterbesprechung 20. Juli 1942," 22 July 1942, T-580, roll 82, folder 394.

153. Hitler, "Verfügung," 12 Aug. 1942, *VI*, no. 57 (18 Aug. 1942).

154. See *VI*, no. 66 (9 Oct. 1942); and Hitler, "Verfügung 7/42," 14 July 1942, *ibid.*, no. 31 (28 July 1942).

155. Hans Schieder, "Vortrag des Leiters des Zentral-Personalamtes [of the Reich treasurer's office] . . . am 20. Juli 1942," p. 30, T-580, roll 77, folder 363; PK, "Anordnung 82/42," 30 Nov. 1942, *RVBl* (A), no. 47 (7 Dec. 1942); and Lingg, "Ämterbesprechung," 18 May 1942, T-580, roll 82, folder 394.

156. The HJ-sponsored "European Youth Congress," staged in Vienna in September 1942, turned out to be a large-scale orgy of corruption and luxurious living. See "Bericht vom Europäischen Jugendkongress, Wien 1942," 29 Sept. 1942, T-81, roll 676, frames 5485531–34.

157. PK, "Verfügung 15/42," 24 Aug. 1942, *VAB*, I, 309.

158. See Himmler's complaints on this score in Himmler to Herff (head of the SS's personnel office) and Berger, 26 Aug. 1942, quoted in Heiber, *Reichsführer*, p. 142.

159. Schwarz to Wächtler, 24 April 1942, BDC/Wächtler (PKC).

160. *VOBl Gau Franken*, nos. 15 and 17 (15 Sept. and 15 Oct. 1942, resp.); and Hitler, "Verfügung 17/42," 18 Oct. 1942, *RVBl* (A), no. 42 (27 Oct. 1942), p. 123.

it took another year to work out the details.[161] The PK and the Reich treasurer's office cooperated largely without friction on the administration of the salary scale.[162] Bormann found the device particularly useful in transferring PLs from the Gau and district offices to the PK and back again, thereby facilitating the multiple field experience that the PK regarded as an important part of its program of in-service training.

Both Goebbels and Ley were at the nadir in their party careers during most of the year; for Goebbels it was a temporary decline, for Ley a permanent rut. As Wegener and others recognized, the NSDAP's propaganda office had been all but eclipsed by the Reich ministry. It was common knowledge within the PO that some of the least capable PLs were assigned to the Reich propaganda office.[163] Their propaganda output matched their creative abilities. It was characterized by a peculiar combination of euphoria and self-deception in which glee over the Allies' "inability" to win the war alternated with an emphasis upon the Reich's good fortunes in fighting its war under the leadership of Adolf Hitler and the NSDAP.[164] Robert Ley certainly shared the euphoria of the propagandists, but his was the result of alcohol rather than incompetence. The ROL's decline had by now reached the stage where he was unable to put together a coherent public address; on one occasion he cited Goethe but told his audience the quote came from Hitler.[165] His loudly trumpeted appointment as Reich building commissioner was another missed opportunity; the number of apartments built in Germany declined steadily under Ley's influence and the effects of Allied bombing.[166] Even his training programs retreated into a vacuum. Although Ley was under the illusion that the *Hoheitsträger* could perform a useful service for the PO,[167] the PK's *Vertrauliche Informationen* had

161. Ulf Lükemann, "Der Reichsschatzmeister der NSDAP" (Dissertation, Free University of Berlin, 1963), p. 126.

162. Schieder, "Vortrag," p. 5.

163. Boelcke, *Kriegspropaganda*, p. 100.

164. See the themes in the *Mitteilungsblatt* of the NS-Gauring in the Gau München-Oberbayern for 1942; and the *Parole* issued by the propaganda office of the same Gau. The Gaurings were administrative devices set up in 1942 to centralize the propaganda efforts in each Gau.

165. See the report of the SD inspector in Danzig to the HSSPF Danzig, 9 Sept. 1942 (top secret), BDC/Ley (PKC).

166. Boelcke, *Deutschlands Rüstung*, p. 91.

167. Ley to Goebbels, 26 June 1942, BA/NS 22/833.

long since replaced Ley's sterile outpourings as a practical aid to PLs in the field. The ROL's elite boarding schools, the order castles and the Adolf Hitler's Schools, continued to supply incompetent PLs, and surely only Ley could explain how either the party's control or its Betreuung functions were enhanced when a group of PLs was sent on a "cross-country hike accompanied by interludes of ideological instruction."[168]

Ley's decline had an obvious effect on the routine work of the PO and on the relative power position of various offices within the NSDAP's territorial administration. The Gauleiters, who had been Ley's allies off and on through the years, gained in social and financial prestige what they lost in political power. It is almost as though Bormann, unable to purge the recalcitrant old paladins, attempted to buy them off. Their salaries were now well above those paid comparable ranks in the civil service; the Gauleiter of Upper Silesia, for example, received a salary of RM 4,070 per month in addition to an expense account of RM 8,000.[169] At the same time, however, the Gauleiters became elevated to a position not unlike that enjoyed by Hess in his last years in office: charismatic and lofty, but absent from the nitty-gritty of decision-making. The Gauleiters issued inspiring appeals at the beginning of every collection of recyclable materials, but the Gau staff office exercised the party's control functions. The establishment of the Gau staff offices was completed by the summer of 1942. Bormann labored hard to fill these agencies with his own select appointees,[170] and increasingly used the Gau staff office as the political nerve center of the PO's provincial administration. The bureau's particular importance derived from the fact that it combined in one agency the Gau-level control functions over both the vertical and the horizontal organization of the NSDAP. The Gau staff office handled draft exemptions, dealt with liaison matters to the state authorities and the Reichsleiters' representatives in the Gau, reported to the PK, and channeled the PK's directives to the district, insofar as Bormann did not communicate directly with the county leaders. Consequently, the Gau staff offices soon became formidable organi-

168. The virtually untranslatable German original is "Querfeldeinmarsch mit weltanschaulichen Einlagen." See *VOBl Gau Baden*, nos. 6 and 9 (15 March and 15 May 1942). For a list of typical training session topics see *VOBl Gau Franken*, no. 20 (1 Nov. 1942), pp. 8–9.

169. BDC/Bracht (SS).

170. Karl Wahl, *Es ist das deutsche Herz* (Augsburg, 1954), p. 149.

zations (the one in Baden-Alsace was manned by thirteen full-time PLs)[171] that superseded the traditional political offices in the Gau.[172]

At the Gau level, state and party affairs were handled essentially by two men, the Gauleiter and the head of the Gau staff office (although in theory the Gauleiters headed both divisions), but in the districts the dual powers were entrusted to the Hoheitsträgers themselves. From Bormann's point of view, there was a great deal of political logic in this scheme. The PK exercised all of the party's control functions at the national level, and the de facto division at the Gau level tended to prevent excessive accumulations of power in the provinces. The concentration could then be resumed in the districts, both as a potential counterweight to the Gauleiters and because the party could exercise its control over societal relations and values most effectively at this administrative level. In consequence, Bormann looked upon the district leaders as the most important PLs below the PK itself in the Nazi hierarchy; on their fanaticism and political ability depended the success of the party's value revolution. As a basic rule, the district leaders received a minimum salary equal to that of the civil service county administrator,[173] but many district Hoheitsträgers were entitled to substantial bonuses because they served in "politically difficult areas." As a result, an official such as the district leader of the well-to-do residential area of Harvestehude in Hamburg took home a gross monthly salary of RM 1,120—equal to the compensation of an undersecretary in a Reich ministry.[174] The district leaders' importance was also underscored by the immediacy of their relationship to the PK. Not only were the *Vertrauliche Informationen* sent directly to their desks, but staff officials of the PK even attended district leaders' meetings so as to link the two institutions even more closely.[175]

The political significance of the district leaders was based not only

171. On the establishment and function of the Gau staff office see *VOBl Gau Baden*, nos. 11 and 14 (1 June and 15 July 1942); and interrogation of GL Kaufmann, 26 April 1947, Forsch. Hbg./PA/12/B.

172. At the same time, the Gau organizational, personnel, and training offices were significantly reduced in scope and jurisdiction. See *VOBl Gau Franken*, no. 4 (1 March 1942), pp. 3–5, and 7–12.

173. Schieder, "Vortrag," pp. 6–9.

174. BDC/Gloy (PKC).

175. "V.I. 108/42," 31 Jan. 1942, *VAB*, I, 172.

upon their contribution to the immediate civilian war effort, but also, and perhaps even more significantly, upon their anticipated role as social controllers in the victorious peacetime future.[176] To some extent, the two strands had by this time merged during the course of the war. In 1942, the Kreisleiters made direct contributions to the war effort in a number of areas. They "managed" (that is, found propagandistically effective explanations for) various shortages. They administered the numerous collections of recyclable materials (from old newspapers to tin cans to acorns, collections were the order of the day in wartime Nazi Germany).[177] And they had a major voice in the policing of POWs stationed in the districts.[178] At the same time, the district leaders could, and did, interfere in the societal life of their districts. The PK wanted to assure for the party "the most far-reaching educational influence possible," and to this end empowered the district leaders to exercise an absolute veto over such basic items as marriage licenses, welfare payments, aid to dependent children, and so on.[179]

As the district leaders made control decisions, the local and sublocal PLs were freed for more positive Betreuung activities. Here the PK hoped eventually to center all public social life on the party organization. To this end, Bormann, somewhat tentatively at first, tried to reactivate the closed membership meeting of the Kampfzeit, with its emphasis on group participation in the discussion period.[180] The party comrades, fired with ideological enthusiasm, would then become the nucleus of sociocultural life in the village or urban quarter. As noted above, party-centered cultural life in the localities was a particular hobby of Bormann's. At the end of 1942, he published a letter to a (probably fictitious) close friend and local leader with whom he had served in the Kampfzeit. The chief of the PK rhapsodized for some eight pages about the party's duty to create a social life that would irresistibly draw the average

176. Wegener in his memo stressed that the entire control of social policy should be turned over to the PO. A "head of the social office" subordinate to the Hoheitsträgers would replace the DAF functionaries. See Wegener-memo, frame 14730.

177. These collections served as popularity gauges since Hitler refused even to hold Nazi-type rigged elections during the war years. See Hitler's speech of 30 Jan. 1942, quoted in Domarus, *Hitler*, II, 1832.

178. PK, "Anordnung 62/42," 26 Aug. 1942, *RVBl* (A), no. 37 (3 Sept. 1942), pp. 110–12.

179. Various directives relating to this area are in *VAB*, II, 85, 89, and 121.

180. PK, "V.I. 156/42," 18 Feb. 1942, *ibid.*, p. 174.

worker or farmer into the programmatic and value orbit of the party.[181]

The plans to make the party the center of social values and mores were failures, not only because of the deteriorating war situation and the consequent disengagement of the German people from the values of the NSDAP, but also because the available PLs, by and large, had not cut their emotional ties to the bourgeois values of their lower-middle-class origins to nearly the extent that Bormann or Himmler had. Most of the district leaders, for example, plainly enjoyed both their social status and the material emoluments of their offices. Many served on the boards of directors of municipal utility corporations; a retail store clerk had become a *Generaldirektor*. In a majority of cases, they identified with the company, not the party,[182] and Hitler early in 1943 issued a directive prohibiting any full-time PL from holding a director's position.[183] In addition, for most political leaders the image of social controller conflicted with the equally, if not more, prevalent value of quasi-militarization. The same Hoheitsträgers who were manipulating family life on Wednesday stood at attention on Sunday and subjected themselves to a meticulous uniform check by the Gauleiter.[184] All of these factors were no less present at the local level, so that the attempt to create local party-centered culture was also a failure. Either the local leaders themselves ignored the directives, or the party had by now so completely alienated the other prominent social personages (particularly the pastor and the teacher) that few residents exhibited any genuine interest in the "NS festivals."[185]

It was fairly obvious that the Nazi revolution would make little head-

181. PK, "Bekanntgabe 16/42," *RVBl* (A), no. 53 (31 Dec. 1942), pp. 158–62. The letter was also printed in the *VOBl* and the *VAB*.

182. Schwarz to Kaufmann, 18 Aug. 1942, BDC/Häfker (PKC).

183. Earlier the PK had prohibited PLs from becoming associated with any economic enterprises, even as private persons. PK, "Anordnung 47/41," 30 Oct. 1941, *RVBl* (A), no. 52 (6 Nov. 1941).

184. *VOBl Gau Baden*, no. 15 (1 Aug. 1942), supplement. Admittedly the contrast is extreme, but these two functions did occupy about equal importance in the life of a district leader.

185. District leader Coburg to GL Bayreuth, 30 July 1942, T-580, roll 362, folder 16. The handwritten comment of a subscriber to the *VI* in the Gau Franken on Bormann's directive to activate village cultural activities in cooperation with the teachers is revealing: "It's a little late when the calf is already drowned" (*jetzt kommt man, nachdem das Kalb im Brunnen liegt*).

way if it had to rely solely on the efforts of its district and local leaders. Both Bormann and Wegener saw that the state as an institutional entity would have to be subordinated to the party as a political decision-making body before the societal revolution could become effective. In his memorandum Wegener pushed particularly for three major and immediate changes in the relationship of party and state. The NSDAP's legal status, which was still that of a public corporation, would have to be changed in order to place the party outside the bounds of civil and criminal law; the party should be accorded the right to issue direct, binding legislation; and most of the powers of the Reich ministries should be transferred to the Gaus.[186] The party was successful in changing its legal status at the end of 1942,[187] but it never succeeded in controlling national legislation directly, and progress toward establishing the Reichsgaus was stymied by Hitler's indecision and the Allied victories at the front. Actually, the establishment of strong Gaus should have occasioned the least difficulties. Hitler had long since expressed himself in favor of the Reichsgau concept, and he continued to stress his approval of the Gauleiters' positions as territorial viceroys throughout the war.[188] The PK in turn continued its planning activities. The future Reichsgaus—like those in the East and Austria—would exercise far-reaching powers to control all societal life in their fiefs.[189] But the necessary territorial readjustments in the Altreich continued to be an insurmountable obstacle. There was general agreement that the present Gaus, based on election district boundaries, could not be turned into viable Reichsgaus, but Bormann's concept of the cultural and racial cohesiveness of an area aroused nothing but the antagonism of the Gau-

186. Wegener-memo, frames 14509–14512. Exhibiting what he called "verbal clout" (*Schnauze*) Wegener referred to the public corporation status of the NSDAP as an "embarrassed solution of calcified jurists." *Ibid.*, frame 14509. For wartime party-state relations see also Wilhelm Stuckart *et al.*, *Verwaltungsrecht* (Leipzig, 1944), p. 14; *VOBl Gau Baden*, no. 15 (1 Aug. 1942), pp. 14–15; and GL München-Oberbayern, "Vorbereitende Massnahmen zur Bekämpfung von Katastrophen bei Fliegerangriffen," T-580, roll 813, box 242, folder 79.

187. See below, p. 410.

188. Picker, *Tischgespräche*, entry for 24 June 1942, p. 252; and Boelcke, *Deutschlands Rüstung*, entry for 7/8 Nov. 1942, p. 199.

189. Klopfer to Siebert, 28 Aug. 1942, BGStA, MA 105282/2; PK, "Rundschreiben 114/42," 31 July 1942, *VAB*, I, 242–43. See also Picker, *Tischgespräche*, entry for 23 June 1942, p. 250.

leiters. As a result, Hitler buried the subject—again. He did issue a decree on January 25, grandiosely entitled "Decree of the Führer Regarding the Continued Streamlining of the Administration,"[190] but aside from permitting the Gauleiters to interfere in the work of the ministries under the guise of increasing efficiency,[191] the directive produced very few results. Indeed, Hitler specifically prohibited any major territorial changes, and even shied away from such relatively minor matters as eliminating some of the smaller counties within the territory of the Reich.[192]

Since Hitler was unwilling to put into effect a scheme he had repeatedly endorsed in public, the chances for the implementation of a far more controversial project, such as assigning to the party the right to legislate directly, were understandably remote. Even Bormann seems to have regarded Wegener's proposal as utopian, and the PK continued relying on the triple levers of personnel control in the civil service, legislative evaluation in the PK's division of state affairs, and influence over the administration of legislation and judicial administration by the Hoheitsträgers to expand the party's control over the state. Bormann kept up the long-standing emphasis in the StdF's office on the separation of civil service positions and PO posts, except in the case of the Gauleiters and in the new Gaus, created from the occupied areas. If anything, he strengthened the separation principle. Even the Gau economic advisors were not permitted to serve simultaneously on such bodies as the Gau chambers of commerce.[193]

This self-imposed modesty served only one purpose: to free the PLs for full-time control functions. Under Martin Bormann the PK constantly refined the evaluation procedures that enabled the party to con-

190. Hitler, "Erlass des Führers über die weitere Vereinfachung der Verwaltung," 25 Jan. 1942, *VAB*, II, 238–41.
191. PK, "Rundschreiben 50/42," 6 April 1942, *VAB*, II, 244. See also Mommsen, *Beamtentum*, p. 120.
192. PK, "Rundschreiben 2/42," 11 Feb. 1942, *VAB*, II, 238. For the fate of the Reichsreform during the war, see also Walter Baum, "Die 'Reichsreform' im Dritten Reich," *Vjh.f.Z.*, III (Jan. 1955), 54–55.
193. PK, "Rundschreiben 121/42," 7 Aug. 1942, *VAB*, II, 223–26; and Bormann, "Aktenvermerk für Pg. Friedrichs und Pg. Klopfer," 14 April 1942, T-580, roll 80, folder 369.

trol appointments and promotions in the civil service. The party's evaluation was of "decisive importance for the professional career of those evaluated."[194] There were a variety of forms of judgment, but the basic criteria never varied: technical competence was important, but political fanaticism ranked above it.[195] At the level of the Reich ministries, Bormann succeeded in installing Hans von Helms, a particularly vigorous advocate of party control over the civil service, as personnel director of the ministry of the interior. Also, the PK's division of state affairs developed a singularly ingenious system of appraising high-ranking civil servants and jurists. The PK commandeered various officials to serve for a time in division III, both to lend their expertise to the PK's review of pending legislation and to be evaluated for their partification tendencies. The officials apparently had no choice in their transfer; refusals brought dismissal from the civil service or the bench.[196] The Gau and district Hoheitsträgers conducted an almost continuous evaluation process of the officials in their areas that hung like a sword of Damocles over the career of all civil servants.[197] District leaders in particular became quite adept at dismissing civil servants who were not persona grata in the party.[198] Looking further into the future, the party envisioned changes in the German civil service that paralleled the restructuring of the teacher-training process. Since the thoroughgoing partification of the civil service was largely prevented by the NSDAP's inability to present candidates for major administrative posts who were both technically qualified and Nazi fanatics,[199] the PK envisioned a significant lowering in the traditional prerequisites for civil service appointments. Instead of a university law degree, a high school education

194. PK, "Grundsätzliche Fragen der politischen Beurteilung," n.d., *VAB*, I, 317–21.

195. The disastrous administrative consequences of this priority listing were recognized even by some of the GLs. See the "Vermerk" by an official of the Reich chancellery on a speech made by Görlitzer, the deputy GL of Berlin, 4 July 1942, BA/R 43 II/421a.

196. See the interrogation of Karl Lang, head of the division's personnel office, IfZ/ZS 1720.

197. PK, "Rundschreiben 15/42," 30 Jan. 1942, *VAB*, II, 304; and Gau personnel office Köln-Aachen, "Rundschreiben," 11 Aug. 1942, BA/R 22/4466 fol. 1.

198. See GL Wächtler to A. Wagner, 13 Feb. 1942, T-580, roll 362, folder 16.

199. Mommsen, *Beamtentum*, pp. 87 and 107.

or officer's commission would suffice for a career in communal and county administration, provided, of course, that the candidate had the party's political endorsement.[200]

The struggle over the civil service went on largely behind closed doors, but the NSDAP's attempt to partify the judiciary in 1942 proved to be a major public issue. The judicial crisis exploded in May, but it had been building up for most of Hitler's adult life. For years, he had railed against lawyers, judges, and legal norms. As the war progressed, his jaundiced eye surveyed virtually all judicial administrations; Hitler criticized the civil, criminal, military, and even the party courts as excessively mild in the pursuit of his enemies.[201] Other party leaders shared Hitler's resentment of administrators and normative codes that resisted political manipulation.[202] With unequaled perversity of logic an editorial in *Das Reich* declared: "The more subjectively a judge clings to the ideas of National Socialism, the more objective and just will be his sentences."[203] The party leaders were opposed to a judiciary that retained even a vestige of independence, since it threatened the party's total freedom from judicial restraint.[204] Bormann and the StdF had been in the forefront of this chorus for some years. In early spring 1942, Bormann recognized the futility of other full-scale partification efforts, and gave judicial reform the highest priority listing.[205] In February and March, as Bormann fed Hitler judicial cases that would arouse his ire, the Führer's attacks on the judiciary grew in frequency and intensity. Finally, in April, the Schlitt case in Oldenburg broke the camel's back. Ewald Schlitt had murdered his wife, and the court sentenced him to an institution for the criminally insane. Hitler immedi-

---

200. Lingg, "Ämterbesprechung 20. Juli 1942," 22 July 1942, T-580, roll 82, folder 394.

201. Dietrich, *Zwölf Jahre*, p. 137; and Hubert Schorn, *Der Richter im Dritten Reich* (Frankfurt, 1959), p. 191.

202. Werner Johe, *Die gleichgeschaltete Justiz* (Frankfurt, 1967), p. 176. See also Curt Rothenberger, "Sechzehn Monate Berlin," p. A, 2 [sic], 4 April 1944. This manuscript is a brief (14 pp.) account of Rothenberger's tenure as state secretary written after his dismissal. A photocopy is in the Forsch. Hbg./PA/12 (Rothenberger).

203. *Das Reich*, 11 Oct. 1942.

204. Schwarz, "Die Verwaltung der NSDAP im Kriege," *Zeitschrift der Akademie für deutsches Recht*, XI (1 Jan. 1942), 4.

205. Rothenberger, "Sechzehn Monate Berlin," p. A, 2.

ately ordered the unfortunate man shot, and turned his wrath on the
Reich ministry of justice.[206]

The incumbent acting minister, Franz Schlegelberger, had seen the
handwriting on the wall for some months and reacted with sheer appeasement to each outburst against his ministry,[207] but judicial reform
mills grind slowly.[208] At any rate, Schlegelberger was expendable because Hitler had found a man ideally suited to carry through a massive
reform of the German judiciary. At the beginning of 1941, the senator
(that is, minister) for justice in Hamburg, Curt Rothenberger, sent a
memorandum on reforms to Lammers, who reacted negatively. Rothenberger was undaunted and sent the same ideas, via Kaufmann, to
Hess, who was interested, but unfortunately had to fly to England.[209] A
year later, the senator reworked the piece into "a short memorandum,
suitable for reading by the Führer."[210] Bormann passed it on to Hitler
at about the same time as he apprised the Führer of the Schlitt case.
Hitler had both a cause célèbre and a plan for remedies.[211]

On April 26, Hitler addressed a special meeting of the Reichstag.
Most of his speech was devoted to an overly optimistic report on the
progress of the war, but spliced into the twenty pages of text was one
page on the judicial crisis. Specifically, Hitler asked the parliament
for "specific confirmation" of his authority to dismiss any judge and
to reform the judicial system without regard to existing laws and
codes.[212] The Reichstag, needless to say, at once approved the necessary
resolution.[213]

206. Domarus, *Hitler*, II, 1855. Johe, *Gleichgeschaltete Justiz*, pp. 172–75, gives
a good account of the connection between the Schlitt case and Hitler's later Reichstag speech.

207. Hermann Weinkauff *et al.*, *Die deutsche Justiz und der Nationalsozialismus*
(Stuttgart, 1968), pp. 141–50.

208. A committee on reform had been meeting in the justice ministry off and on
since July 1941. See Rothenberger, "Sechzehn Monate Berlin," p. A, 2.

209. Johe, *Gleichgeschaltete Justiz*, pp. 228–29.

210. Rothenberger, "Im Kampf um das Recht," pp. D, 1–2 [*sic*]. This is a somewhat longer autobiographical statement written at different dates. Part A was concluded 6 June 1944; parts B–E on 10 Oct. 1944; and part F on 12 Feb. 1945. A
photocopy of the manuscript is in Forsch. Hbg./PA/12 (Rothenberger). See also
Rothenberger's, "Erklärung," March 1944, *ibid.*

211. Lammers ["Vermerk"], 11 May 1942, *ibid.*

212. The entire speech is reprinted in Domarus, *Hitler*, II, 1865–77.

213. *Ibid.*, II, 1874–75. See also Lammers to highest Reich offices *et al.*, 24 June
1942, BGStA, Rsth. 48/1–7.

The immediate administrative consequence of the judicial crisis of 1942 was a complete reshuffling of the top personnel in the Reich ministry of justice. Schlegelberger was dismissed; Hitler commented, "One look at the man is enough for a lifetime."[214] His replacement was Otto Thierack, a close personal friend of Bormann's judicial advisor, Hans Klemm, a former associate of Heydrich's in tracking down Czech resistance fighters, and, most important, one of the most radical partifiers among the professional German jurists.[215] As he had expected, Rothenberger became state secretary (that is, undersecretary) in charge of reforming the judicial system.[216] To his disappointment, however, he was not the only undersecretary. Bormann obviously distrusted a man whose only real relationship to a major party figure was to the Gauleiter of Hamburg, and insisted that his (and Thierack's) friend Klemm become the second undersecretary in charge of day-to-day administration.[217] Even so, the PK insisted on further direct shackles for the justice ministry. Thierack's mandate to overhaul the German judicial system was severely limited by Hitler's specific directive to him to consult with Bormann and Lammers on all major decisions.[218] Lammers was added only when he protested against the exclusion of the Reich chancellery in dealings between the party and a Reich ministry.[219] In addition, Klemm, who kept his rank and position in the PK, routinely reported all internal matters at the justice department to Bormann. Conferences between Bormann and Klemm took place in private; Rothenberger was not privy to their conversations.[220]

214. Picker, *Tischgespräche*, entry for 29 March 1942, p. 212.

215. Höhne, *Orden*, pp. 370–71; Klopfer's interrogation, 24 March 1947, pp. 22–23, IfZ/ZS 352. For Rothenberger's bitter characterization see "Kampf," pp. D, 2 and D, 11.

216. The incumbent, the notorious Roland Freisler, was kicked upstairs to head the Reich's supreme criminal court, the People's Court.

217. Rothenberger, "Sechzehn Monate Berlin," pp. A, 4–5. See also the interrogation of Klopfer, 14 Nov. 1947, IfZ/ZS 352.

218. A copy of the "Erlass des Führers über besondere Vollmachten für den Reichsminister der Justiz," Aug. 1942, is in Forsch. Hbg./PA/12 (Rothenberger).

219. Rothenberger, "Kampf," p. D, 4.

220. Rothenberger, "Sechzehn Monate Berlin," p. A, 9. This appraisal may be overly unfair to Klemm. According to Klopfer (IfZ/ZS 352) the state secretary often opposed Bormann's efforts to prevent corrupt PLs from being prosecuted.

Bormann's primary interest in judicial affairs was in the areas of criminal prosecution and the training of judicial personnel. In both cases the party wanted substantially increased powers of direct interference and supervision. Bormann specifically demanded that the party's Hoheitsträgers have the right to urge punishment for an accused person even if the prosecutor felt that the evidence did not warrant a trial.[221] In addition, he agreed with Himmler that cases against Polish forced laborers in Germany should be handled by the police rather than the courts.[222] Finally, the PK wanted to be apprised of all criminal investigations of PLs[223]—obviously to prevent the judiciary from sitting in judgment on party matters.[224]

In his demands for judicial interference, Bormann was merely the spokesman for the entire party; Hoheitsträgers at every level of the vertical ladder saw Thierack's and Rothenberger's appointments as a license to impose their will on any and all judicial proceedings.[225] Thierack and Rothenberger agreed, although it was their hope to structure the judicial proceedings and sentences so that the PLs would not feel the need to interfere directly. To this end, Thierack not only consulted the Gauleiters almost obsequiously in making judicial appointments,[226] but attempted to provide what were in effect specific sentencing guidelines for the German criminal judges. At first the justice ministry demanded daily telephone communications on politically sensitive cases,[227] and in the fall, the instructions were regularized through the publication of the *Richterbriefe*, a series of critiques by the ministry on the handling and sentencing of typical cases. In almost every instance, the ministry's

---

221. Rothenberger, "Kampf," p. D, 6; Bormann to Lammers, 4 Oct. 1941, BA/R 43 II/1199b. The Gauleiter of Munich put it even more crassly: if the prosecutor and judges did not perform their "duty," "that's what we've got the Gestapo for." A. Wagner, "Rede . . . ," 22 Oct. 1941, BDC/Wagner (PKC).

222. Martin Broszat, *Nationalsozialistische Polenpolitik 1939–1945* (Stuttgart, 1961), p. 153.

223. *VI*, no. 61 (6 Dec. 1941).

224. Rothenberger, "Sechzehn Monate Berlin," p. A, 8; and "Kampf," p. D, 10.

225. For the reaction of the party as a whole see Weinkauff, *Deutsche Justiz*, p. 147.

226. See Thierack, "Besuch des Gauleiters Grohé-Köln," 10 Dec. 1942, BA/R 22/4062 fol. 1.

227. Johe, *Gleichgeschaltete Justiz*, p. 130.

criticism demanded harsher punishments. Still, Thierack had to hand over additional powers to the police. In September, "at the suggestion of Reichsleiter Bormann," Himmler and Thierack concluded an agreement permitting the police to execute a defendant whenever the party protested a milder punishment handed down by the regular courts. In these cases there was no need "to go through the judicial system again."[228] Bormann only abandoned his Hammurabian principles when they reached the PO. Here mercy was far more in evidence than justice. It is symptomatic that the first instance in which the *Richterbriefe* criticized a sentence for being unduly harsh involved a case against a PL. The matter concerned a local party leader who had forced a woman whose husband was at the front into a illicit affair, on the basis of his power to withhold welfare payments. Although the court could find no mitigating circumstances for the PL's behavior, the ministry of justice did: the judge had failed to take into consideration that the defendant was a "soldier in the party."[229]

In the meantime, Rothenberger's "great judicial reform" was making less headway. His mandate from Hitler was unrestrained enough (on August 21, the Führer had told him, "Your ideas, that's my program"[230]), but Rothenberger's day-to-day relationship to Thierack and Bormann grew increasingly uneasy, and as the German armies became bogged down before Stalingrad, Hitler turned to more pressing concerns. Like Thierack, Rothenberger wanted to create a judiciary that would be relatively free from direct political interference precisely because it had become so attuned to the values and aims of the party that it carried out the party's wishes as a matter of course. Specifically, Rothenberger demanded close supervision of judicial training programs by the party, and thoroughgoing cooperation between the judges and the Hoheitsträgers at the Gau and district levels. In addition, he advocated a large-scale simplification and even deprofessionalization of the judicial system. Tribunals at the local level were to be staffed by lay judges whose

228. A copy of the *Vereinbarung* between Thierack and Himmler, dated 18 Sept. 1942 is in Forsch. Hbg./PA/12 (Rothenberger).

229. *Richterbriefe*, no. 2 (1 Nov. 1942), pp. 9–11.

230. Rothenberger, "Sechzehn Monate Berlin," p. A, 6. See also Picker, *Tischgespräche* (Schramm ed.), entry for 31 May 1942, p. 246.

sentences—under the party's influence—would become "legal judgments of the people." In the appeals system, he stressed a greater reliance on the Führerprinzip; single judges would replace multijudge panels in most cases.[231] Up to this point Rothenberger's reform plans had the party's enthusiastic approval. But Rothenberger's zeal carried him further. Along with the emphasis on people's justice came a stress on decentralized legislative processes; the undersecretary opposed directives drafted in both the PK and the Reich ministries because they "lacked connection with the pulse of life."[232] In addition, even Rothenberger was not willing to abandon either codified laws or competent judicial personnel. Despite his willingness to subordinate the judiciary to the party, for Himmler and Bormann Rothenberger remained "a clear representative of the judiciary."[233] Moreover, the judicial crisis was stirring public passions at a time when the regime wanted nothing to disturb the uneasy equilibrium of public morale. Hans Frank, the notorious governor-general of Poland and Hitler's old defense lawyer, was sufficiently shocked by Hitler's attack on the judiciary to rouse himself to a vigorous defense of the remaining rechtsstaatliche aspects of the German judiciary in a series of speeches at the universities of Berlin, Vienna, Munich, and Heidelberg in June 1942.[234] As a result, Frank had to resign as president of the Academy for German Law[235] (which he had created in 1933), but his protests also brought Hitler to the realization that his attack on the judiciary had stirred considerable controversy.

In the end, Rothenberger's efforts were quietly sabotaged. While the undersecretary set to work in the ministry readying his ideas and planning a special conference to publicize the reforms, Bormann subordinated to the PK the Nazi Lawyers' Guild (to which all German at-

---

231. Rothenberger, "Sechzehn Monate Berlin," p. A, 5; and Thierack, "Besprechung mit Reichsführer SS Himmler am 18.9.1942," Forsch. Hbg./PA/12 (Rothenberger). See also Albrecht Wagner, "Die Umgestaltung der Gerichtsverfassung und des Verfahrens- und Richterrechts im nationalsozialistischen Staat," in Weinkauff, *Deutsche Justiz*, p. 351.

232. Rothenberger, "Kampf," p. A, 5.

233. Brandt to Herff, 19 Dec. 1942, T-175, roll 56, frame 2570768.

234. Frank, *Im Angesicht*, pp. 178 and 418; and Weinkauff, *Deutsche Justiz*, p. 74.

235. Hitler, "Verfügung 11/42," 20 Aug. 1942, *VOBl*, no. 236 (Sept. 1942).

torneys had to belong) and the "judicial policy aspects" of the party's official for judicial affairs.[236] Rothenberger found himself increasingly stymied; at the end of 1943 he was rather unceremoniously dismissed on a charge of plagiarism. The accusation was true enough, but it was hardly the major cause of his fall.[237]

Hitler's dislike of judges and lawyers was undoubtedly exceeded only by his hatred of priests and Jews. In these areas, too, the PK enlarged the scope of the party's participation in planning and execution. In the preparations for the extermination of the Jews, Bormann's liaison official to the propaganda ministry, Tiessler, acted vigorously to put the party's propaganda leaders in the forefront of anti-Jewish measures. As early as July 1941 he proposed that all Jews be enrolled in forced labor battalions, and subsequent correspondence between Bormann, Goebbels, and the Gau propaganda leaders pushed for further measures.[238] Similarly, the PK was almost feverishly at work preparing the postwar attack on the churches; for tactical reasons Hitler still refused to disturb the uneasy peace between the party and the churches during wartime. A special department for church affairs in the PK coordinated the plans,[239] while the Gau staff offices handled "confessional matters" in the provinces.[240] As before, developments in the Warthegau and the actions of particularly fanatic district leaders provided revealing portents of the era to come. The head of the Gau personnel office in the Warthegau forced all PLs to sign an affidavit to the effect that they would not join a church either in the Warthegau or upon their return to the Reich.[241] In Eisenach, the district leader insisted that party members whose children received religious training could not speak at party meetings.[242]

236. PK, "Anordnung 61/42," 26 Aug. 1942, *ibid.*
237. Rothenberger describes the intrigues that led to his dismissal in bitter detail in "Sechzehn Monate Berlin."
238. Walter Tiessler, "Rundschreiben an alle Mitglieder des Reichsrings, Verbindungsmänner und Gauringleiter," (draft), 2 July 1941, T-81, roll 676, frame 5485670, and the document in *ibid.*, frames 5485585 ff.
239. PK, "Rundschreiben, 119/42," 2 Aug. 1942, *VAB*, I, 9–10.
240. PK, "Rundschreiben 197/42," 21 Dec. 1942, *ibid.*, pp. 200–01.
241. Paul Gürtler, *Nationalsozialismus und evangelische Kirchen im Warthegau* (Göttingen, 1958), p. 152.
242. District leader of Eisenach to training and propaganda speakers of the district, 29 July 1942; and "Rundschreiben 2/42," 1 Jan. 1942, MiU/GAC, folder 29.

One of the major aspects of public life over which the party's central office had virtually no effective control was economics. Every Hoheitsträger interfered in the economic life of his area with impunity; PLs tried desperately to prevent wartime shortages from leading to popular reactions against their offices.[243] Bormann was determined to secure the PK's influence in the economic life of the nation, not only to prevent a potentially dangerous trend toward autonomy in the Gaus and districts, but also to check the rise of Hitler's newest golden-haired favorite, the new minister of armaments production, Albert Speer. As always, Bormann's basic goal was to exercise control, but not to accept responsibility.[244] At the national level, the chief of the PK obtained Hitler's approval to assign major segments of long-range planning activities to the PK's office of economic affairs,[245] which since June 1940 had been headed by the ruthless and ambitious Hans Bärmann. Bormann's economic chief had no hesitation in entering the thicket of postwar planning. He announced as early as November 1941 that all of the Russian territories west of the Urals would remain under German control and that Germany would tolerate no industrial enterprises in the East that might compete with facilities in the Reich.[246] Unlike Köhler and perhaps Hess, Bormann and Bärmann had no ambitions to destroy the capitalist structure of the German economy. Their ambitions were restricted to securing the party's political control over economic decisions and, particularly, over executive personnel.[247] Immediately after Bormann became head of the PK, the chief of the office for economic policy organized a series of national conferences for the Gau economic advisors, to coordinate their activities. In addition, the PK published the

243. *VI*, nos. 33 and 65 (8 May and 2 Oct. 1942).

244. See the report by Harms (an official in the economics section of the AO) on a national meeting of the Gau economic advisors, Nov. 1941, RvO/GKzbV (Ni)/1b.

245. Picker, *Tischgespräche* (Schramm ed.), entry for July 1942, pp. 262–63. Bormann immediately sent Hitler's remarks on to Lammers. *Ibid.*, p. 262, n. 1. Hitler's opinion became a directive in PK, "Rundschreiben 124/42," 20 Aug. 1942, *VAB*, I, 21.

246. Karl Maurer, "Bericht über die Tagung der Gauwirtschaftsberater in Berlin am 6. November 1941," 21 Nov. 1941, pp. 3–4, RvO/GKzbV (Ni)/1k.

247. See Wegener-memo, frames 14759–63. The Gau economic advisor of Vienna, Walter Rafelsberger, for example, reported to the PK that one member of the board of directors of the Dresdner Bank was a "politically doubtful individual." See the interrogation of Rafelsberger, 22 Sept. 1950, p. 24, IfZ/ZS 1329 (vertr.).

NS-Wirtschaftspolitik, a monthly journal of economic news, simplistic theoretical articles, and decrees.[248]

There was general agreement that the key PLs in the effort to exercise party control over the economy were the Gau economic advisors.[249] To this end, the office of the Gau economic advisor was upgraded to the status of a major party division (*Hauptamt*) in both the Gaus and the districts. At the same time, to prevent the offices from becoming economically dependent upon contributions by business firms, Schwarz took over the financing of their activities.[250] The culmination of these developments came in May 1942, when the private chambers of commerce were converted into quasi-official Gau economic chambers. Although these were in theory subject to the control of the Reich economics ministry,[251] they were in fact executive organs of the Gau administration. A decree issued jointly by Funk and Bormann in December stated specifically that the Gau economic advisor could "on occasion" use the Gau economic chamber "to carry out his duties."[252] Wegener was more honest; his memorandum described the new chambers simply as "control instruments of the Gauleiter."[253]

The party's victory over Funk was less significant than it might have been a year earlier because the major opponent of partification in the economy by now was not Walther Funk, but Albert Speer. In February, Fritz Todt, the Reich minister of munitions and one of Hitler's oldest associates, was killed in a mysterious plane crash in East Prussia. As his successor, Hitler immediately appointed the thirty-eight-year-old Speer, who until then was known chiefly for his architectural and pyrotechnical achievements (he staged fire and lighting displays at the party congresses). Speer was not, however, an unknown entity in the party. He had for some years headed the offices for technology and technical sciences in the DAF. In addition, he numbered at least two Gauleiters,

248. PK, "Rundschreiben 148/41," 28 Nov. 1941, *VAB*, I, 104–05.
249. See Wegener-memo, frames 14764–65.
250. Maurer, "Bericht . . . Nov. 1941," p. 4; and PK, "Rundschreiben 140/41," 3 Nov. 1941, *VAB*, II, 484.
251. Funk's original directive is embodied in PK, "Rundschreiben 70/42," 27 May 1942, *VAB*, II, 491–97.
252. PK, "Rundschreiben 194/42," 19 Dec. 1942, *ibid.*, p. 498. The "Rundschreiben" embodies a joint directive of Bormann and Funk.
253. Wegener-memo, frame 14764.

Karl Hanke and Stürtz, among his personal friends.[254] Nor was Speer without the most prominent character trait among Nazi leaders: ambition for power aggrandizement.[255] He headed already-established branch offices in Paris, Brussels, Den Haag, Oslo, and Copenhagen and saw himself as the master of all of Europe's industry at the end of the war.[256] Most important of all, Speer had a closer relationship and readier access to Hitler than any Nazi leader except Bormann. With Hitler's unhesitating backing, Speer not only eclipsed Göring, who was his nominal superior, but for two years remained "untouchable." Hitler went so far as to announce that he would sign whatever documents came from Speer's office.[257]

Nevertheless, Speer began his career as industrial management genius with a request for cooperation from the party. Using the typical Nazi propaganda approach of dazzling statistics and vast promises (Speer was his own best public relations officer), he appealed to the Gauleiters at the end of February to become his partners in getting more bullets and tanks out of the German armaments industry.[258] The party had no objections to increased production—so long as it did not interfere with the near peacetime economy in most of the Gaus.[259] Speer, on the other hand, could realize his projections only if the German economy as a whole tightened its belt. To be sure, he appeased the party in a number of ways. He aligned the armaments commissions of his ministry with the Gau boundaries, although the commissions' functions were directly related to those of the army commands.[260] Nevertheless, frictions and clashes were not long in coming. Bormann did not take kindly to Speer's suggestion that he reduce the construction activities at the Obersalzberg, and the Gauleiters refused to permit industrial managers in their Gaus to forward suggestions for increased efficiency to Speer's ministry. Moreover, Speer opposed the partification of either

254. Speer, *Erinnerungen*, pp. 37–38, and 437.
255. Boelcke, *Deutschlands Rüstung*, pp. 19–20.
256. Gregor Janssen, *Das Ministerium Speer* (Berlin, 1968), p. 55.
257. Boelcke, *Deutschlands Rüstung*, entry for 23 June 1942, p. 135; and Speer, *Erinnerungen*, p. 227.
258. Janssen, *Ministerium*, p. 39; and Boelcke, *Deutschlands Rüstung*, entries for 5/6 March and 30 May 1942, pp. 70–71, and 130, respectively.
259. Janssen, *Ministerium*, p. 64.
260. *Ibid.*, p. 52.

his ministry or the management of armaments production. Instead he surrounded himself with men who were ambitious and essentially amoral, but not necessarily fanatical Nazis. In general, he regarded his associates' technical ability as far more important than their party records.[261] The system of coordinating the manufacture of munitions lay in the hands of the industrialists themselves, and Speer attempted as best he could to protect the system from direct party interference. No wonder the party quickly became his "most difficult arena."[262]

The gladiatorial combat became even more difficult when the party found a champion of its own in the new general plenipotentiary for labor allocation (*Generalbevollmächtigter für den Arbeitseinsatz*, GBA), Fritz Sauckel. The office of the GBA was yet another attempt in the Third Reich to cut through the intertwining and overlapping layers of jurisdictional competencies by creating a new central office with vast powers to coordinate a major area of the civilian war effort.[263] Bormann had suggested the appointment of a GBA as early as October 1941, but at that time Lammers had been singularly unenthusiastic. He suggested instead increasing the powers of the Reich labor minister, but now Bormann dragged his feet. This solution would give additional authority either to the present minister, Franz Seldte, a weak man who had never prevailed against any force in the Third Reich, or to Robert Ley, who had been clamoring for Seldte's job since 1939.[264] With Speer's coordination of the armaments manufacture, the need for a centralized allocation of labor resources became increasingly acute. Speer suggested his friend Hanke for the post, but Bormann persuaded Hitler that this might represent too great a concentration of power in the hands of one man.[265] Instead, he came forward with the name of Fritz Sauckel, an ex-sailor and since 1927 Gauleiter of Thuringia. Sauckel had never occupied an administrative post outside the party, so that his entire social

261. *Ibid.*, p. 55; and Boelcke, *Deutschlands Rüstung*, entry for 16 March 1942, p. 72.

262. Speer, *Erinnerungen*, pp. 218, 226, and 230.

263. The GBA was one of a series of "Reich commissioners." In May 1942 Gauleiter Kaufmann became Reich commissioner for ocean shipping.

264. Edward L. Homze, *Foreign Labor in Nazi Germany* (Princeton, N.J., 1967), pp. 103–06; and Boelcke, *Deutschlands Rüstung*, entry for 19 March 1942, p. 77.

265. Speer, *Erinnerungen*, p. 233.

and professional frame of reference came from his peers among the Gauleiters. Bormann regarded him as an effective counterweight to Speer. He was right. Since Sauckel shared the Gauleiters' concern for avoiding unpopular measures, he was determined to prevent the mobilization of labor reserves in Germany as long as possible, relying instead on transporting large numbers of slave laborers from the occupied areas to the Reich. Indeed, Sauckel assured the Gauleiters' control over manpower allocation in their areas by appointing them as the provincial representatives of his office with full powers over labor deployment in the Gaus.[266] Speer preferred to rely to a greater extent on German labor supplemented by voluntary or at least semivoluntary foreign workers, but Hitler, always mindful of the specter of 1918, accepted Sauckel's proposals.[267]

The PK's campaign of partification in 1942 also encompassed the armed forces. Relationships between the "two pillars" of the Reich continued to be strained. The Wehrmacht used Hess's flight to create ill-feeling among the officer corps against the party ("Hitler, yes; the party, no"),[268] and the NSDAP blamed the army for the defeat in the battle of Moscow.[269] The Keitel-Rosenberg agreement was a good beginning, but it had not led to a full-scale political indoctrination program in the armed forces.[270] Behind a facade of pious admonitions to cooperate in a comradely spirit, the two major power components of the Third Reich viewed each other with ill-disguised suspicion. The PK laid the groundwork for a new contractual relationship at the beginning of the year. First the PK's representative at the OKW was assured of participation "in all matters that touch upon concerns of the party or that have an ideological character."[271] Some months later, Bormann became the second civilian (Speer was the first) to sit in on the

266. GBA, "Anordnung 1 des Generalbevollmächtigten . . . ," 6 April 1942, *VI*, no. 53 (29 July 1942). This issue of the *VI* contains a collection of Sauckel's directives issued by that time. See also Homze, *Foreign Labor in Nazi Germany*, pp. 115–16.

267. Janssen, *Ministerium*, pp. 77 and 80; and Boelcke, *Deutschlands Rüstung*, entry for 10/11/12 Aug. 1942, p. 171.

268. Picker, *Tischgespräche* (Schramm ed.), p. 132.

269. Boelcke, *Wollt Ihr*, p. 205; and Volker R. Berghahn, "NSDAP und 'geistige Führung' der Wehrmacht 1939–1943," *Vjh.f.Z.*, XVII (Jan. 1969), 68.

270. Wegener-memo, frames 14711–16.

271. PK, "Rundschreiben 22/42," 16 Feb. 1942, *VAB*, III, 261.

military staff conferences at Hitler's headquarters.[272] In June, Bormann succeeded in supplanting the Rosenberg-Keitel agreement with a new treaty in which the OKW recognized the PK's exclusive right to speak and negotiate for the party.[273]

Although the PK used this blanket treaty to issue directives relating to every conceivable aspect of relations between the party and the armed forces,[274] Bormann was particularly concerned with the occupational categories exempt from the draft and the army's political indoctrination program. The army had already acknowledged, presumably somewhat tongue in cheek, the party's low percentage of draft exemptions,[275] but Bormann had wider ambitions for the PLs. Basically, the PK wanted PLs who were eligible for service to spend six months in the army and then return to their posts laden with medals awarded for distinguished service at the front.[276] There was obviously an element of having one's cake and eating it too, but the PK was determined to exhibit decorated PLs. A new potential threat to the party's draft-exempt status came at the end of 1942, but Bormann managed to turn this into yet another opportunity for power aggrandizement. Hitler appointed General Walter von Unruh to head a commission empowered to survey all civilian manpower resources (including the party) and comb out whatever excess, draft-age manpower was available for service in the armed forces.[277] The PK's representative on the Unruh commission was Otto Ifland, an StdF staffer since 1938. His job was twofold: he obviously strove to keep as many PLs as possible out of Unruh's clutches; and at the same time, he made it clear that the party with its "comprehensive knowledge of the people and principles of leadership" would

272. Speer, *Erinnerungen*, p. 551, n. 7.

273. PK, "Bekanntgabe 9/42," 18 June 1942, *VOBl*, no. 234 (July 1942).

274. Pp. 257–738 of the *VAB*'s third volume is concerned with party-military matters.

275. See *VI*, nos. 60, 62, and 64 (3, 10, and 17 Dec. 1942); and the OKW analysis of the party draft exemptees, 12 June 1942, quoted in *VAB*, III, 266.

276. The various decrees are in *VAB*, III, 335 and 337–38.

277. The whole enterprise lent itself to puns. The word *Unruh* itself means "disturbance" in German, but the more colloquial name for the action was *Heldenklau* ("robbing heroes") a play on Goebbels' campaign against *Kohlenklau* ("robbing coal") designed to prevent the wasteful use of fuel.

determine which civilians were expendable on the basis of their political attitudes.[278]

As yet, the party was unable to establish a full-scale political commissar system in the army, but throughout 1942 the PK was laying the groundwork for its introduction. After the battle of Moscow, Hitler became an increasingly enthusiastic supporter of the project. The war was now a war of ideologies, and the task of a chief of staff was not so much to plan strategy ("anybody can do that") as to "educate the army in the spirit of National Socialism."[279] Rosenberg had been put off with the promise that at the end of the war the entire military indoctrination program would be turned over to the party,[280] but Bormann was more concerned with the wartime situation. For the moment, the PK reactivated the so-called service among comrades (Kameradschaftsdienst). This program of legalized snooping by the district leaders had been established in 1940, but the army had succeeded in ignoring it for the last two years. Bormann forcefully resurrected the plan and reminded both the army and the party that any soldier had the right to complain to his district leader, while the Hoheitsträgers, too, would communicate directly with their home town boys at the front.[281]

Much of what was still a groping trend toward full-scale partification in the Altreich became bitter reality in the occupied areas in the course of 1941 and 1942. Despite the setbacks before Moscow, the year 1942 marked both the greatest territorial extent of the Nazi empire in Europe and the development of the most detailed plans for its long-term future. Various and opposing schemes mushroomed: for the colonization of the East, for the establishment of a "Germanic empire" in the West and North, for the virtual absorption of Holland into the Reich,

278. PK, "Rundschreiben 189/42," 12 Dec. 1942, T-580, roll 873, box 799b, folder 2.

279. Domarus, *Hitler*, II, 1813; and Manfred Messerschmidt, *Die Wehrmacht im NS-Staat* (Hamburg, 1969), p. 326.

280. Office of RL Rosenberg, "Niederschrift über die Sitzung der Mitglieder der Reichsarbeitsgemeinschaft für die Schulung der gesamten Bewegung am 20. Juli 1942 . . . ," T-580, roll 842, box 267, folder 348.

281. *VI*, no. 63 (13 Dec. 1941); and "V.I. 499/42," 25 June 1942, *VAB*, I, 68–69. See also *VOBl Gau Franken*, no. 1 (15 Jan. 1942). See also Berghahn, Geistige Führung," p. 68.

and so on. Hitler continued to be vague about his ideas for Europe's future except that he left no doubt about either Germany's later control of the entire continent or the party's prominent role in the administration of the empire. The Nazi leader expressed boundless confidence in the PLs; whatever difficulty might arise, "the men of the party will take care of it."[282] As far as Bormann was concerned, this meant an expansion of the powers of the Arbeitsbereichs.[283] After the establishment of the Arbeitsbereich East for the occupied Russian territories, Hitler granted the PK virtually unlimited political control over the party's administration outside the Reich's boundaries. A decree of August enjoined the Arbeitsbereichs from making any major decision, "particularly in the area of deployment and personnel policy," without consulting the head of the PK. Only Schwarz retained his powers of financial control, much as he had been exempted from Hess's sweeping mandate in 1934.[284]

In addition to keeping watch over the German civil servants stationed in the occupied areas, the Arbeitsbereichs after Bormann's takeover of the PK served as testing grounds for experimental policies and personnel appointments. The PK was particularly eager to use deployment outside the Reich as an integral part of its in-service training program. A persistent pattern emerged as district leaders and district and Gau staff officials were transferred from their Reich positions to one of the Arbeitsbereichs, there to gain experience in administering large amounts of power and new programs, before being sent back to the Altreich. (Their home posts were filled only by acting appointees.)[285] Similarly, the social control aims of the PK were clearly foreshadowed in such matters as the administration of the Winter Help welfare fund

282. Picker, _Tischgespräche_, entry for 1 Aug. 1941, p. 195; and Picker, _Tischgespräche_ (Schramm ed.), entry for 8–10 Nov. 1941, p. 45.

283. The PK's various basic directives relating to the Arbeitsbereichs are reprinted in _VAB_, III, 197–201.

284. Hitler, "Verfügung 8/42," 18 Aug. 1942, _RVBl_ (A), no. 34 (18 Aug. 1942). Schwarz used this directive to prevent the affiliates in the occupied areas from attaining a position of autonomy comparable to the one they had enjoyed in the Altreich. See Lingg to a judge on the OPG's special tribunal, ca. Nov. 1942, IfZ/Fb. 50.

285. _VI_, no. 27 (11 April 1942). The general aim of Bormann's personnel policies became particularly clear in the Netherlands. See esp. RvO/Arb. NSDAP (Ni)/56 D.

and the organization of the staff office in the Arbeitsbereich General-gouvernement.[286]

Indeed, the Arbeitsbereich Generalgouvernement, the oldest of these party institutions, provided some of the most glaring examples of the political bankruptcy inherent in the Nazi Party's rule in the occupied areas. The transition from the StdF's office to the PK was smooth enough,[287] but this in no way lessened the continuing failures of the Arbeitsbereich. In 1942, the occupied areas of Poland were rapidly approaching a state of administrative chaos, and the party's organization contributed significantly to the situation. To be sure, much of the problem could be laid at the doorstep of Hans Frank, and virtually all German officials pressed for his instant dismissal,[288] but since Hitler refused to budge, Frank continued to reside in his castle at Cracow. In addition, his resignation would not have solved the largely self-generated problems of the Arbeitsbereich. For one thing, the Arbeitsbereich's personnel consisted of a superabundance of chiefs with very few subordinates. By this time, there were almost three hundred and fifty full-time PLs in the government-general, and since the number of Reich Germans living there was not large, the Betreuung tasks of the party were simple: the PLs essentially took care of each other. These activities took very little time, and being activists at heart, the functionaries then busied themselves with demonstrations of their status as members of the master race.[289] Ironically, the Arbeitsbereich even had financial difficulties. Approximately 90 percent of the operating expenses were provided by Frank's office, since Schwarz refused to allocate Reich party funds for

---

286. Max Freiherr du Prel, ed., *Das Generalgouvernement*, 2d ed. (Würzburg, 1942), p. 387; and Arbeitsbereich GG, *Anordnungen zur Durchführung des WHW* ([Cracow], 1941), pp. 8–9.

287. In June 1941 Schalk became "representative of the NSDAP to the governor-general." See PK, "Bekanntgabe 22/41," 23 June 1941, *VOBl*, no. 222 (July 1941).

288. Hoffmann (PK) to Friedrichs, 20 Aug. 1942, T-580, roll 80, folder 369; and Berger to Himmler, 21 Oct. 1942, RvO/BDC/H 137. Frank, of course, was not idle; he sponsored an SA unit in the GG to counteract the SS's influence. See Bormann to Wolff (Himmler's office), 11 May 1942, T-175, roll 125, frame 2650371.

289. [Lammers], "Betrifft: Generalgouvernement [note on the visit of Frank's deputy, Bühler, to the Reich chancellry]," 20 March 1943, IfZ/Fb. 50. See also "Merkblatt für die Deutschen im Osten," ca. April 1942, apparently issued by the Polish underground and seized by the SD, T-175, roll 275, frames 2772134–35.

this purpose. Insofar as the government-general, the PK, and Schwarz were bitter enemies, this meant the party in Poland was financially dependent upon its major political adversary.[290] As a result, the Arbeitsbereich's officials in most cases had to do precisely what Bormann strove to avoid in the Altreich, that is, serve as responsible state administrators in addition to being PLs, rather than act merely as control agents and political decision-makers.[291]

Under Nazi plans, the government-general was but a forecourt to the unlimited estates that remained to be acquired in the Russian vastness. The conquest and administration of occupied Russia was to be the single most significant item in the party's revolutionary restructuring of Europe; victory in the West might have been accomplished by the army, but winning in Russia was an ideological achievement impossible without the NSDAP.[292] In theory, policies in the East were the responsibility of Alfred Rosenberg and his ministry for occupied Eastern territories (*Reichsministerium für die besetzten Ostgebiete*, RMO), and in the early months of the campaign the German advance seemed to be accompanied by both political and military success. Collaboration among the Baltic and Ukrainian peoples was at first widespread, and only the reality of the German administration turned collaboration into active and passive resistance. By the time the Arbeitsbereich East was established in April 1942, German rule in Russia was not only recognized as naked oppression, but was substantially endangered by widespread partisan movements.[293]

The Third Reich's rule had also become racked by sharp internal dissensions over basic policy in the regime itself. Like most of Rosenberg's projects, his Eastern policy was grandiose on paper,[294] but weak in both

290. Hoffmann to Friedrichs, 20 Aug. 1942, T-580, roll 80, folder 369; and Rschm., "Aktenvermerk . . . ," 13 March 1942, IfZ/Fb. 50.

291. Odilo Globocnik, "Die Partei im Generalgouvernement," 10 Dec. 1942, IfZ/Fb. 50; and Hoffmann to Friedrichs, 16 Aug. 1942, T-580, roll 79, folder 368.

292. [Joseph Goebbels], "Reichsminister Dr. Goebbels auf der Gauleitertagung am 3. August 1944 in Posen," p. 16, IfZ/276/52/ED 8.

293. Alexander Dallin, *German Rule in Russia, 1941–1945* (New York, 1957), pp. 59–61.

294. For the scope and detail of the Nazi plans at the beginning of the campaign see esp. Rosenberg to Lohse, 21 July 1941, CDJC/CXLV–509; and the letter of an

personnel and administration. Rosenberg's deputy, Gauleiter Alfred Meyer, was a singularly unfortunate choice. Meyer was a weak Gauleiter, who had never excelled at anything, and his only accomplishment in the ministry for occupied Eastern territories was to make an archenemy of Gottlob Berger, the head of the SS's administrative office.[295] Other appointments in the ministry were no more promising. As a group, Rosenberg's associates were "transferred civil servants of the third seeding and more or less unemployed SA leaders and Eastern experts."[296] Part of the difficulty, of course, was that there were simply not enough German officials available, but Rosenberg did his best to aggravate the situation. Although the Reich ministry of the interior offered him some trained personnel, he rejected most of these officials on the grounds that ideological attitude was more important than technical ability. As a result, he was forced to rely on the categories noted above as well as on the dubious products of Ley's Ordensburgen.[297] Needless to say, once it became known that relatively unqualified but politically reliable types would be accepted for service in the East, the various ministries in Germany resolutely dispatched to the RMO both officials who were politically suspect and those who were simply too incompetent to be tolerated further in a well-run bureaucratic establishment.[298] The personnel selected for the East were, as Hitler had intended, fully conscious of their self-proclaimed Herrenmenschen status, and they acted

---

official in the RMO to GL Meyer, 20 Oct. 1941, CDJC/CCXXXII–1. The latter document was already envisioning the "greater Germanic settlement . . . Naugard (Novgorod)." See also Dallin, *German Rule in Russia*, pp. 90 ff.

295. For the appointments of Rosenberg and Meyer see Domarus, *Hitler*, II, 1782; and Dallin, *German Rule in Russia*, p. 86. For Rosenberg's view of Meyer see *Letzte*, pp. 145–46.

296. Helmut Heiber, ed., "Der Generalplan Ost," *Vjh.f.Z.*, VI (July 1958), 286; Dallin, *German Rule in Russia*, pp. 102–03.

297. Otto Bräutigam, *Überblick über die besetzten Ostgebiete während des 2. Weltkrieges* (Tübingen, 1954), p. 25. The territorial commissar of Slonim (Belorussia) thought the *Ordensjunker* were particularly suitable as chiefs of staff. See "Lagebericht," 25 Jan. 1942, CDJC/CXLVa/8. Hoffmann, on the other hand, reported that Ley's products were completely useless as Eastern administrators and should be sent to the army. Hoffmann to Bormann, 22 May 1942, T-580, roll 80, folder 369.

298. See RK Crimea (Schickedanz, one of Rosenberg's long-time associates), "Lagebericht . . . ," 28 Dec. 1942, CDJC/CXLVIIa/17.

in a manner that could only engender hatred among their subject peoples.[299]

Rosenberg's own muddled thinking and political impotence was complemented by Hitler's confused thoughts on the future of the East. The Führer (as well as everybody else in the regime) left no doubt that he wanted Russia exploited for the benefit of the Reich, but he was not very clear on the most effective means of accomplishing this goal. He wanted private enterprise to hold sway in Russia, rather than state-run monopoly organizations; but at the same time the Germans refused to consider breaking up the collective farms, and continued to run them as state enterprises. As always, indecision at the top resulted in additional powers for the men in the field and the entrenched interests in the Altreich. By the end of 1942, the Nazi administration was both cruel and chaotic. When Hitler did eventually decide on a tentative and limited division of the *kolkhozes* (collective farms), the decision was passively sabotaged by the Reich agricultural ministry and the German commissioners in the Ukraine and the Baltic areas.[300] At the same time, the guidelines set down by the commissioners were ignored by virtually every economic organization operating in the East, since each one claimed to be subordinate only to some ministerial office in Berlin or to an industrial enterprise elsewhere in the Altreich and therefore refused to be subject to the political directives of a particular viceroy.[301]

For the NSDAP, the most important decisions in the East were personnel appointments, particularly (now that the ministerial posts had

229. One of the more insightful PLs in the East described both the master race attitude and the level of competence of most officials. As for his own appointment: "One fine day our Gauleiter [Kube] called up: 'I've become commissioner-general for Belorussia; can you manage propaganda . . . ?' I answered immediately, 'Sure I can, but where is Belorussia?' " During the three-week training session "we were told . . . 'you are the master race.' . . . None of us should carry so much as a manila folder by ourselves." See Schröter's remarks in "Protokoll über die Tagung der Gebietskommissare, Hauptabteilungsleiter und Abteilungsleiter des Generalkommissars in Minsk vom 8. April bis 10. April 1943," pp. 38 and 127, IfZ/Fb. 85.

300. Picker, *Tischgespräche* (Schramm ed.), entry for 25 March 1942, p. 208; Boelcke, *Deutschlands Rüstung*, entry for 23 June 1942, p. 135; and Dallin, *German Rule in Russia*, pp. 192 and 331–33.

301. See RKO, "Lagebericht zum 15. Nov. 1942," 29 Nov. 1942; and "Lagebericht Generalkommissar für die Krim—28. Dez. 1942," CDJC/CXLVIIa/3 and 17, respectively. For a "simplified" chart on the administration of the German economy in the East, see Dallin, *German Rule in Russia*, p. 318.

been filled) those of the Reich commissioners (Reichskommissare, RK) and, below them, the commissioners-general (*Generalkommissare*). Under the weak control of Alfred Rosenberg, these promised to become powerful positions with virtually independent administrative powers over areas many times the size of an Altreich Gau. It was obviously of crucial importance whether these men identified with the PO, the SS, the army, or the state. There was actually little danger of an identification with the state or the army, since Hitler named only long-term PLs as Reich commissioners. The coveted RK appointments went to men with widely differing backgrounds in the party; the only thing common to all was a lack of experience and competence in dealing with Eastern affairs. Two of those selected were Gauleiters: Koch of East Prussia and Lohse of Schleswig-Holstein.[302] The first was already a byword for cruelty, corruption, and arrogance; the second had never dealt with anything east of the Elbe. Ex-Gauleiters Kube and Alfred Eduard Frauenfeld represented the category of "rehabs," "old fighters" who had fallen from grace, and who were now given a second chance. Kube was designated commissioner-general for Belorussia, and Frauenfeld would be lord of the Crimea.[303] Kube had been dismissed as Gauleiter of Kurmark (now Brandenburg) in 1936 when he accused Buch's wife of Jewish ancestry, and Frauenfeld had run afoul of the Austrian party intrigues. Understandably, their reemergence did not meet with universal acclaim. Himmler noted that if there had been enough other suitable candidates, one surely would not have had to send Kube.[304] Finally, there were the misfits. This was a grab-bag category of deputy Gauleiters who could not work with their present Gauleiters and "cleansed" SA officials for whom no suitable positions were available in the Altreich. Prominent among this group were the deputy Gauleiters of Bayreuth

302. Rosenberg had proposed Sauckel, though he had no better qualifications. See Rosenberg, *Letzte*, p. 167; and Otto Bräutigam, *So hat es sich zugetragen* (Würzburg, 1968), pp. 340–41. Bräutigam served in the political section of the RMO.

303. For a revealing discussion of personnel appointments, with the various power groups pushing their men, see Bormann, "Aktenvermerk," 16 July 1941, *IMT*/doc. 221-L. The officials present were Hitler, Rosenberg, Lammers, Keitel, Göring, and Bormann.

304. Brandt to Schmidt-Rohr (official in the SS's *Ahnenerbe* office) (draft), May 1944, T-175, roll 117, frame 2642264. See also Dallin, *German Rule in Russia*, p. 204.

and Hamburg, Ludwig Ruckdeschel and Harry Henningsen,[305] and Siegfried Kasche, a long-term SA leader who was now ambassador to the puppet state of Croatia.[306]

Since Hitler was convinced that only the party possessed the proper administrative attitude toward the Soviet Union, he replaced the military administration in the Baltic provinces and the Ukraine as quickly as possible. At the beginning of September, Koch established his headquarters as RKU (Reichskommissar Ukraine) at Rowno, and Lohse moved into Reval as RKO (Reichskommissar Ostland).[307] Throughout his reign Erich Koch administered the Ukraine pretty much as an adjunct to his home Gau of East Prussia, without much regard to Alfred Rosenberg, his nominal superior. He was seldom in Rowno, but spent most of his time in Königsberg. The personnel in the commissioner's office was drawn almost entirely from the Gau East Prussia. Rosenberg complained bitterly about his unruly subordinate, who felt himself shackled by directives from the RMO,[308] but Hitler and Bormann approved of Koch's simplistic and extremely repressive policies.[309] Lohse was an entirely different case. A rather phlegmatic bank employee whose only distinction was winning Schleswig-Holstein for Nazism, the Gauleiter moved his headquarters to Reval, and administered his own Gau as an afterthought to what he obviously felt was a more important post in the Baltic.[310] His relationship to Koch was uneasy, but he shared with the RKU a dislike of the centralized authority in Rosenberg's min-

305. Ruckdeschel was selected as RK of Tula, but the German armies were never able to capture his kingdom for him. See Ruckdeschel to Himmler, 1 Nov. 1941, BDC/Ruckdeschel (SS). Henningsen was appointed to handle relations between the GL, the RMO, and the forced labor battalions working in Germany. See Bräutigam, *Zugetragen*, p. 593. He died in 1944 and was buried with high honors in Hamburg. See Forsch. Hbg./PA/12/H.

306. Kasche was intended as Reichskommissar in Moscow. Dallin, *German Rule in Russia*, p. 296.

307. *Ibid.*, p. 85.

308. Bräutigam, *Zugetragen*, p. 369; Hoffmann to Bormann, 5 June 1942, T-580, roll 80, folder 368.

309. Bormann, "[Besprechungsprotokoll] Streitfall Koch-Rosenberg, 19.5.1943 . . . ," n.d., T-175, roll 275, frames 2772035–43. For Koch's basic attitudes see "Vermerk über die Tagung in Rowno vom 26.–28.8.1942," n.d., CDJC/CXLIV/475.

310. Dallin, *German Rule in Russia*, p. 186; Bräutigam, *Zugetragen*, p. 369.

istry and a penchant for staffing his own office with officials from his
Gau clique in Schleswig-Holstein.[311]

In view of Hitler's preference for party rule in the East, the power
position obtained by the various groups in Russia might well become
decisive levers for achieving their overall power goals in the Reich
itself. As a result, virtually every interest group in the NSDAP attempted
to secure a foothold in the German administration of Russia. Even the
SA rallied itself and proposed something called the "development service East" (*Aufbaudienst Osten*), which turned out to be a euphemism
for the SA's control of the East.[312] The plan was laughable in view of
the combined opposition by the SS,[313] the PK, and the RMO, but it did
indicate the SA's recognition that the road to a political comeback in
Berlin might well pass through Reval and Rowno. The PK drew the
same conclusion as the SA, but its success in implementation was considerably greater. In Bormann's view, the administration of the conquered East was primarily the responsibility of the PO, and he insisted
that there, as in the Altreich, basic policy decisions and all major personnel appointments should be handled by the PK.[314] Bormann exercised his authority, in addition to his direct influence on Hitler's own
personnel appointments and policy decisions, through his roving ambassador in Russia, Albert Hoffmann, and the Arbeitsbereich East. Hoffmann traveled extensively in the German occupied areas in May 1942,
stressing the need for a master-race mentality among the PLs. This was
an integral part of the radical plan of exploitation favored by Bormann,
Koch, Himmler, and, most important, Hitler. The plan had as its goal
the total subjugation of all of the Eastern peoples to the level of helots,
while a small but fanaticized group of party and SS administrators imposed a permanent reign of terror. Hoffmann's lengthy reports point up
the plan's political barrenness. He had a sharp eye out for administra-

---

311. Bräutigam, *Zugetragen*, p. 346.

312. An internal Osaf, "Denkschrift," p. 19, 26 Sept. 1942, noted that the "purpose of the *Aufbaudienst* is . . . comparable to that exercised by the party in the
Reich." See BA/NS 19/1713.

313. For the SS's reaction see Berger to Himmler, 21 Nov. 1942, *ibid*; and Himmler to Lammers, 30 Nov. 1942, in Heiber, *Reichsführer*, p. 169.

314. Friedrich Buchardt, "Die Behandlung des russischen Problems," quoted
in Dallin, *German Rule in Russia*, p. 36.

tive inefficiency, but was absolutely blind to the political consequences of the exploitation, terror, and arrogance he emphasized as desirable traits of German rule in Russia.[315]

The Arbeitsbereich East was the PK's institutional representative in the Soviet Union. It was created on April 1, 1942,[316] "to control politically all Germans in the Eastern territories."[317] Rosenberg functioned as the Arbeitsbereich's nominal head, but day-to-day operations rested with a chief of staff responsible to the PK.[318] As in the Gaus (with which the PK increasingly equated the Arbeitsbereichs[319]), the functional concerns of the party's administration were concentrated in a series of horizontal bureaus within the chief of staff's office, while the vertical administration paralleled the civil administration in the East. All of the territorial chiefs down to the county level were in Personalunion civil commissioners, and also exercised the rights of party Hoheitsträgers.[320] The Arbeitsbereich had ambitions to determine the "ability to serve in the East" (*Ostfähigkeit*) of all Reich German officials,[321] although in practice it never got beyond establishing an organizational scheme on paper. After the Arbeitsbereich's formal establishment in April, no concrete steps to implement Hitler's decree came before September, and as late as October nothing had been done to create offices in the counties.[322] Since the German hold on the East became increasingly tenuous after January 1943, it is obvious that the Arbeitsbereich never achieved any significance as a major control organ. A year after

315. His reports and correspondence are in T-580, roll 80, folder 369. Cf. Schröter's comment that such methods produced the very antithesis of effective propaganda, "Protokoll . . . Minsk . . . 1943," p. 128.

316. Hitler, "Verfügung 3/42," 1 April 1942, *RVBl* (A), no. 14 (7 April 1942).

317. Walter Labs, "Die Verwaltung der besetzten Ostgebiete," *Reich, Volksordnung, Lebensraum,* V (1943), 164.

318. PK, "Bekanntgabe 14/42," 16 Sept. 1942, *RVBl* (A), no. 39 (16 Sept. 1942), p. 117.

319. A. E. Cohen, "Ontstaan en betekenis van 'Der Arbeitsbereich der NSDAP in den Niederlanden,' " p. 8, RvO/Notities, no. 26.

320. Labs, "Verwaltung," pp. 165–66.

321. *Ibid.*; and *IMT*, doc. nos. NG-2720 and NO-5394. Willingness to fraternize with the Russians, particularly sexual relations with Russian women, definitely constituted *Ostunfähigkeit*.

322. GbK. Pernau, "Lagebericht . . . 10. August–10. Oktober, 1942," n.d., CDJC/CXLVII b/13.

its establishment, the ten Ordensburg graduates assigned to the propaganda office in Belorussia had been drafted by the army.[323]

The Red Army was the major factor curtailing the institutional career of the Arbeitsbereich Osten, but the emerging struggle between the PO and the SS certainly helped to delay the birth of Bormann's organizational claim in the East. As noted before, relations between Bormann and Himmler were still quite cordial in 1941, but toward the middle of 1942 Himmler, almost in spite of himself, realized that the PK's chief had ambitions to subordinate the SS along with all the other party components. As late as May 1942, the PK and SS celebrated a joint victory: the de facto dismissal of Walther Darré as Reich minister of agriculture. Darré had long ago fallen out of favor with Himmler, but he retained a tenuous hold on his office through the protection of Hess, who apparently shared Darré's enthusiasm for macrobiotic foods.[324] After Hess's departure, Darré's retirement was only a matter of time.[325] His successor was Herbert Backe, Darré's long-time deputy and erstwhile protégé, who had also inherited his chief's favorable position with Himmler and the SS. Himmler obviously expected that through Backe the SS would retain its strong position in the ministry and the party's office for agricultural affairs. But Backe allied himself with Bormann and the PK. In return for Bormann's willingness to let him occupy the ministerial and the party's agricultural office, Backe agreed to transfer the agricultural office from the SS's influence to that of the PK.[326] As the new minister noted in one of his first major addresses after he became head of the agricultural sector, "It is obvious that agricultural policy in Germany is a function of the NSDAP." In practice, the agricultural office transferred decision-making power from

323. "Protokoll . . . Minsk . . . 1943." p. 128.

324. Darré to Hitler, 7 July 1941, T-580, roll 244, folder 30.

325. According to Darré Göring simply told him in May 1942 that he, Darré, "stood in the way" of Backe and suggested the minister of agriculture take a leave of absence for medical reasons (interrogation of Darré, p. 26, IfZ/ZS 863). Bormann and Darré had been feuding since March 1941. See Darré to Hitler, 26 June 1941; Bormann to Darré, 28 June 1941, BDC/Darré (PKC); and Backe to Darré, 27 June 1941, BDC/Backe (SS).

326. Interrogation of Backe, p. 11, IfZ/ZS 995; Hitler, "Verfügung," 24 Aug. 1942, *RVBl* (A), no. 37 (3 Sept. 1942), p. 109; and *VI*, no. 61 (11 Sept. 1942). See also the interrogation of Darré, IfZ/ZS 863.

the SS-dominated Reich nutritional estate[327] to the party's office for agricultural policy, headed by Backe, who was subject to control by Bormann as chief of the PK.[328]

The Backe coup was not an isolated incident, but part of a systematic effort by the PK to deprive the paramilitary groups in the party, most notably the SS, of their influence over party units that exercised power in the field of social control. At the beginning of the year, the PK had gained control of the ideological training programs for nurses and midwives,[329] and the PK's dynamic new image of the PO was beginning to permeate the lower ranks of the PLs. Symptomatic of this attitude is the self-appraisal of a district leader who claimed that his work was "a great deal more important than the present-day functions of the SA . . . and the other paramilitary groups."[330] Although in 1942 the cooperation between the SS and the PK was still quite good in many areas, Bormann left no doubt that he wanted both a clear separation of the PO and the paramilitary organizations and a recognition of the PO's superior position in the relationship.[331]

The SS was not disposed to suffer the political fate of the SA and fought back. The weapons used in the struggle varied, but the occupied Eastern territories, which in this case encompassed everything east of Danzig, became a major arena of combat. It was not a struggle over policy—Himmler and Bormann agreed strongly on radical measures in the East—but a struggle over power. The SS did its best to paralyze the party's position by pitting the HSSPF's against the Hoheitsträgers. In the Altreich, the Hoheitsträgers were the political superiors of all party units, including SS leaders, but in the East Himmler had secured a much more independent position for his representatives. He

327. Significantly, Wegener wanted the Reich nutritional estate dissolved altogether. See Wegener-memo, frame 14721.

328. Backe's views on his role were expressed in a speech in Hanover, 27 June 1942. Excerpts from the speech were reprinted in the *NS-Landpost*, 3 July 1942, and Himmler had clippings placed in the Backe SS personnel file. BDC/Backe (SS).

329. PK, "Anordnung 1/42 [and] 2/42," 3 Jan. 1942, *VAB*, I, 487–88. Wegener insisted that all kindergartens must be party-controlled. See Wegener-memo, frames 14669–70.

330. District leader Eisenach to Gau staff office Thuringia, 30 July 1942, MiU/GAC, folder 14.

331. Hitler, "Verfügung 18/42," 3 Nov. 1942, *RVBl* (A), no. 44 (4 Nov. 1942); and *VOBl Gau Baden*, no. 8 (1 Nov. 1941).

argued that since the Reich leader of the SS was in charge of Germanization and security affairs in the East, the HSSPFs were independent of the Hoheitsträgers in all matters involving racial policies and the maintenance of law and order.[332] A specific example may illustrate the organizational chaos that resulted: The territorial commissioner for Nikolaiev, an area within the Ostland, was in Personalunion civil administrator and party Hoheitsträger. In his former role, he would normally have been in charge of the police, and in his latter role, the political superior of the SS. In Nikolaiev neither was true. The regular police was subject to the dual control of the HSSPF and of the commander of the regular police, Kurt Daluege. Both recognized Himmler as their direct superior. All other police units were under the sole control of the HSSPF.[333] In addition, there was the problem of Himmler's capacity as RKFDV. As his representative in the field, the HSSPF responsible for Nikolaiev could utilize the party's office for racial affairs to execute his directives. This then led either to the paradox that the territorial office for racial affairs might well order a police action without notification of, much less approval by, the party's Hoheitsträger and main civil administrator, or that the Hoheitsträger might accept appointment as Himmler's RKFDV representative and thus become the SS's direct subordinate. Some of the party leaders in the East attempted to escape the stranglehold of the SS by refusing appointment as Himmler's RFKDV representative, but that, too, was not always possible. Lohse, for example, was reluctant to become the RKFDV's representative in the Ostland, but Himmler forced his hand: the Reich leader SS had already appointed one of Lohse's territorial subordinates as field representative for that district, so that Lohse faced the unthinkable situation of having a direct subordinate become his equally direct superior as far as racial affairs in that district were concerned. Lohse accepted the proffered appointment.[334] The immediate results of this confused situation were a series of bitter feuds between the SS and the

332. Himmler to Bormann, 4 Nov. 1942, T-175, roll 19, frame 2523181. See also Himmler to Rosenberg, 24 June 1941, RvO/BDC/H 196.

333. Gen. K. Nikolaiev, "Lagebericht," April 1942, CDJC/CXIV/474. For the effect of all this on lower police officials see the trial brief of the Leitender Oberstaatsanwalt, Landgericht Hamburg, "141 Js. 1957/62," IV, 744 and XVIII, 3192.

334. Koehl, *RKFDV*, p. 149.

Reich commissioners[335] as well as the delay in establishing the Arbeitsbereich East noted above. Bormann insisted that the party organization
should be in total control of all party units, that is, not only the PO, but
the paramilitary organizations as well. Since this would have undercut
the special powers of the HSSPFs, it is understandable that Himmler
had no interest in the creation of the Arbeitsbereich.[336]

The feud reached continental proportions as both Himmler's and
the Arbeitsbereich's West European power bases became part of the
overall struggle. It was generally conceded by even the most radical
of Nazi colonialists that the "related peoples" of Western Europe would
have to play a major part, under German direction, in the economic
exploitation of the Soviet Union.[337] The SS regarded the selection and
supervision of the personnel sent from Holland, Norway, and so on, to
the East as part of the "Germanization" assignment of the RKFDV,
while the Arbeitsbereichs hoped to arrange these matters through bilat-
eral agreements. The political management of economic exploitation
was the major topic of discussion when the staff leader of the Arbeitsbereich Generalgouvernement paid a formal visit to his counterpart in
Holland in November of 1941.[338]

Actually, the major controversy in the West raged over a far greater
prize, the control of the planned "Germanic Reich." To be sure, Nazi
plans for this elusive entity proceeded in a political vacuum; the peoples of Western Europe "remained, as before, strongly opposed to
Germany; derisive laughter greeted [the announcement of the] battle
against bolshevism."[339] Nevertheless, Hitler was not to be deterred

335. Himmler to Koch, 9 Dec. 1942, quoted in Heiber, *Reichsführer*, p. 161.

336. See Arb. GG [Schalk] to Himmler, 10 Oct. 1941; and Himmler to Schalk,
20 Oct. 1941, BDC/Krüger (SS), I.

337. Dallin, *German Rule in Russia*, p. 285; and Werner Warmbrunn, *The Dutch
under German Occupation 1940–1945* (Stanford, Cal., 1963), p. 26. Relations be-
tween the RKU and the occupation authorities in Holland were taken up in early
1942. Significantly, Koch at first attempted to bypass the RMO in arranging for
Dutch-RKU cooperation. See the correspondence regarding a visit of deputy GL
Siekmeyer (RKU) to Holland in February 1942 in RvO/TB/XXXII. In August a
Dutch economic delegation led by Rost v. Tonningen spent two weeks in the
Ukraine. See *ibid.*, XXXXV.

338. The visit had originally been planned for June. See Schalk to Schmidt, 9
June 1941, *ibid.*, XVIII.

339. Stützpunktleiter Doetinchen to the RK's representative for the province
Gelderland, 17 July 1941, RvO/Arb. NSDAP (Ni)/63 G.

from settling the fate of the smaller nations of Europe with "short and to the point declarations."[340] For some areas, the future had already arrived. After the formal establishment of the NSDAP's organization in Luxembourg, the small duchy became part of the Reich in August 1942.[341] Hitler was somewhat more hesitant in the case of Alsace and Lorraine, but here, too, preparations for reincorporation were well under way by mid-1942. The party was already at work recruiting PLs among the indigenous population.[342] For Belgium, all parties agreed on the establishment of two Reichsgaus, Brabant and Flanders, but since the party and the SS continued to feud over the subsequent control of these resurrected medieval states, the military remained in control.[343]

For Norway and Holland, Hitler did not envision direct annexation; these were the kingpins of the "Germanic empire." Norway proceeded on a relatively straightforward course to satellite status during 1942. The Reich commissioner, Terboven, enjoyed Hitler's full confidence,[344] and as a result, was able to subjugate the rival factions of the SS and the Arbeitsbereich to his own direct control. The Arbeitsbereich, now headed by Hans-Hendrik Neumann, still spent vast sums of money, but did not attempt to usurp Terboven's powers.[345] Instead, the Reich commissioner resolutely created a full-scale collaborationist regime in Norway. At the beginning of the year, Quisling became prime minister, so that on paper at least the Nasjonal Samling's leader exercised formal governmental authority.

340. Picker, *Tischgespräche*, entries for 26 Feb., 28 March, 5 April, and 27 June 1942, pp. 52, 58, 67–68, and 100–01.

341. Paul Weber, *Geschichte Luxemburgs im Zweiten Weltkrieg* (Luxemburg, 1946), pp. 48 and 62.

342. Pierre Crenesse, *Le Procès de Wagner bourreau de l'Alsace* (Paris, 1946), p. 14; and *VOBl Gau Baden*, nos. 4 and 19 (1 Sept. 1941 and 1 Oct. 1942); and Bürckel to Bormann, 18 Feb. 1941, BDC/Bürckel (PKC).

343. Berger to Himmler, 5 Nov. 1942, RvO/BDC/H 139. Abundant documentation on the intrigues of the SS and Schmidt are in RvO/GKzbV (Ni)/8c; Arb. NSDAP (Ni)/9A II, TB/I and LIV; and BDC/H 137 and H 417. See also Konrad Kwiet, *Reichskommissariat Niederlande* (Stuttgart, 1968), pp. 65 and 67.

344. Picker, *Tischgespräche*, entry for 5 May 1942, p. 239; and *ibid.* (Schramm ed.), p. 64.

345. Cohen, "Ontstaan," p. 8. The "political expenses" of the German administration in Norway for fiscal 1942 were RM 4,380,000.00. See Reich chancellery to Reich ministry of finance, 16 March 1942, BA/R 2/11470a. On Neumann see below, p. 449.

Quisling's counterpart in Holland, Adriaan Mussert, although green with envy, never became the Dutch prime minister because his German sponsors, Fritz Schmidt and, more indirectly, the PK, were unable to prevail against the fierce opposition of the SS to the NSB's leader. In the course of 1942 the battle between the Arbeitsbereich Netherlands and the HSSPF in Holland reached its greatest level of intensity. Schmidt continued the buildup of his organization. As noted before, all of the PLs dispatched to Holland were screened by the PK. For the most part they were young men, born around 1910 or 1911. These were not typical "old fighters," but they were bureaucratized and presumably fanaticized administrators. By this time, a more or less formal training system had been developed for PLs assigned to Holland. New appointees served for some time at the Arbeitsbereich's headquarters in The Hague before they were entrusted with a provincial post.[346] Nevertheless, numerous problems remained. Undoubtedly the most significant was the PLs' exaggerated sense of their own importance. In general, transfer to Holland meant a decided upgrading in rank and power. Gau staff officials found themselves entrusted with provinces and block leaders in Germany headed districts in the Netherlands, even though many of those sent had few qualifications other than the indispensable Herrenmensch mentality.[347] No wonder most planned to stay for some years.[348]

The organizational pattern of the Arbeitsbereich reflected the PK's desire to strengthen the PO at the expense of the affiliates. All of the affiliates (and, in theory, the paramilitary groups) were directly subordinate to the political leadership of the Arbeitsbereich.[349] Equally significant, the Arbeitsbereich took steps to align its organization as closely as possible to that of a Gau in the Altreich,[350] although it is clear that the head of the Arbeitsbereich Netherlands never aspired to the

346. On the Arbeitsbereich's personnel policies see Eftger to Hesseldieck, 5 and 17 July and 1 Oct. 1942, RvO/TB, XXV, XLII, and XLVI.

347. For complaints see Arb. NSDAP (Ni), personnel office to lower personnel offices, 10 Feb. 1942, RvO/Arb. NSDAP (Ni)/5 B I. The quality of the PLs sent to Holland may be surmised from the personnel records in *ibid.*,6.

348. Eftger *et al.*, "Betr.: Besuch am 2.10.1942 in München," 2 Oct. 1942, RvO/ GKzbV (Ni)/1e.

349. "Organisationsplan des Arbeitsbereiches der NSDAP in den Niederlanden," ca. Feb. 1942, *ibid.*, 53.

350. OPG, "Anordnung," 20 Feb. 1942, RvO/Arb. NSDAP (Ni)/3 b III.

derivative-agent status of a Gauleiter: his superior was Martin Bormann, not Adolf Hitler.[351] Financially, the Arbeitsbereich was not as well off as its counterpart in Norway, which was able to spend millions while the Arbeitsbereich Netherlands had to be content with thousands. The difference lay again in the person of the Reich commissioner. In both countries, the major source of money was not dues or party funds, but moneys diverted by the Reich commissioner from the indigenous economy. The average monthly budget in Holland in 1941 came to approximately 80,000 Dutch guilders, not an overly large amount.[352]

Within its financial and organizational limitations, the Arbeitsbereich Netherlands attempted to set up full-scale societal control mechanisms for both the Reich Germans living in Holland and, through the NSB, the Dutch themselves. Even the first part of the task was becoming increasingly difficult. Although the Herrenmenschen PLs were presumably unconcerned about their disastrous popularity ratings among the "natives," they could hardly ignore the progressive passive disengagement from Nazism among the Reich Germans. While a majority of the German citizens living in Holland had never joined the party, the membership increase from 1,853 in 1940 to 3,558 in 1942 was at least an impressive percentage gain. In fact, however, the figures were rather misleading. Most of the increase came in 1940 and 1941; by 1942 Reich Germans with an eye for the future did not rush to the Nazi colors. The highest figure in the first half of the year was an increase of sixty-four—for all of Holland—in April.[353] Moreover, activism decreased markedly. In October the party organization in Delft, one of Holland's major cities, was withering away for lack of interest.[354] No doubt recalling the glorious example of the Kampfzeit, the PLs attempted to manage societal relations despite their constituents' apathy. The three main "po-

351. See esp. the documents in RvO/GKzbV (Ni)/1b.

352. Arb. NSDAP (Netherlands), treasurer's office to Rschm., 22 Sept. 1941, *ibid.*, H 696. Detailed budget figures are in *ibid.*, H 1133.

353. The figures are derived from Schmidt's speech to the PL corps in Holland, 12 April 1942, RvO/Arb. NSDAP (Ni), 3aV. For statistics on membership applications in the period January to June 1942, see Arb. NSDAP (Netherlands), treasurer's office, "Einnahmen- und Ausgabennachweise für die Monate Januar bis Juni 1942," n.d., RvO/BDC/H 1133.

354. District leader Den Haag to Strunk, 5 Oct. 1942, RvO/Arb. NSDAP (Ni)/53; and the untitled notes of the local leader Hilversum, dated 24 Aug.–22 Sept. 1942, *ibid.*, 52j.

litical officials" in the Arbeitsbereich were not the traditional offices for personnel, organization, and training, but the PLs responsible for social policy, welfare, and propaganda.[355] Together, these three divisions of the Arbeitsbereich set out to partify the societal relations among Germans living in Holland, so that the party would be in charge not only of the conditions of livelihood but of the very chances of livelihood for these people. Moreover, as noted above, in attempting such broad ranges of social control the Arbeitsbereich was merely a test area for the later application of the PK's plans to the Reich as a whole.[356]

Under the political guidance of the Arbeitsbereich, the Hitler Youth and the DAF became the major mass organizations for Reich Germans. The DAF had a dual task: to separate Reich German employees and employers from their Dutch counterparts[357] and, once this had been accomplished, to control its membership by applying rigid political standards of behavior.[358] The clear subordination of the DAF organization to that of the PO in the Netherlands meant that there would be no parallel lines of authority as in the Reich; instead the DAF's officials would report directly to the Hoheitsträgers.[359] Although an old AO official, B. Casselmann, served for a time as figurehead of the DAF in Holland,[360] the actual head of the organization, Wilhelm Keil, as well as his chief associates, had been selected by the PK's personnel office from among the DAF's functionaries in Berlin. Once in the Netherlands, they

355. See Eftger to all provincial representatives, 27 Nov. 1941 and 30 May 1942, RvO/TB XXVII and XXXVIII, respectively.

356. Arb. NSDAP (Netherlands), "Anweisung 14/41," 8 July 1941, RvO/Arb. NSDAP (Ni)/3c; district leader North Holland to local leaders, 31 March 1942, *ibid.*, 52b; and Schmidt, "Vorlage an den Reichsleiter," 20 Oct. 1941, RvO/GKzbV (Ni), 1d.

357. Eftger, "Vorlage für Pg. Schmidt," 17 Dec. 1942, RvO/GKzbV (Ni)/1e.

358. DAF (Netherlands), "Mitteilung 42," 18 Sept. 1941; and "Arbeitsanweisung 60/41," 16 Oct. 1941, RvO/Arb. NSDAP (Ni)/29 and 29 I, respectively.

359. B. Casselmann (head of the DAF in the Netherlands), "Aufgaben und Pflichten des Orts- und Betriebsobmannes der DAF in den Niederlanden," p. ii [*sic*], (strictly confidential), 16 Oct. 1940, RvO/Arb. NSDAP (Ni)/29 III.

360. Casselmann, like other prewar Nazi leaders in Holland, ended his career on a rather sour note: at the end of 1942 the party court for the Arbeitsbereich ("Beschluss [in Sachen] . . . Casselmann, 12 Dec. 1942, RvO/Arb. NSDAP [Ni]/53) recommended that he be expelled from the NSDAP for a variety of offenses ranging from applying for Dutch citizenship in the thirties to financial irregularities in connection with aryanizations.

looked upon themselves as subordinate to Schmidt and the PK rather than to the DAF.[361] The HJ had in many ways an even more sinister purpose. Not only was it to politicize the children of Reich Germans in Holland and prevent their reimmigration to the Reich (so as not to weaken the German contingent in Holland), but in addition the HJ hoped to alienate "suitable" Dutch youngsters from their heritage and Germanize them through the NSDAP organization.[362]

The desire to strengthen the partified block of Reich Germans in Holland also underlay the party's concern with the Aryanization program. As a prerequisite to the murder of the Jews of Holland, the Reich commissioner seized Jewish-owned business enterprises and stores. Theoretically, the "vacated" properties were to be transferred to politically and economically reliable "Aryans," that is, Dutch or German citizens, although actually the Dutch were virtually excluded from the procedures. Even the NSB was left out of most of the discussions, not to mention the actual decisions.[363] The Arbeitsbereich searched for German "responsible businessmen who were [also] pioneers in the struggle for National Socialist ideas."[364] The Aryanization office established a hierarchy of applicants beginning with German veterans and ending with Dutch Nazis.[365] In actual practice, virtually all of the applicants were Reich Germans selected for political reasons by the Gau economic advisors and then sifted again by the economic department of the PK.[366] The results were not impressive, even by Nazi standards. (It should be noted that the transfers took place only on paper;

361. See Eftger to Hesseldieck, 25 Sept. 1942, RvO/TB/XLVI; and the correspondence in RvO/Arb. NSDAP (Ni)/29.

362. Lindenburger to Möckel, 25 June 1941; and representative of the Reich Youth leadership in the office of the RKFDV to Lindenburger, 21 Jan. 1942, RvO/Arb. NSDAP (Ni)/50 I.

363. Rost van Tonningen to H. Bauer, 5 Dec. 1941, quoted in M. M. Rost van Tonningen, *Correspondentie van Mr. M. M. Rost van Tonningen*, ed. E. Fraenkel-Verkade and A. J. van der Leeuw (The Hague, 1967), I, 740–42. Bauer was an official in the RK's organization office.

364. See Eftger, "Richtlinien für die . . . Aufgabe der für die Entjudung . . . eingesetzten deutschen Verwaltungstreuhänder" (draft), 7 April 1942, RvO/GKzbV (Ni /1e; and Diesselberg (PK IIIB) to Eftger, 17 June 1941, *ibid.*, 5c.

365. Schmidt, "Vorlage an den Reichsleiter," 13 Dec. 1941; and Karl Maurer, "Notiz für Pg. Eftger," 25 Feb. 1942, *ibid.* 5c.

366. Gau economic advisor Pomerania to Eftger, 28 Aug. 1941; Eftger to Diesselberg, 7 Aug. 1941; and Diesselberg to Eftger, 21 Sept. 1941, *ibid.*

the actual property deeds would not be turned over until the end of the war.) In Thuringia, two out of the four applicants were district economic advisors who simply nominated themselves. This was an extreme case, but the remainder of the group distinguished itself primarily by nouveau riche behavior and a lack of either financial or business acumen.[367]

It was no doubt particularly galling even to Dutch Nazis that they were expected to finance in large part the German take-over of great segments of the economy. The Bank voor Nederlandse Arbeid (Bank of Dutch Labor), like its German counterpart a branch of the DAF, was to furnish loans to those among the Aryanization candidates who were unable to continue the businesses on their own.[368] This perverse affront characterized rather well the relationship between the DAF and the NAF (*Nederlandse arbeidsfront*, Dutch Labor Front)—or, for that matter, the other societal affiliates copied slavishly from their Nazi models.[369] The NAF was formally launched on May 1, 1942.[370] From its inception, political control of the NAF rested with the DAF and there were plans to establish the DAF as the formal control organ for the NAF after the war.[371] To preserve at least some leverage against the influence of the Germans, the Dutch civil service organization sought to install as many NSB members as possible in sensitive civil service positions.[372]

367. Eftger, "Notiz für Pg. Bühner," 18 Sept. 1942, *ibid.*, 1e; and Gau economic advisor Thuringia to Bärmann, 8 Aug. 1941, *ibid.*, 5c.

368. Eftger, "Notiz für Pg. Schmidt," 25 June 1941, *ibid.*, 1d. There were no currency problems involved since it was expected that the Dutch national bank would after the war become "a branch office of the Reichsbank." See Rost to Seyss-Inquart, 21 March 1941, Rost, *Correspondentie*, I, 608.

369. These included the Dutch NSV (NVV), the *Winterhulpwerk*, and the organization of civil servants. See, Walter Möller (German representative in South Holland), "Vermerk für Pg. Strankmeyer," 1 Oct. 1941, RvO/BDC/H 1104; and Casselmann to local heads of the DAF, 26 Aug. 1941, RvO/Arb. NSDAP (Ni)/29 III.

370. A simultaneously scheduled establishment of the DAF in Norway "didn't work out." See P. Zimmermann to H. Bockmann, 10 July 1942, RvO/Arb. NSDAP (Ni)/72b. Zimmermann was the German "advisor" to the NAF.

371. *Ibid.*

372. HSSPF, "Bericht 30/41," 28 Aug. 1941, RvO/HSSPF (Ni)/54a. These became pivotal posts after Sauckel appointed Schmidt the GBA's representative in Holland, thus giving the Arbeitsbereich the responsibility for supplying the Dutch slave labor quota. Under these circumstances it was obviously important to staff

The Arbeitsbereich's systematic moves to control every facet of the Gleichschaltung in Holland did not please Heinrich Himmler, the man who had "been given the task by the Führer of carrying forward the concept of the Germanic Reich."[373] There is no doubt that throughout the summer and fall the political initiative in Holland lay with Schmidt and the PK rather than with the SS. Only ten days after Hess's flight, Schmidt and Bormann discussed the possibility of giving the head of the Arbeitsbereich Hoheitsträger status. It took another five months for the actual publication of the directive, but when it was issued, it gave Schmidt sweeping power over the party's organizations in Holland. Only Schwarz's officials were exempted from his supervision; significantly, the SS was not assigned an autonomous status.[374] At the same time, Schmidt and Bormann pushed vigorously for the "Quisling solution" in Holland.[375] Schmidt destroyed the last remnant of a democratic political organization in the Netherlands and seized the exiled queen's property, but he gave no encouragement to the pro-Anschluss forces.[376] That left the NSB as the "sole political will-bearer" in Holland,[377] and the way was cleared for Mussert to become prime minister. Schmidt and his myriad control offices in the Arbeitsbereich would be content to exercise real power behind the scenes.[378] Mussert and the NSB were eager to accept their role.[379] Mussert took the indispensable loyalty oath to Adolf Hitler, and waited for the appointment letter to arrive.[380]

---

the offices with collaborators. For Sauckel's appointment of Schmidt see Schmidt to Sauckel, 30 Oct. 1942, RvO/TB/XXXXVIII.

373. Brandt, "Besprechung des Reichsführers SS mit dem Leider Mussert am 8. Juli 1943," (top secret), n.d., RvO/BDC/H 109.

374. See Walker (staff of the PK) to Schmidt, 19 May 1941, RvO/TB/XVI; and PK, "Verfügung," 15 Oct. 1941, *RVBl* (A), no. 48 (20 Oct. 1941), p. 143.

375. See the resume of Seyss-Inquart's speech to the PL corps, 12 April 1942, RvO/Arb. NSDAP (Ni)/3a V. See also Warmbrunn, *Dutch Under German Occupation*, pp. 31–32.

376. Seyss-Inquart, "Anordnung," 3 July 1941, RvO/GKzbV/(Ni) 1c; Schmidt to Bormann, 15 Sept. 1941, RvO/TB/XXIII; and HSSPF, "Bericht Nr. 23/41 [and] 31/41," 19 June and 15 Sept. 1941, RvO/HSSPF/54a.

377. GKzbV (Ni), "Rundschreiben 2/42," 6 March 1942, RvO/GKzbV (Ni)/2c.

378. Kwiet, *Reichskommissariat*, pp. 147 and 149.

379. See the report (based upon "local NSB sources") of the German police officer in Groningen to Schmidt, 26 Sept. 1941, RvO/TB/XXIV.

380. Lindenburger to Axmann, 2 Feb. 1942, RvO/Arb. NSDAP (Ni)/50 I.

It never came, because the SS bestirred itself and counterattacked. Himmler and his associates fought both Mussert and Schmidt. They objected to Mussert because he resolutely combated the SS's influence in the NSB,[381] but above all Himmler opposed Mussert's grand political design. Mussert still pursued the goal of a united Holland and Belgium. This so-called *Dietschland* had been the NSB's original political platform in the 1920s, but it was the antithesis of plans for the SS-controlled Reichsgaus Flanders and Brabant.[382] Schmidt looked upon Dietschland with considerably greater equanimity, since he saw no particular danger in an enlarged Holland under Mussert's leadership, so long as Schmidt became Reich commissioner of the new entity. The stakes in this power struggle, then, were high: if Mussert became prime minister, he would attempt to destroy the SS's power base in Holland and possibly Belgium; if the HSSPF succeeded in destroying Mussert's control over the NSB, the SS would have eliminated Schmidt's collaborationist scheme and possibly cleared the way for Holland's annexation to Germany.[383]

Since Seyss-Inquart was too weak to play a decisive role in the quarrel (although both sides tried to draw him into it) and Bormann was already in Schmidt's corner, the SS appealed to Hitler to "clarify" the duties of the most loosely defined of Himmler's offices, that of the RKFDV. At issue was the control of racial policy, that extremely vague Nazi concept which encompassed everything from control of the public schools in Czechoslovakia,[384] to issuing permits for marriage under the Nuremberg laws,[385] to political control of the "related" peoples in Europe. The SS's bridgeheads in the "Germanic Reich" were its control of

381. Rauter to Himmler, 30 April and 28 Sept. 1942, RvO/BDC/H 336 and H 28, respectively. See also the report of a *Napola* official in Horst Ueberhorst, ed., *Elite für die Diktatur* (Düsseldorf, 1968), pp. 365–68.

382. Himmler to Heydrich and HSSPF Nord, 16 Feb. 1942; Himmler to Seyss-Inquart, 5 March 1942; and Himmler to Rauter, 24 June 1942, *ibid.*, H 336, H 94, H 836, respectively.

383. Rauter to Himmler, 30 April 1942, RvO/BDC/H 336. See also Kwiet, *Reichskommissariat*, p. 116. The SS was not particularly pleased with Schmidt's dissolution of the NSNAP. See Rauter to Himmler, 3 Oct. 1941, RvO/BDC/H 146.

384. Heydrich and Bormann clashed over this issue at the beginning of 1941; Heydrich won. Detlef Brandes, *Die Tschechen unter deutschem Protektorat* (Munich, 1969), pp. 162 and 237.

385. Lauterbacher to Himmler, 11 May 1942, BDC/Lauterbacher (PKC); and PK, "Anordnung 1/42, Rundschreiben 109/42 [and] V.I. 672/42," 11 Nov. 1941, 3 June and 24 July 1942, *VAB*, II, 85, 12, and 44, respectively.

the Napolas, boarding schools which Himmler hoped to convert into elite training institutes for racially superior Germanic youths,[386] and an organization called the "liaison office for Germanic volunteers" (*Germanische Freiwilligen Leitstelle*). Originally, these offices were simply recruiting agencies for volunteers to the armed SS among the "Germanic" countries of Europe, but under the ambitious direction of Gottlob Berger they assumed a vastly increased significance. Berger regarded them as his personal instrument; he even admonished the HSSPFs that the Leitstellen were not part of their jurisdictional competence.[387] Through the good offices of the SS's agent in the Reich treasurer's office, Willy Damson, Berger persuaded Schwarz to recognize, at least for financial purposes, the SS as the sole spokesman of the NSDAP in its dealings with the Germanic peoples.[388] In March, Himmler succeeded in obtaining from Hitler a directive establishing a "main office for ethnic affairs" (*Hauptamt für Volkstumsfragen*) to coordinate all party activities in this area with the office of the RKFDV.[389] Himmler in turn appointed the HSSPFs in the Western occupied countries as his representatives for "Germanic questions."[390] Finally, Himmler made one of his rare visits to Hitler's headquarters and impressed the Führer immensely with the SS's elite status and the clear direction of its "Germanization" activities.[391] Bormann appears to have been off-guard for the moment. At the time of Himmler's conference with Hitler, Schmidt was little in favor at the PK. The Arbeitsbereich Netherlands was in the midst of his intricate campaign to prepare the NSB for its Quisling role, and to Bormann, Schmidt's moves appeared to be shifty and erratic.[392] As a result, Bormann apparently discounted Schmidt's persistent warnings about the SS's ambitions.

Berger lost no time in seizing the momentum generated by Himm-

386. Himmler to Lammers, 5 March 1942, RvO/BDC/H 247.
387. Brandt to Berger, 8 Nov. 1941, RvO/BDC/H 396; and Berger to Rauter, 4 June 1942, T-175, roll 125, frame 2650301.
388. Berger to Himmler, 27 May 1942, RvO/BDC/H 1174.
389. Hitler, "Verfügung 2/42," 12 March 1942, *RVBl* (A), no. 11 (16 March 1942), p. 27. This was the culmination of one of Berger's systematic campaigns. See Berger to Rauter, 4 June 1942, T-175, roll 125, frame 2650299.
390. Berger to Rauter, 4 June 1942.
391. Hitler, *Tischgespräche*, entries for 5 April and 27 July 1942, pp. 253–56, and 484–85.
392. Bormann to Friedrichs, 16 Feb. 1942, RvO/BDC/H 579.

ler's good standing. At the end of April, he pushed the issue into the open in a speech delivered to the rather obscure "Society of Patrons of the *Germanische Leithefte* (Germanic Instructional Pamphlets)." The address was uncouth, laced with incredibly frank and brutal phrases ("In Denmark, too, we are still saddled with a king we can't beat to death"), but the essential point was clear enough: "The Führer has given the task of guiding Germanic policy to the Reich leader SS. This commission is unambiguous and exclusive." [393] Two months later, Hitler, apparently on his own initiative, [394] formalized Himmler's duties with directive A 54/42, a decree that for a time shifted the balance of power in favor of the SS and, literally, drove Schmidt to suicide a year later. A 54/42 assigned to Himmler the exclusive right to conduct negotiations with *völkische* (that is, collaborationist) groups in Denmark, Norway, Belgium, and Holland. All other agencies needed the SS's prior permission before they could initiate talks. In effect, the decree undermined the position of the Arbeitsbereichs in Western Europe, although A 54/42 in typically illogical fashion also contained a clause that nothing in the decree affected the position of the Arbeitsbereichs. [395]

Neither Hitler nor Bormann seems to have been very clear about the actual intent of A 54/42; presumably, Hitler merely wanted to give Himmler some maneuvering room for his Germanic activities. For Berger, however, the millennium had arrived. Hitler's decree gave political power in Western Europe to the SS, and he had no hesitation in exploiting it. What better way than to shuffle around Reich commissioners? Terboven could move to Belgium, and a HSSPF could take his place in Norway. Seyss-Inquart was thoroughly expendable, Rauter would become Reich commissioner in Holland. [396] The impact of the decree in the occupied areas was immediate. In Holland, the main SS

393. A copy of Berger's speech is in RvO/BDC/H 821. A list of those attending, which included only one GL, Jordan (Magdeburg-Anhalt) is in RvO/BDC/H 824. For sharp criticism of the address see Pancke (HSSPF in Brunswick) to Berger, 5 May 1942, RvO/BDC/H 821.

394. At least Berger thought so. See his "Niederschrift über die Besprechung am 8.10.1942 im SS-Hauptamt," 20 Oct. 1942, RvO/BDC/H 79.

395. Hitler, "Anordnung 54/42," 12 Aug. 1942," *RVBl* (A), no. 34 (18 Aug. 1942); and PK, "Rundschreiben 123/42," 17 Aug. 1942, RvO/Arb. NSDAP (Ni)/3 b III. See also Cohen, "Ontstaan," p. 8.

396. Berger to Himmler, 21 Oct. 1942, RvO/BDC/H 137. This is also in *IMT*, doc. NO-1469.

protégé among the Dutch Nazis, Rost van Tonningen, saw A 54/42 as a signal to attack not only the Mussert wing of the NSB, but Schmidt's person and policies as well.[397] Indeed, rumors of Schmidt's imminent dismissal sprang up quickly, and while Rauter graciously allowed that the head of the Arbeitsbereich could perform his "routine" duties as usual,[398] some of the PLs on Schmidt's staff made haste to desert what appeared to be a sinking ship and climb aboard the SS galleon sailing by.[399] Rauter reported proudly to Himmler that "the political magnetic field of Holland is already turning toward you, Reich leader [of the SS], and that, after all, was the extent of what was to be accomplished."[400] Nor were the consequences restricted to lesser PLs in Holland. The Reich treasurer's office informed Schmidt that in consequence of A 54/42 it would deal with the Arbeitsbereich only in consultation with Berger and Damson.[401]

Schmidt and Bormann were obviously not willing to turn the political future of Western Europe over to the SS. Bormann may have had an inkling of the potential dynamite inherent in Hitler's decree since he asked Hitler to issue simultaneously with A 54/42 a directive specifically subordinating the Arbeitsbereichs to the direct control of the PK.[402] This decree simply restated an already existing status quo, but since it was published at the same time as A 54/42, in the *Reichsverfügungsblatt*, it put Himmler on guard that in dealing with the Arbeitsbereichs he was in fact confronting Bormann. A few days later, the PK moved to weaken the link between Himmler and the party's main office for racial affairs. The office was still headed by Himmler, but at the Gau level Bormann reorganized its organizational status and functions so

397. Rost van Tonningen to Himmler, 22 Sept. 1942, T-175, roll 275, frames 277195–200.

398. Rauter to Himmler, 6 Oct. 1942, RvO/BDC/H 160.

399. Rauter to SS personnel office, 28 Sept. 1942, RvO/BDC/P 60.

400. Rauter to Himmler, 6 Oct. 1942. On the effect of A 54/42 see also Kwiet, *Reichskommissariat*, p. 111.

401. [Schwarz], "Besprechung . . . [Schwarz, Schmidt, Lingg]," ca. 13 Oct. 1942. A copy of this document found its way to Berger (no doubt via Damson), who sent it on to Himmler, 14 Oct. 1942 (RvO/BDC/H 131), along with a covering letter complaining about Schmidt's efforts to escape the effect of A 54/42.

402. Hitler, "Verfügung 8/42," 2 Aug. 1942, *RVBl* (A), no. 34 (18 Aug. 1942). It was a nice touch that a Verfügung stood above an Anordnung in the hierarchy of Hitlerian orders.

that its work came under the supervision of the Gau staff office.[403] Both of these rejoinders could be interpreted as cautious bolsterings of Bormann's defenses. By October, however, it was clear that Himmler and Berger were running amok with A 54/42 and that the time for more direct measures had come. Writing Himmler a "Dear Heinrich" letter, Bormann informed the chief of the SS politely but firmly that A 54/42 was not a license to take over the civil administrations of Holland or Norway. Its sole purpose was to "prevent interference (*Hineinregieren*) by various party offices in the Reich." It did not, then, diminish the authority of the Arbeitsbereichs or of their superior, the PK.[404] Bormann followed this with a series of specific directives narrowing the scope of A 54/42 to exclude the Hitler Youth (thereby undermining Himmler's Napola plans) and religious affairs from Himmler's Germanic rights.[405]

In Holland itself, Schmidt and Seyss-Inquart with Bormann's approval began a race to install Mussert as prime minister before the SS could make full use of its new powers.[406] The Reich commissioner was now firmly on Schmidt's side, undoubtedly because he was aware of his intended fate under Berger's plans. At the end of November, a thousand NSB leaders met secretly at Arnhem and in the presence of Schmidt took an oath of loyalty to Mussert. Shortly thereafter, Seyss-Inquart promised the NSB that it would be consulted in all future personnel appointments in Holland.[407] In early December, Mussert was accorded the singular honor of hearing Hitler's usual monologue to satellite leaders for the second time, and while Mussert marred the visit somewhat by stressing his dietsche plans, the mere fact that Hitler had received him at all made Mussert's position among the available Dutch collaborators all but unassailable.[408] Following his return Seyss-

403. For the organizational chart of the Hauptamt see PK, "Bekanntgabe 13/42," 24 Aug. 1942, *RVBl* (A), no. 38 (8 Sept. 1942), p. 114. See also VI, no. 66 (9 Oct. 1942).

404. Bormann to Himmler, 5 Oct. 1942, RvO/BDC/H 79. See also Hitler, "Verfügung 19/42," 4 Nov. 1942, *RVBl* (A), no. 45 (11 Nov. 1942), pp. 133–34.

405. Seyss-Inquart to the general commissars, 7 Dec. 1942, RvO/BDC/H 1165; and Rauter to Himmler, 17 Dec. 1942, *ibid.*, H 136.

406. Berger to Himmler, 9 Oct. 1942, RvO/BDC/H 218.

407. Rauter to Himmler, 7 Dec. 1942, *ibid.*, H 94; and Seyss-Inquart to Bormann, 5 Dec. 1942, RvO/TB/LII.

408. For the Hitler-Mussert meeting see Dittmar to Seyss-Inquart's press chief, 11 Dec. 1942, *ibid.*; and Himmler to Seyss-Inquart, 16 Dec. 1942, RvO/TB/LIII.

Inquart, in the presence of Schmidt and a special agent from the PK, publicly proclaimed Mussert the "Führer" of the Dutch people as a preliminary step to naming him prime minister.[409] Schmidt had already prepared a laudatory press release to explain the political significance of Mussert's governmental position.[410]

The victories of the Red Army before Stalingrad and the Anglo-American forces in North Africa prevented Mussert's appointment and brought the SS-PK feud over A 54/42 to a temporary halt. Hitler as well as other Nazi leaders[411] realized that the war had taken a decisive turn, and experiments with Germanic policy did not enjoy a high priority at the Führer's headquarters. Indeed, the military crisis at the end of the year signaled a major reversal of Hitler's attitude toward the war and the party's role in it. The Führer's always latent fear of a return of the quasi-revolutionary situation of 1918 became almost pathological. To be sure, public opinion in Germany was indeed at a low ebb at the end of 1942; Bormann complained that the reports reaching him were filled with accounts of war weariness and negativism.[412] Hitler's and Bormann's reaction to these reports was to call forth the party's best efforts to reverse the trend of public opinion[413] and to deny that the people's mood was really that bad: when the flood of negative reports did not abate, Bormann chided the officials of the SD and the PO for generalizing from isolated instances.[414] The Führer's headquarters increasingly became an isolated oasis of make-believe; Hitler was even unwilling to test his charisma in face-to-face meetings with the Reichsleiters and Gauleiters. The gathering planned for November (at the conclusion of

409. Seyss-Inquart's speech was reprinted in extenso in *Deutsche Zeitung in den Niederlanden*, 14 Dec. 1942. For Berger's reaction see his letter to Himmler, 12 Dec. 1942, RvO/BDC/H 94.

410. See Giese (official of the Reich labor service) to Dittmar, 26 Jan. 1943, RvO/TB/LV. The German efforts to keep Seyss-Inquart's announcement from getting into the Reich papers may be followed in Dittmar to press office of the Reich government, 8 Jan. 1943, RvO/TB/LIV.

411. For Goebbels' reaction see Boelcke, *Wollt Ihr*, entry for 10 Nov. 1942, p. 300.

412. PK. "Rundschreiben 198/42," 18 Dec. 1942, *VAB*, I, 395–97. See also Boelcke, *Wollt Ihr*, entry for 20 Nov. 1942, p. 303.

413. Hitler's speech of 8 Nov. 1942, Domarus, *Hitler*, II, 1943. Domarus notes this was "one of Hitler's worst speeches." *Ibid.*, I, 52 and II, 1932.

414. *VAB*, I, 396–97; Boelcke, *Wollt Ihr*, entry for 20 Nov. 1942, p. 303.

the funeral for the Bavarian prime minister) was canceled, ostensibly because Hitler was unable to attend.[415]

Still, crises also brought opportunities. The PK was able to use the deteriorating military situation in the fall to "streamline" the party apparatus, that is, to centralize it further under the PK's control. Hiding behind the fiction that Hitler was his own Reichshoheitsträger,[416] Bormann placed additional restrictions on both the Reichsleiters and Gauleiters. The former could not appoint horizontal staff officials at the Gau level without the approval of the Gauleiter (differences of opinion had to be reported to the PK),[417] and for the first time, Bormann abolished entire offices of certain Reichsleiters as unnecessary to the war effort.[418] The Gauleiters lost their right to interfere in pending court cases. Here, too, only the PK could adjust unsatisfactory sentences.[419] This did not, however, mean that Rothenberger's reforms were entirely dead; the PK still encouraged the district leaders to become actively involved in the "people's justice" movement.[420]

Above all, the PK utilized the 1942 crisis to further its control of the party's personnel policies. At the end of 1942, the party had a total of 242,511 PLs, of whom 85,327 were full-time functionaries. More than one sixth (15,711) of the full-time PLs were of military service age, but presently draft-exempt.[421] Given the party's attempt to control all facets of public life, there was a severe shortage of PLs,[422] but Bormann was determined to use those available without recourse to written regulations or interference by the party offices. Although Ley had laboriously

415. PK, "Rundschreiben" to all RL, GL, and heads of affiliates, HAB/320/22.
416. ROL, *Organisationsbuch der NSDAP*, 7th ed. (Munich, 1943), pp. 98–98a [*sic*].
417. Hitler, "Verfügung 18/42," 3 Nov. 1942, *VAB*, I, 583.
418. See Bormann to Epp (the head of the Reich colonial association), 28 Nov. 1942, T-81, roll 676, frames 5484461 ff.
419. Hitler, "Verfügung 24/42," 2 Dec. 1942, *VOBl*, no. 239 (Dec. 1942). After Hitler's attack on the judiciary the Gauleiters had attempted to assign the right of pardon to their offices rather than to the Reich ministry of justice. See "Notizen aus der Gauleiterbesprechung zum Führervortrag," 11 Aug. 1942, T-84, roll 6, frame 5723.
420. *VI*, no. 79 (18 Dec. 1942).
421. See Wilhelm Zander, "Vorlage an den Reichsleiter," 25 Jan. 1943; and [Friedrichs], "Dem Führer," 13 Feb. 1943, T-580, roll 834, box 799B, folder 4.
422. It was still possible to become a PL trainee without being a member of the party. See *Organisationsbuch* (1943), p. 27a [*sic*].

codified the PO's new list of ranks and their corresponding functions,[423] Bormann issued a circular letter embodying Hitler's views on personnel policy which negated the practical effect of the codification. Promotions within the PO should be based not on seniority and organizational charts, but solely on performance and "personality values."[424] And that judgment was left exclusively to the verticle column of Hoheitsträgers.

Bormann even managed to eliminate the autonomy of the party's judicial system (headed by his father-in-law) as a possible check on the arbitrariness of the Hoheitsträgers and the PK. After falling out of favor in 1936, Walther Buch had continued quietly to head the OPG. His position was not endangered further until the beginning of 1942, when the OPG angered Himmler, Bormann, and eventually Hitler by finding ex-Gauleiter Josef Wagner innocent.[425] As a result, Hitler pointedly did not exclude the party's judicial personnel from his blanket indictment of all jurists. More significantly, the party courts lost the right to try cases involving ideological deviation. The Gauleiters could expel party members who were "not free from ideological error" on their own authority.[426] At the end of November, Buch finally lost most of what powers still remained to him. Hitler issued a short decree emphasizing that the party courts dispensed "political justice," not "right in the abstract." The Hoheitsträgers not only became courts of appeals for the party courts at their level of jurisdiction (with the PK the final appellate division for all cases handled by the OPG), but they could also issue temporary injunctions without consulting the party courts.[427]

In still another breakthrough Bormann shook off the last vestiges of the NSDAP's legal status as a political party. Until December, the NSDAP had been a corporation chartered under public law, but in view of the party's all-pervasive and decisive role in the war effort, Hitler

423. *Ibid.*, pp. 18, 63–64, and 93–98.
424. PK, "Rundschreiben 179/42," 15 Nov. 1942, *VAB*, I, 275–76.
425. See Himmler to Bormann, 5 March 1942; and Bormann to Himmler, 10 March 1942, T-175, roll 125, frames 2650081–82 and 2650080, respectively. The OPG, of course, responded in due course to such high-level criticism and in October 1942 expelled Wagner. See BDC/Wagner (PKC).
426. PK, "Rundschreiben 105/42," 14 July 1942, *VAB*, I, 550. See also Zipfel, *Kirchenkampf*, pp. 110 and 110, n. 149.
427. Hitler, "Verfügung 22/42," 21 Nov. 1942; and Buch, "Richtlinien für die Parteigerichte," 30 Dec. 1942, *VAB*, I, 524–32.

granted what the StdF's and PK's office had long demanded,[428] and declared the NSDAP a unique institution subject only to its own regulations and laws. The party was subject to civil and criminal law only insofar as it chose to be. Lest the phrase "the internal order of the party is governed by party law" imply supervisory rights for the OPG, Hitler specifically noted that only the PK had the power to implement and interpret the December decree.[429]

In a short year and a half, Martin Bormann had weathered the crisis of Hess's flight and significantly strengthened the position of the PO, the PK, and his personal authority in both Germany and the occupied areas. Two revealing indications of the PK's status and self-confidence at the end of the year are Bormann's presence in the troika team of Keitel, Lammers, and Bormann which attempted to filter news reaching Hitler during the Stalingrad crisis,[430] and that, for the first time, Bormann challenged Himmler's use of the SD to spy on the PO.[431] Presumably, Bormann preferred not to recognize the paradox that the Third Reich's defeats had to a large extent brought about his own victories.

428. See Wegener-memo, frame 14509.

429. Domarus, *Hitler*, II, 1957; and Lingg, "Tätigkeitsbericht für das Jahr 1942," 3 Jan. 1944 [*sic*], T-580, roll 834, box 257, folder 274.

430. Speer, *Erinnerungen*, p. 265. Hitler also promoted Lammer's chief assistant and Klopfer to the rank of undersecretary on the same day, 28 November. See Domarus, *Hitler*, II, 1955.

431. Bormann to Himmler, 2 Feb. 1943, T-175, roll 59, frame 2574428. The letter is couched in *Sie* rather than *Du* terms.

Pyrrhic Victories and Paradoxes

For any rational observer, the last two years of the Third Reich are characterized by unprecedented acts of criminality and folly. The defeats at Stalingrad and in North Africa were convincing demonstrations that Hitler had lost the biggest gamble of his life. Still, for two more years the regime sent thousands of soldiers to their deaths and permitted hundreds of thousands to die in the air war, all the while dispatching trains with clockworklike precision to Auschwitz and Treblinka. And something else did not stand still: although it became increasingly meaningless, the struggle for power among the various components of the NSDAP and German society at large continued literally to the very end.

Neither Hitler nor the other party leaders were unaware[1] that the defeat at Stalingrad sent tremors of shock through the fabric of German society. To all but the few soldiers on furlough who had actually been on the Eastern front, the news of Stalingrad came as a total surprise and

1. Despite the absence of a free press or freedom of speech, the Nazi authorities in 1943 were still reasonably well informed of the mood of the country through a series of confidential reports reaching the top offices. Undoubtedly the most complete of these were the weekly SD reports from SD offices around the country and the Reich summary entitled *Meldungen aus dem Reich* ("news from the Reich"). The SD field reports are part of the Bundesarchiv (cited hereafter as BA)/NS 6/244 collection. In addition a selection of the SD's national summaries as well as other SD material is available in printed form in Heinz Boberach, ed., *Meldungen aus dem Reich* (Neuwied, 1965). Boberach also gives a good overview of the history and contents of the SD reports (pp. ix–xxviii). The SD reports were remarkably accurate and candid in their reporting, so much so that the party chancellery toward the end of 1943 began to complain that the SD's agents seemed capable of picking up only negative information. See the marginalia by a PK staffer on the report of the SD office in Berlin, 4 Nov. 1943, BA/NS 6/244.

shock. The Nazi propaganda machine had in no way prepared the population for the defeat, indeed, the leitmotif of the party's propaganda efforts had been to keep the negative effects of the war from reaching the consciousness of the civilian population as much as possible. As a result, public opinion in Germany sank to an all-time nadir; the reports for the month of January uniformly describe a mood ranging somewhere between utter despondency and gallows humor. Since the regime regarded political jokes as a particularly serious indication of popular opposition, jokes like "you probably think this is a blitzkrieg, like the Thirty Years War"[2] did not augur well for the PO's success in containing popular resentment against the regime.

It was fortunate from the point of view of the PO and the PK that immediately after Stalingrad Hitler seemed to disregard his oft-repeated dictum about maintaining morale among the civilian population. Hitler obviously did not want to hear about the true feelings of the people. The Führer isolated himself not only from the masses whose adulation he had so visibly enjoyed in the thirties, but from all but his closest advisors as well. He made only three major public addresses in 1943: a speech on the twenty-first of March, a eulogy for the accidentally killed SA chief of staff in May, and a memorial speech on the anniversary of the 1923 putsch in November. In addition, he spoke on the radio in connection with the Italian crisis in September and met with his Reichsleiters and Gauleiters in February, May, and October. At no point did Hitler visit any of the bombed cities of Germany or travel to a military unit at the front.[3] After the battle of Stalingrad, Hitler took almost all of his meals by himself rather than within the general officers' mess, as he had done previously. Virtually the only persons other than the military staff in daily attendance upon him were his doctor and Bormann.[4]

2. This bitter joke apparently originated in Saxony. It was reprinted in the PK's *Auszüge aus Berichten der Gauleitungen u.[nd] a.[nderen] Dienststellen* (cited hereafter as *GL Auszüge*), 15 Jan. 1943, BA/NS 6/414. The *Auszüge* were a sixteen-page mimeographed publication classified secret and, after 29 May 1943, top secret. They were distributed weekly with a total run of fifty copies. A set is in BA/NS 6/414 and 415.

3. Max Domarus, ed., *Hitler, Reden und Proklamationen 1932–1945* (Munich, 1965), II, 1963.

4. The PK's chief gleefully wrote his wife, "Lammers, Himmler, Ribbentrop, etc., are to stay in their winter quarters, permanently!" Bormann to Gerda Bormann,

Hitler's health deteriorated rapidly. He developed a nervous twitching of the limbs on his left side which ceased briefly after the assassination attempt in 1944 but then became significantly worse. That same summer of 1944, he was ill with jaundice and at the end of 1944 had to have yet another operation on his larynx. During the last months of his life, Hitler was a physical and, to a large extent, a mental wreck.[5]

Hitler could withdraw and leave Göring to explain that the defeat had really been a victory,[6] but for the PLs the political aftermath was not that simple. They could hardly miss the message in the rumor making the rounds in Bavaria, that the Virgin had protected Munich during an air raid and directed the Allied bombers to the housing settlement for PK staffers just outside the city.[7] No wonder the use of "Heil Hitler" greetings diminished noticeably among party members, and many erstwhile activists apparently forgot to put on their party badges when they appeared in public.[8] Bormann's first reaction to such symptoms of disengagement among the party's membership was panic and repression. All leaves for full-time PLs were cancelled for the time being,[9] and the party courts inaugurated a simplified procedure that dealt swiftly with suspected defeatists among the membership.[10]

Hitler seems to have realized rather quickly that in the hour of defeat the party, for better or worse, was indispensable to the continuation of the war effort. He despised the bureaucrats in the ministries, and the army had failed to achieve the goals of the greatest warlord of all times. There remained only the party as "the surest guarantee for the

---

16 Feb. 1943, in Martin and Gerda Bormann, *The Bormann Letters*, ed Hugh R. Trevor-Roper, tr. R. H. Stevens (London, 1954), p. 6.

5. Hildegard v. Kotze and Helmut Krausnick, *Es spricht der Führer!* (Gütersloh, 1966), pp. 329–30, n. 2, gives a summary of Hitler's medical history.

6. Göring, in a speech on 30 January 1943 (the anniversary of the *Machtergreifung*), had compared the German sixth army at Stalingrad with the 300 sacrificed at Thermopylae. See Domarus, *Hitler*, II, 1974–76.

7. *GL Auszüge*, 16 April 1943.

8. Boberach, *Meldungen*, pp. 419–20.

9. PK, "Anordnung 2/43," 20 Jan. 1943, *Verfügungen, Anordnungen, Bekanntgaben* of the PK (cited hereafter as *VAB*), IV, 196.

10. OPG, "Rundschreiben 1/43," 15 Jan. 1943, Rijksinstituut voor Oorlogsdokumentatie, Amsterdam (cited hereafter as RvO)/Arbeitsbereich der NSDAP in den Niederlanden (cited hereafter as Arb. NSDAP [Ni]/9 A II.

preservation of a victory-minded mentality within Germany."[11] As a result, in terms of the power struggle among the components of the Nazi regime, the PO benefited from the disaster on the Volga and those that followed. The more desperate the situation, the more authority Hitler assigned the party to interfere in the operations of the state administration and, later, of the army itself. In turn, it remained to Bormann and the PK to "activate" the PLs so that they made fanatic use of the increased powers[12] which came their way and did not succumb to the general mood of pessimism enveloping the country.

In February, the shock of Stalingrad had been sufficiently blunted to persuade Hitler that his charisma would once again be enough to rally the shaken ranks. After the Reichsleiters and Gauleiters had listened to two days of speeches in Posen delivered by such luminaries as Bormann, Goebbels, Speer, Sauckel, Funk, Backe, and Ley, they traveled to Hitler's headquarters to hear a final appraisal from the Führer himself. (Significantly, Hitler was not willing to remain among his paladins for the two-day conference.) The actual addresses have been lost, but the participants were unanimously convinced that the Reich's situation was not as desperate as it appeared.[13] Buoyed up by new hope and confidence, the top leadership then carried the message back to the PLs in the field: Stalingrad was the near-defeat that had always preceded final victory in the history of the NSDAP. This became the intraparty propaganda theme for the rest of the war.[14] It did not really matter that additional defeats followed the disaster on the Volga. After all, the Machtergreifung had been preceded by a long series of disasters; at the end, those who persevered and made the necessary sacrifices had experienced the triumph of January 30.

Quite aside from the fact that propaganda and charisma alone could

11. Hitler's 1943 New Year's proclamation as quoted in Domarus, *Hitler*, II, 1967.

12. In February Bormann sent out a circular letter emphasizing that as a result of the party's changed legal position the NSDAP had complete autonomy and was not subject to the laws of the state. See PK, "Rechtsstellung der Nationalsozialistischen Deutschen Arbeiterpartei," *Vertrauliche Informationen* of the PK (cited hereafter as *VI*), no. 4 (2 Feb. 1943).

13. Domarus, *Hitler*, II, 1937, n. 104. See also Goebbels, "Reichsminister Dr. Goebbels auf der Gauleiter-Tagung am 3. August 1944 in Posen," pp. 3 and 10, Institut für Zeitgeschichte, Munich (cited hereafter as IfZ)/276/52/ED 8.

14. See *VAB*, IV, 4–19, and 142–49; and Ley, "Rede vor [der] Führerschaft Ostpreussens," *Hoheitsträger*, VII (June 1943), 2–6.

have no appreciable effect on the outcome of the war, the PLs were not a very willing sacrificial group. For most party functionaries the lean years of the 1920s and early 1930s had been a time of sufficient tribulations; they were most reluctant to make further sacrifices. Instead of enthusiastic acceptance, widespread grumbling greeted such restrictions as cancellation of leaves and the shortages imposed by "total warfare." Indeed, the party's powers were frequently used to secure narrow, materialistic benefits for the NSDAP.[15] In addition, the top ranks of the party's leadership corps suffered from an increasingly permanent *crise de nerves*. The unchecked use of alcohol and open corruption testified to the mood of *après moi le deluge* among the NSDAP's territorial and Reich leaders.[16] It did not take observant contemporaries very long to notice that the party was among the rear echelons of those rushing to sacrifice themselves for the Nazi Reich.[17]

The PLs were particularly reluctant to take on new hardships after the surprisingly easy propagandistic containment of the Stalingrad crisis. Both party and people had expected a quick Russian breakthrough after the battle, and when the fronts temporarily stabilized, the party propaganda built up its credibility rating. As early as mid-February, the Gauleiters reported that "the shock has been contained."[18] Goebbels' masterfully staged Sportpalast speech in mid-February[19] and Hitler's radio address on Veterans' Day in March reinforced the temporary return of confidence. By April, the reports coming to the PK noted that the mass of the people were confident of the outcome of the war, and only a minority continued to criticize the leadership. Needless to say, these were very Pyrrhic victories. Hitler had rallied the Gauleiters by force of charisma and Speer's dazzling production figures, but the Nazis were unable to control the flow of events that caused a reversal

15. Oron J. Hale, *The Captive Press in the Third Reich* (Princeton, 1964), p. 287.

16. Schwarz to Bormann, 1 March 1943; and Building Superintendent of the Brown House to Schwarz, 25 Feb. 1943, Berlin Document Center (cited hereafter as BDC)/Amann (PKC).

17. *GL-Auszüge*, 15 May and 19 June 1943, pp. 5–7, and 15–18, respectively. See also Klemm's marginalia on an SD report of 16 Aug. 1943, BA/NS 6/244.

18. *GL Auszüge*, 12 Feb. 1943, p. 2.

19. See Günter Moltmann, "Goebbels' Rede zum totalen Kreig am 18. Februar 1943," *Vierteljahrshefte für Zeitgeschichte* (cited hereafter as *Vjh.f.Z.*), XII (Jan. 1964), 13–43.

of the optimistic mood among the PLs and the people. Hitler's speech to the Gauleiters and Reichsleiters after Lutze's funeral temporarily convinced this group. As Sauckel put it, "We all appeared extremely small. In hours like these one really realizes how immensely great the Führer is."[20] That may well have been his thoughts as he listened to his Führer, but as he returned to Thuringia he was confronted with undeniable evidence that Hitler's greatness seemed unable to prevent either the relentless destruction of his cities by Anglo-American air raids or the steady retreat of the German armies on all fronts. And even if he resolutely shut his eyes to the facts, the mass of the people and the PLs did not. By June, the sour pickle days, to use Goebbels' telling phrase of 1927, had returned.[21] Moreover, thereafter the disengagement of the people from the party continued with almost geometric progression. Each new crisis in the public opinion polls had to be repaired with ever more lavish use of charisma and reckless promises, which led to an even greater credibility gap when new setbacks revealed the party's propaganda lies. The regime then hastened to put forth even more grandiose claims, which quickly suffered a similar fate.[22] It did not augur well for the program of "party activation" that the segment of the German population organized in the party proved to be no exception to these trends. The SD's reports (although not the Gauleiters') revealed a widespread lack of interest in party activities.[23]

The public opinion curve was already in one of its downward trends in the summer of 1943 when the news of Mussolini's overthrow sent it tumbling to new depths. The people gave no credence to the official explanation of Mussolini's retirement for health reasons, but saw only that Germany's single major ally had disengaged itself from the war effort.[24] Indeed, the Italian armistice, even more than Stalingrad, wid-

20. Köhler to Frenzel, 11 May 1943, University of Michigan German Archival Collection (cited hereafter as MiU/GAC), folder 15.

21. This conclusion is expressed in both the SD reports and *GL Auszüge* for this period.

22. See the reports of the SD offices in Schwerin (10 Aug. 1943) and Linz (27 and 30 July 1943), BA/NS 6/243. See also *GL Auszüge* (29 May 1943).

23. Reports of the SD offices in Linz (26 July and 8 Aug. 1943), Berlin (26 Aug. 1943), and Halle (20 Aug. 1943), *ibid.*

24. Reichssicherheits-Hauptamt to PK, 30 July 1943, BA/NS 6/411; and report of the SD office in Berlin, 6 Aug. 1943, BA/NS 6/244. Hitler, fearing Mussolini's

ened the regime's credibility gap to such an extent that the chasm was bridged for only brief periods throughout the remainder of the Third Reich's existence.[25] The certainty that the war was lost became increasingly widespread; the party's propaganda was not read, much less believed;[26] there were even fears of a return of the turnip winter of 1917. There was little overt opposition to the regime (although the SD did note an increasing reluctance to denounce those making anti-Nazi remarks),[27] but the mood of despair turned against the party and its functionaries.[28] By October, under the impact of the continued retreats at the fronts and the poundings of the bombs from above, a stupor settled over the Reich,[29] punctuated only by brief moments of elation or pitiful confidence as Colonel Otto Skorzeny rescued Mussolini from atop the Gran Sasso or Hitler admitted over the airwaves that, yes, the loss of Italy was indeed a setback.[30]

The pattern of few ups and virtually constant downs in the mood of the German people formed both backdrop and decisive factor in the continuing struggle for power among the Nazi leaders in 1943. The overriding need for a stable and productive home front gave unprecedented opportunities for power to several of the Nazi leaders and party segments. Goebbels, Speer, Himmler, and Bormann all competed ruthlessly for Hitler's final laurels. The others had for the most part fallen by the wayside. Rosenberg's ministry for occupied Eastern territories had few lands to occupy, Göring's air force was unable to provide protection from the air raids, Buch's power had passed to Bormann, and

---

fate, ordered surveillance of all members of the Reichstag. Domarus, *Hitler*, II, 1072.

25. This judgment is based upon the information contained in the SD reports for the months of August and September 1943.

26. See the SD reports from Linz, 20 and 27 Aug. 1943, BA/NS 6/243.

27. Report of the SD office in Linz, 12 Aug. 1943, BA/NS 6/243.

28. This is particularly noticeable in the SD's summary report for 31 Dec. 1943, BA/NS 6/244, but the tenor is characteristic of the field office dispatches for December as well.

29. This is particularly apparent in the October SD reports, *ibid.*

30. This is based upon the relevant SD reports from the offices in Schwerin, Linz, and Berlin, 10–28 Sept. 1943, BA/NS 6/243 and 244. The loss of Italy was not a setback for everyone, of course. Despite a sharp letter from Bormann to the three Austrian Gauleiters on 10 September 1943 (BA/NS 6/156), the Gauleiters of Tirol and Carinthia managed to annex considerable Italian territory two days later. See Albert Speer, *Erinnerungen* (Berlin, 1969), p. 321.

Ley spent most of his days in an alcoholic stupor. The first leader to test the new atmosphere after Stalingrad was Joseph Goebbels. The Reich propaganda minister had spent most of the early war years in frustrated impotence, but with the defeat of the Sixth Army on the Volga his talents were needed: next to Hitler, Goebbels was the only Nazi leader with a large store of personal charisma and a high credibility rating among the population at large.[31] His popularity among the PLs was minimal, but that had never mattered; only popularity with Hitler counted.[32] In January, Goebbels set out to become what his enemies called "Führer of the home front."[33] Actually, his preparations had begun some time before Stalingrad. Since December, Goebbels had presided over very informal meetings of a group composed of Funk, Speer and, less frequently, Ley. These functionaries formed something of an elite within the NSDAP leadership, since they were part of the extremely small number of high-level party functionaries with college degrees.[34] This cabal was convinced that Germany's civilian mobilization needed to be significantly increased if the military situation was to be stabilized, and, more than incidentally, the members of the group were also ready allies, since all had been stymied in their ambitions by Bormann and the PO. Goebbels staged his Sportpalast speech of February 18 with its carefully designed audience responses as the climax of his campaign to convince Hitler that the German people were willing to take on new sacrifices in order to provide the means for total victory,[35] and he then modestly suggested himself as the man to take charge of the new era of "total warfare."[36] Goebbels was realistic enough to recognize that further restrictions on the civilian economy alone would not reverse the fortunes of war, but he hoped that evidence of stiffer resistance by Ger-

31. See, for example, the SD's national summary, 29 April 1943, BA/NS 6/243.
32. Willi A. Boelcke, ed., *Wollt Ihr den totalen Krieg?—Die geheimen Goebbels Konferenzen 1939–1943* (Stuttgart, 1967), p. 326.
33. Berger to Himmler, 29 Jan. 1943, in Helmut Heiber, ed., *Reichsführer! . . . Briefe an und von Himmler* (Stuttgart, 1968), p. 185. See also Speer, *Erinnerungen*, p. 271.
34. Speer, *Erinnerungen*, p. 267.
35. Rudolf Semmler, *Goebbels—the Man next to Hitler*, ed. G. S. Wagner (London, 1947), entries for 29 Jan. and 13 Feb. 1943, pp. 68–69. See also Moltmann, "Goebbels' Rede," pp. 27–36, and 40.
36. Boelcke, *Wollt Ihr*, entry for 5 Jan. 1943, p. 318.

many could be used to initiate peace negotiations with the Western
Allies and enable the Reich to turn all of its military efforts to the East.
Goebbels was not unwilling to replace the incompetent Ribbentrop as
foreign minister.[37] Finally, he had at least some vague plans to deprive
Bormann and the Gauleiters of much of their power. The "Goebbels
group" hoped that Hitler would appoint Göring to head a party defense council with full powers to control the Gauleiters.[38]

Perhaps Goebbels should have become suspicious when Bormann,
in a rather sudden about-face, endorsed the plans for greater civilian
mobilization and entered into what amounted to an informal alliance.[39]
While Bormann clearly needed someone with charisma to stabilize the
home front,[40] he in actuality joined Goebbels in order to defeat him.
Goebbels anticipated that a committee of some sort would decide basic
policy guidelines, leaving the administration to him,[41] but to Goebbels'
consternation, the final committee consisted only of Lammers, Bormann,
and Keitel. Goebbels was reduced to the role of originator and propagandist. In addition, Bormann strengthened rather than cut down
the Gauleiters' power. Below the Reich-level committee of three, the
administration of the decrees on total mobilization remained in the
hands of the Reich defense commissioners, in other words, the Gauleiters.[42] Finally, the district leaders and their economic advisors occupied pivotal positions in putting into effect the most important feature
of the new mobilization effort, the registration of all able-bodied German
men and women between the ages of sixteen and sixty for war-related
work assignments. The party chancellery hastened to exempt all full- and
part-time PLs from the duty to register; party work was a sufficiently
important contribution to the war effort.[43] Goebbels could derive little
comfort from Hitler's endorsement of his suggestions in early Febru-

---

37. Wilfred von Oven, *Mit Goebbels bis zum Ende*, 2d ed. (Buenos Aires, 1949),
entry for 1 Sept. 1943, pp. 97–98; and Speer, *Erinnerungen*, p. 270.

38. Speer, *Erinnerungen*, pp. 275–76.

39. Semmler, *Goebbels*, entry for 28 Dec. 1942, p. 68. See also Curt Riess, *Joseph
Goebbels* (New York, 1948), pp. 315 and 339.

40. Semmler, *Goebbels*, entry for 20 March 1943, p. 79.

41. Boelcke, *Wollt Ihr*, entry for 5 Jan. 1943, p. 318.

42. "Erlass des Führers vom 13.1.1943," *VI*, no. 2 (31 Jan. 1943). For Goebbels' reaction see Semmler, *Goebbels*, entry for 18 Jan. 1943, p. 66.

43. PK, "Anordnung 4/43," 29 Jan. 1943, *VI*, no. 6 (10 Feb. 1943).

ary;[44] by this time, the propaganda minister stood impotently[45] on the sidelines, and the Gauleiters even criticized the way he handled the propaganda for the mobilization issue.[46]

Goebbels lost because he misjudged the intensity of Hitler's fear of social revolution and because he failed to appreciate that it was too late to build a power offensive around the person of Hermann Göring. There is no doubt that the "Goebbels group" looked upon social tensions as an effective means of stimulating psychological and material mobilization among the masses.[47] Hitler and Bormann, on the other hand, thought immediately of the protorevolutionary situation in the fall of 1918 and resolutely prohibited any use of social antagonism as a part of "total warfare."[48] Göring was still the titular successor to Hitler, and in the absence of immediate military crises, the Führer loudly voiced his confidence in the *Reichsmarschall*,[49] but he also tended to blame Göring for whatever military defeats happened to take place.[50] Early 1943 was not a good time for proposing Göring's name for new powers.

Goebbels' fall turned out to be temporary, but Ley's was permanent. Ley had already laid plans to participate actively in Goebbels' mobilization efforts. The party training programs would be retooled to provide the PLs and party members, particularly at the district and local levels, with hard-hitting hate sessions against Jews, foreigners, and, presumably, middle-class values.[51] Ley hoped to gain additional influence for the DAF by assigning it primary responsibility for the Betreuung of the population during air raids. It is doubtful that Ley could have realized these ambitions under any circumstances, but his association with Goeb-

44. Boelcke, *Wollt Ihr*, entry for 8 Feb. 1943, p. 334.

45. Privately, Goebbels called Bormann a "primitive Ogpu type." Semmler, *Goebbels*, entry for 20 Nov. 1943, p. 107.

46. *GL Auszüge*, 26 Feb. 1943.

47. Semmler, *Goebbels*, entry for 9 April 1943, p. 82.

48. PK, "V.I. 15/187," 9 April 1943, *VAB*, IV, 125. See also, Semmler, *Goebbels*, entry for 9 April 1943, p. 82.

49. See Hitler's comments on 25 July 1943, quoted in Helmut Heiber, ed., *Hitlers Lagebesprechungen* (Stuttgart, 1962), pp. 306–07.

50. Speer, *Erinnerungen*, p. 275.

51. H. H. Leistritz, "Die Schulung als politisches Instrument des Hoheitsträgers," *Hoheitsträger*, VIII (Jan. 1944), 21–22. The April 1943 issue was devoted to racial policies, those of April and May to ethnic Germans abroad.

bels' plans made it easy for Bormann to destroy even more of Ley's remaining empire. He flatly prohibited additional authority for the DAF, and indirectly encouraged Rosenberg's ambition to replace a number of Ley's Gau training leaders.[52]

As always, it did not take long for other power segments in the Third Reich to join in the attack on Ley's jurisdictions.[53] Schwarz had taken no part in Goebbels' initiative, but he did not hesitate to take advantage of the ROL's vulnerability. By late January, all of the ROL's offices were operating with budgets approved by Schwarz's office,[54] and Ley hastened to assure the Reich treasurer that the DAF and the ROL were administratively very separate entities.[55] Schwarz, with the enthusiastic endorsement of the PK and Rosenberg's office,[56] was also able to move the party further in the direction of an elitist membership definition. A series of directives were designed to eliminate applicants who had been married to Jews (or even those whose present spouse had once been married to a Jew), who had any church ties whatever, or who were likely to become mere dues payers.[57] In the waning days of the Third Reich the old battle between Betreuung and control had been decided; the proponents of an elitist party confidently expected a purge of a million members from the ranks of the NSDAP after the war.[58] Obviously, the administrative future of the NSDAP, if there had been any future at all, belonged not to Ley and his *Organisationsbuch*,[59] but to

52. See, Heinrich Walkenhorst, "Notiz für Pg. Friedrichs," 8 July 1943; and Bormann, "Aktenvermerk für Pg. Friedrichs und Pg. Klopfer," 10 Oct. 1943, BA/NS 6/166 and 156, respectively.

53. Otto Schmidt to Stellrecht (Rosenberg's chief of staff), 30 Sept. 1943, BA/NS 8/231.

54. For an example of a quarterly budget see ROL, administrative office to Reich treasurer, 20 July 1943, BA/NS 22/14.

55. Ley to Schwarz, 5 Feb. 1943, *ibid.*

56. See "Weltanschauliche Erziehung," *Bericht zur weltanschaulichen Lage* (6 Aug. 1943), pp. 22 and 24. The *Berichte* were issued by Rosenberg's representative in Thuringia. A set is in MiU/GAC, folder 36.

57. Reichsschatzmeister (cited hereafter as Rschm.), "Stichworte zur Ansprache des Reichsschatzmeisters . . . am 23.12.43," n.d., T-580, roll 842, box 267, folder 347.

58. "Weltanschauliche Erziehung," p. 22.

59. The personnel office of the Arb. NSDAP/(Ni) ordered the district personnel office of North Holland on 10 April 1943 (RvO/Arb. NSDAP [Ni]/52c) to ignore the *Organisationsbuch* altogether.

Schwarz, with his budget of RM 6 billion, his auditors, and his generous salary scale.[60]

The major political power of the post-Stalingrad era resided with Bormann and the PK. Formally, Bormann expanded his functions only by assuming the title of "secretary of the Führer" in May 1943, and even that, Bormann announced, merely legalized a de facto state of affairs that had existed for some time.[61] In a sense this was true. Bormann had for some years handled Hitler's personal affairs and dealt with such mundane matters as supervising the kitchen staff at the Führer's head-quarters. Nevertheless, Bormann's new title changed the relationship between the PK and state organs. As Hitler's secretary, Bormann had the authority to transmit the Führer's orders to Reich ministers, much as he had done with the Reichsleiters and Gauleiters since May 1941. In effect, the new title placed much of the authority previously held by Heinrich Lammers into Bormann's hands, including the right to mediate disputes among Reich ministers.[62]

Bormann's changing self-image is perhaps an even better indication of his status in the last two years of the war. The PK's chief, who had previously depreciated his talents as propagandist and intellectual, now began to criticize draft speeches by Goebbels[63] and to recommend night-time reading for prominent leaders of state and party.[64] Bormann even discovered talents as a skilled negotiator in himself, although actually his gifts in this area remained more than minuscule, as a series of documents from the late summer of 1943 illustrate. In August Bormann and Ley met to discuss a variety of minor administrative matters. From the minutes of the conversations, it is obvious that Ley did virtually all of the talking. Bormann rejected Ley's proposals, but refused to discuss his reasons, hiding instead behind Hitler's authority. At the end of the

60. For the budget and personnel policies see Rschm., "Stichworte . . . ;" and Schwarz to Greiser, 27 Jan. 1943, BDC/Greiser (PKC).

61. See the enclosure in Bormann to Himmler, 1 May 1943, BDC/folder PK, Staatssekretär–Präsidial-Kanzlei. See also VI, no. 21 (7 May 1943).

62. Enclosure in Kaltenbrunner to Brandt, 26 July 1943, T-175, roll 38, frame 2547871. See also Peter Diehl-Thiele, *Partei und Staat im Dritten Reich* (Munich, 1969), p. 256.

63. See Bormann's and Hitler's comments and changes on Goebbels' draft for a speech in June 1943, BA/NS 6/129.

64. E.g., Hanns Löhr, *Aberglauben und Medizin* (Leipzig, 1943). Löhr's thesis was that organized religion had consistently hindered medical progress.

conversation, Ley had to be satisfied with Bormann's statement that all was being handled according to plan. Yet, when Bormann reported on the meeting to his two chief assistants some weeks later, the head of the PK emerged as a skilled debater who backed his views with long explanations and defeated Ley through the brilliance and length of his arguments.[65] Their chief's arrogance soon communicated itself to his associates. The agency encouraged an image of itself as an omnipotent bureau that could solve whatever problems arose, if only other party offices would turn the difficulties over to the PK as soon as possible.[66] To this end, the PK attempted to stage regular meetings between its staffers and the Gauleiters and Reichleiters. Significantly, these sessions were intended to elicit information from the other agencies, not to become genuine discussions between the PK and its partners.[67]

It is nevertheless an exaggeration to ascribe to Bormann a position in the Third Reich comparable to that held by Stalin in the last years of Lenin's life.[68] Until the very end, the Nazi regime was far too centrifugal to permit the establishment of an all-encompassing, vertical hierarchy of authority. Moreover, although Bormann obviously enjoyed Hitler's confidence, the Führer assigned to the PK primarily preventive and coordinating rather than initiatory powers. Bormann had to be informed of pending plans among the Reichsleiters and Gauleiters, and of anticipated proceedings against PLs formally appointed by Hitler, but the other segments of the party were still relatively free to initiate plans and, consequently, to continue their multifaceted struggles.[69] It is true that the balance of power shifted constantly in Bormann's favor, but this resulted primarily from the PK's systematic drive to increase

65. N.a., "Gespräch-Reichsleiter Dr. Ley mit dem Reichsleiter am 23.8.1943, 14 Uhr," n.d., BA/NS 6/156; and Bormann, "Aktenvermerk für Pg. Friedrichs und Pg. Klopfer," 1 Oct. 1943, *ibid.*

66. PK, "Rundschreiben 11/43," 15 Jan. 1943, *VAB*, IV, 100.

67. Friedrichs, "Vermerk für den Reichsleiter," 21 May 1943, T-580, roll 79, folder 368. Lingg, "Ämterbesprechung—2. Dezember 1943," n.d., T-580, roll 82, folder 394. See also Friedrichs to Witt, 13 Nov. 1943, RvO/BDC/H 1168.

68. Hugh R. Trevor-Roper, "Martin Bormann," *Der Monat*, VI (May 1954), 171–72.

69. Hitler, "Verfügung 5/43," 17 April 1943, RvO/Arb. NSDAP (Ni)/9 A II; and PK, "Anordnung 23/43," 20 March 1943, *Reichsverfügungsblatt* (cited hereafter as *RVBl*) (A), no. 25 (25 March 1943), p. 56; and PK, "Rundschreiben 153/43," 21 Oct. 1943, *VAB*, III, 2–3.

the PO's power not so much by formally controlling other segments in the party (that happened only in the Arbeitsbereichs) but by, literally, eliminating them under the guise of wartime economy. The PK was more successful in the last years of the war than before, because the reverses at the front provided dramatic evidence of the need to curtail many of the far-flung activities of the NSDAP. Bormann and Schwarz systematically shut down or sharply curtailed the activities of a long series of social and professional affiliates.[70] Their assets were transferred to Schwarz's accounts,[71] while the PK and Hoheitsträgers took over the affiliates' control functions for the segments of the population organized in the affiliates.

One of the expected results of the elimination of numerous affiliates was the freeing of some five thousand functionaries[72] for other party work or military service. In view of the continuing and growing instances of incompetence among the PLs at all levels,[73] a supply of relatively well-educated and technically competent administrators from the more specialized affiliates would be more than welcome. These functionaries did not, of course, solve the perennial Gauleiter problem, but their availability speeded the purge of old PLs which a new Gauleiter inevitably conducted. By mid-1943, there was no shortage of potential job openings among the provincial and even Reich leaders. A number of Gauleiters became incapacitated: Sprenger[74] (Kurhessen) had diabetes, Adolf Wagner was paralyzed,[75] and Karl Weinrich (Hessen-Nassau) staged a party for his clique in the bomb-safe Gau bunker during an

70. A summary list of the offices closed or curtailed by early August is in PK, "V.I. 455/43," 5 Aug. 1943, *VAB*, IV, 110–11. For Schwarz's support of Bormann's action see, [Rschm.], "2. Ressortbesprechung am 27. Januar 1943, 15.30 Uhr," n.d., T-580, roll 47, folder 266.

71. Herbert Hänssgen, "Besuchs-Vermerk," 10 Feb. 1943, T-580, roll 244, folder 207.

72. Rschm., "Stichworte . . . ."

73. On the general problem see Berger to Himmler, 10 Oct. 1943, quoted in Heiber, *Reichsführer*, p. 237. In September 1943 Schwarz allocated GL Florian (Düsseldorf) RM 10,000 to pay his personal tax bill.

74. Walkenhorst, "Vorlage," 10 Aug. 1943, BA/NS 6/166.

75. Wagner had been partially paralyzed as a result of a stroke suffered in mid-1942. His actual death did not occur until 12 April 1944. Domarus, *Hitler*, II, 2098, n. 81.

air raid, so that even Hitler admitted he would have to be dismissed.[76] Himmler could not restrain himself from commenting that the acting Gauleiter of Essen, Fritz Schlessmann (Terboven spent all of his time in Oslo), had resigned from the SS and become a PL because he knew he would never rise to become a HSSPF.[77] Then there was the perennial Schirach problem. Again, Hitler agreed that Schirach would have to go, but since a suitable replacement could not be found, the Gauleiter, although rejected by everyone including his Führer, remained at his post until the end of the war.[78] Gauleiter Henlein of the Sudetenland, who was disliked by Bormann and Himmler, prevailed over all of his intrasystem enemies, while Richard Donnewert, his PK-appointed deputy Gauleiter, was dismissed from his post and ended up a drunkard with an SS sinecure.[79]

The list of possible replacements remained pitifully thin, particularly since the PK refused to consider leaders of the affiliates. Bormann wrote "no comment necessary" on a list of Gauleiter possibilities submitted to him in May 1943 after he realized that the names were in fact from a July 1941 list that had been lifted from the files and resubmitted.[80] The PK continued its interest in the HJ as a reservoir of future party leaders. In April, Hitler permitted a direct transfer of HJ leaders to the PO,[81] but since the HJ was already understaffed, the measure could have little practical impact on the NSDAP's present personnel problems. Somewhat more promising was the PK's further centralization of draft exemptions for the party's functionaries. Before January, a number of important offices—among them the Reich treasurer, the NSV, the DAF, the HJ, and the SA—negotiated draft exemptions directly with the army commands, but after Stalingrad this function was transferred to the PK.

76. Oven, *Mit Goebbels*, I, entry for 6 Nov. 1943, pp. 147–50; and Hitler's remarks to Gen. Zeitzler, 27 Dec. 1943, quoted in Heiber, *Lagebesprechungen*, p. 479.
77. Himmler to Rediess, 12 Dec. 1941; and Himmler to Bormann, 10 July 1943, BDC/Schlessmann (SS).
78. Friedrichs, "Vermerk für Pg. Walkenhorst," 12 Aug. 1943; Walkenhorst, "Vermerk für den Reichsleiter," 3 Dec. 1943, and Bormann's marginalia on this document; and Jury to Bormann, 6 Dec. 1943, T-580, roll 80, folder 371.
79. The full documentation on these very involved intrigues is in BDC/Donnewert (SS)/I.
80. Bormann to Friedrichs and Klopfer, 15 Nov. 1943, T-580, roll 80, folder 371.
81. Hitler, "Anordnung 26/43," 7 April 1943, *RVBl* (A), no. 11 (12 April 1943).

Bormann's office was singularly successful in keeping the party's personnel on the job. On June 1, 14,677 PLs were draft exempt, and the PK instructed the Gau staff leaders that further reductions were not possible.[82] The OKW agreed to exempt automatically any individual PL whose party position the PK declared to be indispensable to the war effort.[83] As a result, while the Russians had now reached the Eastern borders of Poland, the PK proudly pointed out that it had been able to protect practically all of the party's contingent.[84] The specific aim of the PK's draft exemption program was not merely numbers, but the safeguarding of PLs who had served at the PK[85] and those who exercised various social control functions: Gau staff officials, district Hoheitsträgers and DAF and NSV district officials. In return for keeping these categories out of the army, Bormann was willing to send some one thousand to twelve hundred less significant functionaries from the dissolved party offices.[86] The in-service training program continued, but it still handled only a small number of men, and at any rate Bormann could not decide where to place these favorites. He wanted to send them back to the Gaus as agents and protégés of the PK, yet at the same time he planned to keep them in Munich so that division II of the PK could finally become "a general staff of the NSDAP."[87]

Under these rather inauspicious circumstances, the accidental death of the SA's chief of staff, Victor Lutze, provided the catalyst for still another massive search for possible replacements for all Gauleiters, deputy Gauleiters, Reich ministers, undersecretaries, and heads of the affiliates and paramilitary organizations. Bormann directed Friedrichs and Klopfer to keep the search very confidential; the reports should not be typed by their secretaries, but submitted directly in their own hand-

82. Kalz (office of the Reich treasurer), "Tagung der M.-Beauftragten . . . 17. und 18. Juni 1943," 19 June 1943, T-580, roll 82, folder 394. The session was chaired by Friedrichs.

83. Friedrichs to all M-officials, 7 April 1943; see also Hitler, "Verfügung 7/43," 12 Dec. 1943, *ibid*.

84. Zander, "[Bericht]," 30 Dec. 1943, *ibid*.

85. See Zander, "Vorlage an den Reichsleiter," 8 Nov. 1943, *ibid*., folder 3.

86. PK to all M-officials, 7 April 1943, *ibid*.; PK to all M-officials, 18 Jan. 1943; and Zander, "Vorlage an den Reichsleiter," 28 Sept. 1943, T-580, roll 874, box 799b, folders 2 and 3, respectively.

87. Bormann to Friedrichs, 11 May 1943, T-580, roll 80, folder 371.

writing.[88] In terms of personnel changes, the results were disappointing. Only two Gauleiters actually took office, and one was already on the scene. In August, Paul Giesler replaced Adolf Wagner. Bormann was also able to install Albert Hoffmann, the old Stillhaltekommissar in Austria and the Sudetenland, and from 1941 to 1943 deputy Gauleiter of Upper Silesia, as provincial Hoheitsträger in the Ruhr Gau Westphalia-South. Hoffmann had been acting Gauleiter of Westphalia since January 1943, but only his permanent appointment in June enabled him to conduct a quiet but extensive purge of PLs in his Gau, replacing older officials with younger, presumably PK-oriented men.[89] Two other prominent PK staffers moved into acting Gauleiter positions. Karl Gerland, until now deputy Gauleiter in Lower Danube, replaced the sick Sprenger, and Neuburg took the place of the disgraced Donnewert in the Sudetenland. As for the group of deputy Gauleiters as a whole, the PK was less than sanguine about their future prospects. A large number were evaluated as "not suitable" and a significant percentage received the notation "no final judgment possible" because they had not yet served at the PK.[90] The latter remark was a revealing if involuntary comment on the insufficiency of the PK's in-service training program. After all, Hess had singled out the deputy Gauleiter corps for special attention almost ten years earlier.

The major results of the 1943 search were procedural ones. Hitler agreed with Bormann that future Gauleiters should not be appointed unless they had served for at least one year in a staff position at the PK.[91] At the end of the year, Bormann issued a lengthy circular detailing the PK's final take-over of personnel policies in the PO. The ROL was reduced to an office providing technical assistance. Drawing a firm distinction between the PL corps and the body of functionaries subject to

88. Bormann to Friedrichs and Klopfer, 15 Aug. 1943, *ibid.*

89. Hans Otto and Otto Schmidt (of Rosenberg's office), "Gedächtnisniederschrift über die Tagung des Hauptschulungsamtes vom 27.9–29.9.1943," 21 Oct. 1943, BA/NS 8/231.

90. Walkenhorst, "Vorlage," 30 Nov. 1943, T-580, roll 80, folder 371.

91. Bormann, "Aktenvermerk," 10 Nov. 1943, *ibid.* Walkenhorst had suggested two years of service, so that the candidates might "become genuine party chancellery men." Walkenhorst, "Vorlage," 30 Nov. 1943, *ibid.*; and Zander, "Vermerk für Pg. Siebel," 27 Dec. 1943, T-580, roll 874, box 799b, folder 3.

the control of the remaining affiliate offices, Bormann emphasized that full-time PLs could be neither appointed to new positions nor dismissed from their present posts without the approval of the party chancellery. In addition, Hitler assigned to the party chancellery and the Hoheits-trägers extensive powers to transfer PLs. At the Reich level, the PK could reassign any PL to Munich, while the Gauleiters could shift PLs to district and local staff offices as they saw fit.[92]

The death of Victor Lutze not only inaugurated a new search for Gauleiters, but also brought about a major change in the relationship between the PO and SA. At the time of the SA chief of staff's car accident, the oldest of the Nazi paramilitary organizations had sunk to an unprecedented low of prestige and influence. Hitler had even begun to reassign the SA's Reichstag seats to other party segments.[93] Lutze himself had done little to reverse the trend; in fact, his death came as he returned from a black-market shopping trip with his daughter. Nevertheless, Hitler ordered all major Nazi party figures to Berlin for yet another of the by-now frequent and lavish "state funerals." Hitler's eulogy went from the seemingly sublime to the certainly ridiculous. He exhorted the NSDAP's leaders too keep their faith in final victory, and prohibited any high party functionary from traveling in a car at speeds faster than thirty-five miles per hour.[94]

Bormann and the PO were obviously more concerned with the appointment of Lutze's successor, particularly since the SS seemed quite willing to take over the SA.[95] Within the SA, sentiment ran high for Paul Giesler, an old SA leader and now acting Gauleiter of Munich–Upper Bavaria.[96] Hitler may have considered a Personalunion between a Gauleiter and the SA chief of staff position, but Bormann won with the nomination of Wilhelm Schepmann.[97] The new chief of staff did not meet with unanimous accolades. The HSSPF in Silesia regarded Mrs.

---

92. PK, "Anordnung 65/43," 1 Dec. 1943, *VAB*, II, 90–98.
93. SA to Fabricius, 11 Feb. 1943; and Bormann to Frick, 28 Feb. 1943, Hauptarchiv Berlin/320/41.
94. The relevant documents are in the two special Lutze folders in the BDC. Domarus, *Hitler*, II, 2011, reprints an excerpt from Hitler's eulogy.
95. Koppe (SS-Ogruf.) to Himmler, 11 May 1943, BDC/Ordner Lutze/II.
96. Frenzel (SA leader in Thuringia) to Köhler, 22 May 1943, MiU/GAC, folder 15.
97. Chief of the SA leadership office to Bormann, 13 May 1943, BA/NS 6/423.

Schepmann as a dangerous philo-Semite, and the Gauleiter of Brandenburg had once branded Schepmann as a man who "with every fiber of
his character was the very opposite of what one would call a National
Socialist."[98]

Schepmann had no illusion about the price he was to pay for his
appointment: the SA had to give up whatever visions it still harbored
about its autonomy as a paramilitary organization, and become subordinate to the PK and the Hoheitsträgers. In one of his first orders as
chief of staff, Schepmann emphasized Bormann's "sincerity" toward the
SA and the close relationship between Hitler and Bormann; the chief
of the PK, he assured the SA's leaders, did absolutely nothing without
the approval of Adolf Hitler.[99] In concrete terms, the SA agreed to carry
out "Kampfzeit-style propaganda of action" at the direction of the Hoheitsträgers. In the districts, the SA leader became an integral part
of the PO's staff organization.[100]

The relationship between the PO and the SS was a less one-sided
affair. As the German armies drew back from the fronts, and the mood
of the public turned increasingly against the PLs, the SS emphasized its
image as the untainted, uncorrupted elite of the dying Third Reich. The
mainspring of the political activist wing in the SS, Gottlob Berger, cease-
lessly bombarded Himmler with letters and memoranda to convince
the SS leader that, apart from Hitler, only Himmler could save the
Reich. Göring, Goebbels, and Ley had lost their "resonance" with the
people, and while Himmler's time "was not yet ripe," Berger had already written off the PO. He noted that the NSDAP and the SS were
for all practical purposes the same, that is, the party was merely a subordinate unit of the SS. And he added, lest the point be missed, that "I

Bormann undoubtedly knew of Adolf Wagner's imminent death and wanted Giesler as full-time Gauleiter of Munich–Upper Bavaria.

98. v. Woyrsch (HSSPF Silesia) to Himmler, 26 June 1942, BDC/Mutschmann
(PKC). Stürtz (GL Brandenburg) to Hitler, 9 July 1934, BDC/Stürtz (PKC).

99. Schepmann, "Richtlinien des Stabschefs" 28 Aug. 1943, T-81, roll 91, frame
104468. Schepmann also made a point of calling upon Schwarz shortly after his
appointment. See *Dresdner Zeitung*, 24 Aug. 1943.

100. See, "Richtlinien des Stabschefs," frames 104467 and 104470–71; "Bericht
über den Gruppenführerappell in Hamburg vom 13. bis 15. Oktober 1943," BDC/
Schepmann (SA); and *Kriegsblätter der Fränkischen SA*, IV (Sept.–Oct. 1943),
2–3.

do not say this arrogantly, but with the sense of deepest conviction."[101]

Despite Berger's purposeful optimism, the power of the SS was based less on the affection of the people than on the reality of its terror organization. Himmler was in direct control of almost every police officer in the Reich; his organization ran the concentration camp system, carried out both the extermination and Germanization programs, and administered a sizable economic empire as well. In August 1943, Himmler became, in addition to all his other posts, Frick's successor as Reich minister of the interior.[102] (Frick had continued to harbor reservations about the total abolition of the rechsstaatliche norms in the civil service, and had been shunted off to become Reich protector in Czechoslovakia.) In his new position, Himmler was the nominal supervisor of most of the Gauleiters, insofar as they served in Personalunion as Reich plenipotentiaries or Prussian provincial governors. Added to the already present irritant of the SD's spying activities among the PO,[103] Himmler's appointment as Reich minister catapulted the open animosity of relatively few Gauleiters—Mutschmann, Stürtz[104]—into a bitter if subdued struggle between the SS and the PO as a whole.[105]

The PK did not yet fully share the PLs' resentment of the SS. Bormann specifically defended the subterranean spying of SD agents on the PO,[106] and routine consultations on personnel appointments produced no major disagreements.[107] On the other hand, there were some

101. The quotations are from two of Berger's numerous letters during these months: Berger to Himmler, 30 July 1943, T-175, roll 124, frame 2599100; and Berger to Himmler, 10 Oct. 1943, quoted in Heiber, *Reichsführer*, p. 237.

102. All SS-controlled sources stressed the joy with which both the man in the street and the "best" among the Gauleiters greeted Himmler's appointment as Reich minister of the interior. See the report of the SD office in Linz, 31 Aug. 1943, BA/NS 6/243; and Daluege to Himmler, 26 Aug. 1943, BDC/Himmler (SS).

103. Himmler to Bormann, 18 March 1943, T-175, roll 59, frames 2574413–22. For a GL's complaints see Weinrich to Bormann, 22 Jan. 1943, T-175, roll 59, frame 2574430.

104. See v. Woyrsch's bitter "[Bericht über die Lage in Sachsen]," 15 Jan. 1944, BDC/v. Woyrsch (SS); and Himmler to Mutschmann (draft), 19 Oct. 1943, BDC/Mutschmann (PKC). On Stürtz see Berger to Brandt, 27 Feb. 1943, BDC/Tittmann (SS).

105. Heinz Höhne, *Der Orden unter dem Totenkopf* (Gütersloh, 1967), p. 394.

106. PK, "Rundschreiben 26/43g," 21 Aug. 1943, *VAB*, IV, 47–48.

107. Himmler to Bormann, 20 Jan. 1943, T-175, roll 59, frame 2574389; and Bormann to Himmler, 10 April 1943, BDC/Zander (SS).

difficulties. The PK's relationship to Gauleiters who were known for their opposition to the SS seemed to be particularly cordial,[108] and the ever watchful Berger even discovered that the PK was systematically sabotaging various SS efforts, though he was relieved to find that these activities were merely the result of the institutional jealousy of subordinate officials at the PK.[109]

Above all, the chief of the PK hoped that the power of the SS, and specifically Himmler's new authority as Reich interior minister, would aid the PK in a major assault on the remaining powers of the state bureaucracy. As far as the party was concerned, the other two major power components in the Third Reich had failed before Stalingrad; whatever previous restrictions had been placed on the party should be nullified in this time of crisis. Since the party had created the state, asked the then-acting Gauleiter of Westphalia-South naively, why should he not ignore whatever legal restrictions stood in his way?[110] Prodded at least in part by such indications of demands for far-reaching party autonomy at the Gau level, Bormann sought to partify the Reich ministries before the centrifugal forces in the NSDAP could partify the state administration in the various provinces. Some ministries presented no problem at all. Thierack continued to place no obstacles in the way of the PK's ambitions in the administration of justice. The ministry offered no objections to the PK's demands for thoroughgoing partification of the entire judiciary process. The party both reserved the right to deny permission for PLs to testify in court proceedings (if such testimony was not in the interest of the party), and insisted that if a PL chose to give "expert testimony," his remarks could not be judged by the normal rules of evidence. At times the party simply had a feeling about a case, and while it might not be possible to supply empirical evidence for this intuitive knowledge, it was nevertheless the definitive judgment in a pending case.[111] Thierack was equally eager to speed the partification of the judiciary personnel. At the end of the year, one of

108. This was especially true of Mutschmann and deputy GL Seeger in Danzig. See the extensive documentation in BDC/Seeger (PKC); and Bormann to Himmler, 15 Feb. 1944, BDC/v. Woyrsch (SS).

109. Berger to Himmler, 9 March 1943, T-175, roll 124, frame 2599560.

110. *GL Auszüge*, 5 March 1943, pp. 17 ff.

111. Dr. Bergmann (an official in the Reich ministry of justice), "Vermerk über eine Besprechung RJM-PK, 22.6.43," 23 June 1943, BA/R 22/vorl. 20672.

the two undersecretaries at the ministry, Curt Rothenberger, was dismissed from office largely because he continued to stress that although the party should be the leading interpreter of the law, the actual dispensing of justice should be in the hands of trained jurists. Bormann insisted that judicial personnel should be incorporated into the PO structure. The party's Reich legal office was eliminated as an affiliate and reorganized as part of the Gauleiters' staff office. Moreover, Thierack replaced a number of chief justices of supreme courts in the Länder with candidates supplied by the Gauleiters, and the new men then served as the judicial staff officials at the party's Gau offices. In this capacity, they were the direct subordinates of the Gauleiters.[112]

At the Reich chancellery, Heinrich Lammers was less disposed to become a handmaiden of the party. Although he had always been one of the most Nazified state officials, he was not willing to be partified, and Bormann's new influence as Hitler's secretary led him to initiate rather futile counterintrigues. If nothing could be done about the present, at least he could prepare for the future. In the fall of 1943, Lammers suggested a secret conclave to choose a successor in the event of Hitler's death. Lammers specifically wanted to exclude the influence of the party in choosing the Führer-designate.[113]

Along with virtually everyone else[114] in the Nazi hierarchy, Bormann continued his efforts to replace Bernhard Rust at the Reich ministry of culture. Rust himself did little to save his position and lamented drunkenly over his powerlessness,[115] but he remained in office. Hitler insisted that a new minister be thoroughly familiar with the Austrian public school and teacher-training system, and Bormann had no ready replacement for any of the Austrian Gauleiters.[116] In the meantime, the

112. Thierack, "Vermerk über Besprechung . . . mit . . . Bormann . . . 6. November [1943]," n.d., BA/NS 22/4062 fol. 1.

113. Walter Baum, "Regierung Dönitz und deutsche Kapitulation," in Andreas Hillgruber, ed., *Probleme des Zweiten Weltkrieges* (Cologne, 1967), p. 347.

114. Oven, *Mit Goebbels*, I, entry for 15 July 1943, p. 161; and Rolf Eilers, *Die nationalsozialistische Schulpolitik* (Cologne, 1963), p. 111.

115. On Rust's drunken performance before the September 1943 conference of university presidents, see Kaltenbrunner's report to Bormann (which the latter passed on to Hitler), Nov. 1943, BDC/Rust (SS); and Helmut Heiber, *Walter Frank und sein Reichsinstitut für die Geschichte des neuen Deutschlands* (Stuttgart, 1966), pp. 641–42.

116. Eilers, *Schulpolitik*, p. 114.

PK pursued its partification program with a series of piecemeal successes. The PK urged greater activism on the part of the PO in all aspects of social control,[117] and Schwarz demanded RM 87 million in Reich subsidies for Volkstumsarbeit in fiscal 1943.[118] A major triumph was the subordination (in April 1943) of two-year nurses' training programs to the control of the PK. The new curriculum, in addition to practical experience, involved almost a hundred and fifty hours (out of five hundred) of ideological and racial indoctrination. The PK hoped this concentration upon the Darwinism of Nazi racial science would replace the traditional Christian humanitarian orientation of the nurses with the hard, fanatic line of the Nazi racial scientists.[119] Somewhat later, similar reforms reshaped the training curricula of midwives and kindergarten teachers—the two professional groups that dealt with children in their most formative stages of development.[120]

Undoubtedly, the most significant target in party-state relations and the pivot of cooperation between Himmler and Bormann[121] was partification of the present and future civil service. On the eve of Himmler's appointment as minister of the interior, Bormann stressed again that the party's judgment must be decisive in the appointment and promotion of civil servants.[122] Schwarz and Bormann were hard at work on plans that would have drastically altered the traditional university-oriented training programs of the Reich bureaucracy. According to the party, for all but the top ranks of the civil service a university degree was not necessary: a graduate of the party-sponsored Hauptschulen could perform the duties equally well.[123]

Bormann's willingness to permit the Gauleiters a wide range of latitude in administering the wartime activities of their Gaus, provided that the PK retained power to influence basic decisions at the center,

117. Friedrichs to Witt, 13 Nov. 1943, RvO/BDC/H 1168.

118. See Reich minister of finance to Reich treasurer, 13 May 1943, RvO/BDC/H 51.

119. See the "Programm der Zweijährigen Krankenpflegeschule a.o. Krankenhaus Znaim/Niederdonau, April 1943–April 1945," BA/NS 6/326.

120. *VAB*, IV, 172 and 173; and ROL, "Anordnung A 16/42," n.d., *Verordnungsblatt Gau Franken*, no. 2 (1 Feb. 1943).

121. Hans Mommsen, *Beamtentum in Dritten Reich* (Stuttgart, 1966), p. 38.

122. Bormann to Schwarz, 26 June 1943, T-580, roll 840, box 265, folder 338.

123. Lingg, "Besuchs-Vermerk 19. Februar 1944–1. März 1944," n.d., T-580, roll 82, folder 394.

led to what was perhaps the most bitter of the many intraregime disputes in the last years of the Third Reich, the monumental battle between Bormann and the party on one side and Albert Speer on the other. At the time of Speer's appointment, Bormann had made a point of requesting the Gauleiters to support whatever measures the minister felt were necessary to increase German armaments production,[124] and while the Gauleiters' response was something less than enthusiastic, there were no major flare-ups between Speer and provincial party leaders until the defection of Italy. Under the impact of this major shift in the diplomatic and military balance of power, Speer called for a far more drastic application of the concept of total warfare. In a speech to the Gauleiters on October 6, the minister devoted most of his remarks to an indictment of mismanagement in the army's logistical support program, but he also accused the Gauleiters of straining to keep a near peacetime economy operating in their areas of jurisdiction and thereby, in effect, sabotaging the war effort.[125] The address was an opening salvo in a struggle that increased in intensity as the situation at home and at the fronts deteriorated. Neither Bormann[126] nor the Gauleiters took Speer's criticism very gracefully, although (or more likely because) it was generally well founded. The popular storm of revenge with which Goebbels threatened the Reich's enemies in his Sportpalast speech of February had turned out to be little more than a mild breeze. Speer supported the mobilization effort wholeheartedly, the party to a much lesser degree, and Hitler, fearing popular reaction gave it virtually no backing.[127] The party's role in the effort was characterized by a revealing schizophrenia. The PO was eager to have on hand a very comprehensive body of laws and regulations governing every conceivable aspect of the mobilization effort,[128] but the PLs made little actual use of the machinery. The regulations served merely to insure the party's

124. Bormann to all GL, "Rundschreiben 6/43," IfZ/PK/Rdschr. geh.

125. Speer, *Erinnerungen*, pp. 289–90, and 326.

126. Bormann accused Speer of striving to become Hitler's successor. Speer, *Erinnerungen*, p. 289. One obvious result of the visible decline of Hitler's state of health was increased concern with his replacement among the paladins.

127. "HMB/OBB," 10 March 1943, Bayerisches Geheimes Staatsarchiv (cited hereafter as BGStA). MA 106671; and Gregor Janssen, *Das Ministerium Speer* (Berlin, 1968), pp. 120–21, and 267–68.

128. See *VI*, nos. 5, 10, and 20 (10 Feb., 10 March, and 4 May 1943, resp.).

permanent control of the entire effort.[129] In actual practice, the PO's contribution to the mobilization drive was a propaganda campaign to combat what was already runaway inflation[130] and, most important, to make sure that PLs were exempt from the general draft of able-bodied Germans into the armaments industry. The Gau economic advisors met once at the beginning of the year to hear Speer, and while Bormann was present at the session (and took copious notes), he made no effort to endorse Speer's views.[131] The head of the PK's economic department also had other priorities: he devoted his major energies to the Aryanization program and various vaguely anticapitalist and anticorporation campaigns.[132]

Like most two-component struggles, the disagreements between Speer and the party reached multicomponent levels as Sauckel, in his capacity as GBA, supported the Gauleiters, while the army gave its backing to Speer.[133] The contest thus provided an additional incentive for the party to increase its influence over the armed forces. Goebbels angrily voiced his conviction that the war could have been won long ago if the party had been in charge instead of the generals,[104] and other party segments echoed his outburst. Bormann insisted that a large amount of personnel fat could be cut from the army, and both the PK's chief and the Gauleiters wanted an expanded political indoctrination program to instill the will to victory in the demoralized German soldier.[135] The party leaders did not hesitate to cite the example of the Soviet political commissar as a model for the partification of the German army. As one Gauleiter put it, there are times when a political

129. *GL Auszüge* (26 Feb. 1943), p. 2; and GL Sudetenland, "Anordnung 633/674g," 26 Feb. 1943, BDC/Donnewert (SS), I.

130. PK, "Rundschreiben 97/43," 30 June 1943, *VAB*, V, 268–69.

131. See Gau economic advisor Vienna to head of the Southeast Europe Society (Vienna), 25 Jan. 1943, T-81, roll 661, frame 5468791; and Dr. Heffter *et al.*, "Aktennotiz über ein Gespräch mit Herrn Dr. Wolff am 20.9.1950," Forschungsstelle für die Geschichte des Nationalsozialismus in Hamburg (cited hereafter as Forsch. Hbg.)/PA/12/T. Wolff was the Gau economic advisor of Hamburg.

132. See, for example, the contents of *NS-Wirtschaftspolitik*, no. 9 (10 Sept. 1943).

133. Janssen, *Ministerium*, pp. 131–32.

134. Oven, *Mit Goebbels*, entry for 10 Aug. 1943, I, 87.

135. PK, "Rundschreiben 3/43g," 12 Jan. 1943, IfZ/PK/Rdschr. geh.; and *GL Auszüge* (26 June 1943), pp. 13–20.

commissar is "not out of place at all."[136] Although the practical application of this concept was still in its infancy, the establishment of the program of National Socialist leadership officer (*Nationalsozialistischer Führungsoffizier,* NSFO) after the battle of Stalingrad constituted a major opening for the further partification of the army.[137] In addition to the NSFO programs, the party concerned itself primarily with personnel appointments in the armed forces. The PK demanded absolute control over the appointment of civilian officials in the army,[138] and sought to infiltrate the officer corps as well. The Hoheitsträgers evaluation became part of the documentation necessary for an officer's promotion, and the PK also tried to speed the advance to officer rank of PLs who served as enlisted men.[139]

It was symptomatic of the increasing vertical partification of the Reich that the centralization of army-party relations at the national level was paralleled by similar controls within the office of the Gau staff leader in the provinces. Indeed, the process of the partification of Germany's regional administration continued at a steady if undramatic pace throughout the year. The developments were most pronounced wherever Reichsgaus had already been established, as in Austria or Danzig,[140] but in the Altreich, too, notable changes occurred. Hitler permitted additional Personalunions between Gauleiters and provincial governors,[141] and as some of the new breed of administratively trained Gauleiters moved into their powerful positions, they increasingly eliminated the distinction between party and state administration in the Gaus.[142] Simultaneously, Klopfer and the PK's division III worked to

136. *GL Auszüge* (2 and 9 April and 19 June 1943), pp. 3, 7–10, and 10–12, respectively.

137. Manfred Messerschmidt, *Die Wehrmacht im NS-Staat* (Hamburg, 1969), pp. 329–30, and 445.

138. Bormann even participated in the appointment of the judge advocate-general. See Bormann to Lammers, 20 May 1943, BA/R 43 II/455c.

139. PK, "Rundschreiben 24/43 g. Rs.," 25 May 1943, IfZ/PK/Rdschr. geh.; and Messerschmidt, *Wehrmacht,* p. 379, n. 1272.

140. With the creation of Reichsgaus, the venerable institution of *Landrats* was abolished; in their place moved Gau administrative directors (*Gauverwaltungsdirektor*). See the interrogation of Bartels (Gau cultural official of Westphalia-North and architect of Himmler's Wewelsburg), IfZ/ZS 1004.

141. See Domarus, *Hitler,* II, 2096–97. See also Peter Hüttenberger, *Die Gauleiter* (Stuttgart, 1969), pp. 153 ff.

142. Speer, *Erinnerungen,* p. 324.

reduce the autonomy of a number of Länder and Reich ministerial agencies and to place their functions under the control of the Reich defense commissioners, who were of course the Gauleiters.[143] In states like Bavaria, where the prime minister was also a Gauleiter, a directive from Hitler gave the Land government far-reaching powers to reassign the jurisdictional parameters of the governmental agencies resident in the territory.[144] Above all, the various directives placed virtually all significant personnel appointments for the Gau—from university teaching posts to public prosecutors—in the hands of the Gauleiters.[145]

In supporting the Gauleiters' virtual control of the state administrative offices, the PK had to tread warily lest the provincial declaration of autonomy include the party's central authority as well. In a number of specific instances, the PK opposed moves toward what it considered excessive independence. A request by the Gauleiter of Pomerania to give him control over draft exemptions in his Gau was rejected out of hand,[146] and both Bormann and Himmler pounced on Gauleiter Wahl when he attempted to set up something akin to a private army.[147] Still, lest he offend his most important collaborators, Bormann welcomed the Gauleiters' suggestion for the most effective way of phrasing the official condolence letters which the local leaders delivered to the next of kin of battlefield casualties.[148]

In addition, the PK relied on the Gau staff leaders to preserve its influence over Gau policies. By the middle of the year, each Gau had a fully established Gau staff office, headed by a PL who, alone among the Gau functionaries, could not be appointed before he had spent at least four weeks at the PK in Munich.[149] The office was deliberately structured as a regional counterpart to the politically most significant agen-

143. Interrogation of Klopfer, p. 7, IfZ/ZS 352. See also the undated "Notiz" on a conference between representatives of the Bavarian state government and the PK, 15 March 1943, BGStA, MA 105418.

144. See Hitler's decree of 7 Dec. 1943 in Domarus, *Hitler*, II, 2063.

145. Rothenberger to GL Hildebrandt, 8 July 1943, Forsch. Hbg./PA/12 Rothenberger); and *VI*, nos. 18 and 32 (22 April and 30 June 1943).

146. *GL Auszüge* (3 March 1943).

147. On GL Wahl's "home guard" see Bormann to Wahl, 18 Oct. 1943, T-81, roll 179, frames 328962–63.

148. *GL Auszüge* (8 Jan. 1943).

149. Walkenhorst, "Vorlage," 18 May 1943, BA/NS 6/166. See also PK, "Anordnung 31/43," 14 May 1943, *VAB*, V, 349.

cies of the far-flung horizontal divisions of the PK's national office (see figures 3 and 4). The office of the Gau economic advisor also exercised significantly greater authority in the last half of 1943. The weak Reich minister of economics suffered increasingly from ulcers, and the Gau economic advisors became the major regional rivals to Speer's ambitions. The advisors, whom Bormann looked upon as "directly responsible to me,"[150] dominated the Gau economic chambers,[151] and interfered directly in the personnel decisions of private business through their powers of political evaluation. This was true particularly of executives traveling abroad, but to a lesser extent the Gau economic advisor also took it upon himself to judge the political and economic performance of executives within his own Gau.[152]

Most of the elaborate social control machinery remained dormant, since the party's activities were increasingly dominated by the twin problems of armaments production and air raids. Hitler and Bormann disliked the bombings' interference with the war effort, but they almost welcomed the political side effect of the raids. Hitler commented that, as in the case of elections in the Kampfzeit, air raids tested a Gauleiter's ability to perform under extreme pressure.[153] The Gauleiters, too, pointed to the effect of the air raids as evidence of their colleagues' incompetence.[154] And for the party as a whole, the air raids proved that only the NSDAP was capable of handling genuine emergencies.[155]

There is little doubt the bombings of German cities had counterproductive propaganda consequences for the Allies. The population as a

150. Martin Bormann to Gerda Bormann, 26 July 1944, in Bormann, *Letters*, p. 68.

151. Dr. Mündich, "Gau Wirtschaftskammer Thüringen—Gestalt und Aufgaben," *Wirtschaftsblätter für den Gau Thüringen*, XVIII (29 Jan. 1943), 303. See also Giesler's address to the "Lehrgang auf der Ordensburg Sonthofen vom 31.5.–5.6.1943," IfZ/Fb. 96.

152. See the relevant documents in BA/NS 6/289 and 290; and Bohle to Bormann, 19 May 1943, BDC/Bohle (SS).

153. See Hitler's remarks to Gen. Zeitzler, 27 Dec. 1943, quoted in Heiber, *Lagebesprechungen*, p. 479; and Seyss-Inquart to Bormann, 14 Aug. 1943, RvO/BDC/H 518. The Gauleiters in turn used the air raids to test their staffs. See Kaufmann to Querner (HSSPF in Hamburg), 23 Sept. 1943, BDC/Kaufmann (SS).

154. *Berichte zur weltanschaulichen Lage* (6 Oct. 1943), pp. 7–8.

155. VI, nos. 28 and 53 (31 July and 9 Dec. 1943); and Grohé's speech (n.d.) to the "Lehrgang auf der Ordensburg Sonthofen vom 31.5.–5.6.1943," p. 32, IfZ/Fb. 96.

FIGURE 3

Gau Staff Office Gau Baden-Alsace

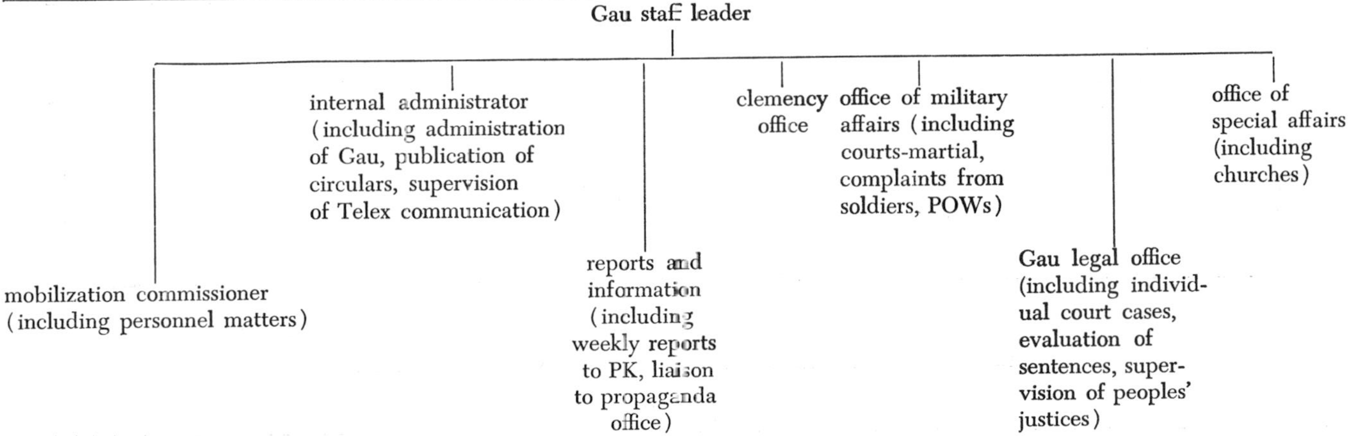

Gau staff leader

internal administrator (including administration of Gau, publication of circulars, supervision of Telex communication)

mobilization commissioner (including personnel matters)

reports and information (including weekly reports to PK, liaison to propaganda office)

clemency office

office of military affairs (including courts-martial, complaints from soldiers, POWs)

Gau legal office (including individual court cases, evaluation of sentences, supervision of peoples' justices)

office of special affairs (including churches)

SOURCES: *VOBl Gau Baden-Elsass*, no. 6 (1 June 1943); PK, "Rundschreiben 7/43," 6 Jan. 1943, *VAB*, IV, 36; and Telschow (GL Osthanover) to Rothenberger, 8 Jan. 1943, Forsch, Hbg./PA/12/(Rothenberger).

FIGURE 4

PK Organization Chart

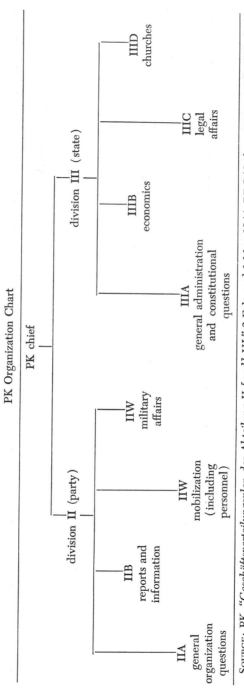

SOURCE: PK, "*Geschäftsverteilungsplan der Abteilung II [und] III*," 2 Feb. and 1 May 1944, BDC/Ordner PK, St., Prä-K.

NOTE: The organization of the PK has been simplified for graphic clarity.

whole did not blame the party for the bombs, but the Allied pilots, and the Hoheitsträgers could well reinforce their popular standing by impressive feats of Betreuung after a severe raid. On the other hand, restrictions originating in Berlin or Munich curtailing the availability of supplies and freedom of movement led to popular dissatisfaction with the Hoheitsträgers. It did not take the PLs long to discover that while Hitler might want morale and armaments, when the two goals were mutually incompatible, the Führer gave priority to the first. Fearing the consequences of reports of poor morale in their areas, the functionaries ignored even the prodding from the PK and Goebbels' office,[156] and all but sabotaged Speer's efforts to mobilize the civilian labor reserves.[157] The PLs rigorously enforced the numerous restrictions on the living habits of foreign workers,[158] but as for the Germans, the party mobilized not production, but propaganda. With a heavy concentration on the offices of the PO,[159] the NSDAP in 1943 attempted to instill its propaganda into all facets of public life,[160] although the major thrust was directed at the PLs and the party membership. There was a significant distinction in the techniques used to belabor these two groups, but the content was essentially similar. The propaganda and training curricula were almost entirely of the morale-uplift variety. The topics and propaganda themes increased confidence by raising unfulfillable hopes among the party's officials and members. There was a heavy emphasis upon the difficulties faced by the enemy, upon the momentary nature of the German setbacks, and above all on the omnipotence and omniscience of Hitler.[161] Anti-Semitic emphases continued to abound. One

156. *GL Auszüge* (12 Feb. 1943), pp. 14–18; and *Propaganda-Parole*, no. 17 (10 Feb. 1943), pp. 1–3, MiU/GAC, folder 56.

157. *GL Auszüge* (8 Jan. 1943), p. 16; and Speer, *Erinnerungen*, p. 299.

158. The total number of foreign workers in Germany in November 1943 was 3,413,225 (Edward L. Homze, *Foreign Labor in Nazi Germany* [Princeton, N.J., 1967], p. 148). About a third of the VIs for the year are concerned with their treatment and supervision.

159. Walter Tiessler, "Keine Aufgabenverschiebung," Gauring München-Oberbayern, *Mitteilungen*, no. 11 (May 1943), pp. 7–8.

160. On the activation of the PO see PK, "Anordnung 55/43," 29 Sept. 1943, *VAB*, IV, 8–10. The scope of the party's activities may be surmised from the list of activity areas in the Gau Baden-Elsass given in T-81, rolls 120–121, frames 141710 and 142163.

161. The propaganda themes for 1943 can be obtained from the issues of the Gauring München-Oberbayern, *Mitteilungen*, and the same Gau's *Parole* for that

propaganda journal put the case with truly unique candor: the Jew must be destroyed both ideologically and physically.[162]

The PK also continued its efforts to strengthen the districts at the expense of the party's Reichsleitung offices. Bormann made no secret of his aim to reduce the party's central offices (other than the PK) to relatively minor agencies, while the freed PLs should be transferred to the district level. He was particularly eager to duplicate the entire horizontal staff organization of the Gaus in the districts, so as to enable the district Hoheitsträgers to act as direct control organs of all party and state activities.[163] Needless to say, the party chancellery regarded the appointment of district leaders as crucial;[164] indeed, the PK on occasion sent one of its own staffers to lead a particularly important district organization.[165] The actual performance of the district organization in the two primary areas of air-raid cleanup and civilian mobilization was rather mixed. On one occasion after an air raid, for example, the party was particularly proud that all of its honorary PLs turned out in response to the party's orders, but it ignored the adverse effect of reducing the municipal work force by two thirds; the same officials who were busy as block leaders for the party were obviously absent from the administrative office of the water department.[166] Similarly, economic control functions were often a euphemism for snooping and

---

year. The organizational scope of the 1943 propaganda effort is apparent from the following figures: in the first six months of the year the Gau Thuringia had staged 94 Gau and district staff sessions, 1,986 local training sessions, 1,845 *Sprechabende*, 132 district staff training sessions, and 1,099 miscellaneous propaganda meetings. See "Volkskunde und Weltanschauliche Feiern," *Berichte zur weltanschaulichen Lage* (6 Aug. 1943), p. 28. Understandably, a large number of PLs had little interest in such sessions. See "Rundschreiben 47/43," 2 Dec. 1943, T-81, roll 124, frame 145894.

162. Gau training office Thuringia, *Rednerschulung*, no. 21 (15 Aug. 1944), p. 5.
163. Lingg, "Tagung der Arbeitsgemeinschaft-Selbstverwaltung 16. November 1943," 24 Nov. 1943, T-580, roll 82, folder 394. See also PK, "Anordnung 34/43," 22 May 1943, *VAB*, IV, 501–02.
164. PK, "Anordnung 53/43," 15 Sept. 1943, *VAB*, III, 77–79. See also the report of the *Völkischer Beobachter* (18 March 1943) on a speech by GL Giesler.
165. This was true of Vienna. Ludwig Jedlicka, *Das Einsame Gewissen*, 2d ed. (Vienna, 1966), p. 11.
166. Hans-Peter Görgen, "Düsseldorf und der Nationalsozialismus" (Dissertation, University of Cologne, 1968), pp. 217–18.

petty interference. In some instances, the district leader took it upon himself to have important industrial workers drafted for political reasons, and both he and the local leaders made widespread use of their authority to "inspect" industrial enterprises.[167] Toward the end of the year, the district leaders were also given what amounted to police powers. They were to cooperate and in fact direct the work of the police in rounding up deserters, foreign laborers, and so on.[168]

In contrast to the districts and Gaus, the locals continued to remain primarily Betreuung organizations. As part of the Backe-Bormann agreement the office of agricultural policy activated its program of "village cultural" policy, while the tired bones of the SA gave the party visibility through frequent propaganda marches.[169] The only major innovation in the activities of the locals was the reintroduction of the *Sprechabend* (discussion evening) for the local party members. The Sprechabend was a propaganda technique that had been used with good effect in the Kampfzeit, and Bormann obviously hoped that the informal atmosphere of a guided discussion would reduce some of the apathy frequent at large-scale propaganda meetings with their set speeches. During a Sprechabend the local leader still delivered himself of a stirring address, presumably of somewhat shorter duration, but then he opened the meeting for questions from the floor—although Bormann warned him to permit no queries relating to military strategy, foreign policy, church-state relations, or questions that contained criticism of the regime.[170]

At the end of the year, the PK expressed its full satisfaction with the activation of the party; the NSDAP was unshakable.[171] Actually, the major results of the year's activities were a further reduction in the

167. PK, "Rundschreiben 17/43g [and] 28/43g," 8 March and 15 June 1943, IfZ/PK Rdschr. geh. The latter practice was prohibited by the PK.

168. PK, "Rundschreiben 57/43g," 27 Oct. 1943, IfZ/PK Rdschr. geh.

169. PK, "Anordnung 17/43," 11 March 1943, *RVBl* (A) no. 18 (13 March 1943), p. 44; *VI*, no. 25 (21 May 1943); and PK, "Anordnung 56/43," 30 Sept. 1943, *VAB*, III, 12.

170. PK, "Anordnung 5/43," 17 Feb. 1943, *RVBl* (A) no. 10 (19 Feb. 1943), pp. 27–28. See also *VI*, nos. 27 and 31 (2 and 23 June 1943, resp.). Unlike many other decrees issued by the center, the *Sprechabend* directive seems to have been implemented in every Gau.

171. PK, "Anordnung 64/43," 11 Dec. 1943, *RVBl* (A) no. 52 (11 Dec. 1943).

autonomous status of the affiliates, with a corresponding increase in the power of the PO's territorial organization,[172] and additional partification inroads into the fabric of German society,[173] rather than a notable growth in the fanaticism of the average party member.

Although the German armies were steadily retreating on all fronts, sizable areas of foreign soil remained under Nazi administration throughout 1943 and into much of 1944. While the party was eager to avoid unpopular measures in the Reich, it hesitated to introduce any concessions in the occupied areas, lest these modify the basic policies of naked oppression and extreme exploitation.[174] The only thing common to the NSDAP's rule at home and abroad after Stalingrad was the conviction that an activated PL corps could save the situation.[175] Almost to the end, neither Hitler nor other major Nazi leaders recognized the possibility of permanent losses in the East. PLs who had become unemployed by the advance of the Red Army did not join the armed forces, but, on Hitler's orders, held themselves ready to move back East as the Wehrmacht reconquered their former bases of operation.[176] Bormann entertained some totally unrealistic hopes for a separate peace between Germany and the Soviet Union, and he encouraged whatever nonefforts were being made in this direction,[177] but he was of one mind with Hitler and Himmler in advocating a continuation of the policies

172. PK, "Rundschreiben 174/43," 24 Dec. 1943, *VAB*, IV, 221–22.

173. PK, "Rundschreiben 164/43," 26 Nov. 1943, *ibid.*, p. 106.

174. See Walter Hewel (the representative of the foreign ministry at Hitler's headquarters) "Auszug aus Notiz für RAM v. 24.5. . . . ," Nuremberg doc. no. NG 3288; and Willi A. Boelcke, ed., *Deutschlands Rüstung im Zweiten Weltkrieg— Hitlers Konferenzen mit Albert Speer 1943–1945* (Frankfurt, 1969), entry for 4 May 1943, p. 252. The best overall analysis of the shifting of Nazi policies after the battle of Stalingrad is Alexander Dallin, *German Rule in Russia, 1941–45* (New York, 1957), pp. 177 ff. On Poland see Martin Broszat, *Nationalsozialistische Polenpolitik 1939–1945* (Stuttgart, 1951), p. 187.

175. *GL Auszüge* (5 June 1943).

176. "Vortrag des Reichsministers Rosenberg beim Führer am 17. November 1943," n.d., Centre Documentation Juive Contemporaine (cited hereafter as CDJC)/CXLII-380.

177. Henry Picker, ed., *Hitler's Tischgespräche im Führerhauptquartier 1941– 42*, new ed. by Percy-Ernst Schramm *et al.* (Stuttgart, 1965), p. 517. This has since given rise to the more than fanciful speculation that Bormann was a Soviet agent. See Richard Gehlen, *Der Dienst* (Mainz, 1971); and, for an effective rejoinder, the letter to the editor by Joseph Wulf, *Der Spiegel*, XXV (25 Sept. 1971), 10.

of extreme repression and Nazification throughout the occupied areas.[178]

In what remained occupied of the occupied Eastern territories, administrative chaos and intraparty infighting reached almost equal levels.[179] Gottlob Berger succeeded in becoming undersecretary[180] at the RMO (replacing Rosenberg's confidant Georg Leibrandt), but the ministry's authority over the territorial lords was virtually extinct. The RKU refused to carry out any of the mild concessions to the Russian people suggested by the RMO,[181] and both Rosenberg and Koch appealed to the SS for support. Berger in turn thought little of either contestant, but welcomed the opportunity to extend the SS's influence.[182] Relations between Rosenberg and Lohse were better, but the RKO's major subordinate, Wilhelm Kube, the commissioner-general for Belorussia, acted very independently. As an ex-Gauleiter, he was Lohse's equal in his status as Hitler's derivative agent, and as a close personal friend of Gauleiter Meyer he incited the wrath of Berger and the SS. Until he was assassinated in September, Kube worked hard to establish something of a benevolent despotism in Belorussia. He had already reached the decision that racially the Belorussians were Aryan and could therefore be treated as a cultured people. In consequence, Kube had ambitions to found a university.[183]

While Bormann used his influence with Hitler to affect the outcome of the multifaceted rivalries of the eastern territorial commissioners the PK's primary institutional concern was with the mass of lower-level PLs in the East, a group describing itself as "politically clear-thinking and fanatical people" as well as very competent administrators.[184] Here Himmler's appointment as Reich minister of the interior inaugurated

178. For Bormann's ideas for judicial reforms in all of Europe see Thierack, "Vermerk über Besprechung . . . mit . . . Bormann . . . 6. November [1943]," BA/ NS 22/4062 fol. 1.

179. Dallin, *German Rule in Russia*, pp. 168 ff.

180. *Ibid.*, pp. 172–74.

181. See the intraoffice memo of the office of the Gauleitung [*sic*] Weissruthenien, 26 Aug. 1944, CDJC/CXLVIIa-3.

182. Berger to Himmler, 27 March 1943 and 22 April 1944, quoted in Heiber, *Reichsführer*, pp. 204–05, and 260.

183. See "Protokoll über die Tagung der Gebietskommissare . . . des General-kommissars in Minsk vom 8. April bis 10 April 1943," pp. 27–44, IfZ/Fb. 85.

184. Wurster (deputy district commissioner in the Arbeitsbereich East) to Michelfelder (chief of staff of the Arbeitsbereich), 14 July 1944, T-580, roll 834, box 257, folder 274.

a potentially major shift of authority in favor of the SS. Since most of the Hoheitsträgers in the Soviet Union and Poland were also civil administrators, the Reich leader of the SS became their immediate superior as civil servants after May 1943.[185] The PK countered this development by a massive buildup and strengthening of the Arbeitsbereichs,[186] which had been previously authorized to control the activities of all Reich Germans working in the occupied areas.

The development was particularly sudden and noticeable in the government-general. Here the primary rivals for power had been Frank and the SS, while the Arbeitsbereich remained somewhat in the background. In the spring and summer came a dramatic change. On paper at least, the party acquired a full-scale vertical and horizontal organization. Particularly noteworthy was the organizational similarity between the Arbeitsbereich's staff office and that of the Gau staff office in the Altreich[187] and the sudden establishment of a "leadership staff" of the SA in Poland—the latter obviously the consequence of the Bormann-Schepmann pact.[188] Like its counterparts in other occupied countries, the Arbeitsbereich had as its major activity the control of all Reich Germans, including members of the SS,[189] through a two-tiered organization of the Arbeitsbereich itself and the mass-membership German Community (*Deutsche Gemeinschaft*, DG). Neither organization had an open membership policy,[190] but co-opted members. Basically, the DG consisted of all Reich and ethnic Germans in Poland, while the

185. Herbert S. Levine, "Local Authority and the SS State: The Conflict over Population Policy in Danzig–West Prussia, 1939–1945," *Central European History*, II (Dec. 1969), 352. For criticism of the *Personalunionen* within the PO see Wurster to Michelfelder, 26 June and 14 July 1944; and Hartmann (Schwarz's representative in the Arbeitsbereich East) to Schwarz, 31 July 1944, T-580, roll 834, box 257, folder 274.

186. The growth may be followed in the issues of the *VOBl Arbeitsbereich Generalgouvernement* (cited hereafter as *VOBl Arb. GG*) for 1943.

187. *VOBl Arb. GG*, III, nos. 1–3 (1943). The complete list of functionaries assigned to the staff office of the Arb. GG amounted to fifty-two PLs by the end of July 1943. See *ibid.*, no. 9 (1943). An incomplete set of the *VOBl Arb. GG* is available in the BA/NSD/1607. The document cited is one issue, not three as the numbering would indicate.

188. *Ibid.*, nos. 4–6 (1943).

189. See Tiessler (deputy head of the Arb. GG) to Koppe (HSSPF in the GG), 5 April 1944; and Berger to Himmler, 26 April 1944, BA/NS 19/1507.

190. The DG, for example, rejected out of hand every person classified in category 4 of the DVL. See *VOBl Arb. GG*, III, no. 8 (1943).

Arbeitsbereich boasted a very select membership of active PLs and certain co-opted dignitaries.[191]

It goes almost without saying that theory and practice differed rather widely. With the Russian armies pounding at the borders, and an incompetent administration from the governor-general on down, the party organization disintegrated rapidly. Corruption remained rampant,[192] and as the Reich and ethnic Germans did their best to refuse volunteer work for the party and disengage from the regime, the Arbeitsbereich's territorial organization existed primarily on paper. Particularly at the lower levels vast areas had no PLs whatsoever.[193]

A similar crash program to activate the Arbeitsbereich East was no more successful. There was no shortage of artfully designed uniforms and organizational charts,[194] but huge administrative areas were virtually without PLs. As in the Altreich and Poland, the most important decision-making center was the Arbeitsbereich's staff office (termed staff chancellery in the East), whose horizontal divisions essentially paralleled those of the Gau staff offices in Germany. And, like its counterpart in the West, the Arbeitsbereich East looked upon itself as an elitist, decision-making entity that shunned public exposure.[195] Nevertheless all was in vain; before the Arbeitsbereich could become a meaningful control organ, the minuscule apparatus had been swept away by the advancing Red Army.[196]

As a result of its geographic position, the Arbeitsbereich Nether-

191. *Ibid.*, nos. 4–6.

192. "Weltanschauliche Erziehung," *Berichte zur weltanschaulichen Lage* (6 Aug. 1943), p. 24.

193. *VOBl Arb. GG*, III, nos. 8–9, and 11–12 (1943); and *GL-Auszüge* (16 April 1943).

194. The staff organizational chart is summarized in Dr. Patutschnick, "Zur Vorlage an den Herrn Reichsleiter [Fiehler]," 29 Jan. 1943, BA/NS 25/1; and Hitler, "Verfügung 2/43," *VOBl*, no. 241 (Feb. 1943). For the territorial divisions see PK, "V.I. 31/387," 23 June 1943, *VAB*, V, 342.

195. The official *Deutsche Zeitung im Ostland* (Reval) published no reports on the activity of the Arb. Osten with the exception of one article on the organization of the Winterhilfswerk (10 Oct. 1943).

196. At the time of its establishment, the Arb. office in the district Weissruthenien consisted of two PLs; a year and a half later the office still had only eighteen functionaries. See Wurster to staff leader Arb. Osten, 14 July 1944, T-580, roll 834, box 257, folder 274. On some of the Arbeitsbereich's less significant welfare–social control functions see the documents in BA/NS 20/84.

lands was active for a considerably longer time. Indeed, the Nazis hoped to use the manpower of Holland to bolster their faltering rule in Russia. Under the organizational auspices of the Arbeitsbereich, the Germans undertook to encourage Dutch colonists and artisans to sign up for service and eventually settle in the East so as to aid the Reich's economic exploitation efforts.[197] The Germans' long-term policy goals, both political and economic, were to associate the Dutch as collaborators with the Reich's Eastern policies,[198] but for the moment, the Nazis had a more immediate interest in forming the Dutch into auxiliary police forces to help fight the Soviet partisans.[199] Like most of the Nazi plans for the East, these never got beyond the stage of discussions and small-scale pilot projects, but it is interesting to note that the two Arbeitsbereichs, East and Netherlands, conducted negotiations entirely on their own, for all practical purposes ignoring the provisions of A 54/42. Neither the SS nor the state administration took an active part in the planning.[200]

The proposed transfer of Dutch settlers to the Soviet Union, with its naïveté and shortcomings,[201] was one of a variety of attempts to deal with the shock of Stalingrad in the occupied areas of Western Europe. That the defeat on the Volga had immense repercussions for the Nazi rule in the West became very evident quite soon. The consequences were perhaps most noticeable in Norway. Here the Germans had established an obvious collaborationist regime, so that Vidkun Quisling and his Nasjonal Samling bore formal responsibility for the increasingly

197. "Vortrag des Reichsministers Rosenberg beim Führer am 17. November 1943," n.d., CDJC/CXLII/380; and Schmier, "Besprechung am 3. Aug. 1943," 12 Aug. 1943, RvO/Generalkommissar zur besonderen Verwendung in den Niederlanden (cited hereafter as GKzbV [Ni])/9d.

198. Schmier, "Vorbesprechung am 5. Juni 1943 in Haag," 12 Aug. 1943 [_sic_], RvO/GKzbV (Ni)/9d.

199. Schmidt to Sauckel, 17 March 1943, RvO/TB/folder 58; and Schmier, "Besprechung bei Gauleiter Dr. Meyer am 1.9.1943 . . . ," 1 Sept. 1943, RvO/ GKzbV (Ni)/9d. Himmler was "flabbergasted"; such a plan would ruin his efforts to obtain Dutch volunteers for the Waffen-SS. See Himmler to Sauckel, 16 March 1943, RvO/BDC/H 94.

200. Schmier, "Vorbesprechung am 5. Juni 1943 . . ."; and "Besprechung am 11. Juni 1943," 12 Aug. 1943, RvO/GKzbV (Ni)/9d. The two Arbeitsbereichs did agree to keep Berger "informed." Schmier, "Besprechung am 15. Juli 1943," 12 Aug. 1943, _ibid._

201. For a report on the failure of the pilot projects see representative in Groningen to Seyss-Inquart _et al._, 31 Aug. 1943, RvO/GKzbV/13b.

repressive efforts of the Germans to mobilize Norway's labor reserves for the Reich's "total war effort."[202] The results were not only sullenness and even some unrest among the Norwegian population, but clear indications that the Nasjonal Samling itself was beginning to disintegrate.[203] The Reich commissioner, Terboven, became morose and blamed fate for his misfortunes.[204] The Arbeitsbereich, on the other hand, saw Terboven's self-effacement as an opportunity to give additional powers to the party's organization in Norway. Wegener's successor as operational head of the Einsatzstab (that is, Arbeitsbereich) Norway, Hans-Hendrik Neumann,[205] was no less ambitious than Wegener had been. Supported by the dubious reasoning that with Quisling at the helm of the country German-Norwegian relations had become an "intra-Germanic" affair, much of the dealings between the Reich authorities and the collaborators in Oslo were channeled directly through the offices of the PK and the Einsatzstab.[206]

There was no Quisling in Holland, but the popularity of the Nazis' policies and presence was no greater than in Norway. On the other hand, the position of the Arbeitsbereich Netherlands was considerably stronger. As Seyss-Inquart's "commissioner-general for special tasks," the head of the party organization, in close consultation with the PK,[207] played a major role in the formulation and execution of the Reich's policies in the Netherlands.[208] In addition, in the provinces, the Reich

202. See Lammers to Seyss-Inquart, 18 Jan. 1943, and the exchange of telex messages between Berlin and den Haag, Jan. 1943, RvO/TB/folders 55 and 56.

203. *GL Auszüge* (5 March and 26 June 1943).

204. Berger to Himmler, 29 May 1943, RvO/BDC/H 103.

205. Neumann was born in 1910 and joined the SA and NSDAP in 1930. A year later he switched to the SS and by 1938 had become Heydrich's adjutant. He moved to Norway with Wegener and served as "advisor" to the Nasjonal Samling. After a term as German police attaché in Sweden he returned to Norway first as head of the AO and after February 1943 as de facto chief of the *Einsatzstab*. See PK, "Rundschreiben 36/43," 27 Feb. 1943, *VAB*, V, 339; and Hans-Dietrich Loock, *Quisling, Rosenberg und Terboven* (Stuttgart, 1970), pp. 505–06, n. 2.

206. *GL Auszüge* (29 May 1943).

207. For examples see Eftger, "Vorlage für Pg. Schmidt," 14 Jan. 1943; Schmidt, "Vorlage an Reichsleiter Bormann," 15 March 1943; and Maurer, "Notiz für . . . Eftger," 19 Oct. 1943, RvO/GKzbV (Ni)/1f, BDC/H 1166, and GKzbV (Ni)/1j, respectively.

208. There were numerous instances of officials holding positions in both the Arb. and the office of the GKzbV. See GKzbV (Ni), "Geschäftsverteilungsplan," 29 Oct. 1943, RvO/GKzbV (Ni)/1a.

commissioner's representatives headed the NSDAP's territorial organization for their area of jurisdiction. As in the case of the other "Germanic" countries, the Nazis' policy aims in Holland after Stalingrad were a morally reprehensible and politically unrealistic blend of mutually incompatible goals. Before the battle of Stalingrad, the Arbeitsbereich had concerned itself primarily with the long-term association of Holland with Germany under Nazi control, but after January 1943 the short-term goal of direct economic exploitation for the benefit of the immediate war needs received increased emphasis. If the Dutch had been passively resistant to the association with Nazi Germany in 1940 and 1941, their opposition to the additional hardships imposed in the name of the Germanic struggle against bolshevism and plutocracy was not only virtually unanimous but active as well. Throughout 1943 measures and countermeasures created almost constant friction between the German occupation forces and the Dutch population. The Nazis insisted upon the return of the already freed POWs to German camps; the Dutch ignored a ban on listening to foreign broadcasts, the Germans seized privately owned radios; the Dutch staged a major strike wave in Overijssell in April 1943; the Germans purged politically suspect mayors.[209] Above all, the year was marked by the roundup of Jews for shipment to the extermination centers of the East and Schmidt's almost fanatical administration of Sauckel's slave-labor goals. The head of the Arbeitsbereich worked particularly hard to exclude both Speer's and Seyss-Inquart's agencies from this drive so that the Arbeitsbereich alone could claim credit for sending fifty thousand Dutch workers to Germany every month.[210]

All of these activities, as well as the ongoing creation of further partified affiliates for social control[211] could not have been carried out

209. Weidlich (representative in Overijssel) to Schmidt, 30 April 1943; Seyss-Inquart to Bormann, 10 May 1943; and Weidlich to Seyss-Inquart, 31 May 1943, RvO/TB/folders 61 and 62, respectively.
210. Schmidt to Timm (office of the GBA), 27 Feb. 1943; and Schmidt to provincial representatives, 5 April 1943, *ibid.*, folders 56 and 60, respectively.
211. The Nazis devoted particular energies to the buildup of the NAF and the Dutch Farmers' Association. See [R. Alt], "Bericht über die Arbeitstagung der Kreishandwerksmeister am 7.4.1943 in Utrecht," 12 April 1943, *ibid.*, 63C. [HSSPF Niederlande], "SD Bericht Nr. 138," 6 April 1943, RvO/GKzbV (Ni)/13p.

without the active participation of the NSB collaborators.[212] Such cooperation, however, became increasingly difficult to obtain as the Germans did their best to alienate their only institutional support in Holland.[213] Joint propaganda marches between NSDAP and NSB and comradely "Heil Hitler's" could not obscure the fact that the Arbeitsbereich for the most part treated the NSB as a subordinate organization which made no major policy decisions.[214] Predictably, the NSB's reaction paralleled that of the Nasjonal Samling in Norway. From Mussert on down, Dutch Nazi functionaries grumbled against their political mentors and some even engaged in measures that bordered on passive sabotage.[215]

It is indicative not only of Schmidt's political insensitivity, but of the prevailing Herrenmenschen mentality among the Arbeitsbereich's functionaries that they were seemingly unconcerned about the growing rift between the NSDAP and the NSB. This is all the more remarkable in view of the fact that Arbeitsbereich's position was by no means unchallenged. After a momentary lull in the spring following the battle of Stalingrad, the SS resumed its attack against the Arbeitsbereich, the NSB, and Schmidt personally. The lines were clearly drawn: Berger wanted to subordinate the Arbeitsbereich to his guidance office for Germanic volunteers for the armed SS (*Germanische Freiwilligen Leitstelle*),[216] while Schmidt argued that as Hoheitsträger all policy strands should be "firmly in [his] hand."[217] Moreover, both Schmidt and Ber-

212. For an example cf. Schmidt to RK's representatives, 5 March 1943, RvO/TB/58.

213. See Arb. NSDAP (Ni), "Wochenbericht," 3 April 1943, RvO/Arb. NSDAP (Ni)/3A I; and Neuburg to main office for racial affairs, 7 April 1943, T-175, roll 72, frame 2589342.

214. Arb. NSDAP (Ni), "Wochenbericht-Niederlande," 15 May 1943, RvO/Arb. NSDAP (Ni)/3 A I; and Ernst (Schmidt's advisor for agriculture), "Aktenvermerk für den Generalkommissar z.b.V.," 8 Oct. 1943, RvO/GKzbV (Ni)/13b.

215. Sellmer (the RK's representative in Drenthe) to Seyss-Inquart, 1 March 1943, *ibid.*, 58; and local leader in Hilversum, "Monatsbericht über Mai, 1943," 7 May 1943, RvO/Arb. NSDAP (Ni)/52j.

216. Berger to main office for racial policy, 22 March 1943, T-175, roll 72, frames 2589360–63; and interrogation of Klopfer, 14 Nov. 1947, pp. 2 and 4, IfZ/ZS 352.

217. Schmidt to PK, Feb. 1943, quoted in PK to main office for racial policy, 23 Feb. 1943, T-175, roll 72, frames 2589345–47.

ger followed incompatible long- and short-term aims simultaneously. What the quota of slave laborers was for Schmidt, SS volunteers were for Berger. Under Berger's auspices, the training curriculum of the Dutch HJ, for example, had but one aim: at the end of the course "it has to appear that whoever does not take up the struggle for the Germanic Reich in the SS is a coward."[218] Each side tried to line up allies in the Reich. Bormann took Schmidt's side, and Berger attempted to absorb the Reich office for racial policy and persuade Ley to endorse the SS's line on the Germanic Reich in the party's training programs.[219]

There was as yet no complete break between Himmler and Bormann at the Reich level (although Berger at one time did resort to literal espionage to obtain a confidential document from the PK's files[220]), but in Holland the HSSPF and the head of the Arbeitsbereich were for all practical purposes at war—and, as Berger said, "often very nasty war." In the middle, and none too steadily at that, stood the hapless Seyss-Inquart. He tilted alternately in the direction of the SS and the Arbeitsbereich. In actual conversation, he often agreed with the HSSPF, but after some reflection, the Reich commissioner tended to recognize again that if the NSB was a small collaborationist base, the pro-SS forces in Holland were infinitesimal.[221] Hitler himself was of no great help in the dispute. After another visit by Mussert to the Führer's headquarters, Hilter decided that while the NSB's leader should not become prime minister, neither should he be dropped; he would remain the Nazis' primary Dutch collaborationist vehicle.[222]

If this Solomonic decision was meant to restore something like an equilibrium to the Dutch political situation, the death of Fritz Schmidt in June brought the return of chaos. On the twenty-sixth, Schmidt

218. Fiessling (staff official of the Reich youth leadership), "Richtlinien für die weltanschauliche Schulung und Behandlung der germanischen Freiwilligen in den W[ehr]-E[rsatz]-Lagern 'Germanische Jugend,'" 19 March 1943, RvO/Arb. NSDAP (Ni)/51 III.

219. Tittmann (of the DAF's racial policy office) to Bruhn (official of the ROL's main training office), 28 July 1943, RvO/BDC/H 1083.

220. Cassel to Brandt, 14 April 1943, *ibid.*, H 398.

221. Rauter to Himmler, 29 May 1943; and Seyss-Inquart to Himmler, 29 May 1943, RvO/BDC/H 125 and H 218.

222. Himmler to Seyss-Inquart, 11 June 1943, *ibid.* At the same time both Berger and Himmler continued their efforts to undermine the effect of Hitler's order. See Himmler's letter to Seyss-Inquart and Rauter to Brandt, 19 Aug. 1943, *ibid.*, H 127.

committed suicide by throwing himself out of a moving train in northern France. He and a group of Gauleiters and deputy Gauleiters were returning from a junket to the coastal defenses when Schmidt decided to end his life. There is little doubt that he did commit suicide, although it took considerable effort on Friedrichs' part to convince Schmidt's widow that her husband had not been murdered by the SS.[223] Indirectly, of course, the SS was responsible. The head of the Arbeitsbereich saw himself blocked in all of his political initiatives by Rauter, and he found it beyond his psychological powers to continue his struggle.[224] Indeed, Schmidt was not the only Nazi leader to break under the strain of the SS-party conflict. In December, the head of the AO in Belgium shot himself for the same reason.[225] Nor did the rivals close ranks over Schmidt's grave. The funeral was a lavish affair, attended by Bormann, Seyss-Inquart, and every major NSB figure, but no leading SS officials made the effort to pay their last respects.[226]

Schmidt's body was hardly cold when the conflict over his successor was won by the PK. Schmidt had died on June 26. Three days later, Rauter wrote Himmler that the new head of the Arbeitsbereich would have to be an SS official. He suggested specifically Robert Thiel,[227] the RK's representative in North Brabant and an official of the Germanische Freiwilligen Leitstelle. Himmler in turn wired Bormann that he wished to speak to the head of the party chancellery before a decision on Schmidt's successor was made.[228] Still, the SS was too slow. On the very day of Schmidt's death, Friedrichs had already suggested a replacement: a rather obscure PK official named Ritterbusch.[229] The new man

223. Friedrichs to Bormann, 26 June 1943; Rauter to Himmler, 29 Nov. 1943, *ibid.*, H 1130 and H 595.

224. Rauter, "Aktenvermerk über Besprechung mit Schmidt und RK," 26 May 1943, RvO/BDC/H 125. See also Bormann's report of his last conversation with Schmidt on 21 June "Aktenvermerk für Pg. Friedrichs und Pg. Dr. Klopfer," 30 June 1943, *ibid.*, H 1147. In addition his brother's recent death may have contributed to the final depression. See PK to Schmidt, 28 June 1943 [*sic*], RvO/TB/64.

225. Jungclauss (HSSPF Brussels) to Himmler, 29 Dec. 1943, T-175, roll 117, frame 2642334–35.

226. *Deutsche Zeitung in den Niederlanden,* 30 June and 3 July 1943.

227. Thiel was born in 1909. Significantly, Schmidt had attempted to dispatch him to the Armed SS in 1942.

228. Rauter to Himmler, 29 June 1943, RvO/BDC/H 106; and Himmler to Bormann, 29 June 1943, T-175, roll 59, frame 2575486.

229. Friedrichs to Bormann, 26 June 1943, RvO/BDC/H 1130. Ritterbusch's

was hardly anyone's first choice,[230] but he was the only official available who had served for some time in Holland (he had been Thiel's predecessor in Brabant) and who could be appointed before, as one PK official put it, candidates from other directions could be nominated. Ritterbusch was a far more passive man than Schmidt (Rauter described him as "a typical elementary school teacher from the country"[231]), but he was as much of a PK man as his predecessor, and during his tenure in North Brabant he had been on particularly good terms with Mussert and the NSB.[232] Above all, the appointment frustrated Berger's ambitions, although the activist SS official was rather slow to realize his defeat. As late as August, Berger urged Rauter to develop the Germanische Freiwilligen Leitstelle as the central decision-making authority for all German policy in Holland, only to be told by the HSSPF that developments along these lines were completely out of the question as long as "the representative of Reichsleiter Bormann is sitting here in Holland."[233] Bormann had won another round over Berger.

Not that it made much difference for the long-range "Germanic" plans of either official. By the end of the year, the Russian army had liberated most of the Soviet Union, and the Western allies occupied the greater part of Italy. The mood of the German people, still faithfully measured by the SD's reports, was correspondingly bleak. It picked up somewhat in the spring of 1944, but these flickers of optimism were the result of a particularly impressive speech or newsreel, and died as quickly as they arose. However, the SD also reported that the decline in morale at home, particularly among women, was not so much a consequence of further military setbacks, which had become a steady occurrence anyway, but of "daily cares" (*Alltagssorgen*), especially the

---

appointment was not made public until 11 July. See *Deutsche Zeitung in den Niederlanden*, 11 July 1943.

230. See the private letter of Brandes (an official at the PK working on the evaluation of SD reports) to Zimmermann (district leader in Eindhoven) 9 July 1943, RvO/Arb. NSDAP (Ni)/72b.

231. Rauter to Himmler, 29 June 1943, RvO/BDC/H 106. See also Werner Warmbrunn, *The Dutch under German Occupation, 1940–1945* (Stanford, Cal., 1963), p. 33.

232. Rauter to Himmler, 28 June 1943, RvO/BDC/H 106.

233. Rauter to Brandt, 19 Aug. 1943, *ibid.*, H 127.

difficulties in obtaining food and household supplies. Moreover, the reports noted a decided lack of interest in such esoteric topics as the future of the Germanic Reich, but a grudging admiration for Stalin's ability to rally the Russians and concentrate their energies on the immediate needs of the war effort.[234]

This last point may well have been an oblique criticism of Hitler, who was not at all willing to risk his remaining store of charisma. The traditional celebration on the anniversary of the publication of the party's program in February was not held in 1944, and a scheduled meeting with the district leaders was postponed and never rescheduled.[235] Hitler still met from time to time with the Reichsleiters and Gauleiters, but the occasions were really little more than pep rallies.[236] As far as the lower ranks of PLs were concerned, Hitler anxiously tried to keep them from receiving information that might cause "mental anguish," such as digests of the foreign press.[237]

Strangely, the morale of the leading PLs was affected to a lesser degree by the constant setbacks of 1944 than by the series of sudden disasters a year before. Indeed, at the Führer's headquarters something like high confidence was the dominant mood for much of the year. As late as March 1944, Bormann refused to curtail the building activities on the Obersalzberg, and in May he became worried lest the war end before the PK had had a chance to work out proposed guidelines for a new personnel policy.[238] Much of the spring was taken up with elaborate preparations for a massive international anti-Semitic congress to be staged under Rosenberg's auspices in Cracow at the end of June. Al-

234. This analysis is a digest of the voluminous SD reports, both field office information and Reich summaries, in BA/NS 6/244 and 411.

235. Domarus, *Hitler*, II, 2088; and Bormann, "Aktenvermerk für Pg. Dr. Klopfer," 5 Feb. 1944, T-580, roll 77, folder 363.

236. See Karl Wahl, *Es ist das deutsche Herz* (Augsburg, 1954), pp. 352–53; and Boelcke, *Deutschlands Rüstung*, entry for 13 May 1944, p. 360. The atmosphere of these sessions is characterized by Wahl's report (*Deutsche Herz*, p. 334) that attendance was required for both the speeches and the film comedy that followed.

237. PK, "Anordnung 10/44," 13 Jan. 1944, *VAB*, VI, 18–19.

238. See Zander, "Vorlage an den Reichsleiter," 31 March 1944, T-580, roll 874, box 799, folder 3; and Bormann, "Aktenvermerk für Abteilung II und IIID," 5 May 1944, quoted in Friedrich Zipfel, *Kirchenkampf in Deutschland 1933–45* (Berlin, 1965), p. 520.

though all of the preparations for the meeting had been made (including the establishment of a brothel staffed with Aryan prostitutes for the delegates' use), the deteriorating military situation forced a reluctant postponement of the congress. It was never held.[239]

In the country at large the PL ranks also held firm. For one thing, most of the party activists believed both the myth of the Kampfzeit victory snatched from the jaws of defeat and the stab-in-the-back legend of World War I.[240] And in contrast to the German people's behavior in the fall of 1918, "our magnificent party" had successfully met the wartime crises and prevented the growth of a protorevolutionary situation.[241] For the quite sizable[242] number of PLs who sought to prepare for the postwar future by dropping out of party activities, Bormann issued a curt reminder that should Germany lose the war, the victors' justice would fall first and most heavily on those who had been active in the PO corps.[243]

Despite the staggering casualties of the armed forces, Bormann continued to keep the PLs at home. In fact, the number of draft-exempt PLs actually increased between December 1943 and the end of January 1944,[244] and Bormann used the renewed crisis atmosphere to develop further the elitist character of the NSDAP. For all practical purposes the membership of the party was no longer open, but co-opted, with the seventeen-year-old HJ graduates almost the sole source of new members.[245] Simultaneously, the PK was able to prevent the establishment of a seniority system in the PO corps. A directive issued over Hitler's signature in March reiterated that only performance and "per-

239. Max Weinreich, *Hitler's Professors* (New York, 1946), pp. 219–35; and Joseph Wulf, *Martin Bormann* (Gütersloh, 1962), p. 93.
240. Oven, *Mit Goebbels*, I, entries for 25 Jan. and 24 May 1944, pp. 178 and 270.
241. See, for example, Goebbels, "Die Partei im Krieg," *Das Reich*, 14 May 1944; and Ley, "Rede in Salzburg," *Hoheitsträger*, VIII (March 1944), 2–3.
242. See the report of the SD office in Schwerin, 11 July 1944, BA/NS 6/407; and "Zur täglichen Arbeit der Partei," *Hoheitsträger*, VIII (Jan. 1944), 18–20.
243. PK, "Rundschreiben 123/44," 31 May 1944, IfZ/PK Rdschr. geh. This top secret circular was sent to all RLs, GLs, heads of the Arbeitsbereichs and the paramilitary organizations.
244. Zander, "Vorlage an den Reichsleiter," 30 Jan. 1944, T-580, roll 873, box 799b, folder 2.
245. PK, "Anordnung 8/44," 8 Jan. 1944, *VAB*, VI, 74–75. See also Köhler, "Rundschreiben 22/44," 29 March 1944, MiU/GAC, folder 30.

sonality values" should guide the appointment and promotion of a PL.[246]

In practice, these measures were part of the PK's drive to weaken the position of the other Reichsleiters. Bormann expanded his moves against Ley with a systematic effort to deprive the ROL of the administration of the party's training programs,[247] while Rosenberg's office led a pathetic and shadowy existence, used and abused by the PK in its struggles with the ROL and the propaganda ministry.[248] Schwarz, who was almost drowning in his budgetary surpluses,[249] retained most of his administrative autonomy, but even he was not immune to the PK's intrusions, and in the first half of 1944 the PK made significant inroads into the management and policy decisions of the party's welfare fund.[250]

The party chancellery's concern in relations with the PO and the party's leaders was to create a reliable,[251] centralized[252] corps of PLs whose foremost loyalty was to the PK, and whose organizational focal point lay in the Gau, district, and local territorial administration.[253] To increase the supply of PK trouble-shooters, staffers continued to roam

---

246. Hitler, "Verfügung 6/44," 10 March 1944, *VAB*, VI, 39; and PK, "Bekanntgabe 80/44," 13 April 1944, *ibid.*, p. 41.

247. Rosenberg's office (Zölffel), "Bericht über die Tagung der Personalsachbearbeiter der Reichsleitungsdienststellen bei der Partei-Kanzlei . . . ," 2 June 1944, T-454, roll 7, frame 4913385.

248. See Payr, "Bericht über eine Dienstreise . . . vom 30.6. bis 2.7.1944," 5 July 1944, BA/NS 30/52. See also Rosenberg's report to Hitler on the tenth anniversary of his appointment as ideological chief of the NSDAP, Jan. 1944, CDJC/CXLII, 380.

249. By 1944 the Reich treasurer's office received a *monthly* subsidy of RM 43,-000,000 from the state, and the budget for 1945 called for a slight increase. The Gau budget of Saxony for 1944 revealed a cash surplus of more than RM 4,000,000. Schwarz, "Ergänzung zu meiner Aufstellung über den Geschäftsbereich des Reichsschatzmeisters der NSDAP—Partei- und Finanzverwaltung," p. 12, T-580, roll 47, folder 266; and Hantzschel (office of the Reich treasurer), "Kriegsetat für das Jahr 1945 . . . Gauleitung Sachsen," 13 Jan. 1945, T-580, roll 842, box 268, folder 250.

250. The documentation is in BGStA, Rsth. 291.

251. In March Friedrichs noted that defeatists had been purged from the party and that discipline had been restored. See Friedrichs "[Rede vor Reichsleitern und Gauleitern 23.3.44]," pp. 9–10, T-580, roll 79, folder 368.

252. Collegiality was not permitted; GL Hoffmann had to dismiss his "Gau senate." Bormann to Walkenhorst, 21 April 1944, T-580, roll 80, folder 371.

253. Zölffel (official in Rosenberg's office), "Bericht über die Tagung der Personalsachbearbeiter der Reichsleitungsdienststellen bei der Partei-Kanzlei . . . ," 2 June 1944, T-454, roll 7, frames 4913380–82.

the countryside identifying promising PLs, and fifty HJ leaders were transferred from the office of the Reich youth leadership to the PK.[254] The special corps of PK men distributed in key posts around the Reich and the occupied areas in turn formed the backbone of Bormann's aggressive campaign to partify the norms of social behavior in the Third Reich. The campaign was particularly noticeable at the grass-roots level. In the latter half of 1944, for example, all of the local leaders in Baden were subjected to four-day training sessions.[255] Upon their return, they presumably acted vigorously to remove yet more vestiges of the old bourgeois, apolitical standards in interpersonal relations. Over Ley's objections,[256] the party encouraged sexual relations (and the resulting illegitimate children) between soldiers on furlough and unmarried girls.[257] Similarly, the party devoted particular attention to the ideological indoctrination of high school and college students.[258] The "National Socialist family evening," a variation of the continuing Sprechabend,[259] was yet another social control mechanism. Its purpose was to "strengthen the wife ideologically" and to prevent "thought deviations between wife and husband and parents and children,"[260] but it does not take a great deal of imagination to discover that such sessions could also be used to encourage denunciations of parents by their newly propagandized children.

With the PO's reputation as an efficient and effective organization secure in Hitler's eyes,[261] the PK was able to achieve significant progress

254. Zander, "Vorlage an den Reichsleiter," 17 Jan. 1944, T-580, roll 874, box 799b, folder 3.

255. See Gau training leader to GL Baden, 14 July 1944, T-81, roll 124, frames 145898–99.

256. For Ley's objections and Hitler's and Bormann's rejoinder see Bormann, "Aktenvermerk für Pg. Friedrichs und Pg. Dr. Klopfer," 5 Feb. 1944, T-580, roll 77, folder 363.

257. Friedrichs, "Rede . . . 1944," pp. 9–10; and *Lage*, nos. 116 B and 118 B (9 June and 7 July 1944).

258. Friedrichs, "Rede . . . 1944," p. 5; and Härtle (one of Rosenberg's closest associates), "Bericht über die Wissenschaftsbesprechung in der Partei-Kanzlei am 17.3.1944," 20 March 1944, BA/NS 30/52.

259. See Dr. Krem, "Sprechabend falsch und richtig," *Hoheitsträger*, VII (Jan. 1944), 9–10.

260. PK, "Anordnung 74/44," 3 April 1944, *VAB*, VI, 26–27.

261. See Friedrichs, "Rede . . . 1944," pp. 7–8; Köhler, "Rundschreiben 21/44," 27 March 1944, GAC/MiU, folder 30; and S[ie]b[el], "Vermerk für Pg. Maurer," 11 Feb. 1944, RvO/BDC/H 1167.

toward its goal of establishing the party as the primary decision-making entity in Nazi Germany. The Führer agreed with the PK's contention that there should be no Personalunions between party and state at the national and regional levels, although the Gauleiters should continue to serve both as Hoheitsträgers and state officials.[262] This decision was not altogether a victory for the Gauleiters. Rather, by combining regional control and authority in the hands of the Gauleiters, it left the PK free to exercise power without responsibility at the Reich level. Basically, Bormann's plan was to endow the Gauleiters with as much state authority as possible, but then to eliminate the direct relationship between regional state authority and the Reich ministries by pushing a super-ministry, the party chancellery (and its vast staff), between the two levels of administration. At the same time, while the PK effectively controlled and coordinated the Reich administrative levels (Lammers found himself almost completely on the sidelines),[263] it did not take responsibility for the decrees emerging from its offices, but relied instead on its authority as de facto Hoheitsträger to enforce its writs.[264] The scheme was almost diabolical: it permitted Hitler and the Gauleiters to maintain the fiction that the Gauleiters were still the Führer's derivative agents,[265] yet it saddled the Gauleiters with the responsibility of enforcing legislative decisions over which they had no control. Moreover, only the Gauleiters themselves held dual positions in state and party; the Gau economic advisors served only as control organs. Bormann specifically prohibited the practice of assigning to them responsible positions in the armaments program.[266]

Most of the Reich ministries put up no more than token resistance to the ambitions of the PK, but the contest between the party chancellery and the Reich ministry for armaments was a far less one-sided affair.

262. Friedrichs, "Rede . . . 1944," p. 8; and Speer, *Erinnerungen*, p. 344.

263. Speer, *Erinnerungen*, p. 265. The decline of Lammers occurred after 17 May; on that date he was still persona grata with Hitler. See Bormann to Schwerin-Krosigk, 17 May 1944, T-580, roll 265, folder 13.

264. Walkenhorst to Fritsch (PK staff official), 21 April 1944, T-580, roll 80, folder 371; PK, "V.I. 2/10," 28 Jan. 1944, *VAB*, VI, 2; and Lammers to highest Reich offices, 28 March 1944, BA/R 22/vorl. 20672. See also Speer, *Erinnerungen*, p. 575, n. 4; and Diehl-Thiele, *Partei*, p. 222.

265. For Hitler's almost fearful loyalty to the GLs see Speer, *Erinnerungen*, p. 355; and Heim, "Vorlage an Pg. Friedrichs," 12 April 1944, BA/NS 30/51.

266. PK, "Rundschreiben 82/44," 16 April 1944, *VAB*, VI, 176–77.

Although he had lost some of his glamor, Albert Speer was still a declared favorite of Hitler and to date Bormann had been unable to sever the frequent and close personal communications between the two men. Both contestants had rather formidable institutional and personal weapons on their side. Speer worked through the closely linked systems of industrial self-government rings and the procurement committees of the armed forces commands to enforce his directives, while Bormann could count on the support of the Gauleiters, the control functions of the Gau economic advisors, and his own ability to foment intrigues against Speer personally. Specifically, Bormann attempted to remove a number of senior officials from Speer's ministry on the grounds that they exhibited an antiparty attitude, and he was successful in recruiting Speer's deputy Xaver Dorsch as an agent of the PK.[267] The struggle took a decisive turn in Bormann's favor when Speer became ill in February and required hospitalization until May. The illness was undoubtedly a heart attack,[268] although there remains some suspicion on Speer's part that he was deliberately misdiagnosed, and given incorrect treatment for a time as well.[269] In any event, Bormann and the PK made effective use of Speer's involuntary absence from the political battlefield. The Gau economic advisors, for instance, moved decisively to contest Speer's control of labor allocation for armaments production in the Gaus.[270]

Speer's administrative autonomy was closely linked to the army's ability to resist its own partification. Until 1944 it had been relatively successful. The Keitel-Rosenberg agreement on political indoctrination in the armed forces was never implemented to a significant degree, but the balance of power shifted at the beginning of the year.[271] Rosenberg had been trying to gain control of the indoctrination program for younger officers during most of 1943, while the OKW, in a move typical of

267. Speer, *Erinnerungen*, pp. 339–40, and 355.
268. See the diagnosis in the papers of Dr. Morrell, Hitler's personal physician, who also treated a number of other prominent Nazis (T-253, roll R 45, frame 1498760).
269. Speer, *Erinnerungen*, pp. 342–43.
270. *Ibid.*, pp. 340 and 369–70. The ministry appealed to Klopfer to restrain the Gau economic advisors.
271. Friedrichs, "Rede . . . 1944," p. 5; and Volker R. Berghahn, "NSDAP und 'Geistige Führung' der Wehrmacht 1939–1943," *Vjh.f.Z.*, XVII (Jan. 1969), 69–70.

Nazi intercomponent infighting, bolstered its defenses by cooperating with the SS. Hitler, equally typically, awarded the victory to neither contestant, but to the PK.[272] In the last days of 1943, Hitler issued a directive giving the PK authority to coordinate the entire program of political indoctrination in the armed forces through a "working staff" established within the framework of the party chancellery.[273] The actual administrator of the new National Socialist leadership officer (NSFO) program was the thoroughly partified General Reinecke,[274] and it is clear from Hitler's initial conversations with him (in Bormann's presence) that the party was far more prepared to run the program than was the army.[275] The NSFO decree was a complete victory for the PK,[276] although the lack of indoctrination personnel and the rapidly deteriorating military situation rendered it yet another Pyrrhic triumph.[277] It is clear, however, that Bormann intended to use the NSFO as the cornerstone of a thoroughgoing partification of the Reich's armed forces.[278] The NSFOs would be fanatical agitators who, as Hitler put it received their faith in victory from their faith in National Socialism.[279] The model was the type of political commissar then in use in the ranks of the Soviet army. To this end, Bormann began almost immediately to undermine Reinecke's authority. The PK insisted that the Gau staff leaders and Gau training officials rather than the OKW should have a deci-

272. Berghahn, "Geistige Führung," pp. 53 ff; and n.a., "Vortrag des Reichsministers Rosenberg beim Führer am 17. November 1943," n.d., CDJC/CXLII-380.

273. Bormann to Rosenberg, 2 Jan. 1943 [*sic*; should be 1944], T-454, roll 7, frames 4913665–66. See also *Lage*, no. 118 B (7 July 1944), 8–10. Hitler's "Befehl," 22 Dec. 1943, is in T-454, roll 7 frames 4913667–68. The new *Arbeitsstab* was part of division II, not the state division, III.

274. See his remarks in Gerhard L. Weinberg, ed., "Adolf Hitler und der NS-Führungsoffizier (NSFO)," *Vjh.f.Z.*, XII (Oct. 1964), 446–47.

275. *Ibid.*, pp. 443–56.

276. Bormann to Rosenberg, 22 Feb. 1944, T-454, roll 7, frames 4913786–88. See also Berghahn, "Geistige Führung," pp. 60 ff.

277. Wahl, *Deutsche Herz*, pp. 344–45; and Wurster to Michelfelder, 14 July 1944, T-580, roll 834, box 257, folder 274.

278. Messerschmidt (*Wehrmacht*, p. 451) quotes from a memo by Ruder, the head of the NSFO Arbeitsstab in the PK, 30 December 1943 advocating that the *Wehrmacht* should become " 'the force of arms (*Schwertarm*) of the PLs.' "

279. See Hitler's speech to OCS trainees, 20 Nov. 1943, Domarus, *Hitler*, II, 2062. See also Berghahn, "Geistige Führung," p. 49.

sive voice in the selection of NSFOs in the various regional army
commands.[280]

June and July were disastrous months for the Nazi regime. The
landings in Normandy proved that "fortress Europe" was something
less than impregnable, and Count Klaus von Stauffenberg's almost successful attempt on Hitler's life in July obviously shook the Führer's confidence even more. Yet for the party and its program of partification neither event was without its brighter side. The PK had already prepared
for the invasion through a decree stipulating that the PO would retain
control over the party functionaries even if an area of the Reich should
become a theater of military operations. The armed forces had no authority to command the party's PL corps; military decision-making power was restricted solely to tactical and strategic matters.[281]

The political aftermath of the assassination attempt had even wider
implications. Hitler's and Bormann's first concern was to retain the
loyalty and confidence of the Gauleiters,[282] both to guard against a
putsch by the army's regional commands and, as far as Bormann was
concerned, to prevent the SS and the Gestapo from pushing the PO into
the background.[283] Stauffenberg's action also stirred to new life the dormant social revolutionary emotions among the PLs. Ley, in what was
obviously a reaction that was representative of many PLs, delivered

280. Messerschmidt, *Wehrmacht*, pp. 453 and 455. For information on the Gau
indoctrination programs see GL Franken, "Rundschreiben 12/44," 3 May 1944,
T-580, roll 921, folder 7; and Volker R. Berghahn, "Meinungsforschung im 'Dritten
Reich': Die Mundpropaganda-Aktion im letzten Kriegshalbjahr," *Militärgeschichtliche Mitteilungen*, I, no. 1 (1967), p. 85.

281. Zander, "Aktenvermerk," 17 Feb. 1944; Stehl (PK official), "Besprechungs-
vermerk: . . . Massnahmen im Falle einer Invasion," 30 March 1944, RvO/BDC/H
530; and PK, "Rundschreiben 123/44," 31 May 1944, IfZ/PK Rdschr. geh. (1944–
45).

282. Hitler held a series of conferences with the Reichsleiters and Gauleiters in
the week following the attempt on his life (Martin Bormann to Gerda Bormann,
29 July 1944, in Bormann, *Letters*, p. 70; and Wahl, *Deutsche Herz*, pp. 340–41);
and Bormann sent a series of seven circular letters to the GLs on the evening of
20 July and for three days thereafter. The first left Hitler's headquarters at 8:30
P.M. See T-580, roll 21, folder 33. Bormann obviously regarded these dispatches
as historically significant; he sent copies to his wife for safekeeping. See Bormann,
Letters, pp. 61–65.

283. Himmler, on the other hand, underscored his belief that he and Goebbels
had saved the situation. T[heodor] E[schenburg], ed., "Die Rede Himmlers vor
den Gauleitern am 3.8.44," *Vjh.f.Z.*, I (Oct. 1953), 383.

a speech a few days after the assassination attempt which was one long and bloodthirsty attack on the German nobility.[284] From beginnings like this started uncontrolled pogroms, and the party had already suffered a setback once when it proved incapable of keeping an organized action of violence from getting out of hand. Bormann saw considerably further than Ley. In the first days after the event, he communicated only with the Gauleiters; the first issue of the *VI* appearing after July 20 contained no interpretation of Stauffenberg's action.[285]

Bormann and Goebbels bided their time, not because they did not share Ley's emotions, but because they wanted a controlled attack on the remaining unpartified elements of German society, rather than a wild but momentary spree. A historical parallel to the July crisis was quickly found in Strasser's resignation of December 1932,[286] and, as had been the case then, the PO had to avoid panic and rally around the miraculously spared Führer. A district leader in Thuringia felt it opportune to remind his PLs of the bloodbath that would have followed among party functionaries had the conspiracy against Hitler succeeded.[287] Instead, the party took its revenge—coldly, systematically, and without interference by other societal forces. The inauguration of the new phase of partification came in a two-day conference of the Reichsleiters and Gauleiters on August 3 and 4 in Posen (Požnan). The first day was devoted to addresses by a number of party leaders; on the second, the party chieftains met Hitler at a reception. Hitler did not deliver a major address. The mood of the conference was expressed in a sentence from Goebbels' remarks: "[the] state and the armed forces have given the Führer only grief . . . that is going to end now; the party will take over."[288]

The speeches for the most part followed predictable lines. Speer dazzled his audience with statistics, and included in his optimistic ap-

284. Semmler, *Goebbels*, entry for 23 July 1944, p. 140. Ley's speech is in *ibid.*, pp. 212–13.

285. *VI*, no. 21 (1 Aug. 1944).

286. Goebbels discovered that Hitler even felt and looked after the assassination attempt as he had felt and looked when Strasser resigned. Oven, *Mit Goebbels*, II, entry for 5 Aug. 1944, p. 109. See also Goebbels, "Rede . . . 3.8.44," pp. 15, 18, 19, and 26.

287. Köhler, "Rundschreiben 45/44," ca. July 1944, MiU/GAC, folder 30.

288. Goebbels, "Rede . . . 3.8.44," p. 56. See also Speer, *Erinnerungen*, p. 405; and Heiber, *Lagebesprechungen*, entry for 31 July 1944, p. 588.

praisal of the military situation several rather oblique remarks criticizing the army and Göring. Himmler was more forthright. His address was one long attack on the German military establishment: it was an "oozing sore." Perhaps for the first time in the history of the NSDAP, a major leader of the party blamed Germany's defeat in the First World War on the incompetence of the officer corps and the general staff. Like Speer, Himmler managed to close on a note of optimism, promising the party leaders that at the end of the war Europe to the Urals would be theirs.[289] Hitler demanded "absolute certainty, faithful trust, and loyalty with work" from his paladins.[290]

Bormann also spoke to the meeting, but his address did not survive the war. At any rate, his activities behind the scenes were more significant. Even before the Reichsleiters and Gauleiters assembled at Posen, he had called a meeting of the Gau staff leaders in Berchtesgaden.[291] The major purpose was undoubtedly to coordinate the aftermath of the assassination attempt in the Gaus and districts and to prevent the full-scale purges that, as Goebbels put it, "we would like to have."[292] Indications of wholesale and indiscriminate attacks on entire social groups were already much in evidence. Individual district leaders, on their own authority, rounded up known former members of the Communist Party and the Social Democratic Party and placed them in concentration camps;[293] and many of the local leaders delivered massive attacks upon the entire officer corps and the nobility during Sprechabende after July,[294] rather than parroting the official line, that the conspiracy had been the work of a small clique of ambitious men.[295] The fires of hatred were hardly dampened by the speeches at Posen. Upon his return to Thuringia, Gauleiter Sauckel informed his district leaders that one hundred and eighty counts had been involved in the conspiracy and

289. Copies of Speer's, Himmler's, and Goebbels' speeches are in IfZ/52 ED 8. Speer reported that his appearance was met by "icy prejudices" on the part of the GLs. Speer, *Erinnerungen*, p. 402.

290. Domarus, *Hitler*, II, 2139.

291. Martin Bormann to Gerda Bormann, 26 July 1944, in Bormann, *Letters*, p. 68.

292. Goebbels, "Rede . . . 3.8.44," p. 21.

293. Köhler, "Rundschreiben 51/44," 25 Aug. 1944, MiU/GAC, folder 30.

294. PK, "Bekanntgabe 254/44," 20 Sept. 1944, *VAB*, VII, 43.

295. PK, "Anordnung 170/44," 27 July 1944, *RVBl* (A) no. 39 (9 Aug. 1944).

that all those guilty of participation would be hanged and their near and distant relatives exterminated.[296]

Bormann, however, systematically pursued the longer-range goal: to partify the army and enlarge the PK's control over the party. Among the important changes immediately imposed on the party-army relationship were the introduction of the Hitler salute throughout the armed forces, an intensification of the NSFO program (Hitler received a delegation of NSFOs on August 3 in connection with the Gauleiter conference),[297] and, most important, permission for soldiers to retain their party membership while on active duty.[298] Earlier, Hitler had confirmed the Gauleiters' exclusive authority to declare martial law in their areas of jurisdiction.[299] The PK also used the July crisis to increase its power at the expense of rival offices. Other party offices saw more significance in Friedrichs' ominous statement that the chancellery bore "full responsibility for obedience to the will of the Führer" than in his assurance that the PK merely wished to "fertilize" the work of the party.[300] Although it seems ludicrous in view of the actual circumstances in the second half of 1944, the PK's rivals were particularly concerned with Bormann's consistent refusal to guarantee the reestablishment of the offices closed down as unnecessary to the war effort—even after peace had returned.[301] Moreover, a party activity that was of marginal significance under the control of one party office became seemingly indispensable to the German war effort when placed under the auspices of the PK.[302]

In the last six months of 1944, the PK reached the apex of its power and influence in the Third Reich;[303] Bormann moved ruthlessly against his fellow Reichsleiters and the remaining positions of autonomy among

---

296. Köhler to his son, 8 Aug. 1944, MiU/GAC, folder 24.

297. Domarus, *Hitler*, II, 2137.

298. PK, "Bekanntgabe 208/44," 30 Aug. 1944, *VAB*, VII, 8–9; and Messerschmidt, *Wehrmacht*, p. 429.

299. Bormann to all RLs and GLs, 24 July 1944, T-454, roll 7, frame 4913312; and PK, "Rundschreiben 232/44," 8 Sept. 1944, *VAB*, VII, 7.

300. Maurer [?], "Vermerk für Pg. Friedrichs . . . Stichworte für Ihre Frankfurter Rede," 20 July 1944, T-580, roll 79, folder 368.

301. Payr, "Bericht über Besprechungen in der Partei-Kanzlei . . . 29.8.44," 30 Aug. 1944, T-454, roll 7, frame 4913242.

302. Payr, "Aktenvermerk für Bereichsleiter Utikal," 16 Oct. and 16 Nov. 1944, BA/ NS 30/ 52.

303. Jedlicka, *Einsames Gewissen*, p. 90.

the state offices. In the area of personnel decisions, even prior to July 20, Bormann, with Ley's and Schwarz's agreement, had begun a policy that made promotion to the upper ranks of the PO corps contingent upon at least four weeks service at the PK.[304] After the assassination attempt, Hitler authorized the PK to terminate any activity or office which the chancellery regarded as superfluous and to reassign the PLs involved.[305] And while some functionaries were sent to the front,[306] for the most part, the PK intended to "utilize these experts to fill the tremendous [number] of vacancies in the Gau and district offices."[307] The PK also took over the direction of the party's training programs, replacing Ley's "theoretical" approach with something described as "ideological compensation for psychological depression resulting from the conduct of total warfare."[308] Of the manifold "ideological" projects previously handled by Rosenberg's office, only anti-Semitic and antibolshevik research remained.[309] However, the PK's staff on its own prepared antichurch propaganda and history texts.[310] A short directive all but eliminated the functions of the party courts: in the future, the Hoheitsträgers could handle all except serious disciplinary cases on their own authority.[311] Finally, the PK for the first time made substantial inroads into the jurisdictional competencies of the Reich treasurer's office. Bormann, over Schwarz's vigorous objections, seized control of the intra-

304. Bormann to Rosenberg, 9 July 1944, T-454, roll 7, frame 4913734.

305. Hitler, "Verfügung 10/44," 16 Aug. 1944, *RVBl* (A) no. 40 (16 Aug. 1944); and PK, "Anordnung 180/44," 14 Aug. 1944, *VAB*, VII, 30. For a concrete example see Rosenberg, "Aktennotiz über die Unterredung mit . . . Friedrichs am 28.8.44," n.d., T-454, roll 7, frames 4913153–62; and Bormann to Rosenberg, 21 Sept. 1944, *ibid.*, frame 4912646.

306. Gau treasurer of Franconia to Gau offices, district offices *et al.*, 15 Aug. 1944, BA/GF/16.

307. Otto (staff official in Rosenberg's office) "Niederschrift über meine Besprechungen . . . 7. und 8. August 1944," 11 Aug. 1944, BA/NS 30/52.

308. Otto, "Niederschrift," 11 Aug. 1944, BA/NS 30/52; and ROL, "Anordnung," 4 Sept. 1944, BA/GF/67.

309. Bormann to Rosenberg, 1 Sept. 1944, T-454, roll 7, frame 4913233.

310. Bormann's marginalia in Gerda Bormann to Martin Bormann, 12 Sept. 1944, in Bormann, *Letters*, p. 111; and Bormann to Rosenberg, 16 Nov. 1944, T-454, roll 7, frame 4913103.

311. PK, "Anordnung 189/44," 21 Aug. 1944, *VAB*, VII, 52. For rumors of bitter enmity between Bormann and Buch at this time see Hermann Buch (Buch's son) to Himmler, 16 Aug. 1944, in Heiber, *Reichsführer*, pp. 280–81.

party system of Telex communications,[312] and the treasurer's office complained that the PK's "streamlining" efforts were actually little more than a pious cover for transferring Schwarz's hitherto sacrosanct powers to the offices of the PK.[313]

The centralization of the party under the authority of the PK found its parallel in the increasingly reckless and desperate measures of revolutionary social control imposed by the chancellery on German society. Although it was obvious that the party's propaganda had lost its last remnants of credibility[314]—even the upturn in public opinion after Hitler's "miraculous" escape from the bomb was quickly dissipated[315]— the PK was determined to ignore the negative feedback,[316] and pressed on with the partification of German life. The Hoheitsträgers took over a larger share of the responsibility for racial policy measures,[317] insuring the strict enforcement of Bormann's dictum that in the future only "genetically healthy (*erbtüchtige*) and deserving" families should receive aid through the NSV.[318] The district Hoheitsträgers also continued their direct interference in the judicial process—despite the min-

312. The documentation is in T-580, roll 82, folder 394. Bormann announced his triumph in a circular to the RLs and GLs, 5 Sept. 1944, T-454, roll 7, frame 4913226.

313. Katz, "Stellungnahme zum Schreiben des Leiters der Partei-Kanzlei vom 7. August 1944," 10 Aug. 1944, T-580, roll 82, folder 394.

314. See the report on the last mass rally of the war in Herne (6 Sept. 1944), in Hermann Meyerhoff, *Herne 1933–1945*, p. 122. For a good indication of the propaganda themes see *Lage*, nos. 115 B and 119 B (31 May and 24 July 1944); and the *Mitteilungen* of the Gauring in München-Oberbayern for the last half of 1944.

315. See the SD's reports in Kaltenbrunner to Bormann, 28 July and 28 Aug. 1944, BA/NS 6/411.

316. In the late summer, after numerous complaints by Goebbels and Bormann that they reported only negative mood indicators, the SD reports ceased publication. See Boberach, *Meldungen*, p. xxviii. Goebbels replaced them to some extent with a system of soldier-agents which reported only from the larger cities. See Berghahn, "Meinungsforschung," p. 87.

317. See Himmler's directive of 16 Aug. 1944, quoted in PK, "Bekanntgabe 266/44," 26 Sept. 1944, *VAB*, VII, 105–07.

318. PK, "Anordnung 197/44," 22 Aug. 1944, *VAB*, VII, 93–101; the quotation is from p. 93. Hitler encouraged these efforts to revolutionize moral values. He wanted the party to mount an "educational" campaign for the acceptance of illegitimate children. See Oron J. Hale, "Adolf Hitler and the Postwar German Birthrate— An Unpublished Memorandum," *Journal of Central European Affairs*, XVII (July 1957), 170.

istry of justice's efforts to appease the party's whim.[319] In its relation with the state, the PK labored to deprive Göring of his title as Prussian prime minister and to transfer the remaining powers of that office to the Gauleiter-governors.[320] This would have indirectly increased the authority of the PK as well, since Bormann had for all practical purposes taken over the jurisdiction of the Reich chancellery. His erstwhile rival, Heinrich Lammers, saw Hitler in person for the last time in late September.[321]

While Lammers moved off the Nazi stage, a new act, "the return of Joseph Goebbels," began. To be sure, the Reich propaganda minister had never been fully out of the limelight, though his influence to date certainly fell far short of his ambitions. The Keitel-Lammers-Bormann alliance had effectively thwarted his bid for control of the civilian war effort, but toward the end of 1943 and the early months of 1944 Goebbels began to make a comeback. His propagandistic[322] and even charismatic talents[323] became increasingly indispensable to Hitler as the war became an unending succession of defeats. Finally, judicious ententes between the propaganda minister, Speer, and a few Gauleiters strengthened Goebbels' position.[324] His relationship with Bormann was ambiguous: the two men worked together against Göring,[325] but Bormann also used Goebbels' deputy, Werner Naumann, to intrigue against the Reich propaganda minister.[326] Above all, however, Goebbels was the only major official to have worked out a fairly concrete and drastic plan for mobilizing Germany's productive capacities,[327] and he had the good luck to send Hitler yet another fifty-page memorandum detailing his

---

319. PK, "Anordnung 332/44," 16 Oct. 1944, *VAB*, VII, 124; *Richterbriefe*, no. 18 (1 Aug. 1944), pp. 169 and 183; and Curt Rothenberger, "Im Kampf ums Recht," p. F, 9 [*sic*], Forsch. Hbg./PA/Rothenberger.

320. Bormann to Klopfer, 30 Aug. 1944, T-580, roll 78, folder 366.

321. Lammers' complaints are in T-580, roll 265, folder 12.

322. Over a special radio network hookup, Goebbels addressed the GLs daily for a half hour at noon. See Wahl, *Deutsche Herz*, p. 321. Hitler also consulted Goebbels before handling the Italian crisis. Domarus, *Hitler*, II, 2033.

323. Hans-Gerd Gisevius, *Bis zum bitteren Ende* (Hamburg, 1960), pp. 469–70.

324. Oven, *Mit Goebbels*, I, entries for 2 Feb., 1 and 16 March, and 6 June 1944, pp. 189–91, 207, 214, 217, and 281.

325. PK, "Bekanntgabe 4/44," 6 Jan. 1944, *RVBl* (A) no. 2 (8 Jan. 1944).

326. Oven, *Mit Goebbels*, I, entry for 11 June 1943, p. 20; and Willi A. Boelcke, ed., *Kriegspropaganda 1939–1941* (Stuttgart, 1966), p. 56.

327. Oven, *Mit Goebbels*, II, entry for 22 Sept. 1944, p. 145.

ideas just before Stauffenberg's attempt on the Führer's life. Hitler was in the mood for radical measures,[328] and on July 22 a high-level conference (Lammers, Goebbels, Bormann, Sauckel, Speer, Keitel, Klopfer and others) concluded that the Keitel-Lammers-Bormann committee had done little to mobilize the Reich's hidden reserves.[329] Lammers lamely defended the three-man committee, but both he and Bormann "acknowledged that a single individual would be more effective."[330] Two days later, Hitler signed a decree appointing Goebbels "general plenipotentiary for total warfare" (*Generalbevollmächtigter für den totalen Kriegseinsatz*, GBK).[331]

Goebbels was convinced that his new office had made him "the first man after Hitler." Indeed, in his euphoria he looked far into the future, and saw himself as both chancellor and foreign minister in a reshuffled cabinet.[332] Indeed, the GBK's powers were extensive. He could issue orders to all Reich agencies, and Hitler had assured him that he would refuse to entertain any complaints against the minister's directives unless they had first gone through the GBK's office. In administering his new powers, Goebbels acted as if he believed his own propaganda: the GBK was essentially a party-run affair.[333] At the Reich level, Goebbels established only a skeleton permanent staff headed by Werner Naumann (planning activities) and Gauleiter Wegener (administration). In the field, Goebbels' orders were handled by the Reich defense commissioners.[334] Clearly, the potential Achilles heel of the scheme was the attitude of the PK and the Gauleiters, insofar as the latter were also Reich defense commissioners. Goebbels was aware of their crucial significance, but he started out very optimistically. He hoped that it would

328. *Ibid.*, II, entry for 25 July 1944, pp. 89–90; and Speer, *Erinnerungen*, p. 399.

329. Goebbels, "Rede . . . 3.8.44," pp. 30–32, and 34.

330. The protocol of the conference has been published in Wolfgang Bleyer, ed., "Pläne der faschistischen Führung zum totalen Krieg im Sommer 1944," *Zeitschrift für Geschichtswissenschaft*, XVII, no. 10 (1969), pp. 1326–29.

331. Domarus, *Hitler*, II, 2132.

332. Oven, *Mit Goebbels*, II, entries for 25 July, 22 Sept. and 16 Oct. 1944, pp. 94, 142, and 162–63.

333. Goebbels, "Rede . . . 3.8.44," pp. 32 and 35; and [Lammers?] "Vermerk über die Besprechung beim Chef der Reichskanzlei am 31.7.44," n.d., BDC/Goebbels (PKC).

334. Oven, *Mit Goebbels*, II, entries for 27 July and 28 Sept. 1944, pp. 97 and 148.

be possible simply to issue basic directives to the Gauleiters, who would then develop detailed measures on their own initiative.[335] His optimism was short-lived; by early September, the newest effort to impose the hardships of war from within had fizzled.[336] Goebbels had been effectively stymied at every level. Although Bormann paid lip service to Goebbels' plans, he had no intention of subordinating his office or the PO corps to the GBK's orders. Instead, the PK treated the decrees issued to Reich and provincial state agencies by the GBK's office as draft directives that were not binding upon the party until they had Bormann's countersignature.[337] In particular, Bormann successfully exempted the PLs from Goebbels' attempt to channel labor reserves into the armaments industry.[338] As for the Gauleiters, they had neither the will to impose hardships on their populations nor the nerves of steel which Goebbels attributed to them. Indeed, there was no shortage of Gauleiters, who in this final stage of their political careers were of little use to the Nazi cause. In desperation Bürckel committed suicide; Schirach had no influence whatever in Vienna; Otto Telschow and his deputy Gauleiter feuded over the Gau Hanover; Weinrich, though dismissed from his post for almost a year, continued, Streicher-like, to interfere in the administration of the Gau Hessen.[339] Despite these obvious shortcomings Hitler refused to authorize a general purge of the Gauleiters.

Goebbels' failure as GBK was aided in large part by the simultaneous decline of Speer's position. Like Goebbels, Speer had become convinced that only a mobilization czar could generate the productive capacity of the Reich's reserves effectively, though a memorandum which Speer submitted on July 20 (before Stauffenberg placed his bomb

335. Goebbels, "Rede . . . 3.8.44," pp. 25, 33, 36, 39, 45, and 52. See also Bleyer, "Pläne," pp. 1316 and 1328.

336. Oven, *Mit Goebbels*, II, entries for 1 and 18 Sept. 1944, pp. 123–24, and 138.

337. See Hitler, "Verfügung 10/44," 30 July 1944, *VAB*, VII, 1; and Hitler's 25 July decree appointing Goebbels GBK.

338. PK, "Anordnung 183/44," 19 Aug. 1944, *VAB*, VII, 172–73. See also Janssen, *Ministerium*, pp. 278–79.

339. Cf. Hüttenberger, *Die Gauleiter*, pp. 209–11; Himmler to Bormann, 2 Sept. 1944; and Bormann to Himmler, 9 Sept. 1944, in Heiber, *Reichsführer*, pp. 286–87; Jedlicka, *Einsames Gewissen*, pp. 67–68, and 93–98.

under Hitler's table) did not envision turning the effort over to the party.[340] Soon after Goebbels' appointment as GBK, significant differences developed between the two men. Speer thought primarily in terms of additional munitions and armaments, while Goebbels was fascinated by the prospect of sending more soldiers to the front.[341] Objectively, Speer's approach undoubtedly promised to be more effective. The continuation of the German war effort, already hampered by severe shortages of critical materials (such as gasoline),[342] became increasingly dependent upon the Reich's own labor force since the supply of foreign labor declined with the liberation of the occupied areas.[343] Dispatching large numbers of ill-trained and superannuated soldiers to the front produced effective propaganda statistics for the GBK, but no battle victories. In addition, Speer remained committed to his system of industrial self-government, while the PK's economic department and the Gauleiters were returning to the social revolutionary ideas of the early Kampfzeit and advocating a trend toward state capitalism under the direction of the PO.[344] Finally, the PK would hardly endorse Speer's suggestion that a significant number of PLs could be used more effectively in industrial production facilities than in the party's offices.

Beginning with Hitler, the entire party phalanx pounced on Speer's policies. Despite the minister's pleas, Hitler was very lukewarm in his endorsement of Speer's emphasis on private enterprise as the backbone of the war effort.[345] Similarly, both Hitler and Bormann rejected Speer's proposal to appoint a commissioner-general to coordinate all mobilization efforts in the crucial Rhine-Ruhr area. Hitler did not wish to offend the sensitivities of his Gauleiters, and Bormann opposed the establishment of any institutions between the PK and the party's provincial

340. Bleyer, "Pläne," p. 1312, n. 1 and 1322; Boelcke, *Deutschlands Rüstung*, entries for 6–8 July 1944, p. 390; and Janssen, *Ministerium*, p. 272.

341. Janssen, *Ministerium*, pp. 274–75.

342. Speer, "Ansprache Reichministers Speer auf der Gauleiter-Tagung am 3.8.1944," p. 20, IfZ/276/52/ED 8.

343. Janssen, *Ministerium*, p. 282.

344. See *NS-Wirtschaftspolitik*, nos. 5/6 (15 Aug. 1944).

345. For Speer's reaction to Hitler's speech of 26 June 1944, see Speer, *Erinnerungen*, pp. 368–71. The speech itself is printed in Kotze and Krausnick, *Es spricht der Führer*, pp. 335–68. See also Speer to Hitler, 20 Sept. 1944, quoted in Janssen, *Ministerium*, p. 172.

chiefs.[346] In fact, Bormann and the Gauleiters formed an impenetrable bulwark against Speer in the last half of 1944. Bormann used the policy differences between Speer and Goebbels effectively to drive a wedge between these two former allies.[347] The Gauleiters, who had never forgiven Speer for his attack on them in the fall of 1943, eagerly grasped each new particle of autonomy that Bormann sent their way.[348] Even before the assassination attempt Hitler had reaffirmed the Gauleiters' sole responsibility for all but actual military operations in case their Gaus became theaters of war.[349] The Gauleiters, under the supervision of the PK, were in charge of building fortifications.[350] It is remarkable that Bormann even encouraged the Gauleiters to sabotage a direct Führerbefehl: Speer won what he thought was a major victory when Hitler ordered the Gau economic advisors not to interfere in the process of armaments production, but Bormann in a prefatory remark to the decree reminded the Gauleiters that there were still ways around Hitler's directive.[351] With that sort of encouragement to stimulate the Gauleiters' deviousness, it was not long before Speer gave in. At the end of the summer he permitted the Gau economic advisors to participate in the control of the production process.[352]

The love-hate relationship between the PK and the SS, which had been smoldering for a year, finally emerged into the open in the last months of the dying Third Reich. In the short time span from the late

346. Boelcke, *Deutschlands Rüstung*, entry for 1–4 Nov. 1944, p. 428. Hitler wavered briefly after 20 July and had already appointed GL Kaufmann regional coordinator for the North Sea area, but Bormann persuaded the Führer to rescind the appointment. See Interrogation of Kaufmann, 14 May 1949, Forsch. Hbg./PA/ 12/K (Kaufmann); and Walther Hubatsch, ed., *Hitlers Weisungen für die Kriegsführung 1939–1945* (Frankfurt, 1962), pp. 276–78.

347. Oven, *Mit Goebbels*, II, entry for 3 Sept. 1944, pp. 128–29.

348. Janssen, *Ministerium*, p. 165.

349. See Hitler, "Erlass . . . über die Zusammenarbeit von Partei und Wehrmacht in einem Operationsgebiet innerhalb des Reiches . . . ," 13 July 1944, and Keitel, "Vorbereitung für die Verteidigung des Reichs," 19 July 1944, in Hubatsch, *Hitlers Weisungen*, pp. 256–64.

350. Hitler, "Verfügung 12/44," 1 Sept. 1944, *VAB*, VII, 2; and Martin Bormann to Gerda Bormann, 3 Sept. 1944, in Bormann, *Letters*, p. 96. See also Hubatsch, *Hitlers Weisungen*, p. 273; *Lage*, no. 120 C (9 Aug. 1944); and Oven, *Mit Goebbels*, II, entries for 5 and 17 July 1944, pp. 51 and 56.

351. See Bormann's preface to Speer's "Erlass," 1 Aug. 1944, *VAB*, VII, 145–46. See also Janssen, *Ministerium*, p. 174.

352. Janssen, *Ministerium*, p. 167.

spring of 1944 to the end of the war, the PK and SS simultaneously entered into their most concrete and far-reaching scheme of cooperation and held each other in the most contempt. Berger was convinced that the PK was a "load of manure,"[353] while Bormann was despondent when Hitler failed to appoint his candidate as head of the SS personnel office.[354] Barracks-room scuttlebutt in the armed SS predicted a massive conflict between Bormann and Himmler,[355] and Bormann's successful expulsion of Himmler from the NSDAP in the final days of the regime showed that the rumors were not without a basis in fact.

Yet, simultaneously, these two bitter rivals were also indispensable allies in a pathetic and hopeless effort to save the regime's existence and partify what remained of German society. Both the SS[356] and Bormann pursued the chimera of a separate peace with Soviet Russia to reverse the military situation, but their most extensive joint effort was the establishment of the totally abortive *levée en masse*, the *Volkssturm* (People's Storm), in the fall of 1944. The Volkssturm was the last and most naive attempt by the Nazis to create a military force controlled solely by the NSDAP. The NSFO program, though administered almost entirely through the PK and headed by a functionary whom Bormann described as "an efficient fellow,"[357] had met with little success, primarily because the armed forces nominated their least able officers for NSFO posts.[358] The Volkssturm was a desperate gamble to substitute élan and fanaticism for military skill and equipment. The idea of a politicized militia was not new; the SA had sponsored such plans under Röhm's leadership and both Gauleiters Wahl and Schirach had toyed with Gau militias,[359] but before July 20 Hitler had had a very low opinion of the

353. Berger to Siebel (PK staffer and SS agent at the PK), 23 May 1944, RvO/BDC/H 215a.

354. Martin Bormann to Gerda Bormann, 14 Aug. 1944, in Bormann, *Letters*, pp. 79–80.

355. Hermann Buch (Buch's son) to Himmler, 16 Aug. 1944, in Heiber, *Reichsführer*, p. 280.

356. Berger to Himmler, 26 Sept. 1944, RvO/BDC/H 324.

357. Martin Bormann to Gerda Bormann, 10 Sept. 1944, in Bormann, *Letters*, p. 107.

358. Boelcke, *Deutschlands Rüstung*, entry for 6–8 July 1944, p. 392.

359. For Wahl's efforts see above, p. 437, Schirach's attempt is described in Friedrichs to Bormann, 23 Sept. 1944, quoted in Karl Stadler, ed., *Österreich 1938–1945* (Vienna, 1966), p. 395.

military effectiveness of militia forces.[360] After he survived the attempt on his life, however, Hitler became convinced that the ideological fervor of the party could also give military strength to a motley array of emaciated old men and frightened young boys. Administrative logic dictated that the military aspects of the Volkssturm should be placed in the hands of the SA, while the personnel and administrative side would be handled by Goebbels as GBK. Indeed, both Goebbels and Schepmann assumed that this would be the case.[361] Bormann and Himmler had other plans. The PK's chief and Goebbels had already developed serious disagreements over the policy patterns of the GBK, and both Himmler and Bormann thought very little of the SA's military ability. As a result, the PK and the SS agreed to share responsibility for the Volkssturm between them. The PK handled administration and indoctrination;[362] Himmler, in his capacity as commander of the German reserves, equipment and training.[363] In addition, Ley was allowed to travel around the Gaus and report on the "work of political and ideological guidance" to the PK.[364] In the provinces, the Gauleiters were in charge of the Volkssturm battalions, a provision that "showed once again the boundless trust which the Führer places in his Gauleiters."[365]

With its formal establishment on September 25,[366] the Volkssturm became the reductio ad absurdum of partification. It was financed by the party,[367] its territorial organization corresponded to the Gaus, and it had no relation to the German military districts.[368] Above all, the Volkssturm was the party's last effort to achieve the social revolution

360. See Hitler's speech of 29 April 1937, in, Kotze and Krausnick, *Es spricht der Führer*, p. 171.

361. Zander, "Aktenvermerk über die am 22.9.44 in Berlin stattgefundene Besprechung," 22 Sept. 1944, T-580, roll 872, box 799b, folder 4.

362. Bormann underscored the importance of the Volkssturm by noting that the functionary handling Volkssturm affairs at the PK could "really earn credits for his future party career in the job." Bormann to Friedrichs, 26 Sept. 1944, T-580, roll 872, box 799 A, folder 4.

363. *Ibid.*

364. PK, "Rundschreiben 346/44," 25 Oct. 1944, *VAB*, VII, 328–29.

365. PK, "Rundschreiben 270/44," 26 Sept. 1944, *ibid.*, pp. 326–27.

366. Domarus, *Hitler*, II, 2151–52. The various decrees and circulars relating to the Volkssturm are in *VAB*, VII, 325–85.

367. Schwarz to all Gau treasurers, 16 Oct. 1944, BA/GF/108.

368. PK, "Anordnung 277/44," 29 Sept. 1944, *VAB*, VII, 361.

envisioned in the Kampfzeit. The ideal of the Volkssturm was the class-less band of fighting men. Significantly, the oath administered to the pseudo-soldiers included "the Volkssturm man would rather give up his life than yield the liberty and consequently the social future of his people."[369] In order to safeguard the Nazis' ideological monopoly in the ranks of the Volkssturm, members of the clergy were rigidly excluded from service.[370]

The first Volkssturm units were inaugurated on October 18 in the "capital of the movement," Munich, and thereafter the Gaus set to work feverishly establishing their quotas of "battalions." This was primarily the responsibility of the Gau and district staff leaders and, in the occupied areas of Europe, the staff leaders of the Arbeitsbereichs. Their successes were impressive enough on paper; the Gau Franconia, for example, came up with one hundred and forty-six battalions.[371]

Needless to say, all of this was shadowboxing. Not only was the Volkssturm miserably equipped,[372] but the unit leaders, each of whom was supposed to be a "believing, fanatical" National Socialist, "a veteran of officer rank and a genuine organizer,"[373] in practice turned out to be draft-dodging friends of the Hoheitsträgers.[374] Since Bormann specifically exempted PLs from all but safe administrative duties in the Volkssturm,[375] the party functionaries soon established vast bureaucracies that administered phantom units across the German landscape.[376] In addition, the SS-PK rivalry permeated all aspects of the Volkssturm venture. Himmler had named Berger to handle the Volkssturm in the SS, and Berger's one-track mind sought immediately to incorporate the

369. See the oath administered to the men in the Volkssturm, *VAB*, VII, 328. See also *Der Politische Soldat*, no. 19 (Dec. 1944), T-580, roll 872, box 799A, folder 3.

370. Bormann to all GLs, 31 Oct. 1944, T-580, roll 872, box 799A, folder 5.

371. Dt. Volkssturm, Gau 7 to the party membership, 15 Dec. 1944, BA/GF/108.

372. Boelcke, *Deutschlands Rüstung*, entry for 29 Nov. 1944, p. 452.

373. PK, "Anordnung 318/44," 12 Oct. 1944, *VAB*, VII, 366.

374. Hans Kissel, *Der deutsche Volkssturm* 1944/45 (Frankfurt, 1962), p. 25; and PK, "Rundschreiben 28/45," 23 Feb. 1945, T-580, roll 872, box 799A, folder 3.

375. PK, "Anordnung 318/44, 379/44 [and] 427/44," 12 Oct., 3 Nov., and 3 Dec. 1944, *VAB*, VII, 330 and 332–34.

376. N.a., "Beobachtungen über die Kampfkraft des Volkssturms" (ca. Feb. or March 1945), BA/NS 30/145. The account relates the experience of a Gau, probably East Prussia or Danzig.

Volkssturm into his armed SS and Germanische Freiwilligen Leitstelle empire. Bormann countered with a series of memos contesting the SS's right to do more than supply the Volkssturm with weapons.[377] Bormann also made one of his rare public appearances at the oath-taking ceremony in Munich, so that the establishment of the Volkssturm would not appear to be solely an SS affair.[378]

What remained of the dwindling Nazi empire in Europe provided an equally fruitful field for the accelerating rivalry of the SS and the PK. The struggle over the East had a positively Alice in Wonderland flavor to it. By the fall of 1944, there were no occupied Eastern territories, but the animosities continued unabated. The Arbeitsbereich East refused to give up its cache of arms to the SS.[379] Koch, Lohse, and Rosenberg were now resident on German soil again, and blamed each other for their forced return.[380] Bormann was particularly anxious to safeguard the PLs freed by the collapse of German rule in the East for party service. Although for the most part these functionaries were relatively young, the PK had no intention of letting more than a few go to the front.[381] In the West, the party won a few more empty triumphs. In Holland, the SS lost. Bormann and Ritterbusch remained in control of the country, though the victory prize was little more than the administration of fortification construction and ditch-digging.[382] The SS shifted most of its operations to Belgium. In July, a week before the assassination attempt, Hitler removed the military administration of Belgium, and appointed Joseph Grohé, the Gauleiter of neighboring

377. See, for example, Bormann to Friedrichs, 29 Oct. 1944, T-580, roll 872, box 799 A, folder 4.

378. Bormann to Giesler, 31 Oct. 1944, *ibid.*

379. See Berger to Himmler, 31 March 1945; and Himmler to Koch, 1 April 1945, T-175, roll 125, frames 2650510 and 2650520. Himmler promised "dear Erich" to return the arms to the Gauleiters after the Ukraine had been reconquered.

380. Particularly ludicrous was Koch's successful intrigue to "take over" the Ostland from Lohse. The documents are in T-454, roll 14, frames 929 ff. See also Dallin, *German Rule in Russia*, p. 626. The Reichskommissariats and Gebietskommissariats were formally dissolved on 10 November 1944. *Ibid.*, p. 637, n. 1.

381. Bormann to Rosenberg, 25 Aug. 1944, T-454, roll 7, frame 4913248.

382. Zander to Ruder, 29 Oct. 1944, RvO/BDC/H 1136; and Hitler, "Befehl über Herstellung der Verteidigungsbereitschaft des Westwalls," 30 Aug. 1944, in Hubatsch, *Hitlers Weisungen*, p. 279 ff.

Cologne-Aachen, as Reich commissioner.[383] The new civilian administration immediately dissolved the AO, and established a regional NSDAP organization. The SS, fearing the creation of yet another Arbeitsbereich—"It's enough to bring tears to your eyes," wrote Berger of that prospect—attempted to prevent a contest for collaborators in Belgium by bribing what pro-Nazi elements remained.[384] The 1944 and (proposed) 1945 budget of the Germanische Freiwilligen Leitstelle earmarked RM 43 million (1944) and RM 42.85 million (1945) for use in Flanders alone.[385]

Neither Berger's bribes nor Bormann's digging in Holland could prevent the end. In the last weeks of the year, Hitler had become a physical wreck and almost a social recluse. In addition to his quack doctor, Theodor Morrell, whom he saw once and at times twice a day, Hitler's daily companions were Bormann and a few of the men with whom he had started his long climb from obscurity, such as Goebbels and Ley.[386] Hitler's force of charisma was no longer automatic: "He had to hypnotize Quisling once more" was his assessment of an unpleasant meeting ahead with the most notorious of his collaborators.[387]

If Hitler had few illusions about the decline of the Nazi regime, the German people as a whole had none; the credibility gap had become a chasm. Significantly, the grumbling was now directed not only against the party and its functionaries, but even against Hitler himself.[388] Goebbels' propaganda continued its variations on the theme "the more desperate the situation, the nearer to victory we are,"[389] but neither the

383. Domarus, *Hitler*, II, 2219; PK, "Anordnung 304/44," 7 Oct. 1944, *VAB*, VII, 227.

384. See Berger's marginalia on a copy of his letter to Friedrichs, 25 Sept. 1944, RvO/BDC/H 79.

385. See the figures for the 1944 and 1945 budgets, RvO/BDC/H 52.

386. Hitler's daily calendar for the period 27 November 1944 to 27 February 1945, drawn up by his personal valet, Linge, is in T-84, roll 22, data sheet 79948. See also Oven, *Mit Goebbels*, II, entry for 22 Jan. 1945, p. 215; and Speer, *Erinnerungen*, p. 433.

387. Heiber, *Lagebesprechungen*, entry for 27 Jan. 1945, p. 862.

388. See the report of the SD office in Vienna, 10 March 1945, BA/NS 6/317.

389. PK, "Anordnung 129/45g," 10 March 1945, *Anordungen, Rundschreiben, Verfügungen.* Goebbels personally ordered the spreading of a rumor that Hitler's long silences were the result of his concern with major military and political decisions, a concern that "would bear fruit in a few weeks." Gau propaganda leader

population nor the majority of PLs paid much attention. Numerous party functionaries panicked as enemy troops came near,[390] while others
were seized by the sense of *après moi le deluge*. Ironically, some of the
toughest Gauleiters were the first to fail in the final crisis. The notorious-
ly cruel and sadistic Gauleiter Greiser left his Gau while the Russian
troops were still some one hundred and twenty kilometers away. He
thoughtfully issued a proclamation asking everyone to stay at his post;
and, taking a large retinue with him, fled to the Altreich.[391] A conference of PLs from the North Seas areas accomplished nothing, but went
through fourteen bottles of genever (Dutch gin), fourteen of cognac,
and 10,900 cigarettes.[392] Matters were no better at the top. Keitel and
Lammers devoted an entire afternoon in February 1945 to a discussion
of the cigars dispensed on the occasion.[393]

But this was not the entire story. If it had been, if the party had disintegrated at the beginning of 1945,[394] the war would have mercifully
ended some months before the final surrender. For one thing, there was
Martin Bormann: "small, corpulent, with a bull-neck, he gives the impression of extraordinary energy and ruthlessness. He has vicious eyes,
set in a red, ugly face . . . His deportment is extraordinarily correct,
indeed charming."[395] Bormann and the PK had by no means reconciled
themselves to defeat.[396] On the contrary, they intensified their efforts
to partify all aspects of government and society. The PK at the end of
the war acted very much like a cancer. From the darkness of the East
Prussian forests and later from the bunker of the Reich chancellery,
the PK directed the PO's subversion of what remained of the Ger-

Bayreuth to district propaganda leaders, 4 Dec. 1944, T-580, roll 872, box 799 A,
folder 2.

390. See the report of an NSFO officer in Ruder to Walkenhorst, 3 March 1945,
T-580, roll 78, folder 366.

391. Oven, *Mit Goebbels*, II, entries for 23 Jan. and 7 Feb. 1945, pp. 216 and
237.

392. Arb. NSDAP (Ni), "[Aufstellung]," 7 Dec. 1944, RvO/Arb. NSDAP
(Ni)/17 B II; and Bockelkamp's undated penciled notations in *ibid.*, 17 B I.

393. Oven, *Mit Goebbels*, II, entry for 25 Feb. 1945, pp. 252–54. The occasion
was a birthday party for the head of the Reich labor service.

394. Domarus, *Hitler*, II, 2179.

395. Oven, *Mit Goebbels*, II, entry for 25 Feb. 1945, p. 251.

396. Martin Bormann to Gerda Bormann, 5 Jan. 1945, in Bormann, *Letters*,
p. 160.

man Rechtsstaat and orderly lines of communication. In February, the PK discovered that the Reich railroads had to be "ideologically permeated."[397] Bormann's representative in the Reich ministry of justice demanded as late as March 1 that the penalties for subversion of the war effort be increased.[398]

With some notable exceptions, Hitler's first group of derivative agents, the Gauleiters, remained loyal almost to the very end. The participants in the last Gauleiter conference saw their Führer as an aged shell of his former self, but they also left his headquarters convinced that victory was still possible.[399] The PK was considerably less content with the Reichsleiters. In March, Bormann ordered his staff to submit yet another list of possible replacements—this time for every Reichsleiter. Walkenhorst did produce a list, though he tactfully suggested no possible successors for Bormann himself.[400] Actually, the PK was also considering the possibility of abolishing the Reichsleiters' offices and incorporating their functions within the chancellery; this would have eliminated the horizontal divisions of the Reichsleitung.[401] Only the Reich treasurer's office would have remained largely intact. But, then, Schwarz had never seriously interfered with Bormann's rise to power and there was no doubt of the treasurer's financial accumen. After all, at the close of his career, the party had "insignificant debts and a cash balance of 1 billion marks."[402]

For the moment, however, the PK was more concerned with the vertical cadres of the PO. Bormann and his men pursued a policy of völkisch nihilism. While destroying the remnants of pre-Nazi norms of behavior, they tried to preserve the PO cadres in order to institute permanent partification of the entire society in the victorious, peacetime Reich that would emerge. As a result, Bormann granted autonomy to

397. Keitel (PK staff official), "Vermerk für Pg. Friedrichs," 23 Feb. 1945, T-580, roll 70, folder 368.
398. See Werner Johe, *Die gleichgeschaltete Justiz* (Frankfurt, 1967), p. 133.
399. Wahl, *Deutsches Herz*, pp. 385–86, and 391.
400. Walkenhorst, "Reichsliste," 10 March 1945, T-580, roll 80, folder 371.
401. *Ibid.*; Hitler, "Verfügung 16/44," 9 Dec. 1944, *VAB*, VII, 59; and Dr. Wagner (deputy head of Rosenberg's Hohe Schule development office), "Aktenvermerk," 13 Oct. 1944, BA/NS 30/52.
402. Schwarz, "Ergänzung," pp. 13–14.

the Gauleiters[403] and district leaders[404] while simultaneously trying to curtail the authority of both the army and Speer's ministry. Speer lost a decisive battle when he had to agree to the "coresponsibility" of the Gauleiters and the Gau economic advisors in the production of armaments.[405] In addition, the NSFO program was for all practical purposes administered solely by the PK.[406] The deployment of the NSFOs changed drastically in the last weeks of the war. Instead of being used as indoctrination officers, the PK sent particularly reliable and fanatic NSFOs (including some of its own staffers) as political commissar–shock troops to places at the front where the German resistance was crumbling—relatively—most rapidly. Political fanaticism was to succeed where military logistics had failed.[407] Moreover, new directives placed PLs in the army's personnel offices and in the offices of the military district commanders.[408] Needless to say, the entire effort was a failure. The German armies vanished into thin air of their own accord; and, perhaps even more frustrating, the officers' mentality refused to be partified. The officers insisted on treating the NSFOs not as political superiors, but according to their military rank—which was usually that of lieutenant or captain.[409] In addition, there was the difficulty that the fifteen hundred

403. Domarus, *Hitler*, II, 2224–25; and Marlis G. Steinert, *Die 23 Tage der Regierung Dönitz* (Düsseldorf, 1967), pp. 157–58.

404. See esp. Josef Luber (an army captain assigned to the PO district office in Innsbruck), "Erfahrungsbericht," 19 March 1945, BA/NS 6/376; and Berghahn, "Meinungsforschung," p. 109.

405. Boelcke, *Deutschlands Rüstung*, p. 21. See also PK, "Rundschreiben 394/44," 10 Nov. 1944, *VAB*, VII, 170.

406. Ulrich (chief of staff of the VII army corps) to field commanders, T-79, roll 24, frame 1077. There are seven folders of NSFO evaluations in T-81, roll 656–58, frames 5461895–5464836. In November Bormann was actually expecting his formal appointment as head of the NSFO program, replacing General Reinicke. See PK, "Bekanntgabe 389/44," 8 Nov. 1944, *VAB*, VII, 240; and Ruder, "Vorlage," 23 Feb. 1945, T-580, roll 78, folder 366.

407. Lichtenberg (official in the PK's dept. II), "Erfahrungsbericht über meinen Sondereinsatz in Oberschlesien und in der Slowakei," 22 March 1945; and Schwund to army group Vistula, 29 March 1945, T-580, roll 78, folder 366. See also Bormann to Henlein, Stürtz, Schwede-Coburg, Schlessmann, Florian, and Grohé, 15 March 1945, T-580, roll 78, folder 366. See also the documentation in BA/NS 6/169 and 377.

408. Plönske (PK staff official), "Vermerk für Pg. Derr," T-580, roll 78, folder 366; and PK, "Bekanntgabe 339/44," 20 Oct. 1944, *VAB*, VII, 233.

409. Gutjahr (NSFO), "Einsatzbericht—Fortsetzung Nr. 2," 15 Feb. 1945, T-580, roll 78, folder 366.

"political tactical commanders" (*politische Kampfkommandanten*) wore the brown PL uniform, and "given the mood of the soldiers at the front, people in party uniform will be beaten to death."[410] As for the Volkssturm, "Hopelessness is the only positive aspect of the situation."[411] The grandiose units simply melted away as soon as they made contact with the enemy. And such post-Volkssturm ideas as the *Wehrwolf* guerrilla organization existed only in the minds of some radio commentators safely tucked away in their transmitting bunkers.[412]

That left the Gauleiters and the vertical cadres of the PO. Despite massive evidence to the contrary, Hitler and, paradoxically, some army leaders[413] were convinced that only the party under the direction of the PK could still keep the country from falling apart.[414] Hitler's distrust of other power components reached ridiculous levels. At one point, he dispatched the Gauleiters to the airfields of the *Luftwaffe* in order to check whether ordered repairs had really been carried out.[415] When all else had failed, Hitler demanded as a final act of loyalty from his Hoheitsträger the physical destruction of their Gaue and districts. In mid-March, he decreed a scorched-earth policy for those sections of Germany still under Nazi control but threatened by immediate Allied occupation, in order to present an industrial wasteland to the advancing Allied armies.[416] That order broke the Hitlerian spell for many of the PLs. A large number of functionaries, including Klopfer and Zander at the PK, became more concerned with their own fate after the Reich's defeat than their oath of obedience to Hitler.[417] The Gauleiters, too, for

410. Berger to Brandt, 18 Feb. 1945, T-175, roll 130, frames 2656814–15. Berger's idea that the SS could manage better was, of course, equally ludicrous.

411. Ernst Jünger, *Strahlungen* (Tübingen, 1949), entry for 5 Jan. 1945, p. 603.

412. See the reports on the Volkssturm and *Wehrwolf* in Herne, in Meyerhoff, *Herne*, pp. 142–43; and the twenty-six page report of the district leader in Küstrin to Bormann, 5 April 1945, T-580, roll 78, folder 366.

413. When Dönitz issued his capitulation announcement, he was convinced that the party still retained immense influence among the German population. See Steinert, *23 Tage*, p. 285.

414. For Bormann's influence over Hitler in the last months and weeks see the de-Nazification proceedings against GL Kaufmann, II, 17–19, Forsch. Hbg./PA/12/K (Kaufmann).

415. Karl Koller, *Der letzte Monat* (Mannheim, 1949), entry for 14 April 1945, pp. 11–12.

416. Hubatsch, *Hitlers Weisungen*, p. 303.

417. Speer, *Erinnerungen*, pp. 445 and 462.

the most part cooperated with Speer's oft-described and largely successful effort to save the remaining industrial capacity of the Reich by
sabotaging Hitler's and Bormann's scorched-earth directives. In the
end, only Florian (Düsseldorf), Grohé (Cologne), and Meyer (Westphalia) refused to heed Speer's advice.[418]

The PLs ended pretty much as they had begun: as an angry, frustrated, atomized, and alienated group of personal failures. It is characteristic that the intrigues continued to the very collapse of the regime
and that, in the final analysis, few were willing to die for the Nazi
values. Even among the Gauleiters, there was a decided shortage of
heroes. In addition to Greiser's desertion,[419] Koch fled to Schleswig-
Holstein and together with Lohse put in a request for a submarine to
take them to South America. In Cologne, Grohé fled, and his city understandably received the Allied armies with a sea of white flags.[420] In
Bayreuth, the Gauleiter was murdered by an SS execution squad on
orders of the deputy Gauleiter.[421] Nor did Bormann's favorites exhibit conspicuously exemplary behavior. Hoffmann in Westphalia-South
plundered the Gau's supply depots and distributed the goods to his
clique.[422] The collapse of the Arbeitsbereich in Holland was characterized by an orgy of senseless destruction and plunder.[423]

While a few Gauleiters, like Hanke, Stürtz, and Goebbels, continued
the useless struggle with fanatical zeal,[424] and an ever smaller number,
notably Kaufmann in Hamburg,[425] took an active part in surrender ne-

418. Janssen, *Ministerium*, p. 310; Speer, *Erinnerungen*, pp. 447 and 453–55;
and Klopfer's interrogation, 21 May 1947, IfZ/ZS 352.

419. Kissel, *Deutsche Volkssturm*, p. 155. There are a number of reports on the
desertion of the Warthegau PL corps in T-580, roll 835, box 252, folder 282.

420. Oven, *Mit Goebbels*, II, entry for 11 March and 12 April 1945, pp. 267 and
294–96; and Speer, *Erinnerungen*, p. 498.

421. *Fränkische Presse*, 18 June 1946. Otto Dietrich, *Zwölf Jahre mit Hitler*
(Cologne, 1955), p. 167, claims the execution took place on Hitler's orders.

422. Schwarz's representative in Westfalen-Süd to Schwarz, 31 Oct. 1944, T-580,
roll 82, folder 394.

423. Himmler to Bormann, 23 Feb. 1945, in Heiber, *Reichsführer*, pp. 308–09.

424. See the report of a propaganda official in Brandenburg (the name is unde-
cipherable) to v. Borcke (an official in the propaganda ministry), 6 Feb. 1945,
T-580, roll 78, folder 366. For Hitler's view of Hanke's defense see Heiber, *Lagebesprechungen*, entry for 2 March 1945, p. 890.

425. Janssen, *Ministerium*, p. 319; Kaufmann's interrogation, 14 May 1949,
Forsch. Hbg./PA/12/K; and *Hamburger Abendblatt*, 2/3 May 1970.

gotiations, Bormann celebrated his final triumph in the abortive pages of Hitler's political testament. At the end of April, Hitler realized that the ring of Russian troops around Berlin would not be broken and determined on suicide. His last days have been described a number of times,[426] and for the final phase in the history of the NSDAP only the justification of Nazism and the list of appointments in Hitler's testament are noteworthy. Hitler admitted no failing; he was a martyr to historical forces whose present failure would be vindicated by future developments. His final writings reaffirmed his belief in anti-Semitism as the ideological foundation of Nazism. Hitler's final list of appointments represented—on paper—the partification of Germany under the direction of the PK. Bormann had succeeded in eliminating his rivals. Himmler was expelled from the party,[427] and Gauleiter Hanke took his place. Most of the functions of the Reichsleiters (including those of the ROL) were absorbed by the PK. Bormann himself became "party minister," and many of his favorites remained or came into the cabinet. Giesler became Reich minister of the interior, Thierack stayed on as justice minister, Naumann succeeded Goebbels, Sauer replaced Speer, Gauleiter Scheel became Reich minister of education, and Goebbels' loyalty was rewarded with the title of Reich chancellor. Seyss-Inquart, who had never offended Bormann, was Ribbentrop's intended successor as Reich foreign minister. It was both a tribute to the technical ministers' cooperation with the Nazis and an indication of the party's inability to supply qualified personnel that most of these ministers were to stay at their posts.[428]

The only seeming anomaly was Hitler's choice of Grand Admiral Karl Dönitz as Reich president. Dönitz had never been conspicuously close to the party or the PK. Yet the admiral had a great deal to recommend him. In the last months of the war, he had distinguished himself by his close adherence to the PK line. In a speech delivered at the beginning of October, Dönitz insisted that steadfast and fanatical loyalty

426. Notably in Hugh R. Trevor-Roper, *The Last Days of Hitler* (London, 1947).
427. For examples of the final conflicts between the SS and the PK see SS-Hauptsturmf. Mewe, "Vermerk für Dr. Brandt," 3 Oct. 1944, RvO/BDC/H 79; and the documents in *ibid.*, H 13.
428. The testament is reprinted in Domarus, *Hitler*, II, 2236–39.

to Hitler would solve all military difficulties.[429] Under these circumstances, it is quite understandable that Bormann attempted to join Dönitz in Flensburg after Hitler's suicide; from the available evidence, the new Reich president was a man with whom the equally new party minister could work in close harmony.

Martin Bormann never reached Flensburg. He vanished. It is conceivable that he eventually found a safe hide-out in South America, Tibet, or Russia, but it is far more likely, and indeed almost certain,[430] that like his Führer and the NSDAP itself, he perished amid the ruins of Berlin.

429. See Bormann's comments on a speech made by Dönitz on 11 Oct. 1944, BA/NS 6/132. Bormann, who described the admiral as "our Dönitz" sent the address to the party archive for safekeeping.

430. Boelcke, *Kriegspropaganda*, p. 56, n. 32.

Postscript

Among the human, moral, and physical rubble left behind by the Third Reich lay what was surely the most unlamented victim of all, the Nazi Party. It is not without irony that the NSDAP accomplished its own demise with greater suddenness and completeness that any other project it undertook during its institutional life. When Field Marshal Keitel signed the Reich's surrender papers at Karlshorst, the Nazi Party's PLs had already committed suicide, gone into hiding, huddled together awaiting the mercy of the Allies, or, in most cases, simply vanished into the obscurity whence they came. Their following had evaporated; their influence on the German people was as much of a *fata morgana* as the Wehrwolf or the alpine redoubt. Gottlob Berger had been right: the party had lost its "resonance." But, then, so had the SS, and every other Nazi organization for that matter.

Even so, the end came with dramatic speed: almost to the day of absolute military defeat, the NSDAP had simultaneously animated and terrorized the German people. On the other hand, the Nazi phenomenon had no success in carrying its political influence beyond the capitulation of the Third Reich. Even such blatantly neo-Nazi constructs as the West German National Democratic Party at the height of its influence had a following that was only slightly larger than the NSDAP's dismal showing in the 1928 elections. In addition, all of the postwar neo-Nazi groups have died quickly of self-generated ills, internal dissension, and lack of effective leadership.

Still, the failure of Nazism to transfer its organizational or political influence beyond the defeat of the Third Reich does not entirely answer the question as to the historical significance of the Nazi Party. Was the

NSDAP a genuinely revolutionary force, or, as might be suggested by the performance of second-rate castoffs after 1945, merely an aggregate of power-hungry individuals led by a historically unique demagogue? And, if the NSDAP was truly revolutionary, why was it so unsuccessful in putting its plans for restructuring societal relationships into effect?

It has been argued in this history of the NSDAP that Nazism was indeed a revolutionary movement. Its ideology, or perhaps mind-set is a more appropriate term, did not, to be sure, derive primarily from the economic dissatisfactions of traditional revolutionary mainsprings. Instead, it was the result of a psychological inability to function in the atomized, post–World War I European social context. The emotional reaction to the lost war gave rise to a set of values that assigned to artificially constructed qualitative differences in the racial makeup of human groups a role as sole causal agent of historical development. From this ideological base that was at best extremely rudimentary the Nazis derived a scheme of racial hierarchization that placed the Aryan, or German, "race" at one end of the scale and the Jews as antiforce at the other. Since the two forces were held to engage in a permanent Manichean struggle for superiority, the Nazis added a belief in the most primitive of social Darwinisms to their list of historical insights. Both within a nation and on the international scene, constant competition and warfare provided a process of racial selectivity which alone could assure the permanent superiority of the self-defined Aryan race. Needless to say, as an intellectual construct these values gained few adherents, but when the Nazis managed to convince groups with genuine socioeconomic grievances that the program had practical relevance for them, the Nazi mind-set became the basis for a revolutionary restructuring, for which the term "partification" seems appropriate, of German and even European society. There is a certain logic in all of the NSDAP's actions and goals after the Machtergreifung; from the Gleichschaltung to the launching of World War II, the Nazi rule from 1933 to 1945 was a series of often desperate attempts to apply the principles of racial qualification to actual societal conditions.

In practice, the Nazis failed in all but the most gruesome of their goals, the extermination of the European Jews. The NSDAP controlled but never wholly partified either Germany or Europe.[1] Paradoxically,

1. Leonard Krieger, "The Inter-Regnum in Germany: March–August 1945,"

the primary reason for the Nazis' lack of success was the belief in their own myths. The recognition of eternal conflict as the primary motivating force of all human endeavors led the party's leaders to tolerate, indeed to encourage, the constant intraparty feuds which diverted much of the movement's energy from revolution to internal warfare. It also contributed to the monumental inefficiency that characterized the party's operations. Following the example of their Führer, with his obsessive fear of a centralized party administration that might revolt against his rule, the NSDAP's major leaders sought to secure their positions through the establishment of elaborate and largely autonomous empires staffed with their incompetent but personally loyal cliques.

These built-in difficulties in turn hindered the NSDAP's take-over of German society. Unlike other revolutionary movements, the NSDAP did not come to power either in a relatively underdeveloped country or during a protorevolutionary situation. German society in 1933 was not only industrialized and technically sophisticated, but also reasonably intact. There was as yet no breakdown in the division of labor by which a modern industrial society functions. The governmental bureaucracy performed its tasks with customary efficiency, the military had not been demoralized, major societal institutions, such as the churches, retained their influence. Moreover, the Nazis needed this intact, technically sophisticated base if they were to attain their goal of European hegemony. Yet they also set out to destroy the old societal relationships because they stood in the way of partification. The result was not only a weakening of Germany's technical and administrative elite through the elimination of all oppositional and Jewish members in these groups, but also the encouragement of the emergence of internal resistance mechanisms to partification within the major societal groupings. The point here is not that any of these groupings actively opposed the Nazis—far from it—but they did resist partification until the very last stages of the Third Reich. In this sense, the Nazi revolution retained almost to the end a putsch-like quality; missing was the massive destruction of the old value-base characteristic of genuine revolutionary upheavals.

The intactness of German society during the Kampfzeit and after the Nazis came to power was the key element in the continuing and self-

Political Science Quarterly, LXIV (Dec. 1949), 509; and Edward N. Peterson, *The Limits of Hitler's Power* (Princeton, N.J., 1969), pp. 427 and 434–35.

destructive struggle over the nature of partification among the various factions of the NSDAP. Beginning certainly with the spectacular electoral victory of September 1930, the party set out to convince various middle-class interest groups in Germany that, after their affiliation with the NSDAP, the party would act as their Betreuer and solve the numerous economic and social problems confronting these groups during the thick of the depression. The NSDAP during the Kampfzeit did not develop a centralized corps of cadre functionaries, and, what is even more important, did not assign the position of decision-making elite to the PO. It was not surprising, then, that the PL corps at the time of the Machtergreifung was staffed primarily with incompetent functionaries who were in no way prepared to serve as the revolutionary elite of an industrialized and technically advanced nation. Rather, the party experienced a series of revolutionary dead ends, which in their combined impact minimized the chances of full-scale partification, if indeed they did not make the prospect altogether impossible. Hitler was unwilling to permit either the realization of the social revolutionary but also chaos-producing aims of the middle-class militant associations or to endorse the buildup and centralization of the PLs to the level of an undisputed control mechanism. Consequently, the NSDAP remained at all times a series of undulating layers of influence, operating simultaneously above, below, and parallel to the other societal institutions.[2]

The first, and perhaps most decisive, of the dead ends came in mid-1933, when Hitler's fear of societal chaos led him to cut off the revolutionary efforts of the middle-class militants. At the same time, he did not wholly endorse the control-concept of partification espoused by the new office of deputy Führer and the Reich treasurer. Instead, Hitler remained an ambivalent onlooker while Hess, Ley, Schwarz, Bormann, and the others continued to feud for some years over the direction of partification in the Reich. The resultant conflicts all but immobilized forceful action by the cadres, but it could not prevent the rise of further revolutionary efforts in the party's paramilitary organizations. The very tentative plans of the SA for some sort of national Bolshevist organization of society were snuffed out with a preventive retaliatory strike—the

1934 purge—but the challenge of the SS, though slower to emerge, was considerably more dangerous to the position of the cadres.

At the end of 1937, the NSDAP had reached the second of its dead ends. To be sure, the deputy Führer had remained relatively victorious in his conflict with the Reich organizational leader (for all the NSDAP's totalitarianism, power struggles in the party seldom resulted in swift and total victories; more often the contestants simply regrouped and resumed the battle with new allies), but the actual partification of Germany made little headway in the years between the Röhm putsch and the Nazi conquest of Austria. Hitler abandoned his brief flirtation with plans for a thoroughgoing structural revolution, the Reichsreform, because it led to a multitude of difficulties he was unwilling to resolve. Moreover, the deputy Führer's limited success in his feud with Ley did not include a rejuvenation of the PL corps. The deputy Führer and Schwarz acted vigorously to remold the PO functionaries, but in the absence of a firm mandate from Hitler their efforts paralleled, but did not supersede, the diametrically opposed and better financed plans of Robert Ley.

The Führer then attempted to substitute success in foreign conquests for the intraparty dilemma he himself had caused. This path was not untrodden. The ill-prepared and unsuccessful Nazi attempt to seize power in Austria in the summer of 1934 was in large part a device to heal the bitter wounds wrought by the Röhm purge. The series of foreign policy successes in 1935 and 1936, however, persuaded Hitler that partification might be accomplished more easily from without than from within. Both the purpose, to prepare Germany for war, and the person of the administrator, Hermann Göring, of the Four Year Plan were evidence that after 1936 Hitler's primary goal in the Altreich would be productivity and stability, not revolutionary experimentation. Hitler's decision, as was the case with so many in his life, was a gamble. He admitted that he began to carry the conflict outside the borders of the Reich without a solid base of Nazification in the Reich itself. There was as yet no new generation of fanatical, partified Germans.[3] But, then, Hitler had always been impatient. And, for a time, the string of terri-

3. Adolf Hitler, *Le Testament politique de Hitler,* tr. François Genoud, intro. by Hugh R. Trevor-Roper (Paris, 1959), entry for 14 Feb. 1945, pp. 58–59.

torial conquests first by diplomacy and then by warfare seemed convincing evidence that Hitler's wager with destiny had succeeded. In
addition, many of the obstacles to partification in the Altreich seemed
much easier to remove beyond the Reich's borders. With the exception
of the Greater Hamburg law, the Reichsreform remained in the planning
stages in the Altreich, but within Austria Reichsgaus quickly made their
appearance. Even more significant, the NSDAP organization in the conquered areas of Eastern and Western Europe, the Arbeitsbereichs, resolved the control-Betreuung conflict in favor of the former from the
very beginning of their operations. Similarly, the Arbeitsbereichs' total
subordination to the office of the deputy Führer provided a degree of
vertical centralization that was still unknown in the Altreich. In terms
of policies, too, the Nazi revolution made considerable headway. The
party-led attacks upon the churches in the Warthegau and the cooperation of the cadres and the SS in instituting repressive population policies throughout Europe were certainly examples of far-reaching social
upheavals.

Still, success also brought renewed failure. Quite apart from the
fact that Hitler's decision to conquer Europe led to a second global conflict and thereby assured Germany's eventual defeat, the price of societal
dynamics was, for most of the war, relative paralysis for the party's
social revolutionary initiatives within Germany. Indeed, the very significance of the party's contribution to the conduct of the war has been
questioned.[4] This seems distorted, for in the last analysis the party increasingly provided the propellant force for the German war effort.[5]
To be sure, internal dynamics limited its effectiveness. Ley and the
other Reichsleiters as well as the Betreuung approach lost further
ground. The ROL's control over such important matters as personnel
policy had already passed to the StdF's office before Hess left for England, and Martin Bormann continued and accelerated the process. To
be sure, even Bormann was never able to command the second set of
Hitler's derivative agents, the Gauleiters, at will,[6] but the party's
Reichsleitung did reach a modus vivendi with the Gauleiters, and their

4. David Schoenbaum, *Hitler's Social Revolution* (New York, 1966), p. xix
[sic].
5. Krieger, "Inter-Regnum in Germany," p. 509.
6. Peter Diehl-Thiele, *Partei und Staat im Dritten Reich* (Munich, 1969), p. 245.

resistance to centralization of the cadres lessened with each year.[7] This was particularly the case as Bormann succeeded in attacking the Reich ministries and transferring much of their authority to the Gauleiters in their role as provincial governors.

Nonetheless, all of these developments were becoming increasingly meaningless as Hitler lost his gambles on the battlefield. By the time Bormann had stabilized the authority of the party chancellery, the German armies had been defeated before Moscow, and the fortunes of war had turned. In addition, Bormann's victories were never in-depth triumphs. The incompetence of the cadre personnel had not been significantly changed. On the contrary, with the territorial expansion of the party's field of operation, the cadres took in PLs who had been rejected for service in the Altreich. Paradoxically, these uniquely unqualified functionaries were in charge of imposing the most far-reaching social changes in German-controlled Europe between the battles of Moscow and Stalingrad.

Radical partification efforts did not come to the Altreich again until early 1943, but, of course, by then it was a revolution in which failure caused success. Much of what Hess and Bormann set out to accomplish in the thirties, Bormann, to the accompaniment of bombs and military defeat, brought to a conclusion, on paper at least, in the years between 1943 and 1945. The vertical centralization of the PO made giant strides forward with the uniform deployment of Gau staff leaders throughout the Gaus. The direct contact between Munich and the districts meant a reduction in the power of the Gauleiters. Similarly, the Gauleiters' appointment as Reich defense commissioners reduced their role as party leaders but hastened the partification of the armed forces. At the same time, the inauguration of the NSFO program saw to it that the party's control of the army remained centralized in the party chancellery. The politization of welfare and social services through the NSV, an area which incidentally has received little attention from postwar researchers, and the introduction of the membership meeting and the "family evening" (*Familienabend*) were advanced means of thought control. Finally, the Volkssturm, for all the lunacy that was characteristic of it militarily, was perhaps the most far-reaching realization of the Nazi

7. Ulf Lükemann, "Der Reichsschatzmeister der NSDAP" (Dissertation, Free University of Berlin, 1963), p. 91.

ideal of a nation as a permanently warring Gemeinschaft. And yet—the history of the NSDAP is full of "and yet's"—even the last two years of the regime were not dominated by the PO alone. The rise and resurrection, respectively, of Albert Speer and Joseph Goebbels, as well as the continuing activities of Heinrich Himmler, prevented the cadres from becoming in any way the sole decision-making force in the Third Reich.

Still, for a brief time the PO had both considerable powers and concepts to establish the beginnings of a society based upon the values of predetermined racial categories. The results were brutal, chaotic, and frightful. But the end was not far different from the beginning: the story of the NSDAP is the saga of a synthetic band of revolutionaries defeated by the logical inconsistency of their own values. The dual myths of racial determination and the overriding importance of struggle as a propellant of human history were both the party's strength and its weakness. They certainly gave the party some dedicated, fanatical leaders who brought the NSDAP to power. At the same time, fanatics seldom possess the technical and administrative skills needed to bring about a value revolution in an industrialized society. The myths of the struggle perpetuated the party's own internal divisions. Time and again, the NSDAP curtailed the partification of German society while its factions feuded over policy direction and personnel composition. On a larger scale, World War II was the logical culmination of the myth's demand for constant strife. In losing the war, in addition to causing untold human suffering and physical destruction, the party also proved that its revolutionary ideology was both objectively and subjectively wrong. It was very possible to destroy societies on the basis of simplistic social Darwinism and racial determination, but these values were incapable of building new societal entities.

Glossary

Agrarpolitischer Apparat	a.A.	Office for Agriculture; the group of Nazi Party officials dealing with agricultural matters
Alte Kämpfer		"Old fighters"; members of the Nazi Party who joined before Jan. 30, 1933
Altreich		Territory of the German Reich prior to the annexation of Austria in March 1938
Angeschlossene Verbände		Affiliated associations; social and economic interest groups affiliated with the NSDAP
Arbeitsbereich der NSDAP		Literally "working sphere of the NSDAP"; the name given to the NSDAP organizations outside of Germany and Austria
Auslandsorganisation	AO	The organization of Nazi Party members living outside the borders of the Reich
Deutsche Arbeitsfront	DAF	German Labor Front; the compulsory union of employees and employers established by the Nazis in 1933
Gauleiter	GL	Functionary of the Nazi Party responsible for party administration in a province or federal state
Generalbevollmächtigter für den Arbeitseinsatz	GBA	General plenipotentiary for labor allocation; Fritz Sauckel's title as slave labor boss during World War II
Generalbevollmächtigter für den totalen Kriegseinsatz	GBK	General plenipotentiary for total warfare; Goebbels' title as coordinator of the war effort after July 1944
Generalgouvernement		Government-general; the Nazi name for occupied Poland

495

Germanische Freiwilligen Leitstelle		Literally "guidance office for Germanic volunteers"; the SS office in charge of coordinating SS activities in Western and Northern Europe
Gliederungen		Literally "divisions"; the collective name for the paramilitary groups and certain other sections, including the Hitler Youth, in the Nazi Party
Hitler-Jugend	HJ	Hitler Youth; Nazi Party organization for boys aged fourteen to eighteen
Hoheitsträger		Literally "bearer of sovereignty"; title given to territorial chiefs in the PO
Höherer SS– und Polizei-führer	HSSPF	Higher SS and police leader; the title of a territorial leader in the SS; corresponds to Gauleiter in the PO
Kampfbund für den ge-werblichen Mittelstand		Militant Association of Commercial Small Businesses; Nazi front organization whose main purpose was to organize retailers' resentment against the rise of chain stores
Landwirtschaftlicher Gaufachberater	LGF	Gau expert on agriculture; the Gau level official of the a.A.
Nasjonal Samling		The pro-Nazi Norwegian political party headed by Vidkun Quisling
Nationaalsocialistische Bewegening	NSB	The pro-Nazi Dutch political party headed by Adriaan Mussert
Nationalsozialistische Betriebszellen-organisation	NSBO	National Socialist Organization of Factory Cells; industrial propaganda units and proto-union wing of the NSDAP, absorbed by the DAF
Nationalsozialistische Deutsche Arbeiterpartei	NSDAP	National Socialist German Workers' Party
Nationalsozialistischer Beamtenbund	NSBB	National Socialist Association of Civil Servants; the Nazi party affiliate that organizes civil service workers
NS-Deutscher Studenten-bund	NSDStB	National Socialist Student Association; Nazi Party affiliate for university students
NS-Frauenschaften	NSF	National Socialist Women's League; name of the NS-Frauenbund after the reorganization of the affiliate in 1932
NS-Handels und	NS-Hago	Parallel and eventual successor organi-

Gewerbeorganisation		zation to the Kampfbund für den gewerblichen Mittelstand; the NS-Hago was founded in May 1933, the Kampfbund dissolved in August
NS-Volkswohlfahrt	NSV	National Socialist Welfare Organization
Oberkommando der Wehrmacht	OKW	High command of the armed forces
Oberstes Parteigericht	OPG	Supreme Party Court; highest court of appeal in the intraparty court system; successor to the Uschla
Partei-Kanzlei	PK	Party chancellery; the party office primarily responsible for administering the PO after May 1941
Politische Organisation	PO	Literally "Political Organization"; general term for the NSDAP's territorial and administrative cadre organization
Politischer Leiter	PL	Literally "political leader"; a functionary in the PO
Politische Zentralkommission	PZK	Political Central Commission; intraparty commission established as part of the reorganization in December 1932; forerunner of the office of deputy Führer
Reichsführer SS	RFSS	Reich leader of the SS; Himmler's title as head of the SS
Reichsgau		Literally "Reich Gau"; name given to the new territorial units in the Reich whose administrative head was directly subordinate to Hitler
Reichskommissar	RK	Reich commissioner; title of a Nazi chief of civilian administration in the occupied areas of Europe; also used as title of an official having administrative responsibility for a function covering the entire Reich
Reichskommissar für die Festigung des deutschen Volkstums	RKFDV	Reich commissioner for the strengthening of Germandom; Himmler's title as administrator of Nazi population policies
Reichskommissariat Ostland	RKO	Reich commissariat Eastland; the Nazi territorial administrative area for the Baltic countries

Reichskommissariat Ukraine	RKU	Reich commissariat Ukraine
Reichsleitung	RL	Reich leadership; top-level bureaucratic decision-making entity of the Nazi Party
Reichsministerium für die besetzten Ostgebiete	RMO	Reich ministry for the occupied Eastern territories
Reichsorganisationsleiter	ROL	Division of the Reichsleitung primarily responsible for training and deployment of the PO functionaries
Reichspropagandaleitung	RPL	Reich propaganda leadership; propaganda office of the Nazi Party
Reichsreform		Literally "Reich reform"; name given to the various efforts to restructure territorial boundaries within the Reich
Reichsschatzmeister	Rschm.	Reich treasurer of the Nazi Party
Reichssicherheits- hauptamt	RSHA	Reich Main Security Office; SS office in charge of administering the SD and the Gestapo
Schutzstaffel	SS	Protection squads; elite bodyguard formations of the NSDAP established in 1927
Stellvertreter des Führers	StdF	Office of the Deputy Führer
Sturmabteilung	SA	Storm troopers, oldest paramilitary unit of the NSDAP
Untersuchungs- und Schlichtungsausschuss	Uschla	Originally an intraparty arbitration committee within the NSDAP, later expanded into a full-fledged system of intraparty courts
Volkssturm		Literally "People's Storm"; the militarily useless militia organization formed near the end of World War II

Checklist of
Less Familiar Nazi Leaders

Amann, Max	Head of the Nazi Party publishing house, 1933–45
Backe, Herbert	State secretary in the Reich ministry of agriculture 1933–42; acting minister of agriculture 1942–45
Bärmann, Hans	Head of the economic section in the party chancellery 1940–45
Berger, Gottlob	Head of the SS's main administrative office 1938–45
Best, Werner	Reich plenipotentiary in Denmark, 1940–45
Bohle, Ernst Wilhelm	Head of the Nazi Party's Auslandsorganisation
Bracht, Fritz	Deputy Gauleiter of Silesia, 1933–41; Gauleiter of Upper Silesia, 1941–45
Brückner, Helmuth	Gauleiter of Silesia, 1933–34
Buch, Walther	Head of the NSDAP's intraparty judicial system, 1933–45
Bürckel, Josef	Gauleiter of the Palatinate, 1933–44; Reich Saar commissioner, 1935; Reich commissioner for the reunification of Austria and Germany, 1938–39; Reich commissioner in Lorraine, 1940–44
Daluege, Kurt	Administrative assistant to Göring, 1933–34; head of the *Ordnungspolizei*, 1936–45
Damson, Willy	Prominent official in the Reich treasurer's office, 1935–43
Darré, R. Walther	Reich minister of agriculture, 1933–42
Dietrich, Otto	Reich press chief, 1933–45
Donnewert, Richard	Deputy Gauleiter of the Sudetenland, 1940–43
Epp, Franz von	Reich governor in Bavaria, 1933–45
Fiehler, Karl	Lord mayor of Munich, 1933–45; head of the NSDAP's office for communal affairs, 1933–45
Florian, Karl	Gauleiter of Düsseldorf, 1933–45
Forster, Albert	Gauleiter of Danzig, 1933–45

499

Frank, Hans   Bavarian minister of Justice, 1933–45; governor-general in Poland, 1939–45

Freisler, Roland   State secretary in the Reich ministry of justice, 1933–42; president of the People's Court, 1943–45

Frick, Wilhelm   Reich minister of the interior, 1933–43; Reich protector in Bohemia-Moravia, 1943–45

Friedrichs, Helmuth   Head of the party division of the party chancellery, 1934–45

Funk, Walther   Reich minister of economics, 1938–45

Gerland, Karl   Deputy Gauleiter of Lower Danube, 1940–43; Gauleiter of Hessen, 1943–45

Giesler, Paul   High SA official, 1933–40; deputy Gauleiter of Westphalia-North, 1940–43; Gauleiter of Munich–Upper Bavaria, 1943–45

Globocnik, Odilo   Gauleiter of Vienna, 1938–39; SS leader in occupied Poland, 1940–41

Greiser, Arthur   Head of the Danzig senate, 1935–39; Gauleiter of the Warthegau, 1939–45

Hanke, Karl   State secretary in the Reich propaganda ministry, 1933–40; Gauleiter of Lower Silesia, 1941–45

Henlein, Konrad   Gauleiter of the Sudetenland, 1938–45

Henningsen, Harry   Deputy Gauleiter of Hamburg, 1933–41; leading official in the Reich ministry for occupied Eastern territories, 1941–43

Heydrich, Reinhard   Head of the SS Security Service (SD), 1933–40; Reich protector in Bohemia-Moravia, 1940–42

Hildebrandt, Friedrich   Gauleiter of Mecklenburg, 1933–45

Hoffmann, Albert   Leading trouble-shooter in the party chancellery; deputy Gauleiter of Upper Silesia, 1941–43; Gauleiter of Westphalia-North, 1943–45

Holz, Karl   Editor of *Der Stürmer*, 1933–45; deputy Gauleiter of Franconia, 1933–40; acting Gauleiter of Franconia, 1940–45

Ifland, Otto   Representative of the party chancellery in the Unruh mission, 1943

Jury, Hugo   Gauleiter of Lower Danube, 1938–45

Karpenstein, Wilhelm   Gauleiter of Pomerania, 1933–34

Kaufmann, Karl   Gauleiter of Hamburg, 1933–45

Keppler, Wilhelm   Economic advisor to Hitler and Hess, 1933 on

Kerrl, Hans   Prussian minister of Justice, 1933–35; Reich minister for religious affairs, 1935–41

Klagges, Dietrich   Prime minister of Brunswick, 1933–43

Klemm, Hans	State secretary in the Reich ministry of justice, 1942–45
Klopfer, Gerhard	Head of the state division of the party chancellery, 1938–45
Koch, Erich	Gauleiter of East Prussia, 1933–45; Reich commissioner in the Ukraine, 1941–45
Köhler, Bernhard	Head of the economic section of the party chancellery, 1933–38
Krüger, Friedrich W.	Leading SA official, 1933–34; head of the SS in occupied Poland, 1941–45
Kube, Wilhelm	Gauleiter of Kurmark, 1933–36; commissioner in Belorussia, 1941–43
Lammers, Heinrich	Head of the Reich chancellery, 1933–45
Lauterbacher, Hartmann	Deputy head of the Hitler Youth, 1933–40; Gauleiter of Hanover, 1940–45
Leitgen, Alfred	Adjutant of Rudolf Hess, 1933–41
Loeper, Wilhelm	Gauleiter of Magdeburg-Anhalt, 1933–35
Lohse, Hinrich	Gauleiter of Schleswig-Holstein, 1933–45; Reich commissioner in the Baltic, 1941–44
Lutze, Victor	Head of the SA, 1934–43
Meyer, Alfred	Gauleiter of Westphalia-South, 1933–45; state secretary in the ministry for occupied Eastern territories, 1941–45
Mutschmann, Martin	Gauleiter of Saxony, 1933–45
Neesse, Gottfried	Deputy head of the Nazi Association of Civil Servants, 1933 on
Oexle, Gustav	Head of Hess's investigative staff, 1935 on
Opdenhoff, Christian	Head of Hess's personnel office, 1936–40; deputy Gauleiter of Upper Danube, 1944–45
Peper, Heinrich	Deputy Gauleiter of East Hanover, 1936–45
Pintsch, Karl-Heinz	Adjutant of Hess, 1933–41
Pohl, Oswald	Reich treasurer of the SS, 1936 on; head of the SS's accounting and business office, 1942–45
Rafelsberger, Walter	Gau economic advisor of Vienna, 1940–45
Rainer, Friedrich	Gauleiter of Salzburg, 1938–41; Gauleiter of Carinthia, 1941–45
Rothenberger, Curt	Senator for justice in Hamburg, 1933–42; state secretary in the Reich ministry of justice, 1942–44
Röver, Carl	Gauleiter of Oldenburg, 1933–42
Ruberg, Bernhard	Head of the Auslandsorganisation in Holland, 1940
Ruckdeschel, Ludwig	Deputy Gauleiter of Bayreuth, 1936–45

Sauckel, Fritz	Gauleiter of Thuringia, 1933–45; Reich plenipotentiary for labor allocation, 1943–45
Schaller, Richard	Lord mayor of Cologne, 1933–37; deputy Gauleiter of Cologne-Aachen, 1940–45
Schepmann, Wilhelm	Head of the SA, 1943–45
Schirach, Baldur von	Head of the Hitler Youth, 1933–40; Gauleiter of Vienna, 1940–45
Schlegelberger, Franz	Acting Reich minister of justice, 1935–42
Schlessmann, Fritz	Deputy Gauleiter of Essen, 1933–45
Schwede-Coburg, Franz	Gauleiter of Pomerania, 1934–45
Seyss-Inquart, Arthur	Prime minister of Austria, 1938; deputy governor-general in occupied Poland, 1939–40; Reich commissioner in Holland, 1940–45
Simon, Gustav	Gauleiter of Koblenz-Trier, 1933–45; chief of Civil administration in Luxembourg, 1940–45
Simon, Heinrich	Ley's chief of staff, 1933–45
Sommer, Walter	Head of the state division of the party chancellery, 1934–38
Sprenger, Jacob	Gauleiter of Hessen-Nassau, 1933–45
Stangier, Peter	Deputy Gauleiter of Hessen-Nassau, 1937–43; deputy Gauleiter of Westphalia-North, 1943–45
Streicher, Julius	Gauleiter of Franconia, 1933–40
Stürtz, Emil	Gauleiter of Kurmark, 1936–45
Terboven, Josef	Gauleiter of Essen, 1933–45; Reich commissioner in Norway, 1940–45
Thierack, Otto	Reich minister of justice, 1942–45
Tiessler, Walter	Liaison official of the party chancellery to the Reich ministry of propaganda, 1940–45
Uiberreither, Siegfried	Gauleiter of Styria, 1939–45
Wagner, Adolf	Gauleiter of Munich–Upper Bavaria, 1933–43; head of Hess's task force on the Reichsreform, 1934 on
Wagner, Gerhard	Head of the Nazi Association of Physicians, 1933 on; close personal associate of Hess; interim head of the Nazi Student Association (NSDStB), 1935
Wagner, Josef	Gauleiter of Westphalia-South, 1933–40; Gauleiter of Silesia, 1934–40
Wagner, Robert	Gauleiter of Baden, 1933–45; Reich commissioner in Alsace, 1940–45
Wahl, Karl	Gauleiter of Swabia, 1933–45
Walkenhorst, Heinrich	Gau organization leader of Weser-Ems, 1935–40; Gau staff leader in Weser-Ems, 1940–42; head

	of the personnel office of the party chancellery, 1942–45
Wegener, Paul	District leader in Bremen, 1934; Bormann's adjutant, 1934–36; deputy Gauleiter of Kurmark, 1936–40; head of the party organization in Norway, 1940–42; Gauleiter of Weser-Ems, 1942–45
Weinrich, Karl	Gauleiter of Hessen, 1933–43
Wulffen, Gustaf A. von	Head of the personnel office of the StdF, 1933–36
Zander, Wilhelm	Head of the party chancellery's section on mobilization affairs, 1937–45

Bibliographic Note

This is in no way intended to be an exhaustive or a definitive bibliography on the subject of the NSDAP from 1933 to 1945. The volume of publications has by now reached such proportions that it would require another book merely to cite them, let alone describe them in any manner. Instead, an attempt is made here to guide the reader toward further exploration of the subject by (1) describing the major collections of unpublished material available and (2) pointing out those published works which are either seminal in nature or have had an impact beyond the narrow confines of specialists. It should also be noted that an exhaustive bibliography on all aspects of contemporary history, including Nazism, continues to appear in the "Bibliographie zur Zeitgeschichte" supplements which accompany every issue of the *Vierteljahrshefte für Zeitgeschichte*.

I. Unpublished Sources

Research in the history of the Nazi Party and Nazi Germany is, of course, greatly facilitated by the availability of large amounts of German archival material, which would have remained classified had not Germany unconditionally surrendered in 1945. The drawback of this feature is, however, that much of the material has been scattered among a large number of archives, and some has become lost entirely. The best overall guide to the present whereabouts of most of the original source collections is Heinz Boberach, "Das Schriftgut der staatlichen Verwaltung, der Wehrmacht und der NSDAP aus der Zeit von 1933–1945," *Der Archivar*, XXII (May 1969), 137 ff.

Relatively few materials have found a permanent home in the German Democratic Republic, but those which have are adequately described in Helmut Lötzke and Hans-Stephan Brather, *Übersicht über die Bestände des Deutschen Zentralarchivs Potsdam* (Berlin, 1957). The largest American depository of Nazi documents is the National Archives in Washington, D.C. The overwhelming majority of the documentation is on microfilm, but the National Archives also has the originals of the voluminous papers collected for the use of the International Military Tribunal in Nuremberg (IMT) and the various American military courts which followed. The major microfilm collections relevant to the Nazi Party are the T-81 materials (miscellaneous German records collection), the T-175 material (SS material), T-454 collection (Rosenberg's office), and above all, the T-580 material. The last is from a variety of sources. Unlike the other collections which were collated and ordered in the United States before being shipped back to Germany, the T-580 material, consisting of some one thousand rolls, remained in Germany and was filmed there. The rolls contain documentation primarily from the Berlin Document Center and unfortunately are not provided with frame numbers. An overall index to the T-580 material is contained in roll 999. A much more detailed description of the other T-material in the National Archives is provided in the *Guides to the German Captured Records Microfilmed at Alexandria, Va.*, some seventy of which have appeared to date. The rare-book room of the University of Michigan Library holds a much smaller but nonetheless important collection of Nazi papers. This is the archive of the Nazi district leader of Eisenach in Thuringia. It is described in Gerhard L. Weinberg, ed., *German Archival Material in the Rare Book Room—The University of Michigan Library* (Ann Arbor, n.d.).

Almost all the captured German documents have now been returned to Germany, with the exception of the IMT material and some items which remain classified. Most of those returned have found their way to the German Federal Archives, which is now the largest depository of Nazi documents. Its holdings are described in considerable detail in Hans Booms and Heinz Boberach, *Das Bundesarchiv und seine Bestände*, 2d ed. (Koblenz, 1969), but it may be useful to indicate here the major archival numbers which were used in the course of the study. They are above all the NS 6 materials (deputy Führer and party chancellery), NS 22 (Reich organizational leader), NS 8 (Rosenberg's office), and R 43 II (Reich chancellery). In addition, there is the so-called Sammlung Schumacher, a rather ill-chosen group of documents taken from various personnel folders at the Berlin Document Center and then rearranged because they seemed to contain no biographical material. Many of these items in turn have been filmed for the T-580 collection, which is available from the National Archives.

Unlike the Bundesarchiv, whose basic purpose is to serve as a scholarly archive, the Berlin Document Center continues to have an essentially judicial purpose. Administered by the U.S. Department of State and the U.S. Mission to Berlin, the BDC contains vast amounts of extremely important material. Its original purpose had been to gather evidence in the various de-Nazification proceedings that occurred in Germany after World War II. As a result, with a few minor exceptions virtually all of its holdings are grouped according to individual names, and the researcher must request a specific individual's folder in order to use the material. In addition, the BDC contains the remains of the party's central membership file, but this material has not yet been made available to scholarly researchers. It should be added that the definition of personnel papers used by the Nazis and the BDC is very broad. Thus folders contain such documents as copies of speeches delivered by particular individuals, as well as newspaper clippings and similar items.

Virtually next door to the BDC in Berlin is the Hauptarchiv Berlin. This archive is the successor organization to the Prussian State Archive, and it retains some papers of the old Prussian ministries and Länder agencies. Much of this material, however, is in the process of being transferred to the Bundesarchiv. (Thus HAB 320 has now become BA R 18.)

At the other end of Germany is the Institut für Zeitgeschichte in Munich. The IfZ was the first German institutional attempt to deal in a scholarly manner with the Nazi past, and while its holdings of unpublished documents remain relatively small, they are nevertheless of considerable importance. In addition to a number of items which were collected by the Institute quite early in the 1950s and which are not available anywhere else, the Institute also retains a large file of so-called *Zeugenschrifttum*. These are interrogation reports and interviews dating from the forties and early fifties involving a number of Nazi leaders and lesser officials. In some cases they are extremely banal, revealing virtually nothing, but in many cases the information is of the utmost importance and quite often much more useful than attempting to interview these people at the present time.

For the history of the party, the Bayerisches Geheimes Staatsarchiv is less significant, but it does contain the papers of Reichstatthalter Epp of Bavaria. The Forschungsstelle für die Geschichte des Nationalsozialismus in Hamburg is one of the best organized and most useful of the German regional archives. Its materials, besides being quite voluminous, are exceptionally well indexed and contain a number of important items. There is considerable documentation on the person and activities of the Hamburg Gauleiter, as well as a large amount of material on the Hamburg minister of justice, Curt Rothenberger, who in 1942 became undersecretary at the Reich ministry of justice and was thus in the center of the judicial crisis of 1942.

It should not be forgotten that large numbers of Nazi documents were originally provenanced outside the borders of the Reich. Many of these have of course become lost or are no longer available, but at least two repositories contain a wealth of materials which is freely accessible to scholarly researchers. One is the Rijksinstituut voor Oorlogsdokumentatie in Amsterdam, which has acquired virtually all that remained of the Nazi rule in the Netherlands and besides has added a large store of photocopied records from the BDC. The other repository, located in Paris, is the Centre documentation juive contemporaine, which holds a quite sizable collection of documents provenanced in Alfred Rosenberg's offices. Most of these deal with the occupation policies in the East, but a number of items are important for the overall history of the party as well. This collection has received a model description in J. Billig,

Alfred Rosenberg dans l'action ideologique, politique et administrative du Reich hitlerien: Inventoire commenté de la collection de documents conservés à CDJC (Paris, 1963).

II. PUBLISHED SOURCES: METHODOLOGY, BIBLIOGRAPHIC, AND BIOGRAPHIC AIDS

Needless to say, most of the items discussed in the section "Literature on the Theory of Totalitarianism and Bibliographic Aids" of the Bibliographic Note for Volume I of this study are equally applicable to the latter part of the Nazi Party's history. Indeed, the controversy over the typology and methodology of classifying totalitarian and fascist political institutions has died down to a considerable extent. Among the few major new contributions is the review article by Tom Bottomore, "Conservative Man," *New York Review of Books*, XV (8 Oct. 1970), 20–24, which draws a clear distinction between political systems in flux and those that remain in equilibrium. Jacques Ellul, *The Political Illusion*, tr. Konrad Kellen (New York, 1967) has continued that author's discussion of the relationship between modern politics and technology. The most important contribution to the discussion is Wolfgang Sauer, "National Socialism: Totalitarianism or Fascism," *American Historical Review*, LXXIII (Dec. 1967), 404–24, which attempts to show that the term *totalitarianism* is less useful as a typological label than is the term *fascism*. Finally, Roland Sarti, "Fascist Modernization in Italy: Traditional or Revolutionary," *American Historical Review*, LXXV (April 1970), 1029–45, shows that far from modernizing Italy, fascism was in fact reactionary and never developed the technological elite needed in a highly industrialized state.

Instead of institutional typologies, much of the recent literature on Nazism and totalitarianism has been devoted to the psychohistorical approach. The lengthiest attempt to deal with the ideas and personality of Adolf Hitler is Friedrich Heer, *Der Glaube des Adolf Hitler—Anatomie einer politischen Religiosität* (Munich, 1968), which attempts to prove that Hitler saw himself as a self-proclaimed Christ figure. The attempt succeeds less than it might have, largely because of the author's unwillingness to go beyond the published sources. Far more incisive is Eberhard Jäckel, *Hitlers Weltanschauung* (Tübingen, 1969). Bradley F. Smith has continued his series of investigations of the youth of Nazi leaders with *Heinrich Himmler: A Nazi in the Making, 1900–1926* (Stanford, 1971), and he presents a considerably more convincing portrait of the Reichsführer SS than does Peter Loewenberg in "The Unsuccessful Adolescence of Heinrich Himmler," *American Historical Review*, LXXVI (June 1971), 612–41, despite the latter's clinical language and strident tone.

A number of important biographical aids on the structure of the Nazi party and the PO are available. The members of the Reichstag are analyzed both by themselves and by recent scholars in Bureau des Reichstags, ed., *Verzeichnis der Mitglieder der Reichstags und der Reichsregierung Abgeschlossen am 20. Mai 1936* (Berlin, 1936) and Max Schwarz, *MdR—Biographisches Handbuch der Reichstage* (Hanover, 1965). These should be used along with the older *Das Deutsche Führerlexikon 1934/1935* (Berlin, 1934) and Great Britain Ministry of Economic Warfare, *Who's Who in Germany and Austria* (London, 1945). For the personnel of the SS officer corps Reichsführer SS, Personal-Kanzlei, *Dienstaltersliste der Schutzstaffel der NSDAP* (Berlin, 1936) is indispensable (as are the later editions of this publication). Finally, Erich Stockhorst's recently published *Fünftausend Köpfe—Wer war was im Dritten Reich* (Velbert, 1967) is by far the most complete compilation of biographical data on Nazi personnel. Reich organizational leader, *Partei Statistik*, 4 vols. ([Munich, 1935]), while not primarily concerned with individual names, is still the best compilation of raw statistical data on the PLs.

Among the bibliographic aids, Otto Neuberger, *Official Publications of Present-Day Germany* (Washington, 1942) is still unsurpassed. The Wiener Library's Ilse R. Wolff, ed., *Persecution and Resistance Under the Nazis*, 2d ed. (London, 1900) remains useful but is by now a bit dated. It should be supplemented with Eugen Weber *et al.*, "Fascisme et National-Socialisme," *Annales*, XXIV (Jan.–Feb. 1969), 195–233.

III. PUBLISHED SOURCES: MEMOIRS, DIARIES, LETTERS, AND COLLECTIONS OF SPEECHES

As one might expect from a movement as historically significant as that of Nazism, the flood of available memoir material, in nature both apologetic and otherwise, is almost boundless. Hitler himself left neither letters, memoirs, nor a diary, but a large number of his speeches have survived and so have most of his incessant monologues. The best collection of Hitler's public speeches as well as his daily activities is Max Domarus, ed., *Hitler, Reden und Proklamationen 1932–1945*, 2 vols. (Munich, 1965). This should be supplemented with Hildegard von Kotze and Helmut Krausnick, eds., *Es spricht der Führer 7 exemplarische Hitler-Reden* (Gütersloh, 1966), a little book that contains not only a masterful analysis of Hitler's style of speaking, but also some of the speeches of the "secret" variety not included in Domarus. Hitler's more privately spoken words must be culled from a variety of sources, but these collections in their entirety do provide a rather complete picture of Hitler's opinions on virtually any subject. Perhaps the earliest of these collections of conversations was Hermann Rauschning, *Hitler Speaks* (London, 1938), whose authenticity had been under some attack until recently, but which has become increasingly accepted as a true historical record. Whereas Rauschning wrote his book in an attempt to arouse the world against Hitler, the various table talk collections were made with Hitler's permission and indeed at the suggestion of Martin Bormann. There are four collections of these; they differ in both the material they contain and the chronological time span covered. The original German edition was Henry Picker, ed., *Hitlers Tischgespräche im Führerhauptquartier 1941–1942*, ed. Gerhard Ritter (Bonn, 1959), which contained only material from the years 1941 and 1942. This is now available in a greatly expanded version with a masterful introduction by Percy-Ernst Schramm in Henry Picker. ed., *Hitlers Tischgespräche im Führerhauptquartier 1941–1942*, newly ed. Percy-Ernst Schramm *et al.* (Stuttgart, 1965). The English language publication Hugh R. Trevor-Roper, ed., *Hitler's Table Talk* covers a longer period, from 1941 to 1945. Finally, Martin Bormann, ed., *Le Testament politiques de Hitler*, tr. François Genoud (Paris, 1959) contains the record of Hitler's last months from the end of February to the beginning of April. The text of Hitler's political and private testament is reprinted in Domarus, *Hitler.*

As could be expected from the much more reticent Rudolf Hess, the record of his speeches and other writings is more meager. There is one thin collection of speeches (Rudolf Hess, *Reden* [Munich, 1937]), but this covers only material up to 1938. In addition, the basically apologetic volume by Ilse Hess, ed., *England-Nürnberg-Spandau* (Leoni am Starnberger See, 1952 [?]), contains some poignant personal letters written by the erstwhile deputy Führer to his wife and son. For Hess's chief of staff the available material is even more disappointing. There is neither a collection of Martin Bormann's speeches nor a diary belonging to him; the only glimpse into his personal feelings is provided by Martin and Gerda Bormann, *The Bormann Letters— The Private Correspondence Between Martin Bormann and his Wife from January 1943 to April 1945*, ed. Hugh R. Trevor-Roper (London, 1954). Similarly, Robert Ley has left only one major record: Robert Ley, *Wir alle helfen dem Führer*, ed. Heinrich Simon (Munich, 1937). Nevertheless this collection of articles and speeches is extremely revealing of Ley's ideas and intentions, precisely because it is both naively and blatantly propagandistic.

Records are not lacking in the case of Joseph Goebbels. The Reich minister of propaganda was a man of great oratorical skill; he also wrote with substantial ability and kept a daily diary. Portions of both his speeches and his diary are available in published form. The diary for the latter half of the 1930s has become lost, but the years from 1941 to 1943 are available in an excellent edition in Joseph Goebbels, *The Goebbels Diaries*, ed. Louis P. Lochner (Garden City, N.Y., 1948). Goebbels himself published a highly censored account of the Nazis' rise to power and their first few months in office (*Vom Kaiserhof zur Reichskanzlei*, 12th ed. [Munich, 1936]). Helmut Heiber is preparing a definitive edition of Goebbels' speeches. The first volume, covering the years 1932–39, has appeared (*Goebbels-Reden Band 1: 1932–39* [Düsseldorf, 1971]). There are several other collections of speeches as well. The minister's wartime addresses for the years 1941–42 are available in Joseph Goebbels, *Das Eherne Herz—Reden und Aufsätze aus den Jahren 1941/42* (Munich, 1943). These should be supplemented with the record of Goebbels' ministerial conferences cited below and with the excellent diaries of two of his closer associates, Rudolf Semmler, *Goebbels— the Man next to Hitler*, ed. G. S. Wagner (London, 1947) and Wilfred von Oven, *Mit Goebbels bis zum Ende*, 2d ed. (Buenos Aires, 1949).

The other self-proclaimed intellectual in the party, Alfred Rosenberg, has left both a diary and an autobiography. His diary covers only snippets of his career in 1934–35 and 1939–40, but it does contain a number of important revelations (Alfred Rosenberg, *Das politische Tagebuch Alfred Rosenbergs 1934/35 und 1939/40*, ed. Hans-Günther Seraphim [Munich, 1964]). The autobiography Alfred Rosenberg, *Letzte Aufzeichnungen* (Göttingen, 1955) is an apologetic tome of little value. Otto Bräutigam, one of Rosenberg's closer associates in the Reich ministry of occupied Eastern territories, has published his memoirs, *So hat es sich zugetragen—Ein Leben als Soldat und Diplomat* (Würzburg, 1968), which is also apologetic, though it does present a rather interesting picture of the chaos that surrounded Alfred Rosenberg.

The published writings of other Nazi leaders are meager. A collection of letters written to and by Heinrich Himmler is available in Helmut Heiber, *Reichsführer! ... Briefe an und von Himmler* (Stuttgart, 1968), but it is only a selection from a large number of letters contained in the T-175 material. As for Göring, his widow has published an account of their life together which is so utterly useless that it almost becomes a model of historical distortions: Emmy Göring, *An der Seite meines Mannes—Begebenheiten und Erkenntnisse* (Göttingen, 1967).

Predictably, the Gauleiters by and large proved to be much less literary-minded than power-hungry. Only two of their number have published memoirs: Karl Wahl, *Es ist das deutsche Herz—Erlebnisse und Erkenntnisse eines ehemaligen Gauleiters* (Augsburg, 1954) and Baldur von Schirach, *Ich glaubte an Hitler* (Gütersloh, 1967). Neither is an important analytical contribution.

On the other hand, a large number of second-rung Nazis have burst into print. Needless to say, those closest (or seemingly closest) to Hitler discovered the greatest urge to publish their experiences. In addition to the older works, the following should be cited: Otto Dietrich, *Zwölf Jahre mit Hitler* (Cologne, 1955); Heinrich Hoffmann, *Hitler Was My Friend*, tr. R. H. Stevens (London, 1955); Albert Zoller, ed., *Hitler privat—Erlebnisbericht seiner Geheimsekretärin* (Düsseldorf, 1949); and Fritz Wiedemann, *Der Mann der Feldherr werden wollte* (Velbert, 1964), an account by Hitler's adjutant. The last book while obviously expiatory in many ways nevertheless views Hitler's personality from a rather novel perspective, that of a simplistic, professional officer. Friedrich Christian Prinz zu Schaumburg-Lippe, *Zwischen Krone und Kerker* (Wiesbaden, 1952) and Walter Schellenberg, *Memoiren* (Cologne, 1956), two works by close associates of Goebbels and Himmler, respectively, are neither new contributions nor of great historical value. Finally, Konstantin Hierl, *Im Dienst für Deutschland* (Heidelberg, 1954) covers only the Reichsarbeitsdienst, and that not very well, while Hans Frank, *Im Angesicht des Galgens* (Munich-Gräfeling, 1953) despite its mea culpa tone is indispensable for an appreciation of the intricacies of Nazi infighting. Understandably, the regime's foreign collaborators have not rushed into print. The only available memoir and letter material in this regard is Robert Ernst, *Rechenschaftsbericht eines Elsässers* (Berlin, 1954), which is highly unsatisfactory, and Minoud Marinus Rost van Tonningen, *Correspondentie van Mr. M. M. Rost van Tonningen*, ed. E. Fraenkel-Verkade and A. J. van der Leeuw (s'Gravenhage, 1967), an excellently edited collection of letters by one of the most radical of the Dutch collaborators.

A separate category is occupied by those individuals who were opportunistic supporters of the regime, but became consciously disillusioned at some point during the twelve-year Reich. Undoubtedly the most important of these is Albert Speer whose recently published memoirs (*Erinnerungen* [Berlin, 1969]) are extremely interesting and indispensable for any study of the Nazi phenomenon. The fact that Speer remained a loyal Nazi until almost the very end does not mitigate his attempt twenty years later to be as objective as possible about the regime. The memoirs of the Reich minister of finances Lutz Graft Schwerin von Krosigk, *Es geschah in Deutschland* (Tübingen, 1951), presented in a series of vignettes of various leaders, are rather lightweight by comparison. Ernst Hanfstaengl's memoirs, *Zwischen Braunem und Weissen Haus* (Munich, 1970), contain little that was not available in his earlier *Unheard Witness* (Philadelphia, 1957), and neither is a very penetrating analysis.

Speer, Schwerin-Krosigk, and Hanfstaengl might be classified as essentially apolitical opportunists; however a special place must be assigned to the conservatives who remained in the Nazi regime to a greater or lesser extent hoping that Hitler would destroy democracy but also restore conservative ideals of law and order. Here the memoirs of Friedrich Hossbach, *Zwischen Wehrmacht und Hitler*, 2d ed. (Göttingen, 1965), are valuable particularly for the 1938 crisis but also for the self-delusion of a conservative, old-line army officer. Hans-Gerd Gisevius, *Bis zum bitteren Ende* (Hamburg, n.d.) is a much more strident and controversial book. It, however, is also relatively unconvincing as to the pure motivation of the old-line conservatives.

Finally, there is the category of what might be called atmospheric contemporaries. The two most important contributions belonging here are the autobiography of Ernst von Salomon, *Fragebogen* (Hamburg, 1951), and the diaries of Ernst Jünger, *Strahlungen* (Tübingen, 1949). Both were men who had done much to undermine the pluralistic structure of the Weimar Republic, but unlike many of their contemporaries they did not succumb to the spell of Nazism and remained intelligent and critical observers of the Nazi

phenomenon. Bruno E. Werner, *Die Galeere* (Frankfurt, 1949) is a fictional-
ized account by a ranking journalist, and it contains a large number of insights. Hans-Georg von Studnitz, *Als Berlin brannte—Diarium der Jahre
1943–1945* (Stuttgart, 1963) and Karl Koller, *Der letzte Monat* (Mannheim,
1949) are diaries of varying length. The first is by a high-ranking official in
the foreign ministry; the second, by the last chief of staff of the German air
force. Koller's contribution covers only the period from April 14 to the end
of May 1945.

IV. Published Sources: Party Publications, Journals, and Newspapers

As befitted a theoretically centralized political institution, the NSDAP
delighted in massive publications of orders, newsletters, and similar items
which were to serve as guidelines for the lower organs of the party. In addition, the Reich offices insisted on a large number of reports from below on
the mood of public opinion. The most important of the latter is the SD's "SD-
Berichte zu Inlandsfragen," a selection of which has been published in Heinz
Boberach, ed., *Meldungen aus dem Reich—Auswahl aus den geheimen
Lageberichten der Sicherheitsdienstes der SS 1939–1944* (Neuwied, 1965).
The PK's "Auszüge aus Berichten der Gauleitungen u.a. Dienststellen" supplies essentially the same information but this time from the point of view
of the Gauleiters.

Among the various collections of orders and directives issued by the
Reichsleitung of the NSDAP and by the office of the deputy Führer as it became more powerful, there are a number of important publications. For the
first years of the Nazi regime, 1932 and following, the *Verordnungsblatt der
Reichsleitung der NSDAP*, ed. Philipp Bouhler, is still important. It lost its
significance as the power of the executive secretary became transferred increasingly to the offices of Ley and particularly Hess, so that the directives
emanating from the office of the deputy Führer supercede to a large extent
those in the *Verordnungsblatt*. In 1937 the deputy Führer issued a compilation of all directives from his office that were still in effect (NSDAP,
Stellvertreter des Führers, *Zusammenstellung aller bis zum 31. März 1937
erlassenen und noch gültigen Anordnungen des Stellvertreters des Führers*
[Munich, 1937]), but this collection is relatively unsatisfactory since it does
not contain orders that were no longer in force by the date of publication. A
complete file of the StdF's directives is available in the NS 6 collection of
the Bundesarchiv (T-580, roll 12, folders 169, 170, and 171). In May of
1940 the office of the deputy Führer began publication of the *Reichsverfügungsblatt*. This continued until the end of the war, though it too became
less important after the party chancellery began publication of the massive
seven-volume collection of *Verfügungen, Anordnungen, Bekanntgaben*
(Munich, 1943) at the beginning of 1943. In addition, after Hess's flight to
England, Bormann started publishing the *Vertrauliche Informationen*, in-

tended primarily as a means of communication between the Reich chancellery and the district leaders.

Robert Ley attempted on a number of occasions to structure the functions of the party both in directive form and through his publications. The earliest of the attempts to define the jurisdictions of the various offices in the Reichsleitung came with the *Dienstvorschrift der P.O.* (Munich, 1933), only a small number of which have survived. Somewhat later the *Organisationsbuch der NSDAP* (Munich, 1936) appeared and went through several editions, the last being published in 1943. Fritz Mehnert and Paul Müller, *Geschäftsordnung der NSDAP* (Munich, 1940) is an attempt dating from the early war years to remedy much of the political insignificance of the *Organisationsbuch*. Among the more propagandistic publications issued by the ROL are the highly popularized *Nationalsozialistisches Jahrbuch*, which appeared annually, as well as the two propaganda journals *Der Schulungsbrief* and *Der Hoheitsträger*. The Reich treasurer's collection of directives was considerably more centralized and presumably more effective. A set of these is available at the Institut für Zeitgeschichte. There are eight volumes of *Rundschreiben des Reichsschatzmeisters* ranging from 1933 to the end of 1941. The OPG published a monthly journal from 1934 to 1940, *Der Parteirichter*. In addition, the directives for a Gau court are available in a wartime version (that is, after the reforms of 1942 and 1943) in Gau Baden, *Richtlinien für die Parteigerichte der NSDAP* ([Strasbourg], 1944).

Goebbels did not have a centralized directive organ, but the party's ideology and propagandistic activities are available in a number of important publications. Of some interest is Reichs-Wahlkampfleitung, *Richtlinien für den Reichswahlkampf zum 29. März 1936* ([Berlin, 1936]), since it is an example of Goebbels' role as campaign manager for the various plebiscites held in Nazi Germany. The variety and radicalization of the propaganda themes throughout the war years can be effectively gauged in three publications: *Die Lage—Zentralinformationsdienst*, ed. RPL and Reich propaganda ministry; the *Mitteilungsblatt*, ed. NS-Gauring of the Gau Munich-Upper Bavaria; and *Die Parole*, ed. Karl Müller (also issued in the Gau Munich-Upper Bavaria).

Beginning with the publication of the *Organisationsbuch* in 1936, the various Gaus were also instructed to publish their own Verordnungsblätter. Much of the information in the Gau publications is merely a reprint of items appearing in various national collections of directives, but in many cases, specific Gau material is also included; hence regional differences can be effectively surmised. The largest of such Gau directive collections is in Munich in the Institut für Zeitgeschichte, which has directives for the Gaus Franken, Berlin, Baden, and Tirol-Vorarlberg. The item for Hamburg, *Gaunachrichten*, is available in the Hamburgische Universitätsbibliothek. A few copies of the very interesting *Pflicht* [for Thuringia], ed. Fritz Sauckel, has been filmed in T-81, roll 661, frames 5475993 ff. For the lower party jurisdictions, the district Verordnungsblatt for München-Oberbayern, *Mitteilungsblatt Kreis*

München der NSDAP, is available in the IfZ. The Gau Bayerische Ostmark, Kreis Pfarrkirchen, *Bekenntnis zum Sieg: Kriegs-Kreistag der NSDAP der Kreise Eggefelden-Giesbach-Pfarrkirchen 15./16. Juni 1940* (Pfarrkirchen, 1940) T-580, roll 362, folder 16, may serve as an example of the slick publications designed to put the district organizations in the center of public social life. Finally, Reichsorganisationsleiter, *Block- und Zellenneuordnung der NSDAP 1936* ([Munich, 1936]) and Kadatz, *Block und Zelle in der NSDAP* (Dresden, 1936) are two important documents on the emptiness of party activity at the block and cell level.

For party activities outside the borders of the *Altreich, Der Ostmarkbrief* is essentially the Verordnungsblatt for Austria after the *Anschluss,* while ROL, *Gau-, Kreis- und Ortsgruppenverzeichnis der NSDAP in Österreich Stand: 1.8.1938* (Vienna, 1938) is a complete listing of the organizational structure of the NSDAP in Austria. After the beginning of the war, the NSDAP organizations in the occupied countries began publishing their own collections of directives. Among those readily available are the *Verordnungsblatt der NSDAP Arbeitsbereich Generalgouvernement* for Poland and the Reich commissioner's *Stimmungsberichte* for Holland. The latter, however, is basically a survey of public opinion reports rather than a collection of directives.

The various Reichsleitung offices also attempted to influence German social and economic life through the publication of a variety of journals devoted to their areas of activity. *Braune Wirtschaftspost* and *Der Gauwirtschaftsberater* document the changing thinking of the Nazis in the field of economics and the progressive take-over of decision-making in this field by the office of the Four Year Plan. In the area of judicial reform, NSDAP, Reichsrechtsamt, *Nationalsozialistische Leitsätze für ein neues deutsches Strafrecht,* 4th ed. (Berlin, 1935) and Reich ministry of justice, *Richterbriefe* are important evidence of the party's persistent interference in the judicial processes.

For the war years, a number of important documentary collections have appeared, enabling the researcher to get a close look at the inner decision-making processes within the Nazi regime. Helmut Heiber, ed., *Hitlers Lagebesprechungen—Protokollfragmente seiner Konferenzen 1942–1945* (Stuttgart, 1962) contains the remains of the massive collection of protocols taken at Hitler's twice-daily wartime staff conferences. Willi Boelcke has almost made a career of publishing the various conference protocols of Joseph Goebbels at the Reich propaganda ministry. His two major and well-edited books *Kriegspropaganda 1939–1941—Geheime Ministerkonferenzen im Reichspropagandaministerium* (Stuttgart, 1966) and *Wollt Ihr den totalen Krieg—Die geheimen Goebbels Konferenzen 1939–1943* (Stuttgart, 1967) cover the available conferences from 1939 to 1943. In addition, the previously cited Boberach collection of SD reports also provides valuable documentation for the war years.

Contrasting sharply to the Weimar Republic, Nazi newspapers reveal very little about the internal workings of the Nazi regime. Moreover, there is virtually no differentiation between the various papers, since all were centrally directed from Goebbels' office. The *Völkischer Beobachter* continued to be published, but it provides no more than a running party line. For the early Nazi era, the *Illustrierter Beobachter* sometimes has quite effective photographic evidence of the *Gleichschaltung* process. The only exceptions to the lack of interest shown by the Nazi papers were the *Frankfurter Zeitung*, which was allowed a pseudoliberal gadfly role until 1943, and *Das Reich*, a weekly publication begun by Goebbels after the defeat of France as the new standard of intellectual journalism for all of Europe.

V. Published Sources, Secondary Material Covering the Entire Period

There is as yet neither a definitive account of the Third Reich nor a full-scale history of the Nazi Party for these years. William L. Shirer, *The Rise and Fall of the Third Reich* (New York, 1960) is a stylistic and interpretive tour de force, but its value as scholarship leaves a great deal to be desired. Karl-Dietrich Bracher, *Die Deutsche Diktatur* (Cologne, 1969) is a brilliant work of interpretive synthesis, but it is intended as primarily that rather than a definitive account based upon contemporary and unpublished sources. There are, however, a number of significant works of a biographical nature on several Nazi leaders. Perhaps the best overall account of the various personality types rampant in the Nazi regime is Joachim C. Fest, *Das Gesicht des Dritten Reiches* (Munich, 1964). This should be supplemented with two accounts of first-hand information on the twenty-two defendants at the International Military Tribunal: Eugene Davidson, *The Trial of the Germans —An Account of the Twenty-Two Defendants before the International Military Tribunal at Nuremberg* (New York, 1966) and Robert M. W. Kempner, *Das Dritte Reich im Kreuzverhör—Aus den unveröffentlichen Vernehmungsprotokollen des Anklägers* (Munich, 1969). On Hitler himself Allan Bullock, *Hitler—A Study in Tyranny* (New York, 1962) remains unsurpassed as a brilliant biography of a political leader. It should be read in conjunction with the photographic record in Jochem von Lang, ed., *Adolf Hitler—Gesichter eines Diktators* (Hamburg, 1968).

The figure of Joseph Goebbels has fascinated observers both during the Nazi regime and after the close of World War II. Curt Riess, *Joseph Goebbels* (New York, 1948) was the first of the postwar biographies to appear, and in many ways it remains important, although it has now been replaced by Helmut Heiber, *Joseph Goebbels* (Berlin, 1962; Eng. ed., New York, 1972). Friedrich Christian Prinz zu Schaumburg-Lippe, *Dr. G.—Ein Portrait des Propagandaministers* (Wiesbaden, 1964), an account by Goebbels' erstwhile adjutant, is a clumsy attempt at whitewashing. Boris von Borresholm and Karena Nichoff, eds., *Dr. Goebbels—Nach Aufzeichnungen seiner Umgebung* (Berlin, 1949) is unsatisfactory as a scholarly work since it has no footnotes or bibliography, but it is obviously the original source of many of the anecdotes used by other authors in later publications. Erich Ebermayer and Hans Roos, *Gefährtin des Teufels—Leben und Tod der Magda Goebbels* (Hamburg, 1952), a biography of Goebbels' wife as well as a story of the minister's extramarital affairs, is based primarily on the revelations of Magda's sister-in-law, the wife of her husband.

Göring has not been copiously studied by biographers. The standard postwar biography is still Willi Frischauer, *The Rise and Fall of Hermann Göring* (Boston, 1951), but it can in no way be called a definitive account. Something approaching an autobiographical statement is contained in Werner Bross, "Gespräche mit Hermann Göring während des Nürnberger Prozesses" (ms. photocopy, Nov. 1946).

There is a desperate need for a full-scale biography of Martin Bormann. Both the account in Hugh R. Trevor-Roper, "Martin Bormann," *Der Monat*, VI (May 1954), 168–76, and the larger work by Joseph Wulf, *Martin Bormann—Hitlers Schatten* (Gütersloh, 1962), suffer from superficiality and a rather strident style.

There is no satisfactory account of any of the other Nazi leaders, but the Reich treasurer's office as an institution has been relatively adequately described in two publications. Anton Lingg, *Die Verwaltung der Nationalsozialistischen Deutschen Arbeiterpartei*, 2d ed. (Munich, 1940) is a wartime account by one of the leading officials of the Reich treasurer's office, but it is rather free from the usual propagandistic jargon. Ulf Lükemann's "Der Reichsschatzmeister der NSDAP—Ein Beitrag zur inneren Parteistruktur" (Dissertation, Free University of Berlin, 1963) is a well-researched if somewhat timid account of the Reich treasurer's office. The PO has fared even less well. Wolfgang Schäfer, *NSDAP—Entwicklung und Struktur der Staatspartei des Dritten Reiches* (Hanover, 1956) was a pioneering work of considerable merit, but its brevity and narrowness of scope make it unsatisfactory as a definitive work on the PO. Karl Astel and Erna Weber, *Die Kinderzahl der 19,000 politischen Leiter des Gaues Thüringen* (Berlin, 1943) has been curiously neglected yet it contains a wealth of statistical information on the PLs of the Gau Thuringia for the later 1930s and early 1940s, information which is not available in the 1935 *Partei Statistik*. Peter Hüttenberger, *Die Gauleiter* (Stuttgart, 1969) is a pioneering but hardly definitive group study of the provincial leaders.

Of the various wings and factions of the Nazi regime, the SS has undoubtedly received the most detailed and definitive treatment. Here the two most important works are Hans Buchheim *et al.*, *Anatomie des SS-Staates* (Olten und Freiburg i.B., 1965) and Heinz Höhne, *Der Orden unter dem Totenkopf—Die Geschichte der SS* (Gütersloh, 1967). The latter is particularly significant in that it demonstrates the validity of a good journalistic approach in the field of contemporary history. Hans-Christian Brandenburg, *HJ—Die Geschichte der HJ* (Cologne, 1968) is the only overall account of the history of the HJ, but it too is rather superficial and in no way definitive.

Lawrence D. Walker, *Hitler Youth—Catholic Youth 1933–36* (Washington, 1970) covers only a minor part of the HJ history in a thoroughly unsatisfactory way.

One of the more controversial aspects of the Third Reich is the degree to which the arrival of the Nazis to power revolutionized everyday life and social relations in Germany. The most far-reaching and interpretive thesis on this theme is the book by David Schoenbaum, *Hitler's Social Revolution: Class and Status in Nazi Germany, 1933–1939* (New York, 1966), which concluded that the party had relatively little influence on social life in Germany and, indeed, that there was no social revolution. Eliot B. Wheaton, *The Nazi Revolution 1933–1935—Prelude to Calamity* (New York, 1969) is a much thinner account but is noteworthy because of the excellent chronological section at the back of the book. The short article by Georges Castellan, "Bilan social du IIIe Reich 1933–1939," *Revue d'histoire moderne et contemporaine*, XV (1968), 502–11, uses a relatively narrow thematic approach, though it is an extremely incisive piece of work documenting clearly that all social groups except the farmers fared worse under the Nazis than they had before. This situation in turn led to the phenomenon of disengagement from the Nazi values, a process which is effectively documented in William Allen, *The Nazi Seizure of Power: The Experience of a Single German Town, 1930–1935* (Chicago, 1965) and Bernhard Vollmer, *Volksopposition im Polizeistaat* (Stuttgart, 1957). The Nazi impact on routine social relations within Germany has been the subject of a number of excellent studies. Hans-Jochen Gamm's, *Der braune Kult—Das Dritte Reich und seine Ersatzreligion* (Hamburg, 1962) is a brilliant account of the Nazi attempt to substitute pseudopolitics for religious exercises, while Franz-Joseph Heyen, *Nationalsozialismus im Alltag* (Boppard am Rhein, 1968) deals more with the everyday totalitarianization of Germany's social life. At least two local situations have been covered in excellent accounts. One, involving the small Westphalian town of Herne is described in Hermann Meyerhoff, *Herne 1933–1945 —Die Zeit des Nationalsozialismus* (Herne, 1963), a report made particularly poignant by the fact that it was written by the town archivist; the other, concerning the large Rhenish city of Düsseldorf, is related by Hans-Peter Görgen, "Düsseldorf und der Nationalsozialismus (Dissertation, Cologne, 1968). Like many dissertations, the latter is rather short on analysis, but the author has done an admirable job of collecting data and presenting it in quite lucid form.

Both the Nazis themselves and postwar researchers realized that the key to the partification of the Third Reich lay in the relationship between the party and the state, as well as the party and various established socioeconomic institutions. The literature on the relationship between party and state is quite extensive. The large-scale work, Hans Frank, ed., *Deutsches Verwaltungsrecht* (Munich, 1937), was an attempt to partify the legal basis of the

NSDAP's role in the Third Reich. The standard Nazi account of the relationship between party and state in the thirties is Gottfried Neesse, *Partei und Staat* (Hamburg, 1936), which is notable for its frankness and its inability to solve the dilemma of party and state. Among the postwar analyses, the most important is Hans Mommsen, *Beamtentum im Dritten Reich* (Stuttgart, 1966), which is both a documentary analysis and an interpretation of the Nazi attempt to take over the civil service. The author concludes that certainly during the war years the party succeeded to a considerable extent in realizing its aim. Peter Diehl-Thiele's *Partei und Staat im Dritten Reich* (Munich, 1969) is devoted primarily to the situation in Bavaria. This is also true of Edward N. Peterson, *The Limits of Hitler's Power* (Princeton, N.J., 1969), a study of the lack of centralization within the regime as exemplified in various local, regional, and Land situations. Finally, Hubert Schorn, *Die Gesetzgebung des Nationalsozialismus als Mittel der Machtpolitik* (Frankfurt, 1963) for all its brevity and emotionalism is a useful catalog of the Nazis' legal basis of their illegal actions.

Probably because the divergence between ideal and practice was so blatantly apparent in the relationship between the party and the churches, this subject has received a great deal of attention among the postwar analysts. The pioneering work in this genre was Hans Buchheim, *Glaubenskrise im Dritten Reich* (Stuttgart, 1952), more a collection of essays than a full-scale work. On the other hand, the two works John S. Conway, *The Nazi Persecution of the Churches, 1933–45* (New York, 1968) and Friedrich Zipfel, *Kirchenkampf in Deutschland* (Berlin, 1965) both give full-scale accounts of the struggle between the party and the churches. Of the two Conway's contribution is in many ways more definitive. Klaus Scholder's "Die evangelische Kirche in der Sicht der nationalsozialistischen Führung bis zum Kriegsausbruch," *Vierteljahrshefte für Zeitgeschichte*, XVI (Jan. 1968), 15–35, presents the situation in the Protestant church from a somewhat different perspective, that of the Nazi leadership itself; it documents why the NSDAP turned from direct interference to pseudoneutrality and indirect attacks. Ludwig Heine, *Geschichte des Kirchenkampfes in der Grenzmark Posen-Westpreussen 1930–1940* (Göttingen, 1961) is primarily a local study of the struggle between church and party with more attention devoted to the church than to the party. The relationship between the party and the Catholic Church has been treated in a full-scale study by Günther Lewy, *Catholic Church and Nazi Germany* (New York, 1964). It emphasizes that the church's anti-Semitic heritage and traditional respect for authority rendered it quite susceptible to collaboration with the Nazis. Nazi foreign policy has only recently received the detailed treatment it deserves. The first volume of Gerhard Weinberg's *Nazi Foreign Policy* (Chicago, 1970) is now the definitive account of the early years of Nazi foreign policy, while Hans-Adolf Jacobsen, *Nationalsozialistische Aussenpolitik 1933–1938* (Frankfurt a.M.,

1968) does the same for the institutional aspects of foreign policy determination. Jacobsen's book is also noteworthy because of its successful integration of the party's role in the formulation of foreign policy.

The Nazi policy toward the Jews continues to be the subject of a large number of scholarly treatises. Among the more recent publications is that of Karl Schleunes, *The Twisted Road to Auschwitz* (Urbana, Ill., 1970), which limits itself to the tracing of the step-by-step replacement of all the free-wheeling anti-Semitic measures of the thirties by the bureaucratic extermination policies of the forties. Helmut Genschel's *Die Verdrängung der Juden aus der Wirtschaft im Dritten Reich* (Göttingen: Musterschmidt, 1966) is an account of the economic measures against the German Jewish population. Needless to say, Raul Hilberg, *The Destruction of the European Jews* (Chicago, 1961), remains the most exhaustive account of the Nazi's anti-Semitic measures leading to the extermination process as well as of the details of that process itself.

With the availability of the mass of army records at the Militärgeschichtliches Forschungsintitut in Freiburg, the spate of books on army-party relationships have mushroomed in recent years. Robert J. O'Neill's *The German Army and the Nazi Party, 1933–39* (London, 1968) is a short but very succinct account of the relations between army and party in the prewar years. In many ways it corrects Wheeler-Bennet's earlier account but is also rather proarmy and subject to a few factual errors. The contributions by Manfred Messerschmidt, *Die Wehrmacht im NS-Staat* (Hamburg, 1969), and Klaus-Jürgen Müller, *Das Heer und Hitler—Armee und NS-Regime 1933–1940* (Stuttgart, 1969), are solid and stylistically rather formidable accounts of the relationship, and are indispensable for understanding it. Of the two, Messerschmidt covers a larger chronological span. Oron J. Hale's *The Captive Press in the Third Reich* (Princeton, N.J., 1964) remains the best account of the Nazi take-over of the press. The immensity of the subject of Nazi economics has hitherto prevented the emergence of a definitive account of this aspect of the Third Reich. Arthur Schweitzer's *Big Business in the Third Reich* (Bloomington, Ind., 1964) is still the best account of the 1930s. Smaller-scale studies by Ingeborg Esenwein-Rothe, *Die Wirtschaftsverbände von 1933 bis 1945* (Berlin, 1965), and Heinrich Uhlig, *Die Warenhäuser im Dritten Reich* (Cologne-Opladen, 1956), cover more specialized aspects of this theme.

Similarly, the Nazi education policies have not received a fully satisfactory treatment. In particular, the Nazis' attempt to establish the *Hauptschule* still needs further investigation. Rolf Eilers, *Die nationalsozialistische Schulpolitik—Eine Studie zur Funktion der Erziehung im totalitären Staat* (Cologne, 1963) is primarily concerned with the party's control of the curriculum. Likewise, the partification of art and culture has not yet been fully explored. Hildegard Brenner's *Die Kunstpolitik des Nationalsozialismus* (Reinbek b.

Hamburg, 1963) is a pioneering but not really exhaustive study; and the contributions by Joseph Wulf, ed., *Bildende Künste im Dritten Reich* (Gütersloh, 1963), and Leon Poliakov and Joseph Wulf, eds., *Das Dritte Reich und seine Denker* (Berlin, 1959), provide a mass of documentation but no genuine attempt to integrate it into an overall interpretation.

The partification of justice in the Third Reich has, on the other hand, received significantly more satisfactory treatment. In addition to the localized study of Hamburg, Werner Johe, ed., *Die gleichgeschaltete Justiz* (Frankfurt, 1967), and Ilse Stoff's documentary collection, *Justiz im Dritten Reich* (Frankfurt, 1967), there is the attempt by Hubert Schorn, *Der Richter im Dritten Reich—Geschichte und Dokumente* (Frankfurt, 1959), to analyze the behavior of the professional judges during the Third Reich, though this work is not thoroughly convincing in its attempt to rehabilitate the profession. Above all, the multivolume work by Hermann Weinkauff *et al.*, *Die deutsche Justiz und der Nationalsozialismus* (Stuttgart, 1968), has provided an exhaustive account of the relationship between Nazism and the judicial processes in the years 1933 to 1945.

VI. Publications Covering Limited Time Periods

A. 1933–1934

The best and most exhaustive account of the first year and a half of the Nazi rule is Karl-Dietrich Bracher *et al.*, *Die nationalsozialistische Machtergreifung* (Cologne, 1960). This account, which covers literally all aspects of public life in Germany, is by far the most important contribution toward any aspect or any phase of the history of the Third Reich. A number of more detailed studies should, however, be mentioned as well. Helmut Krausnick, "Stationen der Gleichschaltung" in Theodor Eschenburg, ed., *Der Weg in die Diktatur* (Munich, 1962) is a good overall account of the phases of the Nazi Gleichschaltung in the early months of the regime's existence. Erich Matthias and Rudolf Morsey, eds., *Das Ende der Parteien 1933* (Düsseldorf, 1960), is a masterful job of collating the death of German political life in early 1933. Anton Ritthaler, "Eine Etappe auf Hitlers Weg zur ungeteilten Macht—Hugenbergs Rücktritt als Reichsminister," *Vierteljahrshefte für Zeitgeschichte*, VIII (April 1960), 193–219, documents the naiveté of the nationalists in dealing with the Nazis. Henning Timpke, ed., *Dokumente zur Gleichschaltung des Landes Hamburg 1933* (Frankfurt, 1964) shows the Gleichschaltung process at a regional level, and Allen's *The Nazi Seizure of Power* provides the best account of the Gleichschaltung at the local level. One specialized and particularly pathetic aspect of the arrival of Nazi rule in Germany is the attempt of the German-Jewish organizations to deal with the Nazis by professing their assimilationist German nationalism. This is especially well documented in Klaus J. Herrmann, *Das Dritte Reich und die deutsch-jüdischen Organisationen 1933–1934* (Cologne, 1970).

The economic and social aspects of the early Gleichschaltung have also been examined in some detail. Kuno Bludau, *Nationalsozialismus und Genossenschaften* (Hanover, 1968) and A. R. L. Gurland, Otto Kirchheimer, and Franz Neumann, *The Fate of Small Business in Nazi Germany* (Washington, 1943) deal with the reaction of the Nazis to the cooperative movement and the small businessmen respectively. Hans-Gerd Schumann, *Nationalsozialismus und Gewerkschaftsbewegung* (Hanover, 1958) covers the Nazi takeover of the unions and their transformation into the Deutsche Arbeitsfront, while the brief article by Raimund Rämisch, "Der berufsständische Gedanke als Episode in der nationalsozialistischen Politik," *Zeitschrift für Politik*, IV, no. 3 (1957), 263–72, shows that the Nazis despite their propaganda were never seriously interested in re-establishing a society based upon Othmar Spann's estate concepts. The Nazi reaction to the churches is presented in two monographs. Kurt Meier gives a full-scale (though somewhat overlong and involved) account of the German Christians, *Die Deutschen Christen* (Halle/Saale, 1965); and Ludwig Volk, *Das bayerische Episkopat und der Nationalsozialismus 1930–1934* is an account of the relationship between Bavarian Catholics and the Nazis. The latter is marred somewhat by the excessively apologetic tone directed toward the Catholic hierarchy. Hitler's early blunders in foreign policy have been brilliantly treated by Dieter Ross in *Hitler und Dollfuss—die deutsche Österreich-Politik 1933–1934* (Hamburg, 1966).

The complex and interrelated developments that led to the Röhm-Putsch a year and a half after the Nazis came to power have been analyzed from a number of viewpoints. Undoubtedly the best account of the rise of the SS machinery in early 1933 is Shlomo Aronson, "Heydrich und die Anfänge der SD und der Gestapo" (Dissertation, Free University of Berlin, 1967). Heinrich Bennecke's two books, *Hitler und die SA* (Munich, 1962) and *Die Reichswehr und der "Röhm-Putsch"* (Munich, 1964), are quite insightful and important accounts despite the fact that the author had been a high-ranking SA official. Among the straight scholarly contributions is the important article by Hermann Mau, "Die 'Zweite Revolution' der 30. Juni 1934," *Vierteljahrshefte für Zeitgeschichte*, I (April 1953), 119–37, and of course the detailed treatment of the entire period in the book by Karl-Dietrich Bracher cited previously.

B. 1934–1936

The period 1934 to 1936, in many ways the most dramatic phase of the struggle between Hess and Ley, has received relatively little attention from the postwar scholarship. The further decline of institutionalized conservatism is analyzed in the collection of documents presented by Volker R. Berghahn, ed., "Das Ende des 'Stahlhelm,' " *Vierteljahrshefte für Zeitgeschichte*, XIII (Oct. 1965), 446–51. Theodor Eschenburg's brief presentation of the 1935 industrial elections, "Streiflichter zur Geschichte der Wahlen im Dritten Reich," *Vierteljahrshefte für Zeitgeschichte*, III (July 1955), 311–16, documents Ley's inability to capture the souls of the German workers. The attempt by Ley to foster and build his elite training system, the Ordensburgen, has been treated both favorably and analytically in a number of accounts. Hans Schwarz van Berk, "Die härteste Schule," *Der Angriff* (26, 28, 31 March and 1 and 2 April 1937) is a court writer's version of the schools and for that reason very revealing. The best analysis of the failure of the Ordensburgen to produce a political elite is Harold Scholtz, "Die 'NS-Ordensburgen,' " *Vierteljahrshefte für Zeitgeschichte*, XV (July 1967), 269–98, which should be supplemented with Dietrich Orlow, "Die Adolf-Hitler-Schulen," *Vierteljahrshefte für Zeitgeschichte*, XIII (July 1965), 272–84. Heiner Lichtenstein's "Schulung unterm Hakenkreuz–Die Ordensburg Vogelsang," in Walter Först, ed., *Menschen, Landschaft und Geschichte* (Cologne, 1965) is a good account of the architecture of the Ordensburg Vogelsang, an aspect of the schools which was an integral part of their curricular endeavors. The NAPOLAs, which always remained more or less in the shadow of the Ordensburgen until they were taken over by the SS in the war, have received a detailed documentary treatment from Horst Ueberhorst, *Elite für die Diktatur* (Düsseldorf, 1968). Finally, there is considerable information in Helmut Heiber's massive *Walter Frank und sein Reichsinstitut für die Geschichte des neuen Deutschland* (Stuttgart, 1966) about a relatively unrelated aspect of the Hess-Ley struggle, Hess's attempt to protect one of his controversial favorites. The same author has published the relevant documents on the Kube scandal of 1936 in "Aus den Akten des Gauleiters Kube," *Vierteljahrshefte für Zeitgeschichte*, IV (Jan. 1956), 67–92.

On the larger societal aspects of the continuing struggle over revolutionary changes in Germany, Walter Baum, "Die 'Reichsreform' im Dritten Reich," *Vierteljahrshefte für Zeitgeschichte*, III (Jan. 1955) 36–56, has provided a lengthy article on the failure of the Reichsreform, while Bernhard Lösener's "Als Rassereferent im Reichsministerium des Innern," *Vierteljahrshefte für Zeitgeschichte*, IX (July 1961), 264–313, is largely an autobiographical account of the formulation of the anti-Semitic laws at the 1935 Nuremberg party congress. For foreign policy, in addition to the works previously cited, Manfred Funke's "7. März 1936–Studie zum aussenpolitischen Führungsstil Hitlers," *Aus Politik und Zeitgeschichte/Parlament* 3 Oct. 1970, pp. 3–34, provides an insightful vignette of Hitler's turning from domestic concerns to the field of revisionist-expansionist foreign policy. The Four Year Plan was of course an integral part of these renewed preparations for war, and its formulation has been studied in a number of accounts. Basic are Wilhelm Treue's publication of Hitler's original memorandum of the Four Year Plan, "Hitlers Denkschrift zum Vierjahresplan 1936," *Vierteljahrshefte für Zeitgeschichte,* III (April 1955), 184–203, and Burton H. Klein, *Germany's Economic Preparations for War* (Cambridge, Mass., 1959). The struggle between Schacht and Göring is the subject of an article by Amos E. Simpson, "The Struggle for Control of the German Economy, 1936–37," *Journal of Modern History,* XXI (March 1959), 37–45, while Martin Wolfe has subjected Nazi fiscal policy to succinct analysis in "The Development of Nazi Monetary Policy," *Journal of Economic History,* XV (no. 4, 1955), 392–402.

C. 1937–1939

The overall renewed confidence felt by the party after the successes of 1936 and 1937 is well expressed in Hess's "confidential" speech to the PL corps at the 1938 party congress (*Rede auf Reichsparteitag 1938 vor Reichs-, Gau- und Kreisleitern* [Munich, 1938]). A copy is available in MiU/GAC, folder 51. Party aspects of the Anschluss of Austria are covered in two Austrian contributions, Ludwig Jedlicka, "Der 13. März 1938 in Sicht der historischen Forschung," *Donauraum,* XIII (Nr. 3), 144–55, and Karl Stadler, *Österreich 1938–1945 im Spiegel der NS-Akten* (Vienna, 1966). Jedlicka's article is also significant for its bibliographical contributions and for attempting to put the Anschluss into the overall perspective of developments in southeastern Europe.

The 1938 progrom has received particularly detailed treatment. The earliest and in many ways the most complete account to date of the preparations and the pogrom itself is Hermann Graml, *Der 9. November 1938* (Bonn, 1953). A somewhat later version Heinrich Uhlig, "9. November 1938," *Aus Politik und Zeitgeschichte/Das Parlament,* 6 Nov. 1963 adds to Graml's account and provides additional details. The best English presentation is Lionel Kochan, *Pogrom 10 November 1938* (London, 1957) while Wilhelm Treue's publication of Hitler's triumphant speech the day after the progrom, "Rede Hitlers vor der deutschen Presse (10. November 1938)," *Vierteljahrshefte für Zeitgeschichte,* VI (April 1958), 175–91, illustrates the relationship between the pogrom and Hitler's continued aggressiveness and war preparations. The Nazis' last peacetime conquest, that of Czechoslovakia, has recently been the subject of two masterful treatises, one in German and one in English: Detlef Brandes, *Die Tschechen unter deutschem Protektorat,* vol. 1 (Munich, 1969) and Vojtech Mastny, *The Czechs under Nazi Rule* (New York, 1971). Brandes's contribution is to appear in two volumes; the one published to date only covers the story up to 1942.

D. 1939–1941

The literature for the wartime aspects of Nazi Germany is of course particularly voluminous, but few of these works concern themselves in detail with the study of any aspect of the party's history during the conflict. For example, Andreas Hillgruber's very valuable essay collection, *Probleme des Zweiten Weltkrieges* (Cologne, 1967), not only lacks any articles on the role of the party but fails to mention the party on any of its pages. Louis de Jong, *The German Fifth Column in the Second World War*, tr. C. M. Geyl (Chicago, 1956) is also relatively unconcerned with the Nazi Party, except insofar as the German minorities in Europe were at this time subject to Nazi Party control. The book is particularly noteworthy for its demonstration of the relatively insignificant influence of the minority groups in the Nazis' conquest of their host countries.

The Nazi economy has been treated in two major studies. One, Alan S. Milward, *Die deutsche Kriegswirtschaft* (Stuttgart, 1966), is based on a Western point of view, while the collaborative work by Dietrich Eichholtz et al., *Geschichte der deutschen Kriegswirtschaft 1939–1945* (Berlin [East], 1969), is a multivolume study from a Marxist point of view. Many of the latter's interpretations are of course highly tendentious, but the East German study is noteworthy for its very careful documentary work. The administration of the party itself became the subject of a contribution by Franz X. Schwarz, "Die Verwaltung der NSDAP im Kriege," *Zeitschrift der Akademie für deutsches Recht*, XI (1 Jan. 1942), 2–5. Though it is not exhaustive, it is a good compendium of information about the party's internal administration at the beginning of the war.

The war was, of course, the most important prerequisite for the rapid rise of the SS to a position of challenging importance. The SS's role in determining Nazi policy in the occupied areas of Europe was the basis of much of Himmler's power in the Third Reich. Nazi population policy and the role of the SS in this area are the subjects of Robert L. Koehl's pioneering monograph, *RKFDV—German Resettlement and Population Policy, 1939–1945* (Cambridge, Mass., 1957). Herbert S. Levine in a much briefer contribution contrasts the position of the HSSPFs in the occupied territories with their position in the Altreich, in "Local Authority and the SS State: The Conflict over Population Policy in Danzig–West Prussia, 1939–1945," *Central European History*, II (Dec. 1969), 331–55. In addition, Helmut Krausnick's "Denkschrift Himmlers über die Behandlung der Fremdvölkischen im Osten (Mai 1940)," *Vierteljahrshefte für Zeitgeschichte*, V (April 1957), 194–98, should be consulted for the origins of Nazi population policy in the East.

A number of important works with a regional focus have appeared. Basic for Poland are two works by Martin Broszat: *Nationalsozialistische Polenpolitik 1939–1945* (Stuttgart, 1961) and the more narrow, unpublished "Verfolgung polnischer Geistlicher, 1939–45" (mimeographed *Gutachten* of the Institut für Zeitgeschichte; Munich, 1959). Somewhat further to the West, Paul Gürtler has written about the Nazi attack on the churches in the Warthegau in *Nationalsozialismus und evangelische Kirchen im Warthegau*

(Göttingen, 1958). Finally, while Max Freiherr du Prel, ed., *Das General-gouvernement*, 2d ed. (Würzburg, 1942) is a clear work of propaganda, it is still useful for the organizational aspects of Nazi rule in occupied Poland. Hans-Dietrich Loock's *Quisling, Rosenberg und Terboven—Zur Vorgeschichte und Geschichte der nationalsozialistischen Revolution in Norwegen* (Stutt-gart, 1970) is a masterful study of the intrigues that led to the establish-ment of the Nazi rule in Norway, although unfortunately it does not carry the story beyond September 1940. For Holland, Werner Warmbrunn, *The Dutch under German Occupation, 1940–1945* (Stanford, Calif., 1963) and Konrad Kwiet, *Reichskommissariat Niederlande* (Stuttgart, 1968) cover much the same material, although Warmbrunn deals with more than just the administrative aspects and Kwiet's presentation of the various competing factions of Holland is rather more sophisticated. A somewhat popularized yet very poignant account is the well-illustrated *Bezetting*, ed. Louis de Jong (Amsterdam, 1966). That author's own definitive multivolume history of the Netherlands in the Second World War, *Het Koningrijk der Nederlanden in de Tweede Wereldoorlog* (The Hague, 1969–), three volumes to date, has not as yet reached beyond 1940. For Luxemburg, Paul Weber, *Geschichte Luxemburgs im Zweiten Weltkrieg* (Luxemburg, 1946) is an emotion-filled account of the Nazi rule, and while it contains a great deal of information, the book is marred by the absence of scholarly apparatus. It also suffers from having been written in the immediate postwar era. The best accounts of German rule in France are Eberhard Jäckel, *Frankreich in Hitlers Europa—Die Deutsche Frankreichpolitik im Zweiten Weltkrieg* (Stuttgart, 1966) and Pierre Crenesse, *Le Procès de Wagner bourreau de l'Alsace* (Paris, 1946), with Jäckel being much more balanced of the two.

Understandably, ever since the 1940s the subject of Hess's flight to England has fascinated scholars and journalists alike. Neither have been fully able to integrate Hess's personality and overall activities into the seemingly solitary decision to undertake his flight, but the most recent con-tribution to the subject, James Douglass-Hamilton, *Motive for a Mission* (New York, 1971), undoubtedly provides as much information on this in-volved subject as we are ever likely to have.

E. 1941–1943

The years which saw both the German triumphs in Russia and the turn-ing point of the war are covered in many of the larger-scale works, but a num-ber of more specific monographic treatments might be cited at this point. Friedrich Wilhelm Lampe's *Die Amtsträger der Partei* (Stuttgart, 1941), though it pretends to be scholarly, is a superficial analysis. It is of interest only because it reflects the uncertainty that had seized Nazi political scientists in the aftermath of Bormann's arrival at the party chancellery. The two most dramatic events during these years were the German rule in Russia and the arrival of Albert Speer in the pantheon of Nazi leaders. The best contemporary account of Nazi rule in Russia is Walter Labs, "Die Verwaltung der besetzten Ostgebiete," *Reich, Volksordnung, Lebensraum,* V (1943), 132–66. Among the post-war publications Otto Bräutigam, *Überblick über die besetzten Ostgebiete während des 2. Weltkrieges* (Tübingen, 1954) is useful primarily because it is the account of a high official in the Reich ministry for occupied Eastern affairs. Helmut Heiber, ed., "Der Generalplan Ost," *Vierteljahrshefte für Zeitgeschichte,* VI (July 1958), 281–325, shows some of the more grandiose preparations for the Nazi rule in Russia. All of these are eclipsed and surpassed by Alexander Dallin's massive *German Rule in Russia, 1941–1945—A Study of Occupation Policies* (London, 1957), the definitive account of the Nazis' occupation policies in the East. For the extermination policies against the Jews, in addition to the works cited above, it may be useful to add Hermann Langbein, . . . *wir haben es getan* (Vienna, 1964), a collection of letters and original documents particularly useful for the party's participation at the local and district levels. The arrival and activities of Albert Speer may be followed in his own memoirs, but this material should be supplemented with two other major sources: the first is Willi A. Boelcke, ed., *Deutschlands Rüstung im Zweiten Weltkrieg —Hitlers Konferenzen mit Albert Speer 1942–1945* (Frankfurt a.M., 1000), which is the record of Speer's conferences with Hitler from 1942 to 1945. This raw documentary material has in turn been subjected to a scholarly analysis by Gregor Janssen in his monograph *Das Ministerium Speer— Deutschlands Rüstung im Krieg* (Berlin, 1968), which provides in many cases a needed corrective to the account in Speer's memoirs. Sauckel's role as GBA and his conflicts with Speer are detailed in another recent monograph, Edward L. Homze, *Foreign Labor in Nazi Germany* (Princeton, N.J., 1967).

F. 1943–1945

The last two years of the Nazi rule in Germany were marked by a decided acceleration in the partification measures, and much of this new policy of social control is reflected in both documentary and monographic publication. Oron J. Hale, "Adolf Hitler and the Post-War German Birthrate— An Unpublished Memorandum," *Journal of Central European Affairs,* XVIII (July 1957), 166–73, is a good overall introduction to the entire policy of social control in these last two years. In addition, the introduction of the NSFO program is examined in the following publications: Gerhard L. Weinberg, ed., "Adolf Hitler und der NS-Führungsoffizier (NSFO)," *Vierteljahrshefte für Zeitgeschichte,* XII (Oct. 1964), 443–56, which provides the protocol of Hitler's original appointment of General Reinicke, and Volker R. Berghahn, "NSDAP und 'Geistige Führung' der Wehrmacht 1939–1943,"

Vierteljahrshefte für Zeitgeschichte, VII (Jan. 1969), 17–71, a more general, but very good article on the failure of Rosenberg and the success of Bormann to take over the program.

The July 1944 assassination attempt has been dealt with so often that it has almost acquired a historiography of its own. Rather than cite all the available material, it may suffice to note that the most exhaustive and also most recent account is Peter Hoffmann, *Widerstand, Staatsstreich, Attentat— Der Kampf der Opposition gegen Hitler* (Munich, 1969), which also contains a massive bibliography. This should be supplemented for the somewhat different circumstances of the July assassination in Vienna with Ludwig Jedlicka, *Das Einsame Gewissen—Der 20. Juli 1944 in Österreich* (Vienna, 1966).

A description of the immediate aftermath of the July plot, the appointment of Goebbels as *Generalbevollmächtigter für den Kriegseinsatz*, and the August 1944 Gauleiter conference is available in two publications. One is the protocol of the ministerial conference appointing Goebbels, published in Wolfgang Bleyer, "Pläne der faschistischen Führung zum totalen Krieg im Sommer 1944," *Zeitschrift für Geschichtswissenschaft*, XVII (no. 10), 1312– 29; and the other is Himmler's speech at the Gauleiter conference, Theodor Eschenburg, ed., "Die Rede Himmlers vor den Gauleitern am 3.8.44," *Vierteljahrshefte für Zeitgeschichte*, I (Oct. 1953), 357–97. Additionally, the other speeches made at the Gauleiter conference—Speer's and Goebbels'—are available in photostatic form at the Institut für Zeitgeschichte. The chaos and ludicrousness of the Nazis' final months have given rise to a large amount of often sensational literature, much of which can be disregarded. The only monographic treatment of the Volkssturm is by the military officer in charge of tactical administration, Hans Kissel. His *Der Deutsche Volkssturm 1944/ 45—Eine territoriale Miliz im Rahmen der Landesverteidigung* (Frankfurt, 1962) is notable primarily for the general's naiveté in continuing to treat the Volkssturm as a viable military force. The simultaneous attempt both to gauge public opinion and to mold it in the final months of the Third Reich is treated in Volker R. Berghahn, "Meinungsforschung im 'Dritten Reich': Die Mundpropaganda-Aktion im letzten Kriegshalbjahr," *Militärgeschichtliche Mitteilungen*, I (1/1967), 83–119, and in Erich Murawski, *Der deutsche Wehrmachtsbericht—Ein Beitrag zur Untersuchung der geistigen Wehrmachtsführung* (Boppard am Rhein, 1962). The latter work is primarily a reproduction of the communiqués of the OKW during the period from 1 July 1944 to the end of the war. The breakdown of regular administrative procedures within Germany is discussed in some detail in Speer's memoirs and in Willi A. Boelcke, "Hitlers Befehle zur Zerstörung oder Lähmung des deutschen Industriepotentials 1944/45," *Tradition*, XIII (1968), 301–16; Leonard Krieger, "The Inter-Regnum in Germany: March– August 1945," *Political Science Quarterly*, LXIV (Dec. 1949), 507–32; and Hans Mommsen, ed., "Ein Erlass Himmlers zur Bekämpfung der Korruption in der inneren Verwaltung von Dezember 1944," *Vierteljahrshefte für Zeit-geschichte*, XVI (July 1968), 295–310.

Finally, the Dönitz aftermath of the Third Reich has been described by the admiral himself in his very apologetic *Mein Wechselvolles Leben* (Göttingen, 1968) [Engl. ed.: *Memoirs*, tr. R. H. Stevens (London, 1959)] and in the equally uncritical account by one of his younger associates, Walter Lüdde-Neurath, *Regierung Dönitz* (Göttingen, 1950). A useful corrective to these two laudatory books is Marlis G. Steinert, *Die 23 Tage der Regierung Dönitz* (Düsseldorf, 1967). The best treatment of Hitler's own final days remains Hugh R. Trevor-Roper, *The Last Days of Hitler* (London, 1947).

Index